REUSE BASED SOFTWARE
ENGINEERING

REUSE BASED SOFTWARE ENGINEERING
TECHNIQUES, ORGANIZATION, AND MEASUREMENT

HAFEDH MILI
University of Quebec, Montreal

ALI MILI
West Virginia University, West Virginia

SHERIF YACOUB
Hewlett Packard Laboratories, California

EDWARD ADDY
Logicon Inc., Florida

A Wiley-Interscience Publication
JOHN WILEY & SONS, INC.

Library of Congress Cataloging-in-Publication Data:
Mili, Hafedh.
  Reuse based software engineering / Hafedh Mili . . . [et al.].
    p. cm.
  ISBN 0-471-39819-5 (cloth : alk. paper)
  QA76.76.R47 M35 2001
  005.1—dc21   2001024246

10 9 8 7 6 5 4 3 2 1

To Amel, may she realize all her hopes
H. M.

To Noor, may her star shine ever brighter
A. M.

To our first instructors, Aicha and Taieb
H. M., A. M.

To my parents and family
S. Y.

To my wife, Eleanor, and to my daughters, Rachel and Rebekah
E. A.

Contents

Preface

Software productivity has been steadily increasing since 1970, but not enough to close the gap between the demands placed on the software industry, and what the state of the practice can deliver. Today, as software costs continue to represent an increasing share of computer system costs, and as software faults continue to be responsible for many expensive failures, nothing short of an order-of-magnitude improvement in software quality and development productivity will save the software industry from its perennial state of crisis. Reuse-based software engineering has been touted, since the late 1960s, as the only practical and realistic approach that can deliver such improvements "in the short term." This book provides a state of the art and the practice of all aspects of reuse-based software engineering, and attempts to explain why the "short term" keeps eluding us, and how to catch up.

Despite decades-long intensive research in software engineering and artificial intelligence, software generation remains an elusive goal. Progress has been made, of course, but the target has continued to move even faster, outdistancing the kind and scale of software that generative techniques can deliver. Hence, short of sufficiently understanding the process we use to build software from imprecise and contradictory user needs, subject to all the contradictory constraints of cost, reliability, time to market, and portability—to name a few—to encode it into a generator, we could try to reuse the products or repeat the development processes, of previous developments efforts. The underlying hypotheses are that (1) the computer systems that we develop today have a lot in common and (2) by reusing the process and products of previous development efforts to solve new problems, we increase productivity and improve the quality of the resulting system.

Reuse is not only natural but may be the key to progress. Psychologists and cognitive scientists have long argued that we humans seldom solve problems from first principles. When faced with a problem to solve, we first perform a "rote recall," just in case this problem was already solved. When that fails, we perform "approximate recall," with the hope of identifying an already solved problem that is so close that its solution can be adapted, locally, to address the new problem. Only when that fails do we fall back on analytic problem solving, at least as far as decomposing the initial problem into a set of more manageable subproblems. The key to progress, some would argue, is to reuse (learn from past experiences), and to communicate (be able to transmit knowledge to new generations).

In the early days of the profession, because of the scale of the systems to be built (small), the expressiveness of the programming languages (low level), and the cost distribution of computer systems (machines and machine time predominant), it was felt that much benefit would accrue from reusing *executable programs*. Much research effort in software engineering in general and software reuse in particular went into software packaging issues, and more specifically, language features that support modularization and abstraction. A lot of progress has been made along these dimensions, but again, the target has continued to move; as the size and complexity of typical software systems kept increasing, organizational aspects of both the software product and the teams building it began to dominate the software development process, in terms of complexity, cost, and impact in general. This meant that software reuse research needed to focus on ways to encode, package, and organize software artifacts of a granularity that is bigger than the procedure or routine, and at a stage of development that is earlier than code. Simultaneously, as the number of stakeholders increased, and the financial stakes grew higher, there was a need to focus on the organizational and economic aspects of reuse.

Since the 1970s, a number of organizations have recognized the potential for software reuse to improve productivity and enhance the quality of the products being built. In the early 1980s, the (U.S.) federal government in general, and the Department of Defense in particular, have launched a number of initiatives to help understand, organize, and promote software reuse, within its software providers community, and throughout the software industry in general. A number of organizations had embarked on software reuse initiatives since the 1970s. The results varied widely, and in those cases where reuse was successful, the approach used was sometimes not repeatable, not scalable, or both, and its benefits were nonmeasurable. Nowadays, it is widely recognized that in order to attain worthwhile, predictable, and repeatable reuse levels at the scale of the enterprise, we must address software reuse at three levels:

- A set of techniques for developing and packaging high-quality software artifacts that are widely applicable, and cost-effectively usable
- An organization that has the mandate, the discipline, the skills, and the resources for producing, *consuming*, and managing a shared repository of reusable artifacts

- A set of control and management tools for planning, controlling, and evaluating the degree to which such an organization attained its objectives

This book covers all three sets of issues, and the breadth and depth of coverage that we strove for in all three areas has made this book worth writing and we should hope will make it worth purchasing, and perhaps even reading!

There has been much research, and a growing body of codified practical knowledge in all three areas. However, the three areas have not attained the same level of maturity, and the contents of this book reflect that reality. Perhaps the most mature area is the technical field; research on reuse-enabling software packaging technologies has been ongoing since the late 1960s, with practice increasingly closing the time lag—and sometimes reversing it, by producing techniques and tools faster than researchers can conceptualize. Here the challenge is simply to keep up! In this area, we built on our collective experiences from learning about, doing, consulting, mentoring, and teaching various reuse-enabling technologies. For this knowledge to have a shelf life that is longer than that of the latest fad, be it a language, tool, technique, or method, we have to look for, and try to codify, some of the fundamentals of modeling and programming for reuse. We hope that this material will help complement the more practical skills and techniques that this book contains, by tooling the "introspective professional" with some of the skills to consume, if not develop, the next generation of techniques.

The organizational aspects of software reuse have received increasing attention since the late 1980s, both as a distinct body of knowledge and in relation to more general issues such as process maturity frameworks and issues related to process reengineering and change management. Input for organizational models has come both from (1) synthesizing known success stories of reuse organizations in the industry and (2) by analytically building such models by drawing on general knowledge from process reengineering, risk management, and change management. The result has been a set of more or less elaborate organizational models drawn up by public (e.g., government), parapublic [e.g., Software Engineering Institute (SEI)], and industry consortia [e.g., Software Productivity Consortium (SPC)]. Each one of these—relatively similar, and invariably commonsensical—models would warrant a full book in its own right. We chose to synthesize this knowledge, and focus on the commonalities, but provide pointers to the individual sources, as well as to known cases where such organizational models—or variants thereof—were successfully used.

The area of economic modeling of software reuse is perhaps the least mature of the three. Central to economic modeling is the issue of reuse measurement. Software measurement has, for a long time, been the lot of a small community of determined software engineering researchers and professionals, but not afforded the sexy status of the more mainstream research subjects. In practice, it is one of the main reasons why most software organizations are not above level 1 of the capability maturity model (CMM); very few software organizations measure software and the processes that produce it, and even fewer know what to do with the data. The area of software measurement is witnessing a boom of sorts, mostly in terms of software quality measurements, and in relation to reengineering and maintenance. However, this boom is not likely to benefit the economic modeling of software reuse in the short run, because in economic modeling, we are interested in functional size measurements, to which software reuse adds layers of complexity. The material related to the economic modeling of software reuse is a mixture of a tutorial and a literature survey, although the models that we describe can be valuable simulation tools for the reuse strategic planner and/or manager.

The intended audience for this book is technical. The material in this book is either irrelevant or too detailed for most managers. There are a number of excellent books out there whose contents and style of delivery is targeted at the hurried manager who needs bullet points to include on next day's plan review meeting.

We strove to make this book useful to both the academic and the professional by including foundational material as well as practical and tutorial material. We have also included review questions and exercises to support the teaching of the material in an academic (mostly) or professional training setting.

The Professional. The material covered in this book will be useful to developers and technical managers and leaders. A developer can skip right up to Part III, read Chapters 7 and 8, and then on to Part IV, where the introduction gives a detailed roadmap for Chapters 10–14. Chapters 15 and 17 in Part V are also a must read; Chapter 16 (on component retrieval) may be skipped. Curious developers can read the one chapter in Part VII (specialized forms of reuse) that is more relevant to their organizations or projects. Technical managers would benefit from Parts I–III (except Chapter 9), the last two chapters of Part IV (application frameworks, Chapter 13; architectural frameworks, Chapter 14), and all of Part VII. Technical leaders (e.g., architects) would benefit from Parts I and III–V (possibly skipping some of the foundational material in Part IV; see the introduction to that part), and the chapter that most corresponds to their development practice from Part VII.

The Academic. This book is suitable for a sixth- or seventh-semester advanced software design course. We recommend Chapter 1, Chapters 6 and 7 of Part III, the entire Parts IV and V, and, depending on how much general software engineering background the students has, perhaps Chapter 19 (component-based software engineering). The book is also recommended as a graduate course in computer science or management information systems (MIS). For computer science students, Part VI could be left out entirely, and some of the introductory material on object oriented (OO) techniques (Chapter 9) could be skipped. For MIS students, we could cover Parts I and II, all of Part III except Chapter 9, the introductions to Parts IV and V (Chapters 10 and 15), and Parts VI and VII. Some chapters include review questions and exercises. The uppercase letters in Exercise sections indicate level of problem difficulty or complexity: (A) easiest, (B) intermediate or medium difficulty, (C) hardest or maximum difficulty, and (R) research problem.

We hope that you will have as much fun using the material in this book as we have had writing it.

HÁFEDH MILI, ALI, MILI, SHERIF YACOUB, AND EDWARD ADDY

August 2000

Acronyms and Symbols

AA	assessment and assimilation
ACT	annual change traffic
ADL	architecture description language
ADN	adaptive dynamic network
AFMC	Air Force (U.S.) Material Command
AI	artificial intgelligence
AOP	aspect-oriented programming
API	application program interface
APL	Array Programming Language
ARBV	average return on book value
ARC	Army (U.S.) Rescue Center
ARR	average rate of return
ASL	application-specific language
ASSET	Asset Source for Software Engineering Technology
ATA	architecture tradeoff analysis
ATM	Automated Teller Machine
AWT	abstract windowing toolkit
BIDM	basic interoperability data model
BS	behavioral sampling
CAD	computer-aided/assisted design
CARDS	Comprehensive Approach to Reusable Defense Software (proprietary to USAF–NASA)
CASE	computer-aided/assisted software engineering

Common abbreviations (i.e., CPU, IEEE, R&D, etc.) omitted here. Proprietary definitions are capitalized.

CBSD	component-based software/system development
CBSE	component-based software/system engineering
CCC	credit card company
CCL	Command Center Library
CCPL	command and control product line(s)
CIM	Center of Information Management
CLOS	Common LISP (list processing) Object System (language)
CM	Configuration Management (proprietary to SEI)
CMM	Capability Maturity Model
COCOMO	constructive cost model
COM	Component Object Model (Microsoft)
CORBA	Common Object Request Brokerage Architecture
COTS	commercial off-the-shelf [product(s)]
CRA	car rental agency
CRC	cyclic redundancy check
CT	coding and (unit) testing
CTA	Computer Technology Associates
C2AI	Command and Control Architecture Infrastructure
DADP	domain analysis and design process
DARPA	Defense Advanced Research Projects Agency
DBMS	database management system
DCE	distributed computing environment
DD	detailed design
DII	dynamic invocation interface
DISA	Defense Information Systems Agency
DLL	dynamically linked library
DM	design modification
DSRS	Defense Software Repository System
DSSA	domain-specific software architecture
EAF	effort adjustment factor
EJB	Enterprise Java Beans
ESC	Electronic Systems Center [U.S. Air Force (USAF)]
FAST	family-oriented abstraction, specification, and translation
FIFO	first in/first out
FODA	feature-oriented domain analysis
4GL	fourth-generation language
FSP	full-time software person/programmer
GUI	graphical user interface
IC	investment cost(s)
IDL	interface definition language
IM	integration modification
IMS	information management system
IIOP	Internet Inter-ORB Protocol
IRR	internal rate of return
ISO	International Standardization Organization

IT	information technology; integration testing
JDBC	Java database connectivity
JIAWG	Joint Integrated Avionics Working Group
JODA	joint object-oriented domain analysis
KAPTUR	knowledge acquisition for preservation of tradeoffs and underlying rationales
KLOC	kiloline(s) of code
LNCS	Lecture Notes in Computer Science
LI	library insertion
LM	labor-month(s)
LMFS	Lockheed Martin Federal Systems
LMTDS	Lockheed Martin Tactical Defense Systems
LOC	Lines of code
MIL	module interconnection language
MIS	management information system
ML	machine language
MVC	model view conroller
NPLACE	National Product Line Assessment Center
NPV	net present value
NTT	Nippon (Japan) Telegraph & Telephone Corporation
ODBC	object database connectivity
ODM	organization(al) domain modeling
OLE	object linking and embedding
OMA	Object Management Architecture (proprietary to OMG)
OMG	Object Management Group
OMT	object modeling technique
OO	object orientation
ORB	object request broker
ORRA	organizational engineering for reuse assessment
OSI	Open Systems Interconnect (protocol)
PASTA	process and artifact state transition abstraction
PBV	payback value
PCTE	portable common tool interface
PD	product design
PDL	Program Design Language
PI	profitability index
PLA	product-line architecture
PLAF	pluggable look and feel
PLE	product-line engineering
PLP	product-line practice
PRISM	Portable Reusable Integrated Software Module
PROLOG	programming in logic
PuLSE	Product-Line Software Engineering (proprietary to Fraunhofer Institute for Experimental Software Engineering)
QA	quality assurance

RA	requirements analysis
RAASP	Reusable Ada (language) Avionics Sofware Package(s) (U.S. Air Force)
RBP	relative blackbox price (default value 0.40; see Chapter 19).
RCA	relative cost of adaptation (default value 0.67; see Chapter 19).
RCDE	relative cost of domain engineering (default value 0.20; see Chapter 19)
RCM	reuse capability model
RCR	relative cost of reuse (of software) (default value 0.20; see Chapter 19)
RCWR	relative cost of writing for reuse (default value 0.15; see Chapter 19)
REBOOT	reuse based on object-oriented techniques
RIC	Reuse Information Clearinghouse
RICC	Reusable Integrated Command Center (proprietary program)
RLIG	Reuse Library Interoperability Group (also abbreviated RIG)
RLPM	reuse library process model
RMI	remote method invocation
ROI	return on investment
RPC	remote procedure call
RSL	reusable software library (a, generic)
RWP	relative whitebox price (default value 0.20; see Chapter 19)
SAAM	Software Architecture Analysis Method
SA/SD	Stucture Analysis/Design
SAIC	Science Applications International Corporation
SCAI	space command and control architectural infrastructure
SCM	service control manager
SD	start date; standard deviation
SEI	Software Engineering Institute
SEL	Software Engineering Laboratory
SLA	savings & loan association (a, generic)
SORT	Software Optimization and Reuse Technology (NASA)
SPARC	Scalable Processor Architecture
SPC	Software Productivity Consortium
SQL	Structured Query Language
SRI	Software Reuse Initiative (proprietary program)
SRSC	software reuse support center
STARS	Software Technology for Adaptive and Reliable Systems
SU	software understanding
SWSC	Space and Warning Systems Center
TCP/IP	Transmission Control Protocol/Internet Protocol
UML	Unified Modeling/Medical Language
URL	uniform resource locator
V&V	verification and validation
VBX	Visual Basic Controls (Microsoft)

| WAP | Wireless Application Protocol |
| WVHTCF | West Virginia High Technology Consortium Foundation |

$\rho(P)$	Cost of developing product P with reuse (see Chapter 19).
$\pi(A)$	Cost of purchasing reusable asset A (see Chapter 19).
$\sigma(S)$	Cost of developing product S from scratch (see Chapter 19).
$\theta(W)$	Cost of (whitebox) reusing asset W (see Chapter 19).
$\beta(B)$	Cost of (blackbox) reusing asset B (see Chapter 19).
$\tau(S,B,W)$	Cost of integrating components S, B and W (see Chapter 19).
$\omega(P)$	Labor overhead incurred by the development of project P as a result of practicing software reuse

REUSE BASED SOFTWARE
ENGINEERING

Part I

Introduction

... reuse is neither a silver bullet nor a magic weight loss pill.
It is a diet and exercise program ...
PAUL G. BASSET, 1997

In this part, we familiarize the reader with the culture of software reuse, and lay the groundwork for the rest of the book. Chapter 1 introduces the terms and concepts that arise in the practice of software reuse. Chapter 2 discusses the state of the art and the state of the practice in software reuse, covering in turn managerial issues, technical issues, and current or recent reuse infrastructures. Chapter 3 discusses the multidisciplinary nature of software reuse, and covers the field one aspect at a time, serving as an introductory overview of the whole book.

Chapter **1**

Software Reuse and Software Engineering

Software development cannot possibly become an engineering discipline so long as it has not perfected a technology for developing products from reusable assets in a routine manner, on an industrial scale. As a discipline, *software reuse* must define and promote the managerial, organizational, and technical standards that are required to achieve this goal. The very idea that *software reuse* is a legitimate topic for a book (does your library have a book on hardware reuse?), let alone one that is the focus of many annual conferences and of much debate, is a paradox: in all other engineering disciplines, reuse is an integral part (so integral, it is not even noteworthy) of good engineering design. This paradox raises two issues, which we discuss briefly:

- *Why is software reuse an issue, and not, for example, hardware reuse?* A question as wide as this can elicit a different answer from each respondent. Perhaps the common denominator of all possible answers is that software assets are typically very information-rich; hence it is very difficult to characterize them, match them, and capture their relevant properties.

- *How is software reuse different from software design?* There is more to software design than software reuse; even if all the building components of a system were available as reusable assets, we still would have the task of deriving the system architecture, combining the components, integrating their interfaces, and testing the aggregate system. Also, there is more to software reuse than software design. Not only do we need good reusable assets (to reuse) and a good discipline of software design (that exploits the benefits of reuse); we also need a wide range of measures, procedures, and guidelines that allow us to optimize the production, storage, retrieval, and exploitation of reusable assets.

3

In this chapter, we introduce some terminology related to software reuse, and discuss relevant products, processes, and paradigms.

1.1   CONCEPTS AND TERMS

1.1.1   A Definition of Software Reuse

While we all have an intuitive understanding of software reuse, in a number of instances it is difficult to determine whether we are dealing with genuine software reuse or some other software development situation. Hence, before we define software reuse, we consider a number of examples and analyze them to determine whether we want to consider them as instances of reuse.

> An Ada programmer writes a menu-driven management information system (MIS) application and in this application offers to sort (1) an array of permanent employee records by increasing social security number, by decreasing hourly salary, or by increasing age and (2) temporary employee records by decreasing hire date. The programmer then writes a single sort routine, and in this routine makes the array entry, the array size, the ordering key and the ordering relation generic; the programmer then (re)uses this single sort routine for all applications, parameterizing it as necessary.

Question: Is this an instance of reuse? We recognize that this programmer uses many of the Ada features that are known to promote reuse but is merely using good programming discipline to enhance program quality and thus is not practicing reuse per se. Hence, ideally, we do not want to consider that there is reuse unless there is some measure of *independence* between the process of producing reusable artifacts and that of exploiting them.

> What if the same programmer needed, a few weeks later, to sort an array of spare part records, while keeping records with the same part number in their original order (e.g., because they represent successive batches of the same part), and used the same sort routine as above?

Question: Do we consider the use of the Ada sort routine as an instance of reuse? Again, we would not want to consider this as software reuse, because we feel that a prerequisite for this title is that the process of producing and consuming reusable artifacts be *systematic*. This instance is sometimes referred to as *incidental reuse* or, less formally, as *code scavenging*. Ideally, the producer of a reusable asset is expected to have some cognizance of the possibility that his code will be reused, and some idea of the application domain within which it is expected to be reused.

> A C programmer acquires a C compiler from a vendor and uses it to write a graph traversal algorithm, then to write a simulation program, then to write a numeric analysis procedure.

Question: Do we consider that the repeated use of the C compiler is an instance of software reuse? The answer is no, for a simple reason—the programmer is not using the compiler for *development* activities but rather is using it as a final product. Hence an additional condition for reuse is that the reusable asset be integrated into a larger software system, in the context of a software development process.

> A C programmer writes a program to solve trigonometric equations and invokes the sine function 12 times throughout the program.

Question: Do these repeated uses of the *sine* function qualify as software reuse? The answer is no; irrespective of what the C standard provides, this function can reasonably be considered as part of the language—in the same way as C functions *read*, *write*, *reset*, and so on. Had the programmer actually developed the *sine* function, this would still not be an instance of reuse but merely an instance of good procedural design.

> A Fortran programmer writes a program to solve trigonometric equations and needs to invoke the sine function 12 times throughout the program. Because the version of Fortran he is using is very old, it does not provide for library functions. However the programmer's organization has an off-line repository of Fortran routines from which programmers can extract a sine routine; the programmer then inserts the code of the sine routine into the program as a procedure declaration, checks that this creates no conflict with program names, and compiles the whole program.

Question: Do we have software reuse? If so, how many instances? The answer is that we have software reuse, a single instance (the procedure declaration). Note that the production and the use of the *sine* function are independent, and that the consumer of the function proceeded through all the steps of the software reuse process: requirements identification, library search, asset retrieval, and asset integration within a system under development.

> An Ada programmer writes a simulation program that involves queues of processes and an array of processors and to this effect looks up generic Ada packages for queues and arrays, includes them in the running Ada environment and instantiates the queue twice (ready queue, blocked queue) and instantiates the array once (processor array).

Question: Do we have software reuse? If so, how many instances? We consider that we have two instances of software reuse, one for each abstract data type that is invoked. The programming language Ada supports the practice of reuse by providing ADT libraries; library assets are provided as part of the language environment, and can be augmented by the user organization.

To summarize the lessons we have learned from these examples and counterexamples, we can say that software reuse is contingent on the following general provisions: a measure of independence between the processes of asset development and asset use; a systematic process that governs the production, storage, and retrieval of reusable assets; a cognizance of the form of the reusable asset (if not its source code, at least its invocation protocol within a host system); and finally, the condition that the retrieved assets be used as part of a development process. We attempt to capture these ideas in the following definition:

> Software reuse *is the process whereby an organization defines a set of systematic operating procedures to specify, produce, classify, retrieve, and adapt software artifacts for the purpose of using them in its development activities.*

Undoubtedly, there are cases when this definition is not sufficiently precise to rule one way or another; it is adequate for our purposes, however.

1.1.2 Software Reuse: Potentials and Pitfalls

Like any other engineering discipline, software engineering stands to gain a great deal from a sound discipline of reuse; but unlike most other engineering disciplines, software reuse does not arise naturally in software engineering, and when it does, it does not come without costs and risks. We briefly review some of the benefits and pitfalls of software reuse.

Software reuse benefits can be classified into three categories, which we discuss in turn below:

- *Gains in Productivity*. Gains in productivity are the main motivation for software reuse; by reusing existing assets, we save the manpower required to develop them again.
- *Gains in Quality*. Gains in quality stem from two sets of measures: (1) when a component is developed for reuse, one can rationalize large investments in its quality, on the premise that these investments will be amortized over its multiple uses; (2) when a reusable component is used by a larger community, it gets debugged more thoroughly.
- *Gains in Development Schedule*. By using reusable assets, we save not only on manpower (person-months) but also on development schedule (months). This translates into shorter time to market, which may in turn mean a bigger market share.

For all its promise, software reuse has not been a matter of routine practice, for a number of reasons:

- *Limited Reuse Potential*. Software assets are very information-rich; this limits the likelihood of a match between a specific query and an available asset. Modern programming disciplines, which emphasize information hiding, and modern programming languages, which support information hiding, help us control this problem, but do not overcome it entirely.

- *Nonnegligible Overheads.* It is easy to be misled by the reuse *propaganda*, and to overlook the nontrivial costs associated with software reuse. We will see in subsequent chapters that, even under the best conditions, the margin of benefits of software reuse is fairly limited.
- *Nonnegligible Risks.* We will see in subsequent chapters that it is also possible for a poorly planned reuse initiative to actually cost more than it saves.
- *Nonnegligible Obstacles.* The introduction of reuse requires rather profound changes in the operational procedures of an organization; these changes are usually met with resistance. Also, reuse requires healthy investments and does not bring returns immediately; hence it requires long-term managerial support.

In light of this background, one must remember that software reuse is no panacea; it requires careful planning, realistic expectations, and a long-term perspective. It is more akin to a diet and exercise program than to a magic weight-loss pill.

1.1.3 Exercises

1. (B) Benefits of software reuse include productivity gains, quality gains, and development schedule gains. Discuss how to quantify these gains, possibly using a uniform unit. Also discuss how to measure them in practice.

2. (B) To illustrate how information-rich software assets can be, consider a hashing algorithm, and describe it fully for the benefit of a potential (re)user. This includes not only all the representational aspects (input formats, output formats, calling protocols) but also all the semantic aspects (explain how the algorithm handles collisions).

1.2 SOFTWARE REUSE PRODUCTS

1.2.1 Reusable Assets

The most common form of reusable artifact is, of course, source code in some programming language, but it is not the only one. In this section, we review some of the common reusable artifacts, and discuss in turn their essence, representation, and indexing keys.

- *Executable Code.* The essence of a piece of executable code is the function that it computes; executable code is typically represented in machine-readable form, and is indexed by means of its functional properties.

- *Source Code.* Much of what we said above about executable code applies to source code, to the extent that source code embodies a *function*. But to the extent that it also embodies structural information, source code can be viewed as problem-solving knowledge. Source code is, of course, represented by programming languages, and can be indexed by means of its structural properties, as well as its functional properties.

- *Requirements Specifications.* Whereas code assets are executable, requirements specifications are not; rather, they are the products of eliciting user requirements and recording them in some notation. Specifications can be represented in natural language, in formal notation (logic, axiomatic systems, formal languages), or in a mixture thereof. Specifications are indexed by means of the functional properties that they capture, and may be reused to build either compound specifications or (after modification) variations on the original product.

- *Designs.* Designs are generic representations of design decisions; their essence is the design/problem-solving knowledge that they capture. In contrast to code assets, designs are not executable; in contrast to specification assets, they capture structural information rather than functional information. They are represented by *patterns* that can be instantiated in different ways to produce concrete designs. Unlike functions or modules, designs cannot be indexed by their functional properties; rather, they can be indexed by features of the family of problems that they solve.

- *Test Data.* Imagine that we have developed a software system and that we have integration-tested this system using some test data. We may want to reuse the same test data to test the system subsequently, following a maintenance operation; also we may want to use the test data to test a similar product, which has a similar set of inputs but different output conditions (consider, e.g., that the same test data can be used to test a procedure that sorts arrays in increasing order, and a procedure that sorts arrays in decreasing order). For this reason, test data are a perfectly legitimate reusable asset. Representation of these data is straightforward, and the data can be indexed by a description of the input domain of the software system, or possibly some general indication of the function of the system.

- *Documentation.* Natural-language documentation that accompanies a reusable asset can conceivably be considered as a reusable asset itself; in addition, many reusable assets (specifications, designs) can be represented as natural-language documentation. Documentation is most typically represented in natural language and can be indexed via the asset that it documents; other indexing mechanisms for documentation include information retrieval techniques and tools, as well as hypertext tools.

- *Architectures.* A software *architecture* defines the structure of a software system as the aggregate of a set of components that exchange data. The constructs by which building blocks are usually combined in an architecture have a higher level of abstraction than do programming language constructs, and are of a different nature; they prescribe information flow, control flow, or communication protocols between components. Architectures are represented by means of specialized notations, and are indexed by means of their architectural features.

Executable code and source code will be referred to as *software components* or simply as *components*. In this subsection, we have reviewed the various forms that reusable software assets may take; in the next subsection, we discuss means to organize reusable assets into *reuse libraries*.

1.2.2 Reuse Libraries: Vertical versus Horizontal Sets

In order to be useful, a reuse library must have a simple characterization of the assets that are included therein. In order to make effective use of a reuse library, a reuser must have a clear understanding of its contents, so as to determine whether his needs are likely to be adequately met by the library. The contents of a library may be defined in one of two ways. Before we discuss these, we make the following observation about the makeup of a typical software application: If we analyze the volume of code of a typical application, we find that it can be divided into three categories:

- *Generic components*, which provide general-purpose programming support on top of the programming language. Such components include abstract data types, graphic utilities, mathematical routines, and menu drivers. These components are typically useful across application domains, and are known to account for up to 20% of the size of a typical application. These are exactly the kinds of components that are typically provided as part of the Ada environment; they build a software layer on top of the programming language.

- *Domain-specific components*, which fulfill functions that are specific to the application domain of the software product. If the domain is, say, data processing, such components may include sorting packages, file management packages, and hashing functions. If the domain is systems programming, such components may include device handlers, resource managers, and specialized priority queue handlers. These components are typically specific to the application domain at hand, and are known to account for up to 65% of the size of a typical application.

- *Application-specific code*, which serves the purpose of the specific application at hand and can hardly be useful across applications. Application-specific code may perform such functions as customizing domain-specific components, combining domain-specific components, or providing specific functionality. Typically, application-specific code is not expected to be useful in applications other than those in which it is written, and is known to account for up to 15% of the size of a typical application.

This observation leads us to consider two possible characterizations of a reuse library:

Horizontal Definition. We may want to build a library that contains *generic* components, which augment the expressive power of the programming language without committing to a specific application domain. The advantage of such a library is that it is useful across several application domains, and hence potentially several development projects. The drawback of such a library is that its leverage is limited to about 20% of the size of the application, as we discussed earlier.

Vertical Definition. We may want to build a library that contains *domain-specific* components. The advantage of such a library is that reusing its assets can reduce the amount of code that we must develop by up to 65%. The drawback of such a library is that it can be used only within a single application domain, and hence potentially few projects. Vertical libraries are particularly useful for organizations that develop and maintain large scale, long-lived software products.

The contrast between horizontal libraries and vertical libraries, and their role in building applications, is illustrated in Figure 1.1. The X axis represents component genericity, and the Y axis represents component functionality. A horizontal library offers great domain variation but limited functionality (and hence accounts for a small percentage of the functionality, and size, of any given application); a vertical library offers more functionality but limited domain variation. An application (represented by the vertical rectangle in the center) cuts across both libraries, borrowing much more from the domain-specific vertical library than from the generic horizontal library. An application that falls outside the application domain would use little reusable code.

Chapter 16 of this book deals with the technical aspects of reusable component classification and retrieval.

1.2.3   Exercises

1. (A) Consider the following collections of software products; indicate whether they represent vertical or horizontal libraries. For vertical libraries, give a characterization of the application domain that they serve.

  (a) A collection of ADT implementations, with varying characteristics, written in a common language (e.g., Ada).

  (b) A collection of numeric routines, written in Fortran, that compute common numeric functions (sine, cosine, log).

  (c) A collection of operations research programs (linear programming routines, dynamic programming routines, nonlinear optimization routines, integer programming routines).

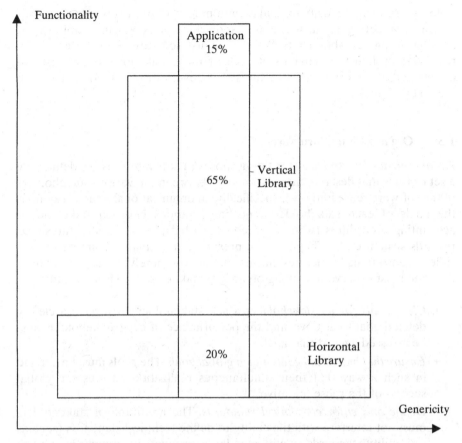

FIGURE 1.1   Library definitions: horizontal versus vertical.

(d) A collection of data processing functions that operate on main storage and secondary storage (sorting, searching, hashing, merging).

(e) A collection of linear algebra routines that perform matrix operations (matrix inversion, determinant, eigenvalues, eigenvectors) and are written in C. Same question, if the routines are written in APL (A Progamming Language; a matrix manipulation language).

1.3 SOFTWARE REUSE PROCESSES

It is possible to identify three stakeholders in the process of software reuse: corporate management, which initiates the reuse initiative and monitors the attending costs and benefits; the domain engineering team, which is responsible for producing, classifying, and maintaining reusable assets; and the application engineering team, which is responsible for producing applications, possibly using reusable assets. We can discuss software reuse processes by reviewing in turn the activities of each of these stakeholders; but first, we discuss some organizational structures that govern the interactions between these stakeholders.

1.3.1 Organizational Structures

An *organizational structure*, for the purposes of software reuse, is defined by a set of rules that describe the relationships between the various stakeholders of the software reuse initiative. Specifically, an organizational structure defines the goals of each stakeholder, reporting relations between stakeholders, accounting procedures (who gets credit for what), incentive structures, and rewards structures. In Chapter 4, we present and evaluate a number of possible organizational structures; in this section, we merely discuss the criteria that one must observe in making organizational decisions. These include

- *Clear goals for all stakeholders*. Each stakeholder must have a clearly defined goal to achieve, and the performance of each stakeholder must be assessed against that goal.
- *Ensure that individual goals match global goals*. The goals must be defined in such a way that their simultaneous realization ensures the global success of the reuse initiative.
- *Define and enforce technical standards*. The multitude of stakeholders must not interfere with the ability to define technical standards (such as reusability standards, quality standards, productivity standards), and to uphold them across the corporation; this can be achieved by appropriate assignment of responsibilities and prerogatives.
- *Provide adequate incentives for all stakeholders*. Reuse will not happen as a result of lecturing or preaching. The best way to ensure that it happens is to define appropriate incentives for all stakeholders; for example, producers of reusable assets must have concrete motivations to produce, and consumers must be duly motivated to consume reusable assets.

One of the most important organizational decisions—that having the greatest impact on reuse operations—is whether the organizational structure is *domain-centered* or *application-centered*. Under a *domain-centered* organization, the domain engineering team decides the development of reusable assets, leaving it to application engineering teams to adjust their design discipline or activity to take the best advantage of available reusable assets. Under the *application-centered* organization, the application engineering team delegates development tasks to the domain engineering team, to serve the goals of their application development activity. Talent within the organization must be distributed according to the type of organization that is selected. Organizational structures are discussed in Chapter 4, and somewhat in Section 6.1.

1.3.2 Domain Engineering

The *domain engineering* team is responsible for producing, maintaining, and cataloging reusable assets, to make them available to application engineering teams; by and large, *producing reusable assets* can be interpreted to include acquisition of assets developed outside the corporation, such as commercial off-the-shelf (COTS) products. The success of the domain engineering team can be measured by how much their assets are being sought by the application engineering teams. The prerogatives of the domain engineering team depend a great deal on whether the organizational structure is domain-centered or application-centered; under a domain-centered structure, these include the following tasks and responsibilities:

- *Domain Analysis.* This task consists in defining an application domain, and analyzing it to determine whether it is worthwhile to develop a reuse infrastructure for the domain. The domain analysis proceeds by characterizing, extensively or intensively, the applications that belong to this domain. Then, it involves cataloging the commonalities and variabilities that exist among the applications of the domain, so as to determine whether the overhead involved in developing the reuse infrastructure for this domain can be justified in light of the expected volume of application development within the domain. There are a number of industrial-strength methodologies that support the domain analysis phase. Chapter 8 deals with domain analysis; in addition to characterizing the discipline of domain analysis, we discuss heuristics for commonality and variability analysis, and describe some of the major domain analysis methodologies.

- *Domain Engineering.* If the domain analysis phase is conclusive, then the domain engineering team proceeds to build the reuse infrastructure that is required to support application development within the domain. This includes a generic architecture, which captures the structural commonalities identified during the domain analysis phase, and a set of reusable asset specifications, which fit in the generic architecture, along with protocols that prescribe how the assets fit in the architecture, and how they can be parameterized to account for the variability that was identified in the domain analysis phase.

- *Asset Acquisition.* This phase consists of *development for reuse*, with possibly some external procurement of reusable assets (such as COTS products). Development for reuse differs from traditional software development, due to all the additional measures that are needed to meet the requirements of genericity, reliability, maintainability, and documentation; also, it is known to cost significantly more, as we will see in Chapter 19.

- *Asset Classification.* This task is in effect a *database administration* task; it consists of cataloging and storing reusable assets, so as to facilitate their retrieval and assessment by application engineering teams. Chapters 10–14 present (mostly) object-oriented techniques for building reusable software component.

- *Asset Maintenance.* This task is in effect a maintenance task, merged with a *configuration management/version control* task. As components evolve through corrective maintenance (correcting bugs) and perfective maintenance (producing successive upgrades), the applications that use these components may be affected, and may need to be modified. Chapter 5 deals with some of the infrastructure issues related to configuration of reusable components from the perspective of the asset provider.

In application-centered organizations, the specification of reusable assets is done by the application engineering function rather than the domain engineering function. The activities of the domain engineering team are then concentrated on the last three functions: *asset acquisition*, *asset classification*, and *asset maintenance*.

1.3.3   Application Engineering

The focus of the application engineering team is to develop applications using reusable assets. A measure of success of the application engineering function is how well they exploit the available reusable assets in their development work. In application-centered organizations, the application engineering function includes the following tasks and responsibilities:

- *Development with Reuse.* The adoption of reuse has a great impact on the development process; this impact depends on whether the prevailing development discipline is top–down or bottom–up. Generally speaking, a reuse-based top–down discipline of application development proceeds through the following phases: requirements specification, whereby the application's requirements are specified; product design, whereby the system's design is refined to the point where it is possible to identify design units that can potentially be found in the reuse library; retrieval, whereby the units are looked up in the reuse library and then assessed to determine whether they are adequate for the purposes of the design at hand; coding of the missing units (that were not found in the library); and subsequent integration and testing. A reuse-based bottom–up discipline is different in that the reuse library is visited before, rather than after the design. After the requirements specification, we proceed to *browse* the library, that is, to familiarize ourselves with its content; then we proceed to develop a design that takes the best possible advantage of the assets we have seen in the library. Subsequent steps proceed in the same manner as top–down design. Chapter 15 outlines a development with reuse process; Chapter 16 discusses issues raised by development with reusable components.

- *Specifying Reusable Assets.* Under an application-centered organization, the application engineering team is mandated to commission the development of reusable assets; these may be commissioned for the purposes of a specific project, with the understanding that they have long-term reuse potential.

- *Reengineering for Reuse.* As byproducts of development projects, the application engineering team may take components developed for a specific application and select them for reuse. They are selected on the basis of their (perceived) reuse potential; before they are integrated into the reuse library, they need to be reengineered to meet the reusability standards of the library.

Under a domain-centric organization, only the domain engineering team decides which assets to produce; hence the application engineering team tasks do not include *specifying reusable assets*. Also, under this organization, the domain engineering team is (in principle) the sole provider of reusable assets; hence the application engineering team tasks do not include *reengineering for reuse*. Under a domain-centric organization, the application engineering team focuses on *development with reuse*.

1.3.4 Corporate Oversight

The role of the *corporate oversight* function is to oversee the deployment of the reuse initiative; this includes planning and executing the reuse initiative, budgeting costs, monitoring costs and benefits, and facilitating coordination between the stakeholders. An important role of the corporate oversight function is also to arbitrate between the domain engineering and the application engineering teams. In domain-centered organizations, the domain engineering team may drift away from the immediate needs of the application engineering team; in application-centered organizations, the domain engineering team may end up merely subcontracting development work (that has little potential for long-term reuse).

1.3.5 Exercises

1. (B) There are three ways to define the boundaries of a domain for the purposes of domain engineering:

- *Common Expertise.* This criterion identifies a field of domain expertise and attempts to cater to it through specialized development of software assets that span the range of applications of the expertise at hand. This criterion is producer-focused, and could be a natural criterion for a domain expert.

- *Common Design.* This criterion identifies a problem-solving pattern that is embodied in some generic software assets and attempts to cater to it through the development of generic assets that can be specialized for specific needs. This criterion is product-focused, and could be a natural criterion for a programming expert.

- *Common Market.* This criterion identifies a segment of the software market and attempts to cater to it through specialized development of software assets that cover the range of needs of the market; its rationale is to be a one-stop shop for the selected market segment. This criterion is consumer-focused, and could be a natural criterion for a (marketing) manager.

Each of these criteria can be justified by an economic rationale; it makes economic sense to invest resources to develop this domain, because of future gains in process productivity and product quality. Derive and compare the rationale for these three criteria.

2. (B) In reference to the three criteria that can be used to define the boundaries of a domain, consider the following domain definitions and tell which criteria apply to each (there may be more than one criterion for a given domain):

   (a) A family of queue simulation applications (see Appendix B).

   (b) A family of operations research programs.

   (c) A family of numerical analysis applications.

   (d) A family of compilers for different versions of a programming language.

   (e) A family of CPU (central processing unit) scheduling algorithms.

3. (B) In reference to the three criteria that can be used to define the boundaries of a domain, for each criterion, give an example of a domain that embodies the criterion. Illustrate the economic rationale of the criterion on the example.

4. (B) In reference to the phase of *development with reuse* under the application engineering function, consider the two development disciplines of top–down design and bottom–up design. Which is more consistent with software reuse? Why?

5. (B) There are two ways to avail oneself of the assets in a library of software components. In top–down design, we visit the library with specific requirements in hand, and search the library for assets that satisfy these requirements; this is called *retrieval*. In bottom–up design, we visit the library without any predefined concept of desirable functional properties

but with some general relevance guidelines that we may apply, such as application domain, computing platform, structural features, and problem-solving knowledge. Characterize the difference between browsing and retrieval. Is browsing an instance of retrieval, where the selection criterion is non-functional? Is it a form of retrieval where the emphasis is on recall rather than precision? Is it a form of retrieval where the emphasis is on application domain rather than functionality? Do we apply retrieval when we are familiar with a library and browsing when we are not?

1.4 SOFTWARE REUSE PARADIGMS

The processes we have discussed in the previous section can be applied within a variety of paradigms, which we review in this section. We will discuss in turn paradigms for software retrieval, software adaptation, and software composition.

1.4.1 Paradigms for Software Retrieval

It is possible to distinguish between two paradigms for using a software library: *browsing* and *retrieval*. These can be contrasted as follows:

- *Browsing* consists of navigating the software library to acquaint oneself with its holdings. Browsing is performed before product design, at a time when designers have no precise definition of what they need—but do have some idea of what kinds of assets may be useful.
- *Retrieval* consists of navigating the library to find assets that satisfy (in a sense to be defined) prespecified requirements. Retrieval is performed after product design, when the designer has clearly specified requirements to fulfill. Retrieval methods can, in turn, be divided into two classes: methods of *exact* retrieval, whereby we seek to identify library assets that precisely fulfill our requirements; methods of *approximate* retrieval, whereby we seek to identify assets that almost fulfill all the requirements, or fulfill almost all of the requirements. Inherent in methods of approximate retrieval is the idea that we wish to minimize postretrieval adaptation effort. In some cases, approximate retrieval is performed as a compromise once it is determined that exact retrieval fails. In other cases, approximate retrieval is performed systematically, on the assumption that any asset that satisfies the criteria of exact retrieval will prove to optimize the criteria of approximate retrieval.

1.4.2 Paradigms for Software Adaptation

It is common to recognize two distinct patterns of software reuse, which differ mostly by their adaptation step. We review them in turn below:

- *Blackbox* reuse, whereby retrieved assets are integrated into host systems *verbatim*, without modification. Blackbox reuse does not require that the user know about the design or implementation details of the asset—only its function and its invocation protocols. We consider as *blackbox* reuse instances where the user must set some parameters as part of the invocation protocols.

- *Whitebox* reuse, whereby retrieved assets are analyzed and modified before being integrated into a host system, because they do not necessarily satisfy the requirements of the host system. Whitebox reuse does require that the user analyze and understand the implementation details of the asset; this understanding effort is commensurate with the impact of the modification. In order to distinguish between the changes made under blackbox reuse (such as setting parameters, options) and those made under whitebox reuse (modifying source code), we mandate that all the changes for which the asset designer has planned and made provisions for at design time fall under blackbox reuse.

We refer to the component adaptation activity performed under blackbox reuse as *instantiation*; under whitebox reuse, as *modification*. Issues in component adaptation are discussed in Chapter 17.

One can justifiably argue that whitebox reuse is not a viable reuse alternative, and must be avoided at all costs. The rationale for such a case is that asset modification, which arises in whitebox software reuse, poses a serious challenge to the key rationale of software reuse, by posing a threat of losing program quality and programmer productivity.

- *Loss of Productivity.* In order to modify a component with any degree of reliability, one must first read it, analyze it, and understand it thoroughly. This is known to be a time-consuming and potentially frustrating process, which must be justified against the alternative of merely deriving a new component from scratch. It is not difficult to imagine situations where it is easier to write a component from scratch than to try to adapt a similar component. As a (pathological) example, imagine trying to derive a quicksort program by modifying an insertion sort program—and this is a case when the two programs compute the same function.

- *Loss of Quality.* All the effort one may have invested in verifying a component is lost the minute a modification, any modification, is done on the program. Regression testing techniques and structural testing techniques do enable us to take advantage of previous testing efforts to reduce the amount of testing that is required, but their potential is limited.

Generally speaking, blackbox reuse occurs less often but produces greater benefits, whereas whitebox reuse occurs more often but has smaller benefit margins.

1.4.3 Paradigms for Software Composition

It is possible to distinguish between two paradigms of reuse-based software development, depending on the nature of the reusable software assets:

- *Compositional Development.* Compositional development is applicable whenever the reusable assets are finished software products in compilable/executable form, and consists in composing these assets to produce larger software systems. As an example, we consider a reuse library that contains a set of database operations, including operations to perform the storage, modification, retrieval, and deletion of entries, as well as operations to reindex, sort, or back up the database. An instance of *compositional development* would consist of building an application by defining a sequence of menus that invoke these functions according to user selections.

- *Generative Development.* Generative development is applicable whenever the reusable assets are represented *intensively* in terms of instanciable *patterns* rather than as finished products. Generative development consists then of instantiating the pattern that embodies the reusable asset by providing specification-level parameters; a *generator* uses those specification-level parameters to generate a usage specific instance of the pattern, possibly leaving stubs to be filled out by hand in an application-specific way.

It is possible to characterize generative development as a more advanced evolutionary stage of reuse; it is possible in fairly stable (and typically, narrow) application domains that are so well understood that their variations have been embodied in a handful of specification-level parameters. Of course, a generator will occasionally stub out some application-specific function(s), to be filled out by hand, but the overall structure of applications within its scope is automatically generated. It is possible to contrast generative development versus compositional development by observing that generative development reuses the upper layers of the design structure, occasionally leaving some of the lower-level components to be filled out by hand, whereas compositional development reuses the lower layers of the design structure, leaving the glue code to the developer. We discuss application generators briefly in Section 7.2.

1.4.4 Exercises

1. (A) We have encountered two properties that enhance the reusability of a software asset: *generality* and *genericity*.
   (a) Define and contrast these two concepts.
   (b) One of these is a feature of the asset's specification; the other is a feature of the asset's design. Map them accordingly.

(c) One of these is a semantic property of the asset; the other is a syntactic property. Map them accordingly.

(d) One of these affects the software retrieval phase; the other affects the software adaptation phase. Map them accordingly.

(e) How can a programming language support genericity? How can a specification language support generality? (Or, can it?)

2. (B) We have encountered two paradigms for software adaptation: *instantiation* (in blackbox reuse) and *modification* (in whitebox reuse). Compare these options with respect to the following criteria:

(a) Productivity gains

(b) Quality gains

(c) Development schedule gains

(d) Likelihood of occurrence (which is dependent on the likelihood of a match under blackbox and under whitebox reuse).

3. (A) We consider a library of Ada functions, to which we submit a query for a function that adds the elements of an integer array. We retrieve an Ada function that takes three parameters: an array, a binary operation, and an integer value. If the integer value is the neutral element of the binary operation, this function returns the result of applying the binary operation to all the elements of the array. We take this function, and provide it with operation + and value 0 for the second and third argument. Is this an instance of blackbox reuse or whitebox reuse.

4. (A) We consider a library of Pascal functions, to which we submit a query for a function that adds the elements of an integer array. We retrieve a Pascal function that computes the product of all the elements of the array, which we modify by replacing the initialization by 0 and the product by +. Is this an instance of blackbox reuse or whitebox reuse?

1.5 FURTHER READING

Software reuse was first envisioned by McIlroy [1969] (all references cited in text are listed in the Bibliography at the end of the book) in 1968 as a manufacturing-like process of production and consumption of off-the-shelf software components. The view of reusable products has since evolved to include nowadays a number of other assets [Deutsch 1989, Freeman 1987, Prieto-Diaz 1993]. Different researchers use different criteria to categorize reusable knowledge, but by and large, most classifications rely on one of three factors, or a combination thereof: (1) stage of development at which the asset is produced and used, (2) the level of abstraction of the asset, and (3) the nature of the asset (concrete artifact vs. skills vs. abstract knowledge). Capers Jones [1984] identifies four types of reusable artifacts: (1) data, involving standardization of data formats; (2) architectures, which describe standard design and programming conventions; (3) detailed designs, which are generic patterns for common business applications; and (4) programs, which are executable source code units. Horowitz and Munson [1984] consider several kinds of reuse processes that are based on the use of high-level program generation systems. It is possible to identify three general classes of reusable assets:

- *Reusable program patterns* [Biggerstaff and Richter 1987, Horowitz and Munson 1984], where code or design patterns are used to instantiate specific code fragments; a typical example is illustrated by the programming clichés and design clichés of the Programmer's (and Design) Apprentice project at MIT [Rich and Schrobe 1976, 1978; Rich and Waters 1988, 1990; Waters 1981, 1982].
- *Reusable processors* [Horowitz and Munson 1984], which are interpreters for executable formal specifications.
- *Transformation systems* [Baxter 1992, Biggerstaff and Richter 1987, Horowitz and Munson 1984, Mostow and Barley 1987, Partsch and Steinbruggen 1983], which embody programming and software development knowledge in transformation systems.

Krueger [1992] proposes a multilevel classification of reusable assets based on levels of abstraction, and uses this classification to account for a wide variety of reusable assets and reuse paradigms. Prieto-Diaz [1993] classifies reusable assets into six families: source code, designs, specifications, objects, text and architectures. With minor modification, this is the classification we have presented in this chapter.

The breakdown of applications into *generic* components, *domain-specific* components, and *application-specific* code is due to Poulin [1997]. The distinction between *horizontal* libraries *vertical* libraries is due to Prieto-Diaz [1993]. The definition of organizational structures for software reuse is due to Basili et al. [1992], and Caldiera and Basili [1991]. The distinction between blackbox reuse and whitebox reuse is widely acknowledged [Poulin 1997, Prieto-Diaz 1993].

Chapter 2

State of the Art and the Practice

The purpose of this chapter is to present the state of the art and the state of the practice in software reuse, as well as to sketch future prospects of this discipline. We will review three aspects of this discipline in turn, namely: software reuse management, software reuse techniques, and software reuse initiatives.

2.1 SOFTWARE REUSE MANAGEMENT

As with many areas of software engineering, managerial aspects play a crucial role in software reuse. It is a matter of common knowledge that software reuse cannot happen without strong commitment from the managerial structure of the organization. In this section, we investigate in turn the state of the art and the state of the practice in managerial aspects of software reuse, then we discuss some outstanding issues therein.

2.1.1 State of the Art

In order to present the state of the art in software reuse management, we discuss in this section an integrated reuse management discipline that epitomizes the state of the art in the field: it is the reuse based on object-oriented techniques (REBOOT) approach, which stems from a 4-year (1990–1994) European research project. The REBOOT methodology recognizes that despite its promises (in terms of gains in product quality, programmer productivity, and time to market), the technology of software reuse has not delivered in practice. Also, this methodology recognizes that this poor performance can be traced back to the following observations about reuse practice:

- An emphasis on technical aspects, at the expense of managerial and organizational aspects
- An emphasis on sophisticated technical solutions which, for all their technical merit, can be deployed only at the expense of disruptive adjustments in the organization's operational procedures

To avoid the pitfalls of traditional software reuse solutions, the REBOOT methodology emphasizes technology consolidation rather than innovation, and integrates technical and managerial aspects.

To streamline *reuse introduction*, the REBOOT methodology defines a set of activities, along with associated roles to carry out the activities, and models to provide frameworks for these activities. These are summarized in Figure 2.1. The managerial discipline of REBOOT recognizes five issues that must be addressed when we introduce and operate a software reuse program: *reuse organizations*, which deals with the distribution of responsibilities between the various agents in an organization that practices reuse; *project management*, which deals with how development projects are managed to accommodate, and benefit from, software reuse; *development for and with reuse*, which deals with managerial guidelines for developing reusable assets, and for developing software products using reusable assets; *library organization*, which deals with the classification, storage, and retrieval of reusable assets; and *metrics*, which

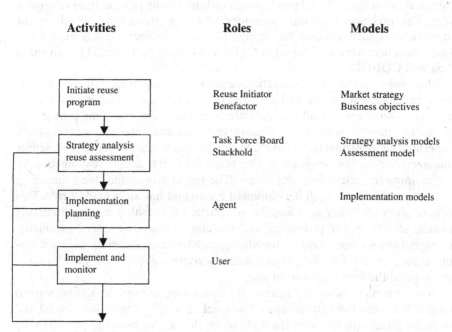

Activities	Roles	Models
Initiate reuse program	Reuse Initiator Benefactor	Market strategy Business objectives
Strategy analysis reuse assessment	Task Force Board Stackhold	Strategy analysis models Assessment model
Implementation planning	Agent	Implementation models
Implement and monitor	User	

FIGURE 2.1   REBOOT's reuse introduction process.

deals with quantifying, monitoring, and controlling process features and product features.

A key managerial issue in the REBOOT discipline is *reuse organization*: how to divide labor, define responsibilities, define reporting structures, and set up reward structures, among all the agents who make reuse happen in an organization. REBOOT distinguishes between three types of reuse organizations: *project-centered* organizations, where reusable assets are generated as byproducts of development projects; *production-centered* organizations, where a dedicated team produces reusable assets for the benefit of development projects; and *domain-centered* organizations, where teams of domain experts develop domain-specific reusable assets for the benefit of the domain.

Overall, REBOOT recognizes that software reuse introduction is a painstaking, long-term process that involves important investments and a long investment cycle. Hence software reuse cannot happen without the long-term dedication and support of the organization's management.

2.1.2 State of the Practice

To illustrate the state of the practice in software reuse management, we consider a 4-year project conducted at Nippon Telegraph and Telephone Corporation (NTT). This project focuses on managerial aspects of software reuse, and illustrates the premise that software reuse is inherently a managerial issue. This project involves 100 NTT engineers and 500 staff members from contracting companies, and produces an estimated one million lines of code a year. The products that were developed by this project are development support tools, such as compilers, design tools, and project management tools. These products were developed in C and SYSL (a dialect of PL/1), with some Ada and COBOL.

The project adopted a production-centered organization, with seven software development groups and a reuse group. The reuse group is made up of a *reuse support group* and a *reusability committee*. The reuse support group produces reusable assets and monitors, validates, and catalogs assets that are generated as byproducts of development projects. Also, it reports to senior management on the progress of the reuse initiative and is responsible for maintaining the reusable assets library. The reusability committee is made up of one member from each development group and has an oversight role. This role consists of: defining validation standards for reusable assets; discussing reward structures for producing and consuming reusable assets; producing reuse guidelines, operational procedures, and manuals; defining and monitoring reuse targets for the project; and coordinating between development groups and the reuse support group.

After the first year, the reusability committee started to define annual targets for *reuse ratio* (to measure the level of usage of reusable assets) and *deposition ratio* (to measure the level of production of reusable assets). Also, the committee defines reward structures to encourage the production and use of reusable assets. Both the reuse ratio and the average size of reusable asset increased from year to year, to reach the values of 16% (reuse ratio) and 600 lines of code (size of reusable asset) in the fourth year; the reuse ratio fell short of the management's expectation and of the goal set by the reusability committee—which was 20%.

The *average usage frequency* of the library (defined as the ratio of the yearly sum of reuse frequencies to the number of modules stored in the library) reached the value of 0.28 in the fourth year, and the size of the library at the end of the 4-year period was 800 assets. Of course, the 800 assets are not equally likely to be referenced (the 20/80 rule). The *active module ratio*, defined as the ratio of assets that were referenced at least once in a year over the total size of the library, stayed constant throughout the four year period at about 0.2. From a managerial point of view, this may suggest that one must be very careful with defining incentive mechanisms for producing reusable assets. If the incentive is too strong or the deposition target is too high, asset producers may be compelled to submit assets that do not really qualify, yet will end up filling the library with useless assets.

Another interesting outcome of the NTT experiment pertains to the size of reusable modules. The study finds that average-size modules (between 300 and 2000 lines) account for the greatest share of reused code, because frequently used modules are usually very small and large modules are seldom used. Also, the experiment highlights the pitfalls of ad hoc asset gathering and advocates instead a systematic, carefully planned domain engineering effort. In order to be successful, a domain engineering effort must meet the following criteria: be relatively small, be well understood, pertain to a static technology, and have extensive development plans.

Finally, the NTT experiment highlights the paradox of software reuse management, which is illustrated in Figure 2.2. It is hard to achieve gains in software reuse without considerable investment in time and labor; it is difficult to justify spending large amounts of time and labor without short-term tangible gains. In summary, one can draw the following conclusions regarding software reuse management:

- In order to maximize reuse ratio, a software reuse program must focus on a narrow application domain, that has considerable commonality.
- In order to amortize investment costs, a reuse program must involve a large volume of software development.
- In order to account for the time required to introduce reuse-specific procedures and to populate the reuse library, a reuse program must be planned over a long period of time.
- In order to maintain an acceptable active module ratio, a reuse program must exercise caution when defining producer incentives, and must apply strict quality criteria for including assets in the library. Another means to ensure the uniformity of quality standards in the library and to maintain

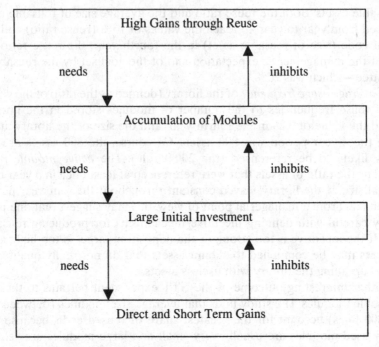

FIGURE 2.2   The paradox of software reuse management.

a good active module ratio is to focus on domain engineering rather than ad hoc gathering.

- In order to maintain adequate control of the costs, benefits, and trends associated with the reuse initiative, it is important to have an appropriately defined metrics program.
- In order to ensure that the reuse initiative is given the time and resources needed to mature and start producing results, senior management commitment is required.

2.1.3 Perspectives

There is little doubt that managerial issues are critical to the success of a software reuse initiative. What is needed in the future are analytical and practical investigations of the following managerial issues:

- An assessment of the various team organizations in software reuse, and their impact on productivity and quality. It is quite likely that an optimal team organization depends a great deal on many factors, such as the size of the corporation, the width of the target application domain, the expected volume of software development activity, the objective function (quality, productivity, time to market), and the application domain (information systems, systems programming, command and control)—so that no single team organization emerges as the universal choice.

- An investigation of metrics that allow software reuse managers to monitor the progress of the software reuse initiative. Typical metrics include, for example, the reuse ratio and the deposition ratio; issues include the derivation of target values for these metrics, and means to achieve these targets.

- An investigation of cost models that quantify the costs and benefits of software reuse, as well as an investigation of the controllable factors that allow a manager to control costs and benefits.

2.1.4 Exercises

1. (B) Consider the SEL (Software Engineering Laboratory) experiment reported by Caldiera and Basili [1991]. Analyze and compare it to the experiment of NTT presented above.

2. (B) Consider the IBM experiment reported by Poulin [1997]. Analyze and compare it to the experiment of NTT presented above.

3. (B) Consider the Hewlett-Packard experiment reported in Lim [1994]. Analyze and compare it to the experiment of NTT presented above.

2.2 SOFTWARE REUSE TECHNIQUES

In this section we focus on technical aspects of software reuse. Technical issues can be divided into two broad classes: *application engineering*, which involves developing with reuse; and *domain engineering*, which involves developing for reuse.

2.2.1 State of the Art

Research on software reuse techniques focuses on the specification, the validation, the design, the implementation, the certification, the classification and retrieval, and the composition of reusable software assets—most typically executable assets. Domain engineering deals with the first six steps (specification, validation, design, implementation, certification, classification), and application engineering deals with the last two (retrieval, composition). We review these eight steps in turn, and discuss the current state of the art pertaining thereto, in light of the most recent research; for more concrete and more detailed information on the state of the art, consult the bibliographic references cited in Section 2.4, or in the "Further Reading" sections in the relevant chapters of this book.

Specification. The specification of (functional) requirements of a software product has been an active area of research for a very long time (since the late 1960s) for a variety of reasons. Requirements specification is a difficult problem (hence it is difficult to find general solutions thereof); it is crucial to the success of software development projects (hence it remains at the forefront of technical concerns), and it poses interesting technical challenges (hence it excites the interest of researchers). The specification of reusable assets is, if anything, even more challenging, for at least three reasons:

- *Defining the Product and the Specification Concurrently.* In traditional requirements specification, the product to be specified is (at least supposedly) well known and well understood; by contrast, in domain engineering the definition of the reusable asset and its specification take place concurrently, and may conceivably influence each other. Studies of software reuse economics find that the cost of producing a reusable asset from a product definition is 20% higher than the cost of producing the same asset for single use, and that the cost of producing a reusable asset including domain engineering costs is 100% higher than the cost of producing the same asset for single use. The 80% differential accounts for the cost of product definition.

- *The Stakes of a Reusable Asset Are Bigger.* Because a reusable asset is expected to be reused in several applications, the stakes involved in its quality are much greater than those of an asset that is produced for single use. Because the quality of a software asset begins with the quality of its specification, this places a special emphasis on the need for quality specifications.

- *Requirement for Generality.* One of the most important requirements of a reusable asset is *generality*: the more general the asset, the wider its range of applications, hence its reuse potential. Finding the right concepts, that are sufficiently general to be widely used, and represent a sufficiently large development effort that their use improves productivity, is an important challenge of domain engineering.

Validation. Validation consists of ensuring that the product definition does represent a recurrent concept in the application domain, and that the specification does reflect the selected definition.

Design. One of the main challenges of reusable asset design is to provide *genericity*: the ability to specialize a general asset into any one of its many possible instances, in a quality-preserving and cost-effective manner. Whereas generality (discussed above, under asset specification) deals with the definition of the product, and advocates that its function be as general as possible so as to enhance the reusability potential, genericity deals with the representation of the product's design, and advocates that it be easily instantiated to specific contexts. In other words, generality is a semantic property while genericity is a syntactic property; an alternative view is that generality is a property of the specification while genericity is a property of the design (hence, a fortiori, the implementation). The most typical way to provide genericity relies on the mechanism of *parameterization*, namely, the ability to represent the asset in such a way that all its intended instantiations are achieved by setting predefined parameters. Current work attempts to achieve parameterization by borrowing ideas from *parameterized programming*, and elaborating on them by taking advantage of the premise that design languages do not have to be executable. Chapter 11 is dedicated to abstraction and parameterization techniques in object-oriented analysis and programming.

Implementation. The implementation of reusable assets differs from traditional single use implementation in that a special emphasis is placed on product quality, and that the tradeoff between quality and cost is typically decided in favor of quality. Other implementation issues include the emphasis on principles of modularity (information hiding, low coupling) as well as the preservation of genericity. The reader will find in Chapters 11 and 12 an arsenal of component-level techniques for building parameterization and composability into reusable components.

Certification. In the context of domain engineering, component certification includes not only functional certification (i.e., correctness with respect to the asset specification), but also adherence to the quality standards that are in effect for the asset library at hand; Chapter 16 gives a synthesis of some of these quality standards. Also, as with implementation, the tradeoffs of quality versus cost are resolved in favor of quality, because the stakes of good quality are higher for a reusable asset than for an asset developed for single use. Current work in this area attempts to define quality criteria, as well as methods to ensure that these criteria are met.

Classification. This issue consists in indexing and classifying a reusable asset once we have determined that it meets the quality criteria of our library. *Indexing* consists in deriving the characteristic features of a given asset for the purpose of future reference; *classification* consists in determining how to store the asset so that future relevant references can address it (and irrelevant references do not address it). This matter has received widespread attention in software reuse research, to the point where it was equated with software reuse; more recently, there has been an increasing recognition that classification is not the bottleneck of software reuse technology—hence research needs to focus on other aspects for the time being.

Retrieval. Classification and retrieval go hand in hand, of course, since they influence each other to a large extent. Hence much of what we said about the classification of reusable assets applies to asset retrieval. Current research trends stress *blackbox reuse* over *whitebox reuse*. These trends stem from the observation that code modification (implied in whitebox reuse) is both costly (hence defeats the gains in productivity) and error-prone (hence defeats the gains in quality that are associated with software reuse). To maintain the benefits of software reuse in terms of productivity and quality without sacrificing the ability to adapt retrieved components to specific usage contexts, current research trends advocate the production of general, generic reusable assets. The difference between instantiating a generic reusable asset and modifying the source code of an asset is that the former is provided by the very design of the asset, and is done under the warranty of the product, while the latter is done under the responsibility of the reuser who may or may not understand all the details of the asset's design.

- An important issue to understand about the retrieval of reusable software assets is that a reusable asset may abstract either a *structure* or a *function*; consequently, the retrieval query may either be *find an asset that has this structure* or *find an asset that has this function*. An example of a structural abstraction is a pattern for array reduction, which, given an array and a binary operation, will return the result of applying the operation to all the elements of the array; such an asset is parameterized by the binary operation and the neutral element. Instances of this asset include a routine to return the sum, the product, the maximum element, or the minimum element of the array. All the instances of this abstraction have the same structure, but have widely varying functions. An example of functional abstraction is a sorting routine, which is parameterized by the size of the array, the structure of array records, the key on which the ordering is defined, and the direction of the order (increasing, decreasing). The essence of this asset is its function, which is used to index it (identify it); whether it sorts the array by quick sort or insertion sort makes no difference.

- Another issue to consider is the contrast between *retrieval* and *browsing*. Retrieval consists in submitting a predefined query (whether functional or structural); browsing consists in navigating the library to inspect its contents. Current research trends advocate that browsing is the predominant pattern of library search, because a designer does not design an application *then* formulate and submit queries to the library; rather, the designer consults the library to see what is available and then designs the application in such a way as to take the best advantage of current library holdings. This is not unlike the role of programming languages in software design. A programmer does not design a program and *then* worries about how to articulate the design in the selected language; rather, the programmer gets acquainted with the language then designs the program in such a way as to take the best advantage of the language's features.

Composition. The discipline of asset composition draws on three areas of software engineering research: software architecture, software generators, and programming languages. In some narrow application domains, for some restricted families of problems, it is possible in today's technology to automate the production of software applications from specifications. Chapter 12 describes a set of programming and design techniques for building object-oriented software components that are composable by design and/or construction.

2.2.2 State of the Practice

We review the eight steps we have discussed in the previous section and discuss the state of the practice as it pertains to these steps.

- *Specification.* There are two aspects to the specification of reusable assets in a particular application domain: the *definition* of product requirements, and the *specification* of the requirements once they have been defined. The latter step does not differ significantly from traditional requirements specifications; many organizations are sufficiently mature nowadays to practice requirements specifications at an advanced level, on nontrivial examples, using formal specification notations and automated tools for specification vallidation. As far as defining product requirements, many organizations nowadays recognize the crucial role of *domain analysis* in their reuse initiative, and invest significant amounts of time and resources into this task.
- *Validation.* The validation task is a mere extension of the specification task; it is applied equally widely in industry.
- *Design and Implementation.* Principles of modular programming (information hiding, separation of specification from implementation, provisions for low coupling, concern for weak context requirements, etc.) are practiced fairly widely in industry. Advances in programming language design and programming discipline provide incentives to observe these principles as well as (limited) means to enforce them. Chapters 11–14 reflect the state of the practice in terms of programming language constructs, design patterns, and integration frameworks.
- *Certification.* The definition and enforcement of certification standards for inclusion in reuse libraries is standard practice in industry, although the rigor and the nature of the certification criteria vary somewhat. Typical criteria include correctness, reliability, as well as some quality features.
- *Classification and Retrieval.* There is a wide gap between the state of the art and the state of the practice in asset classification and retrieval. While research prototypes provide sophisticated solutions to enhance the precision and recall of queries, most practical reuse initiative shun these solutions in favor of low-key library science inspired solutions. Library science relies on information retrieval technology, which, for all its inad-

equacies with respect to software assets (as opposed to books), is an
established technology with reliable support tools. Two more observations explain this gap between state of the art and state of the practice:
(1) the distinction between retrieval and browsing, and the premise that
the most prevalent paradigm in practice is browsing (for which precision
and recall are not relevant); (2) the observation that classification and
retrieval is not the bottleneck of software reuse, and hence has little
impact with respect to the success or failure of a reuse project in
practice.

- *Composition.* There are practical reuse initiatives nowadays where applications are developed nearly automatically from formal specifications,
  using existing reusable assets. These initiatives can be characterized by
  some common features: a narrow application domain; an exhaustive
  domain analysis, resulting in an extensive domain library; an automated
  software composition/generation capability; and sophisticated classification and retrieval mechanisms. Without these conditions, it is still
  possible to develop applications by composing reusable assets, but much
  of the work is done by hand; many current initiatives proceed under these
  conditions, but all rely on good domain analysis.

2.2.3 Perspectives

Among the issues that appear to merit the attention of researchers in the
future, we mention the following:

- *Domain Engineering.* Domain engineering appears to be the predominant technical issue in software reuse, as it is the key to successful deployment of software reuse initiatives. It is difficult to imagine generic
  research issues on domain engineering; the best way to make progress, it
  seems, is to practice domain analysis on new application domains and to
  attempt to synthesize general principles pertaining thereto.
- *Reusability Packaging Techniques.* Under this category, we group language design research as well as research into module interconnection
  languages and integration infrastructures, in general. Some of the work
  described in Chapters 11–14 is still work in progress, both in terms of
  research ideas, and in terms of tool or language support.
- *Reusability Assessment and Certification.* It is not uncommon to observe
  that reuse libraries have a fairly low ratio of active assets (e.g., percentage of assets retrieved in a given year). This can be traced, at least in part,
  to a technical problem. In the absence of clearly defined criteria of when
  an asset is reuse worthy, it is tempting to include an asset whenever we
  have doubt about its reuse worthiness; this results in a situation where
  the library is cluttered with assets that have little reuse potential but drive
  the effectiveness and the efficiency of the library. A possible remedy to

this situation is the definition of quantitative metrics that reflect the reuse worthiness of an asset, as well as means to assess these metrics cost effectively.

- *Browsing and Retrieval.* Much of the past research into software reuse libraries focused on *retrieval* as the prevailing form of a query. The library user submits queries of the form *find an asset that has this function* or, sometimes, *find an asset that has this structure.* In the context of bottom–up programming, the user has no preconceived idea on what function or what structure is needed; rather, the user wishes to get acquainted with the contents of the library prior to designing a solution, precisely because the contents of the library is expected to influence the solution. Under these conditions, the prevailing forms of a query are: to find all the assets that (1) pertain to this application domain (for vertical reuse) or find all the assets that (2) operate on this platform or virtual machine (for horizontal reuse). This has an impact on the organization of asset libraries; new organizations and new navigation and/or retrieval mechanisms must be explored.

2.2.4 Exercises

1. (C) Consider the four patterns of library queries:
   (a) Find all the assets that have this function.
   (b) Find all the assets that have this structure.
   (c) Find all the assets that have this application domain.
   (d) Find all the assets that run on this platform.

For each pattern, derive an efficient library organization; for each organization, assess how the other patterns of queries are performed.

2.3 SOFTWARE REUSE INITIATIVES

2.3.1 Software Reuse Libraries

2.3.1.1 Comprehensive Approach to Reusable Defense Software (CARDS)
The Comprehensive Approach to Reusable Defense Software (CARDS) is a U.S. Air Force–National Aeronautics and Space Administration (NASA) program that is dedicated to further pursue the U.S. Department of Defense (DoD) objectives of achieving widespread institution of systematic software reuse. The main mission of the CARDS program is to design operational reusable software libraries that support multiple domains and serve as a model for the construction of other domain specific reuse libraries that can be integrated to the CARDS library system. CARDS includes a set of domain-specific libraries such as the reuse library framework (RLF), which is developed by the Software Technology for Adaptable and Reliable Systems

(STARS) program. It also hosts other operational libraries such as the Command Center Library (CCL) and the Portable Reusable Integrated Software Modules (PRISM) Distributed Library (PDL).

In addition to the set of domain specific libraries, the CARDS library system contains various library maintenance and browsing tools supported with an end-user Web-based interface. The web-based interface offers access to CARDS libraries, documentation, and information on CARDS reuse programs. CARDS main function is to maintain general library operations and is not specific to particular domains. Because it is a model-based reuse library, CARDS has encoded models that facilitate tailoring of the library software and introducing new domain-specific libraries into the system.

The CARDS program focuses on the transition of advances in the techniques and technologies of domain-specific software reuse into mainstream software acquisition. The approach that CARDS takes is to develop and operate a set of domain-specific libraries and the necessary tools to operate these libraries. It draws on technologies derived from the field of knowledge-based representation and relies on a model-based formal approach to reuse libraries that is believed to be richer than lower-level data modeling of the information stored in the libraries.

Building on the results drawn from the CARDS program, several domain-specific reuse programs have been initiated. For instance, the National Product Line Asset Center (NPLACE) was initiated. NPLACE is managed by the West Virginia High Technology Consortium Foundation (WVHTCF) and sponsored by the Air Force Electronic Systems Center (ESC). The establishment and operation of NPLACE is a direct support for product line engineering, it builds on and extends the work done in this area by the CARDS and PRISM programs. A product-line engineering (PLE) process produces a product-line infrastructure that includes a generic software architecture and a collection of reusable off-the-shelf components. NPLACE envisions that COTS software will help reduce development lifecycle through reuse of architectures and components, reduce development costs, and improve quality and reliability through application of trusted components. NPLACE focuses on testing off-the-shelf software and presenting decisionmaking information in an interactive Web-based repository. This specific program is concerned with using COTS components in the PLE context.

2.3.1.2 Defense Software Repository System (DSRS)

The Defense Software Repository System (DSRS) is a software reuse library initiative dedicated to developing a network of software reuse support centers (SRSCs); each is a library of defense reusable assets. DSRS provides an automated distributed library that supports storage and retrieval. DSRS has a central site at the Defense Information Systems Agency (DISA) and several other remote sites that include the Army Reuse Center (ARC), Air Force DSRS, Defense Logistics Agency, Marine Corps Software Reuse Branch,

Navy Software Reuse Support Center, and the National Security Agency DSRS.

DSRS is the responsibility of DISA/Joint Interoperability and Engineering Organization for Information Management Software Reuse Program, which is concerned with promoting software reuse within the U.S. DoD information management systems. The DSRS is a library approach to promote reuse that offers users the capability of searching for reusable assets that can decrease development time. The distributed library supports assets of various nature including requirements, specifications, architectures, designs, source code, documentation, and test suites. DSRS was initially introduced to support Ada software assets then extended to support storage and retrieval of any reusable asset. DSRS holds commercial, defense, federal government, and public domain categories of reusable assets.

DSRS is a deployed, operational repository with multiple interoperable locations across several sites. Specifically, in November 1993, seven DSRS locations supported nearly 1000 users and listed nearly 9000 reusable assets. The main site listed 3880 reusable assets and had 400 user accounts. We expect that the number of users and the number of reusable assets have since grown enormously. DSRS is adaptable to additional types of reusable assets and approaches to describing them. The long-term objective of the DoD Software Reuse Initiative (SRI) is supporting a virtual repository where location of libraries and retrieval mechanisms are virtual to the end user. DSRS interconnected repositories provide the ability to locate and share reusable components across domains and among services.

2.3.1.3 Asset Source for Software Engineering Technology (ASSET)

The Defense Advanced Research Projects Agency (DARPA) has originally initiated the program of Asset Source for Software Engineering Technology (ASSET) as a subprogram of the STARS program. The purpose of the program is to provide an on-line repository for reusable software assets. Initially, the program was devoted to developing, operating, and maintaining assets and systems needed to operate the repository for the purpose of serving the STARS program.

In 1995, the Science Applications International Corporation (SAIC) turned the ASSET program into a commercial site on the World Wide Web. The major core capabilities and experience of ASSET are centered around software reuse and Web technology. The site provides a repository of free and commercial assets in digital libraries, database management, object-oriented systems development, software configuration management, distributed information systems, and Internet/Web-based systems. ASSET offers services and products in digital library support, electronic commerce, World Wide Web solutions, and software engineering, specifically reengineering and reuse technologies. These services are provided through a worldwide software resource discovery that contains over 1000 assets available to the public via the World

Wide Web. ASSET also supports reusable software asset brokerage service that provides access to commercial high-technology software and tools via electronic commerce. It also provides services in developing custom digital libraries and training and education services on software reuse.

2.3.1.4 Perspective

The U.S. DoD has invested intensively in developing the three main reuse libraries; Asset Source for Software Engineering Technology (ASSET), Comprehensive Approach to Reusable Defense Software (CARDS), and Defense Software Repository System (DSRS). The virtual interoperability of these libraries is another research subject that is under investigation. A prototype has been completed for an advanced library interoperability capability model. This prototype uses the Common Object Request Broker Architecture (CORBA), which has been developed and matured as a standard for distributed object-oriented computing. The objective of the interoperability prototype is to enhance existing interoperability services and to provide Internet access to library services provided by the three main DoD libraries.

The Reuse Library Interoperability Group (RLIG; also known as RIG) has expended much effort in building the interoperability system that has been in place among the three libraries since late 1993. The CORBA-based prototype builds upon the original prototype to allow users of any of the member libraries to browse through reusable assets (typically software components or documents) located at the other libraries, view descriptions of the assets, and retrieve the actual asset.

2.3.2 Software Reuse Methodologies

2.3.2.1 The DoD Software Reuse Initiative (SRI)

The DoD Software Reuse Initiative (SRI) responds to the DoD software reuse vision that calls for a technology-based investment strategy which identifies and communicates appropriate reuse processes and technologies. It is an alliance of several DoD reuse activities with main participation from three major software reuse programs: the Air Force's Central Archive for Reusable Defense Software (CARDS), DARPA's Software Technology for Adaptable Reliable Systems (STARS), and the Defense Information Systems Agency's (DISA) Software Reuse Program. SRI builds on these efforts through strategic planning, focusing activities, and achieving a common goal of systematic software reuse.

The SRI program envisions that the productivity gains promised from reuse can come only from a systematic approach that emphasizes the reuse of conceptual software assets throughout the whole development lifecycle (requirements, architectures, components, etc.) rather than opportunistic code reuse. The DoD SRI mission includes three major goals that address both complex and challenging technical and nontechnical issues: transitioning of reuse technology into the DoD mainstream practice, developing infrastructure support for reuse that reduces the cost and risk of adopting reuse, and promoting development paradigm shifts so that actions that increase effective software reuse are encouraged and institutionalized.

The SRI program introduces reuse processes into early development and maintenance activities. For instance, reusing specification and design and reverse engineering existing systems will produce great benefits throughout a development project, such as productivity and cost savings. The SRI approach is process-driven and aims at the integration of reuse as a disciplined systematic software engineering process. New technologies and tools are required to support the new activities introduced by adopting software reuse as a disciplined software engineering process. The SRI program envisions that domain-specific, architecture-centric, process-driven, and technology-supported approaches are essential to provide the infrastructure for systematic reuse.

The SRI program advocates a product-line approach to systematic software reuse using two key elements: domain engineering and application engineering. Domain engineering develops the infrastructure for building applications. Domain engineering processes includes domain analysis and modeling, architecture development, organization, and storage of reusable components and defining mechanisms used to develop products based on the domain architecture and elements. Application engineering develops the products and addresses the instantiation of reusable components and any domain infrastructure (including specifications, code, test, etc.) for the purpose of developing an individual product. SRI has an ultimate vision of fusing systematic reuse and software engineering to make reuse a mature engineering discipline through architectures and parameterized designs. The DoD SRI emphasized the selection of technologies for investment and the strategy for implementing the recommended research.

In summary, the SRI reuse strategy capitalizes on systematic reuse and envisions that the way to do this is to define processes to

- Identify domains where the greatest opportunities exist to apply systematic reuse.
- Identify the domain assets and the domain-specific architectures.
- Define the criteria for deciding the ownership of reusable assets.
- Integrate reuse into the overall system lifecycle.
- Develop and apply new business models that encourages organizations to practice reuse and define evaluation criteria for reuse success.
- Define and implement a technology transition plan to a reuse-based paradigm

2.3.2.2 Software Optimization and Reuse Technology (SORT)

The DoD has demonstrated its commitment to take advantage of reuse technologies through the Software Reuse Initiative (SRI) program. Along the same line, the National Aeronautics and Space Administration (NASA) has realized that in order to successfully utilize software reuse technology there must be a focused effort that is dedicated to the institutionalization of software reuse within the agency. The Software Optimization and Reuse Technology (SORT) program (1995–2000) is NASA's focused effort for achieving and applying software reuse technology to selected NASA centers. The SORT program assists multiple NASA technical centers to foster the development of reuse techniques and the adoption of systematic software reuse. The SORT Program was created in collaboration between the NASA's Ames Research Center and the West Virginia High Technology Consortium Foundation (WVHTCF). Other industrial partners include DN American and Lockheed Martin.

The SORT program is composed of two main complementary tasks:

1. *SORT Domain Engineering.* This task involves the evaluation of NASA's domains and the selection of domains in which there is a good potential for reuse efforts. The objective is to scope a selected set of domains of interest to guide the focus upon which resources will be expended. The program then focuses on applying reuse techniques to the selected domains to produce reusable assets. A domain engineering framework will be developed to identify these reusable assets. The SORT program takes a model-based, domain-specific approach to applying software reuse technology.

2. *SORT Technology Transfer.* This task investigates how to use information and lessons obtained from the domain engineering task to assist the adoption of reuse techniques within NASA's domains of interest. The objective is to communicate the domain engineering methodologies and technologies that were developed in the first task throughout NASA centers in order to foster reuse techniques that are applicable to NASA centers and to introduce a product-line strategy within the NASA agency.

2.3.2.3   Software Technology for Adaptable Reliable System (STARS)

The STARS program is sponsored by DARPA and is contracted through the Air Force Electronic Systems Center (ESC). The prime STARS program was initiated in 1988. The project involves three prime corporations; Boeing, Lockheed Martin Federal Systems (LMFS), and Lockheed Martin Tactical Defense Systems (LMTDS). The STARS program integrates modern software development processes and reuse concepts within a software engineering environment technology to increase software productivity, reliability, and quality. STARS focuses on accelerating a change in the way software is developed within the Department of Defense (DoD). This change represents a shift to reuse and product-line engineering technologies that is process-driven, domain-specific, and technology-supported.

The major objectives of the STARS program are

- Apply a reuse-based product-line approach to the development of DoD software systems.
- Develop quantitative and qualitative metrics for the development effort conducted in the product-line approach and the resulting product.
- Develop experience reports documenting the lessons learned in applying product-line approaches.
- Motivate organizations developing projects under the STARS program to utilize product-line technology and to continue using and applying the product-line approach to other projects.

The STARS project (1988–1995) developed more than 291 assets in the ASSET collection emphasizing that the future roadmap for software development should be architecture-based. Systems should be built using system composition techniques, domain-specific languages, components provided by service oriented suppliers, and a systematic product-line approach. Systems should evolve seamlessly from prototyping through product lifecycle.

Three demonstration projects have been developed to apply the STARS research results: the Air Force Command and Control Infrastructure, the Navy Flight Instrument Trainer, and the Army Guardrail Common Sensor 4 (GRCS4). The successful completion of these projects demonstrates the feasibility of large-scale reuse and product-line engineering approaches to the development of software systems.

To address existing shortcomings identified by the STARS research program, the Air Force Materiel Command's (AFMC) Space and Warning Systems Center (SWSC) undertook an initiative to create an architecture-based approach to achieve their desire to provide new capability to the warfighter more rapidly, efficiently, and cheaply. The AFMC recognizes the importance of disciplined software engineering development process that is reused-based. Stovepipe implementations preclude reuse and prevent resource sharing. The SWSC maintained in excess of 12 million lines of code on 34 separate operational systems written in 27 languages. In 1990, the SWSC initiated an effort to develop a strategy to move to a common reusable domain architecture. The SWSC achieved large-scale reuse by producing a set of architectural components called the *Command and Control Architecture Infrastructure* (C2AI), which promised to significantly reduce systems development time and cost while increasing quality. C2AI was implemented in a pilot program called the reusable integrated command center (RICC). The RICC technology yielded the first set of reusable artifacts supporting a new common architectural approach including domain reusable components.

Being able to achieve large-scale reuse through the C2AI, the Air Force and the STARS program agreed to launch another project, known as *space command and control architectural infrastructure* (SCAI), to prove the transition to product-line engineering. This project aims at accelerating the SWSC progress toward a product-line paradigm for producing and maintaining the systems in its domain, thus systematizing large-scale architecture-based reuse.

The technologies to be demonstrated were STARS product-line technology and RICC technology.

To accomplish these goals, the project combined architectural infrastructure innovations from the Air Force and SWSC and new product-line concepts from STARS. Following the success of the SCAI project, other SWSC programs transitioned to use the new technologies. The goal for building a real system was to develop a space mission capability and reusable domain assets (architecture, models, components, processes, etc.) that could be applied to future product-line applications.

2.3.2.4 FAST: Family-Oriented Abstraction, Specification, and Translation

FAST is a software development process focused on building families of software products. Originated by David Weiss at AT&T and applied at Lucent Technologies, the FAST methodology reported decrease in development time and cost for members of the family by 60–70% [Weiss and Lai 1999]. A central feature of FAST is planning and structuring for change by searching for abstraction mechanisms and applying them for the design and implementation of components. The schema for abstraction is developed by asking software engineers to define abstractions that are useful in defining the family and then translating these abstractions into a language for specifying and modeling family members. The language is further checked for completeness, consistencies and other properties and as a result engineers can build tools that generate the software for a family member using its description in these tools.

FAST also has a mechanism to track the production progress. The *process and artifact state transition abstraction* (PASTA) process description method is used in FAST to precisely describe the processes the engineers are using to develop a new family member or have used to develop other members. PASTA models the artifacts used in the production process, the activities performed during a process, the operations used to manipulate the artifacts, and the role played by people in the process. The PASTA process can also model concurrent and sequential activities.

FAST, including its process modeling technique PASTA, is a software reuse methodology that focuses on the production of several products in a family that constitutes a product line. The product line approach to software development is further discussed in Chapter 22. FAST is one product-line approach that enables organization to transit from software *development* to software *production* by organizing teams and following product family development processes.

2.3.2.5 Software Reuse Business

The reuse-driven software engineering business is a framework developed by Ivar Jacobson et al. [1997] to define a set of guidelines and models that help ensure success with large-scale object-oriented reuse. The framework is referred to as *reuse business*. It deals systematically with business, process, architecture, and organization issues in a product line. Reuse business processes are categorized under three main categories: (1) component system engineering, (2) application family engineering, and (3) application system engineering. Component system engineering is responsible for creating component systems. Each component system is a set of customizable configurable software components where a component is a type, class, or any work product that has been specially engineered to be reusable. Application family engineering creates the overall system architecture and identifies the component systems that will be used with the architecture to develop applications that belong to the same domain. Application system engineering is the process of creating a specific application that belongs to the domain by selecting, specializing, and assembling components from component systems. Reuse business does not have an explicit domain engineering process, but distributes the main domain engineering processes between application family engineering and component system engineering.

2.3.3 Software Reuse Standards

The Reuse Library Interoperability Group (RLIG) (sometimes abbreviated RIG) is a working group that focuses on the interoperability between reuse libraries. The purpose of RLIG is to propose and produce drafts for standards for interoperability between software reuse libraries. The group then submits these standards to be formally standardized by organizations such as IEEE. With the increasing number of reusable software libraries and assets, it becomes inconvenient to application developers and library users to maintain separate access procedures and account for each individual library. The user should be able to virtually access and retrieve assets irrespective of their location. Therefore, libraries should provide a method for interoperation with other libraries so that a user of any one library could obtain the services offered by other libraries. RLIG has the objective of proposing standards that facilitate reuse library interoperation.

Initially RLIG was founded in 1991 as a volunteer organization, and currently RLIG membership consists of over 20 organizations, agencies, reuse library programs, and institutions. The group started as a collaboration between the STARS program and the Air Force Reusable Ada Avionics Software Packages (RAASP) to achieve interoperability between these two libraries. In 1992, the ASSET and CARDS reuse libraries joined the interoperability program and in 1993 the DSRS joined the network.

RLIG developed a glossary for the reuse library terms and acronyms, and a basic interoperability data model (BIDM) for library interoperability. The proposed data model abstractly specifies the data that can be shared across multiple libraries. In 1994, the IEEE approved the first standardization project proposed by RLIG.

Among RLIG's technical reports that have been standardized by the IEEE are the IEEE P1430, *Guide for Information Technology: Software Reuse: Concept of Operations for Interoperating Reuse Libraries* and IEEE P1420.2,

Standard for Information Technology: Software Reuse: Data Model for Reuse Library Interoperability: Basic Interoperability Data Model (BIDM). RLIG has several technical committees working on standardization of reuse library interoperability issues. Additional standards under development by RLIG technical committees include data model extensibility, asset evaluation and certification, metrics, and interoperability protocols and architecture.

2.3.4 Exercises

1. (B) Compare the three reuse library initiatives (CARDS, ASSET, and DSRS) discussed in Section 2.3.1 with respect to the types of assets supported by the library, the retrieval and storage mechanism, support for distributed environment, technical approach to construct the library (information-based, model-based, etc.), and size of the library in terms of the number of assets and asset categories.

2. (B) Software reuse initiatives discussed in this section are categorized under software reuse libraries, methodologies, and standards. There are several other approaches to classify software reuse initiatives such as industrial versus governmental, component reuse versus process reuse, and so on. Illustrate with justification your perspective of organizing software reuse initiatives.

3. (A) Compare the software reuse methodologies discussed in Section 2.3.2. Base your comparison on each program's objective and goals, approach, scope (specific to an organization or general), product (or expected results), and source (government or industrial).

4. (D) Refer to the documentation of the STARS demonstration projects[1] and identify the lessons learned in the U.S. Army, Navy, and Air Force demonstration projects. Categorize the lessons learned under technical, management, and organization categories.

5. (B) Consider some industrial initiative to software reuse such as Hewlett-Packard initiative[2] and McClure research,[3] and compare to governmental initiatives such as SORT or STARS.

2.4 FURTHER READING

Further information on the REBOOT methodology is available in the literature [Faget and Morel 1993, Karlsson 1995, Sindre et al. 1995]. The NTT

[1] Software Technology for Adaptable, Reliable Systems (STARS) Web site: http://www.asset.com/stars/.
[2] Systematic Software Reuse and Component Based Software Engineering. Hewlett-Packard Laboratories Research Web site: http://www.hpl.hp.com/reuse/.
[3] Software Reuse Resource Center for Business, Extended Intelligence, Inc. Web site: http://www.reusability.com/home.html.

experiment reported in Section 2.1.2 is due to Isoda [1995]; other reports on the practice of software reuse management and its impact on productivity and quality, are also available [Caldiera and Basili 1991, Poulin 1997, Lim 1994]. Work on the state of the art and the state of the practice in the technical aspects of software reuse includes the RESOLVE project [Edwards 1993; Ernst et al. 1991, 1994; Harms and Weide 1991; Sitaraman 1992; Sitaraman 1994; Weide et al. 1994], the GenVoca project [Batory 1996; Batory and Geraci 1997; Batory et al. 1995, 1998; Jimenez-Perez and Batory 1997; Smaragdakis and Batory 1998], and the Amphion project [Lowry et al. 1994]. Provisions for critiquing and assessing component-based designs are available in the literature [Batory et al. 1995, 1998; Batory 1996; Batory and Geraci 1997; Jimenez-Perez and Batory 1997; Smaragdakis and Batory 1998; Reubenstein and Waters 1991; Rich and Schrobe 1976, 1978; Rich and Waters 1990; Waters 1981, 1982]. For information on parameterized programming, consult Goguen [1984, 1996]. For a fairly recent and reasonably exhaustive survey of methods of storage and retrieval of software assets, consult Mili et al. [1998] (see also Chapter 16). Nada [1998] has also given a survey of software reuse practice. An overview of software reuse perspectives can be found in the report by Zand and Samadzadeh [1998], which synthesizes the discussions of a recent panel session at the *Symposium on Software Reuse* [Harandi 1997].

For more information on the CARDS library concepts and development, see the reports by Estep and Hissam [1994] and Quick and Cortes [1994]. For further information about the DSRS initiative and library systems, consult the DSRS Web site[4] or contact the Customer Assistance Office of the Software Reuse Program at 500 North Washington Street, Falls Church, VA 22046. For more information about the interoperability of the DoD software reuse libraries, consult the RLIG or CORBA Web site.[5,6] Information about the CCPL program can be found on the CCPL Web site,[7] and information on the NPLACE program can be found on the NPLACE Web site.[8]

For more information about the DoD Software Reuse Initiative program and its status, consult the Web site for the SRI.[9] Further information about NASA's Software Optimization and Reuse Technology (SORT) program can be found at the program Web site.[10] For more information about the STARS program and its demonstration projects consult the STARS Web site (see

---

[4] Defense Software Repository System Information. DoD's Corporate Information Management (CIM) Information Technology Management, U.S. Department of Defense Web site: http://www.c3i.osd.mil/bpr/bprcd/0104.htm.

[5] Reuse Library Interoperability Group Homepage: http://www.asset.com/rig/home.html.

[6] CORBAReuseLib, (CORBA and Library Interoperability between Reuse Libraries) Web site: http://source.asset.com/stars/darpa/Newsletters/Mar-1995/9.html.

[7] Command and Control Product Lines (CCPL) Web site: http://www.ccpl.com.

[8] National Product Line Asset Center (NPLACE) Web site: http://www.nplace.wvhtf.org/.

[9] The Department of Defense Software Reuse Initiative program Web site: http://dii-sw.ncr.disa.mil/ReuseIC/.

[10] Software Optimization and Reuse Technology (SORT) Web site: http://sort.wvhtf.org/.

footnote 1). The FAST methodology is discussed by Weiss and Lai [1999], and the reuse business methodology is discussed by Jacobson et al. [1997]. Information about RLIG history, technical committees, current activities, and their relation to IEEE standards can be found on the RLIG and ASSET Web sites (see footnotes 6 and 7).

Chapter 3

Aspects of Software Reuse

We can credit much of the progress achieved in software engineering to the realization that this field is multidisciplinary, and that focus on one aspect of this field is not effective in practice unless it is matched by commensurate efforts in the other aspects. Likewise, software reuse is multidisciplinary, and we need to study all the aspects of this discipline. In this chapter we discuss in turn three broad aspects of software reuse, referring the reader to parts of the book where these aspects are covered.

3.1 ORGANIZATIONAL ASPECTS

At the organizational level, two sets of measures are required for the smooth operation of a software reuse initiative: a *managerial infrastructure* and a *technological infrastructure*. Because such structures involve nontrivial changes to the corporate operational procedures, they must be phased in progressively; we must also consider the process of *institutionalizing reuse*.

3.1.1 Managerial Infrastructure

The managerial infrastructure is the set of functions, responsibilities, reporting requirements, and reward or incentive mechanisms that are required to ensure the seamless operation of reuse processes. The organizational measures that are taken for the sake of software reuse must be merged with existing measures for traditional software development. This may involve adding new functions (e.g., those dealing with library management and domain engineering) and altering existing functions (e.g., those dealing with application engineering). Managerial infrastructures are discussed in Chapter 4, where we discuss in turn organizational structures, then reuse-specific skills and job descriptions.

3.1.2 Technological Infrastructure

The technological infrastructure includes all the corporatewide technical functions that must be provided to support reuse operations. Chief among these is the library support function, which includes a *configuration management* function; as various versions of the same product are used in more and more applications, the configuration management function must keep track of the versions in existence, along with their host systems. Also, a *quality assurance* function must be supported along with the configuration management function, to define, monitor, and enforce product and process standards; these standards apply to the reusable asset level, as well as the application level. Likewise, *testing* standards, *verification and validation* standards, and *certification* standards must be established and enforced at the asset level and the application level; at both the asset and the application levels, these standards differ from traditional development standards, because of the special requirements of software reuse. Finally, standards for risk assessment and risk analysis must be established and enforced by the technological infrastructure function; risks pertaining to development for reuse include excessive development costs and overestimated reuse potential, while risks pertaining to development with reuse include excessive reuse overheads and poor-quality reusable assets. Chapter 5 discusses technological infrastructure in some detail; Chapters 19 and 20, which discuss economics of software reuse, offer means to quantify reuse risks in economic terms.

3.1.3 Reuse Introduction

Because the introduction of software reuse in software development organizations is accompanied by nontrivial organizational changes, it must be carefully planned and executed. It is usually dependent on a *reuse champion*, who must secure the cooperation of all the parties involved to bring about the necessary organizational changes. To be successful, the reuse champion must have clearly specified goals, must be able to articulate these goals to relevant parties, and must be able to measure progress toward these goals in objective terms. This individual must also have a sound cost/benefit analysis of the initiative, along with the risks involved and their impact on the analysis. Reuse introduction is dependent on a precise plan of action, and on solid managerial support; software reuse requires a long investment cycle, and does not produce benefits unless management is willing to consent the time and resources needed for the return on investment. Reuse introduction is also dependent on the willingness of asset developers to work within the domain engineering paradigm, and the willingness of application developers to give reusable assets serious consideration, and eventually to contribute to the organization's asset capital, by occasionally producing or adapting reusable assets. The stepwise introduction of reuse mandates the recruitment of specialized staff, the evolution of development processes toward reuse-based models, and long-term procedures for monitoring and measurement. Reuse introduction is the subject of Chapter 6.

3.1.4 Exercises

1. (A) In what way does the configuration management function under software reuse differ from traditional software development?

2. (A) In what way does the quality assurance function under software reuse differ from traditional software development? Discuss this issue for development for reuse, and for development with reuse.

3. (A) In what way does the certification function under software reuse differ from traditional software development? Discuss this issue for development for reuse, and for development with reuse.

4. (A) In what way does the verification–validation function under software reuse differ from traditional software development? Discuss this issue for development for reuse, and for development with reuse.

5. (A) In what way does the testing function under software reuse differ from traditional software development? Discuss this issue with respect to development for reuse, and development with reuse.

3.2 TECHNICAL ASPECTS

Technical aspects of software reuse can be divided into three classes: domain engineering aspects, component engineering aspects, and application engineering aspects. We review these in turn, below.

3.2.1 Domain Engineering Aspects

The most common (and most successful) paradigm of software reuse involves developing applications within a predefined application domain; individual applications within the domain typically differ in terms of specific functional options (e.g., supporting a variety of services to choose from) or operating details (e.g., same functionality offered on different platforms) but share a common product architecture and draw on a common pool of reusable assets. *Domain engineering* consists of scoping the domain, deriving the domainwide product architecture, specifying the reusable assets along with means to specialize them for specific applications, and generally preparing the application development activities. The most crucial step of domain engineering is *domain analysis*, which consists in scoping the domain and deciding whether it is worthy of being developed. If it is determined to be worthwhile, then a domain architecture and a set of asset specifications are derived. Chapter 7 discusses general issues in domain engineering, Chapter 8 discusses domain analysis, and Chapter 9 assesses programming paradigms from the viewpoint of reusability.

3.2.2 Component Engineering Aspects

Component engineering is the discipline that deals with how to develop reusable software assets. What makes an asset reusable are two features: its usability and its usefulness. While usability is a domain engineering issue, usefulness is a component engineering issue:

- *Usefulness* refers to how often the asset is expected to be reused; this matter is debated during the domain analysis phase, and an asset is selected for development for reuse if its expected frequency of reuse is found to justify its development cost. Clearly, genericity is an important ingredient for usefulness, because it enhances the frequency of reuse of an asset by enabling the user to tailor the asset to specific needs in a controlled manner.
- *Usability* refers to how little it costs to reuse this asset; this matter is usually decided at component engineering time. An asset is all the more useful that the context which it requires to run is simpler, and that its coupling with host systems is smaller. Clearly, modularity is an important ingredient for usability, because it emphasizes simple interface specifications and low coupling.

Object-oriented programming is known to foster reusability, because it enhances usability (through modularity/genericity). Part IV presents a detailed discussion of object oriented reusability techniques; it covers, in particular, architectural considerations in component engineering, as well as emerging standards in the development and deployment of reusable assets.

3.2.3 Application Engineering Aspects

Application engineering is the discipline of developing system applications from reusable assets. This discipline raises three issues that are (at least in part) foreign to traditional software development: asset retrieval and assessment; asset composition; and asset integration. Chapter 16 discusses the storage and retrieval of software assets for the purpose of software reuse; to this effect, it presents means to characterize and means to assess storage and retrieval methods. Then it uses characterizing features to classify existing methods, and uses assessment features to evaluate and compare them. Finally, it discusses means to build and maintain software libraries. Chapter 12 discusses object-oriented techniques for ensuring component composability. Chapter 17 discusses how to integrate reusable assets in host systems.

3.2.4   Exercises

1. (A) What means do object-oriented programming languages have to promote or support genericity? Illustrate by an example how provisions for genericity provide support for usefulness.

2. (A) What means do object-oriented programming languages have to promote or support modularity? Illustrate by an example how provisions for genericity provide support for usability.

3.3   ECONOMIC ASPECTS

Economic analysis enables managers to quantify, justify, and document their decisions, thereby providing a sound basis for their decision making processes. One may argue, with some merit, that all software metrics are, in fact, economic functions; they reflect quality features or operational features, on which one can, ultimately, place a monetary value. We divide economic aspects into three broad classes: software metrics, which reflect attributes that increase the market value of an asset; software reuse cost estimation techniques, which derive costs and benefits for software development for reuse, and with reuse; and software reuse return-on-investment (ROI) models, which quantify reuse related decisions as investment-like decisions.

3.3.1   Software Reuse Metrics

Software engineering metrics usually try to quantify product attributes by means of quantitative functions; software engineering metrics can be conveniently divided into structural metrics, which reflect structural attributes of assets, and functional metrics, which reflect functional attributes. For software reuse, it is possible to distinguish between component engineering metrics, domain engineering metrics, application engineering metrics, and corporate level metrics. These are discussed in some detail in Chapter 18.

3.3.2   Software Reuse Cost Estimation

We have argued above that software metrics can reasonably be interpreted as economic functions; yet they are sufficiently distinct from traditional economic functions (that focus on costs and benefits) to warrant separate consideration. While metrics reflect abstract attributes such as product quality or process maturity, cost models quantify concrete lifecycle costs, which are measured in person months. In Chapter 19, we briefly discuss some traditional software cost estimation formulas, which we then use to estimate reuse costs at the component level and at the application level. For each of these cost models, we quantify, in turn, development costs, then the benefits gained from reuse; these are divided into quality gains, productivity gains, and time-to-market gains.

3.3.3 Software Reuse Return on Investment

It is possible to structure reuse processes as the superimposition of four decision cycles: corporate decision cycle, domain decision cycle, application decision cycle, and component decision cycle. Furthermore, it is possible to model each of these decision cycles as an investment cycle, involving all the ingredients of an investment decision: an upfront investment cost, an investment cycle length, a discount rate, and an expected yearly benefit that stems from the investment. Using the cost modeling information gained in Chapter 19, we derive, in Chapter 20, quantitative economic functions that characterize the four investment cycles of interest. These four models can be used to give meaning to the evasive notion of *making reuse happen*. The way to make reuse happen is to identify the controllable factors in ROI models, and to fine-tune these factors so as to make all the ROI functions positive. If each stakeholder in the reuse process (corporate manager, for the corporate decision cycle; domain manager, for the domain engineering cycle; project manager, for the application decision cycle; and component developer, for the component decision cycle) is given the responsibility to maximize its ROI function, then in doing so they will all contribute to *making reuse happen*.

3.4 FURTHER READING

Reifer [1997] provides a detailed discussion of software reuse introduction in governmental and industrial organizations, based on his longstanding experience as a consultant.

Part II

Organizational Aspects

As discussed in Chapter 1, one of the key characterizing features of software reuse is the fact that it is a systematic process. A number of measures must be taken, at the institutional level, to ensure that the production and the consumption of reusable assets take place in a carefully planned and carefully executed manner. This part considers these organizational matters: Chapter 4 reviews the various organizational sructures that can be adopted to streamline reuse processes; Chapter 5 presents the technical infrastructure that must be provided to support reuse processes; and Chapter 6 discusses the stepwise introduction of reuse processes within a software development organization.

Organizational Aspects

Chapter 4

Software Reuse Organizations

Software reuse is about producing and consuming reusable assets; a *software reuse organization* defines the roles, responsibilities, functions, reporting structures, incentive structures, reward structures, and resources, of the various stakeholders in the process of producing and consuming reusable assets.

4.1 SOFTWARE REUSE TEAM STRUCTURES

In this section, we survey existing organizational structures for the production and consumption of reusable assets. These organizational structures can be characterized and classified by means of a set of features, which we review first.

4.1.1 Characteristic Features

We have found that the following features offer a fairly complete (if not necessarily orthogonal) characterization of software reuse organizations.

- *Team Cohesion.* A software reuse organization can be characterized by the cohesion of the teams that it defines. Team cohesion has an impact on productivity, because it fosters loyalty to the team's fellow members, dedication to the team's goals, and pride in the team's achievements.
- *Reporting Structure.* A software reuse organization can also be characterized by its reporting structure. Under some reuse organizations that

we discuss in the sequel, some stakeholders may report to more than one manager, creating the potential for ambiguity and tension.

- *Communications Overhead.* A software reuse organization can be characterized by the communication overhead that it creates; this is clearly an important evaluation criterion, as it has an impact on productivity.

- *Turnover Impact.* A software reuse organization may be judged by the impact that high personnel turnover may have on the viability of its software reuse program. A good organization is one that ensures immunity of the corporate reuse program from personnel turnover. An organizational structure that relies too heavily on the expertise or experience of a single individual, for example, becomes vulnerable to the departure of that individual.

- *Loyalty Conflict.* A producer of reusable assets who is dedicated to a specific development project (as some organizations provide) is really serving two goals at once: the goal of the project, which is to complete the proposed product within the available resources; and the goal of the organization, which is, in addition to the project's goal, to produce reusable assets and to make use of existing corporate reusable assets (so as to amortize their cost). A producer who is overly dedicated to the project may choose to focus on achieving the project's objective, and become in effect just another programmer on the project's team; a producer who is overly dedicated to corporate goals may fail to acknowledge the immediate needs of a project in favor of long-term corporate needs, thereby stalling the project. A good organization is one that avoids divided loyalties or integrates checks and balances to make sure that adequate tradeoffs are worked out between various imperatives.

- *Project Competition.* Some software reuse organizations may produce a situation where project teams are competing for the attention of the producer team, to produce reusable assets for their project. A good organization is one that avoids such situations or provides a mechanism for a fair management of the producers' resources.

- *Library Cohesion.* Library cohesion is achieved by enforcing a uniform representation of reusable assets, a uniform quality standard between assets, and a uniform procedure for including assets. It is easier to achieve library cohesion if a single entity (person or team) is mandated to affect its content; not all organizations provide for this criterion.

- *Producer Incentives.* In order to enrich its library, a corporation must provide incentives for producers. Such incentives may include a well-crafted and well-tuned reward structure and protocols of career development for asset producers, as well as protocols of professional recognition. Typically software personnel get promoted and gain recognition on the basis of their success in completing development projects; because asset developers do not directly develop projects, alternative means must be put in place to recognize their contributions and reward their performance. A good software reuse organization is one that provides these means.

- *Consumer Incentives.* If reusable assets are as good as they are claimed to be, then it should not be difficult to convince project managers to make use of reusable assets. But making the commitment to use reusable assets on a given project is not without risk: if the reuse library does not have the right assets for a given project, attempts to use it will only distract development personnel and delay the project. This is another instance where a project manager faces a conflict between project goals (to complete the proposed product within the allocated resources) and corporate goals (to make use of reusable assets, so as to amortize the corporate investment in the reuse program). To mitigate the risks involved, a software reuse organization may provide consumer incentives over and above the gains in productivity and quality that are reaped from reuse— for instance, under the form of recognition for reuse percentage achieved on a project.

- *Byproduct Incentives.* Under *producer incentives*, we discussed incentives that designated producers may have to produce reusable assets (vs. contributing to current development projects). We now consider incentives that individual project teams may have to contribute to the corporate reuse library as a *byproduct* of carrying out their project. We will see in subsequent chapters that the development of a reusable asset is significantly more costly than the development of an asset for single use, usually 50% more costly. Hence, if we want project teams to make an effort to contribute reusable assets, we must provide tangible substantial incentives to that effect; an additional benefit of such incentives is that the same project team is more likely to consume reusable assets in subsequent development projects.

4.1.2   Software Reuse Team Structures

4.1.2.1   Lone Producer

The *lone producer* organization provides that a single unit, the *lone producer*, is responsible for producing and maintaining reusable assets for the organization. Typically, the organization includes two or more project teams, which are the *consumer teams*. A flowchart for the lone producer organization is shown in Figure 4.1.

As lone producers are responsible for catering to their project teams, they report directly to the level 2 manager but also report to both project managers. Lone producers also interact with the project teams at a technical level to discuss interface details of the assets that they produce.

4.1.2.2   Nested Producer

The *nested producer* organization attempts to address the weaknesses of lone producer by providing one producer for each project team; a flowchart of this

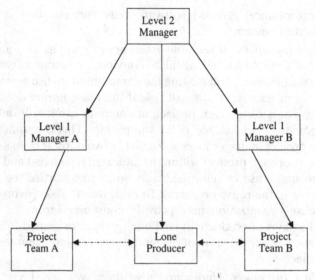

FIGURE 4.1 Lone producer flowchart.

organization is given in Figure 4.2. All nested producers are considered as members of the project team to which they are assigned; they report to the team's manager, participate in achieving the team's goals, and share in the credit of the team's success. However, because the goals of individual project teams (to complete assigned projects within time and budget constraints) are not the same as the overall corporate goal (to nurture the corporate reuse program and keep it focused), the nested producers report to a *reuse manager* in addition to their respective project managers. Reuse managers are trustees of the corporate reuse initiative; they ensure continuity of the reuse initiative as projects are phased in and out, maintain the focus of the corporate reuse goals, and are responsible for operating (enriching, enhancing, and maintaining) the software reuse library. The reuse manager must ensure that nested producers balance the short-term goals of individual projects against the long term goals of the corporation—that they do not, in effect, become *just another programmer* in their respective projects. Also, as the trustee of the corporate reuse library, the reuse manager must define quality standards for the library, as well as operational procedures for enforcing these standards. The performance of nested producers is assessed by project managers, to reflect their contribution to project goals, and by the reuse manager, to reflect their contribution to corporate reuse goals. Requests for reusable assets are submitted by project managers to the reuse manager, who determines whether the requested asset has reuse potential; in case of conflict, the arbitration of the level 2 manager may be required.

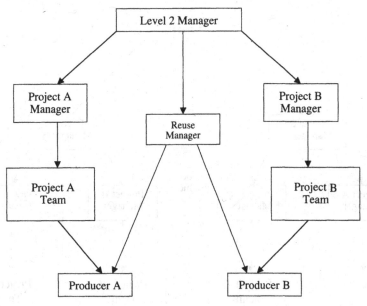

FIGURE 4.2   Nested producer flowchart.

4.1.2.3 Pool Producer

The *pool producer organization* combines features of the lone producer (a single producer unit) with features of the nested producer (project-dedicated producers) into an organization that involves project-specific producer units pooled within a corporate level reuse structure; of course it typically involves more people than either lone producer or nested producer. A flowchart of the pool producer organization is given in Figure 4.3. In the pool producer organization, each project team has a dedicated producer team; on the other hand, for the sake of corporate-wide consistency, the producer teams pool their resources to produce a unit that is responsible for managing the corporate reuse policy. This unit is responsible for carrying out the corporate reuse program; in particular, it maintains the corporate reuse library. Because the structure of the producers pool is fairly loose (none of the producer teams is specifically responsible for the reuse program), this organization is not well adapted for long-term reuse plans; it is, however, suitable for geographically distributed teams, for the same reasons. The pool producer organization works best for two to three teams; for more than three teams, the communications overhead between producer teams becomes prohibitive. Also, because the reuse structure (made up of the loose combination of producer teams) is not tightly knit, the pool producer organization cannot handle long term reuse initiatives, with large asset repositories.

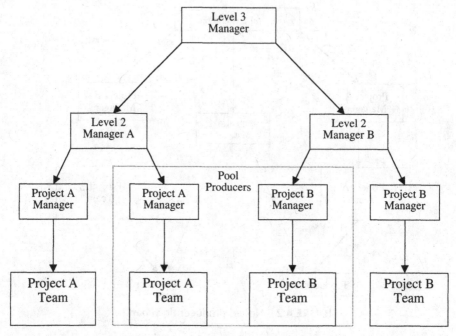

FIGURE 4.3   Pool producer flowchart.

Among the requirements for a successful deployment of this organization, we mention the need (1) to articulate a *reuse vision*, which serves as the focal point of the pool producers (which must be balanced against the goals of project teams); (2) to clarify ownership and responsibility for the joint repository of reusable assets; and (3) for conflict resolution strategies, to provide for the conflicts that may arise between project goals, and between development versus reuse goals.

4.1.2.4   Team Producer

The *team producer organization* provides for separate teams for project development and reusable asset production. A flowchart of the team producer organization is given in Figure 4.4. The producer team serves as the trustee of the corporate reuse initiative: It focuses on the corporate long-term reuse goals; enforces the corporate reuse policy; and creates, updates, and maintains the corporate base of reusable assets. Team members report to the producer manager, who reports directly to the corporate management, rather than to development project managers. The producer team produces reusable assets on the basis of two distinct thrusts: (1) its own domain analysis, if it determines that such assets are sufficiently useful to warrant being developed and packaged for reuse; and (2) requests from project teams, if it deems that the requested asset bears sufficient general interest for the corporation at large

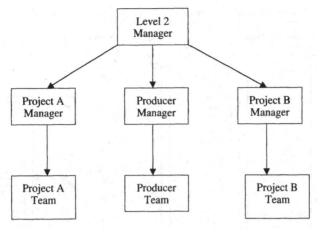

FIGURE 4.4   Team producer flowchart.

(rather than a narrow immediate goal of the project team) to justify its effort. In the team producer organization, project teams are not expected to contribute to the corporate base of reusable assets, but are expected—indeed, encouraged—to make the best use of it. Once the organization is operating at cruising speed, it is possible to view each project team and the producer team as separate, self-sustaining, units. The producer team earns its keep by charging its services to the project teams and is motivated to produce quality reusable assets so as to maximize the dependence of project teams on its services. The project teams earn their keep by producing software products at the lowest possible cost, and hence have ample incentives to take advantage of the assets offered by the producer team.

4.1.2.5   The Experience Factory
The *experience factory* organization is an instance of the team producer organization. We discuss it separately because it has very specific features, and has been the subject of extensive empirical investigations in the past. A flowchart of this organization is given in Figure 4.5. The experience factory is a special form of the generic *team producer organization*, which can be characterized by the following premises.

- *Reusable Assets.* The most discriminating feature of the experience factory is its emphasis on software development *experience* as the most general form of reusable asset. Whereas reusable assets are traditionally equated with executable components, the experience factory takes the position that any form of software development experience can be packaged into a reusable asset. Among the forms of assets, we mention equations between process or product parameters, histograms or pie charts of

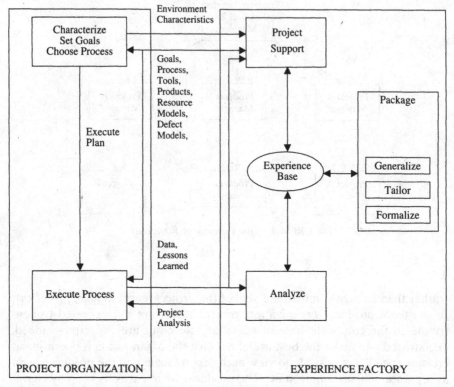

FIGURE 4.5 Experience factory flowchart.

project data, ranges of normal project data, and lessons learned from past development projects.

- *Packaging.* Packaging is the process by which some information resulting from past development experience is compiled into a reusable form, by abstracting away details that pertain to the specific project and focusing on the essence of the experience. This process applies to all forms of reusable assets; if the asset is executable code, then packaging it consists in shedding all the features that pertain to its usage in the system for which it was originally developed and generalizing it to prepare it for future reuse in other systems. Examples of packages produced by the experience factory include *product packages*, which are abstractions of lifecycle products (programs, designs, architectures, specifications, test data); *process packages*, which are abstractions of lifecycle processes (process models, methods, test data generation method); *relationship packages*, which abstract relations between various product parameters and process parameters (cost models, defect models, reliability models); and *tool packages*, which assist the generation or analysis of software products and processes (code generators, planning and cost estimation tools, static analyzers, regression testers). Packaging these various kinds of information consists not only in abstracting away project specific details but also in representing and storing packages in a way that facilitates their indexing and their retrieval.

- *Separation of Producer and Consumer Functions.* The experience factory stands out by the specific protocols that it defines between the project organization and the experience factory. These are two separate units, having distinct goals and distinct agendas, but reporting to the same level of upper management. While the project organization earns credit on the basis of successfully completed projects, the experience factory earns credit for maintaining and enriching the corporate experience base, and for keeping the corporate reuse program on track.

Unlike all other organizations we have discussed so far, the experience factory organization has no cognizance of the multitude of project teams: all project teams are lumped into a single unit, the project organization. A corollary of this situation is that the experience factory does not deal with project competition, because any conflict between project teams is resolved within the project organization. Also, the project organization is not expected to make any direct contribution to the corporate experience base; rather, it is focused on project delivery. Of course, the experience factory does collect information and lessons learned on projects developed by the project organization; but we assume that this takes place in a non-intrusive manner, so that it causes little or no overhead on the operations of the project organization.

4.1.3 Determining Factors

In the previous section, we discussed the possible organizations that a corporation may adopt to carry out its reuse initiative; in this section, we turn our attention, to the parameters that affect the choice of an organization. We briefly review these parameters below and discuss how they influence the choice of an organization.

- *Size of the Corporation.* Large corporations are more likely to afford the heavy upfront investment costs that are inherent to some of the reuse organizations.
- *Size of the Development Team.* Some reuse organizations are not feasible unless the development team is large enough.
- *Yearly Production.* Some reuse organizations cannot be justified unless the volume of yearly software production warrants it.
- *Homogeneity of the Product Line.* If the corporation has a heterogeneous product line, then it may be better to adopt a reuse organization that is consumer centered (e.g., nested producer or pool producer); if the corporation has a homogeneous product line, then it may be better to

adopt a reuse organization that is producer centered (e.g., lone producer, team producer, or experience factory).

- *Homogeneity of Development Platforms.* As with product lines, the homogeneity of development platforms favors producer centered organizations whereas the heterogeneity of development platforms favors consumer-centered organizations.

- *Software Reuse Maturity.* Some reuse organizations cannot be justified unless the corporation has reached a high level of reuse maturity (e.g., its reuse library has reached a certain size).

- *Software Reuse Scope.* Some organizations (lone producer, nested producer) are best adapted to project-level reuse; others are best adapted to corporate wide reuse (pool producer, team producer); yet others are best adapted (or can accommodate even) reuse across corporate boundaries (consider, e.g., that the experience packaged by the experience factory may come from outside the corporation).

- *Geographic Distribution.* The teams of a reuse organization may or may not be considered as geographically distributed depending on the bandwidth of communication between them.

- *Reuse Mandate.* If the corporate reuse program is mandated by management, then strong incentives must be put in place across the board (producer incentives, consumer incentives, byproduct incentives) to drive the reuse initiative. If the reuse initiative is driven by technical staff, then it is best to adopt a reuse organization that involves few extra incentives.

4.1.4   Exercises

1. (C) Consider the characterizations discussed in Section 4.1.1 and the organizational structures discussed subsequently. Characterize each organizational structure with respect to the features put forth.

2. (B) In chapter 2, we discuss the REBOOT methodology, which distinguishes between three families of team organizations: *component centered*, *production centered*, and *domain centered*. Consider each organization discussed in this chapter and determine which family it belongs to.

3. (B) In reference to the criteria set forth in Section 4.1.3, derive a situation for which the *lone producer* organization is ideally suited (or at least the best suited among all the organizations we have discussed in this section). Analyze all the determining factors that pertain to this situation and assess how the lone producer organization fares with respect to the criteria set forth in Section 4.1.1.

4. (B) In reference to the criteria set forth in Section 4.1.3, derive a situation for which the *nested producer* organization is ideally suited (or at least the best suited among all the organizations we have discussed in this section).

Analyze all the determining factors that pertain to this situation and assess how the nested producer organization fares with respect to the criteria set forth in Section 4.1.1.

5. (B) In reference to the criteria set forth in Section 4.1.3, derive a situation for which the *pool producer* organization is ideally suited (or at least the best suited among all the organizations we have discussed in this section). Analyze all the determining factors that pertain to this situation and assess how the pool producer organization fares with respect to the criteria set forth in Section 4.1.1.

6. (B) In reference to the criteria set forth in Section 4.1.3, derive a situation for which the *team producer* organization is ideally suited (or at least the best suited among all the organizations we have discussed in this section). Analyze all the determining factors that pertain to this situation and assess how the team producer organization fares with respect to the criteria set forth in Section 4.1.1.

7. (B) In reference to the criteria set forth in Section 4.1.3, derive a situation for which the *experience factory* organization is ideally suited (or at least the best suited among all the organizations we have discussed in this section). Analyze all the determining factors that pertain to this situation and assess how the experience factory organization fares with respect to the criteria set forth in Section 4.1.1.

8. (B) Consider the *center of excellence* organization discussed by Coulange [1998, Chapter 12]. Present this reuse organization and assess it using the criteria set forth in Section 4.1.1. Characterize a situation where such an organization is most appropriate.

9. (B) Consider the *advisory group* organization discussed by Coulange [1998, Chapter 12]. Present this reuse organization and assess it using the criteria set forth in Section 4.1.1. Characterize a situation where such an organization is most appropriate.

4.2 REUSE SKILLS

The organizations that we have discussed above involve a number of job descriptions that are alien to traditional software development; we review these in turn, and discuss the skills that such job descriptions require.

4.2.1 Librarian

The function of a librarian is akin to that of a database manager: providing access to library assets for a community of users; as a service provider, the librarian must ensure that the library service is useful, usable, and efficient.

But there is more to the function of a librarian than database (asset base, experience base) management:

- Unlike database entries, which are typically identified by a meaningful key (social security number, employee number), assets in a reuse library do not necessarily have such a key. Their retrieval becomes a major issue that has a profound effect on the usefulness and the efficiency of the library; this matter is discussed in more detail in Chapter 16. Finding the appropriate representation for library assets and the appropriate indexing mechanisms for these assets requires a great deal of expertise in a wide range of software topics (information retrieval, natural language processing, formal specifications, programming languages, formal semantics, logic, etc).

- As the trustee of the corporate reuse library, the librarian must control all the entries that are included in the library, for such aspects as: generality, correctness, reliability, clarity. This requires a good mastery of software quality as well as software metrics.

4.2.2 Reuse Manager

A reuse manager is, first, a software manager and hence must have a good understanding of the traditional software management issues, such as programmer motivation factors, programmer productivity, software project planning, software project cost estimation, and software process models and lifecycles. In addition, the reuse manager must be fluent in the following aspects of software reuse management:

- *Software reuse organizations*: the means to assess their effectiveness for any particular set of circumstances, and the factors that affect the choice of an organization.
- *Software reuse economics*: the costs and benefits associated with all reuse-related products and processes.
- *Software reuse metrics*: means to measure the quality of reusable assets, assess the maturity of reuse processes, define reuse goals, and monitor their attainment.
- *Software reuse products*: defining what constitutes a reusable asset, how to package it, how to represent it, and how to assess its worth for the corporation.
- *Component engineering frameworks* and the attending component based software development disciplines.

4.2.3 Domain Engineer

The *domain engineer* probably is the most novel job description and also has the greatest influence on the success or failure of a reuse initiative—especially for producer-centered organizations. The domain analyst investigates an application domain and determines, on the basis of past application development within that domain, what items of development experience are worthy of packaging for the purpose of future reuse. The domain analyst synthesizes, compiles, packages, and archives units of knowledge that capture past software development experience; such units may deal with programming knowledge and also deal with domain knowledge, project management knowledge, and a variety of other pertinent kinds of knowledge. Depending on the scope of the reuse program, such knowledge stems from (and is packaged for) project experience, corporate experience, or experience in the software engineering discipline at large.

Domain analysis has emerged as an autonomous discipline, and has become to a large extent textbook material. Most of the existing work on domain analysis focuses on capturing domain knowledge, perhaps combined with programming knowledge. Because of the recognition that other forms of software engineering knowledge are equally worthy of packaging and reuse, more work is required in the future to extend domain analysis to cater to these other forms.

4.2.4 Application Engineer

There are two broad families of software development methodologies: *top–down* software development and *bottom–up* software development. It is fair to view object oriented programming as a bottom up programming discipline where the programming language provides active support for the discipline's premises. It is also reasonable to consider that software reuse is better adapted to a bottom–up discipline than to a top down discipline of programming. In top–down programming, the programmer/analyst decomposes the specification that must be solved into subspecifications and then consults the library for components that satisfy the unfulfilled subspecifications. The likelihood that randomly generated subspecifications would match reusable library components is very small, given the amount of functional detail carried by typical specifications and components.

The bottom–up discipline of software development is better adapted to software reuse, to the extent that the consumer (programmer/analyst) builds a solution to the specification at hand using assets that are known to be available, while perhaps adding extra project-specific code or self-contained assets that may qualify to be reused in the future. The contents of the reuse library influences the consumer in the same way as a programming language influences the programmer's thought process; the consumer derives software solutions to take the best advantage of existing assets in the same way as a programmer derives a programming solution to take the best advantage of the programming language's strengths. Consumers who have adapted their problem-solving skills to an existing reuse library no longer need consumer incentives.

In addition to general knowledge of development with reuse, an application engineer may also need to know about current technology in component-based software development. This is an evolving technology that is very rich in new frameworks and support tools.

4.2.5 Component Engineer

Whereas the domain engineer analyzes a domain, derives reference architectures, and specifies reusable assets, it is the task of the *component engineer* to develop reusable components from specifications produced by the domain engineer. In addition to the obvious requirements that stem from development for reuse (emphasis on quality, integrity, traceability, genericity), the component engineer must be fluent in the evolving frameworks of component-based software development, and their attending standards and tools. Part IV of this book deals with reusable component engineering issues.

4.2.6 Exercises

1. (A) Consider current standards for component based software engineering (such as CORBA, COM, DCOM). For each reuse skill or function covered in this section, discuss what information the agent who fulfills that function must know about these standards.

2. (A) Consider a programming assignment that consists of writing a simulation program for a CPU dispatcher. The dispatcher involves the queue datatype (e.g., for the ready queue) and the set datatype (e.g., for the set of blocked processes).

   (a) Discuss how you would design such a system if your target programming language were standard C, which provides no components library.

   (b) Discuss how you would design it if your target language is Ada, which is provided along with an extensive library of common datatypes, along with a random-number generator.

   (c) What would you want to know about the components library before you perform your design? In what sense does the components library influence your design?

   (d) Discuss the skills of an application engineer in light of this example.

4.3 FURTHER READING

Fafchamps [1994] discusses four reuse organizations that are used by Hewlett-Packard. Coulange [1998] discusses six reuse organizations, including the four that Fafchamps has observed at HP. Basili and others [Basili and G. Caldiera 1992, Basili et al. 1994] discuss an experimental software reuse organization, and McClure [1995] gives general managerial recommendations about the organization of software reuse. Further information on domain analysis, is available in the literature [Hess et al. 1990, Jawarski et al. 1990, Kang et al. 1990, Prieto-Diaz 1991a, 1991c; Tracz 1992, Vitaletti and Chhut 1992].

Chapter 5

Support Services

The infrastructure that supports a systematic software reuse program must support all areas of the software development process, including the supporting activities of software engineering that ensure appropriate quality in the final software product. Areas of software engineering that must be incorporated into a commercial-level reuse-based process include these support services: configuration management (CM), quality assurance (QA), testing, verification and validation (V&V), risk management, and certification.

The IEEE standards and guides that address the six activities above either explicitly or implicitly define the process in terms of the development of a single application system [IEEE 1993, 1995, 1997, 1998a–1998d]. To meet the needs of industrial use, each of these supporting activities needs to be adapted to a development environment based on the reuse of software components, and supporting the development of software systems based on these components.

5.1 CONFIGURATION MANAGEMENT

Software configuration management (CM) includes activities related to identification, documentation and control of the artifacts under configuration control. The functions of a general CM process are configuration identification, configuration control, status accounting, configuration audits and reviews, interface control, and subcontractor/vendor control [IEEE 1998b]. CM is the focal point for managing and controlling the variants of the many types of software artifacts, both during initial development and in the subsequent evolution during deployment of the software systems.

The existence of a systematic software reuse environment increases the demands on a CM program by an order of magnitude, because the software components will now be used in multiple systems rather than in an individual system. For every version of a system, the CM process will need to track the version of each component used in the development of that particular system, along with all the dependencies of that version of the component with other components in the system. The increase in complexity of the CM process for reuse-based software engineering is based on two considerations [Edwards and Weide 1997]:

- Any change to a component must be considered in terms of all systems that use (or may potentially use) the component.
- Multiple versions of a component must be stored, maintained, and available for use, due to compatibility issues with other components.

While an individual system may pass on an upgrade to a component once or twice, continuing to forego upgrades indefinitely is not a viable option. If the component is obtained from outside the organization, the developer will not continue to support older versions of the component. Even if the component is controlled by the organization, backward compatibility cannot be maintained indefinitely, and failure to upgrade means that the organization must support a growing number of versions, with a geometric growth in version dependencies. Another aspect of the need to accept version upgrades is that most upgrades contain multiple improvements, including performance improvements and error correction in addition to functional additions. Passing on an upgrade means that the system will not obtain the collateral improvements to the functional enhancements. Hence the CM process within reuse-based software engineering must address the issue of maintaining multiple versions of a component and the decision basis for installing a new version of a component.

An example will serve to illustrate the impact of software reuse on the CM process. The configuration control function of a traditional system application involves the evaluation, coordination, approval, and implementation of approved changes to an item under configuration control [Berlack 1992]. A principal requirement is the development of the plan by which the revised configuration item will be moved into the development or operating environment. The plan will usually include a design review to determine the impact of the change and a review by a control board to determine the fitness of the revised item for deployment. The design review within the systematic software reuse environment must now consider the effect of the change on every system that uses the item and on any common software architecture. The impact on other configuration items that have dependencies on the item proposed for change must also be considered, as well as the level of assurance needed by the item because of its criticality within the software systems and the nature of the change. After an approved change has been implemented, the control board must determine the sufficiency of the revised item for all systems using the item, and for any common software architecture. The plan for deploying the revised item must address each system, and must consider dependent revised items that must be simultaneously deployed in each system.

The software library, which is discussed in Chapter 16, is the focal tool for performing configuration management. For a software library serving an architecture-based reuse effort, as in a software product line or a family of related systems, the task of configuration management may easily dominate the task of component storage and retrieval. The software library must provide the means to enable the user to identify component dependencies (including version dependencies) and to access component-related information such as known defects, level and methods of assurance, test configurations, cases, and results, design rationale, and identification of systems using the component. Ideally, the CM function of the software library will be associated with a system composer or checker who will enforce rules related to component or component version dependencies.

5.2   QUALITY ASSURANCE

The quality assurance (QA) process ensures that the software development (and software evolution) process and the software products conform to established standards. This process normally uses activities such as peer reviews, inspections, and QA team reviews to ensure conformance, rather than the level of analysis and testing performed by a V&V process or a testing process. The QA effort is generally directed more toward process than product [Glass 1992]. Obviously the QA process must adapt to any change in the development process, and so it must adapt to the implementation of a reuse-based software engineering environment. QA must ensure that the development process is well defined, documented, and followed. Although this is not new to QA, what differs is that there are now two processes: the domain or product-line process and the system process. The two processes interact but have different goals and products. QA must ensure not only that the individual processes are defined and followed but also that the process interaction is defined and followed.

Since the QA process evaluates all lifecycle products (not only development products but also the products of the other support engineering processes), QA must adapt to the changes in all software processes related to a systematic software reuse environment. The QA plan should specify the documents that should be produced and the general format of all documentation. This role plays an important part in ensuring that the proper information is duly recorded, and made available for future reference.

5.3 TESTING

Testing includes activities at various stages of development, from unit testing to integration, system, and acceptance testing. Reuse-based software engineering will not impact the activity of structural testing, since this type of testing is based on the structure of the individual code module. (Note that the code is tested against its specification, and the specification of a reusable component will probably differ from a component designed for an individual system, but the activity of structural testing against specification remains the same.) However, scenario-based testing and functional testing will need to have test cases that consider all systems for which the component is intended. Care should be given to error and boundary conditions that could differ between the systems. Test outputs will need to be classified by the system, since the same set of inputs could result in different outputs in different systems.

At a minimum, careful representation of the testing that was performed must be recorded to indicate exactly how the component was tested. Test documentation from domain-level testing and from testing within individual systems pertaining to a component should be available to system developers to enable them to determine whether further testing for a particular component is necessary for individual systems. This implies a need for uniform test documentation throughout the product line, including test cases, test inputs, and test results.

There should be little impact due to a reuse-based software engineering environment on system and acceptance testing, as this activity is system-specific. While integration testing in the sense of integration of the complete system is obviously system-specific, the normal approach to testing the integration of parts of the system should be accomplished with the reusable components.

5.4 VERIFICATION AND VALIDATION

Software V&V methods are used to increase the level of assurance of critical software, particularly that of safety-critical and mission-critical software. Software V&V is a systems engineering discipline that evaluates software in a systems context [Wallace and Fujii 1989]. The term *verification* refers to the process of determining whether or not the products of a given phase of the software development cycle fulfill the requirements established during the previous phase; *validation* is the process of evaluating software at the end of the software development process to ensure compliance with software requirements [IEEE 1990].

V&V must be extended into the reuse-based software engineering process by activities analogous to those in application-level V&V being performed on the domain model, the generic architecture, and the software components. In

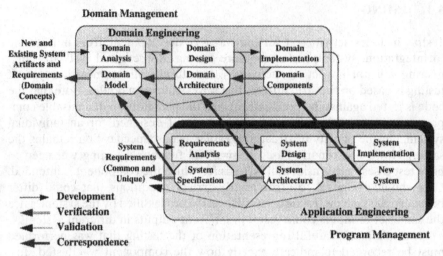

FIGURE 5.1   Framework for V&V within reuse-based software engineering.

addition, new V&V activities must be employed to ensure the proper transition between domain engineering and application engineering [Addy 1998].

Domain-level V&V tasks are performed to ensure that domain products fulfill the requirements established during earlier phases of domain engineering. Correspondence tasks in the transition between the domain level and the application level provide assurance that an application artifact correctly implements the corresponding domain artifact. Traditional application-level V&V tasks ensure the application products fulfill the requirements established during previous application lifecycle phases. Figure 5.1 depicts the relationships of the activities and artifacts within domain engineering with the activities and artifacts of application engineering. Table 5.1 lists the different V&V

TABLE 5.1   V&V Tasks for Lifecycle Phases at the Domain and Transition Levels

Level	Phase	Tasks
Domain engineering	Domain analysis	Validate domain model
		Model evaluation
		Requirements traceability analysis
	Domain design	Verify generic software architecture
		Design traceability analysis
		Design evaluation
		Design interface analysis
		Component test plan generation
		Component test design generation

TABLE 5.1 (*Continued*)

Level	Phase	Tasks
	Domain implementation	Verify and validate components
		Component traceability analysis
		Component evaluation
		Component interface analysis
		Component documentation analysis
		Component test case generation
		Component test procedure generation
		Component test execution
Application engineering	Requirements	Software requirements traceability analysis
		Software requirements evaluation
		Software requirements interface analysis
		System test plan generation
		Acceptance test plan generation
	Design	Design traceability analysis
		Design evaluation
		Design interface analysis
		Component test plan generation
		Integration test plan generation
		Test design generation
		Component testing
		Integration testing
		System testing
		Acceptance testing
	Implementation	Source code traceability analysis
		Source code evaluation
		Source code interface analysis
		Source code documentation evaluation
		Test case generation
		Component testing
		Integration testing
		System testing
		Acceptance testing
		Test procedure generation
		Component testing
		Integration testing
		System testing
		Component test execution
Transition	Requirements	Correspondence analysis between system specification and domain model
	Design	Correspondence analysis between system architecture and generic software architecture
	Implementation	Correspondence analysis between system implementation and generic reusable components

activities that should be performed during domain engineering, during application engineering, and in the transition between domain engineering and application engineering.

5.4.1 Domain-Level Tasks

Domain-level tasks are analogous to application-level tasks, in that the products of each phase are evaluated against the requirements specified in the previous phase and against the original user requirements. Domain-level tasks can be divided into the three phases of domain analysis, domain design, and domain implementation, which correspond to the application phases of requirements, design, and implementation.

During domain analysis V&V, the V&V team should ensure that the domain model is an appropriate representation of the user requirements. (The singular term "model" is not intended to imply that only one model will be constructed; this term is used to denote the one or more models that express the domain requirements.) Note that ensuring that user requirements are satisfied implies that the requirements of the domain must be explicitly stated. Criticality analysis is performed to ensure that high-risk requirements are appropriately addressed, either mission-critical requirements or those related to properties such as safety and security. The criticality analysis should also determine critical functions that will be performed by software. The domain model is evaluated to ensure that the requirements are consistent, complete, and realistic, especially in the high-risk areas. The model is evaluated to determine responses to error and fault conditions and to boundary and out-of-bounds conditions. As the domain engineering progresses into later phases, the requirements are traced forward. This will allow evaluation of the impact of changes to the domain artifacts.

Domain design V&V tasks focus on ensuring that the domain architecture satisfies the requirements expressed in the domain model. Each requirement in the domain model should trace to one or more items in the domain architecture (forward traceability), and each item in the domain architecture should trace back to one or more requirements in the domain model (reverse traceability). The domain architecture is evaluated to ensure that it is consistent, complete, and realistic. Interfaces between components are evaluated to ensure that the architecture supports the necessary communication between components in the architecture, users, and external systems. Planning and design of component testing are performed during this phase. The component testing should include error and fault scenarios, functional testing of critical activities, and response to boundary and out-of-bounds conditions.

Domain implementation V&V tasks ensure that the domain components satisfy the requirements of the domain architecture and will satisfy the original user requirements. The components should have a forward and reverse tracing with the domain architecture. Components that are involved with performing critical actions should receive careful consideration. The interface implementation, both within components of the architecture and with systems outside the architecture, is evaluated to ensure that it meets the requirements of the domain architecture. Component test cases and test procedures are generated, and component testing is performed.

Integration test activities are explicitly omitted from the domain-level tasking, since integration testing is oriented toward application-specific testing. Some form of integration testing might be appropriate within domain-level V&V in the case where the architecture calls for specific domain components to be integrated in multiple systems. This limited form of integration testing could be done along with the component testing activities.

5.4.2 Correspondence Tasks

Correspondence analysis is a term not found in [IEEE 1998d]. The term is used within this book to describe the activities that are performed to provide assurance that an application artifact corresponds to a domain artifact; specifically the application artifact is a correct implementation of the domain artifact. Four activities are to be performed during correspondence analysis:

- Map the application artifact to the corresponding domain artifact.
- Ensure that the application artifact has not been modified from the domain artifact without proper documentation.
- Ensure that the application artifact is a correct instantiation of the domain artifact.
- Obtain information on testing and analysis of a domain artifact to aid in V&V planning for the application artifact.

Correspondence analysis is performed between the corresponding phases of the domain engineering and application engineering lifecycles. The system specification for any system within the domain should correspond to the domain model. The system specification could involve instantiating, parameterizing, or simply satisfying the requirements expressed in the domain model. Any system-unique requirements should be explicit, and the rationale for not addressing these system-unique requirements within the domain model should be stated. Although some degree of correspondence analysis should be at least implicitly performed for all systems developed in accordance with the domain architecture, more care should be taken for systems with critical functions and for their critical areas of software.

The system architecture is analyzed to ensure that it satisfies the requirements specified in the domain architecture. Any variations should be documented along with the reason for the variation. The rationale for parameters chosen or options selected in constructing the system architecture from the domain architecture should be recorded. The system components are analyzed to ensure correspondence to domain components. Again, variations, parameters, and options should be recorded along with their rationale. Baseline testing might be appropriate in order to compare variants of a domain component.

5.4.3 Communicating Results

Communicating V&V work products and results is vital to avoiding the repetition of V&V tasks and to ensuring that potential reusers can properly assess the status of reusable components. V&V work products and results should be associated with the component and made available to domain and application engineers. In some cases, V&V efforts might be directed at a group of strongly related components rather than at an individual component, and this information should also be available. Groupings might include components that are expected to occur together in multiple applications, or might include variants of one domain artifact.

The information on similar components within the domain should be consistent in content and format, in order to allow the information to be easily used by both domain engineers and application engineers. The information that should be communicated includes the following:

- V&V planning decisions and rationale.
- V&V analysis activities.
- V&V test cases and procedures.
- V&V results and findings.

5.5 RISK MANAGEMENT

Risk management is a process that involves identifying, assessing, and controlling risks in the software development process [Charette 1990]. The risks can be development risks that prevent the system from being completed on time, within budget, and with full functionality, or operation risks that cause damage (e.g., human injury, loss or corruption of data, unauthorized access to data) when the system is in deployed operation. Identifying risks is a daunting task within single system development; this task is even more difficult as components are developed with the intent of their use in multiple systems. Risk management often involves a tradeoff between conflicting interests, such as increasing the time to market in order to perform additional testing to increase assurance that the product meets certain requirements, with a potential loss of market share due to the delay. Risk management within a reuse-based environment must consider not only the viewpoints of different stakeholders in a system but also those of different stakeholders in multiple systems as well as the stakeholders in the product-line assets. Although not necessarily different in substance, the magnitude of risk management has increased dramatically.

Criticality analysis, which is a form of risk analysis, is used to determine the level of assurance required for an individual application system or for the components in a system. Criticality analysis also needs to be extended to include consideration of multiple application systems developed using a reuse-based approach, to guide the level of effort for the various components. Four aspects should be considered in determining the level of assurance for reusable components [Edwards and Weide 1997]:

- *Span of application*—the number of components or systems that depend on the component.
- *Criticality*—potential impact due to a fault in the component.
- *Marketability*—degree to which a component is likely to be reused by a third party.
- *Lifetime*—length of time that a component will be used.

5.6   CERTIFICATION

The IEEE standard definition for *certification* is "the process of confirming that a system or component complies with its specified requirements and is acceptable for operational use" [IEEE 1990]. (Actually, this is the third of three definitions, where the first two address a written guarantee and a formal demonstration, respectively, of this confirmation.) The confirmation of compliance of an item with its specification can be performed by assessing some combination of the personnel developing the item, the process by which the item is developed, or the quality attributes of the item itself [Voas 1998]. The concept of software certification is in itself a controversial topic, with debate on certification of software engineers, the relationship between a good process and a good product, and the ability to assess the quality attributes of software products.

These issues apply to software that is developed under any methodology, including reuse-based software engineering. However, reuse-based development introduces further issues into the certification process. The reliance on previously developed components [often commercial off-the-shelf (COTS) components] means that the quality of the developers and the development process of the component may be unknown, leaving product certification as the only approach. Needing to understand the implementation of each component undermines much of the advantage of incorporating reusable components in a blackbox manner, through an understanding of the interface and functional descriptions. Even if the component is thoroughly understood, knowing and describing the exact conditions under which the component may be used without violating the conditions of assurance is a daunting task. The legal implications on warranty and liability from certification of a reusable component or of a system developed with reusable components are not as yet resolved, and can impact the developer of the component, the (re)user of the component (who is the developer of a software system), and the acquirer of the system.

5.7 EXERCISES

1. (A) How does configuration management in system development differ from configuration management in a reuse-based software engineering environment?

2. (A) Why is it important within a software reuse environment to document what was performed during testing and V&V?

3. (B) Why is each of the aspects important in determining the proper level of assurance for a software component?
   (a) Span of application.
   (b) Criticality.
   (c) Marketability.
   (d) Lifetime.

4. (B) Give an example of an operation risk. Give an example of a development risk. What are the similarities and differences between these two types of risk?

5.8 FURTHER READING

The texts and papers by Berlack [1992], Charette [1989], Hetzel [1993], Lewis [1992], Perry [1991], and Wallace and Fujii [1989] provide more information on the various software support activities, usually in reference to application engineering.

Chapter 6

Institutionalizing Reuse

The most difficult part of implementing a software reuse program within an organization may not be identifying and addressing technical issues, but rather cultural and organizational issues [Aharonian 1991, Bassett 1998, Hunter 1996, Jacobson et al. 1997]. Software reuse requires that developers, and development and acquisition organizations, approach software development from a different perspective. This change in perspective must involve changes in many areas of the operation of the organization, including organizational structure, incentives, funding, training, and attitude.

The goal of institutionalizing software reuse is to make reuse simply a part of the way that the organization develops and manages its software, rather than as a separate effort apart from other software activities. Software needs to be treated as an asset rather than as an expense, and reuse needs to be interwoven into the operational processes of the organization. Institutionalization of software reuse, as with any other organizational changes of any magnitude, will not occur quickly, and will be a separate focus of the organization for some period of time.

6.1 ORGANIZATIONAL READINESS

One of the first steps to be performed when deciding whether to implement a software reuse program within an organization is to determine the current status of the organization and its ability to manage and control its processes. A systematic approach to reuse requires that an organization be able to define, use, and refine processes. Several reuse maturity models, similar in approach to the Software Engineering Institute's Capability Maturity Model for Software (CMM-SW) [Paulk et al. 1993], have been developed to assist organizations in assessing their practices relative to software reuse.

Koltun and Hudson [1991] presented their draft reuse maturity model in a position paper at the Fourth Annual Workshop on Software Reuse (WISR4). Their model is designed to assess organizational processes that are necessary for achieving high levels of software reuse. The model contains five levels: initial/chaotic, monitored, coordinated, planned, and ingrained. Ten dimensions or aspects were mapped against the five levels to produce a *reuse maturity framework*, as shown in Table 6.1. The organization's readiness to incorporate systematic reuse is determined by a series of questions related to the *dimensions of maturity*.

Lim [1998] developed an organizational reengineering for reuse assessment (ORRA) tool for collecting benchmark data on software development with reusable assets. The assessment collects data from the organization considering the aspects of management, personnel, economics and metrics, technology, process, and reusable assets and products. A set of questions is used in interviews to compare the respondents' ratings of the importance to software reuse of areas within the aspects with how well the organization performs in that area. Both the importance and the current performance are evaluated on a scale of 1–5. The results are used to identify those areas that need attention because they are important to software reuse but the organization does not currently perform well in those areas.

The Software Productivity Consortium [SPC 1993a] includes a reuse capability model (RCM) within its reuse adoption process. The RCM is a self-assessment and planning aid for the organization. The RCM consists of an assessment model to understand the present state of the reuse practices within the organization and an implementation model to guide the implementation of the reuse program within the organization. The assessment model, which is summarized in Table 6.2, contains a set of critical success factors, each of which has one or more goals. The organization evaluates each goal using two criteria:

- The extent to which the organization meets the specified goal
- The expected impact on the organization's reuse capability from fully satisfying the stated goal

6.2 BARRIERS TO REUSE

Many authors on the subject of software reuse have included a list of issues or barriers that must be resolved in order to implement software reuse within an organization. While the details of the lists vary from author to author, they share a great deal in common. Table 6.3 summarizes the barriers discussed by several authors.

TABLE 6.1 Reuse Maturity Framework

			LEVEL		
Dimensions of Maturity	1 Initial/Chaotic	2 Monitored	3 Coordinated	4 Planned	5 Ingrained
Motivation/culture	Reuse is discouraged	Reuse is encouraged	Reuse is incentivized, reinforced, rewarded	Reuse is indoctrinated	Reuse is "the way we do business"
Planning for reuse	Nonexistent	Grassroots activity	Targets of opportunity	Business imperative	Part of a strategic plan
Breadth of reuse involvement	Individual worker	Workgroup	Department	Division	Enterprise wide
Responsibility for making reuse happen (advocacy + day-to-day management)	Individual initiative (personal goal; as time allows)	Shared initiative	Dedicated individual	Dedicated group	Corporate group (for visibility not control) with division liaisons
Process by which reuse is leveraged	Development process chaotic; unclear where reuse comes in	Reuse questions raised at design reviews (after the fact)	Design emphasis placed on reuse of off-the-shelf parts	Focus on developing families of products	All software products genericized for future reuse
Reuse inventory (assets)	Salvage yard (no apparent structure to collection)	Catalog identifies language- and platform-specific parts	Catalog organized along application-specific lines	Catalog includes generic data processing functions	Planned activity to acquire or develop missing pieces in catalog

TABLE 6.1 *(Continued)*

Dimensions of Maturity	LEVEL				
	1 Initial/Chaotic	2 Monitored	3 Coordinated	4 Planned	5 Ingrained
Classification activity	Informal, individualized ("in the head," "in the drawer")	Multiple independent schemes for classifying parts	Single scheme, catalog published periodically	Some domain analyses performed to determine categories	Formal, complete, consistent, timely classification
Technology support	Personal tools, if any	Lots of tools, e.g., CM, but not specialized to reuse	Classification aides and synthesis aides	Electronic library separate from development environment	Automated support integrated with development system
Metrics	No metrics on level of reuse, payoff, or cost of reuse	Number of lines of reuse code factored into cost models	Manual tracking of reuse occurrences of catalog parts	Analyses performed to identify expected payoffs from developing reusable parts	All system utilities, software tools, and accounting mechanisms instrumented to track reuse
Legal, contractual, accounting considerations	Inhibitor to getting started	Internal accounting scheme for sharing costs, allocating benefits	Data rights and compensation issues resolved with customer	Royalty scheme for all suppliers and customers	Software treated as key capital asset

Source: Koltun and Hudson [1991].

TABLE 6.2   Reuse Capability Model

Critical Success Factors		Goals
	Application Development Factors	
Asset awareness and accessibility	AA-1	Developers are aware of, can find, and have access to any relevant reusable assets and external sources of assets
	AA-2	Developers are aware of and reuse assets that are specifically acquired or developed for their application
Asset identification	AI-1	Developers identify potential reusable assets in each major activity in the development life cycle that might satisfy their development needs
	AI-2	Developers identify potential reusable assets before establishing constraints that limit reuse opportunities
	AI-3	Developers identify and reuse early lifecycle assets that result in the reuse of corresponding later lifecycle assets
	AI-4	Developers identify and reuse designated high-payoff, reusable assets
Asset evaluation and verification	AE-1	Developers understand and evaluate reusable assets against their needs before committing to reuse and asset
	AE-2	Developers verify asset quality before selection
Application integrability	AN-1	Technologies applied in developing applications (i.e., processes, methods, tools) facilitate the integration of reusable assets
	Asset Development Factors	
Needs identification	NI-1	Current developer needs for solutions are identified
	NI-2	Anticipated developer needs for solutions are identified
	NI-3	Current customer needs for solutions are identified
	NI-4	Anticipated customer needs for solutions are identified
	NI-5	Identified needs are used as a basis for acquiring or developing reusable assets to meet the specified needs
Asset interface and architecture definition	AD-1	The relationships of an asset to its external environment are defined

TABLE 6.2 (*Continued*)

Critical Success Factors		Goals
	AD-2	The relationships between assets within the same major activity (e.g., requirements analysis, design) of the development lifecycle of a product are defined
Needs and solutions relationships	NS-1	Transformation relationships between needs and their corresponding solutions are defined (e.g., from requirements to design, from design to code)
	NS-2	Identified transformation relationships between needs and solutions are used as a basis for acquiring or developing broad-spectrum assets.
Commonality and variability definition	CV-1	Commonality and variability relationships between needs are defined and used to acquire or develop assets to meet multiple needs
	CV-2	Commonality and variability relationships between solutions (assets, architectures of assets) are defined and used to acquire or develop adaptable solutions for meeting multiple needs
Asset value determination	AV-1	The net value of an asset is estimated on the basis of experience data and identified needs
	AV-2	The estimated net value of an asset is used as a basis for focusing the organization's resources on acquiring or developing high-payoff assets for reuse
Asset reusability	AR-1	Technologies applied in developing reusable assets facilitate their integration into applications
Asset quality	AQ-1	Reusable assets are under configuration control
	AQ-2	Feedback on reusable assets is collected and used to maintain and enhance the reusable assets
	AQ-3	Sufficient data are provided for an application developer to understand, evaluate, and apply reusable assets
	AQ-4	Reusable assets are verified against their specifications
	AQ-5	Reusable asset quality goals or standards are established and tracked
		Management Factors
Organization commitment	OC-1	Management commits to defining, implementing, and improving the organization's approach to reuse and demonstrates its commitment to the staff

TABLE 6.2 (*Continued*)

Critical Success Factors		Goals
	OC-2	Management commits funding, staffing, and other resources to define, implement, and improve the organization's approach to reuse.
	OC-3	The staff supports the organization's approach to defining, implementing, and improving the organization's approach to reuse
	OC-4	Management structures its organization, policies, procedures, and standards to facilitate a standard reuse process supporting multiple product development efforts
Planning and direction	PD-1	Reuse strategies are defined for product development efforts in support of product objectives, and product development activities are planned and directed in accordance with the product development's reuse strategy
	PD-2	Product-line reuse strategies are developed to maximize the benefits of reuse over sets of related products, and the product-line activities are planned and directed in accordance with the strategies
	PD-3	Management develops a long-term strategy for improving the organization's reuse capability, and the organization's improvement efforts are planned and directed in accordance with the improvement strategy
	PD-4	New business opportunities are created that take advantage of the organization's reuse capability and reusable assets
Costing and pricing	CP-1	Reuse cost accounting procedures are defined and enhanced
	CP-2	Management establishes a long-term plan for funding reuse activities and improvement efforts
	CP-3	Product pricing and funding strategies take into account expected costs and anticipated benefits of reuse over the product or product line
Legal and contractual constraints	LC-1	Reuse legal on contractual constraints are identified and enforced
	LC-2	Legal and contractual constraints on reuse are removed or reduced to increase the potential for reuse when feasible

TABLE 6.2   (*Continued*)

Critical Success Factors		Goals
Intergroup coordination	IC-1	Application and asset development activities are coordinated between and among application and asset development groups to identify, track, and resolve intergroup issues
Process and Technology Factors		
Process definition and integration	PI-1	Reuse activities and resources are identified in the product software development plan
	PI-2	Standard reuse processes are defined and integrated with the organization's standard software development process
	PI-3	Standard reuse processes provide sufficient flexibility for tailoring the standard processes to the unique needs of the product development efforts
	PI-4	The standard reuse processes have sufficient flexibility to adapt to new product environments (markets)
Measurement	MS-1	The impact of reuse on cost, schedule, and product is estimated during development planning; then actual impacts are recorded as the development proceeds
	MS-2	Reuse experiences from past and current projects are collected and made available
	MS-3	The effectiveness and efficiency of reuse technologies are measured and used as a basis for determining the most suitable technologies for given situations
Continuous process improvement	CI-1	Performance of the standard reuse processes is measured and analyzed to increase understanding and identify strengths and weaknesses
	CI-2	Plans are established to systematically address weaknesses identified in the standard reuse processes
Training	TR-1	The knowledge and skills necessary to effectively apply an organization's reuse technologies are determined, gaps in the staff's knowledge and skills are identified, and a plan is developed and enacted to fill the gaps
	TR-2	The effectiveness of training to fill the gaps in necessary reuse technology knowledge and skills is measured and analyzed to identify weaknesses

TABLE 6.2 (*Continued*)

Critical Success Factors		Goals
	TR-3	Plans are established to systematically address the weaknesses identified in reuse technology training
Tool support	TS-1	Reuse tools are used to support defined reuse activities and methods for which they are effective
	TS-2	Reuse tools are acquired, developed, or tailored to support the standard reuse processes
	TS-3	Reuse tools are integrated with the organization's software development environment
	TS-4	Reuse tools provide sufficient flexibility to adapt to new process or product environments
Technology innovation	TI-1	Management and staff are aware of new and evolving technologies and standards that may affect their products and reusable assets
	TI-2	New technologies are identified that will meet or drive customer needs, have a clear benefit, and take advantage of the organization's reuse capability; selected technologies are inserted into the organization's process or product

Source: SPC 1993a.

TABLE 6.3   Barriers to Implementing Software Reuse

Koltun and Hudson [1991]	Aharonian [1991]	Hooper and Chester [1991]	Bassett [1997]
Cultural	Economics	Organizational management and structure	Conceptual
Institutional	Management	Organizational behavior	Technological
Financial	Technology transfer	Contractual and legal considerations	Managerial
Technical	Training	Financial considerations	Infrastructural
Legal	Legal issues		Cultural
	Politics		
	Tradition		
	Continual advancements in technology		

6.2.1 Cultural

Any change to an organization or its processes will face resistance, since it is easier to just continue to do things the way they are done now. Change requires effort, and without the proper motivation people will stay focused on the day-to-day effort of getting the job done. Table 6.4 lists a number of attitudes that can resist implementing software reuse within an organization [Bassett 1997].

6.2.2 Managerial

Project managers are generally tasked and incentivized to ensure the success in development of particular systems. This provides a framework for managers to resist any activities or restrictions that they perceive to detract from their goal of developing that system within budget and schedule. Managers with this type of incentive will balk at committing resources to find common solutions with other systems or adhering to common standards that seem burdensome to their system.

6.2.3 Technological

Legacy, stovepipe systems have led organizations into point solutions, lacking in common standards, common tools, and common business processes. The choice of the next tool or solution is often made with an eye toward staying on the cutting edge, without considering the impact on compatibility or inter-operability.

Even though architectural description languages are available, the architectures used to describe complex software systems are still depicted with box and line diagrams. The architectures are brittle, nonflexible, and non-extensible. Architectures that support software reuse should address the need for component architectures that are adaptable.

TABLE 6.4 Attitudes that Resist Implementation of Software Reuse

Fear of tests/measures
Entrenched apathy
Compensation based on size of staff
Lack of commitment
Cowboy or loner mentality
Plagiarism is bad
Incompetence
Fear of the unknown
Peer rivalry
Fear of failure
Gadgeteers
Everything we do is unique

Despite emphasis and improvements in software metrics since the late 1990s, many organizations fail to implement a systematic and thorough metrics program. Without the ability to measure both the product and the process, it is very difficult to control current activities much less improve them or project them into the future.

6.2.4   Infrastructural

If common processes are to be implemented within an organization, the knowledge of those processes and the tools that support them must be distributed across the organization. On-line information and help-desk support should be available in all areas.

The organization's processes must adapt as technology support enables particular activities to be performed more efficiently. An activity that lies on the critical path may be improved by a new tool or process, and force an activity that was not previously on the critical path to become critical. Management must be aware of the organizationwide implications of technological improvements.

6.3   OVERCOMING THE BARRIERS TO REUSE

A survey of European industrial reuse projects concluded that the key factors for a successful reuse project are the commitment of management, the existence of training and awareness actions, and an effort to find a reuse approach that fits the context of the company [Morisio et al. 1999].

6.3.1   Executive Support

Executive support for software reuse seems to be a key ingredient for the successful implementation of systematic software reuse, to the point of being a necessary (while not sufficient) factor for success. This is not surprising, since systematic software reuse requires initial funding, organizational restructuring, new processes, and revised business practices, none of which can occur without the commitment of top-level management. The management must be willing to allow time for its investment to mature, and for the organization to make the necessary behavior and attitude changes.

6.3.2   Training

Academic preparation of software engineers does a good job of teaching languages, methods, and tools, and most computer science graduates understand software at the code level. However, our educational system is focused on the individual student, and is not oriented to teach the team concepts that are required for system development, much less the component-based processes of software reuse. An organization that is committed to implementing software reuse must devote resources to provide training to its developers and managers, not only on the tools but also on the processes of software reuse.

6.3.3 Incentives

Project managers, in particular, must receive incentives to move their attention from their own system development activities to the greater needs of the organization. Their contribution to the efficiency and performance of the overall development organization, and not just to their own project, needs to be explicitly a part of their job evaluation. The organization should also provide adequate incentives for developers that produce reusable components and for developers that use those components, and not allow either group to become second-class citizens.

6.3.4 Incremental Approach

A phased or incremental approach to the introduction of software reuse can be used to reduce the risk of failure from using a big-bang approach. This type of approach is recommended by the large majority of software reuse implementers. Several incremental approaches are described below.

The approach advocated by Hooper and Chester [1991] includes nine phases for implementing a software reuse program within an organization. The phases are listed below, with the recognition that there are implied feedback loops and iterations.

PA1: Assess current software engineering practices and remedy major shortcomings.

PA2: Obtain top-level management support to undertake investigation of reuse feasibility.

PA3: Identify one or more application areas (if any) that are important to the organization's mission, are well understood, and have recurring similar software requirements.

PA4: Conduct an inventory of reusable assets for the identified application area(s).

PA5: Establish an initial library of reusable components.

PA6: Determine and conduct a pilot software project employing reuse.

PA7: Evaluate experience/success with reuse in the pilot project, present results to management, and obtain a decision whether to proceed.

PA8: Expand reuse activities to additional application domains and organizational segments, as success and management approval warrant.

PA9: Conduct the following activities as part of the practice of software reuse (in the pilot project and in all succeeding reuse efforts):

- Institute management policies and practices to encourage reuse.
- Institute or carry out a software engineering process incorporating the creation and use of reusable products.
- Adjust the organizational structure and staffing as appropriate to support reuse.
- Implement or update library mechanisms.
- Perform domain analysis of selected domains and develop or acquire enough reusable components to conduct reuse for the domains.
- Continually assess the effectiveness of the reuse-based process and adjust or augment it as appropriate.

A Reuse Working Group formed as part of an effort to establish a software reuse program within Motorola recommended a plan of action for its software managers [Joos 1991]. The plan consisted of eleven steps:

1. Find a champion (for reuse) for each role in the reuse organization (i.e., manager, reuse engineer, reuse architect, and librarian). They must have strong software engineering backgrounds.
2. Provide these personnel with reuse training (i.e., object-oriented analysis and design, software reuse, and domain analysis).
3. Analyze the initial target domain.
4. The reuse working group should establish standards (templates, documentation, classification), and the department personnel should initiate them.
5. Select and obtain state-of-the-art tools for the department.
6. Have the personnel become expert with the tools.
7. Populate a reuse repository.
8. Collect and record the baseline metrics data.
9. Start training other software engineers how to use the tools.
10. Begin designing all software with reuse and for reuse from day 1.
11. Provide incentives for reuse.

Jacobson, Griss, and Jonsson [1997] argue that a systematic, incremental transition will reduce the risk of stalling the transition process because of the large number of simultaneous changes in multiple aspects of the organization. They describe an incremental transition process that leads an organization through a five-step process:

TRA1: Creating a Directive to Reengineer the Software Business. The management of the company creates and publicizes a reengineering directive, as a clear statement of the high-level reuse business goals and their rationale. The directive defines and communicates the initial business, process, architecture, organization, and reuse goals. It defines the scope of the changes and establishes accountability. Management empowers an initial group of people (the transition team) to envision the reuse business.

TRA2: Envisioning the New Reuse Business. According to business needs and the initial application family engineering efforts, the transition team develops a high-level vision of the new architecture, software business processes, and organization. They identify stakeholders, champions, and early adopters. The specific goals are documented in an objective statement. Some transition plans are developed in which several versions of a reuse business might be defined as intermediate points for incremental adoption. Significant communication begins and key stakeholders are engaged in the transition.

TRA3: Reverse-Engineering the Existing Software Development Organization. The transition team identifies and studies the existing architecture, software assets, software processes, organization, tools, and baseline measures. The goal is to understand and baseline current software engineering practice, identify assets, determine the status of reuse, and understand organization issues.

TRA4: Forward-Engineering the New Reuse Business. Develop the desired software engineering processes, organization, and appropriate software engineering environment and tools.

TRA5: Implementing the New Reuse Business. The new model is installed into the business. People are trained, and processes, organizations, architectures, and systems are (incrementally) replaced.

TRA6: Continuous Process Improvement. As the new business becomes operational, collect and analyze reuse process and product metrics to measure progress, identify key areas for further improvements and then make small process changes.

Software Productivity Consortium. One portion of the RCM discussed in Section 6.1 is the implementation model. The implementation model constitutes a prioritization and partitioning of the critical success factors by mapping the goals of the critical success factors to the four stages in the model: opportunistic, integrated, leveraged, and anticipating. This mapping provides guidance on the goals that must be achieved in order for the organization to function at a certain stage, and hence provides the increments that should be achieved by the organization. The mapping provided in the RCM is presented as one possible implementation model, and allows for different possible mappings to produce alternative implementation models.

6.4 EXERCISES

1. (A) Why should organizational assessment be one of the first steps in implementing software reuse within the organization?

2. (A) Do technical or nontechnical issues pose greater barriers to institutionalizing software reuse?

3. (A) What are some disadvantages to implementing software reuse using a phased approach?

4. (A) Why is it important to the success of software reuse for senior management to support its implementation? How can senior management demonstrate support for software reuse?

6.5 FURTHER READING

The text by Tracz [1995] provides an entertaining look at the nuts and bolts of institutionalizing software reuse. The texts by Jaffe and Scott [1999] and Lim [1998] and the SPC guidebook [SPC 1993a] provide more information on organizational change issues and on software reuse adoption. The article by Williamson [1997] discusses cultural issues in implementing software reuse from the perspective of the chief information officer.

Domain Engineering: Building for Reuse

Domain engineering is the set of activities involved in developing reusable assets across an entire application domain, or a family of applications. Domain engineering differs from application engineering in terms of *intent*, *process*, and *product*. The *intent* is to develop reusable components. With application engineering, we are concerned mostly with developing a component that addresses the specific needs of the application at hand; reusability of the component is a desirable by product, but not the focus of the development activities. The *process* of domain engineering is distinctly different from that of application engineering in terms of both the inputs and the individual activities that make it up. Domain engineering also differs from application engineering in the product to the extent that the product of domain engineering is (or should be) reusable by design, and it may not be concrete enough to be used within an application as is; it may require well-defined tailoring mechanisms to make them usable for a specific application. In this part we discuss the process and product of domain engineering.

In Chapter 7, we define the desirable characteristics of reusable assets, and provide an overview of the various approaches to acquiring them. In particular, we recognize reusability as the combination of *usefulness*, and *usability*. The usefulness of a reusable asset within an application domain refers to the frequency with which the component may be needed. Its usability refers to the ease with which it may be used and integrated into applications within the domain.

Chapter 8 is concerned with domain analysis, a set of activities aimed at identifying the common aspects to applications within an application domain. Broadly speaking, the output of domain analysis is a set of software specifications for those parts that are common to the domain. Those specifications serve as input for domain design and implementation, which aim at building more or less concrete realizations of these reusable assets so that they may be instantiated, adapted, and integrated into the development of applications within that domain. Domain analysis is concerned with the identification of *useful components*, while domain design and implementation is concerned with the *usability* of the artifacts that implement domain components. Identifying commonalities within an application domain relies on *abstraction*. Chapter 8 takes a look at *abstraction* and factorization, from an ontological point of view, regardless of the representation within which reusable components are described.

Chapter 9 attempts to compare programming paradigms from a reuse point of view. The premise of the chapter is that commonalities occur in the natural world and that a reuse-oriented development paradigm should express those commonalities in a way that maximizes their usability, that is, that minimizes the effort required to instantiate and integrate a reusable component. We take a look at the three programming paradigms (declarative, procedural, and object-oriented) in terms of abstraction and composition, with the lofty goal of characterizing the situations in which a particular paradigm is preferable to the others. We fall short of that goal, but in the process, advocate multiparadigm development.

Chapter 7

Building Reusable Assets: An Overview

Building custom software remains the default development paradigm. This is done by crafting individual components and assembling new and existing components into modules, subsystems, and entire applications. The purpose of software reuse practice may be seen as an attempt to reduce the number of individual components that need to be crafted for each new application or system to be built, and an attempt to raise the level of the component assembly language (see, e.g., frame-based software engineering by NETRON [Basset 1987]). In this chapter, and in Chapters 8–14, we are concerned with the problem of building those reusable components and the component assembly language in such a way that the custom part of software development required for new applications be reduced to a minimum. This requires a set of skills, work methods, and work tools that are distinctly different from those required by application engineering, with or without reusable components.

We first start by defining reusabiliy characteristics in general terms of essence and form. We discuss reusability characteristics in more detail for specific reusable assets; development paradigm-dependent reusability characteristics are discussed in more detail in Chapter 9. In Section 7.2, we provide an overview of the various ways in which reusable assets may be acquired, taking into account economic and businesswide issues. In particular, we provide a brief discussion of reengineering as a way of identifying reusable components, or enhancing their reusability, and of application generators, as a special kind of reusable artifacts. We discuss domain engineering lifecycles in Section 7.3, and conclude in Section 7.4.

7.1 REUSABILITY

What makes a software asset reusable? What is the difference between a custom component and a reusable component? Notwithstanding the differences in terms of external packaging of reusable assets, reusability is a continuous spectrum along which software assets might fall—the purpose of domain engineering is to ensure that the products of the engineering process fall *systematically* and *consistently* within the reusable end of the spectrum. We like to define reusability as the sum of two characteristics: (1) *usability*, which assesses the extent to which a software asset is "easy" to use, regardless of its functionality; and (2) *usefulness*, which is the extent to which a reusable asset will *often* be needed, regardless of its packaging. Naturally, the two characteristics aren't completely orthogonal, and we will illustrate the dependencies where important. Both characteristics depend on the nature of the asset (product vs. processor), its granularity (component vs. subsystem), its stage of development (e.g., analysis vs. design), and the development paradigm (object-oriented vs. procedural vs. logical). In this section, we focus on the most common features of these characteristics; more specific features are discussed throughout this chapter and in Chapters 8 and 9.

7.1.1 Usability

Usability is the extent to which a reusable asset is "easy" to use. Regardless of the nature of the reusable asset, reuse involves four steps, in one form or another:

1. *Selection*, which is the process of identifying a reusable asset as a potential candidate for fulfilling a need at hand
2. *Analysis*, which is the process of understanding how to use the asset in general, and the customizations required to adapt it to the problem at hand
3. *Customization*, which is the process of adapting the reusable asset to the problem at hand, if need be
4. *Instantiation*, which is the process of integrating the—possibly customized—reusable component into the system at hand

"Ease of use" concerns all four steps. The first two steps have to do with what might be called *extrinsic packaging*, that is, essentially accompanying documentation, whereas the last two steps are affected by the *intrinsic packaging* of the asset, which consists of the particular choice of language constructs that define the usage interface of the reusable asset. To the extent that the documentation helps one understand the intrinsic packaging, we discuss intrinsic packaging first.

Krueger has proposed a valuable way of thinking about reusable components [Krueger 1992]. We think of reusable components as a combination of two things: a *specification* or *definition*, and one or several *concrete realizations* or *implementations*. For the time being, we will not worry about the realization part, as that part is often hidden from the user—a developer—especially in the case of blackbox reuse. The specification part consists of two things: a *fixed part* and a *variable part*. The fixed part consists of the part of the reusable asset that must be used as is. The variable part is that part of the asset that depends on the particular use, and may either be provided along with the reusable asset or have to be supplied by the user. Figure 7.1 illustrates this point.

Finding the separation between the variable part and the fixed part is probably the most significant engineering decision of a reusable asset, and involves several tradeoffs. First, there is the issue of identifying the variable part in the application domain, *regardless of any packaging considerations*. Karlsson and Brantestam [1995] consider that the identification of the functionality of a reusable asset starts with the identification of the functionality for a specific use, which is then followed by a generalization step, where such requirements are adapted to handle a variety of needs. To start with, anticipating those needs in advance is a nontrivial task, which is discussed in Section 7.1.2. Once those needs have been anticipated, the goal is to account for all those variations while keeping the size of the fixed part at a maximum (see Fig. 7.2), and that of the variable part to a minimum. For example, assume that we wish to design a car platform that will handle four-cylinder, manual-transmission, front-wheel drive, four-door sedans; four-cylinder, manual-transmission, all-wheel drive, four-door sedans; and four-cylinder, automatic-transmission all-wheel drive four-door sedans. If we view the car as the combination of a "power bloc" (the subsystem that makes the car move) and a chassis, then we end up with one chassis (fixed part), and three different "power blocs" (variable part), with no reuse between the power blocs. If we break down the power bloc into an engine, a transmission, and a powertrain, then we recognize that the same

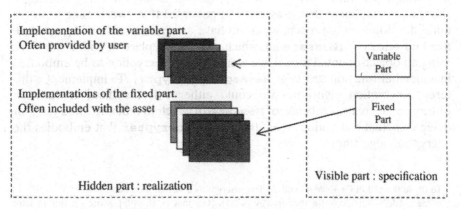

FIGURE 7.1 Anatomy of a reusable asset.

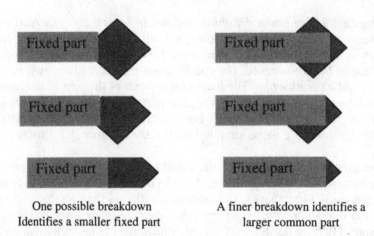

One possible breakdown   A finer breakdown identifies a
Identifies a smaller fixed part   larger common part

FIGURE 7.2   A better breakdown maximizes the size of the fixed part.

engine can power all three models, and that only two models of transmission and powertrain are needed to power all three car models.

What is at issue is not simply finding the right size or *granularity* level for the components in the application domain; if we start off with the "wrong" boundaries, we may have to break our applications into much smaller pieces before we start identifying common pieces.

The second challenge, once the variability in the target domain has been properly identified and circumscribed, is to find an implementation-specific packaging that keeps in one part, all of the variable part *and as little of the fixed part as possible*; and in the other part, the remainder of the fixed part. Suppose that we are dealing with a network application that handles messages transmitted using different encryption algorithms. From an application domain point of view, the variability is a well-defined *encryption algorithm*. How can we package that variability in such a way that we isolate the encryption algorithm in a component that is as small as possible? If we were using a procedural development approach, we could have a single function with signature **String** encrypt(**Message** m), which we could replace at will. If we were using an object-oriented model, we would expect encryption to be embodied in a member function **String Message**::encrypt(). To implement a different encryption algorithm, we could either edit the member function encrypt, or create a subclass of **Message** in which to redefine encrypt,[1] or delegate actual encryption to another object **Encrypter** that embodies the encryption algorithm.[2]

---

[1] To those trained in C++, we should declare encrypt as a virtual method.
[2] Some readers will recognize the *strategy pattern* [Gamma et al. 1995]. More on this in later chapters.

As we can see, different development paradigms put the boundary between the fixed part and the variable part differently. Further, within the same paradigm, different solutions may be used that differ in many respects, including the cleanliness of the separation between the fixed part and the variable part, the effort required to customize the variable part, and some other design-level considerations.

The third challenge consists of striking a good balance between generality and adaptation effort. An abstract reusable component will be usable in more situations than will a functionally equivalent concrete component. However, a concrete component will require little or no adaptation effort *where it is usable* whereas an abstract component will require more significant adaptation effort across its usability range. Figure 7.3*a* makes that point. Different abstraction techniques have different profiles (see Fig. 7.3*b*) and different associated costs.

Abstraction that is based on "fuzziness" and incompleteness is low-cost, but comes with a high level of adaptation efforts. For example, a sort component packaged as an algorithm in pseudocode may be sufficiently general to apply to any collection of data, but will require writing the actual code for every specific use. Abstraction that is based on using advanced parameterization and composition techniques is costlier to implement (intellectually or resource-wise), but yields lower overall adaptation efforts. In the "sort" example, generality similar to that for the informal pseudocode may be achieved with an ingeniously coded function template. Generally speaking, new technological advances in software reuse help push the generality–adaptation effort curve toward lower efforts. Chapters 11 and 12 deal with such techniques.

Let us now talk about the *external packaging* of reusable components. This is the kind of information required to support *selection* and *analysis*. Selection requires information that can be matched against a developer's need expressed in the form of a query. This information can be in the form of a

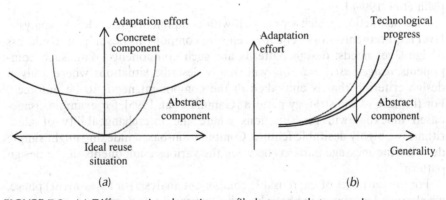

FIGURE 7.3 (a) Difference in adaptation profile between abstract and concrete components; (b) new reuse technologies Help push the generality vs. effort curve towards the origin.

textual description, a list of terms taken from a specific controlled vocabulary, or a set of specifications of the component [Mili et al. 1995a]. We have devoted an entire chapter to reusable component search and retrieval (Chapter 16), and we will not elaborate on the various indexing and retrieval techniques. In this section, we focus on issues related to documentation.

First, there is a general issue related to the *style* of *indexing*, or more generally, the style of description of the "functionality" of reusable components. We distinguish between two styles:

- *Usage-based indexing*, which describes the different potential uses of a component in terms that are close to the way developers might *first* express their needs

- *Computation-based indexing*, which describes the intrinsic properties of the component, regardless of any particular use

We illustrate the difference through a simple example of a sort component. *Usage-based indexing* might stipulate that the component could rank students on the basis of their grades; employees, their salaries; salespeople, their sales; and so on. *A computation-based description* might say that the component takes as input a collection C and reorganizes it in such a way that for all $c \in C$, we have $f(c) \leq f(successor(c))$, for some user-supplied function $f()$. With usage-based indexing, we must anticipate *all* the different ways that the component can be used so that the component can be retrieved where it can be used. However, usage-based indexing has the advantage of being expressed in the same language in which developers first express their needs, and will not require a *translation* effort by the developer. With computation-based indexing, developers have to express their needs (a *problem*) in a way that can be matched against the description of how a component behaves (a *solution*); in other words, they have to solve the problem in their heads first, before they can start searching for a component that *implements* that solution [Mili et al. 1995a].

This distinction, which works well with components that address analysis-level requirements, works equally well with components developed to address design-level needs; design patterns are such components. With such components, *usage-based indexing* will simply describe situations where a given design criterion that is embodied in the component needs to be enforced. For the case of the strategy pattern [Gamma et al. 1995], for example, usage-based indexing will list situations where the interchangeability of algorithms is a highly desirable feature. Computation-based indexing might simply describe the message patterns between the various components of the design pattern.

For the purposes of the reusable component analysis (or assessment) phase, we also need information about *how* the component performs its function, and *how* to use it. Information about *how* a component performs its function or fulfills its role, in general, depends on the kind of component (analysis, design, design pattern), on the kind of reuse (whitebox vs. blackbox reuse), and on those aspects of its structure that may be of concern to the reuser. For example, if performance is an issue, it may be important to know either the algorithm or its complexity, to know how much swapping space is required, and so forth. Generally speaking, the information can be either *intrinsic* or *structural* in the sense that we show, to varying degrees of detail, the actual component arti- facts and their interrelationships, or *extrinsic* or *attributive* in the sense that we include values of various measures such as performance metrics, quality metrics, and so forth. The kind of information that is included depends on the kind of reuse; if the component is meant to be reused in a blackbox fashion, then *extrinsic* information will suffice—otherwise, we need both.

Information about *how* to use a component must include several informa- tion items, including at least the following:

- *Environmental Requirements.* Such requirements may include a software platform, an infrastructure component [e.g., an object request broker (ORB), or some other software bus], a development paradigm (e.g., if the component is a model fragment), a service (e.g., persistence), and so forth.
- *Contextual Bindings.* This means the various settings we need to perform so that the component satisfies the need at hand (e.g., connecting the component to a database driver, setting the proper environment vari- ables, using the proper terminology).
- *Adaptation Procedure.* This includes information about the operations needed to custom-tailor the component to the application at hand. The adaptation procedure can be more or less constrained, depending on the type of the component, and the maturity of the reuse framework. On one end of the spectrum, we have informal guidelines for adapting highly abstract reusable components (e.g., user requirements). On another end of the spectrum, we have specific tools that transform the reusable com- ponent into a concrete form, based on the specification of handful of parameters. We have everything in between.
- *Instantiation and Assembly.* Instantiation and assembly are related to the *operation* of the reusable component within its reuse context, once it has been adapted to that context, namely, its *integration* within its host envi- ronment. This is best understood in the context of component frame- works where the construction of the individual components, and the *knowledge of how these components are related once assembled*, is not enough to know how to use the framework. We also need to know how to create *instances* of the components, and how to *connect* them to enact the collaborations inherent in the framework. If we are dealing with an executable component, then instantiation and assembly correspond to launching the component and setting the right command arguments, and

so on. For the case of an analysis model fragment, this consists of importing the model fragment and setting the right connections.

- *Example Uses*. The importance of examples cannot be overstated, especially for sets of related or interacting components (see, e.g., Maiden and Sutcliffe [1992]). Examples act like traces of a complex algorithm or procedure; the algorithm is the adaptation, instantiation, and assembly. As such, they help reusers form *mental models* of what is to be done (see, e.g., Stacy and McMillian [1995]) and understand the solution better. Examples that are framed as miniature case studies have been shown to help students learn design skills in an academic setting [Linn and Clancy 1992], confirming both our intuitive understanding of the value of case studies, and similar results obtained in other disciplines. The frameworks and design patterns communities have recognized the importance of this aspect of documentation, which is present in the documentation patterns they advocate (see, e.g., Johnson [1992] and Gamma et al. [1995]).

The relative importance of items in this list depends on the kind of component, and on the kind of reuse targeted. In particular, if the reuser is a "passive reuser," the description of the *how* of the solution might be limited to those aspects that impact its reuse and integration in the problem at hand; an "active reuser" might want to "reverse-engineer" the component to extend it to other nonplanned or nondocumented uses [Johnson 1992]. Butler et al. [1998a] identified six (re)use types of frameworks, ranging from simple use in an application to framework maintenance and reuse in *the development of other frameworks*, and proposed a framework for documentation that attempts to identify what we called *documentation primitives* required to support a particular use type Butler et al. [1999].

Good-quality documentation is hard to develop, may be fairly costly, and is hard to evaluate directly, let alone quantitatively. It may very well constitute the major technical bottleneck to effective reuse. Ultimately, the answer may lie in reducing the need for documentation, and moving progressively away from reuse by assembly toward reuse by generation.

7.1.2 Usefulness

A reusable component is also one that is *often* needed. We should first stress the fact that our separation of *usability* from *usefulness* is a simplification for presentation purposes. For instance, a good *software* packaging of a component will make it *more often* usable because it will lower the modification barrier, specifically, the cost of adapting it to a particular use. What is meant by "good" can mean a whole range of abstraction, generalization, and composition techniques that could make, for example, an *application-specific* component into a *domain-independent* component (see, e.g., Mili and Li [1994]).

That being said, there are a few things we can say about the *usefulness* of software components that does not involve packaging. One view on the nature of reusable components is based on an idealized layered view of application software, as shown in Figure 7.4. Ideally, the *actual* software architecture would match this conceptual view. The application layer corresponds to those aspects of the application that are *specific* to this application (e.g., remote transfer payments), and that may not apply to other applications within the domain (e.g., banking). The domain layer corresponds to those aspects that are domainwide (banking). The services layer corresponds to general infrastructure services, such as persistence and distribution, which are application domain–independent. The language layer consists of any extensions to the language that may be developed to support applications developed in that language. We consider low-level utilities such as container classes as language-level extensions because they provide higher-level "language idioms" but are otherwise general-purpose, and may be used at the upper layers. The Smalltalk language is a crying example whereby the entire language is a library. The operating system layer deals with the underlying platform, including the file system, the windowing system, and input devices.

We can define usefulness in terms of stability across vertical domains, as well as through time. According to the layered view of Figure 7.4, the lower the layer the greater the stability across vertical domains, and the more general the applicability of the component. In terms of stability through time, the answer may be surprisingly different; domain aspects may very well be the most stable, with the language layer coming in second.[3] Time resilience is not a sufficient measure of usefulness: it all depends on how many times a component will be needed during one time period. Thus, it may be worthwhile to develop a reusable component today that may become obsolete next year, pro-

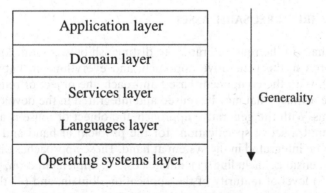

FIGURE 7.4 A layered view of application software.

---

[3] Notwithstanding the Java tidal wave, it is true that new languages spring up only once in a while, and they evolve very little—thank god—once they come into regular use. Libraries are also fairly stable, although they used to change, when nobody took them seriously.

vided it will be used repeatedly over the course of the coming year! Favaro and Favaro [1998] compared decisions on investments in reusable assets to financial options, and compared protection against technological obsolescence to *hedging*. We discuss return-on-investment (ROI) studies in more detail in the context of reusable assets in Part VI; we will be content for the time being to raise the issue.

We stress the fact that Figure 7.4 represents a conceptual view of the functionalities within an application. A good *architectural design* of that application would use the same functional layers to correspond to actual software layers, with well-defined communication protocols between them. For example, software engineering manuals have long advocated the separation of the user interface from that of the application logic's code, to keep the application logic portable across various interface styles and platforms (see, e.g., Myers [1989] and Harston [1989]). Modern user interface frameworks go a long way toward enforcing such a separation by clearly separating the various computational tasks with a graphical application and providing separate reusable components. Smalltalk's model view controller (MVC) framework is an example of such a framework—until interface generators surfaced and wiped out decade-long progress in graphical application engineering, that is. We could also mention CORBA, which made it possible, in principle, to separate business logic from the implementation language itself by allowing applications written in different languages to interoperate over an object request broker. Generally speaking, packaging software in such a way as to match the separation between the various functional layers is no easy technical feat, although progress is being made regularly. We will describe various packaging techniques throughout Part IV of the book that will help develop those layers separately, and compose them effectively.

7.2   ACQUIRING REUSABLE ASSETS

It is customary in the reuse literature to distinguish between the component-based approach, the generative approach, and everything in between (see Chapter 1). With the component-based approach, the object of reuse is a set of software artifacts that may be reused and integrated in the development of new systems. With the generative approach, the object of reuse is a tool that takes as input a set of specifications for the problem at hand and produces artifacts to be integrated in the system at hand. These approaches differ along several dimensions, including (1) initial cost of implementation, (2) reuse leverage, (3) level of maturity of the application domain, and (4) the technical prowess required to implement them. Most current approaches to reuse are hybrid and use different mixes of components and generation. Some of the issues in acquiring reusable assets do not depend on the reuse approach, and those are discussed in the next two subsections. Issues specific to generation are discussed last.

7.2.1 Build versus Buy

Reusable assets are "software objects" that must be acquired at a certain cost, and that must be used a number of times to amortize that cost. There are different ways of acquiring reusable assets, and the major deciding factor in choosing one way over another is ultimately an economic one. One of the first major distinctions is between, (1) *buying* them from outside organizations, and (2) *building them* in house. Barnes argued that the decision must ultimately be based on economic factors. As a general rule, an organization should consider purchasing reusable components in areas that do not represent its main line of business. For example, an organization specializing in banking management information systems (a vertical market) should probably purchase existing distribution frameworks (technological components), rather than build its own. Not only is it *not* likely to have the best competencies in distributed computing, say; even if it did, it would cost it much more to develop a distributed computing framework than to purchase it from a software vendor that made its living out of these frameworks, and that spreads its development costs on *hundreds*, *thousands*, if not *millions* of customers. An organization should *only* build in house those assets that (1) correspond to its core business, (2) are not available on the market, and (3) for which it has competitive advantage in terms of either quality or cost, or both.

There are some issues that may qualify these purely economic factors. There are some risks inherent in depending on third-party software for critical components. These include rapid evolution of the components, lack of (or poor) technical support, and poor quality control. For example, the U.S. DoD procurement practices include a number of development standards to which its subcontractors must adhere for both the software they develop *and* the software they reuse. Evolvability is also an important factor to consider; it may be more cost-effective to adopt a third-party solution in the short term, but much costlier to evolve the system to an emerging standard, for example, in the long run, if the third-party vendor does not choose that route. Voas [1998a] has identified and analyzed five sources of headaches in dealing with library components.

In the remainder of this section, we first look at general issues in building reusable assets in house, and then talk about a specific kind of reusable assets, namely, application generators. Application generators are worth studying on their own because they fall on one end of the component-oriented–generative spectrum of reuse approaches. As such, they bring to bear a unique set of skills, and they provide unusually high leverage, when done properly.

7.2.2 Building Reusable Assets in House

We now consider the issue of building reusable assets in house. An organization that has some experience in a given application domain will have accumulated some reusable experience in that domain. That experience may be in the form of tacit expertise accumulated in the heads of developers, project managers, sales and customer relations people, and others. It may also be in the form of project-specific development artifacts that may be more or less reusable in their current form. Both kinds of experience may be used as a starting point for developing reusable assets. Generally speaking, the construction of readily reusable assets consists of organizing and repackaging existing artifacts that are either generally useful, but not usable, or readily usable but not useful enough, to turn them into generally useful and readily usable assets. The actual method used depends on several factors, including

- *The Reuse Readiness of the Source Artifacts*. More work needs to go into artifacts that are either too general but not directly usable (e.g., domain knowledge) or immediately usable but too specific (e.g., a procedure that sorts a fixed-size table).
- *The Reuse Readiness of the Target (Reusable) Artifacts*. Reusable artifacts vary from general guidelines or statements about a particular domain, to application frameworks, to code templates, to executables or DLLs (dynamically linked libraries) that can be invoked within an application. Naturally, the greater the gap between the source and target artifacts, along either the usefulness or the usability dimension, the greater the effort required to bridge the two.
- *The Level of Automation Desired (or possible)*. Naturally, if good-quality reusable artifacts can be derived automatically and cost-effectively, then all the better. In practice, automation is feasible and cost-effective only for the labor-intensive, knowledge-poor stages of reengineering; correctness-preserving abstraction in software is even more difficult than in other domains because of the brittleness of software.

At the low-tech(nology) end of the spectrum, the reusable asset "acquisition method" consists of simply organizing project-specific potentially reusable artifacts in a public space, and providing content search and browsing tools to access them. Such was one of the deliverables of the PRACTITIONER project, an ESPRIT-funded university–industry reuse project [Mili et al. 1994a]. Not too surprisingly, users of that deliverable—called PRESS—felt that it had more palpable benefits than some of the more sophisticated tools and methodologies of the project[4] [Mili et al. 1994a].

A second acquisition strategy consists of reengineering or preemptive maintenance to enhance the reusability and maintainability of existing systems to make them more reusable and more maintainable. Automated tools may be used in this case to

---

[4] As we will see later, this is a critical factor for the success of an institutional reuse initiative; end users (i.e., developers that reuse) have to start seeing benefits early on to buy into the more investment intensive stages of a reuse initiative.

- Identify those parts of a system that have good quality and complexity attributes, to package them (manually) as reusable assets [Caldiera and Basili 1991, Sahraoui et al. 1998], or, on the contrary, those that indicate potential fault lines and that warrant reengineering or preemptive maintenance [Yeh et al. 1991].

- Perform some low-level code transformations to parameterize or simply port existing code. An example of the former is processors that remove platform (operating system, libraries, etc.) dependencies from existing code. Tools in this category may also simply assist in the modification by performing data and control flow analysis on existing code to help reusers assess the impact of the modifications they are undertaking.

- Extract development information at abstraction level i from component representations at abstraction levels $j < i$, to support maintenance, migration, or reengineering. The idea here is that existing artifacts embody domain knowledge, which is reusable, but is embedded into—and somewhat inseparable from—the artifacts of a solution, which are not reusable or are of poor quality, or of the wrong platform, and so on. This is a notoriously difficult process because as we work our way through development steps (or transformations), domain knowledge becomes less and less explicit. Further, the structure of the artifacts reflects more the technical solution's framework and the nonfunctional requirements of the system than the structure of the application domain.

Wide-spectrum reverse engineering, in which the difference between the source and target levels of abstraction is fairly wide (e.g., from code to conceptual models), remains an elusive research goal. Existing research tools often rely heavily on user intervention. Alternatively, they rely on encoded domain knowledge in the form of reference models against which components are "parsed."

The popularity of object-based methods has spurred a lot of interest in object-related re-engineering and reverse engineering. First, there is the issue of reengineering existing legacy code into object-oriented code, with the expectation that the new code be of a better quality and more easily maintainable. A number of methods have been proposed in the literature that construct classes by clustering procedures around the data that they manipulate (see, e.g., Liu and Wilde [1990], Livadas and Roy [1992], Ogando et al. [1994], Harris et al. [1995], Sward and Hartrum [1997], Sahraoui et al. [1999]). These methods use different kinds of interprocedural data flow graphs and different heuristics to identify the object-centered procedure clusters.

Now that object-oriented software development has matured, we may start talking about *legacy* object-oriented systems, which may themselves have been poorly designed from day 1, or simply corrupted through repeated and poorly managed maintenance. There have been a number of research efforts aiming at reengineering or supporting the reengineering of object-oriented code with varying degrees of automation in the actual reengineering effort. At one end of the spectrum, we have approaches that *measure* software quality attributes related to maintainability and reusability, identifying potential problem areas (see, e.g., Schwanke, [1991]). At the other end of the spectrum, we have approaches that perform some measure of reengineering. One such approach is that of *refactoring* [Opdyke 1992] whereby class hierarchies are rearranged to maximize the factorization of data and behavior.

The domain engineering guidelines that have been put forth by software engineering research organizations (Software Productivity Consortium, Software Engineering Institute, etc.) focus on the high-level process and on high-level heuristics regarding high level domain engineering tasks (see, e.g. [SPC 1993a]); it is understood that different sources of information may be used as an input toward the development of reusable assets—including existing systems—and that tools may be used to support the reengineering process, either from existing systems or from general domain knowledge (see, e.g., Lubars [1990]). We will be looking at domain engineering processes in more detail in the next section.

7.2.3 Building Application Generators

Generally speaking, an application generator may be defined as *a tool or a set of integrated tools that inputs a set of specifications and generates the code of an application within an implementation language.* What distinguishes application generators from compilers of high-level and very high-level languages, or automatic programming systems, are the "specifications" or "programs" input by the developer: (1) partial—the tool completes them by a set of domain-dependent reasonable defaults, and (2) partially or totally nonprocedural—declarative, graphical, and so on [Martin 1985]. Martin enumerated a number of mostly behavioral properties that application generators should exhibit, including (1) user-friendliness, (2) usability for nonprofessional programmers, (3) support for fast prototyping, (4) capacity to run applications that take an order of magnitude less time to develop than with traditional development [Martin 1985]. It is next to impossible to give a more precise operational definition of what constitutes an application generator without excluding known classes of application generators. This is because the specification language used—and hence the generation technique—depends very heavily on the application domain. For the same reasons, it is difficult to design a development methodology for application generators that is appropriate for all application generators, and the development of application generators *in general* has received little attention in the literature; by contrast, developing *with* application generators has received a fair amount of attention (see, e.g., Misra and Jalics [1988], Verner [1988]). The material presented below is based mostly on the work of Levy [1986] and Cleaveland [1988], describing work at AT&T Bell Labs.

Viewed as translators, application generators have a fairly standard architecture (system design). Further, the programming techniques for implementing translators (detailed design) are well understood and fairly standardized. In fact, the design and implementation of translators is so well understood and standardized that application generators themselves can be built using application generators [Cleaveland 1988]! The major difficulties in building generators reside in: (1) recognizing cases when they are appropriate [Levy 1986, Cleaveland 1988]; (2) defining their requirements, in terms of defining the input language, the output language, and the "transformation grammar" [Levy 1986, Cleaveland 1988]; and (3) validating their outputs, that is, verifying that the code generated does what it is supposed to do [Intrator 1994]. The first two difficulties are methodological in nature. Defining the input language involves striking the proper balance between a language that is sufficiently abstract to be usable by noncomputer experts, but also concrete enough so that executable code can be efficiently generated. Validating the generated code poses a number of technical—and theoretical—challenges [Intrator 1994].

Levy identified a coarse three-step methodology for developing with application generators (what he calls *metaprogramming* [Levy 1986]): (1) identifying the requirements of the generator, (2) building the generator, and (3) using the generator. Cleaveland proposed a breakdown of the requirements phase into six subphases briefly summarized below [Cleaveland 1988]:

Recognizing Domains. This step consists of assessing whether an application generator approach is appropriate. According to Levy, application generators are appropriate for applications that embody a "complex synthetic set of rules" [Levy 1986]: complex in the sense that no notation is known within which they can be described succinctly, and synthetic in the sense that they are human-made. This implies that the rules will probably not be right the first time and that they will keep evolving. This makes it appropriate for prototyping. Or, if we look at the full half of the cup instead, application generators are needed when several similar systems have to be built and maintained. This makes it suitable for stable and well-understood application domains. Cleaveland proposed a number of "appropriateness heuristics" including [Cleaveland 1988] (1) recognizing recurring patterns between applications (code, design, architecture), (2) a "natural" or "emergent" separation between the functional (declarative) requirements and the implementation (procedural) of applications, or (3) a fairly systematic procedure to go from one to the other.

Defining Domain Boundaries. This consists of identifying the parts of applications that will be generated, the parts that will have to be built by hand, and the interfaces between the two [Cleaveland 1988]. There is a tradeoff between the range of applications that can be built with the generator (breadth), and how much of these applications will be automated (depth); the decision should be based on economic considerations [Levy 1986, Cleaveland 1988].

Defining an Underlying Model. This step consists of defining an abstract computational model for the application domain. It is abstract in the sense that it does not depend on a particular implementation technique. Different computational models are appropriate for different application domains [Levy 1986]. For example, a computational model appropriate for reactive systems could be finite-state machines, while one appropriate for database applications could be relational calculus or algebra. Computational models are important for consistency, understandability, and validation [Cleaveland 1988]. They also make it easier to systematize the implementation of a generator, and the generation of a family of generators.

Defining the Variant and Invariant Parts. The invariant part of an application family consists of the implementation details of the application, and all the defaults assumed by the generator; the variant part consists of those aspects that the developer has to specify. The variant part includes input specifications as well as *code escapes* [Cleaveland 1988]. Code escapes are used when a part of the application cannot be captured concisely or at all within the computational model; they defeat some of the advantages of generators (maintainability at the specification level, traceability, testability, etc.) and should be avoided whenever technically possible [Cleaveland 1988] and economically justifiable [Levy 1986].

Defining the Specification Input Method. The input method is essentially the user (developer) interface of the generator. Input methods depend on the underlying computational model and the target user (developer) community. Input methods include (1) textual inputs (expressions), (2) graphical inputs (e.g., for user interface builders [Myers 1989]), and (3) interactive template-filling [Cleaveland 1988].

Defining the Products. Generators can generate programs, documentation, tests programs or data, and even input to other generators [Cleaveland 1988]. Issues such as packaging for readability and/or integration and performance are important for code fragments [Cleaveland 1988].

A major concern with application generators is their testing: checking that they do generate the correct code. One common way to test programs is to compare their actual outputs to expected outputs. With program generators, we are not certain that the expected output is correct; it, itself, has to be tested. This additional level of indirection makes it that much harder to validate generators [Intrator 1994]. The problem is more acute than with traditional high-level language compilers, which translate imperative code into imperative code, and where there is an easier correspondence between source code and—nonoptimized—target code.

7.3 DOMAIN ENGINEERING LIFECYCLES

A software lifecycle is a model for organizing, planning, and controlling the activities associated with software development and maintenance [Peters 1987]. For the most part, a lifecycle identifies development tasks, and identifies and standardizes intermediary work products (deliverables), and review and evaluation criteria. The known lifecycles are mostly geared towards the development of single applications, or *systems*. By contrast, domain engineering may be defined as the process of building reusable artifacts for an entire application domain, and it is legitimate to ask whether the same lifecycles may be used for domain engineering.

The answer to this question depends on many factors, including how we define and view domain engineering. We start our discussion by highlighting some of the underlying issues. Next, we describe two domain engineering *frameworks*. The first, SYNTHESIS, is a domain engineering framework developed by the Software Productivity Consortium (SPC) within the context of a far reaching software reuse initiative. SYNTHESIS is typical of the work of organizations that focus on defining formal processes by either scientific tradition (e.g., SEI) or obligation, to the extent that these organizations (or their clients) deal with customers that insist on having formal repeatable processes (e.g., the U.S. DoD). The second is a framework developed by Jacobson, Griss, and Jonsson, and is more representative of the view in the object-oriented community, which is more technology-driven. We conclude this section by attempting a synthesis of the emerging domain engineering principles.

7.3.1 Issues

7.3.1.1 Domain Engineering as a Standalone Activity versus as a Side Show to Application Engineering

Depending on the authors, domain engineering may be seen as a standalone process—some would say, *business*—with its own organization, process model, resources, and skills [Prieto-Diaz 1987, Moore and Bailin 1991, SPC 1994]. The view from the trenches has it that such a view is unrealistic, and can only work, if ever, in large organizations that can free the required human resources and garner the required financial resources to build an organization whose only mandate is to build assets that *may* be reused in specific *application* engineering projects (see Fig. 7.5). Indeed, this approach is often deemed high-risk, and the time required for a return on investment may exceed top management's patience or horizon. A lower-risk approach, but one with arguably nonoptimal payoffs in the long run, considers domain engineering as a process driven by application engineering; the construction of a reusable asset is initiated only from the need to fulfill an application-specific need. In this case, there isn't much of a domain engineering process, except spending more time on some of the steps of application engineering (e.g., design, code documentation), or adding reuse-specific steps, such as generalization, robustness

Domain engineering activities   Application engineering activities

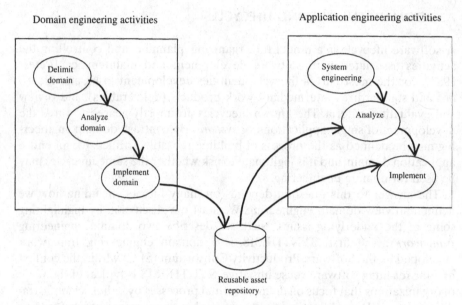

FIGURE 7.5   A producer–consumer model of domain engineering.

analysis that goes beyond the needs of the current application, and documenting the *use/reuse* of the asset. Figure 7.6 shows one such process in which domain engineering activities rendezvous with application engineering around common deliverables, yielding a much more synergetic relationship between the two; the various application engineering activities *use* and *contribute* to the base of reusable artifacts for that step. The process shown in Figure 7.6 is close to that proposed by Caldiera and Basili [1991] for the *experience factory* in which the teams devoted to servicing individual application needs are kept separate from the team responsible for building and maintaining reusable assets, but the two teams work synergistically.

7.3.1.2   *Source for Reusable Assets*

As mentioned in the previous section, there is a wide spectrum of approaches to the engineering of reusable assets, depending on the extent to which an organization has software artifacts and processes that it can mine for reuse, and the quality and readiness of those assets for reuse. All approaches rely on available domain expertise in various forms, whether in the form of documents or human expertise. However, the approaches differ in their level of reliance on existing assets. An approach centered around the existence of potentially reusable assets will have a lifecycle centered around mining legacy systems for potentially reusable assets and reengineering those assets to make them more reusable [Moore and Bailin 1991]. Such approaches tend to be more inductive and synthetic in nature. When no such legacy systems base exists, such as in a

Reusable assets base   Project deliverables

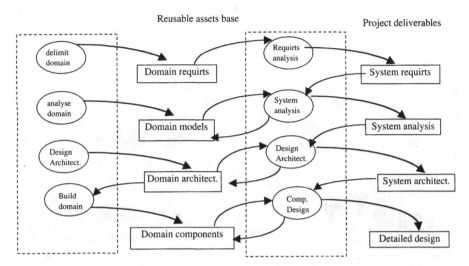

FIGURE 7.6 A more synergetic relation between domain engineering and application engineering.

new domain for the organization, the domain engineering approach is much more analytical or forward-engineering-oriented [Jacobson et al. 1995]. The same is true when a legacy asset base exists, but is hopelessly out of sync with the current needs of the organization. For example, there is little to be gained from mining a mainframe-based COBOL application that uses a hierarchical database, if the target implementation technology is a multitier client–server system using relational technology or, better yet, a CORBA-based object-oriented distributed architecture. Generally speaking, as object orientation has become the default development paradigm, there seems to have been less interest in the community in approaches to domain engineering that focus on reengineering existing systems. However, there is still interest in *reverse-engineering* legacy systems as a way of extracting *domain knowledge* but not so much as a way of uncovering potentially reusable *concrete artifacts* (see Fig. 7.7).

7.3.1.3 Production versus Management of Reusable Assets
Reuse-oriented software development relies on the existence of a base of reusable assets that developers can consult for the needs of specific applications or systems. Some authors have focused on the process of constructing reusable assets, while others covered the entire lifecycle of reusable assets, from creation to insertion into the reuse repository, to updates, and possibly even the removal of such assets from the repository. In the "early days" of software reuse in general, and domain engineering in particular, there was a marked focus on the management of the reusable assets base [Prieto-Diaz

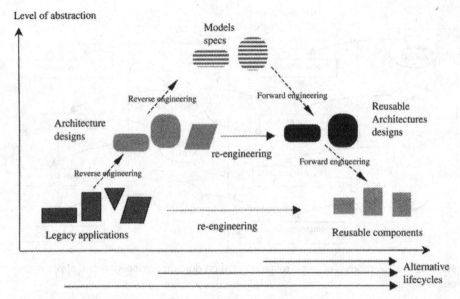

Level of abstraction

Models
specs

Reverse engineering   Forward engineering

Architecture
designs

Reusable
Architectures
designs

re-engineering

Reverse engineering   Forward engineering

Legacy applications

re-engineering   Reusable components

Alternative
lifecycles

FIGURE 7.7 The many possible activities of domain engineering. Depending on the availability and quality of legacy systems, domain engineering can involve a mix of reverse-engineering activities, reengineering activities, and forward-engineering activities.

1987]. This reflected both our understanding of the field at the time, and the nature of reusable assets considered at the time. In the earlier days of reuse, reusable assets were mostly small-size code components. Applying reuse at a large scale generally meant having *many* such components, and the issue of *indexing* (or *classifying*) them and *retrieving* them was a major concern. In its simplest form, domain analysis consisted of building domain taxonomies and classification to support the classification of reusable components [Prieto-Diaz and Freeman 1987, Reboot 1993]. For example, if components are character-ized by a search attribute "application domain," describing the areas in which the components may be applied, a taxonomy of application areas may be used to organize components, and support various retrieval algorithms [Frakes and Pole 1994]. Figure 7.8 shows one such lifecycle described by Prieto-Diaz [1987]. More complex forms, evolving out of automatic programming and transfor-mational systems, used more complex representations for reusable compo-nents (see, e.g., DRACO [Neighbors 1991], LASSIE [Devanbu et al. 1991]). Such representations—sometimes referred to as *application-specific high-level specification languages*—usually embed abstract descriptions of components within software architecture glue (e.g., module interconnection languages), and quite a bit of generation technology [Basset 1987]. Domain engineering in this case is as much *software* engineering as it is *knowledge* engineering [Neighbors 1991, Devanbu et al. 1991].

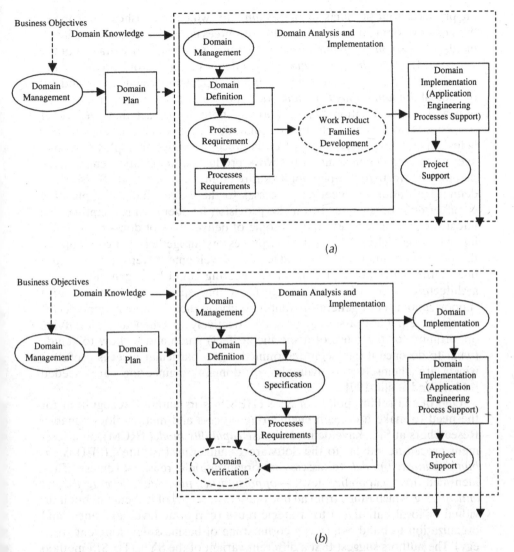

FIGURE 7.8 SYNTHESIS processes: (a) opportunistic reuse; (b) leveraged reuse.

7.3.2 A Sample of Domain Engineering Lifecycles

The Software Productivity Consortium (SPC) proposed a domain engineering *framework* in the form of a tunable domain engineering methodology called *SYNTHESIS* that can be adapted to the context of a particular organization. In SYNTHESIS, domain engineering is recognized as an incremental activity that benefits from feedback from application engineering. Domain engineering produces four products: (1) a *domain plan*, which establishes the scope of domain development and the tasks and resources needed for the various increments; (2) a *domain definition*, which defines the scope and orientation of the domain; (3) a *domain specification*, which defines a set of work product families whose implementation would facilitate application engineering; and (4) the actual *domain implementation*. An important aspect of domain specification and implementation that is worth of note is the fact that they cover *processes* as well as artifacts. In particular, domain engineering relies on *and* helps define the application engineering process. It relies on application engineering to help define some of the work products of application engineering that may be worth developing for an entire family of applications. It also helps define application engineering processes to the extent that (1) application engineering processes need to make provision for identifying, adapting, and integrating reusable assets and (2) some of deliverables of domain engineering may be guidelines, procedures, or processors, altogether, that cover one of the more labor-intensive, knowledge-poor development steps. For example, one of the deliverables of domain engineering could be a generic product architecture, a set of standard interfaces that specific applications must support, and a set of generators that help bridge them to application-specific interfaces. For these assets to be used effectively, a "when to" (identifying opportunity for the reuse of a specific artifact) guide and a "how to" guide (what to do once it has been determined that a particular asset is useful)— which are themselves deliverables of domain engineering—are needed [Moore and Bailin 1991].

One of the selling points of SYNTHESIS is its authors' recognition for the need to make a domain engineering process and methodology tunable. Researchers at SPC have defined a *reuse capability model* (RCM), an assessment procedure similar to the Software Engineering Institute's (SEI) *capability maturity model* to assess an organization's reuse readiness. They identified four capability levels—*opportunistic, integrated, leveraged*, and *anticipating*, which range from ad hoc reuse (awareness of its benefits, but individual or local initiatives) to strategic reuse (corporate-level awareness and organization to build assets as a cornerstone of business development strategy). The authors suggest that a different variant of the SYNTHESIS method may be appropriate in each case, reaching a different tradeoff between speed of return, and overall long-term payoff, depending on the organization's ability and willingness to stomach high-volume slow-return investments. Figures 7.8*a* and 7.8*b* contrast the domain engineering process for opportunistic reuse with that for leveraged reuse.

The reader may notice that in the opportunistic process, there is no explicit attempt to specify the domain (the family of applications) as *an integrated whole*; we learn just enough about the domain to develop (or reengineer) the components that are likely to be of use, or that are *explicitly* demanded. In the leveraged process, a conscious effort is made toward specifying the domain first, from which requirements for individual components *as well as infra-*

structures and processes are identified. Jacobson, Griss, and Jonsson state in their book that they do advocate a domain engineering per se, but propose two processes to which they refer as *component system engineering* and *application family engineering*, which correspond closely to SYNTHESIS's opportunistic and leveraged version, respectively [Jacobson et al. 1997]. For illustration purposes, we reproduce a brief description of both processes, to highlight the difference in focus (architecture vs. components). The application family engineering process goes as follows:

1. *Capturing requirements that have an impact on the architecture.* The idea here is that, by focusing on those requirements of the family members that could affect the architecture, we could, quickly and cost-effectively, arrive at a generic and stable architecture,
2. Performing robustness analysis. This is a validation stage.
3. Designing the layered (architecture) system. This involves choosing the architecture as well as identifying the pieces that could be reused and integrated into that architecture (legacy subsystems, third-party software, etc.).
4. Implementing the architecture as a layered system. This involves implementing the fixed (common) layers or components of the architectures, and specifying the interfaces of the others.
5. Testing the layered system. Validate the architecture against representative applications of the application family.

By contrast, the component system engineering process goes as follows:

1. Capturing requirements focusing on variability. The focus here is on variability in *function* in order to identify the widest range possible of functional requirements within the application domain.
2. Performing robustness analysis.
3. Designing the component system. Start with analysis object models, and design according to implementation environment.
4. Implementing the component system.
5. Testing the component system.
6. Final packaging of the component system. This includes documentation and organization or classification into a reuse repository.

The two processes appear to be utterly complementary, with the first focused on the architecture and the second on populating a target architecture—albeit not formally defined. Further, it would make sense for the application family engineering process to come *before* the component system engineering process. In practice, the two processes correspond to two maturity levels of the organization or the application domain, and component system engineering comes first during the maturing process.

Finally, we should mention the case of application generators as the ultimate point in the maturation process of the domain design and implementation phases of the domain engineering process. We described in the previous section a process for building application generators, which embodies the widely accepted phases of domain scoping, specification and/or analysis, design, and implementation. Application generators also illustrate the relationship between application engineering and domain engineering; the use of application generators, as a reusable workproduct, has its own lifecycle, which is different from conventional application engineering. Specifically, application generators shorten the conventional analysis → design → implementation → testing cycle, for those parts covered by the generator, by allowing the production of code that is correct by construction, from analysis-level information.

7.3.3 Summary

Generally speaking, there seems to be wide recognition within the reuse community of the following principles:

Principle 0. We need an organization (a structure and resources), a process, and methods to develop software assets that are reusable by design. While this may sound as a truism to software reuse aficionados, we found, in our consulting practice with small to midsize development organizations, that a number of midlevel managers hold the naive belief that project managers can manage to "squeeze in some domain engineering" if they could just be better "team players." Worse than no reuse awareness is an awareness of the benefits but not of the costs; organizations where a first reuse initiative failed to deliver—all too predictably—will put it off indefinitely.

Principle 1. On the other hand, the rigid separation of domain engineering organizations and processes from the application engineering organizations and processes is neither realistic nor the most effective. In addition to the psychological hurdle for managers who have to fund the domain engineering organization with no *directly* or *immediately* measurable benefits, it is important that the relationship be a two-way relationship to make sure that the domain engineering organization develops assets that are *useful*—both *immediately* and in the foreseeable future—and *usable* [Arango 1991].

Principle 2. We need a customizable domain engineering practice. The domain engineering organization, processes, and methods must be tailorable to accommodate (1) the application domain, (2) the size of the adopting organization, (3) its development practices (maturity level), and (4) the nature of the reuse mandate it has. By *mandate* we mean both the objective and the freedom to act. If reuse, as a technology, is on trial, then we should focus on minimizing risk, alas at the expense of payoff. If, on the other hand, the question is not "whether" but "how," then a higher-risk/higher-payoff approach might be tried.

Principle 3. We need a domain engineering process that is well integrated with the application engineering method. This is to be understood two ways. First, domain engineers should *accommodate* existing application engineering processes by making sure that the artifacts they produce can be easily found, understood, adapted, and integrated into application development, and for this, they have to provide guidelines, procedures, and tools to help application developers perform all these reuse tasks within their normal workflow. Second, they should *enhance* existing application engineering processes to better take advantage of the available reuse infrastructure. For example, assume that domain engineering had produced a generic architecture for applications in the family and identified interchangeable functional and infrastructural components that cover most of the applications in the family. Provided a complete enough coverage of the application family by the domain engineering, application engineering *could* be reduced to a selection process centered around identifying the characteristics of the application that would warrant the use of one specific architectural variant, and the integration of a specific set of components. This illustrates how domain engineering can *potentially* enhance the application engineering process. In order to effectively support such a process, domain engineering must develop a selection tool, which can be anything from a set of decision guidelines to actual generators, illustrating another relation between the two.

Principle 4. Domain engineering is work in progress. A number of authors have stressed the *incremental* and *iterative* nature of domain engineering. This is not only a matter of convenience (e.g., minimize upfront costs) but there is no other way: the constant interaction between application engineering and domain engineering provides domain engineering with both a priori and a posteriori evaluation of reusable assets. In our view, *incrementality* refers to scope, that is, the extent to which an application domain is covered. *Iterativeness*, on the other hand, refers to the gradual improvement in individual assets' quality: individual assets become more reusable as they are put through real tests. Arango [1991] argued forcefully against what he called "pure domain engineering," which aims for the development of reusable assets *that are effectively reusable on their first trial* because, in addition to having delayed payoffs, there is no way to evaluate reusability a priori! In fact, he defines the purpose of domain engineering as enhancing the performance of developers in application engineering.

In addition to incrementality and iterativeness, some authors have stressed the *participatory* nature of domain analysis and design [Karlsson 1995]. Participatory design, or any approach based on consensus building, find their justification in the fact that analysis and design that are hard enough for individual applications where we always have to reconcile competing considerations, then become virtually intractable when we try to accommodate the competing needs of *several* known and *anticipated* applications.

7.4 SUMMARY AND DISCUSSION

In this chapter, we introduced reusability, and gave an overview of the strategies and processes we need to put in place to acquire reusable assets. The points of the chapter may be summarized in the following checklist:

- *Reusability*. Reusability is the combination of two characteristics: (1) *usefulness*, which is the extent to which an asset is often needed; and (2) *usability*, which is the extent to which the asset is properly packaged for reuse. Roughly speaking, *usefulness* refers to functionality whereas *usability* refers to packaging. Generally, there is a tradeoff between usefulness (generality) and immediate usability (with no adaptation). Technological advances in software packaging techniques help reach better ⟨usefulness and usability⟩ optima. Finally, usefulness and usability are interdependent to the extent that the judicious separation of the fixed part of an application from its variable parts help make the fixed part more useful and more easily usable.

- *Acquiring Reusable Assets*. There are two general strategies to acquire reusable assets: (1) build them in house or (2) buy them. The decision should be based on economic factors: which is more cost-effective. This involves both the cost of the initial acquisition as well as future maintenance and updates. Further, it should be qualified with some long-term risk factors inherent in depending on a third party for a potentially critical component of one's software. If the decision is made to build in house, then there is a whole spectrum of technical approaches that rely more or less heavily on existing legacy software, going from making such legacy software publicly accessible, to reverse-engineering specific modules, to reengineering them, to straight tabula rasa engineering of reusable assets. This depends on the availability, intrinsic quality, and appropriateness (for new developments) of legacy software. We studied the case of application generators as an extreme point along the spectrum.

- *Domain Engineering Lifecycles*. Application engineering is the process of building high-quality software solutions within the allotted time and budget. Domain engineering is the process of building reusable assets to help application engineering achieve its goals. And yet, in day-to-day operations, application engineering and domain engineering have conflicting imperatives, and thus should be separated. That being said, we should be dogmatic about the nature of domain engineering and its relationship to application engineering; it should be (1) tailored to the context of the organization, (2) well integrated with application engineering in terms of methods as well as processes, and (3) incremental and iterative.

In Chapter 9, we will compare the three classical programming paradigms, logical, functional/procedural, and object-oriented, for the extent to which they support reusability, and more specifically, usability and those aspects of usefulness that depend on usability. As Part IV is devoted *mostly* to object-oriented techniques, Chapter 10 provides a brief tutorial on object-oriented software development. This tutorial will not suffice for the reader who is not sufficiently familiar with object orientation to assimilate the material in the subsequent chapters, and is meant both as a guide to the object oriented literature, as representative of where we stand in the areas where no consensus yet exists. Subsequent chapters of Part IV address different packaging technologies with an overriding interest in object-based techniques.

Chapter 8

Domain Analysis

Domain engineering is the collection of activities required to establish and maintain a body of knowledge and a technical infrastructure necessary to effectively develop and maintain a family of applications within a given problem domain. Domain engineering in general, and domain analysis in particular, have been recognized as essential to obtaining systematic, scalable, and provably beneficial software reuse. The basic premise of domain analysis (and domain engineering in general) is that organizations usually develop computer systems that have a number of commonalities related to either their application domain (e.g., billing, payroll), or the technical solutions that they require (or that the organization knows how to deploy), or to the required packaging of the software solution. Domain analysis methods propose more or less formal processes that attempt to capture those commonalities, and capitalize on them by developing reusable software artifacts that embody those commonalities.

Good domain analysis depends on several kinds of skills, but by and large, a domain analysis method has to address three sets of issues:

- How to organize domain analysis activities into a systematic and controllable process
- How to integrate them into the normal application development process in such a way that both benefit, and in a way that optimizes the use of the resources of the organization
- How to find widely useful components, and how to package them in such a way that they are easily usable

The first two sets of issues are more organizational and process-oriented, while the third is purely technical. The literature abounds with domain analysis methodologies, covering a wide spectrum of process and organizational approaches, and some of them are discussed in this chapter. However, most methodologies are usually short on the technical guidelines for finding generic components, and most rely on specific development methodologies' claims regarding abstraction. Precisely, most domain analysis methodologies rely on object-oriented (OO) modeling, and hence, refer us to the claims of OO modeling regarding abstraction. In this chapter, we make an attempt at describing what abstraction is, and propose some general, paradigm-independent guidelines regarding abstraction and separation of concerns. Both will be addressed in much greater detail in subsequent chapters that deal exclusively with object techniques (Chapter 11, on abstraction and parameterization in OO, and Chapter 12, on composition techniques).

We start with a general introduction to domain analysis. In Section 8.2, we discuss the issue of defining the boundaries of the domain of analysis. Section 8.3 presents the general issue of identifying domain requirements, and distinguishing them from application-specific requirements, as a first step toward defining domainwide reusable artifacts. Section 8.4 proposes a reference model for reusable artifacts, and discusses general issues related to both the development *and* reuse of such artifacts. Section 8.5 discusses abstraction, from a general knowledge/information modeling point of view, and from a software engineering point of view. Section 8.6 contains brief descriptions of some of the major domain analysis methodologies. We describe select domain analysis tools in Section 8.7, and conclude in Section 8.8.

8.1   BASIC CONCEPTS

8.1.1   A Domain

A general definition of a domain is an area of knowledge or activity characterized by a family of related systems. A domain is characterized by a set of concepts and terminology understood by practitioners in that specific area of knowledge [Bass et al. 1997]. A domain can also be defined by the common managed features that satisfy specific market or mission.

The SEI [Domain 1999] has characterized a domain by its scope, its information (objects), its features and uses, and its behavior or operational characteristics. We characterize a domain by one of three criteria [Mili et al. 1999b]:

Common Expertise. This criterion identifies a field of domain expertise and attempts to cater to it through specialized development of software assets that span the range of applications of the expertise at hand. This criterion is producer-focused, and could be a natural criterion for a domain expert.

Common Design. This criterion identifies a problem-solving pattern that is embodied in some generic software assets and attempts to cater to it through the development of generic assets that can be specialized for specific needs. This criterion is product-focused, and could be a natural criterion for a programming expert. Domains under this criterion are related to solution artifacts.

Common Market. This criterion identifies a segment of the software market and attempts to cater to it through specialized development of software assets that cover the range of needs of the market; its rationale is to be a one-stop shop for the selected market segment. This criterion is consumer-focused, and could be a natural criterion for a (marketing) manager. Domains under this criterion are related to business logic and goals.

Of course, these criteria are not mutually exclusive; an ideal domain is one that satisfies all three criteria. If such an ideal domain exists, then the expected return on investment is maximized because the business goals are well defined, the commonalties between solutions are maximal, and the domain experts have the sufficient knowledge and experience to build the common solutions.

8.1.2 Domain Analysis

Domain analysis is the process of capturing, analyzing, and modeling information about applications in a domain, specifically, common characteristics and reasons for variations. It is a process by which we are able to exploit similarities in applications (products or systems) in the domain, capture experiences, and identify variabilities. Domain analysis is accomplished by reengineering techniques and domain analysis methods. The useful product of domain analysis is the creation of a body of knowledge that will be used for the rest of the domain engineering activities as well as the application-engineering activities. Domain analysis is [Kang et al. 1990] "the process of identifying, collecting, organizing, and representing the relevant information in a domain, based upon the study of existing systems and their development histories, knowledge captured from domain experts, underlying theory, and emerging technology within a domain." Activities of a domain analysis method often include

- Defining a glossary of terms for the domain
- Documenting domain assumptions and technical risks
- Identifying domain stakeholders
- Identifying problems within the scope of the domain and their variations
- Identifying legacy system artifacts that reflect current deployed applications and implement functionality required in the domain applications
- Identifying commonalties and variabilities in the family of applications lying within the domain

There is a growing literature on domain analysis methods. We briefly discuss the main features of these approaches later in this chapter. Domain analysis activities produce domain models, which capture the relationships between applications within the same domain.

8.1.3   Domain Models

Domain models are the terminologies and semantics that characterize elements and relationships within a family of related applications. Domain models include

Domain Definitions. This is a list of terms that are specific to the domain. One of the main benefits of domain analysis is providing a shared vision of the domain. This shared vision is usually provided by a common vocabulary (glossary) that improves communication among domain experts.

Commonalties. This is a set of services and functionalities that are common across various applications in the same domain. These functionalities are often related to user requirements. These commonalties further derive commonalties in the design and implementation of the domain components.

Variabilities. Variabilities define how each application differs from another within the same domain in terms of services and functionality. These variabilities further derive the design and implementation of domain components such that they are adaptable to different needs of applications developed within the domain scope.

Rules and Constraints. Domain models include definitions of constraints and rules that are driven by the nature of applications in the domain. These rules include structuring rules (constraints about the structure of the application), potential implementation constraints (imposing specific technologies), and business rules.

Environmental Boundaries. In domain analysis, we define boundaries between the applications and the environment. These boundaries define the stimuli, events, inputs, and outputs, which define the information flow between each application and its environment and the semantics of that information. Context diagrams, or similar models, are often used to identify these boundaries.

Requirements. These are the behavioral and qualitative requirements to be met by each application in the domain. This includes the set of features offered by each application. Requirements do not include common requirements only, but examples of application-specific requirements as well. Use cases are modeling constructs that capture the user requirements into an aggregation of functionalities, operations, and services.

They are often associated with scenarios that specify the details about how a use case will be implemented.

Decision Models. Decision models define what is in the domain and what is outside the scope of a domain on the basis of the decisions taken by the domain analyst.

Issues. Domain models often include a documentation of the issues identified during the analysis of the domain. This documentation is a recorded list of problems that arose during domain analysis and possibly their resolutions or ideas about how they can be solved.

8.1.4 Exercises

1. (A) Given the domain of "simulation of waiting queues" discussed in Appendix B.1, define an example for each category of the domain models defined in Section 8.1.3.

2. (A) Given the domain of "library systems" discussed in Appendix B.2, give three definitions of this domain using the taxonomy: common expertise, common design, and common market, as defined in Section 8.1.1.

3. (B) Given the nonexhaustive list of domain models in Section 8.1.3, give examples of modeling artifacts that can be used for each category and identify why these models are suitable. For example, context diagrams can be used to capture environmental interactions.

8.2 DOMAIN SCOPING

8.2.1 Scoping Criteria

Domain scoping could be derived mainly by economic factors. Bayer et al. [1999] discuss a business-driven process to derive the scope of a domain. This approach is part of a product-line engineering approach called PuLSE (product-line software engineering) [Debaud and Knauber 1998]. To define the scope of a domain, the domain analyst characterizes business objectives that are gathered from several stakeholders and calculates their benefit functions. Characterization functions define characteristics of each application in the domain. Benefit functions use the characterization functions to come up with a domain scope. A product map is developed for the domain. Product maps include existing applications, future applications, and potential applications. These maps also show characteristics and benefit functions. From the product map, the analyst identifies common business objects and functionalities as application commonalties. A separate process is used to investigate the variabilities.

A similar way to scope the domain is to use an attribute/product matrix [Bayer et al. 1999]. This matrix is used to define the variabilities in the domain, where each application in the domain is assessed with a set of attributes that the analyst identifies to be common features. As a result, a matrix is developed whose columns are the applications and its rows are the attributes. Developing common scenarios can be a key practice in defining the domain scope. Use cases and scenarios have proved to be good practices in domain analysis methods. Domain analysis in a product-line engineering context is more scoped. This is because the definition of the domain is guarded by a set of products that we should be able to produce for this domain. This is discussed further in Chapter 22.

One way to scope the domain is to use the set of commonalties and variabilities between applications in the domain. The set of allowed variabilities could limit the extensibility of the domain. However, it is usually hard to explicitly capture commonalties and variabilities as reported by several experiences [Bass et al. 1999]:

Commonalties include common set of assets and their common features, common structure, common control and data flow between assets, and common usage scenarios. When identifying commonalties, functional/nonfunctional commonalties (e.g., performance issues) should be considered. Commonalties also include capturing common requirements for the domain. These requirements serve as the information repository for the whole domain.

Variabilities include optional modes, tasks, services, and variabilities in assets and architectures. It is usually beneficial to define some variations required by specific applications in the domain that are not of exactly the same nature as with other applications. These variabilities can include variations in a common problem (requirement, functionality) or variations in the solutions. Variations in the problems are helpful for application engineers to identify specific application problems for which they seek solutions. Variations in the solution space facilitate the task for application engineers to identify which solution is applicable to their specific application.

8.2.2 Over- and Underscoping

Finding the boundaries of the reusability domain—domain scoping—is a particularly challenging task because of the tradeoffs involved. If domain analysis is too wide in scope, then we might face a problem of overscoping. *Overscoping* refers to the situation in which a lot of effort and budget is put in developing domain models to be very general and such effort is not justified by the applications developed on the basis of these models. The other end of the spectrum is *underscoping*, where the domain artifacts that we develop are not general enough to be instantiated in applications that belong to the domain or they are difficult to adapt. This is the case when domain artifacts that we produce during domain analysis activities need immense instantiation and adaptation effort to develop a specific application within the domain.

Scoping is a critical practice in domain analysis. There is always a tradeoff in defining the domain scope, namely, the number of applications to be included within the domain [Bass et al. 1999]. Widening the scope has the potential for greater cost avoidance, but an increase in the complexity may wipe out this advantage. This tradeoff is sometimes referred to as the *economy of scope*. For instance, Boeing reports on its experience in choosing between tightly focused domains and a single somewhat more generic domain in producing avionics software for three types of aircraft [Bass et al. 1999]. The first alternative recognizes each craft as a domain on its own, while the second recognizes the three crafts as one domain. Similarly, Raytheon reports on choosing a domain for radar-guided missiles, a domain for infrared guided missiles, or a single domain for all missiles. Cummins reports on choosing separate domains for high-horsepower, medium-horsepower engines, and so on, or one domain for all engines. Many companies advocated a broader single domain rather than multiple focused ones because they perceived that benefits occur faster when the scope is broader.

8.2.3   Exercises

1. (B) Given the domain of "simulation of waiting queues" discussed in Appendix B.1:
   (a) Identify a set of functional commonalties and variabilities among applications in the domain.
   (b) Identify a set of nonfunctional commonalties and variabilities among applications in the domain.
   (c) Study the attribute/product matrix as defined in the PuLSE approach [Debaud and Knauber 1998], and construct the matrix for the domain "simulation of waiting queues."

8.3   DOMAIN VERSUS APPLICATION REQUIREMENTS

A domain analysis approach to software intensive systems requires that the system analysts distinguish between those requirements that are common to all applications in the domain and those that are specific to a particular application. In addition to this distinction in the nature of a requirement, a requirement traceability mechanism should be used to identify the relationship between requirements and to trace requirements to software assets used in the development across applications in the domain.

So, how does requirements engineering practice differ in the context of domain analysis?

Distinguishing Domain and Application Requirements. Domain engineering is concerned with both domain requirements and application-specific requirements. The outcome of the domain engineering phase is a set of domain assets. These assets should satisfy the essential baseline commonalties (domain requirements) and at the same time provide a flexibility mechanism to accommodate variances for specific applications (application requirement). There is always a problem of assessing whether a requirement is a reference requirement, that is, a standardized requirement for a family of applications, or an application-specific requirement.

Satisfying Customer Requirements. Requirements can be satisfied by the development of software assets that are used across applications in the domain (a domain requirement). On the other hand, some requirements are completely satisfied by application-specific development at the application engineering phase.

Traceability. Requirement traceability in a domain analysis context becomes more complex. Several traceable threads exist. For example, tracing an application-specific requirement or a common requirement (domain) to the core asset (domain) or to an application-specific asset developed in the application engineering phase.

Nonfunctional Requirements. Managing nonfunctional requirements becomes harder. To achieve a certain quality level of the final product, it is not obvious how to distinguish the quality assessment process during the development phases (domain engineering and application engineering) such that the overall quality of the application is achieved.

Gathering Requirements. Domain requirements constitute a long list that could be generated by gathering requirements of the individual applications in the domain and developing an abstraction that expresses a specific behavior in terms of variation points. This approach to gathering requirements is straightforward; however, it is tedious and time-consuming. It also hinders the benefits reaped from initiating a domain analysis approach.

Abstracting a set of common requirements for the applications in the domain can aid in identifying assets at the domain engineering phase and determining the suitability of the asset at the application engineering phase. These abstractions should accommodate further refinement and instantiation. Domain requirements may include abstract requirements that are common to the applications in the domain but can also include an enumeration of specific solutions, which are considered variations in the requirements to suit specific applications. These variations are hard to collect at the domain engineering phase. However, the application engineering phase can produce these variations and add them to the domain engineering library. Reengineering existing applications and abstracting their requirements can be a potential source for domain requirements, however they may not be cost effective.

An example of domain versus application requirements [Bass et al. 1999] is the noise generation that is used to simulate an engine noise in flight simulators. The domain requirements may say that the noise generation is required in every system and that the generated noise depends on engine conditions and atmospheric conditions. Additionally, we may say that the generated noise has a pitch, intensity, and duration. Instantiating this requirement in specific applications would say something about the values of these attributes. Challenges in requirements engineering in the context of domain engineering include

- Managing various application requirements as a function of common domain requirements and specific application requirements
- Managing requirements in the commonality/variability context and the relationship between domain requirements and specific application requirements
- Managing requirement traceability along the domain and application engineering lifecycles

Figure 8.1 illustrates an example of requirement traceability in a domain engineering context.

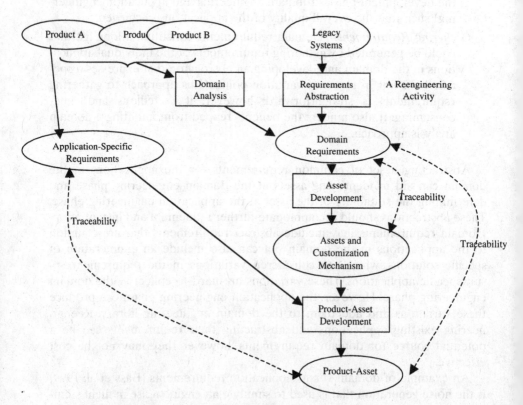

FIGURE 8.1   Requirement traceability in domain engineering.

8.4   ANATOMY OF A DOMAIN COMPONENT

Domain analysis aims at maximizing the reusability of domain models and artifacts in multiple applications within the same domain. The next phase in domain analysis is the design and implementation of domain components. Given a set of commonalties and variabilities as identified in the domain analysis phase, domain components are designed and implemented such that we maximize the common parts of the component used in multiple applications, minimize the variable parts, and provide flexibility to easily adapt the component. In so doing, we are able to maximize the application commonalties that are captured in the common parts of the component, and minimize the effort required to adapt the domain component to suit applications within the domain. Domain components are essentially the main domain artifacts with high potential of reuse and maximal gain when reused. In this section, we discuss the anatomy of a domain component design to achieve reusability.

8.4.1   A Model for Component Families

We defined reusability in Chapter 7 as consisting of two related properties, usefulness, and usability. Recall that usefulness concerns the extent to which a particular reusable artifact is applicable to a wide variety of problems, whereas usability relates to the packaging of the component in a ready-to-use fashion. A reusable component has an intent or a role that it plays within the scope of its applicability or usefulness. The realization of that intent or role consists of a fixed part, which is the part that has a common implementation over its applicability range, and a variable part, whose role is the same over that same range, but whose implementation differs from one point to another. Figure 8.2 illustrates this point.

   To some extent, domain analysis deals with *usefulness* whereas domain design and component realization deals with *usability*. In domain analysis we identify common needs. Given a set of common needs, domain design and component realization define how to package the solution in such a way that the overall cost of using the component over its operating range is minimized. Generally speaking, the cost of reusing a component is a function of the cost of reusing the fixed part, plus the cost of implementing the variable part. Extending the fixed part usually means moving some levels of abstraction higher to hide lower-level "nonessential" differences. At the same time, the cost of reusing the fixed part depends on its *use readiness*, which is a function of its *concreteness*; an abstract component needs some adaptation or instantiation effort—possibly automated—before it can be integrated. Hence, as we saw in Chapter 7, reusable component packaging involves finding a tradeoff between range of applicability in its current form, and the effort required to use it in each case within that range. Advances in programming languages and packaging techniques help enhance the tradeoff and enable us to reach better optima. Figure 8.3, also taken from Chapter 7, illustrates this point.

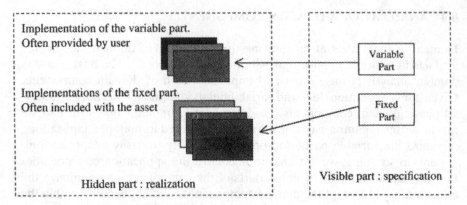

Implementation of the variable part.
Often provided by user

Implementations of the fixed part.
Often included with the asset

Hidden part : realization

Variable
Part

Fixed
Part

Visible part : specification

FIGURE 8.2 Anatomy of a reusable asset.

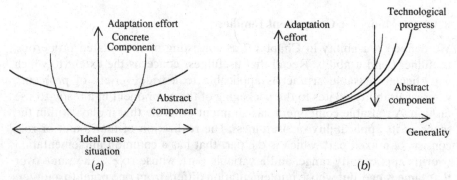

Adaptation effort

Concrete
Component

Abstract
component

Ideal reuse
situation

(a)

Adaptation
effort

Technological
progress

Abstract
component

Generality

(b)

FIGURE 8.3 (a) Difference in adaptation profile between abstract and concrete components; (b) new reuse technologies help bring down the effort–generality curve.

The model of reusable assets that we use (see Fig. 8.2) is based on Krueger's definition of a reusable component, called *component abstraction*. According to Krueger, a *component abstraction* may be described using an *abstraction specification*, and *abstraction realizations* [Krueger 1992]. The abstraction specification embodies both the shared properties among the elements, called the *fixed part* of the abstraction, and the ones that distinguish between them, called the *variable part* or *parameters* of the abstraction [Krueger 1992]. The *abstraction realizations* represent the different instances of the abstraction, however it is convenient to represent them [Krueger 1992]. Much of the AI (artificial intelligence) work on automatic programming is based on instantiating or specializing "reusable" program templates [Balzer 1985] (sometimes called *frames* [Bassett 1987] or *cliché's* [Rich and Waters 1988]), which may also be considered as *component families* of sorts, whose members consist of the different ways in which the component may be used.

8.4.2 Concerns in Designing Component Families

There are a number of factors to consider when designing a component family. Component families have the potential of

- Savings on development and maintenance for the *common aspects* of the family members.
- Savings on the development and maintenance of the family members, above and beyond the savings resulting from the implementation of the common aspects.

Savings on the common parts are maximized if the common aspects are properly (not necessarily physically) separated from the variable parts of the family members. Savings on the variable parts are gained from reducing the *conceptual complexity* of individual members and minimizing the complexity of developing the variable part and integrating it with the fixed part. For instance, given a conceptually "clean" separation of the common and variable parts, the user of a component family need not see the implementation details of the common parts and has to deal only with the variable parts. And with some ingenuity, the "implementation" of the variable parts can be reduced to specifying parameter values.

Component families have to be evolutive in the sense of allowing for the specification or derivation of new unanticipated family members without too much changes to the family description—provided they are members of the same component family, that is, share the same common parts. The contrary would be symptomatic of a conceptual gap between the expression or description of the family and its *intent*. This is the case where we intended to develop a component family, but the way we described or abstracted the common parts and their separation from variable parts may prevent us from adding a new member to the component family. We may refer to this property as *completeness*.

Conversely, component families have to be safe in the sense that they should not allow for the (inadvertent) creation of components that are not within the family. We refer to this property as *soundness*. Component families also have to be evolutive in the sense that new families can be derived from older ones, either through specialization (e.g., by optimizing the implementation of a subfamily) or through generalization (by parameterizing a fixed aspect of the current family members). Ideally, this sharing between families extends beyond creation and into maintenance; specifically, maintenance of the common aspects between a family and its derivatives is centralized, in essence building a family of component families!

Addressing the issues raised above involves a mix of methodological design guidelines and packaging techniques for designing and implementing component families. In packaging terms, these issues may be translated into the following requirements, which we group under three major categories:

Ergonomy. A clear separation of the fixed part from the variable part of the component family description, from the point of view of both the developer of the family (designer) and the user (the "instantiator" of the members).

Safety. "Constants should be": that is, enforcing the constancy of the fixed part of the family during the "legal" derivation of the members. Another requirement is to specify the parameters or variable parts intensionally (e.g., in terms of obligations) and support the proof of conformance of particular values, rather than enumerate the different values and matching instantiation values against them.

Evolvability. Incremental parameterization or resolution: the specialization or generalization of an existing family should involve *local* and *conservative*[1] changes to the existing family. Another requirement is shared maintenance of common aspects to a family and its derivatives.

8.4.3   Exercises

1. (B) Using the example of the waiting queues simulation in Appendix B, give examples of the fixed and variable parts as well as how to minimize the dependencies between the fixed and variable parts for each of the two components: the service facility and the queuing facilities.

8.5   ABSTRACTION AND DOMAIN ANALYSIS

To maximize reusability and to adhere to the component model described in Section 8.4.1, we have to find a way to identify commonalties in the design of the component family, abstract the component design, and use this abstraction to define the common (fixed) parts of the component. This section addresses this issue.

8.5.1   Abstraction and Commonality Analysis

The Webster dictionary defines abstraction as the act of "separating, removing, summarizing, reducing," and its product, *abstract*, as "that which comprises in itself the essential qualities of a larger thing, or of several things; a summary." Assume that we have a set of descriptions for a corresponding set of concepts, systems, or programming artifacts. If we wanted to say everything there is to say about each concept, the descriptions would be *infinite* in length [Hautamaki 1986], and untractable. Abstraction seems to involve two operations: (1) *for a given concept*, being able to focus on the properties (qualities) that are essential to a particular purpose, and (2) being able to describe *a set of concepts* simultaneously in a way that is more economical than enumerating their individual descriptions.

---

[1] Conservative in the sense of not requiring undoing of previous work [Lubars et al. 1992].

We can think of descriptions in terms of multidimensional vectors along a number of descriptive dimensions. *Abstraction* means being able to say the same or a close amount of information with much fewer dimensions, to describe single concepts, or to describe several concepts *collectively*.

Let $C_1 = \langle u_{1,1}, \ldots, u_{1,j}, \ldots, u_{1,n} \rangle$, $C_2 = \langle u_{2,1}, \ldots, u_{2,j}, \ldots, u_{2,n} \rangle, \ldots, C_i = \langle u_{i,1}, \ldots, u_{i,j}, \ldots, u_{i,n} \rangle$ be i concepts with the corresponding vector descriptions. Abstraction can mean one or a combination of operations to be described below.

- Being able to describe any of the concepts $C_1, \ldots, C_i$ by a fewer than the n dimensions, without losing (much) information for the viewpoint of interest.

For example, one of the "properties" of a software component could be the name of its developer. The name of the developer has no bearing on the functionality described, and can be omitted without loss of functional information. This kind of abstraction corresponds to a simple projection [Hautamaki 1986].

There is another kind of abstraction that will reduce the number of dimensions required to describe a concept simply by taking advantage of some of the relationships and dependencies that exist between the dimensions. In effect, this is like recognizing that a vector of dimension n has fewer than n independent variables (*rank* lower than n) and can be written in terms of other, fewer independent vectors. In software terms, we can describe a distributed component/artifact in terms of the underlying security service, and in terms of a particular ORB vendor. Assuming that each ORB implementation comes with a single security service, it is not necessary to describe *both* the ORB implementation *and* the security service. We call this *dimensionality reduction*. Cases of dimensionality reduction do occur in the code where the challenge is to recognize that pieces of the code depend on each other *and* evolve in mutually consistent ways. For example, in a portable graphical application, we could have the choice of a scroll bar class, and a composite pane class, but we have to pick them from the same library package; the *abstract factory* pattern recognizes this dependency and codifies it in a way that guarantees its enforceability [Gamma et al. 1995]. The reverse operation, called *splitting*, is described below.

- Being able to represent a set of concepts by a single description that is more economical than an enumeration of their individual descriptions.

The idea is to replace a set of individual descriptions by a more concise description of the set, possibly by losing some information about specific individuals. There are a number of techniques that can be applied here. Going back to our set of concepts $C_1 = \langle u_{1,1}, \ldots, u_{1,j}, \ldots, u_{1,n} \rangle$, $C_2 = \langle u_{2,1}, \ldots, u_{2,j}, \ldots, u_{2,n} \rangle, \ldots$, and $C_i = \langle u_{i,1}, \ldots, u_{i,j}, \ldots, u_{i,n} \rangle$, assume that all the descriptions have exactly the same values along the first j dimensions. In this way, the set may be described symbolically as the concatenation $\langle u_{1,1}, \ldots, u_{1,j} \rangle$.

$\{\langle u_{1,j+1}, \ldots, u_{1,n}\rangle, \langle u_{2,j+1}, \ldots, u_{2,n}\rangle, \ldots, \langle u_{i,j+1}, \ldots, u_{i,n}\rangle\}$, we call this *grouping*. Thus, instead of having to represent i concepts with $n*i$ values, we only need $j + (n - j)*i$ values. Of course, we could decide that the variables from $j + 1$ to n are not interesting for our purposes, and be content with $\langle u_{1,1}, \ldots, u_{1,j}\rangle$ as the description for the set. As applied to component families, the vector $\langle u_{1,1}, \ldots, u_{1,j}\rangle$ would be the abstraction of the common parts of components in the family and the vectors $\{\langle u_{1,j+1}, \ldots, u_{1,n}\rangle, \langle u_{2,j+1}, \ldots, u_{2,n}\rangle, \ldots, \langle u_{i,j+1}, \ldots, u_{i,n}\rangle\}$ are the variabilities in each component.

Alternatively, we could try to decompose or split some dimension, if we think that the similarities between values are to be found at a smaller granularity. Assume that we are able to express $u_{k,j+1}$ as a two-dimensional vector $\langle v_{k,j+1}, w_{k,j+1}\rangle$, for all $k = 1, \ldots, i$, and assume that $v_{k,j+1}$ has the same value for all $k = 1, \ldots, i$—call it $v_{1,j+1}$. Then, we can describe the set of concepts with the concatenation $\langle u_{1,1}, \ldots, u_{1,j}, v_{1,j+1}\rangle \cdot \{\langle w_{1,j+1}, u_{1,j+2}, \ldots, u_{1,n}\rangle, \langle w_{2,j+1}, u_{2,j+2}, \ldots, u_{2,n}\rangle, \ldots, \langle w_{i,j+1}, u_{i,j+2}, \ldots, u_{i,n}\rangle\}$. While we still need the same number of variables to describe the differences, we have reduced the overall scope of the variable part by splitting one variable dimension into subdimensions, one common and fixed and one variable. We call this technique *splitting*. Figure 8.4 illustrates a case of splitting. Here, by going further down the granularity hierarchy to look at the insides of methods, we were able to identify a commonality that was not captured by the initial method boundaries.

We could also try to capture further similarities between the different individuals by seeing if there is a way to describe the different values along one dimension more concisely. For example, we could find that the set of values $\{u_{1,j+1}, \ldots, u_{i,j+1}\}$ is best captured in terms of a property $P_{j+1}(.)$ such that $P_{j+1}(u_{k,j+1})$ is true for all $k = 1, \ldots, i$. In that case, the set will be described in

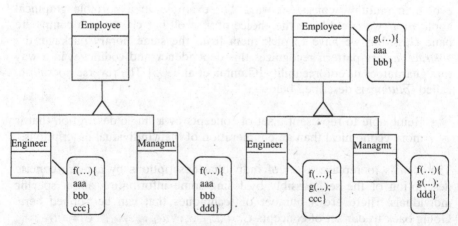

FIGURE 8.4 By splitting the method $f(\ldots)$, we were able to factor out the common parts between the two implementations of engineer and management.

terms of the concatenation $\langle u_{1,1}, \ldots, u_{1,j}, P_{j+1}(.)\rangle \cdot \{\langle u_{1,j+2}, \ldots, u_{1,n}\rangle, \langle u_{2,j+2}, \ldots, u_{2,n}\rangle, \ldots, \langle u_{i,j+2}, \ldots, u_{i,n}\rangle\}$.[2] We call this operation *intensionalization*. To some extent, *intentionalization replaces a difference by a higher-order commonality*; it constrains the range of variability.

There could be several intensionalizations for the same set of values (*extension*). For example, assume that $i = 3$, and that $\{u_{1,j+1}, \ldots, u_{i,j+1}\} = \{1, 2, 4\}$; we can describe the set as the set $\{2^k\}_{k=0\cdots2}$. This predicate may be "extensionally sound," but perhaps unlikely to be the "real" common thread between 1, 2, and 4. What we have to consider when we replace a set of values (an *extension*) by a predicate (an *intension*) is

- To account for all of the known occurrences (*extensional completeness*)
- To not account for any of known counterexamples (*extensional soundness*)

Of course, the predicates (intensions) may include values that were not anticipated, in effect resulting in a bigger set of concepts than the original set $\{C_1, \ldots, C_n\}$. But this is the bread and butter of classification[3] and categorization approaches in statistics and machine intelligence; the important thing is that the newly described concept or set makes sense [Gennari et al. 1990].

For example, assume that we start out with two implementations of sorted lists; one that stores integers, and one that stores real numbers. Assume that the two list structures use the same insertion algorithm; one that uses a comparison operator <= between the values contained in the list. There are many ways to describe these two data structures. One way is to describe them both as ordered lists of numerical values, which would be accurate, and satisfy both the *extensional completeness* and *extensional soundness* principles. Another description of the same set could be an ordered list of data values supporting a boolean operation <=. This description also satisfies the *extensional completeness* and *extensional soundness* properties, for the set consisting of the two sorted list types, but includes yet to be defined things such as sorted lists of strings, employee records, and stock values. Obviously, the second description is more useful, although perhaps a bit riskier as there may be adverse side effects, yet to be uncovered, which apply only to some types that are outside the initial set of two. What this means is the predicate in question does not properly capture all the constraints that needed to be imposed on the parameter type.

Coplien noted an interesting—and all too occurring—case of commonality analysis when dealing with a family of components (programs): the case where

---

[2] In $\langle u_{2,1}, \ldots, u_{2,j}, P_{j+1}(.)\rangle$, we combined values and predicates that values must satisfy in the same tuple. We could view a value $u_{2,j}$ as the predicate $P_i(x): [x = u_{2,i}]$.

[3] Classification is used here in the sense of grouping instances in classes.

the commonality *knowingly* does not characterize *all* the members of the family; instead, the common abstraction describes the *dominant* characteristics of the family, with exceptions handled explicitly [Coplien 1999, p. 67]. He takes the example of the "email message" abstraction, which should handle content-bearing messages as well as acknowledgment messages. A message *typically* has a body, but acknowledgment messages don't. At first glance, they may be considered as messages with empty bodies. However, this simplifying assumption may end up costing a lot downstream, as all the message handling programs have to handle the special case of empty bodies. In the end, it comes down to a tradeoff between the simplicity of keeping a single abstraction (a message), but propagating the complexity of handling empty messages to *all* message handling code, or to have two different abstractions (content-bearing *message* vs. event notification messages or the like) with their separate message-handling logic. Coplien calls this *negative variability* in the sense that the variations within the family may invalidate or negate the characteristics of the family, as opposed to the other, *positive variability*, which adds detail to, or binds variables of the family descriptions[4] [Coplien 1999].

Discussion

In practice, when we try to build a reusable component, we aim for a component that is as applicable as possible to all applications within a domain. There are two ways to achieve this goal:

- By analyzing several components that have similar goals and functionalities, and extracting from these a common description, or a description of a single component, with potential variants, that will fulfill all the needs of the original components. This is the method advocated in domain analysis, which takes as input a set of already built systems in the given application domain. Coplien calls this *inductive commonality* [Coplien 1999, p. 31].

- By extrapolating from a single component description. The idea here is to identify those aspects of the component that can be made variable and that would extend the most the applicability of the component. For example, given a component implementing an array of integers that supports a QuickPort sorting algorithm, we could extend the component by parameterizing its sort algorithm or its stored data type, or both. Clearly, the type parameterization will make the array component far more applicable than the algorithm parameterization, and if cost and complexity are an issue, we may go for only the type parameterization. Coplien calls this *deductive commonality* [Coplien 1999, p. 31].

[4] Coplien argues that we have traditionally handled commonality by embodying the family description in abstract classes, and the family members as derived classes from the family description. Positive variability is typically reflected in the fact that the family members are subclasses but also subtypes. Negative variability is reflected in the use of method cancellation and other nonkosher artifacts such as conditional compilation [Coplien 1999]. See Cook [1992] and Godin and Mili [1993] for a critical study of the Smalltalk80 collection library.

In either case, the full range of the "abstraction strategies" presented above (projection, grouping, splitting, and intensionalization) applies, and may be applied repeatedly to the same reusable component.

8.5.2 Abstraction Dimensions

Having identified abstraction strategies in terms of manipulations on multi-dimensional vectors, we now turn to what those dimensions might be. Which dimensions should we consider? The short answer is that there are many dimensions that one could and *would want to* consider; separation of concerns has been a software engineering problem solving tool—and a elusive goal [Tarr et al. 1999]. Coplien proposed a hierarchical breakdown of problems into domains, subdomains, and then parts, where subdomains may themselves be made of other subdomains [Coplien 1999, Chapter 4]. Domains are the object of *domain analysis* and refer to *application* or *business domains*. Subdomains are reusable chunks of business logic that may be useful in many kinds of applications. For example, in the domain of order entry systems, there are subdomains dealing with customer files, inventory, on-line catalogs, and so on. Shlaer and Mellor [1992] use the notion of domain to break a system into a set of coherent and relatively weakly coupled subsystems [Shlaer and Mellor, 1992]; for them, domains partition the set of objects that make up an application:

- An object is defined in exactly one domain.
- The objects in a domain require the existence of other objects in the same domain.
- The objects in one domain do not require the existence of objects in other domains.

They argue that there are typically four types of domains within systems:

1. Application domains, dealing exclusively with business logic
2. Service domains, which embody things such as user interfaces, communications, event messaging, and other general utilities
3. Architectural domains, which embody architectural choices in terms of specific metalevel artifacts (templates, patterns, etc.) and guidelines
4. Implementation domains, which include programming languages (and language constructs), networks, operating systems, and common class libraries

It is fair to say that there are different views of what domains are and how they interrelate. Two major distinctions stand out: (1) domains and subdomains that are related to the business or application logic and (2) domains that are related to the solution artifacts (the last three for Shlaer and Mellor). The second distinction is related to the relationships between the domains and sub-domains that make up an application. For Shlaer and Mellor, for example, domains partition objects—no overlap. For Coplien, domains (or subdomains) may share subdomains [Coplien 1999]. For the role modeling and separation of concerns community (subjects [Harrison and Ossher 1993], role models [Reenskaug 1995], views [Mili et al. 1999b], aspects [Kiczales et al. 1997], hyperslices [Tarr et al. 1999]), domains overlap heavily as they represent different facets of the same objects, and there is a lot of research attempting to separate those domains physically—insofar as a CASE tool can manipulate a representation of them—so that they may be developed and evolved independently.

A related aspect to overlap is whether the subdomains of a given domain are mutually exclusive or whether we can have one or more subdomain within the same system. There does not appear to be a general rule. All the (four) domain types described by Shlaer and Mellor are to be present in a finished application.[5] However, within the application domain, any combination of subdomains may be present—unless there are domain-specific reasons that prevent two subdomains from coexisting. For example, in the domain of service charges for discount brokers, some brokerage houses charge a flat service fee as a percentage of the amount invested, and allow customers to move funds around free of charge, while others charge a smaller amount, but per transaction. Thus, in the domain of service charges, we have two alternative and mutually exclusive subdomains: (1) fixed per investment charges and (2) per transaction charges. Generally speaking, when a domain is decomposed into subdomains consisting of required *roles* within the domain, all the subdomains must coexist. However, when the subdomains consist of alternative implementations of a particular role, then it is often the case that two sudomains from the same branch cannot exist. Going back to our vectorial representation of software artifacts, *domains that correspond to roles will constitute different dimensions that need to be described*, and along which the software artifact may be abstracted. However, *alternative implementations of the same role constitute different values along the same dimension*.

Figure 8.5 illustrates the structure of domains. It is tempting here to equate the four domain types to the typical layered architectures, where we separate the user interface, the application logic, the services (persistence, remote access), and the underlying operating system/virtual machine. However, in our minds, *domains correspond to distinct concerns within the same software artifact, rather than (necessarily) different artifacts*. Typically, a *finished* software artifact (e.g., a code component) would involve "selecting" one "entity" (or value) from each of the domains. For example, a COM component that implements a "customer server" is the combination ⟨**Customer**, messaging/DB, COM-bus, C++ class⟩, where **Customer** is the analysis-level meaning of

---

[5] We can imagine an application that is still at the analysis stage to have only the application domain and the services domain known, with the others still to be decided.

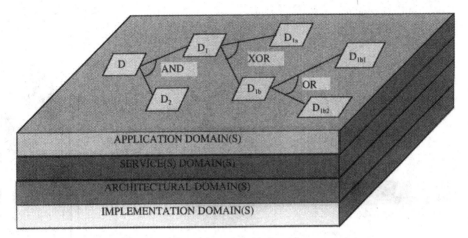

FIGURE 8.5 Domains and relations between them.

a `Customer` (application domain), which uses persistence and the COM messaging service (services domain), a COM bus (architectural domain), and is implemented as a C++ class (implementation domain). Figure 8.6 illustrates this point.

All three components C_1, C_2, and C_2' are completed software artifacts. Thus, their descriptions contain entries along the four domains (application, services, architectural, and implementation). We assume that they are all written in the same language, to use the same services, and based on the same architectural style; they will only differ along the dimensions that are within the application domain. C_1 and C_2 belong to two different subdomains, and thus do not have the same descriptive properties and unit vectors within the application domain ($v_1 v_2 v_3 \ldots v_n$ vs. $v_3 v_5 v_8 \ldots v_j$)—although they may have dimensions in common ($v_3 v_5 v_8$). However, C_2 and C_2' belong to the same subdomain (have the same set of properties), and C_2' is a specialization of C_2. The reader may notice that C_2 has no values along the dimensions v_3 and v_j whereas C_2' has specific values for those (3 and 6, respectively). *In this case, we would say that C_2 is an abstraction of C_2' along the $\langle v_3, v_j \rangle$ dimensions.*

Generally speaking, we should be able to generalize/abstract a software artifact along any of the dimensions within any of the domains. For example, we could make a component independent of the implementation language by making it CORBA-enabled—by providing a *paradigm-independent* IDL interface to it. We could make it independent of the architectural style, either by providing several interfaces to it, one per style, or by providing an interface generator with built-in templates that could generate one of those interfaces on demand. Abstraction can also occur within the services domains: on Windows platforms, we can make a component independent of the underlying relational database by accessing the data through Open or Java Database Connectivity (ODBC or JDBC) Drivers.

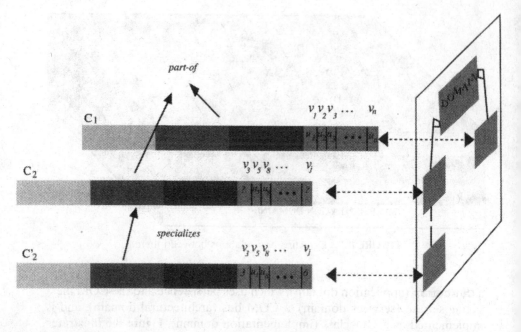

FIGURE 8.6   An example vectorial representation of three finished components.

Note that, generally speaking, we would gain much from building artifacts corresponding to the various domain types (e.g., application, services, architectural, implementation), or domains within those types, and combining those artifacts as late in the lifecycle of the software as possible. For example, most development methodologies are adept at keeping the four domain types fairly separate, early on in the development lifecycle (analysis and architectural design), but start binding the artifacts together from detailed design onward. Shlaer and Mellor are good at separating analysis-level considerations from design-level considerations up to the code generation phase; instead of designing classes one by one, they argue, one must design implementation molds (templates) that are then applied to different types of objects to generate code [Mellor 1993]. Mili and Li [1993] proposed an approach to class design that maps analysis-level classes to separately developed and maintained generic data structures to generate implementation-level class representations (data definitions, accessors, and some domain-specific functions). Role modeling and the OORAM methodology [Reenskaugh 1995] are concerned with keeping behavioral concerns separate throughout the analysis phase, and only synthesizing the various behavioral roles that objects play prior to moving to design. To some extent, subject-oriented programming [Harrison and Ossher 1993], aspect-oriented programming [Kiczales et al. 1997], and view programming [Mili et al. 1999] all aim at delaying the binding of the various behavioral roles that objects may play, even further in the lifecycle; until *compile time*, for subject-oriented programming and aspect-oriented programming, until *linking time*, for an earlier (limited) implementation of subject-oriented programming [Ossher et al. 1994], and a combination of *compile time* and *runtime* for view programming [Mili et al. 1999]. A number of design patterns use programming language constructs to separate concerns *across* objects and object relationships—with construct-specific binding times. Chapter 11 deals with such language constructs, and talks about some of the design patterns in terms of the concerns that they separate.

8.5.3 Exercises

1. (B) Using the waiting queues example in Appendix B, give examples of each of the following abstraction strategies: dimensionality reduction, projection, grouping, splitting, and intensionalization.

8.6 DOMAIN ANALYSIS METHODS

In Sections 8.3 and 8.4, we discussed issues pertaining to the design of domain components and the role of abstraction in defining commonalties between components in a component family. In this section, we take a more general perspective of domain analysis by looking at existing methodologies to analyze a domain.

The literature abounds with descriptions of domain analysis methods that share the same objectives: analyzing the domain and developing domain models. However, each technique defines a particular way of understanding the domain and capturing domain information as domain models. In general, a domain analysis method can be characterized by the process (steps to conduct the analysis), the product (usually domain models), and supporting tools. In the following, we summarize the general approaches taken by some well-established domain analysis methods.

8.6.1 Feature-Oriented Domain Analysis (FODA)

The feature-oriented domain analysis (FODA) method was developed at the Software Engineering Institute (SEI), [Kang et al. 1990, FODA 1999]. FODA focuses on identifying features that characterize a domain and hence gives the approach its name. Applications in a domain provide several capabilities. These capabilities are modeled in FODA as features. To model these features, FODA defines a process for domain analysis that is based on three activities:

Context Analysis. The context analysis activity defines the bounds of a domain with the objective of scoping the domain under investigation. Scoping is done by identifying the relationship between the applications in the domain and the elements that are external to the domain. Variabilities are identified in terms of different data requirements and operation requirements imposed by the external environment. Context analysis is used to define the inputs and outputs to and from the domain. The results of context analysis are usually context diagrams and structure diagrams. Context diagrams relate the domain to the environment, while structure diagrams relate the domain to other domains, which could be part of the original domain. Defining domain interaction with the external environment and with other domains helps in defining the set of capabilities (features) that the domain encloses.

Domain Modeling. The domain modeling activity identifies commonalties and variabilities that characterize applications within the domain, by modeling the functions, data, and relationships between applications in the domain. The resulting models usually define what the applications are, what they do, and how they work. Domain modeling is composed of feature analysis, information analysis, and operational analysis, which produce features, information, and operational models, respectively. A features model describes what the applications do in terms of operations (functions). An information model describes the applications in terms of entities and their relationships. An operational model relates the information model and features model to the behavior and function of applications. Operational models are described in terms of entities, functions, and behavior charts such as state machines. In addition, an extensive domain dictionary is developed, which contains the terms and abbreviations that are used in describing the domain model and a textual description of the features and entities themselves.

Architecture Modeling. The architecture modeling activity creates the software architecture that defines a common solution structure for applications in the domain. Architectural modeling defines a framework for constructing applications in the domain. It identifies concurrent processes and common assets. It also allocates features, functions, and data objects to the processes and assets. As a result, the architecture model is developed, which defines the basic partitioning and interconnections necessary for constructing applications in the domain. The common architecture is defined in terms of component interfaces, the nature of the interconnections (specification of architecture connectors), model initialization, and model execution (possibly execution scenarios).

8.6.2   Organization Domain Modeling (ODM)

Organization domain modeling (ODM) [Simos 1995, ODM 1993] prescribes a general method for conducting domain analysis in an organization. ODM offers a domain analysis method that is part of a larger domain-engineering lifecycle. Considerable support and collaboration in refining the ODM method has come from Hewlett-Packard and Unisys Corporation, as a prime contractor for the Defense Advanced Research Projects Agency (DARPA) Software Technology for Adaptable and Reliable Systems (STARS) program [ODM 1993].

Although ODM focuses mainly on organizational issues and transition to reuse discipline, it defines domain engineering technical activities. ODM has three main processes: domain analysis, architecture development, and asset implementation. The domain analysis approach focuses primarily on explicit descriptive and prescriptive analysis phases. "An explicit distinction is made between domain modeling activities that are descriptive, 'as is,' and prescriptive, 'to be.' This distinction aims to prevent a modeler from unconsciously modeling aspects of legacy systems in terms of how (the modeler believes) they should be designed rather than how they were actually designed" [ODM 1993]. A descriptive domain model is developed from legacy systems, artifacts, and past experiences. This descriptive model is transformed into a prescriptive domain model that documents the features that the domain architecture will support. A domain architecture is then created and represented in a concrete and analyzable format. Finally, domain assets are developed that conform to the architecture.

The domain analysis method of ODM is mainly a descriptive/prescriptive approach that focuses on reengineering existing legacy systems. It also provides iterative scoping of the domain where a set of applications is used as examples for the domain scoping activity.

8.6.3 Joint Object-Oriented Domain Analysis (JODA)

The joint object-oriented domain analysis (JODA) method advocates the idea that software objects are more understandable and customizable than traditional functions and subroutines. JODA was developed by the Joint Integrated Avionics Working Group (JIAWG) reuse subcommittee [Holibaugh 1992]. JODA defines domain models using the Coad–Yourdon object-oriented analysis technique. These domain models are then used to define the domain architecture. Domain models are developed using the Coad–Yourdon whole–part and inheritance diagrams. Domain models are defined in terms of objects, their attributes, and their services. Variations in the domain are reflected as variations in the objects' attributes, services, and relationships with other objects in the domain models.

JODA is the domain analysis part of the reuse-based software development approach defined by JIAWG. This approach also includes business and methodological planning. Business planning identifies the high-level domain to which the analysis approach will be applied. This definition of the domain usually includes the domain scope and technology dependencies, and whether domain expertise is available. Methodological planning defines the domain engineering activities, application engineering activities, and how they integrate. The JODA domain analysis method defines the domain structure and requirements, and captures them in domain models. These domain models are implemented and stored as a repository of reusable software objects.

JODA consists of three phases: preparing the domain, scoping the domain, and defining domain models. Preparing the domain is concerned with collecting information about the domain under consideration either by interviewing domain experts or by reengineering existing systems. The preparation process in JODA also includes investigating the stability and maturity of technologies in the domain and their anticipated future. The domain scoping in JODA includes definition of the domain glossary, services, dependencies, and the development of a high-level whole–part, subject, and inheritance diagrams. The last phase in JODA is modeling the domain by defining the object life histories and state-event response, investigating operation scenarios, and packaging and grouping reusable objects. The domain analysis activities within JODA are iterative. Figure 8.7 shows the JODA analysis process.

8.6.4   Reuse Library Process Model (RLPM)

The reuse library process model (RLPM) [RLPM 1991] was developed as part of the STARS program. RLPM process defines a domain analysis activity as a part of the domain engineering phase of the process model. The domain analysis process in RLPM is concerned with

- Domain knowledge acquisition
- Classification and keywords analysis
- Developing functional models
- Developing domain architectures

The domain analysis process within RLPM has specific features that distinguish it from other domain analysis methodologies. The RLPM domain analysis method is heavily process-based. There is little to say about the domain models that are produced. It is a combined top–down and bottom–up process. The top–down analysis process produces functional models, whereas the bottom–up analysis process is concerned with the classification and keywords

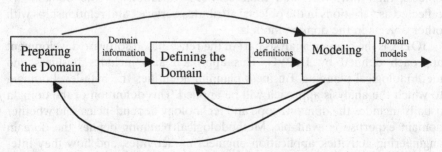

FIGURE 8.7   JODA domain analysis method.

analysis. This combined approach is unique to the RLPM. The RLPM is based on Ruben Prieto-Diaz's work [Prieto-Diaz 1991]. This method adapts many principles from library science to the organization and implementation of a reuse library.

8.6.5 Domain Analysis and Design Process (DADP)

The domain analysis and design process (DADP) [SofTech 1993] is developed by the Defense Information Systems Agency (DISA) Center of Information Management (CIM). The activities described in DADP are similar to those described in the RLPM approach with more emphasis on the description of domain models that are produced from the analysis phase. The DADP method takes a problem/solution space approach. The domain is defined in the problem space where system engineers are mostly involved. System engineers define the problem and the system constraints. Software, hardware, and human-factor engineers are then involved to define and evolve a solution space. The analysis aspect of DADP is concerned with identifying and defining problems within a group of related systems in the same domain. Domain analysis develops generic requirements to address frequent requirements in the domain and ensure the flexibility of these requirements in a changing environment in terms of both technology and management. The design aspect of DADP is concerned with the development of domain-specific solutions in terms of architecture and reusable assets.

DADP has four phases:

Identifying the Domain. The outcome of this step is a set of business models, definitions of system capabilities, domain models, definitions of external interfaces, known reuse opportunities, groups of systems sharing same capabilities, and some descriptions and documentation of current systems and anticipated systems.

Scoping the Domain. The domain is scoped with more than three systems in mind. In this phase, the domain analyst also identifies opportunities for reuse among systems in the same domain and reuse across other domains. The domain knowledge and team experiences are also documented.

Analyzing the Domain. This step involves analyzing the problem space information. Commonalties and common object adaptation requirements are identified. Domain models are constructed and verified.

Designing the Domain. At this step the solution space is addressed by providing solutions in terms of common designs and implementations of domain objects.

The DADP advocates an object-oriented technology approach where most of the diagrams are based on the old object-oriented analysis models of

Coad–Yourdon [Coad and Yourdon 1991]. However, no particular process is emphasized. The main advantage of this method is that it corrects much of the vagueness in the STARS process, particularly in domain model construction and definition.

8.6.6   Domain-Specific Software Architecture (DSSA)

The DSSA [Braun 1992] domain models are developed by DARPA for command and control (C2) applications. The DSSA domain analysis method is more concerned with defining the models to be produced rather than the analysis process. These domain models are function, dynamic, and object models:

Function and Dynamic Models. Function and dynamic models describe the functional processes in a manner similar to the structured analysis diagrams. These diagrams include data flow diagrams and control flow diagrams. These models offer a hierarchical decomposition of the domain functionality.

Object Models. Object models are developed using the object modeling technique (OMT) of Rumbaugh et al. [1991]. These models include class diagrams containing class attributes, class methods, and generalization and association relationships.

The choice of object-oriented analysis diagrams in the DSSA application seems flexible. Any of the current object-oriented analysis methods contains diagrams capable of describing the information contained in the DSSA C2 object model.

8.6.7   The SYNTHESIS Domain Analysis Method

Domain analysis is a part of the SYNTHESIS approach that was developed by the Software Productivity Consortium [SPC 1993]. As a part of both the opportunistic and the leveraged approach, domain analysis activity is defined as the scoping and specification of a domain based on the analysis of the needs of a targeted project in an organization. The activities of domain analysis include

Domain Definition. The domain definition activity is concerned with identifying an informal description of the applications in the family and related application engineering that constitutes a domain. It defines how applications in a domain are similar and how they differ

Domain Specification. The domain specification activity includes subactivities for identifying process requirements, application requirements, decision models, and abstracting the application design.

Domain Verification. Domain verification is concerned with ensuring correctness, consistency, and completeness of domain engineering products. It includes verifying domain definitions, specifications, and implementation.

The output of the domain analysis phase is the domain definition and specification. Domain definition includes

Domain Synopsis. An informal description of the domain scope.

Domain Glossary. A definition of the vocabulary used by experts in the domain.

Domain Assumptions. Definitions of what is common and what is variable among systems in the domain.

Legacy Products. A collection of work products from existing systems.

The domain specification consists of

Decision Models. A decision model identifies the application engineering requirements and decisions that determine how members of the family may vary.

Product Requirements. Product requirements describe the abstracted content of the members of the family.

Process Requirements. Process requirements describe the established process for application engineering with a domain.

Product Design. A product design determines the structure and composition of solutions provided by members of the family.

8.6.8 Reuse Business Methodology

The *reuse-driven software engineering business* is a framework developed by Ivar Jacobson et al. [1997] to define a set of guidelines and models that help ensure success with large-scale object-oriented reuse. The framework is referred to as *reuse business*. It deals systematically with business, process, architecture, and organization issues in a product line. Reuse business processes are categorized under three main categories: (1) component system engineering, (2) application family engineering, and (3) application system engineering. Component system engineering is responsible for creating component systems. Each component system is a set of customizable configurable software components where a component is a type, class, or any work product that has been specially engineered to be reusable. Application family engineering creates the overall system architecture and identifies the component systems that will be used with the architecture to develop applications that belong to the same domain. Application system engineering is the process of creating a specific application that belongs to the domain by selecting, specializing, and assembling components from component systems. Reuse busi- ness does not have an explicit domain engineering process, but distributes the main domain engineering processes between application family engineering and component system engineering.

8.6.9 Comparison

To gain insight into how to perform domain engineering, we need to analyze and compare existing domain engineering methods using controlled experi- ments and case studies. In an attempt to study domain analysis methods, we set up a controlled case study in a *classroom* environment [Mili and Yacoub 2000]. We used the example of waiting queue simulation described in Appen- dix B. As part of their evaluation, students are required to work on term projects, which include a domain engineering task and an application engi- neering task. Students are organized in teams; each team turns in a collective domain engineering deliverable, and each student subsequently turns in a selected application developed using the team's domain engineering deliver- ables. The assignment of applications to students is not done until *after* domain engineering is complete, and is done by the instructor so that when students perform domain engineering, they do not know which application they will end up developing; this ensures that they make their assets as generic as possible. Student teams select a domain engineering methodology from a set of six candidates; generally, they have no prior knowledge of these method- ologies. For the purposes of this study, student teams are asked to fill out questionnaires. The teams chose to work with FODA, JODA, SYNTHESIS, and Reuse Business Methods. The purpose of the experiment is to analyze and compare the candidate domain engineering methods with respect to the following criteria:

Rationale for Domain Definition. We are interested to find out whether the domain analysis method emphasizes a definition of the domain as a common expertise, common design, or common market as we defined earlier in Section 8.1.1.

Processes for Domain Definition. A domain may be defined in one of two ways: by increasing commonality or increasing variability. In an *increas- ing commonality* approach, we start from a comprehensive definition, which includes a wide range of (possibly heterogeneous) applications, and we reduce this set in a stepwise manner, until we are satisfied with the level of commonality of the applications that remain. This process can also be referred to as *stepwise exclusion*. In an *increasing variability approach*, we start from a small set of applications, which have presum- ably a great deal of commonality, and we expand the set until we are satisfied that the domain is fairly large, while still maintaining adequate commonality. This process can also be referred to as *stepwise inclusion*.

Guidelines for Domain Architecture. We are interested to know, for each method, whether the method advocates a specific architectural style (e.g., layered, client–server, or pipes-and-filters architectures), and whether it provides constructive guidelines for how the architecture is derived. In particular, does the method provide guidelines for mapping commonalties and variabilities into architectural features? Are the architecture guidelines *product-based*, that is, describe what the architecture is, and how is it represented, or *process-based*, that is, describe how to create the architecture?

Domain Engineering Deliverables. Each domain analysis method produces a set of deliverables, which include domain definition, assumptions, and analysis models. We are interested in analyzing the deliverables of each method, and assessing the extent to which these deliverables capture information about the domain of the applications family.

Reusable Assets. We are interested in cataloging the set of reusable assets that are produced for this application domain. An analysis of this set for each method and a comparison across methods should give us some insights into the design features of each method.

Domain Engineering Lifecycle. We are interested in analyzing the lifecycle advocated by each method, and assessing the extent to which the life-cycle gives concrete guidelines in producing the deliverables of domain engineering.

Domain Engineering Effort. How much effort was needed to conduct the domain engineering phase? How was this effort distributed on the various activities/phases? The cost of domain engineering cannot be used in isolation to assess a domain engineering method; a method may cost more than another, but may also produce better reusable assets, thereby reducing application engineering costs. Hence we consider that it is the sum of domain engineering costs and application engineering costs that reflects the cost effectiveness of a domain engineering method.

Technology Dependency. Some domain engineering methods advocate a specific technology, and can be applied only within that technology.

Language Dependency. Some domain engineering methods advocate a specific set of languages (for specification, architecture description, design, implementation, etc), and can only be applied using these languages.

In the following paragraphs we summarize the results found in this study under some of the categories described above. For more details about the experiment and results under other categories, the reader is referred to Mili and Yacoub [2000].

8.6.9.1 Rationale for Domain Definition

FODA defines the domain by instantiating a structure diagram and a context diagram. The common characteristic among all applications in a domain is the aggregate of a structure diagram and a context diagram. The structure diagram maps events and concepts, and the context diagram shows the data flow between service stations, customer queues, and the simulation program. Clearly, FODA's rationale for domain definition is *common design*.

The SYNTHESIS domain analysis team argued that SYNTHESIS domain analysis emphasizes the *common market* characterization of a domain definition, because SYNTHESIS emphasizes a business reuse level solution. As part of the domain definition, SYNTHESIS documents the domain status, which includes an endorsement that the domain synopsis and assumptions define a viable domain. It also defines the confidence and risks associated with the endorsement. To meet the common market rationale defined by the SYNTHESIS process, the team considered themselves a company targeting the market with this product line and analyzed their background and experiences in the field. The team considered the other teams as market competitors and analyzed the market from that perspective.

The JODA domain analysis method is a part of a larger reuse lifecycle that is composed of: business planning, methodology planning, domain engineering, and application engineering. JODA identifies the domain as part of its business planning phase. The criteria for identifying a domain are as follows. Is the domain well understood, is the technology predictable, and is the domain expertise available to support domain engineering? These criteria are mostly related to our *common expertise* classification. Although the JODA team did not have the specific domain expertise in our case study, the team managed to relate the project to their previous experience in simulation of queuing networks.

Reuse Business defines an application family as a set of applications with common features. These applications work together to help some users accomplish their work. Reuse Business also considers the same application systems that need to be reconfigured, packaged, and installed differently for different users as a family. In addition, a family is a set of fairly independent application systems that are built from the same lower level reusable components and the same architecture. Therefore, we consider this method a *common design*.

Table 8.1 summarizes the observations made by the teams. Domain analysis methods differ in the criteria by which they characterize and define a domain. The teams were able to use the classification of *common design*, *common expertise*, and *common market* to characterize the domain of our case study differently according to the analysis method that they used.

TABLE 8.1   Rationale for Domain Definition

FODA	SYNTHESIS	JODA	Reuse Business
Common design	Common market	Common expertise	Common design

8.6.9.2 Processes for Domain Definition

FODA advocates defining the domain by collecting relevant information, based on the study of existing systems and their development histories. Hence its approach to domain definition appears to be driven by *increasing variability*.

The SYNTHESIS team pursued a bottom-up approach based on sample applications and *increasing variability*. However, the SYNTHESIS method itself does not imply an increasing commonality or increasing variability process. The team reported that because the domain in our case study is limited, they pursued the increasing variability approach. They also tried to increase variability by adding other applications to the domain such as train unit dispatchers and telephone waiting queues.

The JODA method relies heavily on domain expertise and interviewing and reengineering existing systems. We tend to classify this as an *increasing commonality* approach because the method collects a wide amount of information and uses this information to narrow down the domain.

The Reuse Business team found that the process is better described as *increasing variability*. They point out that the main feature of the method is modeling with use cases. They started with the set of common applications, given in Section 8.2, from which they identified use cases.

We note that the teams found it hard to characterize the domain analysis process as *increasing variability or increasing commonality* [Mili and Yocoub 2000]. They were inclined to use the *increasing variability* approach. This may reflect more on the way the domain was described than on meaningful differences between methods.

8.6.9.3 Guidelines for Domain Architecture

The guidelines provided by the FODA team about the domain architecture are *product-based*. The architecture is defined in terms of component interfaces, model execution (scenarios), and nature of interconnections (specifications of architecture connectors). The FODA team developed a *layered* architecture style for the domain such that reuse can occur at the layer appropriate for a given application. In general, FODA advocates a layered architecture that has four layers:

1. The *domain architecture layer*, which is a set of processes and their interactions

TABLE 8.2 Process for Defining a Domain

FODA	SYNTHESIS	JODA	Reuse Business
Increasing variability	Both	Increasing commonality	Increasing variability

2. The *module structure chart layer*, which shows the packaging of functions, features, and data into modules that are common to applications in the domain

3. The *common utilities layer*, which defines utilities that are general across several domains

4. The *subsystem layer*, which defines operating system, languages, and so on

The FODA team also identified some guidelines for creating the architecture, which include defining concurrent processes, defining common modules, and then mapping features, functions, and data to these processes and modules.

The SYNTHESIS team developed the architectures as a consequence of activities for defining commonalties and variabilities. The SYNTHESIS team described a *process-based* guideline for creating architectures. An interesting result that the SYNTHESIS team found is that they can map commonalties into components and variabilities into parameters to these components. The SYNTHESIS method is flexible on representation and definition of the architecture style. The team used the Unified Modeling Language (UML).

The JODA team found that the guidelines for creating architectures are mostly *process-based*. The team used scenarios for developing subject diagrams and whole–part diagrams and further refined these diagrams by analyzing detailed scenarios of each part. There are no restrictions on how JODA represents the domain. The team emphasized the role of scenarios in deriving the domain architecture and identifying components.

The Reuse Business team found that the architecture guidelines are *product-based*. In an OO context, the team described the architecture as a set of subsystems, their interfaces, and nodes on which these subsystems are executing. The Reuse Business domain analysis method produces a layered architecture where a layer is defined as a set of subsystems with the same degree of generality. Upper layers are application specific and lower layers are generic. Thus the representation of the architecture is more emphasized than the process of developing it.

Table 8.3 illustrates the observations made by the teams on the architecture guidelines that they inferred from their selected domain analysis methods. The table shows whether the guidelines are process-based or product-based.

TABLE 8.3 Guidelines for Domain Architecture

	FODA	SYNTHESIS	JODA	Reuse Business
Product-based	Layered			Layered
Process-based		Mapping commonalties and variabilities to components	Scenarios	

It also shows the main characteristic of the architecture style or the main guideline for the creation process.

8.6.9.4 Technology and Language Dependence

The FODA team reported that the method is heavily based on structure analysis and design (SA/SD). The domain models that the team produced are based on context diagrams, data and control flow graphs, structured charts for module designs, and function and operation models. Therefore we can consider FODA technologically dependent on structured design and programming. FODA does not advocate a specific implementation language. The SYNTHESIS team reported that the method does not advocate a particular technology nor a specific implementation language. JODA is based on the assumption that objects are more understandable and customizable than traditional functions and subroutines. Therefore, the method is heavily based on the object-oriented technology. The notations and models used are the Coad–Yourdon models. These models are now integrated into UML models. Reuse Business has an object-oriented domain analysis method and therefore it is heavily based on OO analysis and design models such as use cases and scenarios. The implementation language is only restricted to be object-oriented. Table 8.4 summarizes the dependence of the domain analysis methods on technology and programming languages.

None of the domain analysis methods involved in our case study is programming-language-dependent, although most are technology-dependent (object-oriented or structured). SYNTHESIS is the only method that is neither technology- nor language-dependent; the team selected object-oriented models and languages nonetheless.

Even though this study is preliminary, we can discern some distinct trends in the way the different methods approach a given problem. Some methods focus on processes, while others focus on products and deliverables; some methods focus on business considerations, whereas others focus on technical considerations; some methods propose guidelines, whereas others impose standards; also, some methods require more detailed deliverables, and it remains to be seen whether more detail is synonymous with better quality or merely with larger overhead. Interestingly, these differences have a profound influence on the deployment of each method and these differences permeate the whole lifecycle and the deliverables. The comparisons we make between the methodologies must be qualified with three premises. First, many of the

TABLE 8.4 Dependence of Domain Analysis Methods on Technology and Programming Languages

	FODA	SYNTHESIS	JODA	Reuse Business
Technology dependence	Yes	No	Yes	Yes
Language dependence	No	No	No	No

features we observe on the deployment of the four distinct methodologies on a common application domain stem, not from the methodologies, but from the domain. Second, some of the variances we observe between the methodologies stem, not from the different methodologies, but from the different skill levels and interest levels of the student teams. Third, some of the features that we observe are dictated solely by the methodology, and do not depend on the example on which the methodology is applied.

8.6.10 Exercises

1. (A) Given the various domain analysis methods summarized in this section, identify a set of activities that you perceive in a domain analysis process.

2. (B) Construct a table comparing the support of the analysis methods summarized in this section to the activities that you identified in the first exercise.

3. (A) Characterize, using two keywords, each domain analysis method described in this section. Select the keywords based on the most salient features of the approach, for example, process-based, product-based, reverse engineering approach, or architecture-based.

8.7 DOMAIN ANALYSIS TOOLS

To improve the practice of a domain analysis method, the analysis steps should be automated when possible. We consider here two examples of what a tool support for a domain analysis process could possibly do.

8.7.1 KAPTUR, a Knowledge-Based Tool

The knowledge acquisition for preservation of tradeoffs and underlying rationales (KAPTUR) is a knowledge-based tool that supports several domain analysis activities. KAPTUR supports domain analysis by extracting the knowledge from applications developed in that domain. First, a set of basic structures and functions are provided to the application developer based on the knowledge of previously developed systems in the domain. Whenever a new function, subsystem, or modification is encountered in the new application, this information is fed to the KAPTUR tool. The tool uses this information to automatically build knowledge-based relationships between different systems sharing some common properties and functions.

The KAPTUR tool supports entity relationship and data flow diagrams as models to capture domain information. It also stores information about design choices and rationales behind the selection of specific architectures. KAPTUR is briefly discussed by Sodhi and Sodhi [1999] and is the product of Computer Technology Associates [CTA 1990].

8.7.2 GENESIS, a Builder for Database Management Systems

The GENESIS system is a domain analysis approach that is heavily supported by tools. The system is concerned with developing database management system (DBMS) applications. The GENESIS system realizes the benefits of developing reusable components and collecting prewritten components to manage the creation of new DBMS applications. GENESIS can generate new centralized relational DBMS applications with considerable configuration flexibility. The GENESIS method defines a generic architecture as the main product of the database domain analysis phase. This generic architecture is used to construct DBMS systems. The user of the GENESIS tool can plug in modules with well-specified interfaces into the generic architecture.

The GENESIS system was developed by Don Batory [Batory et al. 1988]. The system emphasizes a domain analysis process with tool support. The process is architecture-centric in which building blocks are used to construct the application structure. The tool facilitates the analysis process. The effort on the GENESIS system and tool support is also extended to support object-oriented and distributed databases.

8.7.3 Exercises

1. (B) Define a set of features that you perceive as essential in a tool that supports domain analysis. In enumerating the features, consider what a domain analyst would expect from a domain analysis tool. Give the rationale behind each feature you select.

8.8 FURTHER READING

For more information about domain analysis approaches and their influence on software reuse practice, consult the domain analysis and design process book by Sodhi and Sodhi [1999]. The FODA analysis method is discussed further elsewhere [FODA 1999], the JODA method is discussed in further detail by Holibaugh [1992], and the organization domain modeling (ODM) method is discussed by Simos [1995] and in another report [ODM 1993]. A comprehensive discussion of the SYNTHESIS approach is also available [SPC 1993]. Jacobson et al. [1997] discuss the reuse business approach with examples. We refer to a more recent paper [Mili and Yocoub 2000] for a classroom experiment to compare that application of FODA, JODA, SYNTHESIS, and reuse business to the waiting queues example in Appendix B.

Chapter 9

Programming Paradigms and Reusability

The more one thinks and talks about software reuse, the more one realizes that software development shouldn't be done any other way but with reuse in mind. Building for reuse should and often is the default development paradigm, although without the proper guidelines and the proper discipline, factors such as time and budgetary constraints, and sheer intellectual laziness or lack of know how, result in poorly reusable software. In this chapter we look into the different software development paradigms, and examine the extent to which they support reuse. The three paradigms we will be looking at are *logic*, *procedural*, or *functional* programming, and *object-oriented programming*. We start by defining those characteristics that a programming paradigm must support to facilitate the reuse of artifacts developed using the paradigm. Later, we examine, in turn, the three paradigms, and then conclude with general observations on ways to combine the three paradigms in actual system development.

9.1 USABILITY ATTRIBUTES

We have seen in the previous chapter that *reusability* is a combination of usefulness and usability, where *usefulness* refers to the extent to which an artifact is needed, and *usability* refers to the extent to which the artifact is packaged in a way that facilitates its use. The usability of artifacts depends on two factors: (1) the constructs of the language or notation used to represent the artifacts and (2) the judicious use of those constructs to package reusable artifacts. In this section, we are interested in the constructs of the representation language, regardless of the way in which they are used, or, perhaps more accurately, we assume that those constructs are used to their full potential.

160

9.1.1 Reusability–Abstraction Boundaries

The first premise of this endeavor is that the nature of the problems that software developers have to solve lends itself to reusability. In other words, few systems need to be built from first principles, and there is a lot of commonality that can be taken advantage of. The second premise is that there are some *intrinsic* boundaries within those systems that encapsulate common or reusable chunks of knowledge, data, or functionality. Underlying this hypothesis is the intuition that there exists a set of boundaries that are optimal in the sense that *for the given granularity*, there is no other boundary that better isolates the constant parts of the system from the variable parts. The key concept here is the granularity, because if we go at a lower level of granularity, we might be able to get more fine-grained reusability. However, the cost of assembling components of such granularity may be neither interesting, nor efficient. At the extreme, a programming language is utterly reusable but the level of reuse afforded by high-level programming languages (syntactic constructs and low-level built-in operations) is not interesting. We are hard pressed to further formalize what those intrinsic boundaries might be, but the important thing is that we have a reference model against which we can compare the various paradigms. We might call these a system's "fault lines," and we assume that these fault lines are optimal in the sense that a modeling and/or programming paradigm benefits from supporting packaging techniques that can *at least* match those natural boundaries, but could also go to lower levels of granularity. Further, we assume that the assembly of components of that granularity does not force us to resort to using components or constructs of lower granularity.

The intuition behind natural boundaries comes from physics, and more specifically, solid-state physics. In solid-state physics, we deal with the behavior of continuous, malleable, and elastic bodies. However, traditional physics theory provides us with a number of *mathematical abstractions* that allow us to treat two solid objects as *point masses*. Consider the bodies shown in Figure 9.1. If we wanted to compute the attraction between the two objects, we would have to add the sum of attractions between each pair of chunks of volume, one from each object. The magnitude of the elementary force would be $\delta f = -(\delta v_1 \times \rho_1) \cdot (\delta v_2 \times \rho_2)/r^2$, and it has the same direction as the line joining the two chunks; we assume that ρ_1 and ρ_2 are the densities of bodies 1 and 2, respectively, at those positions. To compute the attraction force between the two bodies, we need to sum over the volumes of B_1 and B_2:

$$F = -\iint_{B_1 B_2} \frac{\rho_1 \times \rho_2}{r^2} \delta v_1 \delta v_2 = -\frac{\rho_1 V_1 \times \rho_2 V_2}{R^2}$$

where V_1 and V_2 are the volumes of bodies 1 and 2, respectively, and where R is the distance between their centers of gravity; we assume that the two bodies have constant density (are homogeneous). The force here has the direction of the line joining the two centers of gravity.

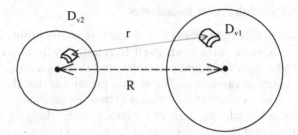

FIGURE 9.1 The point mass abstraction in physics.

In other words, for the purposes of gravitational forces, solid bodies can be treated as *points*, located at their (geometric in this case) center of gravity, whose mass equals the total mass of the body. For the purposes of gravitational forces, there are no other interactions between the two bodies that are not accounted for by the point mass abstraction.

Different utilisations require different abstractions. It may be that for centrifugal forces within a rotating object, an abstraction consisting of a planar disk, perpendicular to the rotation axis, with the cumulative mass, may be appropriate. Generally speaking, the physics domain supports a number of abstractions based on

- Formal and *exact* abstraction operators that are built-into the underlying mathematical theory; in this case, various integral/summation operators for intensive variables (e.g., density) or "linear" (e.g., "proportional to volume") extensive variables
- Reasonable approximations in which "gross" object abstractions account for *most* of the interactions within a system, and between systems, and in which we ignore low-level and low-intensity interactions [Simon and Ando 1961]

The questions that we ask are

- What are the abstraction boundaries in the systems that we typically model and implement?
- How well do the various programming paradigms accommodate those abstraction boundaries?

By analogy from physics, the abstraction boundaries depend on the kind of process that we try to model. We try to answer this question by being a little bit more precise about the *modeling* problem.

Modeling consists of mapping constructs of the modeled world to constructs of the modeling world. Modeling is a projection in the sense that the constructs. of the modeling world have fewer dimensions than the constructs of the

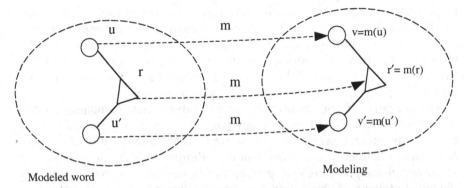

FIGURE 9.2 A good modeling formalism needs to be a homomorphism.

modeled world. We can have several projections, each focusing on some properties of the modeled world, and ignoring the others. An important property
of modeling formalisms or representations, is what we call *homomorphism*.
Let U be the modeled universe and V its model. For all u belonging to U, we
call $v = m(v)$ the *model* of u. Let R be a binary relation on U, that is, elements
of R are pairs $\langle u, u' \rangle$ where u and u' are elements of U. The homomorphism
property says that there exists a binary relation R' on V such that

$$\forall \langle u, u' \rangle \in R \rightarrow \langle m(u), m(u') \rangle \in R'$$

Figure 9.2 illustrates this point. The homomorphism property is important only
for those relations in the modeled world that we want to represent.

The homomorphism property for relationships should be understood in
very general terms. The relationship r could be a static relationship between
two entities of the same system, a function where u is the input and u' is the
output, or a transition between two states of the same system.

With the goal of comparing the three programming paradigms with regard
to reusability, we need a paradigm-neutral metamodel of *modeled worlds*. This
is not an easy intellectual exercise as even the most abstract mathematical representations carry with them a paradigmatic bias. For example, algebraic specifications of systems are biased toward the encapsulation of data and functions,
and hence, object orientation, whereas set-theoretic or logic-based representations are biased toward functional (procedural) and logic programming,
respectively.

9.1.2 Abstraction and Composability

Composability is an important property of reusable components, and is closely
related to abstraction boundaries. The intuition behind composability is that,
if in the real world, the behavior of a system is obtained by arranging two subsystems in a particular way, possibly constraining their interactions, it should

be possible to find a corresponding arrangement between their models, that would result in a model of the real world aggregate. Referring back to Figure 9.2, the relation *r* in this case is that of aggregation. What is important in the model composition is the notion of *conservative extension* [Lubars et al. 1992] whereby the composition of the two models should be done without opening up the two models, and by adding as little glue as possible.

This is a rather strong condition because the abstraction boundaries around the two subsystems and submodels inevitably filter out details that may be relevant to the interactions between the subsystems. Put another way, *abstraction boundaries are useful to the extent that they abstract all of the detail irrelevant to the useful compositions, and only those*. This can be expressed in terms of the commutativity of abstraction and composition, as shown in Figure 9.3. In this example, we used geometric composition and the smoothing operation of the graphics package of the text processor used for this very chapter. By composing and then smoothing, we get a different (and better, smoother) result from the path "smooth, then compose." A closely related example from the computer world is the roundoff in arithmetic calculations.

Symbolically, composability may be expressed with the following mathematical identity. Let S_1 and S_2 be two systems, and m the modeling operator, we define composition in terms of two operators $\otimes$ and $\oplus$ such that $m(S_1) \otimes m(S_2) = m(S_1 \oplus S_2)$, where $m(S)$ is the model of system S. In this equation, it is understood that S_1 and S_2 will interact in many ways, and it is understood that $m(S)$ will embody a limited perspective of S. The composition operator on models is useful to the extent that it composes the models in such a way

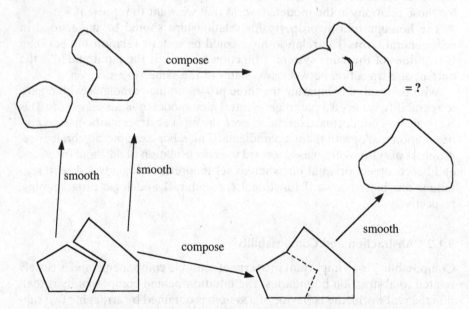

FIGURE 9.3   Abstraction (smoothing) can be bad for some compositions!

that the composition corresponds to the model of the actual real-world composition between the two systems. This means that the composition and the modeling are independent of each other. Without going into the details of this relationship, let us just say that this depends on the nature of the modeling or representation. For example, if the modeled world and the modeling world are both multidimensional vector spaces, and if the composition operator is vector addition, then models are composable by virtue of the distributivity of multiplication with respect to addition: $M \otimes (v_1 \oplus v_2) = (M \otimes v_1) \oplus (M \otimes v_2)$. Other combinations of modeling and composition operators may be analyzed along the same lines.

The "composability through modeling" problem manifests itself again when we deal with abstraction: within the *modeling* world itself, abstraction or aggregation boundaries need to be such that the interactions between the components of two systems may be expressed in terms of the aggregates. Figure 9.4 illustrates this point. On the lefthand side, we show two groups of "objects" that are good candidates for *abstraction*, namely, for packaging as single units. We also have a relationship that ties elements of the first group to elements of the second group. If we put an abstraction boundary around the two groups of objects, we need to be able to express the relationship between those subcomponents, through the two groups' abstraction boundaries (righthand side). In this case, a relationship (R) between components is now represented by three relationships:

- Two *internal relationships IR* and *IR'* that are part of the *definitions* of the two aggregates, and that relate the attributes of the components to those of the aggregates (see, e.g., Mili et al. [1990]),
- An external relationship R' between the two aggregates.

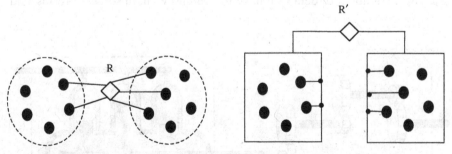

The interactions between low level components are represented in terms of those components.

Those same interactions are abstracted through the abstraction boundaries of the two aggregates.

FIGURE 9.4 Abstraction boundaries force us to represent low-level interactions between components in terms of (1) relations between components and aggregates, and (2) relations between aggregates.

Symbolically, let X be the aggregate with components $x_1, x_2, \ldots, x_m$ and Y the aggregate with components $y_1, y_2, \ldots, y_n$; the equivalence mentioned earlier may be stated as follows:

$$R(x_1, \ldots, x_i, y_1, \ldots, y_j) \equiv IR(x_1, \ldots, x_i, X) \cdot R'(X, Y) \cdot IR'^{-1}(y_1, \ldots, y_j, Y)$$

If the same abstraction operator had been used for both aggregates, then IR and IR' would be the same relationship.

From a methodological point of view, starting with a relation R (or a set of such of relations), we look for abstraction operators (relations IR) and the corresponding relationships between aggregate (relation R') such that the previous equation is satisfied. We say that IR is an *R-valid abstraction* of the system [Mili 1989].

R-valid abstractions can be found trivially: by exposing the components in the interface of the aggregate. For example, assume that we have a model for a car's motor system in terms of the individual components such as cylinders (combustion chambers), pistons, camshaft, and crankcase, as well as the gearbox, the stick shift, the clutch, and the powertrain, with connections between various components. We can divide all of these components into two subsystems, the *engine*, and the *transmission*, and then a single relationship between two components, one belonging to the engine and the other belonging to the transmission, will be sufficient to represent all the interactions between the engine and transmission. If we were to encase the engine and the transmission, one component will have to stick out of that case to assure the connection between the two (see Fig. 9.5).

The real test for abstractions ("encasings") comes when we have to preserve several interactions through the aggregate's interface (encasing); if we are forced to export (make visible) most of the inner components, then our abstraction is not very useful as it doesn't reduce the complexity of the aggregate, or the amount of detail we have to contend with. In software terms, bad

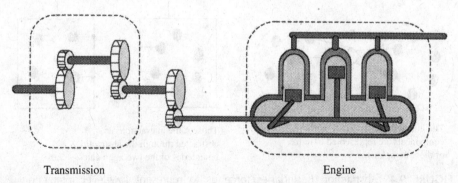

Transmission   Engine

FIGURE 9.5 Good abstractions enable us to represent the important interactions with a few (or none) component exports through the interface of the aggregate.

abstractions may manifest themselves in many ways. Assume that we have a class **Car** with component classes **Engine**, and **Transmission** (see Fig. 9.6 for a Java example).

In this example, we are exporting nearly all the attributes of **Engine** and **Transmission** through the interface of **Car**, thereby achieving no noticeable reduction in complexity or detail. A less obvious but equally symptomatic approach is one where access methods return the individual components, and where most useful behavior of the class **Car** starts by first getting a handle on a component, and then working directly on the component.

In the next section, we study the various representation paradigms, to later assess them in light of the factors discussed in this section.

9.2 REPRESENTATION AND MODELING PARADIGMS

9.2.1 Declarative versus Procedural Representations

The issue of how best to represent knowledge had been a recurring theme in knowledge representation. It is fair to say that knowledge representation research has been concerned with two distinct, but not unrelated goals. The first goal was to gain understanding into the structure of human cognition, both in terms of memory structures, and in terms of cognitive processing. Foremost of the preoccupations of this research are cognitive plausibility and experimental validation. Cognitive plausibility is concerned with a concordance of the representation models with what we already know about cognition and semantic memory. For example, while first-order logic is a good formal representation for deductive reasoning, it is not a plausible one from a cognitive perspective, simply because human inference processes are fairly "qualitative," but also robust in the case of uncertainty or lack of information; they are not as cut and dry as logic [Rumelhart and Norman 1983]. A second aspect of cognitive plausibility is *experimental* empirical validation. Typically, cognitive scientists would design a processing model of human cognitive processes, which can explain paradoxes, responses times, and the like. They design and conduct experiments to validate the model, accounting for old paradoxes and creating new ones, and so goes the research. All of this is done without taking into account the actual implementation hardware (neurons, synapses, electric jolts, etc.[1]). The second goal of knowledge representation research is the construction of heuristic computer programs that can solve difficult and ill-defined problems by manipulating a partial representation of the knowledge that is germane to the problem at hand. Researchers in this area are not concerned with cognitive plausibility, although knowledge of cognitive

---

[1] Although some epistemologists have relied on the actual hardware and on physical theory to prove, or disprove, the possibility of *true* artificial intelligence by using computability arguments [Penrose 1989].

```
public class Engine{
    private int volume;
    private int power;
    public int
        getVolume()~...}
    public void
        setVolume(int I){...}
    public int
        getPower(){...}
    public void
        setPower(int I){...}
    ...
}
```

```
public class Transmission{
    private int firstRatio;
    private int secondRatio;
    public int
        getFirstRatio(){...}
    public void
        setFirstRation(int I){...}
    public int
        getSecondRatio(){...}
    public void
        setSecondRatio(int I){...}
}
```

```
public class Car {
    private Engine engine;
    private Transmission trans;
    public int getVolume() {
        return engine.
            getVolume();}
    public void
        setVolume(int I){
        engine.setVolume(i);}
    ...
    public int getFirstRatio(){
        return
            trans.getFirstRatio();}
    public void
        setFirstRatio(int i){
        trans.setFirstRatio(i);}
    ...
}
```

FIGURE 9.6 A poorly designed "abstraction": the aggregate (needs to) exposes all the details of its components to offer the desired functionality.

processes often helps inspire problem-solving strategies *in the very early stages* of the research, or to spice up one's account of one's research with the in-laws or at mundane cocktail parties.

An age-old—and somewhat artificial—debate in knowledge representation is whether knowledge is best represented *declaratively*, or *procedurally*. In declarative representations, knowledge is represented in terms of statements and propositions, supported by a general-purpose inference engine that performs the required cognitive tasks at hand. In *procedural* representations, the cognitive tasks in question are embodied in procedures whose *sole* purpose is to perform a given cognitive task. These procedures may be seen as "black-box" in the sense that the internal representation of the data or knowledge that they manipulate is of no interest to the observer, and no system-level properties depend on the organization of data that is internal to a given procedure. Typically, *declarative* methods have been used to support inferences consisting of verifying properties of objects or to verify some statement about the world being modeled. Figure 9.7 shows two alternative declarative representations of a knowledge base that answers questions about categories (classes) and individuals. In the semantic network representation, the inference procedure consists of an algorithm that traverses labeled links in the network and collects the relevant information. In the logical representation, a theorem prover establishes new facts by plugging values into variables and using logical inference rules. In both cases, a single inference procedure is used no matter what is to be verified.

When we talk about procedural representations, we are really talking about two things. First, we have the representation of procedures or *skills*. Procedures may be represented by entities that describe what they do, how to invoke them, the inputs they require, and so on. Second, we have the *representation of knowledge in the form of procedures*, regardless of the nature of the knowledge being represented, whether it is procedural (a *skill*) or propositional (statements about the world). An example of the latter is to write special-purpose procedures that can answer a specific set of questions about the world

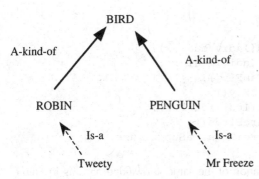

For all x, ROBIN(x) -> BIRD(x)
For all x, PENGUIN(x) -> BIRD(x)
For all x, BIRD(x) -> CAN-FLY(x)
ROBIN(tweety)
PENGUIN(Mr Freeze)

FIGURE 9.7   Two alternative declarative representations of the same knowledge base.

being modeled. To take the previous example, we can have a procedure to check whether an individual is a bird, another to check whether an individual can fly, and so forth. Figure 9.8 shows what such a representation might look like.

Which is better? An advantage of the latter representation is that we can optimize the performance of some operations, instead of using a general-purpose engine that enacts the same generic algorithm to answer all sorts of questions, no matter how obvious or complex.

The declarative versus procedural debate was raging in the mid 1970s, at a time when knowledge representation researchers started coming up with hybrid representation languages such as *frames* [Minsky 1975], *plans* [Abelson 1975], *scripts* [Schank 1975], and *actors* [Hewitt 1975]. Simula was about one generation old, and the first version of Smalltalk (Smalltalk72) was nearing the end of its lifecycle [Goldberg and Robson 1989].

Terry Winograd summed up the advantages of the two representations as follows [Winograd 1975]:

Declarative Representations

- *Flexibility and Economy.* The major argument against procedural representations is that they have to specify, for each bit of knowledge, how it is to be used, *for all the potential uses*. In the previous example, the property can fly for birds can help answer a bunch of questions; we provide a procedure for each question. With declarative representation, the facts are specified once, and a general-purpose inference procedure helps answer all sorts of questions,

- *Understandability and Learnability.* Specifying knowledge in a declarative fashion yields a more understandable representation, and one that is easier to acquire/learn from outside sources. This is not the case with procedural representations.

- *Accessibility and Communicability.* Winograd stated that much of what we know can be stated as a set of explicit facts and rules, with important implications on resoning system *construction* and *maintenance* (incrementality and traceability?).

```
boolean isABird(Individual x);
boolean canFly(Individual x);
boolean robinsCanFly();
boolean birdsCanFly();
boolean isRobin(Individual x);
boolean robinsAreBirds();
boolean robinsAre(Class aSuperClass);
. . .
```

FIGURE 9.8 A procedural representation of the same knowledge base as in Figure 9.7.

Procedural Representations

- *Procedural Modeling.* There are obviously some problems for which procedural representations are more appropriate. One such problem is robot control. It is easier to solve a problem by specifying an operation as a series of steps with built-in constraints (e.g., to not knock off other objects on its way) that *constructs* the solution, rather than solving it by (1) specifying the result in terms of a desired end state, and the constraints that a solution must satisfy, and (2) applying a general search procedure that will search for a general solution. One well-known problem with declarative representation of evolving/dynamic systems is the *frame problem*, whereby we have to *explicitly* specify the things that remain true while objects within the system change state.[2] We have to do this with declarative systems for two reasons. First, because of inevitable knowledge gaps,[3] we don't state everything that is known to be true or false; we state what we think will be relevant to our problem. Second, because of the knowledge gaps, we don't infer all of the dependencies between the facts and rules that are stated, and thus we have to explicitly state those dependencies. With procedural representations, we just specify what is changing, and it is implicitly understood that what is not affected by the procedure will not change.

- *Second-Order Knowledge.* An important aspect of knowledge is "knowing about it" and knowing when to enact it. It is theoretically possible to represent second-order or *metalevel* knowledge with declarative methods, but much easier to do in procedural representations where the same procedure first decides what to do, and then dispatches the work to be done accordingly.[4]

- *The Need for Heuristic Knowledge.* We rarely solve problems from first principles, and often have heuristics that avoid "blind search" in the solution space as declarative approaches would typically do. Procedural approaches typically construct solutions that are known to satisfy the desired properties, which is a lot more efficient and easy to control than logical inferences.

---

[2] Truth maintenance systems address this problem by *precompiling* the relevant dependencies in a network.

[3] Interestingly, such knowledge gaps are what causes expert systems to be brittle (see, e.g., Lenat et al. [1991]).

[4] This is still possible to do in first order logic where context variables are used to control inferences. For example, in response to a planning problem where the initial state is at(here,x), the final state is at(airport,x), we can enact different methods to reduce the distance between x and the airport, depending on the order of magnitude of the distance between here and the airport (less than 2 kms, between 3 and 10, etc.). We do this by posting or stating context variables as in

```
CurrentGoal(at(here,x),at(airport,x), distance(here,airport)> 3)
   → appropriateMethod(cab)
CurrentGoal(at(here,x),at(airport,x), distance(here,airport)> 3)
   AND appropriateMethod(cab) → CurrentGoal(catchcab(here,airport)
```

Rumelhart and Norman consider the procedural versus declarative representations as two points on a continuous spectrum of approaches [Rumelhart and Norman 1983]. They view representations as made up of a representation language and an interpretation procedure, with knowledge distributed in different proportions between the two, as illustrated in Figure 9.9. We would argue that choosing a representation method along this spectrum is as much a matter of organization as it is a matter of description of knowledge. For example, the procedures within a procedural system may themselves be implemented by a generic inference procedure applied to a small declarative knowledge base. To some extent, the different representations are styles of organization at a given level of abstraction. A representation system consists of a vocabulary, and an organization principle. Those same atoms, which embody a piece of knowledge, may themselves be organized according to the same or a different organizational principle. For example, consider the following rule within a knowledge base:

```
if alarmIsRaisedOn(A,X) ∧ OperatingAt(X,Y) ∧
   Capacity(X,Z) ∧ (Y > 0.8* Z)                        →
MajorAlarm(A)
```

We do have to evaluate the predicate `OperatingAt(X,Y)` for system X and value Y, and that is probably evaluated procedurally. Similarly, in the procedure

```
void BoilerController::handleEvent(Alarm a) {
  if (shouldRaiseMajorAlarm(a))                         {
    . . .
  }
  else {
    ...}
}
```

we don't know how the logical expression `shouldRaiseMajorAlarm` (. . .) is evaluated, and it may well be some piece of a logic-based system.

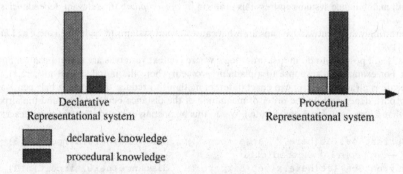

Declarative
Representational system

Procedural
Representational system

declarative knowledge
procedural knowledge

FIGURE 9.9 Declarative versus procedural representations.

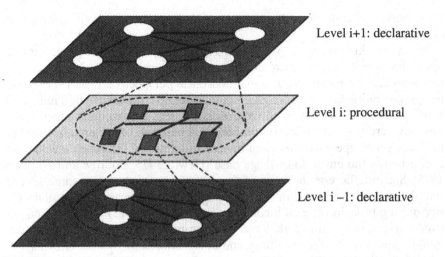

Level i+1: declarative

Level i: procedural

Level i −1: declarative

FIGURE 9.10 Using different representation paradigms at different levels of abstraction or granularity.

Figure 9.10 illustrates this interleaving of modeling paradigms at different levels of abstraction. In Chapter 11, we will see examples where the rule-based and object-oriented paradigms can coexist in peace.

Now that we have established the fact that the declarative versus procedural attributes are two values on a continuous spectrum, and that we can actually mix and match the two paradigms within the same system, we can go back and try to address the questions raised earlier without the need to commit to a particular style for an entire system. Before we do that, we introduce object-oriented programming as an evolutionary descendant of both declarative and procedural representations.

9.2.2   Object-Oriented Modeling

Object-oriented programming, as we know it today, is the confluence of several developments in knowledge representation, in simulation, and in software engineering. From the software engineering end, it represents the embodiment of algebras, or, more familiarly, the notion of abstract data types. At some level, algebras may be seen as tuples $(S, op_1, \ldots, op_n)$, where $op_1, \ldots, op_n$ are closed operations on the set S; elements of S could themselves be tuples. The language-level packaging of the definition of the datatype (the set S) and of the operations that manipulate elements of S is akin to *classes* (*modules*, or *packages*) (see Chapter 10). Languages such as Modula-2 and Ada 83 are part of that tradition. From the simulation field, the language Simula [Dahl and Nygaard 1970], often considered the common ancestor of object-oriented languages, represented simulated objects using classes, that is, grouping of state variables and operations that manipulate those state variables; interactions between simulated objects are represented by messages exchanged between them.

From the knowledge representation end, object-oriented programming appeared as both a theoretical imperative and an implementation packaging and optimization technique. From a theoretical perspective, two observations led to the emergence of object representations. First, the distributed nature of some of the lower-level cognitive processing (e.g., recognition) suggested a model whereby tasks are accomplished by a network of communicating but not very smart agents, rather than by an "all-knowing" inference mechanism that accesses the entire knowledge base [Hewitt 1975, Bobrow and Norman 1975]. Second, there is the issue of *frames* or *scripts*, which are some sort of template knowledge structures that account for two observed phenomena: (1) performing tasks in cases of incomplete knowledge and (2) speed of recognition. For example, assume that you are touring a college building. The tour guide takes you through a hallway, and opens doors one by one, showing you what is inside. If you are in the computer laboratories wing, you expect the rooms to be full of computer equipment and computer documentation. If you walk into faculty or graduate student offices, you expect to see a big messy desk, a desktop computer, and bookshelves overflowing with magazines and books. The idea of recognition through frames is that we start "instantiating" a frame corresponding to what our expectations are of what lies behind that door. We can fairly quickly determine if the room into which we walked is a lab, or an office: the two candidate frames will "activate" their "frame component checkers," which should evaluate quickly if the present room is a lab or an office, by focusing on specific aspects or components of the room. Identifying those components will proceed recursively in the same fashion that we instantiated the frame for the room: a computer frame will look for a keyboard, a monitor, and possibly a CPU unit nearby. However, if the office occupant has just moved in, the computer will be packaged, and it will be a matter of recognizing a computer package (typical size, computer brand name written somewhere on the package, drawing, etc.). To distinguish between an office and a computer lab, usually the size of the room and the number of computers give us a clue. However, we can have labs with single computers in them, in which case we should focus on smaller level details such as personal belonging suggesting that the room is a private space (e.g., family pictures, personal correspondence) not shared by many people. And so on and so forth.

This recognition pattern, combining a top-down approach (hypothesizing a general frame, and validating it by checking the expected components) with a bottom-up approach (recognizing a low-level object, which suggests a possible set of enclosing frames) seems to pervade most recognition tasks, including program understanding (see, e.g., Maiden and Sutcliffe [1992]). Further, it points to two fundamental characteristics of knowledge: (1) chunking and (2) activeness, whose combination is found neither in declarative representations nor in procedural representations. "Chunking" refers to the extent to which related pieces of knowledge are packaged into a unit together. Figure 9.11

```
category Robin is
                boolean robinsCanFly();
                boolean isRobin(Individual x);
                boolean robinsAreBirds();
endcategory
```

FIGURE 9.11   Packaging knowledge about a category into a single unit.

shows a packaging of all knowledge about robins into a category of individuals called `Robin`.

"Activeness" refers to the fact that individual pieces of knowledge *react* to external stimuli to solve problems, instead of offering themselves up as knowledge stores to a central inference engine. This marks a difference in control paradigms and intelligence distribution: with declarative methods, a single inference engine embodies the *general, task-independent* intelligence of the system, with an essentially hierarchical control. With procedural methods, intelligence is distributed among a set of procedures customized to handle a *single* (or *fixed set* of) *task-dependent* processes; in that sense, intelligence is "hardcoded" and can hardly be called intelligence. Further, control is hierarchical. With object-oriented systems, we have distribution of *knowledge*, *control*, and *intelligence*.

In terms of control, the object-oriented model is more complex than either the declarative model, or the procedural model. Control is not deterministic in the sense that procedural systems are, and in principle it is difficult to design new behaviors by combining existing ones [Aksit and Bergmann 1992]. In practice, three things make behavioral design easier: (1) we can compromise on some tenets of the paradigm to get things done (e.g., using *synchronous* remote procedure calls rather than message passing); (2) while, in principle object systems are *synthesized* from low-level components, *analysis* remains the main way of producing objects; and (3) we can add constructs to the object paradigm to help make global behaviors easier to specify from individual components behavior (e.g., constraints and constraint programming); see Chapter 12.

9.3   ABSTRACTION AND COMPOSITION IN DEVELOPMENT PARADIGMS

We defined reusability attributes of the different modeling paradigms in terms of two properties, *abstraction boundaries*, and *composability*. Notwithstanding differences in modeling prowess between individual developers, we are interested in *paradigmatic* differences in terms of intent and in terms of linguistic constructs. In this section, we study the abstraction boundaries and the composability characteristics of the three programming paradigms, declarative, functional, and object-oriented.

9.3.1   Declarative Representations: The Case of Logic Programming

We distinguish between two kinds of operations: *composition*, and *abstraction*. Composition consists of combining two programs or knowledge bases in order to obtain the combined behavior of the two. *Abstraction* consists of deriving a more synthetic representation of a program or knowledge base, possibly for a specific purpose, generally reducing complexity and level of detail, often at the expense of flexibility of usage. In logic-based declarative representations, *composition* is done simply by putting together two (or more) knowledge bases, KB_1 and KB_2: *an inference engine will be able to infer everything that results from knowing* KB_1 *and* KB_2 (including contradictions between the two), *with no additional work required.* This is perhaps logic programming strongest point: effortless composition.[5] This is true of all declarative representations where a general-purpose inference engine operates upon a passive knowledge base. Of course, for the composition to be profitable, the two knowledge (rule) bases that we are putting together should have the same granularity and the same vocabulary. If one rule base talks about `sibling(x,y)`, and another about `brother(x,y)` and `sister(x,y)`, we would need to add rules that connect the two. For example, using a PROLOG style:

```
sibling(x,y):- brother(x,y)
sibling(x,y):- sister(x,y)
```

The issue of structure and nomenclature is a common problem in composing knowledge based systems, and software systems in general [Garlan et al. 1995]. It was one of the motivations for the CYC project:[6] providing a common base to which the various expert systems can relate, in order that their expertise may be combined. It was also the motivation behind UML, the *Unified Medical Language*, sponsored by the (U.S.) National Library of Medicine, which consisted of a modeling language for representing medical concepts (a *meta language*). We will come back to the issue of bridging structural differences later in Chapters 11 and 12.

In terms of abstraction, we may think of logic-based declarative representations as having two abstraction procedures. The first procedure groups

---

[5] The closest thing to effortless composition in procedural or object representations is the blackboard model whereby *actors* or *agents* post events on a shared "blackboard" for other agents to grab and react to. Less esoterically, event-based systems where components register for events come close to achieving the same level of composability.

[6] The CYC project [Lenat and Guha 1990] aimed at developing a common sense knowledge base with the "reasoning capabilities of a 5-year-old" but that can learn from reading (i.e., can "go to school"). The CYC knowledge base "knows" that a person is at least 14–15 years younger than its parents, that people who live at place X and work at place Y normally find a way of getting from X to Y. It has no expert knowledge but expert systems that are built on top of its ontology can interoperate and share expertise [Lenat et al. 1990]. See the website of Cycorp (http://www.cycorp.com).

together the rules that have the same consequent. Consider the following rule base, written in a PROLOG style this time:

```
cousin(x,y):- parent(x,z),parent(y,t),sibling(z,t)
cousin(x,y):- parent(x,z),parent(y,t),cousin(z,t)
cousin(x,y):- parent(x,z),cousin(z,y)
cousin(x,y):- cousin(y,x)
```

The lefthand side contains the "goals" or the "consequences"; and the right-hand side contains the antecedents. In PROLOG, clauses that have the same consequent are collectively referred to as a procedure (the "cousin" procedure). Logically, we have $[(A \to B) \wedge (C \to B)] \Rightarrow [(A \vee C) \to B]$. This abstraction mechanism enables us to represent complex relationship definitions concisely and results in no loss of information. The second abstraction procedure consists of what might be called *closure*, and it consists of stringing along implications. Logically, $[(A \to B) \wedge (B \to C)] \Rightarrow [A \to C]$. If we use the two abstraction rules, we might be able to compile an entire proof procedure into a single implication. For example, we can compile three implications into one, as in $[A \to B, C \to D, B \wedge D \to E] \Rightarrow [(A \wedge C) \to E]$. If the goal was to prove E, then once the proof has been made, we no longer need to go through the various steps, and the implication $[(A \wedge C) \to E]$ becomes part of the rule base.

The issue now is whether we should encapsulate the original implications under the compiled implication or rule, that is, whether we should mask or hide the rules that were used to prove the rule $[(A \wedge C) \to E]$. In other words, should *composition* necessarily be accompanied with *abstraction* (i.e., hiding the components). Viewed in these terms, the first composition procedure (proceduralization) does not result into a loss of information, but doesn't abstract (hide) much detail, either. The second composition procedure (closure) does abstract lots of the details, and does result into a loss of information: by just keeping $[(A \wedge C) \to E]$, we no longer know that $A \to B$, or that $B \wedge D \to E$. This may not be relevant if E was the goal we are interested in, and A and C are the only hypotheses that we can directly verify. However, it may be important if our rule base contained the following additional rules $F \to G, B \wedge G \to I$, because keeping $A \to B$ means the difference between being able to prove $[A \wedge F \to I]$ or not. Figure 9.12 illustrates this point.

The knowledge "item" $A \to B$, when exposed, may contribute to various proofs. When encapsulated within a particular proof procedure, we could potentially preclude its use within other proofs. It is interesting to note that the language PROLOG does not have modularization concepts as part of its semantics: specific implementations do provide their own. In this context, a module is a physical packaging of a set of rules with *an interface* that consists of a subset of rules to be *exported*, that is, shared with other modules. Thus, the only way to make a given rule visible is to *explicitly* export *it*, or a set of

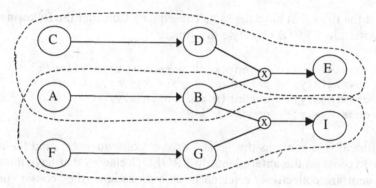

FIGURE 9.12   The rule base may yield two overlapping abstractions.

rules that allows us to infer *it*. The notion that something is only true "if you know about it" is foreign to mathematical logic and may be why some implementations of PROLOG prefer not to include modularization.

Modularization in PROLOG illustrates the tension between faithfulness to a well-understood mathematical formalism, on one hand, and addressing software engineering imperatives such as modularization, abstraction, reduction in complexity, and so forth, on the other hand. This tension notwithstanding, abstraction through composition illustrates *one way declarative knowledge can be made procedural*. The starting point was a set of rules, and some general-purpose inference procedure. When that general purpose procedure is used to answer a specific question (prove a statement), we get a trace which we then hardcode or hardwire into a single rule, saying in effect, "with this rule base, if you know $S_1, \ldots, S_n$, you will eventually be able to prove C, so let us say that $S_1 \wedge S_2 \ldots \wedge S_n \to C$ and use that directly." Now, we have a piece of knowledge that is efficient, that embodies some rich but nondecodable or shareable background knowledge, but that can answer a "single question."

If we recast the discussion in reuse terms—the initial purpose—we get to consider the point of view of the reusable component *developer* and the reusable component *user*. For the reusable component user, what is important is to have a set of high-level, noncomplex but powerful components with flexible and effortless composition; how the components are built is of little concern to the reuser, except perhaps the performance implications. To the developer of the reusable component, the availability of the building blocks (individual rules) used to build more complex components (individual rules) is the most important factor. In other words, the reusable component developer might want to deliver two reusable components abstracted as [$A \wedge C \to E$] and [$A \wedge F \to I$], but have all the ingredients available at all times. To the developer, abstraction is a delivery mechanism. The developer versus reuser relationship may be applied at different levels of abstraction of the reusable components; the reuser of components of level n is also the developer of components of level $n + 1$.

Finally, we note that the two abstraction procedures discussed above group rules on the basis of some consequent, that is, an n-ary, predicate. If the predicate is unary, it describes a category (set) of objects. If the predicate is n-ary, with $n > 1$, then the predicate describes a relationship. By compiling into a single rule all that is relevant to deriving a predicate, we are, to some extent, organizing the rule base around definitions (*intentions*) of *categories* (classes?) and *relationships* (associations?).

In summary

- Notwithstanding the differences in vocabulary and in knowledge structure, the composition of declarative knowledge bases is effortless; we don't need to do anything to make sure that the obtained behavior of the composed system is the behavior that results from composing the behavior of the two component systems.

- Abstraction procedures ("proceduralization" and "closure") turn general-purpose but inefficient declarative knowledge into efficient special-purpose knowledge, which is less flexible.

- Abstraction should hide the ingredients or components from the reuser to reduce detail and complexity. However, it should not hide the ingredients from the reusable component developer, who can use them to build other abstractions; both should coexist.

This last point applies to all the paradigms, and we will see how it translates for the case of procedural (next) representations and object-oriented ones (last).

9.3.2 Procedural (Functional) Programming

Whereas declarative programming achieves goals, given a set of known facts and rules, by applying a general inference procedure, procedural programming achieves each goal by providing a specific procedure for that goal. How the procedure operates from the inside is, in principle, of no interest to the outside. In particular, the procedure may be the result of applying a generic inference procedure to a special-purpose knowledge base! Notwithstanding the performance implications of such an *implementation*, the implementation itself is of no concern to the invoker of the procedure. By contrast to declarative representations—and logic-based representations in particular—where abstraction consisted of a bottom–up operation grouping the atomic knowledge units that participate in a given goal into a unit, the starting point for procedural representations is the goal or task to be achieved. Subsequent operations may break a task into several subtasks.

How can we break up a task into subtasks? The first objective of decomposition is reducing complexity. Assume that we have a procedure that we decompose into two subprocedures: A and B. In addition to providing an implementation of A and an implementation for B, we need to provide a glue to connect them. Generally speaking, it is expected that the complexity of either component, or of the piece needed to connect them, be smaller than that of the original procedure. However, overall, we may have increased the complexity, compared to the case where the system is to be developed in one piece. There is the implicit assumption that development effort is not a linear function of complexity. Thus, if we break a system into subsystems that, collectively, may have more components and more lines of code, we may still save on development time because each piece of functionality will take much less time to develop, stand alone, than as a piece of a bigger functionality. As a result, we may *overall* save on development time. Generally speaking, we may postulate the following minimal conditions for a decomposition to be effective:

- `Complexity(A + B)` ≥ `Complexity(A)`
- `Complexity(A + B)` ≥ `Complexity(B)`
- `Complexity(A + B)` ≥ `Complexity(Connection(A,B))`

We should add to these inequalities the one relating development efforts in both cases:

$$\text{DevEffort}(A + B) \geq \text{DevEffort}(A) + \text{DevEffort}(B) \\ + \text{DevEffort}(\text{Connection}(A,B))$$

To illustrate this point, let `size(A)` be the size of system or procedure A, and assume that the development effort for a given system S is given as follows:

$$\begin{aligned}\text{DevEffort}(S) &= \alpha \times \text{size}(S)^2, \text{ if S is atomic} \\ &\quad \text{(developed in one shot)} \\ &= \text{DevEffort}(\text{Connection}(S_1, \ldots, S_n)) \\ &\quad + \Sigma_i \; \text{DevEffort}(S_i)\end{aligned}$$

Then, if we assume that there is a linear overhead in decomposing, that is, if we assume that `size(Connection(S`$_1$`, . . . ,S`$_n$`))` $+ \Sigma_i$ `size(S`$_i$`)` $= (1 + \beta) \times$ `size(S)`, for some positive β, then it is easy to see how decomposition could save development time, despite its overall complexity (and size) overhead.

The second criterion for decomposition is reuse. We decompose a system into two (or more) subsystems in such a way that the subtasks may be useful for other purposes. With that prospect, we are able to relax all the above mentioned inequalities. In particular, `DevEffort(A+B)` need no longer be larger than the development of the components and of the glue. We have an entire section dedicated to software reuse metrics, and we won't go any further. Rather, what we are looking for here are criteria for decomposing such that the resulting components are reusable.

Let us first look at the abstraction mechanisms in procedural programming to gain insights into how to use those mechanisms to package reusable functionality. We distinguish between two abstraction mechanisms: one for data and one for process. *Data abstraction* is the process of parameterizing a task by the data on which the task is performed. The following example illustrates three levels of parameterization[7] of the same task:

```
boolean robinsAreBirds();
boolean robinsAre(Class aSuperClass);
boolean inheritsFrom(Class class1, Class class2);
```

This *abstraction* or *parameterization* recognizes the fact that the same goal can be achieved on different data by applying the *same* computation on the corresponding data structures. Note that declarative programming goes much further in this direction, and stipulates that the *same process* may be applied to *all kinds of data* to accomplish *any task*. Here, we are just saying for *a given task*, the *same computation* may be applied to all kinds of data. Of course, practically, "all kinds of data" is limited to *certain* kinds of data.

The second abstraction mechanism is what we might call *functional parameterization*, whereby we isolate a piece of computation that fulfills a specific role toward the accomplishment of the overall task, and package it as an interchangeable *function*. Figure 9.13 shows a functional parameterization of an ML function that merges two sorted lists of integers (Fig. 9.13a) into a function that can merge sorted lists of anything (Fig. 9.13b). In this case, the comparison operation was "abstracted" into a function comp.

Functional parameterization is an important ingredient of functional polymorphism in ML. Underlying functional parameterization is an important distinction between two aspects of functions:

- Functions fulfill certain roles within computations.
- Functions can have different implementations depending on the data they manipulate.

```
fun merge(L1,L2) =                      fun merge(L1,L2,comp) =
  if hd(L1) < hd(L2) then                 if comp(hd(L1),hd(L2)) then
    hd(L1)::merge(tail(L1),L2)              hd(L1)::merge(tail(L1),L2)
  else                                    else
    hd(L2)::merge(L1,tail(L2))             hd(L2)::merge(L1,tail(L2))
             (a)                                      (b)
```

FIGURE 9.13 A recursive function for merging sorted lists of (a) numbers (things to which "<" applies) and (b) lists of anything.

---

[7] Or, seen in the other direction, the functions robinsAre(Class) and robinsAreBirds() result from "currying" the function inheritsFrom(Class,Class) [Ullman 1998].

Functional parameterization extends the applicability of a given procedure—like merge(.,.) in Figure 9.13—to a larger domain (input parameter types) by replacing a piece of computation by a function that embodies the role (the essence of) played by that computation.[8] If we make that function as a parameter of the procedure (merge(.,.)), we extend the applicability of merge(.,.) to all those situations where both its own function and part of its implementation (everything but the functional parameter, e.g., all the code except the comparison in the example of Fig. 9.13) are applicable. For the purposes of the ongoing discussion, we liken the distinction between the *role* of a procedure (or its *function*) and its *implementation* to that between *specification* and *implementation*.

To see what functional parametrization does, let f be the definition or specification of a procedure, and impl(f) one of its implementations. We have domain(impl(f)) $\subseteq$ domain(f). Further, let impl(f) consist of a set of statements $\langle S_1, \ldots, S_n \rangle$. Then, each statement imposes some restrictions on the set of values to which the procedure applies. Symbolically, this would be

$$\text{domain(impl(f))} = \cap_i \text{domain(S}_i)$$

We can easily see that by encapsulating a set of statements—say, $S_1, \ldots, S_j$—into a function g, the implementation of our function becomes $\langle g, S_{j+1}, \ldots, S_n \rangle$, and its domain is now:

$$\text{domain(impl}'(\text{f)}) = \text{domain(g)} \cap [\cap_{i \neq j} \text{domain(S}_i)]$$

where impl'(f) refers to this new implementation of f. However, because $\langle S_1, \ldots, S_j \rangle$ is only one of many possible implementations of g, we have domain(impl(f)) $\subseteq$ domain(impl'(f)). This illustrates how functional parameterization *could potentially* enlarge the domain (applicability) of a procedure. In practice, it is not clear that such an enlargement has taken place. For instance, if

$$\cap_{i \leq j} \text{domain(S}_i) \supseteq \cap_{i > j} \text{domain(S}_i)$$

then no widening occurs by using the function g(. . .) instead of the statements $S_1, \ldots, S_j$. Consider the example of Figure 9.14, where in addition to merging the two lists, we add one to each element.

In this case, the types of L1 and L2 were bound by lists of floats, because of the instructions hd(L1) + 1.0 and hd(L2) + 1.0, which remained after the functional parameterization. Therefore, replacing > by the generic

---

[8] Philosophers of science distinguish between *function* and *computation*. The word *function* has a purposeful connotation, while *computation* is "goal-neutral." A *computation* that is performed within the context of a bigger or enclosing computation *plays a particular role within that enclosing computation*. In other words, *computation within context is a function* [Darden and Rada 1987].

```
fun merge(L1,L2) =                  fun merge(L1,L2,comp) =
  if hd(L1) < hd(L2) then             if comp(hd(L1),hd(L2)) then
    (hd(L1) + 1.0)                       (hd(L1) + 1.0)
        ::merge(tail(L1),L2)                ::merge(tail(L1),L2)
  else                                else
    (hd(L2) + 1.0)                      (hd(L2) + 1.0)
        ::merge(L1,tail(L2))                ::merge(L1,tail(L2))
          (a)                                   (b)
```

FIGURE 9.14 Two implementations of a recursive function for merging sorted lists of floats and incrementing them. Replacing < (in (a)) by comp (in (b)) didn't widen the domain of the function.

comp(.,.) function didn't broaden the domain of the function merge. Practically speaking, this means that when we group computations (instructions) within a procedure into functions (and function parameters), we can optimize the broadening of the applicability of the procedure by choosing functions with *orthogonal* or independent domains. This is a general property, and applies to all kinds of parameterization techniques. A computational object (data structure of function) with parameters (type parameters or function parameters) $p_1, \ldots, p_n$, is generic to the extent that the parameters are independent or orthogonal. Any dependence between the parameters will limit the applicability of the computational object.[9]

We should note that functional (and data) parameterization does not change the procedural nature of knowledge. By abstracting long sequences of computations into short sequences of *functions*, we are still achieving goals by executing a goal-specific sequence of operations—although that sequence is more generic. If the nature of the task to be performed requires a change in one of its steps, we have to find the smallest "function" that contains that step, and replace its implementation by another one that fulfills the same function. Ideally, a small change in the task to be performed or in the data operated on should require a commensurably small change in the implementations of the functions. In particular, by applying functional parameterization to the steps that access the data being manipulated, we are able to keep the changes small—this is *data abstraction* in the object-oriented sense, and will be discussed in the next subsection as well as in the next chapter.

Let us summarize. In procedural programming, tasks are accomplished by enacting a special-purpose computation. We use decomposition for two reasons: (1) to reduce complexity by distributing it among more easily manageable components and (2) to reuse those components. These two criteria are

---

[9] The *Factory* design pattern is used in situations where two such parameters are mutually dependent and need to be chosen together, as a pair [Gamma et al. 1995]. Why use two parameters in that case? In general, there are two reasons for that: (1) there are *other* aspects for which the parameterized components are independent, and (2) so that each may be used in other structures.

used in the context of an analytic (top–down) approach, where we perform the decomposition/modularization in the process of implementing the computation.

We have also seen that functional programming supports two abstraction mechanisms:

- *Data abstraction*, which generalizes computations from a specific set of objects of interest to all those objects whose structure allows them to support those computations.
- *Functional abstraction*, which replaces a subset of a given computation by a function that fulfills the roles played by that subset, hence broadening the applicability of the enclosing computation to other objects supporting that *function*, possibly using different computations. In particular, we have seen criteria for identifying such subsets in a way that broadens the applicability of the enclosing procedure to its maximum extent.

The two abstraction (parameterization) procedures are to be used in a synthetic bottom–up fashion, once a solution to the problem at hand has been found. In simplistic practical terms, the two abstraction mechanisms may be used to reengineer existing systems to make them more generally applicable, that is, reusable.

With regard to the goals of this chapter, we ask to what extent do the abstraction boundaries of procedural programming correspond to the natural boundaries of reuse with the represented systems. As mentioned earlier in this chapter, it is difficult to answer this question in the absolute since any attempt to answer this question has to go through a modeling of the systems we are representing, and this modeling cannot be paradigm-neutral. We are hard-pressed to define what a "good" procedure might be without referring to objective (and domain-neutral) criteria such as complexity, functional reuse, and computational genericity.[10] In practice, it is a combination of these criteria, along with accumulated experience of what worked and what didn't, that enables us to model functions effectively, both analytically and synthetically—there is nothing "natural" about 99% of the procedures that we typically model.

---

[10] In an earlier paper [Mili 1996a], we sought criteria for identifying a minimal set of methods that objects must support, some sort of a behavior that is *minimal* in the sense that it embodies all of the "atomic behaviors" of an object, and nothing more. Our definition of an atomic behavior was that one that was either purely functional (returns no value no side effects) or purely side-effectal (no return value). Further, side-effectal behaviors had to leave the object in a valid state, but have no intermediary valid states; that is, they cannot be decomposed into a sequence of two (or more) side-effectal behaviors where the first leaves the system in a consistent state [Mili 1996a].

9.3.3   Object-Oriented Development

We will be devoting two entire chapters to discuss abstraction (Chapter 11) and composition (Chapter 12) mechanisms in object orientation. For the purposes of this chapter, we will discuss the paradigmatic aspects. Roughly speaking, object orientation supports two, nearly orthogonal, abstraction dimensions. The first dimension is behavioral in nature, and consists of the view of object-oriented programs as collaborations between interacting objects. The second dimension is definitional in nature, and views objects as belonging to specific classes and types, with set-theoretic relationships between them. While both dimensions yield powerful abstraction mechanisms, a major difficulty in object orientation is our insistence on believing that these two dimensions are correlated, and on devising methodologies that attempt to build on this relation or correlation. We start this section by looking at the behavioral view. Next, we look at the definitional view and at the structure-function relationship. Next, we discuss an experiment that attempted to test the abstraction boundaries of object orientation.

9.3.3.1   *The Behavioral View*
We mentioned in Section 9.2.2 that things get done in the object-oriented paradigm through the collaboration of interacting objects with limited intelligence toward the accomplishment of a given function. Starting with the definition of some global behavior to implement, object modeling may appear as an equation with two unknowns. Given a multivariable function $f(x_1, x_2, \ldots, x_n)$ to implement, find a set of objects Y_1, Y_2, Y_m and a function $g(p_1, p_2, \ldots, p_m)$ such that $g(Y_1, Y_2, \ldots, Y_m) = f(x_1, x_2, \ldots, x_n)$. In this case, the function $g(\ldots)$ embodies interobject behavior.

This is a difficult problem, and probably in part because of this, the object-oriented modeling problem is seldom framed in this way. Most methodologies avoid the problem by prescribing that we find the objects first, and then distribute the required functionality between those objects. This stems from the belief that objects "exist in the natural world," and are just waiting to be found. Unfortunately, this view was common in the early generation development methodologies (*data-driven* methodologies [Fowler 1993]), and often led to suboptimal boundaries both at the object and subsystem level [Aksit and Bergmans 1992], even in those application areas with a long tradition in information modeling. A **Customer** class whose only functionality is limited to read/write access to its attributes may be widely useful, but is not worth reusing.

If objects have no existence of their own, then it is no longer an issue of checking whether they define optimal reuse boundaries: optimal reuse boundaries become the very definition of what objects are all about. Software engineers who work in nontraditional MIS (management information system) areas where objects are simply service providers with state, will argue that that is what objects are. A print spooler, a process dispatcher, or an ORB do not exist in the "natural world," they are pure software abstractions. What is it exactly that we are trying to optimize, and how do we go about it? One view of this considers object abstraction as a clustering problem. We assume that we have identified the functions, possibly decomposed, and the data that these functions operate on, and we are trying to put boundaries around clusters of functions and data in such a way that (1) what is inside the cluster is highly cohesive and strongly interdependent, (2) clusters are loosely coupled, and (3) the glue that binds clusters together is contextual and of relatively small size compared to what binds the elements of a cluster. Figure 9.15 illustrates this idea. Cyberneticists have a name for such systems: *nearly decomposable systems* [Simon and Ando 1961]; they would be *perfectly decomposable* if we could find boundaries such that no coupling remains between clusters.

Of course, for these clusters to reflect good (stable and resilient) reuse units, we have to vary the input to our clustering algorithm; we have to cover a wide range of functions and data within a particular application domain, and hence, domain analysis! Interestingly, a number of reengineering methods that aim at migrating procedural code into object code use exactly this paradigm.

In our view, functional abstraction and object abstractions are two sides of the same coin. At the most fundamental (atomic or granular) level, we have simple functions and simple (scalar) data. From there on up, functional

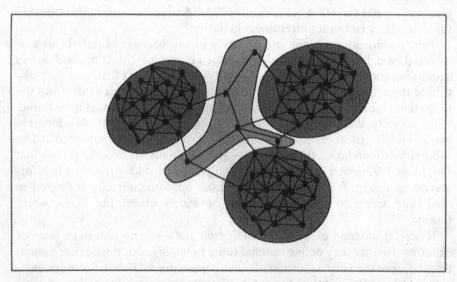

FIGURE 9.15 Finding object boundaries is a clustering problem. Clusters of function and data (dark gray ellipses) become classes, and what remains outside (shapeless blob) is interobject behavior.

abstraction and data abstraction just repackage the same basic elements differently (see Fig. 9.16). Functional abstraction starts from several sample computations, to identify a recurring group of elementary functions, and wrap them within functional boundaries making the overall function more general by making, among other things, some temporary results of the computation private to the function. Object abstraction, on the other hand, uses several sample computations that manipulate similar data and groups them into an object package, by the same token simplifying the expression of functions involving that data. In the case of Figure 9.16, the sample computation, involving eight variables and five functions becomes a function (f'_3) involving three objects, where f'_3 uses a modified protocol from that used by f_3. Note that we can apply object abstraction to the results of functional abstraction, and we would end with bigger objects, having bigger functions.

Having generated first-level clusters to obtain more aggregate data with functionality (i.e., "reactive data"), we can reiterate this clustering operation at will, getting (1) *increasingly higher-level clusters* and (2) *increasingly looser clusters*. Thus, the first application of our clustering procedure identifies the most strongly cohesive clusters, which would then correspond to the most widely useful classes. As we move up the cluster/aggregation hierarchy, we get weaker and more application-dependent clusters. Figure 9.17 illustrates this idea. The paler shade of gray of the upper cluster reflects its weaker cohesion. Most readers will probably be surprised to know that we have just described

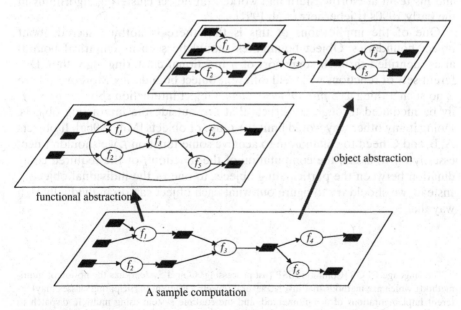

A sample computation

FIGURE 9.16 Functional programming and OO programming package the same functions and data differently.

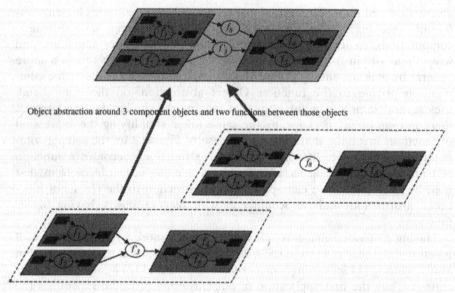

Object abstraction around 3 component objects and two functions between those objects

FIGURE 9.17 How aggregate objects are born.

the general idea behind an actual development methodology, the *cluster method*, which *was* floated around in the late 1980s (see Henderson-Sellers [1993]; also, Section 15.2, below, elaborates on this idea). Further, Lieberherr and his team at Northeastern had worked on object clustering algorithms in the early 1990s [Lieberherr et al. 1991].

One of the implications of this is that there is nothing sacred about object boundaries. Object boundaries should be seen as empirical boundaries identified through some sort of a functional clustering algorithm. Different sets of functions will yield different object boundaries. Moreover, there is no such a thing as a *pure object system*. Object interaction should necessarily be mediated through constructs that are outside the interacting objects. Doing it any other way would limit the reuse of objects [Mili 1996a]. If objects A, B, and C need to collaborate to achieve some function f, we shouldn't necessarily try to assign the computation of the function f or the required coordination between the participating objects, to one of the individual objects.[11] Instead, we should try to figure out what each object can do individually, in a way that

---

[11] The language CLOS [Common LISP (list processing) Object System] has the notion of multimethods, which are methods that involve several objects. Different participating classes may different implementations of a multimethod, and the runtime system using multiple dispatch to execute a multimethod.

- Helps with the computation of f
- Can help with the computations of many other functions involving the object

There are many wrong ways to divide an inter-object behavior between the participating objects. One obviously wrong way consists of using objects as data stores and embodying all of the behavior in outside functions. In this case, we are back to functional programming territory in terms of abstraction and composability, but often worse off because less care is usually taken in designing those functions than with straight procedural programming.

The other less obviously wrong way consists of assigning interobject behavior either to a single object, making that object context dependent and the other objects less worth reusing, or to divide it up entirely between the participating objects, with one object responsible for the coordination. There are degrees of badness in this scenario, with the worst scenario being that all the participating objects depend on each other, and the best scenario being that all but the coordinator doing exactly what they should, no more and no less, and the coordinator doing their part, as well as the coordination, preferably in separate methods.

In the perfect scenario, once we have identified objects' individual responsibilities, we should be left with the code that is responsible for coordinating the objects and for computing the things that are not the exclusive competencies of any object in particular. That code can be implemented declaratively or procedurally, with the advantages and disadvantages discussed in Sections 9.3.1 and 9.3.2. A good implementation of interobject behavior not only ensures the independent reusability of the interacting objects, but also the reusability of the inter-object code itself. In particular, if that code is polymorphic (the notion of data abstraction), it may be used to coordinate different sets of objects, provided that they support predefined sets of services. Chapter 12 of this book is devoted almost entirely to flexible ways of implementing inter-object behavior. Chapter 13 illustrates some of the abstraction and composition techniques that enable us to compose independently developed objects to achieve higher-level functionality.

9.3.3.2 The Definitional View

So what is the deal with inheritance? Inheritance has a muddy relationship to object-oriented development. Chapters 10 and 11 look into the various facets of that relationship for both programming and modeling. For the purposes of our discussion, we consider the paradigmatic issues. Notice that the behavioral view of objects does not mention inheritance, or even classes. Inheritance may have ended up in objects because of object orientation's knowledge representation ancestry. In knowledge representation, inheritance has two meanings: (1) it is a relationship that describes concept subsumption and (2) it is a logical inference procedure. Both meanings will be discussed in more detail in Section 11.1.2. But in both cases, it relates to concept *definitions*, which may be seen as membership predicates. For example, we could define the concept (class) of Dog by the predicate $P_{Dog}(x)$ defined as follows:

$$P_{Dog}(x) \equiv Mammal(x) \wedge Barks(x) \wedge HasWaggingTail(x)$$

Subsumption between concepts is then just the implication relationship between their membership predicates. For example, we can define Chihuahua dogs with the predicate:

$$P_{Chihuahua}(x) \equiv Mammal(x) \wedge Barks(x) \wedge HasWaggingTail(x)$$
$$\wedge SpeaksSpanish(x)$$
$$\equiv P_{Dog}(x) \wedge SpeaksSpanish(x)$$

and thus

$$P_{Chihuahua}(x) \Rightarrow P_{Dog}(x)$$

or, Chihuahua is a subtype of Dog. In object orientation, the meaning of classes is not always clear. Typically, at the analysis level we think of them as *definitions*, but at the design and implementation levels we think of them as *templates* for instantiating individuals of the class, in a way that supports the *implementation of the definition* (e.g., providing for the various state variables that are needed by the functions to implement their behavior).

Object-orientation has struggled with this distinction at the analysis level, where some methodologists insist on the distinction between type and class [Martin and Odell 1997], and at the programming language level, where, in our opinion, only Java has addressed the distinction adequately. Subtyping and subclassing are discussed in Section 10.2.4.

The confusion between structure (templates) and behavior (definition) is not without merit, of course. Philosophers of science have long argued for the existence of structure–function relationships [Darden and Rada 1988]. At the most basic level, protein structures in DNA molecules (genes). That relationship can be very degenerate, however, with different structures generating the same behavior (redundancy, fault tolerance, etc.), or similar structures generating different behaviors in different contexts. One manifestation of this degeneracy is the trouble object-oriented methods have in characterizing behavioral specialization *structurally*! Formally, we know how to characterize behavioral specialization. If types are defined by algebras, then we extend those algebras by adding new operations (new methods), or by replacing some of the existing operations with more specific conformant ones (e.g., contravariance). But how do we *construct* the specialization of an operation from that operation? We know of a few simple patterns, but those patterns don't come near to covering the range of behavioral specializations. We show below one such pattern—let us call it the **super** pattern:

```
class A {
        public Type1 f(Type2 x) {...}
}
class B extends A {
        public Type1 f(Type2 x) {
                doSomethingWith(x) ;
                return super.f(x); }
}
```

In this case, the specialization of f(...) adds a preprocessing to the original version.

So, what do we make of inheritance or generalization–specialization as an abstraction mechanism in object orientation? We share the view that *inheritance* is not an essential aspect of object orientation, but polymorphism is. The next two chapters take us through a thorough examination of inheritance, from a number of viewpoints, but for the purposes of this chapter, suffice it to say that inheritance does not contribute to defining abstraction boundaries; as a typing mechanism, it simply supports the reuse of definitions. As a class (implementation) mechanism, it is simply a mechanism for code sharing. According to Bertrand Meyer, inheritance is a mechanism for the developer of reusable components, and not for the reuser of that code [Meyer 1990]. However, polymorphism is, whereby a function that can take several types of objects can be used for any of those objects, without adaptation.

9.3.3.3 An Experiment

An often-cited advantage of object-oriented models is their presumed resilience to evolution, which, translated in our terminology, means that objects define good abstraction boundaries. In 1992, Lubars et al. set out to test the claim that object-oriented models are stable [Lubars et al. 1992]. They defined model stability in terms of three properties: (1) *localization*, meaning that changes should be localized in the model, even if they require considerable rework in a localized area; (2) *conservative extension*, meaning that the effect of a change on the work already done should be minimal, that is, that we should, as much as possible, extend existing work but not redo it; and (3) *model independence*, in the sense that changes to structural (data) models have little impact on behavioral models, and vice versa. The authors modeled the ATM (automated teller machine) application using Rumbaugh et al.'s object modeling technique (OMT) [Rumbaugh et al. 1991], and considered two "small" change scenarios to assess the stability properties. Lubars et al. observed that the structural model—called *object model* in OMT—was well behaved, but that the behavioral models[12] were not. This confirms the observation we made to the effect that we don't

---

[12] OMT uses several complementary notations to represent behavior, including event flow diagrams to represent messages exchanged between objects, and Harel state charts for individual objects to represent objects' individual behaviors.

have the right tools to incrementally construct more specialized behaviors by modifying existing ones. They also observed that the models were somewhat interdependent because in one scenario, changes to the behavioral models led to revising the object model [Lubars et al. 1992]. In other words, the object boundaries they had in their original model were not good enough abstraction boundaries. According to our discussion on the behavioral view, this may be due either to the fact that OMT is data-driven (objects are identified *before* system functionalities are explored) or because the authors— clearly—didn't consider enough functions to crystallize the object boundaries, or both.

The authors recognized that theirs was not a controlled experiment, and that no definitive conclusions could be drawn. We believe that some of the difficulties were specific to OMT, and to data-driven methods in general, but concur with their observation that ease of evolution may conflict with ease of description. The authors mentioned two modeling tricks that would have stabilized the models: (1) the use of abstract classes to leave room for future specialization or factoring of existing classes and (2) the use of "mixins"[13] to separate concerns and to reuse them independently; both techniques have no meaning to the end user [Lubars et al. 1992].

9.4   TOWARD MULTIPARADIGM DEVELOPMENT

We set out to study the three development paradigms, declarative, functional, and object-oriented, from the point of view of reuse. In particular, we tried to answer two questions. The first, and most important, is: in what way does each paradigm support reuse. To this end, we defined two criteria that we believe to be crucial: (1) what *abstraction boundaries* (what kind of chunks) are supported by each paradigm, and (2) how easily and freely can we compose such chunks, once we have wrapped them with the appropriate constructs. The second, more difficult—but thankfully much less important—question had to do with choosing a paradigm that is best suited for a particular situation. We wanted our comparison to be *objective* and independent of any human factors, such as the purported intuitiveness or naturalness of one developing paradigm versus another. Objects exist in the natural world (physics, society) but rarely in the abstract world of systems software (e.g., a switching software). We believe that a fair comparison would need to focus on the properties of the different paradigms as *computational* paradigms, regardless of *application areas*, which may favor one paradigm over another, and regardless of *implementations* of the paradigm, which may also favor one paradigm over another.

When we strip objects bare of their knowledge representation and cognitive heritage, on one hand, and their made-to-measure application areas

---

[13] Broadly speaking, mixins correspond to "mixing in" the features inherited from two different superclasses (multiple inheritance) each representing a view of the class.

(modeling and implementation of natural processes) where objects are easy to identify, and when the application domain provides us with its own set of abstractions, we are left with *a packaging technology for behavior and data that optimizes reuse*. If we are open-minded about the way functions are computed, then we can choose the right paradigm for implementing objects' intrinsic behavior (within the clusters) as well as inter-object behavior.

From our discussion in Sections 9.3.1 and 9.3.2, declarative programming has the advantages of flexible and effortless composition. However, it does not abstract away details, and suffers from poor performance. Procedural programming, on the other hand, is faster, abstracts away detail, and offers less opportunities for composition. Because interobject behavior is contextual, and usage-specific, it seems appropriate for the declarative paradigm: an application that uses a given set of objects will specify declaratively the "functions" that these objects have to implement, which can often be specified in terms of structural relationships or functional dependencies to be maintained. Chapter 12 discussed inter-object behavior more thoroughly, in terms of both (1) declarative language constructs (e.g., *contracts* [Helm et al. 1990], *constraint objects* [Mili et al. 1990], and *advisory aspects* [Kiczales et al. 1997]) and (2) design patterns.

When objects are often used together with the same set of interobject behaviors, it pays to

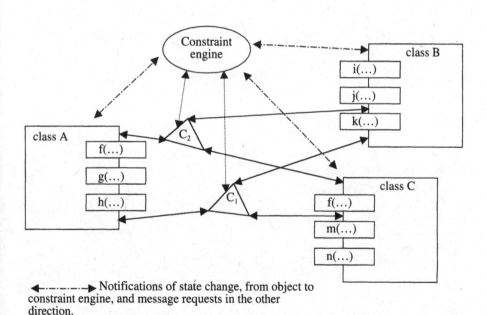

←·—·—·—·→ Notifications of state change, from object to constraint engine, and message requests in the other direction.

FIGURE 9.18 A multiparadigm application mixes objects with functions and constraint programming.

- Abstract the objects, with the interobject behaviors, into an aggregate *opaque* object (higher-level cluster),
- Perform the *closure* of the declarative specification of the behaviors to obtain a more efficient functional equivalent (see Section 9.3.1).

In other words, the declarative paradigm is a convenient evolutionary step toward stable and firmed-up objects with functionally implemented methods. Figure 9.18 illustrates the coexistence of objects, functions, and declarative constructs (constraints) that are enforced by a central constraint engine. Researchers at the University of Washington have proposed such hybrids in the early 90's (see, e.g., Freeman-Benson [1990]). In a subsequent study [Mili and Sahraoui 1999], we proposed a model of frameworks based on this paradigm, where interobject behavior is specified and enforced declaratively, but where a *closure* operation encapsulates a framework instantiation into an aggregate whose behavior is the "proceduralization" of the various interaction sequences of the framework. This proceduralization may be seen as a non-editable deployment-specific transformation [Mili and Sahraoui 1999].

Part IV

Object-Oriented Domain Engineering

Part III discussed technology independent technical issues in domain engineering. In this part, we study object-oriented techniques for developing reusable software, or object-oriented domain engineering.

This part contains five chapters that discuss a set of object-oriented techniques for modelling and implementing software components in a way that makes them *usable*, that is, easily customizable and easily composable. These chapters are fairly technical in nature, and aren't meant just to "give an idea." There are two kinds of material in these chapters: (1) *foundational material*, which attempts to address the *why* of things; and (2) *practical material*, which handles the *how*. The hurried reader may skip some of the foundational material on to the more practical material. The leisurely reader (are there any left?) may want to study the material in the sequence given.

Chapter 10 provides a pragmatic introduction to object-oriented programming. Although we expect most readers of the book to be object-savvy, at least in general terms, some of the technical details about object-oriented languages and language constructs are needed for the more advanced material of Chapters 11–14. We discuss the ways in which different OO languages (C++, Java, Smalltalk, Eiffel, Ada) implement specific constructs. Advanced OO practitioners can probably skip the entire chapter altogether. Intermediate objecteers can probably skip right into Section 10.2.4. Beginners are urged to go through the whole thing. Technical managers may read up through Section 10.2.3, and pick up the discussion later in Section 10.3, which compares programming languages.

Chapter 11 deals with abstraction techniques in both modelling and programming. Some of these techniques are built into existing object analysis methodologies (programming languages). Others are powerful combinations of built-in techniques. Others yet are design-level constructs that support abstraction and that can be implemented using existing constructs. In particular, we have a section that discusses some abstraction design patterns. Section 11.1 contains a lot of foundational material. The hurried reader and technical managers may want to read only Sections 11.1.4 (metamodeling) and 11.1.6 (metamodeling in practice). Advanced OO developers and technical managers may want to skip Section 11.2. The rest of the chapter is a recommended read for everybody.

Chapter 12 deals with composition techniques. Section 12.2 is more foundational in nature, and may be skipped by technical managers and hurried readers. Section 12.3 is a must read for everybody because it surveys emerging software packaging and composition technologies (subject-oriented programming, aspect-oriented programming, and some other less mature approaches). Section 12.4 is a must read for all except the technical managers who may not have to design software themselves.

Chapter 13 deals with object frameworks—object frameworks with coarse granularity, and complex, high-payoff customizable reusable assets. These assets are worth knowing about and good ones are excellent lessons in design. This chapter discusses what they are, the range of abstraction and composition techniques that are usually employed to make them customizable, and presents example fragments of a successful framework (the Java SWING framework). Technical managers may want to limit their reading to Sections 13.1 and 13.3. Others should read the entire chapter.

Chapter 14 deals with architecture in the context of reuse. We start with an introduction to architectures (architctures, architectural styles, and connectors). Section 14.2 deals with the role of architecture in reuse, both as a reusable product and as a reuse-enabling infrastructure. In particular, we discuss a special kind of framework, which we call *architectural frameworks*: frameworks that implement the computational or interaction infrastructure of architectural styles (meaning middleware). The remaining sections discuss CORBA, Java technologies (RMI and EJB), and COM. Our presentation of these technologies is by no means complete; plenty of reference material and plenty of overviews in the literature are cited. We chose to focus on a small subset of each technology, but address it in enough detail that technical people get a feeling for the way these frameworks are implemented, or, can implement the services that they offer. As such, they also provide good lessons in design. The entire chapter should be accessible and useful to all the intended readers of this book.

Chapter **10**

A Pragmatic Introduction to Object Orientation

Since the mid eighties, object-oriented software engineering has gone from a curiosity preached and practiced by a few researchers and European software specialists with Nordic-sounding names, to the mainstream software development paradigm. For a while, object-oriented programming had come to be considered a panacea for all computing aches. Nowadays, most experts would agree that object orientation is a powerful *packaging technology* for creating reusable software components. However, as Chapter 9 showed, object orientation is not the sole—or even a necessary—condition for reusability. Chapters 11–14 take pains to show that by using objects, reusability comes neither ineluctably nor easily; a lot more ingenuity has to go into using the object paradigm to achieve high-level reusability.

In Chapter 9, we discussed object-orientation from a knowledge representation or modeling perspective. In this chapter, we take a look at object orientation from a programming perspective, introducing the various tenets of object-oriented programming in a fairly mechanical, decidedly nonanthropomorphic fashion, by the same token emphasizing its merits as a packaging technology. Understanding these concepts is important for us to assimilate the more advanced programming techniques shown in the coming chapters. We assume no prior knowledge whatsoever with objects and object orientation, for two reasons. First, we expect that some of the readers of this book will be practicing engineers who are busy maintaining successful legacy applications and who haven't had the chance to indulge into object fare. Second, those who don't know anything but objects will find a pseudohistorical justification for some of the features of object-oriented languages.

Section 10.1 provides a general introduction to object orientation and presents an example that will be referred to in this chapter and throughout the book. Section 10.2 includes a discussion of the major tenets of object orientation, namely, encapsulation and information hiding, overloading, genericity, subtyping, inheritance, polymorphism, and dynamic binding. In Section 10.3, we discuss criteria for comparing programming languages, assuming that we really do make rational choices based on objective feature-by-feature comparisons between languages. We conclude in Section 10.4.

10.1 INTRODUCTION

10.1.1 Overview

Dahl and Nygaard [1970] introduced the concept of "object" in programming in their language Simula. Simula was designed as a language for simulating dynamic physical systems. Physical objects were modeled by structures containing state variables and procedures used to manipulate them. Using today's jargon, we would say that objects are compilation units that encapsulate data with the procedures that manipulate them. One advantage of such structures, from a programming language point of view, was to separate the visibility of variables from their lifetime; in other words, a variable could be active outside the scope of its visibility. This is the basic idea behind information hiding. Information hiding enables us to build modules that are easier to understand and more reusable. Because of information hiding, "objects" can be manipulated only through public interfaces—sometimes called *protocols* or simply *interfaces*—specifically, a set of procedures that are "publicly" visible. This makes it possible to change the implementation details of an object without affecting its clients.

Intuitively, a class is (the description of) a collection of objects that share the same data structure and support the same operations. The description of a class includes a data template and a definition of the operations supported by the objects (called *instances*) of the class. In some object-oriented languages and modular languages (e.g., Modula and Ada), a distinction is made between the specification of a class (e.g., package specification in Ada) and its implementation (e.g., implementation module in Modula). Typically, the specification of a class corresponds to its public interface.[1] An abstract class is a class that has a specification but no implementation. Overloading makes it possible for several classes to offer or implement the same operations; the compiler disambiguates operation references using the parameter or operand types.

Polymorphism makes it possible for a variable to hold objects belonging to different classes. Dynamic binding delays the resolution of operation ref-

---

[1] This is the case in the Modula and Ada families of languages. In C++, however, the specification must list the procedures and data variables that are not visible outside, but say so.

erences until runtime when the actual type of the variable is known; this allows for greater flexibility in programming [Meyer 1988]. Overloading and polymorphism make it possible to develop general-purpose client code that is indifferent to the reimplementation and extension of server code. Classes can be organized along hierarchies supporting different kinds of "inheritance." The parallel with natural taxonomies, whereby a natural category "inherits" a number of properties from its ancestors, is tempting, sometimes useful, and often misleading [Intrator and Mili 1994]. For the time being, let us just say that inheritance in programming languages is a built-in code-sharing mechanism that, without polymorphism and dynamic binding, would not be much different from various module import mechanisms in traditional languages.

In the next section, we introduce the tenets of object orientation as mechanisms that enable us to enhance the reusability of our code. The code samples shown in that section are mostly written in known modular or object-oriented languages, but we will occasionally write something in an imaginary extension of familiar languages. A good many code samples are taken from the domain of financial institutions. We will refer to this domain in later chapters of the book. We describe the domain next.

10.1.2 The Financial Domain

The example described in this section deals with a confederation of savings and loans associations (SLAs) which are financial institutions that offer a similar set of products, and that cater to the same type of customers, namely, small businesses and individuals. Typically, SLAs offer small business loans to family-owned businesses, and manage low-risk investments for individuals—typically, low but guaranteed return savings accounts.[1] Taking advantage of the similarity between the products they offer, SLAs get together for several reasons, including sharing costs (e.g., shared information system infrastructure, shared marketing), risks (e.g., deposit insurance), and the customer base (serving customers no matter how far they are from home base). By buying into a confederation, the various SLAs would typically relinquish some of their independence, and are obliged to adhere to a set of operating and product standards. This translates, among other things, into a particular information infrastructure.

Figure 10.1 shows a very high-level architecture of the information technology (IT) infrastructure of such a confederation. For the time being, we are not so much concerned about the actual physical distribution of the data as with the data ownership. We assume that the confederation owns a database containing confederationwide product definitions (types of loans, approval criteria, reimbursement policies, schedules, etc.) and operation guidelines and parameters (fees, template organizational charts, quality control, handling client complaints, unclaimed balances, etc.). In addition to this data, the confederation will store data about customers that can be shared by the other institutions. Specific SLAs will have their own definitions of products, which

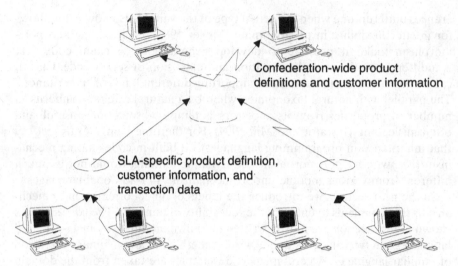

FIGURE 10.1 The information infrastructure of a confederation of SLAs.

are subsumed by that of the confederation. Further, they will have information about customers who have opened accounts in their SLAs, which won't be found elsewhere. We will come back to the data and process architecture in later chapters.

10.2 THE TENETS OF OBJECT-ORIENTED PROGRAMMING

We introduce the tenets of object-oriented programming as mechanisms to enhance the reusability and maintenance of code. We describe one such piece of code next. The example starts out as a Modula-2 program which has a familiar Pascal-like syntax. As we introduce new OO constructs we will occasionally use constructs that are not part of the language (or any language), to keep the presentation simple. Sections 10.2.2–10.2.5 introduce, in turn, encapsulation and information hiding, overloading and genericity, subtyping and class inheritance, and late binding and polymorphism.

10.2.1 A Sample Program

For the time being, we are interested in a small piece of code that processes payments made at an automatic teller machine. We assume that the payments are read one batch at a time. Each batch consists of, first, the account that must be debited, then by a sequence of triples representing (1) the amount of the payment, (2) an identification of the payer (e.g., the customer account number for a utility), and (3) the bank account number for the beneficiary.

The processing part of this module is shown between lines (22) and (31) in Figure 10.2. It consists of a main loop over some input file f from which the

```
(1)   MODULE handlePayments;
(2)   FROM accounts IMPORT Account, getAccountWithNum,....;
(3)   ...
(4)   TYPE Payment =RECORD
(5)   amount: REAL;
(6)   debitorAccount : STRING;
(7)   creditorAccount : STRING;
(8)   END;
(9)   ...
(10)  VAR currentPmnt: Payment;
(11)  payerAccount : Account;
(12)  payerAccountNum : STRING;
(13)  ...
(14)  PROCEDURE registerPayment(VAR debitAccnt: Account, aPayment:
      Payment);
(15)  VAR
(16)    credAccount: Account;
(17)  BEGIN
(18)    credAccount = getAccountWithNum(aPayment.credAccountNum);
(19)    debitAccnt.balance = debitAccnt.balance - aPayment.amount;
(20)    credAccount.balance = credAccount.balance + aPayment.
        amount;
(21)  END registerPayment;
(22)  ...
(23)  BEGIN
(24)    ...
(25)    WHILE not(eof(f)) DO
(26)      payerAccountNum = readln(f);
(27)      payerAccount =getAccountWithNum(payerAccountNum);
(28)        WHILE hasOneMorePayment(f) DO
(29)          currentPmnt = readPayment(f);
(30)        registerPayment(payerAccount,currentPmnt);
(31)        END;
(32)    END;
(33)    ...
(34)  END handlePayments.
```

FIGURE 10.2   A first-cut program that handles payments.

payer account number [line (26)] and the corresponding batch of payments [lines (28)–(31)] are read and processed. Line (30) shows a call to a procedure that is defined in lines (14)–(21) that updates the account of both the payer (customer) and the creditor (e.g., the local phone company). This procedure takes no parameters; it operates on the global variables payerAccount and credAccount, which are declared in the "main" module. Finally, we assume that some external module called **accounts** contains the definitions of the *type* **Account** and of the procedure getAccountWithNum(String)— hence the **IMPORT** directive in line (2). This program is in Modula-2. It is poorly designed, and we hope that first- or second-course computer science students are taught to know better! We will use it, however, to introduce the sometimes all-too-obvious and commonsensical nature of the tenets of object-oriented programming.

10.2.2   Encapsulation and Information Hiding

First, from a functional point of view, the procedure `registerPayment` has a great potential for reuse as a procedure for registering any kind of transaction involving money transfer from one account to another. However, the way it is written reduces its applicability. Indeed, the procedure is aware of, and *uses*, the structure of both the **Account** and the **Payment** type. This kind of coupling has been called *stamp coupling* (see, e.g., Pressman [1992, pp. 336–338]). If we change the internal representation of **Account** or **Payment**, we will need to change the implementation of `registerPayment`. For example, if **Payment** is now represented as follows:

```
(1)  TYPE
(2)  TypeOfData = (Amount,DebitorAccount,CreditorAccount);
(3)  Payment =ARRAY[Amount..CreditorAccount] OF STRING;
```

Then, we need to change `registerPayment` to the code shown in Figure 10.3.

We showed in bold the code fragments that need to be changed to accommodate the new type implementation. *Similar changes need to occur in all the programs that access the data type* Payment. To minimize the impact of a data implementation change on client programs, we need to

1. Create entry points to the structure of the data that abstract away the details of the implementation.
2. Forbid access to the structure of the data by means other than those entry points.

```
(1)  PROCEDURE registerPayment(VAR debitAccnt: Account,
     paymnt: Payment);
(2)  VAR
(3)    credAccnt: Account;
(4)  BEGIN
(5)    credAccnt = getAccountWithNum(paymnt[CreditorAccnt]);
(6)    debitAccnt.balance= debitAccnt.balance -
       value(paymnt[Amount]);
(7)    credAccnt.balance= credAccnt.balance +
       value(paymnt[Amount]);
(8)  END registerPayment;
```

FIGURE 10.3 New version of `registerPayment()` to accomodate new implementation of type Account.

The solution to (1) is encapsulation: grouping data structures with the functions/procedures that manipulate them. The key to (2) is information hiding: a set of language mechanisms and software design guidelines that relieve clients (and prevent them) from having to know or use the implementation details of a data type to be able to use it.

Encapsulation and information hiding have been offered by a number of *modular* but non-object-oriented languages such Modula-2 and Ada 83. In Modula-2, we might define the data type **Payment** as listed in Figure 10.4. Whereas the definition module defines the type and the signatures of the procedures that manipulate variables of the type, the implementation module contains the actual implementation.

With the definition of getAmount(...) shown in Figure 10.4b, a user of the **Payment** type need not know how the amount property of payments is stored, and that knowledge is localized in the procedure getAmount(). The new implementation of registerPayment(...) that uses the access functions will resemble the format listed in Figure 10.5.

```
(1)   DEFINITION MODULE Payment;
(2)   TYPE Payment = RECORD
(3)     amount: REAL;
(4)     date: Date;
(5)     debitorAccount : STRING;
(6)     creditorAccount : STRING;
(7)   END;
(8)
(9)   (* Read/write procedures for amount *)
(10)  PROCEDURE getAmount(aPayment: Payment): REAL;
(11)  PROCEDURE setAmount(VAR aPayment: Payment; newAmount: REAL);
(12)
(13)  (* Read/write access for debitor account number *)
(14)  PROCEDURE getDebitorAccount(aPayment: Payment): STRING;
(15)  PROCEDURE setDebitorAccount(VAR aPayment: Payment, aNumber:
      STRING);
(16)  ...
(17)  END Payment.
```
(a)

```
(1)   IMPLEMENTATION MODULE Payment;
(2)
(3)   PROCEDURE getAmount(aPayment: Payment): REAL;
(4)   BEGIN
(5)     RETURN aPayment.amount;
(6)   END getAmount;
(7)   ...
(8)   END Payment.
```
(b)

FIGURE 10.4 (a) Definition module for the type Payment; (b) implementation module for the type Payment.

```
(1)  PROCEDURE registerPayment(VAR debAccnt: Account, paymnt:
     Payment);
(2)  VAR
(3)    credAccnt: Account;
(4)  BEGIN
(5)    credAccnt = getAccountWithNum(getCreditorAccount(paymnt));
(6)    setBalance(debAccnt,getBalance(debAccnt)- getAmount(paymnt));
(7)    setBalance(credAccnt, getBalance(credAccnt)+getAmount
       (paymnt));
(8)  END registerPayment;
```

FIGURE 10.5 Protecting registerPayment() from implementation changes in Payment and Account.

As it turns out, the preceding definition (Fig. 10.4*a,b*) of the data type **Payment** gives client programs the possibility of accessing the internals of the data structure using access functions, but doesn't *force them* to. To make the internals truly inaccessible, we use an *opaque type declaration*—a *private* data type declaration in Ada. In Modula-2, this means putting an anonymous type declaration in the definition module, and expliciting the type in the implementation module (see Fig. 10.6).

Those familiar with Ada will recognize about the same style and constructs, modulo a few syntactic differences. Surprisingly, this separation between definition and implementation is not a built-in feature of some of the better-known OO languages such as C++, Smalltalk, and Eiffel. In C++, it is possible to write a class definition in one header file and the actual method bodies in another. However, there is no *privileged* relationship between the two files; it is like any other relationship between a .h (header) file and a .cpp file. Figure 10.7 shows excerpts of the two files.

Note that although we include all the type information—the visible and the hidden—in one file (payment.h), the qualifiers **private** and **public** determine the visibility. Note also that we need to include the <payment.h> file in the payment.cpp file, as we would any other file, whereas for Modula and Ada, where the separation between definition/specification and implementation is supported, the "import" is implicit. The (unfamiliar) reader will also note that the type **Payment** does not show up as a parameter of the functions. That is because these functions are invoked using the "dot" notation, as in

```
(1)  Payment aP;
(2)  aP.setAmount(2.5);
(3)  aP.setDebitorAccount("S213-765-7890");
```

Hence, the **Payment** parameter is implicit, and its fields (data members) can be referred to in the body of the function without qualification as in the statement "**return** amount" of the function getAmount(). We will consider other features of C++ as we go along.

```
DEFINITION MODULE Payment;
FROM accounts IMPORT . . .;
TYPE Payment;

(* Read/write access for amount *)
PROCEDURE getAmount(...): REAL;
PROCEDURE setAmount(...);
...
(*Read/write access debitor accnt *)
PROCEDURE getDebitorAccount(
..):STRING;
PROCEDURE setDebitorAccount(...);
...
END Payment.
```

```
IMPLEMENTATION MODULE
Payment;
TYPE Payment = RECORD
  amount: REAL;
  date : Date;
  debitorAccount : STRING;
  creditorAccount : STRING;
END;
PROCEDURE
getAmount(aP:Payment):REAL;
BEGIN
  RETURN aP.amount;
END getAmount;
...
END Payment.
```

FIGURE 10.6   Opaque/private-type declaration: enforceable information hiding.

```
#include<account.h>
class Payment {
private:
  float amount;
  CDate date;
  CStringdebitorAccount;
  CString creditorAccount;
public:
(* Read/write access for amount *)
  float getAmount();
  void setAmount(floatanAmount);
  ...
(*R/w access debitor accnt *)
  CString getDebitorAccount();
  void setDebitorAccount(CString n);
  ...
}
// contents of payment.h file
```

```
#include<payment.h>
#include <iostream.h>

float Payment::getAmount() {
  return amount;
}

void Payment::setAmount
(float aMt){
  amount = aMnt;
}

CString
Payment::getDebitorAccount()
{
  return debitorAccount;
}
...
// contents of payment.cpp file
```

FIGURE 10.7   The same declaration in C++.

We should mention that neither Smalltalk nor Eiffel supports this *physical* (different files) or *logical* (different compilation units) separation between definition and implementation.[2] Java is somewhat in between; the specification of `classes` is similar to that of Eiffel—declaration and definition are intertwined. However, if we think of `interfaces`, which are *implementationless type declarations*, then we do have this separation, which is more powerful than

---

[2] In Eiffel, the code browser might offer the possibility of filtering out the code body, but that is not a language feature. The same applies to Smalltalk browsers.

that in Modula and Ada. We will have plenty of opportunities to talk about it in later chapters.

We should stress the advantages of the separation between specification and implementation. Consider the following model segment showing the classes **Customer**, **Account**, and **Transaction**. A **Customer** can have 0, 1, or several accounts, but each account is associated with one customer. An **Account** can have 0, 1, or several transactions on it, and a transaction (e.g., withdrawal or deposit) takes place on 1 or several accounts (transfer). If we were to implement this part of the model, we could implement **Customer** first, then **Account**, then **Transaction**.

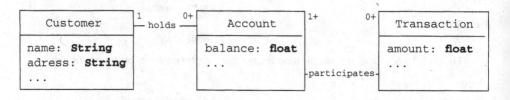

Breaking this into modules, by separating the definition and the implementation, we get the following module dependencies.[3] The arrows indicate the direction of the dependency. As we can see, the definition

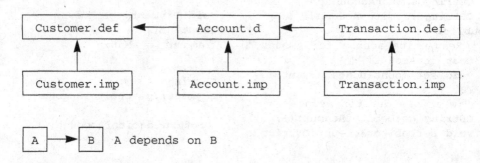

and implementation of **Account** needs *only* the definition of **Customer**; it doesn't need its implementation. Similarly, the definition and implementation of **Transaction** needs *only* the definition of **Account** (and hence, that of **Customer**) but not its implementation. With this breakdown, we are able to have three subteams work on different parts of the implementation, *in parallel, as soon as an agreement has been reached on the definition of the classes.* The definition of a particular entity/class represents, in effect, *the contract between the implementer and the user of the class* [Meyer 1988].

---

[3] We assume here that variables of type **Customer** do not have references to variables of type **Account**, but that there is some other way of getting the set of accounts held by a customer. The same applies to the relationship from **Account** to **Transaction**.

Practically, in C++, we are able to write and compile code as soon as the header files have been finalized. Only the linkage and execution have to wait for the implementations to complete (although sometimes, we can also stub some of the functions if need be). This also means that different implementations can be tested for the same code base, without having to recompile anything: we simply need to link with different libraries. With the concept of interfaces, Java goes even further, thanks to its late binding: we can link different implementations *during runtime*.

10.2.3 Overloading and Genericity

```
DEFINITION MODULE
ListOfStrings;

TYPE Node = RECORD
  value: STRING;
  next : SortedList;
END;
  SortedList = POINTER TO
                    Node;

PROCEDURE init(VAR
          sl: SortedList);

(* Insert value val into list
sl and return pointer to its
node *)
PROCEDURE insert(VAR sl:
    SortedList,
  val : STRING): SortedList;
...
END ListOfStrings.
```

```
IMPLEMENTATION MODULE
ListOfStrings;

PROCEDURE init(VAR sl: SortedList)
BEGIN
  sl := NULL;
END init;
PROCEDURE insert(VAR sl: SortedList,
    val:STRING):SortedList;
VAR nodePtr,cur,prev: SortedList;
BEGIN
  ALLOCATE(nodePtr,size(Node));
  nodePtr^.value := val;
  IF (sl == NULL) THEN
    sl := nodePtr;
    return nodePtr;
  END;
  IF less(val,sl^.value)THEN
    nodePtr^.next := sl;
    sl := nodePtr;
  ELSE
    cur := sl; prev := NULL;
    WHILE (cur != NULL) DO
      IF less(val,cur^.value)
      THEN
        nodePtr^.next := cur;
        cur := NULL;
      ELSE
        prev := cur;
        cur := cur^.next;
      END;
    END;
    prev^.next := nodePtr;
  END;
  return nodePtr;
END;
END ListOfStrings.
```

Assume now that each time a payment is made from a particular account, that payment is recorded within the account. Practically, this will often mean that variables of type **Account** will have a data field/member that points to a list of payments. Further, we would probably want that list to be sorted by increasing dates. Assume that we happened to have, by chance, an implementation of a sorted list of **String**s, as shown above. Very little in that implementation depends on the fact that what we are storing are **String**s, with the exception (1) the explicit declaration of the type of the field "value" of the **Node** record, (2) the declaration of the type of the parameter to insert(...), and (3) the call to the function less(.,.), which returns true if the first parameter is smaller than the second. Thus, if we want to use the list to store payments sorted by date, we need to

- Replace the type declaration of "value" from **String** to **Payment**.
- Replace the type declaration of the "val" parameter of "insert(.,.)" from **String** to **Payment**.
- Write a different version of "less(.,.)" as follows:

```
(1)   PROCEDURE less(payment_1: Payment; payment_2: Payment):
      BOOLEAN
(2)   BEGIN
(3)     RETURN anterior(getDate(payment_1),getDate(payment_2));
(4)   END less;
```

where we assumed that anterior(.,.) checks whether the first date is anterior to the second one.

Not only is this too much work; we couldn't use two sorted lists of different value types within the same program. We will need to use a different type name for each kind of sorted list, *and we couldn't use the function name* less(.,.) *to compare things other than* **STRING**s, *forcing us to change the code of the function* insert *itself.* Object-oriented languages offer us two mechanisms to handle this:

- Overloading—the possibility of using the same name for different functions, *provided the compiler has enough type information to disambiguate them*
- Genericity—the possibility of defining data structures that are parameterized by one or several member types or functions that can be specified on a per use basis

Overloading is the mechanism through which the compiler can distinguish between the two versions of less(.,.), based on the types of parameters. For example

```
(1)   VAR string1, string2 : STRING;
(2)      payment_1, payment_2 : Payment;
(3)   BEGIN
(4)      ...
(5)   IF less(string1, string2) THEN
(6)      WriteLn("String 1 is less than String 2");
(7)   END;
(8)   IF less(payment_1,payment_2) THEN
(9)      WriteLn("Payment 1 is anterior to Payment 2");
(10)  END;
(11)     ...
```

A compiler for a language that supports overloading is able to disambiguate the calls to less(.,.) in lines (5) and (8) according to the types of the parameters used in each case; there is no doubt which version is meant in each case. Generally speaking, two functions that have the same name must differ by the number of parameters, the types of the parameters,[4] or both. The reader should note that nearly all languages support overloading. In Pascal, when one writes

```
(1)   var
(2)      birthyear, thisyear, age: integer;
(3)      weightAtBirth,weightGained, newWeight: real;
(4)   begin
(5)      thisyear := birthyear + age;
(6)      newWeight := weightAtBirth + weightGained;
```

the "+" operator used in statement (5) is different from that used in statement (6). Anyone who has done assembly knows that the machine code for the addition of integers is different from that for floats. A Pascal compiler determines which version of "+" to use on the basis of the operands. What distinguishes object languages is *user-defined overloading*. The C++ language is the all-category champion in terms of overloading—although some would argue that Smalltalk is that champion.[5] In C++, one can redefine the *binary opeators* such as "+", "<", and "<<" (the left shift operator), the *assignment operator* ($a = b$), the *array reference operator* (the "[ ]" in $a[i]$) and the function call operator (the "( )" in $f(x)$). However, it doesn't support the overloading of the "new" operator. Smalltalk supports the overloading of all of the above, including the new operator, with the exception of the assignment operator. Smalltalk is

---

[4] This is not always easy. When the two functions have the same number of parameters, and the formal parameters of the two versions are in a pairwise subtype relationships, it may be difficult to disambiguate a call, especially when we throw in polymorphism, and a language's built-in *automatic* type conversion.

[5] Smalltalk's flexibility comes from its (nearly) fully reflexive architecture. More on this in the next chapter. C++'s flexibility comes from the genius and "recklessness" of its designer.

written mostly in Smalltalk, with the exception of some basic functions that are written in C/C++. As a general principle, anything that is written in Smalltalk is overloadable. Some things that are coded in C/C++ (but with a Smalltalk interface) are also overloadable. Ada enables developers to overload their own definitions. In addition, it supports the overloading of the binary operators, including "+", "<", and the like. Java is perhaps the language with the most restricted overloading.

Genericity applied to our case would mean that the type of values stored in the nodes would be a "dummy" parameter to be specified only when the list is to be used for something. In Ada, the definition of the sorted list *generic package* would look like this:

```
(1)  GENERIC
(2)    TYPE T IS PRIVATE;
(3)    WITH FUNCTION less(a,b:T) RETURN T;
(4)  PACKAGE SortedList IS
(5)    TYPE SortedList IS PRIVATE;
(6)
(7)    PROCEDURE init(sl: IN OUT SortedList);
(8)
(9)    --Insert value val into list sl and return pointer to
       --its node
(10)   PROCEDURE insert(s: IN OUT SortedList;val:T) RETURN
       SortedList
(11)   ...
(12)  END SortedList.
```

The implementation itself would look like this:

```
(1)  PACKAGE BODY SortedList IS
(2)  TYPE SortedList IS ACCESS Node;
(3)  TYPE Node IS RECORD
(4)    value: T;
(5)    next: SortedList;
(6)  END RECORD;
(7)  PROCEDURE init(sl: IN OUT SortedList) IS
(8)  BEGIN
(9)    sl := NULL;
(10) END init;
(11) PROCEDURE insert(sl: IN OUT SortedList,val:T) RETURN
     SortedList IS
(12)   nodePtr,cur,prev: SortedList;
(13) BEGIN
(14)   nodePtr := NEW Node;
(15)   nodePtr.value := val;
(16)   IF (sl == NULL) THEN
(17)     sl := nodePtr;
(18)     RETURN nodePtr;
```

```
(19)    END IF;
(20)    IF less(val,sl.value) THEN
(21)       nodePtr.next := sl;
(22)       sl := nodePtr;
(23)    ELSE
(24)       cur := sl; prev := NULL;
(25)       WHILE (cur /= NULL) LOOP
(26)         IF less(val,cur.value) THEN
(27)            nodePtr.next:= cur;
(28)            cur := NULL;
(29)         ELSE
(30)            prev := cur;
(31)            cur := cur.next;
(32)         END IF;
(33)       END LOOP;
(34)       prev.next:= nodePtr;
(35)    END IF;
(36)    RETURN nodePtr;
(37) END insert;
(38) END SortedList.
```

With this definition, we could use the sorted list as follows:

```
(1)  PACKAGE ListOfString IS NEW SortedList ( T =>
     Strings.String,
(2)        less => Strings.less);
(3)  PACKAGE ListOfPayments IS NEW SortedList ( T =>
     Banking. Payment,
(4)        less=> Banking.predates);
(5)  TYPE Account IS RECORD;
(6)     owner: Customer;
(7)     balance: float;
(8)     payments: ListOfPayments.SortedList;
(9)  END RECORD;
(10) ...
(11) myAccount : Account;
(12) onePayment : Payment;
(13) listOfStrings: ListOfStrings.SortedList;
(14) ...
(15) BEGIN
(16)   ...
(17)   insert(myAccount.payments, onePayment);
(18)   insert(listOfStrings,"hello");
```

Lines (1)–(2) and (3)–(4) show two *instantiations* of the generic package **Sort-edList**, into two packages **ListOfStrings** and **ListOfPayments**. The instantiation shows the values to which the type and function parameters of the generic package **SortedList**, are bound. Line (8) shows the declaration of field "payments" as the package **ListOfPayments** 's specific version of type **SortedList**. The same for line (13) shows the declaration of a list of strings. Line (17) shows a call to the "insert(.,.)" function with the parameter types (**ListOfPayments.SortedList, Payment**), and line (18) shows a call to the "insert(.,.)" function with parameter types (**ListOf-Strings.SortedList, String**). This is an instance of overloading.

Compilers handle instantiations differently, but the easiest (and most often used) way is to generate internally and compile different code versions of the package, one for each instantiated type parameter; in some sense, treating type parameters like code macros.

Genericity—also called *parametric polymorphism* by language theoreticians [Cardelli and Wegner 1985]—is supported by Ada (83 and 95), Eiffel (*deferred classes*), and C++ (*templates*). Other languages such as C, Modula, CLOS, Smalltalk, and Java do not support genericity, each for its own reasons. C does not support it probably simply because the language is too old, and because both its usefulness and the underlying theory were not known at the time of its creation. Modula, which stresses data abstraction and modular design, was meant as an introductory teaching language, and it was perhaps felt that genericity was not needed or was too difficult to teach. CLOS and Smalltalk are untyped, and there is no need for parametric polymorphism to be able to use the same code with different component types. Only Java has no excuse for *not having* genericity. It does get around it, awkwardly. We will talk about that later.

A C++ template for the SortedList type (class) might look like the following:

```
(1)  template⟨class T⟩
(2)  class SortedList {
(3)  private:
(4)    T value;
(5)    SortedList⟨T⟩* next;
(6)  public:
(7)    // constructor
(8)    SortedList();
(9)
(10)   // initialize
(11)   void init();
(12)   ...
(13)   SortedList⟨T⟩* insert(T val);
(14)   ...
(15) }
(16)
```

To use a C++ template, we enclose the parameter between ⟨⟩ as in:

```
(1)  SortedList⟨Payment⟩* listOfPayments, currentPayment;
(2)  Payment onePayment;
(3)  // initialization code
```

```
(4)  ...
(5)  currentPayment = listOfPayments→insert(onePayment);
(6)  ...
```

C programmers have managed to build generic functions and data structures thanks to a powerful but dangerous combination of "void" or "char pointers" (in effect, pointers to bytes, i.e., with no word alignment requirements), function parameters, and nearly unrestricted type casting. The following shows excerpts from the man page of the C function qsort(.,.,.,.):

```
(1)  SYNOPSIS
(2)     qsort(base, nel, width, compar)
(3)       char *base;
(4)       int (*compar)();
```

The input array is base (base is a pointer to the first element), nel is the number of elements, width is the size (in bytes) of elements in the array, and compar is a function used to compare two elements of the array and that returns an integer (int). The troubles with such a solution are numerous. For instance, such functions are hard to code (the first C libraries have been coded by gurus and "artists" like Brian Kernighan, James Gosling, etc.). Also, there is no static type checking to ensure that the function passed as an argument does indeed handle values of the type contained within the table. Finally, there is no easy way of finding the functions appropriate for a particular type, *because of lack of encapsulation!*

In some nonflattering way, Java handles genericity the way C used to emulate it; to make a Java container class (Vector, List, etc.) "generic," we use a component type that englobes all types—much like our C type char*; which is byte pointer—namely, **Object**, which is the necessary ancestor of Java classes. Then we have the potential of putting objects of different types within the same container (e.g., List). Further, if we want those objects to do anything useful, we have to use explicit casts, and run the risk of getting a runtime exception if the type of the stored objects is not the one expected. More on this later.

We now bid farewell to Modula and Ada'83, and move into mainstream object-oriented languages to talk about the remaining features.

10.2.4 Subtyping and Class Inheritance

10.2.4.1 Subtyping in Non-OOP Languages

The theory of data structures and abstract data types has its roots in algebra. Algebraic structures are defined in terms of a *domain* D or set of values, and a set of operations defined on the domain, namely, a pair $\langle D, Op \rangle$. Without going into the details of the formalism of algebraic specifications (and risk offending formalists), let us just say that there is an intuitive understanding of what *subtyping* means. We will come back to typing in later chapters, and go a little more in depth than here. For the purposes of this chapter, we will be content to highlight the salient features and stress the difference between subtyping and subclassing.

We say that a type $T = \langle D,Op \rangle$ is a subtype of type $T' = \langle D',Op' \rangle$, if

- $D \subseteq D'$, and
- For each operation op_i in Op', there is a corresponding operation op_j in Op that is identical to or "more specific"[6] than op_i.

Practically, this means that all the values of the subtype are also values of the supertype, and that all the operations of the supertype apply to values of the subtype.

Subtyping is supported in programming languages, essentially limited to subtypes of the type INTEGER, and usually, in the form of intervals of integers. In Modula-2, for example, one might write:

```
(1)   TYPE  DaysOfTheWeek = {Monday, Tuesday, Wednesday,
                             Thursday, Friday, Saturday,
(2)         Sunday};
(3)         WorkDays = DaysOfTheWeek[Monday..Friday];
(4)         HoursWorked = ARRAY[WorkDays] OF INTEGER
(5)         DaysOfTheMonth = INTEGER[1..31];
```

Lines (1) and (2) define an enumeration type, which, for all purposes, is just a set of successive integers that happen to have "named values." This point is made clearer with the definition of the WorkDays type, which is an interval of enumeration values, namely, **INTEGER**s! Line (5) shows a potential use for this type: a range of indices for an array.

Line (5) above defines the type DaysOfTheMonth as the set of **INTEGER**[7] values ranging from 1 to 31. Because DaysOfTheMonth is a subtype of **INTEGER**, all of the operations that apply to **INTEGER**s, apply to DaysOfTheMonth. For example

```
(1)   VAR
(2)       day1, day2, day3 : DaysOfTheMonth;
(3)       value1, value2, value3 : INTEGER;
(4)   BEGIN
(5)       value3 := value1 + value2;
(6)       day3 := day2 + day1;
(7)       day3 := value3;
(8)       day1 := 33;
(9)       day2 := day3*day1;
```

---

[6] We say that op_j is more specific/defined than op_i if and only if, for all, $x \in Dom(op_i)$ then $op_j(x) \subseteq op_i(x)$. This means, among other things, that $Dom(op_i) \subseteq Dom(op_j)$. If op_i and op_j are functions, that is, to each x, they associate a single value, which simply means that the functions return the same values over $Dom(op_i)$.

[7] In modula-2, we also have the type CARDINAL, which is made up of positive integers, hence the need to specify the base type when we define an interval of positive integers.

The use of the operator "+" on DaysOfTheMonth [line (6)] is legitimate because DaysOfTheMonth *are* **INTEGER**s. We have all grown accustomed to accept that a C function with signature:

```
(1)  int whatever(int arg1, int arg2)
```

will accept any pair of arguments that are *assignment compatible* with int, including subtypes of int[8]. Thus, in some sense, the type DaysOfTheMonth inherits the operations defined on **INTEGER**. A programmer might choose to define functions that take DaysOfTheMonth as arguments; those functions will *not* accept general integers as arguments. Note that from a memory representation point of view, programming languages usually don't bother optimizing the representation of subtypes of **INTEGER**s. The type DaysOfTheMonth, with 31 values, needs no more than a byte—5 bits, to be exact; nobody bothers with the trouble anymore. However, compilers would flag statements (7) and (8) as typing errors, and the runtime system may flag the statement (9) with an error if at that moment the product day3*day1 happens to go out of bounds.

To summarize, programming languages support subtyping for **INTEGER**s and integer-mappable types (enumerations, the **CHARACTER** type). Subtypes inherit the operations of the supertype, in addition to whichever operations were defined specifically for the subtype. Typically, subtypes have the same internal memory representation as the base types, which reduces their utility to the—all too-important, if not overriding—goals of program readability and correctness.

In addition to supporting subtypes on **INTEGER**s and other integer-mappable types, non-object-oriented languages may support type *renaming*. In this case, the set of values for a type and its "supertype" are identical. In most

```
DEFINITION MODULE Queue;
TYPE Queue;
PROCEDURE init(VAR q: Queue);
(* Enqueue *)
PROCEDURE enqueue(VAR q:Queue;
          val : INTEGER):Queue;
...
PROCEDURE dequeue(VAR q: Queue):
                        INTEGER;
END Queue.
```

```
IMPLEMENTATION MODULE Queue;
FROM List IMPORT List,
addFirst(),...;

TYPE Queue = List;
...
PROCEDURE enqueue(VAR
q:Queue;val: int):Queue
BEGIN
  RETURN addLast(q,val);
END enqueue;
PROCEDURE dequeue(VAR q:
Queue):INTEGER
BEGIN
  RETURNremoveFirst(q);
END;
END Queue.
```

[8] Assignment compatibility usually means subtyping (the right handside is a subtype of the left handside), but can be muddied with typecasting followed by regular assignment (e.g., assigning an int to a float in C), or, polymorphism as will be explained later.

cases, renaming is used for readability and for managing visibility. For example, in Modula-2 or Ada, one might define the type **Queue** as a private type (i.e. whose implementation is not visible), and offer only methods to "enqueue" and "dequeue," which would call the appropriate methods on **List**. In this example, we can call on the functionality of **List** within the implementation of **Queue**, but not make that visible outside.[9] In this case, we can't say that **Queue** is a subtype of **List** (or at least, we can't say that publicly), but **Queue** reuses the implementation of **List**, and may offer additional functions not available in **List**.

10.2.4.2 Subclassing and Subtyping in OOP Languages

Let us go back to our banking example, and assume that our SLA decides to offer *credit margin* accounts. A credit margin is halfway between a credit card and a checking account. It is like a credit card in the sense that its normal state is to be in the read. The interest rate is higher than that in typical savings accounts. And usually, customers have to pay at least the interest on the balance each month. However, just like a checking account, one can withdraw cash or make checks or payments against it. We show below the C++ definition of **Account** next to that for **CreditMargin**.

```
class Account {                        class CreditMargin {
  Customer _owner;                       Customer _owner;
  float _balance;                        float _balance;
  SortedList<Payment>*                   SortedList<Payment> _payments;
_payments;                               float _minBalance;
public:                                public:
  Account():_owner(null),                CreditMargin()
  _balance(0.0){                           :_owner(null),_balance(0.0),
    _payments = new                        _minBalance(0.0)  {
      SortedList<Payment>();               _payments = new
  }                                          SortedList<Payment>();
  ...                                    }
  void setBalance(float b) {             ...
    _balance = b;                        void setBalance(float b) {
  }                                        _balance = b;
  void addPayment(Payment pt){           }
    _payments->add(pt);                  void addPayment(Payment pt){
  }                                        _payments->add(pt);
  ...                                    }
}                                        ...
                                       }
```

The reader will note that **CreditMargin** has the same attributes as **Account**, except for an additional attribute _minBalance. Somewhat

---

[9] C++ aficionados are probably on the edge of their seats: yes, that is pretty much what **private** subclassing in C++ does.

expectedly, the functions that access the common attributes (setBalance(.), addPayment(.), etc.) are the same for both classes. Why, one would ask, can't we take advantage of the similarity to avoid redundancy between the two classes, and to create a single code base to contain the common aspects between the two classes? Subclassing is the answer. We show below the new definition of the **CreditMargin** class in C++ style, and in Java style.

```
class CreditMargin: public          class CreditMargin extends
Account {                            Account {
  float _minBalance;                   private float _minBalance;
public:                                public CreditMargin(){
  CreditMargin()                         super();
    :Account(),                          _minBalance = 0.0;}
    _minBalance(0.0)  {  }             ...
  ...                                }
}
```

The first line shows the declaration of **CreditMargin** as a subclass of **Account**. In C++, we have the option of declaring this relationship in the open (**public**), only to family and friends (**protected**, which makes it known to subclasses and their friends), or private (**private**) to the class and its friends. In the example of **List**s versus **Queue**s above, one might want to declare a **Queue** as a *private* subclass of **List** so that **Queue** may inherit functionalities of **List** to implement its own functionalities, but so that "nobody else" would know about it, and abuse it (e.g., removing elements from the tail of the **Queue**). Note that Java does not provide such a finely tuned control over the visibility of inheritance, in part because it has different constructs for implementation inheritance (the one shown above) and subtyping (inheritance of *interfaces*; more on this later).

When we declare a class to be a subclass of another, we only specify the things that distinguish the subclass from the superclass. As a first approximation—notwithstanding the visibility issues of the previous paragraph—all the things defined in the superclass are inherited or applicable to the subclass. A subclass may, in addition, define *new attributes* and *functions*; in our example, **CreditMargin** introduces the attribute _minBalance and the corresponding access functions to access it. Finally, a subclass may *override* inherited functions. In our example, we might consider that the function addPayment() will first check whether the credit margin (_minBalance) wouldn't be exceeded if the payment goes through.

```
(1)  class CreditMargin extends Account {
(2)    private float _minBalance;
(3)    public CreditMargin(){
(4)      super();
```

```
(5)        _minBalance = 0.0;}
(6)     ...
(7)     public void addPayment(Payment pt)throws
        NotEnoughFunds {
(8)       if (_balance - pt.getAmount() < _minBalance) {
(9)         throw new NotEnoughFunds(this,pt);
(10)      }
(11)      super.addPayment(pt);
(12)    }
(13)    ...
(14)  }
```

The new and more realistic[10] version of addPayment() checks first whether there is enough money, before recording the payment. Since we are inheriting a method that does the recording (**Account**'s version of addPayment()), we can invoke it from within the redefined method using the keyword **super** to distinguish the call to the inherited version from that of the locally available version. In essence, the class **CreditMargin** added an input validation step to the inherited version of addPayment().

In C++, we can refer to a method at any level in the inheritance hierarchy. The same method would be written as

```
(1)     public void addPayment(Payment pt)raises
        NotEnoughFunds {
(2)       if (_balance - pt.getAmount() < _minBalance) {
(3)         raise new NotEnoughFunds(this,pt);
(4)      }
(5)      Account::addPayment(pt);
(6)    }
```

The notation Account::addPayment in line (5) specifies the version of addPayment by referring explicitly to its implementing class. This is a mixed blessing. On the positive side, it allows developers a finer-grained control over the method resolution. On the negative side, it ties the code into a particular *implementation hierarchy: this code will work only if there is a superclass of* **CreditMargin** *that is called* **Account** *and that has access to a method called* addPayment. Thus, when evolving and maintaining such code, one must be concerned with preserving not only the functionality of the software, which should be the overriding—if not sole—criterion but also the idiosyncracies of its implementation.

10.2.4.3 Subclassing–Subtyping Distinction
The issue of distinguishing between subtyping and subclassing should be a fairly easy one, if it weren't for the fact that programming languages don't

---

[10] In Java, exceptions are user-defined classes and objects. Java's redefinition rules prescribe that the parent version of addPayment *also* raise the exception NotEnoughFunds, or some superclass thereof.

always have the constructs to distinguish between them, or the flexibility to support full-fledged subtyping. First, at a fairly intuitive level, we say that A is a subtype of B if the following is true:

- All the elements (instances) of A are also elements of B.
- A program that functioned in some way with instances of B will continue to function in a similar way if we replace the elements of B by elements of A.

We may refer to the second principle as that of *behavioral substitutability* or *behavioral conformance*. Subclassing was defined *operationally* above in terms of what it allows and what it does. We start by taking two examples that illustrate the extreme cases. The first case, shown in both C++ and Smalltalk, is an example of subclassing that does not entail subtyping. The base class **List** supports methods for adding and removing elements from either end of the list. The subclass **Queue** permits to add elements in one end, and remove them from the other. Theoretically, a **List** and a **Queue** do not support the same set of operations, although a **Queue** may be implemented using a **List**. In C++, to accommodate *implementation reuse* and "behavioral nonsubstitutability," we use the **private** subclass mechanism whereby the subclass relationship between **List** and **Queue** is visible only to **Queue**, which may use the attributes and methods from **List** to implement its own behavior. We can see how the method enQueue refers to the inherited method insertLast. However, we cannot invoke insertLast directly on a **Queue**. The following code excerpts illustrate this:

```
(1)  List* aList = new List();
(2)  Queue* aQueue = new Queue();
(3)  aList->insertLast("hello");       // legal
(4)  aQueue->enQueue("Bonjour");       // legal
(5)  aQueue->insertLast("Whatever");   // ILLEGAL
(6)  aQueue->removeFirst();            // ILLEGAL
```

```
class List {                      Object subClass: #List
 void* _value;                      instanceVariableNames: 'value
 List* _next;                     next'
public:                             classVarNames: ''
 // constructors                    ...
 List();                          !Class methods for: 'instance
 List(void* val);                creation'
                                  !!
 //inserting and removing        new: val
 //elements                        "create new instance & assign
 List* insertFirst(void*         val"
 val);                             | newInst |
 void* removeFirst();              newInst := self new.
```

```
List* insertLast(void*
val);
void* removeLast();
};
// class Queue inherits
//from List
class Queue: private List {
public:
  // constructors
  ...
  // inserting/removing
  //elements
  Queue* enQueue(void* val){
    return insertLast(val);
  }
  void* deQueue(){
    return removeLast();
  }
}
```

```
newInst setValue: val.
∧newInst.!
...
!Instance methods for:'inserting
...'!
!
insertFirst: val
"create new node with val at
head"
  ...!
removeFirst
  ...!
"------------------"
List subclass: #Queue
  instanceVariableNames: ''
  ...
!Instance methods for: 'inserting
...'!
!
enqueue: val
  "add element to end of Queue"
  ∧super insertLast: val.!!
dequeue
  "remove element from head
                   of Queue"
  ∧super removeFirst.!!
insertLast: val
  "should not be called"
  self shouldNotImplement.!!
removeFirst
  "should not be called"
  self shouldNotImplement.
```

For the case of Smalltalk, there is no such thing as *private subclassing*, and if we declare a class as a subclass of another, "everybody can see it." Thus, unless we do something about it, all of the following are legal:

```
(1)  | aList aQueue |
(2)  aList := List new.
(3)  aQueue := Queue new.
(4)  aList insertLast: 'hello'.       "legal"
(5)  aQueue enQueue: 'Bonjour'.       "legal"
(6)  aQueue insertLast: 'Whatever'.   "legal"
(7)  aQueue removeFirst.              "legal"
```

Accordingly, in order to prevent programmers from calling **List** methods on **Queue**s, but at the same time, allow **Queue** methods to use **List** methods, we do the following:

- Redefine **List**'s methods in such a way that they raise an exception (**self** shouldNotImplement), and
- Write **Queue**'s methods in such a way that they use **List**'s versions of the same methods—we do that by invoking these methods using the **super** keyword.

This is often referred to as *method cancellation* in Smalltalk, and is fairly common in the Smalltalk library. This example illustrates a case where we have *subclassing* but where the relationship of the two classes is not one of subtyping. As we saw from the C++ code excerpts, we cannot mistake a **Queue** for **List**. This has been thoroughly criticized in the literature as poor class hierarchy design [Cook 1992, Godin and Mili 1993] that makes class use or reuse, and maintenance difficult.

Intuitively, typing concerns the *public* or *external* behavior of objects. Types are then defined in terms of a set of method signatures and a set of behavioral axioms that describe *what* methods are supposed to do, and not *how* they do it. When we talk about types, we seldom bother with the distinction between attributes and methods; we equate each attribute with a pair of read/write methods, and can thus consider everything as methods. Lest we raise the hair of theorists, let us represent a type by a pair $T = \langle S, A \rangle$, where S is a set of method signatures (operations) and A a set of behavioral axioms (equations involving compositions of methods). We say that a type $T_1 = \langle S_1, A_1 \rangle$ is a subtype of $T_2 = \langle S_2, A_2 \rangle$ iff

- $S_2 \leq S_1$, that is, T_1 has all the operations of T_2 and possibly more.
- $A_1(S_2) \Rightarrow A_2(S_2)$, that is, if a common operation satisfies the behavioral requirements and axioms of type T_1, then it necessarily satisfies the behavioral requirements of T_2.

The first condition ensures that the types "look the same"; the second, that they "behave the same." In principle, we don't require that the operations of the supertype be found *as is* in the subtype: we require that they have a *type conformant*[11] equivalent in the subtype [Meyer, 1988]. In practice, because of the difficulty of distinguishing between type conformant redefinitions and overloaded functions, programming languages will consider any change in signature from a class down to its subclasses as overloading.

Let us now consider an example of subtyping but where there is no subclassing relationship. Consider the example of a **Set** and a **Bag**. A set is an unordered collection of objects that allows the addition and removal of elements, and various tests for membership and containment. A bag is also an unordered collection of objects that allows the addition and removal of elements, and tests for membership and containment. However, a bag can store

---

[11] Let f be a method defined on T_2 that takes input I_2 and produces output O_2. If we redefine f in T_1 to take input I_1 and produces output O_1, then we must have $I_1 \supseteq I_2$, and $O_1 \subseteq O_2$.

several occurrences of the same object (allows "duplicates"). We show below the interfaces for the two structures.

```
interface Set {                    interface Bag {
  //inserting and removing elts      //inserting and removing
  Set insertElement(Object ele);     //elements
  Object removeElement (Object       Set insertElement(Object ele);
  ele);                              Object removeElement(Object
                                     ele);

  // testing for membership/
  // containment                     // testing for membership/
  boolean hasElement(Object          // containment
  ele);                              boolean hasElement(Object ele);
  boolean contains(Set aSet);
  boolean intersects(Set aSet);      // testing for size
                                     boolean empty();
  // testing for size                int cardinality();
  boolean empty();
  int cardinality();               }
}                                  // A Java definition of type Bag
// A Java definition of type
//Set
```

We showed in *italics* the operations that are defined on the type **Set** but not on the type **Bag**. On the basis of the signatures alone, we might say that **Set** is a subtype of **Bag**. We also have to make sure that the operations of **Set** are consistent with those of **Bag**. Mathematically speaking, a **Set** is a special case of a **Bag** (or multiset). The difference may be described in terms of the number of occurrences of any given element in a **Set** (0 or 1) versus in a **Bag** (any positive integer). Let $count(x,X)$ be the number of occurrences of element x in X. We can define the semantics of the various operations in terms of $count(x,X)$. For example, the effect of $insert(x)$ on sets may be expressed as follows:

$$S.insert(x) \; :- $$
$$count(x,S') = min(count(x,S) + 1,1) = 1$$

where S stands for the receiver (set S) *after* the operation has completed. By contrast, the effect of $insert(x)$ on **Bag** may be expressed as follows:

$$S.insert(x) \; :- $$
$$count(x,S') = count(x,S) + 1$$

The effects of the operation $remove(x)$ may be defined in a similar fashion. On sets

$$S.remove(x) \; :- $$
$$count(x,S') = max(count(x,S)-1,0) = 0$$

and for bags

```
        S.remove(x)  :-
                count(x,S') = max (count(x,S) -1,0)
```

and so forth. We have thus established that **Set** is a subtype of **Bag**:[12]

```java
class Bag {                              class Set extends Bag {
  private Hashtable table;                 //constructor
  //constructor                            Set(){
  Bag(){table= new Hashtable();}             super();
                                           }
  Bag insertElement (Object el){
    Integer cnt =                          Object removeElement(Object
      (Integer)table.get(el);              el){
    int num = 1;                             if hasElement(el){
    if (cnt! = null)                           table.remove(el);
      num = cnt.intValue()+1;                  return el;
    table.put(ele,new Integer(num));         }
  }                                          return null;
  Object removeElement(Object ele)         }
{
    Integer cnt =                          // testing for membership/
      (Integer)table.get(ele);             // containment
    int num = -1;                          boolean contains(Set s) {
    if (cnt != null){                        ...
      num = cnt.intValue()-1;              }
      if (num > 0)                         ...
        table.put(ele,new Integer
          (num));                        }
      else
        table.remove(ele);
      return ele;
    }
    return null;
  }
  ...
}
```

Implementationwise, it is not clear what the relationship between a class implementing **Bag** and a class implementing **Set** should be. We will show one implementation of **Bag** and two alternative implementations of **Set**. In the first, **Set** will be implemented as a subclass of **Bag**. In the second, there is no relation between the two implementations because we choose an implementation of **Set** that minimizes memory usage, at the expense of computing time.

---

[12] The subtype relationship depends, in part, on what operations we choose to attach to both types. This choice depends, in part, on *intrinsic* and *fundamental* properties that objects satisfy, as well as on patterns of usage of the objects. For example, we could very well have included the operation count(**Object** ele), which makes sense for a **Bag** but not for a **Set**. Had we done that, we would have broken then subtyping relationship. Mili [1996a] proposed a way of identifying a canonical set of behaviors that a type or class must support.

In the first case, shown above, we inherit all of the methods of **Bag** in **Set** as is, with the exception of the removeElement(**Object** ele) operation, which is written to remove an element from the table, instead of decrementing the number of its occurrences. By not redefining the inherited version of insertElement(**Object**), we let successive calls to the method with the same element increment the counter for that element. That is okay, considering the fact that **Set** does not need to know or care about that counter.

In the second case, we assume that **Bag** is as defined above, and that we already have a class **SortedList** that inserts elements (instances of **Object**) based on the integer value returned by the function hashCode()—in Java, **Object** is the mother of all classes, and hashCode() is defined in **Object**.

```
(1)   class Set {
(2)     private SortedList container;
(3)     public Set() {
(4)       container = new SortedList();
(5)     }
(6)
(7)     public Set insertElement(Object element) {
(8)       container.insert(element);
(9)     }
(10)
(11)    public Object removeElement(Object element) {
(12)      return container.removeElement(element);
(13)    }
(14)
(15)    public boolean hasElement(Object ele){
(16)      return (container.search(ele) != null);
(17)    }
(18)
(19)    public boolean contains(Set another) {
(20)      Enumeration elements = another.getElements();
(21)      while (elements.hasMoreElements()) {
(22)        Object next = elements.next();
(23)        if (! hasElement(next)) return false;
(24)      }
          return true;
(25)    }
(26)
(27)    private Enumeration getElements() {
(28)      ...
(29)    }
(30)    ...
(31) }
```

In this case, **Set** wraps the functionality of **SortedList**, and adds a few set-specific functions, including some utility functions that are not part of the public interface (e.g., the function getElements()).

Through the last two examples, we wanted to illustrate the difference between subtyping and subclassing. Subtyping is a relation between specifications, whereas subclassing is a relation between implementations. In general, it is reasonable to assume that similar specifications would lead to similar implementations, and hence, expect subclassing to follow from subtyping. In practice, *differences in non-functional requirements may compel us to choose unrelated implementations for two related types*. What cannot be tolerated are cases where *subclassing is used between implementations of unrelated types*.

10.2.5 Method Resolution, Late Binding, and Polymorphism

Let us go back to our banking example, and consider the **Account** and **CreditMargin** classes again. Figure 10.8 shows the class hierarchy, and an object of class **CreditMargin**. We showed in blue the attributes and methods of **Account**, all of which are inherited by **CreditMargin**, with the exception of setBalance() which has been redefined (shown in bold in **CreditMargin**). We showed in italics the new attributes and methods of **CreditMargin**. Now consider the following code excerpts:

```
(1)  CreditMargin aCM = new CreditMargin ();
(2)  aCM.setOwner('Martin');
(3)  aCM.setMinBalance(-5000.0);
(4)  aCM.setBalance(-1432.5);
```

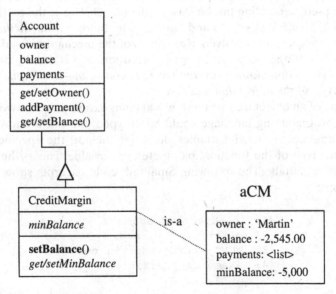

FIGURE 10.8 Method resolution scenarios.

Line (2) shows a call to setOwner() on an instance of **CreditMargin**. Because of overloading, there may be several methods with the same name. We have to find the most appropriate version for this call—this is called *method resolution*. The default method resolution mechanism starts by looking at the class of the receiver (aCM)—in this case, **CreditMargin**—to see if that class offers the method. If it doesn't, then we climb up the inheritance hierarchy until we find a class that does offer that method, and then use its version. In this case, **CreditMargin** has no method setOwner(), but its superclass **Account** does. Line (3) shows a call to a method that is only defined in **CreditMargin**, and that version will be used. Line (4) shows a call to setBalance(), which has been defined in **Account** and redefined in **CreditMargin**. Because the receiver is a **CreditMargin**, it is the version of **CreditMargin** that will be executed.

Now, we address the related questions of *who* is responsible for method resolution and *when* it takes place. The answer depends on the programming language, and for some languages, it may depend on which options or features we choose to use. Generally speaking, method resolution may take place during compilation—referred to as *early binding* or *static method resolution*. In this case, the *compiler*, having in its various symbol tables the definitions of the various classes, their relationships, and the types of the various variables, will perform the inferences we showed above, and identify the appropriate versions of the methods to use for each call. This is the default method resolution mechanism in C++, in Ada'95, and for some methods in Java.[13]

Method resolution can also be done during runtime, by the runtime environment or the *virtual machine*. In this case, a "method dispatcher" will determine dynamically, for each method call, which version of a particular method should be used, depending on the class of the object. This is the method used in Smalltalk, Java, Eiffel, CLOS, and some C++ methods (*virtual methods*) with a variety of mechanisms involved. Regardless of the mechanism used, runtime method resolution slows down program execution, and is usually done for a reason: *When we don't know—or don't want to constrain—at compilation time, the exact type of the object that will execute.*

The type of an object may be unknown at compilation time for two reasons. First, the programming language could be untyped; the declaration of functions, parameters, or local variables does not include the specification of the (return) *type* of the function, parameter, or variable. This is the case for CLOS and Smalltalk. The following Smalltalk code excerpts show untyped declarations:

```
(1)    | aList aCM aName |
(2)    aList := List new.
(3)    aCM := CreditMargin new.
(4)    aName := 'Martin'.
```

---

[13] In Java *final* methods.

```
(5)   anElement setOwner:aName.
(6)   aList insertFirst: aCM.
(7)   aName := aList.
```

Line (1) shows the declarations of the variables used in this code. Variable declarations consist of enclosing the *names* of these variables between two |; we don't say what kind or type of object those variables will hold. If we analyse the code, we will realize that aList will hold an object of class **List**, but that requires knowing that (1) **List** is the name of a class and (2) the method **new** as available to **List** (i.e., defined in **List** or inherited) returns an instance of **List**. The same kind of inference can be made in line (3). In line (4), because we assign a literal to aName, we know that it has the type of that literal, namely, a **String**. From the **List–Queue** example shown earlier, we reproduce the definition of the insertFirst: method.

```
(1)   insertFirst: val
(2)     "create new node with val at head"
(3)     ...!
```

The signature of the method is seen in line (1). The important thing here is what we *do not* see—we don't see a type for the parameter val, and we don't see a return type. We can guess what the return type of insertFirst: is by looking at the type(s) of the objects returned by the function. We can guess the type of the argument by looking at the methods called on that variable within the body of insertFirst:. For example, if we see that length and subString: are called on val, we might be able to say with certainty that val is a **String**—provided the program is correct, of course—because only the class **String** has available to it those two methods, directly or through inheritance. We can also guess what the type of val is, by looking at the pieces of code that call the method insertFirst: and see what gets passed as argument. And so on and so forth. What this shows is that

- We can infer the types of the objects without resorting to declarations.
- Type inference consists of resolving a network of type constraints.

We should add that for correct programs, the network of typing constraints will have solutions. However, there may not be a single solution.[14]

The result of all of this is that Smalltalk compilers don't bother with type validation, and hence method resolution is done at runtime. To reduce the runtime overhead, Smalltalk's virtual machines will "cache" associations between methods and classes in the form of dispatch tables that are updated

---

[14] SML, a functional language, does not require type declarations, unless the type system has more than one solution, in which case the developer has to supply types to reduce the solution space.

only when methods or classes are added or removed. CLOS uses a similar approach.

The second reason why we wouldn't know or want to constrain the type of an object at compilation time is illustrated through the following example. Let us revisit our batch program that handles payments, and recast it in object-oriented terms (see Fig. 10.9). We assume the implementation language to be C++. We assume here that customers can make their payments either from a regular checking account (**Account**) or from a credit margin account (**CreditMargin**). The program is able to tell which it is according to the account number:

In this case, we assume that each type of account will handle payments differently—that is, will have a different implementation for registerPayment (. . .). However, we wouldn't know before reading the account number

```
(1)   #include ⟨account.h⟩
(2)   #include ⟨cmargin.h⟩
(3)   #include ⟨payment.h⟩
(4)   ...
(5)   void main(int args, char** argv) {
(6)     PaymentInputStream f = ....;
(7)     CString payerAccountNum;
(8)     Account anAccount;
(9)     CreditMargin cm;
(10)    ...
(11)    while (!f.eof()) {
(12)      f >> payerAccountNum;
(13)      if (payerAccountNum.prefix(2).eqstr("CM")) {
(14)        cm = f.getCreditMarginWithNum(payerAccountNum);
(15)        while (f.hasOneMorePayment()){
(16)          currentPmnt = f.readPayment();
(17)          cm.registerPayment(currentPmnt);
(18)        }
(19)      else {
(20)        anAccount = f.getAccountWithNum(payerAccountNum);
(21)        while (f.hasOneMorePayment()){
(22)          currentPmnt = f.readPayment();
(23)          anAccount.registerPayment(currentPmnt);
(24)        }
(25)      }
(26)    ...
(27)  }
```

FIGURE 10.9 An (awkward) object-oriented version of the program that handles payments.

from which kind of account the payment is being made. We assume that the input is read from an instance *f* of the class **PaymentInputStream** that is a subclass of **istream** [see line (6)] that has specific methods for reading account and payment information from an input stream. To accommodate both **Account**s and **CreditMargin**s, we would need two methods that have the following signatures:

```
CreditMargin PaymentInputStream::getCreditMarginWithNum
  (CString number)
Account PaymentInputStream::getAccountWithNum(CString number)
```

which would return instances of the proper classes [lines (14) and (20)], depending on the account number [line (13)].

If we had several kinds of accounts—such as a complex subtree under **Account**, then we would need as many branches in the code, one per kind of **Account**. Thank god there is a better way: *polymorphism*. Polymorphism means that we can assign a variable of type T_1 to a variable of type T_2:

```
T₁ v₁;
T₂ v₂;
v₂ = v₁;    // polymorphic assignment
```

Different languages allow more or less permissive relationships between T_1 and T_2. In Smalltalk and CLOS, there need not be any relationship between T_1 and T_2, because the compiler does not know the types of the variables, anyway! In Eiffel, C++ and Java, T_1 *has to be a subtype (subclass) of* T_2. With this in mind, we can rewrite our program as shown in Figure 10.10.

Here, the variable anAccount of type **Account** may stand for both *instances of* **Account** as well as *instances of* **CreditMargin**. Hence, instead of having two methods with signatures:

```
CreditMargin PaymentInputStream::getCreditMarginWithNum
  (CString number)
Account PaymentInputStream::getAccountWithNum(CString number)
```

a single method is needed with the second signature above, which will return an instance of the proper type, based on the account prefix number or such, and that method is called in line (12). In line (15), depending on the actual (runtime) type of anAccount, the proper version of registerPayment is or should be called. For example, if getAccountWithNum(...) returned a **CreditMargin**, then we would make sure that it is the version of **Credit-Margin** that is called in line (15).

The question is how we can do that. This depends on the method resolution time (and the language). If the language does method resolution at

```
(1)   #include ⟨account.h⟩
(2)   #include ⟨cmargin.h⟩
(3)   #include ⟨payment.h⟩
(4)   ...
(5)   void main(int args, char** argv) {
(6)     PaymentInputStream f = ....;
(7)     CString payerAccountNum;
(8)     Account anAccount;
(9)     ...
(10)    while (!f.eof()) {
(11)      f >> payerAccountNum;
(12)      anAccount = f.getAccountWithNum(payerAccountNum);
(13)      while (f.hasOneMorePayment()){
(14)        currentPmnt = f.readPayment();
(15)        anAccount.registerPayment(currentPmnt);
(16)      }
(17)    }
(18)  ...
(19)  }
```

FIGURE 10.10 A much better version of the program that handles payments.

runtime, the runtime environment will check during runtime the *actual* type of the object referenced by anAccount—called *dynamic type*. This is the method used in Smalltalk, CLOS, Java, and Eiffel. In C++, the *default* method resolution time is compile time. This means that in line (15) above, it is **Account**'s version of registerPayment that will be called on anAccount, no matter what getAccountWithNum(...) returned. If we want C++ to perform runtime method resolution (*dynamic binding*), then we have to declare that particular method as *virtual*.[15]

The combination of polymorphism and dynamic binding is a powerful technique for writing "client code" that is relatively independent of the "server code" and its evolution. Through polymorphic assignments, new and more specialized versions of servers may be provided without invalidating the old ones, and without requiring any change in the client code. This, rather than inheritance per se, is, in our opinion, the most powerful feature of object-oriented programming languages because of the flexibility it affords in the "client—server relationship" between system components; it is a key technique in the development of reusable component frameworks.

---

[15] In C++, objects have a *virtual function table*, which is a table indexed by method signatures that point to the compiled versions of those *virtual functions*. By declaring a method as virtual, we are telling the compiler's code generator to look up the method in the virtual function table of the object during runtime, instead of copying in the address of a specific method (that of the class of declaration), as is done with non-virtual functions.

10.3   THE LANGUAGE WARS

"We called it Smalltalk so that nobody would expect much from it"—ALAN KAY
"C++ is an object-oriented assembly language"—
OVERHEARD BY PANELISTS AT OOPSLA
"Eiffel is a very good language for implementing provably correct stacks"—
PROBABLY A C++ PROGRAMMER
"Ada is a language that was designed by a committee"—ANONYMOUS QUOTE
"Java is a crippled Smalltalk for C++ programmers"—SMALLTALK PROGRAMMERS

These are some of the comments about some of the better known OOP languages, and not the worst at that—actually it is much worse to not be made fun of. It is fairly reasonable to assume that all the object languages have been developed by fairly intelligent people working with a constantly evolving theory and an evolving set of practical concerns and opportunities, under some constraints, and we can safely say that all these people did a fairly good job at that.

There are different ways to compare languages. In the preceding sections, we got a glimpse of the major object-oriented languages through an implicit feature-by-feature comparison. The set of features supported by a particular language combine to offer a particular style of programming that may be suited for different kinds of applications, and different deployment environments, and different development competencies, with concerns ranging from ease of learning to the ease with which designs can be translated into programs, to concerns for portability and interoperability. It is fair to say that our way of looking at languages has undergone two major shifts in focus from the early days of structured programming. While the Algol generation was more concerned with structure for programming in the small (structured programming, program verification, etc.)—we refer to these as the *microstructures of the language*—the subsequent generation was more concerned with modular designs where modules are the size of functional or infrastructure subsystems; we refer to these as the *macrostructures of the language*. Of issue were things such as scalability, module interconnection constructs, and support for team development. With recent advances in software packaging and runtime architectures, allowing components written in different languages and running on different machines to run as if they were written *in the same language*, and *on the same machine*, the focus shifted back to *micro* or *local* properties of languages.

With that in mind, we present a set of dimensions along which programming languages may be compared. We may divide those dimensions along the steps of the lifecycle: (1) accessibility, (2) use, (3) quality control, and (4) deployment. Accessibility has to do with both the material accessibility of the language and the corresponding development tools, and its accessibility in terms of ease of learning, purity of paradigm—or lack thereof, depending on what is sought—consistency of syntax and style, and so on. It is fairly easy to agree on the material accessibility of a language (although zealots of all lan-

guage stripes will argue with facts and numbers), but the "intellectual accessibility" of a language is harder to agree on. For example, most would agree
that Smalltalk has the simplest and most consistent syntax of the major languages (C++, Smalltalk, Eiffel, Java, CLOS)—except perhaps the Eiffel
people—but there is little agreement as to which language is easiest to learn.
The Java people would argue that the evolutionary nature of Java from C/C++,
and more generally speaking, the structured programming languages, would
make it easier to learn than Smalltalk, say. The Smalltalk people would counter
that the well-known Smalltalk learning curve is due to a *true* paradigm shift,
and to the fact that one learns the Smalltalk library in the process of learning
the language,[16] with the byproduct that advanced Smalltalk programmers tend
to be extremely efficient.

The "use" dimension of a language is more concerned with (1) its expressiveness, (2) the ease with which analysis and design models may be translated
into code, and (3) the extent to which its packaging and modularization
mechanisms support reuse and facilitate maintenance. Expressiveness may be
likened to the set of features of the language. Obviously, different combinations of features will yield the same expressive power, making even a technical comparison sometimes a bit difficult. In terms of distinct constructs, it is
fair to say that Smalltalk may be the most feature-poor language, with no
support for templates or generic classes, abstract classes, multiple inheritance,
or multiprocessing (threading, synchronization, etc.). However, the combination of its "typelessness," its late binding, and its support for metaclasses, more
than make up for the lack of those constructs in terms of power—enough to
make us forgive Smalltalk's unsafety. Java suffers more seriously from the lack
of genericity because of its strong typing, but does very well in the multiple
inheritance arena with its separation between interfaces (types) and classes
(implementation). C++ and Eiffel compete for first place with richness of features; C++, with private versus protected versus public subclassing, virtual
versus regular methods and subclassing, friends, function templates, and a
much wider range of overloadable operations; and Eiffel, with pre- and postconditions, assertions, renaming, and export interfaces. C++ is loaded with features aimed at optimizing code volume and efficiency, whereas Eiffel is more
geared toward code correctness and safety.

The ease with which analysis and design models may be translated into code
depends in part on the richness of the features of the language but also on its
level of abstraction. For example, multiple specialization is a legitimate occurrence in analysis models—although perhaps not as frequently legitimate as
one may be led to believe; a language that does not support multiple inheritance will require contortions and lead to less than optimal code sharing and
potential semantic problems.[17] Most Smalltalk programmers will boast an iter-

---

[16] In Smalltalk, iteration constructs are (overridable) operations on **Collections**. Hence, one
cannot learn iteration without learning about **Collections**.
[17] An example is the famous broken delegation problem. More on this in later chapters.

ative analysis, design, and code cycle starting in the code browser![18] This is due in part to the richness of the library, allowing the developer to focus on the higher-level constructs of the problem domain. It is also due to the "typeless-ness" of the language and its late binding, which allows developers to write, compile, and test incomplete programs, enabling them to focus, first, on the critical parts of an application, and to iteratively branch outward, completing the skeletons of programs, much like the spiral model. The Eiffel camp might see it differently.

In terms of packaging for reuse and maintenance, we have to consider abstraction and modularization mechanisms. The distinction between types and classes is an important abstraction mechanism facilitating both reuse and maintenance. Java's explicit constructs give it an edge. To some extent, C++'s subclassing qualifiers (private, protected, vs. public) enable us to do the same thing, although they do not prevent us from abusively and ambiguously mixing the two—a common reproach leveled at C++; it does not have enough safeguards. Genericity is another powerful abstraction mechanism in support for reuse and maintenance. Packaging-wise, we have to distinguish between physical packaging and logical packaging. Physical packaging is concerned with the physical level modularization or large programs into files, directories, and the like. Logical packaging is concerned with modularization constructs that are part of the language or the runtime environment. Physical packaging often revolves around the notion of a file, and the various languages offer about the same possibilities. With regard to the logical modularization, we have to consider the richness of the modular structure, and the expressiveness of the intermodule interfaces. C++ offers the notion of namespace, which is a compile time notion useful for resolving naming conflicts. Modula offers a recursive module structure. Ada's packages are more limited. In terms of spec-ifying interfaces, Ada and Modula offer equivalent filtering (import/export) facilities. Eiffel offers a powerful perclass filtering mechanism. Smalltalk80 offers no logical modularization mechanism. Subsequent add-ons such as the team development environment Envy[TM] [19] introduced the notion of *applica-tion* and dependencies between applications. Java is perhaps the richest lan-guage with respect to logical modularization with the package notion.

The third dimension along which languages could be compared has to do with quality control. By quality control, we mean two things: (1) the ability to statically verify a program and (2) the ability to detect problematic situations during runtime, and to recover from them gracefully and methodically. On the subject of static verification, clearly, the stronger the typing, the better the lan-guage. In this sense, Ada is probably the safest language to use, given its strin-gent typing system, followed by Eiffel, then Java, then C++, then Smalltalk and any LISP derivatives (e.g., CLOS). This type safety comes at the expense of flexibility, with Smalltalk and CLOS topping the list, with Java reaching new

[18] If you are from the Software Engineering Institute, you are supposed to scream just about now.
[19] Envy is a trademark of Object Technology International (OTI), Inc.

heights for a typed language. On the issue of runtime error detection and handling, Eiffel appears to be the safest language to use, thanks to its boolean assertions in the form of preconditions, postconditions, and invariants. These assertions can be activated or deactivated on demand, through a compiler switch. Some C++ compilers also offer the assert mechanism, which checks runtime invariants. In terms of error handling, Ada was the first among the typed languages to offer exceptions, but we feel that Java has the best mix of discipline and flexibility, offering a consistent and flexible framework for defining *typed* user exceptions, since exceptions are classes like any other user-defined classes. Also, because exceptions are part of method signatures, the Java compiler makes sure that client programs are aware of the exceptions that are raised by the code they use, and ensures that exceptions raised by subclasses are always properly handled. Smalltalk offers a generic exception mechanism where the error-handling code must be provided along with the code that performs the normal processing. For example, the method that retrieves a value from a table has the following two variants:

```
jInc := incomesTable at:'John'.
mInc := incomesTable at:'Mary' ifAbsent:[log nextPutAll:
        'No Mary'].
```

The first variant will raise an error (exception) in case the key provided as argument (string John) is not found; that error will go all the way up. The second variant will evaluate the block of code passed as an argument ([log nextPutAll: 'No Mary']) if it fails to find the key.

The last dimension of comparison is related to the deployment of applications. At issue are things such as portability across platforms and vendors, interoperability with other languages, and ease of deployment and of updates. Portability benefits from two factors, language standardization, and compiler and runtime technology. Eiffel and Ada are probably the most stable of the languages, Eiffel because the language definition was held by a single company until the late 1990s, and Ada because it was developed in a top–down fashion (both the Ada'83 and Ada'95 versions) by language committees and because there was no unbearable market pressure to produce an object-oriented version ahead of the standard. With Smalltalk and C++, standardization came as an industry imperative, and was relatively long in the making—although still work in progress for the case of Smalltalk. Java was once again the exception because of the unique strategy used by Sun to introduce the language, making both the specification of the language, and Sun's implementation tools and libraries public domain. The basic premise of "write once, run everywhere," which is the major selling point of Java, pressured tool vendors to stick to the language and virtual machine specifications put out by Sun.[20] In terms

---

[20] Only a vendor with the clout of Microsoft can venture to develop a different, albeit faster, virtual machine.

of compiler and runtime technology, both Java and Smalltalk benefit from the virtual machine paradigm: by compiling source code into an intermediary version that runs on a virtual machine, we ensure that the compiled code itself may be executed on any platform that provides an implementation of the virtual machine. By contrast, C/C++ compilers generate machine-specific machine code, and that code is not portable across hardware or firmware platforms. System programmers go to great lengths to make C++ binary code portable across runtime environments and hardware platforms; Microsoft's component object model (COM; discussed in Chapter 14, Section 14.5) was developed in part for that purpose [Box 1998].

In terms of interoperability with other languages, there are two degrees of interoperability, in-process interoperability, and interprocess interoperability. With in-process interoperability, compiled code from different languages interacts in the same memory space. In-process interoperability is difficult to achieve for a variety of reasons; the chief reasons are the differences in memory layout and differences in calling conventions. The usual way of handling this is to resort to the lowest common denominator between the two languages, and to find a way (a macro, a preprocessor directive) to let the compiler know that a particular call is made to a function written in a different language so that the proper mapping is generated. Also, it is generally much easier to link code from an earlier bound language to a later bound language, rather than the other way around. For example, LISP, Smalltalk, and Java all can link up to C/C++. Most of LISP/Smalltalk/Java is written in LISP/Smalltalk/Java, but ultimately, something needs to happen on the real machine, and that usually happens by escaping into some native code, usually written in C/C++. That native code is usually compiled directly into the virtual machine, with a LISP/Smalltalk/Java interface. For example, Smalltalk has a default nonoverrideable constructor (**basicNew**) that is a Smalltalk front for the C/C++ function that performs the actual call to allocate (...) and returns the pointer. This method is one of many *user primitives* (called *native methods* in Java). The virtual machine has reserved codes for these operations, and calls the corresponding C/C++ function when the corresponding operation code is encountered in program bytecode. To link C/C++ code into Smalltalk, we normally have to treat those functions like the other user primitives, and rebuild the virtual machine executable with these new functions. We can only pass simple arguments back and forth (strings, numbers, and arrays of numbers). Advances in linking and loading technologies make it possible nowadays to link external C/C++ code into applications without having to rebuild the virtual machine.

Interestingly, interprocess interoperability between languages is not much more difficult to implement than is interprocess interoperability of programs written in *the same language*. Indeed, the major difficulty in either case is to manage object identities across memory spaces, and the issue of passing structured data back and forth as bytestreams via the underlying communication infrastructure. Chapter 14 deals with such *distribution infrastructures*, but suffice it to say that such infrastructures are valuable as integration tools as much as they are valuable as distribution tools.

Finally, in terms of ease of deployment and updates, Java is the easiest to deploy and update, by virtue of everything we have said about it so far. However, component and distribution technologies are bridging the gap for the other languages, making it possible to replace program components during runtime, with more or fewer restrictions (e.g., waiting until all the objects created by a particular component have died before removing a particular component). Ease of deployment has been a major selling point for Web-based client–server applications. Further, the ability to upgrade applications while they are running is a critical one in mission-critical applications. For example, the FCC (Federal Communications Commission) mandates that companies that manufacture telephone switching guarantee *less than one second of downtime per serviced phone line, per year*; clearly, a shutdown for maintenance is out of the question.

10.4   DISCUSSION

In this chapter, we provided an introduction to object-oriented programming concepts and languages. Our description of language features focused on the most widely known languages. There are a number of research-oriented languages, and niche languages that we didn't address. Further, for the languages presented here, we focused only on their object orientation, insofar as their object orientation makes them candidate packaging technologies for reusable software components.

The next two chapters will look at additional constructs that support reuse. Some are language-based, some are design constructs, and some are modeling constructs. The programming and design constructs seen in the coming chapters build on the mechanisms shown in this chapter. Chapters 13 and 14 show examples of uses of combinations of these techniques to yield flexible and reusable object-oriented software.

Chapter 11

Abstraction and Parameterization Techniques in Object Orientation

We defined reusability as consisting of two related properties: usefulness and usability. Recall that usefulness has to the do with the extent to which a particular reusable artifact is applicable to a wide variety of problems, whereas usability concerns the packaging of the component in a ready-to-use fashion. To some extent, domain analysis deals with *usefulness* whereas domain design and component realization deal with *usability*: given a set of common needs, how to package the solution in such a way that the overall cost of using the component over its operating range is minimized.

The cost of reusing a component is a function of the cost of reusing the fixed part, plus the cost of implementing the variable part. Obviously, the bigger the fixed part, the better. Extending the fixed part usually means moving some levels of abstraction higher to "intensionalize" lower-level "nonessential" differences (see Section 8.5). At the same time, the cost of reusing the fixed part depends on its *use readiness*, which is a function of its *concreteness*; an abstract component needs some adaptation or instantiation effort—possibly automated—before it can be integrated. Hence, as we saw in Chapters 7 and 8, reusable component packaging involves finding a tradeoff between the range of applicability of a component in its current form, and the effort required to use it in each case within that range. In this and subsequent chapters, we are concerned with packaging techniques that help extend the range of applicability of a component (i.e., the relative size of the fixed part) without unduly increasing the cost of its use over that range. Figure 11.1, also taken from chapter 7, illustrates this point.

The systems that we model and implement may be apprehended from a variety of viewpoints or perspectives, including the user viewpoint (or viewpoints, one per user community), the viewpoint(s) of the problem domain, the

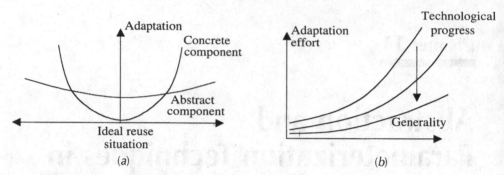

FIGURE 11.1 (a) Difference in reuse effort profile between concrete and abstract components; (b) new reuse techniques help lower the adaptation effort required for components, that is, improve their usability-given a certain level of generality-usefulress.

viewpoint(s) of the solution domain, and so forth. Within each viewpoint, several subviewpoints may be germane or needed to describe and understand the system (the process view, the data view, the structure view, etc.). The description along any view is seldom *complete*, that is, doesn't say everything that can and needs to be said to describe the system. It is also the case that the description along one viewpoint may not be suitable for another viewpoint, as the viewpoints may have different reference models. Systems require representations along several viewpoints both for completeness and for ergonomics. Abstraction may be defined as a viewpoint-specific transformation that, when applied to the description of system, yields a description that preserves the aspects that are essential to that viewpoint and deemphasizes (or eliminates) those aspects that are not essential or relevant to that viewpoint. The description of a system may be seen as a *contract* between its developer or *provider*, and its user or *client*. The more abstract the description *that a reuser can work with*, the more *freedom the developer will have to implement that contract*.

In this chapter, we are concerned with the representation and packaging constructs provided by object orientation to support abstraction, regardless of the domain (services, architectures, business or application). Coplien proposed three properties of objects, as computational entities, that we may wish to vary and/or abstract:

- *Algorithms.* We can abstract algorithmic differences by using the same function name to refer to different algorithms for performing the same operation. Coplien argues that the language mechanism to support abstraction along this dimension is *overloading*.
- *Behavior.* We can abstract behaviors by finding a common, more general, shared expression. Coplien argues that the (C++) language mechanism used to support abstraction along this dimension is generalization/ inheritance. Other language mechanisms include Java's interfaces, which abstract behavior, independently of implementation.

- *Data Structure.* We can abstract data structures by finding a common "data denominator" that embodies the shared data between two (or more) entities. The mechanism used to represent data commonality consists of embodying such data in an object, and making that object a component of the data structures that share its fields.

These are only *some* of the abstraction techniques used to handle variability and commonality along *some* of the tenets of object-oriented programming. Some are applicable at both the modeling and implementation levels (e.g., aggregation, name overloading), although they may have different expressions. There are other dimensions of commonality/variability of objects, as computational entities, that are not directly expressible as language constructs. Such commonalities and variabilities are often expressed in terms of *design patterns* [Coplien 1999]; these are generally commonalities or variabilities that involve relations between several objects. We study abstraction techniques for OO modeling in the next section. Programming language constructs are discussed in Section 11.2. Section 11.3 deals with abstraction and parameterization *design patterns*. We conclude in Section 11.4. The contents of this chapter include material in papers by Mili and Intrator [Intrator and Mili 1994] and Mili and Pachet [2000], and on the *excellent* book titled *Multiparadigm Design in C++*, by James Coplien [Coplien 1999]. We will draw heavily on the material presented in Sections 8.4 and 8.5.

11.1 ABSTRACTION TECHNIQUES IN OBJECT-ORIENTED MODELING

In order to identify the abstraction mechanisms appropriate for object-oriented modeling, we propose to use an approach similar to Coplien [1999], and identify the various properties of objects as computational entities, but at the modeling level. If these properties are sufficiently independent, it is reasonable to attempt to treat them as separate dimensions (or domains; see Section 8.5), and to explore modeling language mechanisms that allow us to "abstract away" differences along these properties. This would allow us a packaging of reusable components that accommodates variations, and circumscribes them to small and identifiable parts of a software artifact. We start our discussion by studying object representations, as a description language, namely, by studying the *ontology* of object-oriented modeling. Next, we discuss one particular aspect of that ontology: inheritance. We discuss inheritance both from the point of view of formal knowledge representation (Section 11.1.2) and from the more informal point of view of object modeling methodologies (Section 11.1.3). Sections 11.1.4 and 11.1.5 deal with *metamodeling*. Roughly speaking, *metamodeling* refers to reflection in the context of object *modeling*. We see examples in Section 11.1.4, and a formalization in Section 11.1.5. We conclude this section with some practical abstraction heuristics (Section 11.1.6).

11.1.1 An Ontology of Objects

Object-oriented modeling views programs as sets of collaborating objects. An object is a cohesive computational entity embodying a set of a related services and the relevant data and state information. The very notion of an *object* is a convenient computational abstraction to package related functionality and state or data. We consider that this is the basis on which abstraction mechanisms are built. Figure 11.2 shows a first-level ontology of objects, reproduced from Chapter 9. Note that we refrained from the notion of classes and operations attached to classes. This serves two purposes. First, not all object-oriented models and languages are class-based; prototype languages are not [Ungar and Smith 1987, Malenfant 1995]. Second, the idea of operations attached to objects is not a universal one, neither from a modeling point of view, nor from a programming point of view. From a modeling point of view, class responsibility collaboration (CRC) cards, responsibility driven design [Wirfs-Brock et al. 1990], and to some extent, Fusion [Coleman et al. 1994], first model system-level functions (called **Function** in Fig. 11.2), then carve up the responsibilities of each object.

Reenskaugh's OORAM methodology considers the notion of a class as secondary to the notion of *role* describing the capacity in which an object participates in achieving a specific goal. From a programming point of view, some languages consider nontrivial operations as extraneous to objects (e.g., constraint object programming languages) while others use multiple dispatch to distribute an operation among several classes.

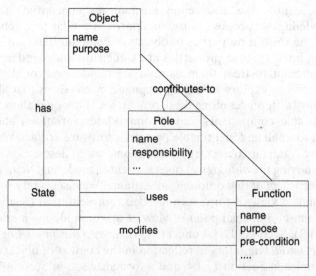

FIGURE 11.2 A first-cut ontology of objects.

The association between function and state (data) that is shown in Figure 11.2 illustrates the fact that the system is memory-bearing and that functions affect its memory. The association between object and state reflects the fact that some of that memory is encapsulated in objects. The functionality of an object (its behavior) consists of the set of roles that it plays in the different system functions [Reenskaugh 1995].

We can build a number of abstraction mechanisms on top of the ontology of Figure 11.2. The first one is the notion of a class as a repository for the definition of state and operations for objects with like behavior. Hence, instead of describing a system by describing *all* of its objects, with their states and the functions to which they contribute, we describe a system by describing the classes of objects it comprises, and the *typical* operations to which they contribute. Figure 11.3 shows the extended ontology.

As we are at the analysis level, we don't have the distinction between type and implementation; it is all types. We will use the terms *type* and *class* interchangeably. The left part of Figure 11.3 shows how things (system functions, represented by the class **Function**) get done (functional view); the right part shows what things are (structural or *definitional* view). To say that system functions are *external* combinations of *intrinsic*, context-free behaviors of the individual objects is itself an abstraction—and sometimes, the only valid one (see, e.g., Mili et al. [1990]), one that is not shared by the object orthodoxy that views any system behavior as the result of triggering some method of some object or entity of the system. As shown in Chapter 9, it is generally useful to

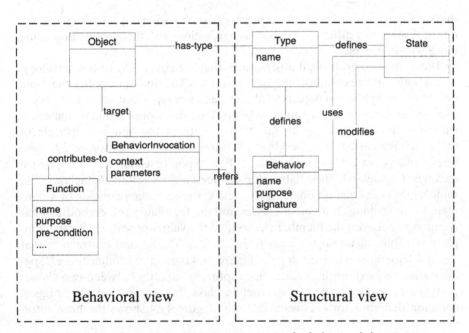

FIGURE 11.3 Recognizing types as repositories for behavioral descriptions.

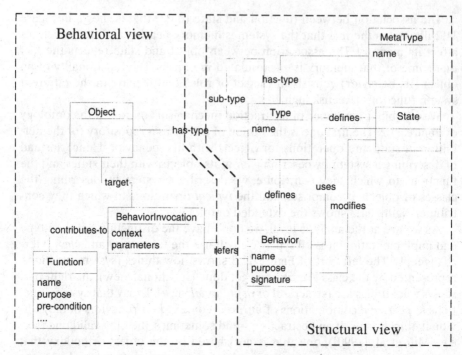

FIGURE 11.4 Extending the previous ontology with subtyping and metaclasses.

think of computational models in terms of combinations of paradigms at different levels (and different kinds) of aggregation, and this view is becoming more widely accepted.

There are two additional abstractions that we could add to this ontology, which both capture commonality between types. The first one applies the same operation we applied to objects to obtain classes or types, but this time to types themselves. Given a set of similar types or type descriptions, find a characterization of this set (a *type* or *class*) that captures the common aspects of the types. We called this operation *intensionalisation* in Section 8.5. A type (class) whose values (instances) are other types (classes) will be called a *metatype* (*metaclass*). The relationship between a class and its metaclass is the same as that between an object and its class; the metaclass consists of a template for describing its member classes, and the template itself embodies what is common between the member classes, and the values or settings for the template variables distinguish a class from another. The second abstraction that we could operate on the ontology of Figure 11.4 is good old "inheritance": specialization and extension. Inheritance captures similarity between two classes or types by embodying it in a typelike class that consists of the "biggest common denominator" between the two.[1] Figure 11.4 shows the new ontol-

---

[1] Logically, it is also the "biggest common denominator." See below.

ogy. We didn't explicit the structure of metatypes any further. Nor did we consider the fact that metatypes may have metametatypes of their own. We come back to these issues later.

In the next section, we start by studying inheritance in knowledge representation. Section 11.1.3 deals with specialization and extension in object-oriented analysis. Section 11.1.4 deals with what we call *metamodeling*. In Sections 11.2 and 11.3 we see how metamodeling abstractions can be implemented in object languages.

11.1.2 Inheritance in Knowledge Representation

Inheritance is perhaps the most commonly misunderstood and least agreed-on concept in object orientation. There are several reasons, including object orientation's rich and diverse ancestry [Wegner 1987a] and its simultaneous use of all those "inherited" meanings in analysis, language design, and programming. For the purposes of this chapter, we present three interpretations of inheritance, with particular attention to its uses as an implementation technology for program families: (1) *generalization*, per knowledge representation; (2) *subtyping*; and (3) *subclassing* as a code-sharing mechanism. Issues of formality and safety are central to our discussion. In this section, we are concerned with inheritance from a modeling point of view, specifically, per knowledge representation.

In knowledge representation, the term "inheritance" is used to refer to both *generalization relationships* between concepts or classes, and to the default *inference mechanism* that ensues from such relationships [Mili 1988]. Broadly speaking, concepts have *intensions*—what they "mean"—and *extensions*—what they refer to. For example, the concept of the "morning star" *means* (*intention*) "the star that shines in the morning," and *refers to* (*extension*) the planet Venus.[2] In logical terms, we can think of the *intension* of a concept C as a one-place predicate $P_C(.)$ *that returns true for instances* of the concept, and its *extension* as the set E_C *of such instances*. In this context, generalization is *equivalent* to logical implication between concept intensions and implies set inclusion between their extensions. Let C_1 and C_2 be two concepts, and $P_{C_1}(.)$ and $P_{C_2}(.)$ their corresponding intensions, and E_{C_1} and E_{C_2} are their corresponding extensions. We have

C_1 is more general than $C_2 \equiv (\forall x)[P_{C_2}(x) \Rightarrow P_{C_1}(x)]$, which implies $E_{C_2} \subseteq E_{C_1}$

Inheritance *as an inference process* has received considerable attention in the knowledge representation community [Thomason et al. 1986]. In its simplest form, inheritance can be expressed by the following informal rule:

---

[2] Incidentally, the "evening star" *means* (*intension*) "the star that shines in the evening" and happens to also *refer to* (*extension*) to the planet Venus.

Let C_1 and C_2 be two concepts such that C_1 is more general than C_2, then whatever is true for C_1 is also true for C_2.

We can't make the description of inheritance—as an inference mechanism—more explicit without adhering to one particular definition or school of thought. In one interpretation, let $F(.)$ be a one-place predicate such that $P_{C_1}(.)$ $\rightarrow F(.)$. We may say that $F(.)$ is a *property* of C_1. Inheritance in this case consists of using the implication $P_{C_2}(.) \rightarrow P_{C_1}(.)$ to infer that $P_{C_1}(.) \rightarrow F(.)$, or, in other words, that F is also a property of C_2. All would be peachy keen if penguins could fly,[3] but they can't and knowledge representation languages must handle this problem one way or another. In this case, the implication $P_{\text{Bird}}(x)$ $\rightarrow \text{Flies}(x)$ is obviously not true, since some birds—namely, penguins!—do not fly. This led researchers to distinguish between essential or definitional properties, which are always inherited without exception, and nondefinitional (or normative, or prototypical) properties, which may be cancelled or overridden by subconcepts [Rumelhart and Norman 1983]. Others have questioned the logical interpretation of generalization relationships themselves within natural taxonomies, and proposed what amounts to nonmonotonic/nontransitive generalization relationships [Rosch 1978, Mili and Rada 1992].

Some knowledge representation languages such as the KL-ONE family [Brachman and Schmolze 1985] do not allow the representation of "cancelable properties" and support such monotonic inferences as hierarchical classification, while others are based on nonmonotonic logics and support a number of defeasible inferences (see, e.g., Lenat's discussion of CYC [Lenat et al. 1990]). The underlying differences, from a knowledge representation point of view, are both philosophical–epistemological (essence of knowledge) and pragmatic (representing imperfectly coded knowledge). In KL-ONE, the intension of a concept is described by the (logical) conjunction of a number of "noncancelable," inheritable properties. For example

$$P_{C_1}(.) \equiv F_1(.) \wedge F_2(.) \wedge F_3(.)$$

A subconcept C_2 may either *extend* the set of applicable properties, as in

$$P_{C_2}(.) \equiv F_1(.) \wedge F_2(.) \wedge F_3(.) \wedge F_4(.) = P_{C_1} \wedge F_2(.)$$

or specialize one (or more) of the properties of C_1, as in

$$P_{C_2}(.) \equiv F_1(.) \wedge F_2(.) \wedge F_3'(.), \text{ where } F_3'(.) \rightarrow F_3(.)$$

or both, as in

---

[3] Intuitively, **Penguins** are **Birds** $[P_{\text{Penguin}}(.) \rightarrow P_{\text{Bird}}(.)]$, **Birds** fly $[P_{\text{Bird}}(.) \rightarrow \text{Flies}(.)]$, and yet, **Penguins** don't fly [it would be enough to find some penguin that does not fly, but here, $P_{\text{Penguin}}(.) \rightarrow \neg \text{Flies}(.)]$.

$$P_{C_2}(.) \equiv F_1(.) \wedge F_2(.) \wedge F_3'(.) \wedge F_4(.), \text{ where } F_3'(.) \rightarrow F_3(.)$$

Classification in KL-ONE compares the properties that make up concept descriptions [Lipkis 1982], and its transitivity depends on the fact that properties are noncancelable. The specialization of properties in KL-ONE [e.g., the relationship $F_3'(.) \rightarrow F_3(.)$] covers a number of relationships, from the simple *value restrictions* for simple scalar properties (e.g., restricting the domain of a particular property to fewer possible values) to a recursively defined specialization relationship between property values—which, incidentally, makes classification *undecidable* [Lipkis 1982].

If we go back to Coplien's commonality and variability analysis, let C_1 and C_2 be two concepts or classes with membership predicates $P_{C_1}(.) \equiv F_1(.) \wedge F_2(.) \wedge F_3(.) \wedge F_4(.)$ and $P_{C_2}(.) \equiv F_1(.) \wedge F_2(.) \wedge F_3(.) \wedge F_5(.)$, respectively. Finding the common superconcept between the two consists of finding the most "restrictive" predicate that they both imply, and that would be $P_{C_{1,2}}(.) \equiv F_1(.) \wedge F_2(.) \wedge F_3(.)$. The ways in which $P_{C_1}(.)$ and $P_{C_2}(.)$ differ from $P_{C_{1,2}}(.)$ is what Coplien called *positive variability*. If we decided, instead, to use C_1 as a reference, and represent C_2 in relation to C_1, then we would have a case of *negative variability*: C_2 differs from C_1 in a way that is part of C_1's own definition [Coplien 1999]. Thus, if C_2 is to be implemented as a subclass of C_1, we would have to resort to things such as cancellation, conditional compilation, and the like [Coplien 1999].

11.1.3 Inheritance in Object-Oriented Analysis

There is surprisingly precious little about the semantics of inheritance in object-oriented modeling techniques, with a few notable exceptions (see, e.g., Champeaux et al. [1992], and Martin and Odell [1997]. The one aspect of the semantics that did receive attention in the literature is the issue of whether specializations of the same class are mutually exclusive, and whether they cover the entire domain of that class. Figure 11.5 illustrates some of the nuances. Some methodologies have distinct notations for the various cases (filled vs. hollow triangle, bounding the specializations of a partition within a box, etc.).

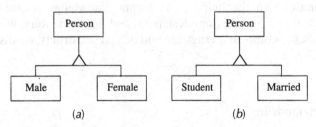

FIGURE 11.5 Cases where subclasses (a) constitute a partition of the subtype (disjoint, and covering) and (b) overlap and do not cover the superclass entirely.

One of the difficulties in using the full-fledged semantics of specialization in knowledge representation languages is that it does not map very nicely to object-oriented languages. For example, while inheritance in knowledge representation supports the specialization of attributes, there is no corresponding programming language mechanism for data members: a data member can be inherited only as is. The semantics of an attribute (reflected only in the type) cannot be changed, and any restrictions in the domain will have to be enforced by writing different access methods. We also have cases where programming languages do handle specialization concepts, but the modeling notations don't; object-oriented modeling notations make no provisions for specifying that an operation associated with a type is specialization of another operation defined in a supertype. This is a much-needed relation, and one that ends up represented at the design and code level. It is a shame that it shouldn't appear at the modeling level; the purported traceability of object-oriented methods depends on it.

The relative poverty of object-oriented analysis with regard to specialization manifests itself also in the process. A number of methodologists prescribe an inductive (learning) approach to identifying generalizations, and most come with their own set of heuristics for recognizing generalization relationships and for factorizing the common aspects. However, there are a few formal tools that can help in the discovery. One of the first such tools is the Demeter system [Lieberherr et al. 1991]. Cook [1992] and Godin and Mili [1993] proposed formal methods for organizing classes into generalization hierarchies and lattices based on a description of their attributes and methods. The method proposed by Godin and Mili [1993] has the advantage of being optimal in the sense of yielding a hierarchy or lattice with no redundancy; each feature (attribute or method) is defined in a single place in the lattice. Later versions of the classification algorithms took into account specialization relationships between attributes and methods belonging to different classes, yielding more realistic generalization hierarchies [Godin et al. 1996].

In summary, it is fair to say that while generalization/specialization offers a formal and powerful knowledge organization and abstraction tool, object-oriented analysis methods use only a fraction of its modeling power, and rely on little, if any, of the formal tools for building domain knowledge hierarchies. We advocate the use of the full expressive power of generalization in the modeling phase, with the help of the formal knowledge organization and classification tools, and letting designers and implementers worry about mapping such structures into language and design constructs; we discuss those in Section 11.3.

11.1.4 Metamodeling

We use the term *metamodeling* to refer to the act of *intensionalizing* (see Section 8.5) a set of similar or related types. We first describe instances where this intensionalization is needed or useful, and then propose a formali-zation of metamodeling.

11.1.4.1   *Intensionalizing Domain Knowledge*

Consider our example of a confederation of savings and loans association (SLA) from Chapter 9. This is a simplified version of an actual modeling problem, for an actual such institution, on which one of the authors has worked. Generally speaking, different types of loans have different payment formulas. The association between types of loans and payment formulas is practically industrywide. For example, all student loans have an initial defer-ment period, after which regular payments must be made at a minimum pace, but a student may pay the remaining balance in full at any point in time. It is also almost always the case that mortgages are to be paid back accord-ing to some regular payments, and full payments usually carry a penalty because lending institutions usually turn around and sell mortgages to poten-tial investors with a guaranteed rate of annual return. For each one of these modes of payment, there are a number of parameters such as frequency of payment, ranges of allowable percentages, and so on. Different member institutions of an SLA may offer different subsets of these ranges. For example, institution A will offer 6-month, 1-, 2-, and 3-year fixed-rate mortgages, while institution B will offer 1-, 2-, 3-, and 5-year fixed-rate mortgages. An individual who walks into a particular institution (e.g., A) will get a mortgage with a single value from these parameters, for example, a 3-year fixed-rate mortgage.

A first-cut object model for this problem looks like Figure 11.6. This model says that a "loan" is payable according to a "payment schedule" and that there are many types of loans, and many types of payment schedules. What it fails to say is which schedules of payment are appropriate for which types of loans, in general, and for individual institutions. If we had one payment schedule per

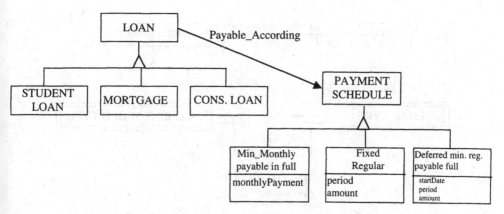

FIGURE 11.6 A simplistic model of loans and payment schedules.

loan type, we could represent this easily within this model by specializing the association "payable according" into three (or more) more specific associations. However, the combinations can be numerous, and when we take into account the specifics of individual institutions, they become unwieldy.

What is really at issue here is the fact that we are attempting to represent information about two aspects: (1) account *types* and (2) specific *accounts* of these types; the latter have to abide by the constraints and parameters of the former. The object model of Figure 11.6 shows a model of the associations between individual accounts and individual payment schedules but very little about account types in general; if we restrict ourselves to a single institution, it may show which payment schedules apply to which accounts for this particular institution. We would need a separate model for each institution. The way of handling this consists of representing information explicitly about types of loans, types of payment schedules, and institutions, explicitly. Figure 11.7 shows such a model.

The upper part of the model is equivalent to the model of Figure 11.6. The lower part is the metamodel. The classes **LoanType** and **Payment ScheduleType** represent types or classes of loans and payment schedules, respectively, i.e., classes whose instances are themselves classes. The fact that a particular institution uses a specific subset of the set of payment schedules practiced by the industry at large is represented by the subset relationship ($\subseteq$ in Fig. 11.7) between the association that is specific to individual institutions and the general one. The information that would have been embodied in separate models, one per institution, is now represented by a single (meta)model (lower part of Fig. 11.7), and some specific instances of that model (e.g., a table).

The explicit presence of this information is valuable for the purposes of coding the desired behavior concisely and generically.

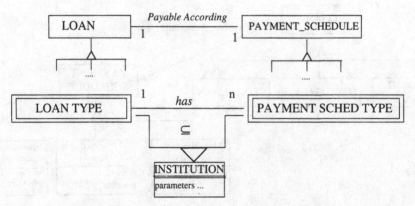

FIGURE 11.7 A complete model including a metamodel.

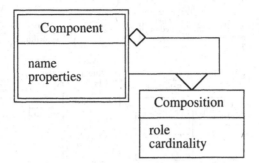

FIGURE 11.8 A partial model for bills of material.

A very common instance of this general problem is the bill of materials problem in a manufacturing organization. For each nonelementary product, the organization would have a recipe for the product indicating its composition. For example, a table is created for a **Board** and four **Legs**. A **Chair** is made of two **Boards**, four **Legs**, and two **Armrests**. These recipes need to be stored and manipulated in the same way that we need information about LEG123402 and CHAIR2364315, in which warehouse they are stored, and whether LEG123402 is a component of CHAIR2364315. In this case, the recipes are represented by a metamodel, and they are themselves models of the data (database). The metamodel is shown in Figure 11.8.

11.1.4.2 Powertypes

James Odell first coined the term "powertype" [Odell 1995]. For Odell, a powertype is to a type what a powerset is to a set: the type of types that are subtypes of a given type. Huh? Let us consider the type **Tree**. **Tree** has many subtypes, with lots of commonalities, and lots of differences between them. The set of subtypes of **Tree** defines a type, and that type is called the powertype of **Tree**. The types **LoanType** and **PaymentScheduleType** are both powertypes, in Odell's jargon. Figure 11.9 illustrates examples of powertypes taken from different domains [Odell 1995].

This diagram illustrates, again, the possibility of representing meta-types, types, and relationships between them (between types, between metatypes, and between types and metatypes), all in the same diagram. This also means that we represent a class (e.g., **LoanType**) and its instances (**Mortgage**, **StudentLoan**, etc.) in the same diagram.

Powertypes are only a special case of metatypes; the instances of the metatype are further constrained to have the same supertype.

11.1.4.3 Process Abstraction

Metamodeling may appear as a design optimization technique, or stronger yet, as a design imperative. Broadly speaking, class behavior that is dependent on the definitional structure of the class may be decomposed into a structure

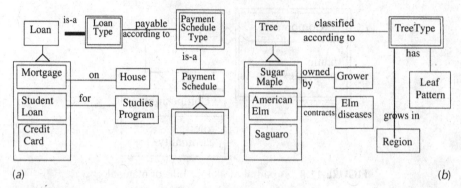

(a)   (b)

FIGURE 11.9 (a) **LoanType** and **PaymentScheduleType** are powertypes; payable_according_to is an assoc.between powertypes; **Mortgage, House**, and so on are types; on and for are associations between types. (b) **Treetype** is a powertype; **Tree, SugarMaple, AmericanElm, Region, Grower**, and **LeafPattern** are all types [Odell 1995].

access part, and a computation part [Mili and Li 1993]. The idea of collection class iterators may be seen as a simple example of this, where we separate the iteration part from the actual computation to be performed on the individual elements of the collection. The following C++ sample code illustrates the idea:

```
(1)   T Collection<T>::average() {
(2)     CollectionIterator<T> it(this);
(3)     T average;
(4)     int n = 0;
(5)     Node<T> current;
(6)     while (! current = it.next()) {
(7)       n = n + 1;
(8)       average = average + current.value();
(9)     }
(10)    return average/n ;
(11)  }
```

In this case, the same function average() may be used on all the subclasses of **Collection**, independently of how they are structured, provided that each subclass provides an iterator. We could go one step further, if the structure of the class were available during runtime; even the iteration part may be written once for all. This approach may be used to define a generic shallow copy operation, for example, a generic comparison operation or a generic persistence operation. The following code excerpts show a generic shallow copy operation:

```
(1)   RootObject* RootObject::shallowCopy(){
(2)     RootObject* copy = oneJustLikeMe();
(3)     DataMemberIterator it(this);
```

```
(4)    MemberNameType name;
(5)    while ( ! name = it.next())
(6)      copy → setValueOf(name,this → getValueOf(name));
(7)    return copy ;
(8)  }
```

We assume that `setValueOf(MemberNameType, void*)` and `void* getValueOf(MemberNameType)` will do the "right thing," and that users of `getValueOf(..)` will do the proper typecasting with the returned value, and so forth. Note that the class **DataMemberIterator** knows how to access the list of data members of the current object.

Figure 11.10 illustrates the new ontology of objects that takes into account the decomposition of behaviors into structure access and computation. While this ontology refers to implementation constructs, it is useful to keep in mind those constructs during analysis so that the specification of those behaviors may be written independently of those constructs. We earlier proposed [Mili and Li 1993] guidelines for writing analysis-level behavioral descriptions without committing to a particular implementation.

In addition to reducing the amount of code that needs to be written, our approach to process abstraction may be almost mandatory in applications

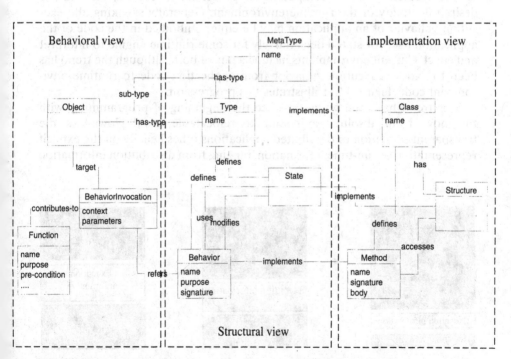

FIGURE 11.10 An augmented ontology incorporating the distinction between models and implementations.

where "new classes" are added to the system during runtime. In nontyped languages such as Smalltalk and CLOS, new classes may be added, queried, instantiated, and manipulated during runtime, and this is not a problem. With Java, new classes that satisfy a precompiled interface may be linked during runtime, but we cannot extend the interface. With C++, neither is possible, and a metamodeling approach is required, notwithstanding the advantages of code reuse mentioned above. In Section 11.3 we show design patterns for implementing this for the case of C++ and like languages.

11.1.4.4 Computational Metamodeling

Under computational metamodeling, we group descriptions of objects as computational entities, or processes, that may have a location (memory space), resources scheduled for it, priorities, and the like. This is to be contrasted with what me might call *structural metamodeling* and *behavioral metamodeling*, which includes the kind of metamodeling described so far, which involves the explicit description of the structure and behavior of objects (during runtime) or classes (during "modeling time"). Computational reflection may be seen as a special case of computational metamodeling where the meta-language for describing behavior is the programming language itself.

Behavioral metamodeling may manifest itself to varying extents depending on the variability in the computational properties of the objects and the desired flexibility of the runtime environment. Generally speaking, the execution behavior of an application may be either embodied in the code of the application itself, or stated declaratively for some runtime engine to interpret and enact. Current environments include a mix of both, although the trend has been to extract execution behavior from application code to runtime environment code. Figure 11.11 illustrates this progression.

This trend has been going on since the beginning of programming, with the move from absolute addressing to relocatable code! Nowadays, the transparent execution of distributed applications relies heavily on the explicit representation of run-time information, ranging from distribution information

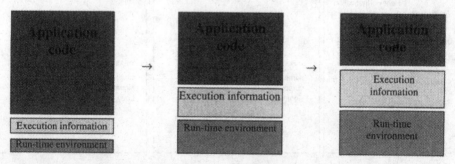

FIGURE 11.11   The runtime environments have been shifting toward an explicit (declarative) description of programs' runtime characteristics.

(e.g., the location of database tables) to information usable by ORBs (interfaces and locations of individual objects). Figure 11.12 illustrates this point.

An even more advanced use of behavioral metamodeling is the explicit representation and "execution" of execution models. This is particularly valuable in distributed concurrent applications where different mechanisms for message sending, message handling, synchronization, resource allocation strategies, and so on [Briot and Cointe, 1996] may be used or tested. Partially or fully reflective programming languages like Smalltalk make it possible to describe those mechanisms in the language itself as in Actalk [Briot 1989; see also Kuwabara et al. 1995].

This approach has several advantages. By separating the execution model from the application logic, it considerably reduces the size of applications. Further, it yields reusable executable models that may be combined with other applications, and far more reusable domain objects, which may then be used under different circumstances (single-user system; multiuser; multiuser, distributed; multiuser, multiprocessor; client–server, etc.).

11.1.5 Understanding Metamodeling

11.1.5.1 *Metamodeling = Factorization + Intensionalization*
Metamodeling is an abstraction mechanism. As such, it involves two steps:

1. Factorization to isolate concerns, and more specifically, to isolate a fixed part from a variable part
2. Intensionalization, or the replacement of extensions by intensions

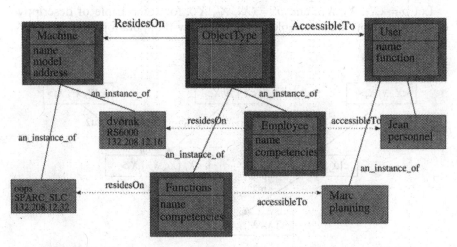

FIGURE 11.12 Representing location and access information explicitly.

By *intensionalization*, we recognize a set of disparate values as a coherent class that can be described by a definition (intension). We now look at the two classes of metamodeling use cases in this light.

In the first case, we needed to represent classwide constraints (permissible payment schedules for a given loan type), and we thus distinguished between instance properties and class properties. This distinction is not always easy to make, especially when class properties rather directly influence instance properties. Permissible payment schedules are class properties, whereas actual payment schedules are instance properties. Generally speaking, specifying the domain of an attribute is a class description activity, whereas picking a value from that domain for a given instance is an instance description activity. With regard to intensionalization, it is embodied in the recognition of such a thing as a **LoanType**, a **SchedulePaymentType**, and a relationship between the two. These three entities accounted for all sorts of associations between subclasses of **Loan**, and subclasses of **PaymentSchedule**.

In the second class of cases, the factorization allowed us to separate essential, domain-specific computation, from execution specifics (distribution of data, concurrency, etc.). Intensionalization consisted of parameterizing execution models by identifying a generic execution *engine* that refers to an explicit/declarative execution model.

Note that we can "go meta," that is, move from instance to class, along any dimension. In the example above, we "went meta" along the application domain (e.g., going from **Loan** to **LoanType**). We could go along the execution model, and get classes of computational objects whose instances differ from an execution model (parameter) point of view. We could also go meta several times, along the same or several dimensions. Figure 11.13 illustrates this point. Here, X_1, X_2, X_3 represent three different dimensions of description. Starting with three tuples $\langle X_1, X_2, X_3 \rangle$, $\langle X'_1, X_2, X_3 \rangle$, and $\langle X'_1, X_2, X_3 \rangle$, we first get two opportunities from going from instances to classes.

Let $p = \langle X_1, X_2, X_3 \rangle$, and $p' = \langle X'_1, X_2, X_3 \rangle$, for some triple of descriptive dimensions. Note that by replacing p and p' by the metaobject $p_m = \langle C_1, X_2,$

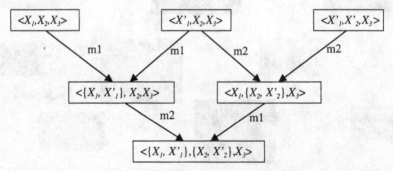

FIGURE 11.13 Intensionalizing ("going meta" along) different dimensions.

$X_3\rangle$, where C_1 is the intension of the set $\{X_1, X_1'\}$, we lose some information. For this transformation to be information lossless, we need to keep the knowledge that X_1 and X_1' are known to satisfy C_1, or are the ones we are interested in. In the loans example, in addition to saying that there exists an association between **LoanType**s and **PaymentScheduleType**s, we still need to say *which* payment schedule types are associated with which loan types. In other words, we replaced several instance level descriptions with one class level description, and several new instance level descriptions. Where did the economy of representation occur, if any?

In fact, the economy of representation occurs at two levels. First, the new instance-level descriptions are much simpler than the original ones. In the p/p' example, we traded the description of entire triples (e.g., complete models) for an enumeration of domain values (X_1 and X_2'). Second, the class-level model C_1 may be reused with new instances, and tailored for other purposes.

Finally, recall that any one of the dimensions can be further separated into any number of dimensions (see Section 8.5), giving that many more ways of going meta. In the SLA example, financial institutions offer a number of products that are sensitive to a variety of rates, including interest rates, currency exchange rates, and stock rate of return. Some products may have floating rates, while others have agreed-on fixed rates. This concerns both loans and various kinds of deposits (mutual funds, savings account, etc.). In addition to the metaclass **LoanType**, which describes the products where the institution lends money to the customer, we could have another metaclass **FloatingRateProductType**, which describes those products that use a floating rate. For each product type, we have to specify what that (floating) rate is (e.g., interest rate, bond rates, currency exchange rates), and the premium the institution charges depending on the status of the customer [regular, special, and VIP (very important customer)]. The class **FloatingRateProductType** may have the following data members in a C++-like syntax:

```
(1)  class FloatingRateProductType {
(2)      String productName ;
(3)      RateName floatingRate ;
(4)      Dictionary<CustomerStatusValue,RateValue>* premiums ;
(5)      ...
(6)      // access methods to these attributes
(7)  }
```

A specific product, for example, **FloatingRateMortgage**, would have the attribute values productName = FloatingRateMortgage, floatingRate = InterestRate, and premiums = {⟨REGULAR,2.0⟩, ⟨SPECIAL,1.5⟩, ⟨VIP,1.0⟩}. The values of these class attributes may show up as static data members of the class, or encoded directly in the methods of the class, if that code is generated automatically (more on the generation in

Section 11.3). The class **FloatingRateMortgage** might look something like this in C++:

```
(1)  class FloatingRateMortgage {
(2)    static String productName= "FloatingRateMortgage";
(3)    static float InterestRate ;
(4)    static Dictionary(CustomerStatusValue,RateValue)*
(5)    premiums =...;
(6)  }
```

In this example, the class properties/attributes showed up as static data members, and as data member values.

The class **FloatingRateMortgage** is an instance of both **LoanType** and **FloatingRateProductType**. This deserves several observations. First, programming languages do not support multiple classification—an object cannot be of several non-ordered (subtype) types; what they do support is multiple inheritance whereby we create a type for each combination of types an object might have during its lifetime. Second, this kind of situation is usually handled with multiple inheritance; instead of **LoanType**, we would use the class **Loan**, and instead of **FloatingRateProductType**, we would have a class called **FloatingRateProduct**, and both would be superclasses of **FloatingRateMortgage**. The class **FloatingRateProduct** would have a data member that is of type float with a generic name such as floatingRate. In addition to yielding more complex class hierarchies, with generic and heavily overloaded data member and function names, whichever static data members we factor out will be shared by all the subclasses, which opens another can of worms. If the language does support metaclasses and multiple inheritance, but no multiple classification, we can have multiple inheritance of metaclasses; that is, we would define a type **FloatingRangeLoanType** of which the class **FloatingRangeMortgage** is an instance. So, a word to the can-do-that-in-Smalltalk crowd—no, you can't! And even if you could, the multiple inheritance of metaclasses raises a number of issues regarding the compatibility of the metaclasses [Graubé 1989, Forman et al. 1994].

11.1.5.2 is-a versus is-a-model-of
We refer to the relationship between an instance to a class with the commonly used (and sometimes confused) name is-a, or "is an instance of." My mortgage is an instance of the class **Mortgage**, and the class **Mortgage** is itself an instance of the class **LoanType**. In object orientation, a class definition is "a model of its instances," in the etymological sense, sort of like a template. However, the definition or intension of a class need not be under the form of a template. We could conceivably imagine the definition of the class **Person** as the one-place predicate:

$$Person(x) \equiv LivingCreature(x) \land Race(x, 'Human')$$

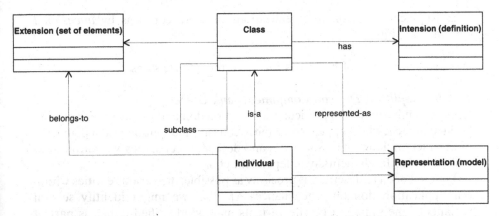

FIGURE 11.14 The distinction between classes, intensions (definitions), and representations (models).

However, we could provide a template for the class **Person** with attributes name, age, gender, and other details. The confusion results because we assume that the provided attributes determine the class, in the sense that

$$\texttt{Person(x)} \equiv \texttt{HasName(x)} \wedge \texttt{HasAge(x)} \wedge \texttt{HasGender(x)}$$

This confusion is inherited from knowledge representation languages based on features [Rosch 1978] or attributes. The is-a-model-of relationship implies a *representation* act, which is a *projection* of the actual definition. Figure 11.14 attempts to illustrate these distinctions. For the sake of simplicity, we distinguish between **Individual** and **Class** whereas, in fact, it is the same entity.

11.1.6 In Practice—a Summary

When modeling an application, a number of things can be done to take advantage of the observations and techniques that we showed in Sections 10.1 and 10.2. We will refrain from proposing a yet another object analysis process: (1) there is some fairly good competition in this area, and (2) the techniques proposed here may be seen as refinement techniques to be applied to a first-cut object model. We will, however, give a set of heuristics based on the observations and techniques discussed earlier.

The two major steps in parameterization are:

1. Splitting components or objects along independent or loosely coupled concerns

2. Replacing the concrete realizations of these concerns by *intensional* abstractions

We give below a set of heuristics for performing these steps.

11.1.6.1 Splitting Domain Components and Objects

Lack of familiarity with a particular application domain usually breeds coarse-grained objects, which appear to be fairly cohesive and reusable, at a high level of abstraction. However, as analysis and design proceed, they will turn out to embed lots of fundamentally independent choices.

First, we need to describe, as precisely as possible, the various entities within our application domain. The chances are that we might identify several variants of the same entity. The variants may be identified either as part of the problem statement, or inductivley, by asking "what if" questions, and considering alternative choices for some of the characteristics of our components/objects. For example, in the banking domain, we might describe a **Loan** account in general terms, and then describe a few dozens types of loan accounts, from credit card loans, to consumption loans, to credit margins, to mortage credit margins, and so on. For example, a **Loan** account may be characterized by the term (fixed term, versus flexible), by the payment mode (see earlier discussion in Section 11.1.4), by type of interest calculation, and so forth. If these (three) criteria influence the *qualitative* behaviour of objects of type **Loan**, then that may be ground for embodying the difference in different classes. The first inclination of novice analysts is to use a single dimension—that of **Loan** type—and account for all of these variations using inheritance. If we have three differentiating criteria (loan term, payment mode, and interest calculation), and two possible choices for each one of these criteria, then we could potentially end up with 2^3 (8) classes. Figure 11.15 shows two alternative organizations for these eight classes.

If we look at the lefthand hierarchy, the one classified by term of loan, then payment mode, then interest calculation frequency, we notice that some functionality will be duplicated in several places. For example, if we assume the hierarchy to be a full binary tree of depth 3, then each type of interest calculation will be repeated 4 times (here, we showed only the variable-term loan branch). If interest calculation is independent of the other criteria (fixed versus variable term, and payment mode), then it is unnecessary duplication. If we perform our classification based on interest frequency calculation *second* (righthand side of Fig. 11.15), then the interest calculation logic will be coded "only twice." If we start classifying by interest calculation, then each type of interest calculation will be coded only once—at the expense of coding other pieces of logic several times.

Classification based on several *independent* criteria is usually indicative of a good opportunity for splitting the object/class in question. An alternative to the above classification is a breakdown of the **Loan** object into a new smaller **Loan** object, a **Payment** object, an **InterestCalculation** object, and a

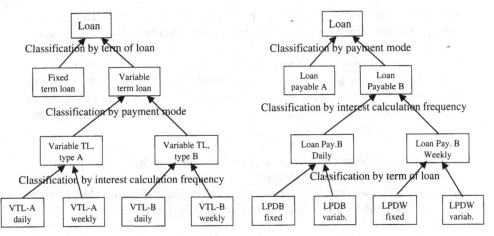

FIGURE 11.15 Two alternative multicriteria classifications of domain classes.

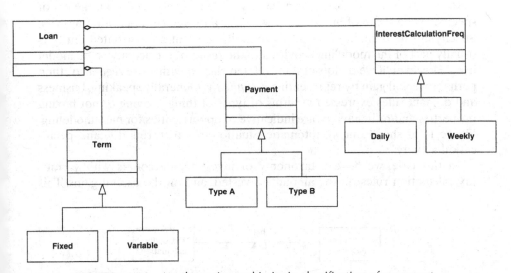

FIGURE 11.16 An alternative multicriteria classification of a concept.

Term object (see Fig. 11.16). Each component will contain the data and the functionality to handle the particular aspect of the object. The interesting thing here is that we were able to make the **Loan** abstraction, as a whole, more reusable (now a single class handles all sorts of loans), but in exchange, we extracted a set of three smaller subabstractions that are allowed to vary.

This kind of situation has many other remedies, including multiple inheritance. Our solution is akin to the *strategy pattern*, and the reader can find a thorough discussion of the symptoms, and a comparative discussion of the alternative solutions in the patterns book [Gamma et al. 1995]. The strategy pattern is concerned with separating algorithm/operation specification from its implementation—the latter is implemented with the strategy object. In our case, our objects describe complete facets (data + behavior) of the object **Loan**. A yet finer-grain decomposition than *strategy* further breaks down algorithms into *policies* (control aspects) and *computation* (data transformations). Such concerns are more at the level of detailed design, and are discussed later.

11.1.6.2 Identifying Occurrences of a Common Intension: When Generalization Is Too General

In Section 11.1.4 we saw various cases of metamodeling. We would like to highlight the cases that are relevant to analysis, and how to detect them.

Specifying Attribute and Association Domains As mentioned earlier, the *act* of specifying the domain (the range) of an attribute, or the type of an associated entity, is a class description activity, or to be contrasted from the act of specifying the *value* of an attribute, which is an instance description activity. Specifying the domain of an attribute or the type of an associated entity is usually part of the modeling activity, and the result of the activity is the model itself. However, if we do lots of it for related classes, with some *regularity*, then perhaps we will gain by representing it *explicitly*. Generally speaking, business and domain rules expressed in terms of types of things, having or not having properties and/or behaviors, are indicative of opportunities for metamodeling. Figure 11.17 shows one symptomatic situation of a recurring domain specification activity.

In this case, we have a taxonomy of investment accounts with various tax calculation rules on the amounts invested, and on the capital gains. This

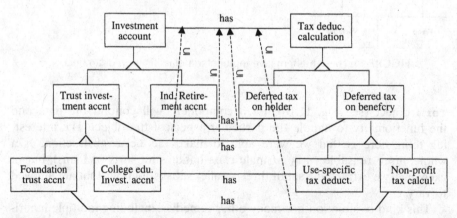

FIGURE 11.17 An association defined at the higher levels of the hierarchy needs to be specialized.

model is not supposed to reflect reality in any particular country, and some domain specialists may find it hair-raising. The sloppy way of doing this would be to be content with a general association between the top classes (i.e., **InvestmentAccount** and **TaxDeductionCalculation**) and perhaps some text annotation somewhere to show the correspondence between the various kinds of accounts, and the corresponding tax calculation rules. A conscientous modeler, on the other hand, would capture the generalization, but would want to explicit domain knowledge in the actual model. In this caricatural case, there is a one-to-one correspondence between types of investment accounts, and types of calculation procedures. We recognize this as a case where metamodeling would be appropriate. The rule might be described as follows:

> If you have several class hierarchies that are connected at various places by associations with similar semantics, there may be room for reducing the complexity by "metamodeling" the association.

In loose mathematical terms, we could call such hierarchies as being *quasihomomorphic*. Note that this rule works if we bother to represent all of the associations between the classes precisely. As mentioned above, the sloppy modeler would not bother with such a precision, and this opportunity for metamodeling will go uncovered.

Finally, if we feel the need to place restrictions on the domain of an attribute as we go down a class hierarchy, then that, too, can be handled by metamodeling, and the attribute might actually be transformed into an association where the type of the associated entity is the domain of the attribute.

Handling Explicit Requirements on the Runtime Behavior of the Software Components The nonfunctional requirements usually deal with a variety of issues, including the static properties of the software, as a whole, or relative to specific components (coding standards, portability, maintainability, etc.), and the runtime behavior of the *system* in terms of performance, execution medium, distribution, parallelism, access rights, and other parameters. System flexibility requires that all these criteria be parameterizable and modifiable. That may be an explicitly stated requirement, in which case it needs to be satisfied, or it may be a desirable property, in which case its benefits need to be balanced against its costs in terms of conceptual complexity and performance overhead. It is not very clear in our minds whether these issues are exclusively architectural or design issues, or whether they may be tackled as soon as the analysis level. It depends, in part, on whether these variabilities are part of the problem (requirements) or part of the solution (an optimal design).

In the remainder of this section, we give examples of variations and how they can be handled. In most cases, we provide an additional level of indirection that enables us to provide an abstract view of a component to its clients and/or users. Typically, a program or component goes from being an active component with embedded runtime behavior (e.g., distribution policy) into some sort of an interpreted program being "interpreted" by some *virtual machine*:

- *Parameterizing Control Strategies.* Instead of having the control strategy embedded in the implementation code, we use a generic control model which may be parameterized to yield specific control styles.

- *Location Transparency.* We talk to objects or components through "abstract" components that may execute the operations locally or delegate to a remote object or component. CORBA provides location transparency through the use of proxies that implement the same interfaces as local objects.

- *Parameterizing Access Rights.* Traditional database management systems have an explicit representation of user access rights to elements of the data. The notion of accessibility in object orientation—and more specifically, OO programming—is not as fine-grained as that in the more traditional DBMSs: they are static (code level) and are class-based (e.g., things accessible to a class, versus to the class and its subclases, vs. to the world). We can reintroduce a flexible access management system by intercepting messages before they are executed, and validating them with regard to the requester by consulting some shared repository. The same mechanism used for locating transparency may be used here.

- *Parameterizing Functional Interfaces.* In heterogeneous systems, different components may provide the same set of services under different names, or using different signatures or protocols. If we don't have the exact signature of a method or service, we can access it through a description of its semantics. The CORBA trader service offers such a mechanism. The underlying mechanism that enables it is the notion of an interface registry and of a dynamic invocation interface.

More patterns are described when we discuss design and programming patterns.

11.2 ABSTRACTION TECHNIQUES IN OBJECT-ORIENTED PROGRAMMING LANGUAGES

In this section, we study two abstraction constructs in object-oriented programming languages: *abstract classes*, and *generic classes*. We will study these constructs for the extent to which they enable developers to (1) express commonalities in a centralized fashion, making it possible to develop and maintain those common aspects in one place; and (2) accommodate variations among objects in a circumscribed and constrained fashion. Both constructs rely on inheritance, to varying degrees. We refer to the reader to the discussion of inheritance in Chapter 10.

11.2.1 Abstract Classes

According to Goldberg and Robson [1989], "[An abstract class is] a class that specifies protocol, but is not able to fully implement it; by convention, instances are not created of this kind of class." Using the usual separation between *specification* and *implementation* in data abstraction, an *abstract class* consists of a class specification, and an incomplete implementation. Fully abstract classes have no implementation. Fully concrete classes have all of their specified methods implemented. Because they are not fully implemented, abstract classes cannot be instantiated, and they are created to be subclassed. In actual applications, abstract classes appear as internal nodes of class hierarchies, where all the leaf nodes are fully implemented. In reusable libraries and frameworks, abstract classes may appear as leaf nodes of class hierarchies, but it is understood that they need to be subclassed and fully implemented before they can be instantiated (see, e.g., Mili and Sahraoui [1999]). Abstract classes may appear in class hierarchies for two reasons. First, from a technical point of view, abstract classes may be used to support polymorphism and dynamic binding in typed—and otherwise early-bound—languages such as C++ [Stroustrup 1986] and Eiffel [Meyer 1988]).

Consider the following example of the savings and loans association (SLA) again. The SLA may offer a number of account types such as **Checking-Account**, **SavingsAccount**, or **CreditMargin** accounts. The processing of a payment differs from one type of account to another. With checking accounts, a payment simply results into decrementing the balance by the amount of the payment, and charging a transaction fee to the account. With savings accounts, it is a withdrawal like with checking accounts. Further, we take note of the transaction date and calculate the cumulated interest since the last transaction. With credit margin, it is the same principle except that it is interest charged rather than credited. Because the same file will contain payments relevant to different kinds of accounts, we don't know which kind of account will be returned by getAccountWithNum(...) [line (10) in Fig. 11.18].

Thanks to polymorphism, we can group all three kinds of accounts under a common class **Account**, and the same function (getAccountWith-Num(...)) can return any of its subclasses [line (10) in Fig. 11.18]. Figure 11.19 shows a sample (and somewhat naive) implementation of getAccount-WithNum(...) for illustration purposes.

Returning to Figure 11.18, line (13) shows a call to the method registerPayment(**Payment**), which could be an *abstract method* of **Account**, with each of its subclasses defining their own version. In C++, this would look as shown in Figure 11.20. In this case, the method registerPayment(...) is defined as a *pure virtual method* in **Account**

```
(1)   #include <account.h>
(2)   ...
(3)   void main(int args, char** argv) {
(4)     PaymentInputStream f = ....;
(5)     CString payerAccountNum;
(6)     Account* anAccount;
(7)     ...
(8)     while (!f.eof()) {
(9)       f >> payerAccountNum;
(10)      anAccount = f.getAccountWithNum(payerAccountNum);
(11)      while (f.hasOneMorePayment()){
(12)        currentPmnt = f.readPayment();
(13)        anAccount→registerPayment(currentPmnt);
(14)      }
(15)    }
(16)    ...
(17)  }
```

FIGURE 11.18 A polymorphic handling of payments using abstract classes and methods.

```
(1)   class PaymentInputStream {
(2)   ...
(3)   public:
(4)     Account* getAccountWithNum(CString num) {
(5)       if (num.prefix(2).eqstr("CM")) {
(6)         CreditMargin* cm = CreditMargin::getAccount(num);
(7)         return cm;
(8)       };
(9)       if (num.prefix(2).eqstr("SA")) {
(10)        SavingsAccount* sa = SavingsAccount::getAccount(num);
(11)        return sa;
(12)      };
(13)      if (num.prefix(2).eqstr("CA")) {
(14)        CheckingAccount* ca=CheckingAccount::getAccount(num);
(15)        return ca;
(16)      }
(17)    }
(18)    ...
(19)  }
```

FIGURE 11.19 A method that manufactures objects of different types.

to *force* the subclasses (**CheckingAccount**, **SavingsAccount**, **Credit-Margin**) to define their own version. The equivalent construct in Java would qualify the declaration of the method (and the class) with the keyword

```
class Account {                     class SavingsAccount:public
  float _balance;                   Account{
  ...                                 ...
  public:                           public:
    virtual void registerPayment(     virtual void registerPayment (
      Payment aPayment) = 0;            Payment aPayment) {
  ...                                   ...
}                                     }
                                      ...

class CheckingAccount: public     }
Account{                            class CreditMargin:public Account{
  ...                                 ...
public:                            public:
  virtual void registerPayment(      virtual void registerPayment(
    Payment aPayment) {               Payment aPayment) {
    ...                                 ...
  }                                   }
  ...                                 ...
}                                   }
```

FIGURE 11.20   An abstract class in C++.

abstract as in

   (20)   **abstract void** registerPayment(Payment aPayment);

to the same effect.

An abstract class is not only used for typing purposes; it may factor out the common aspects to its subclasses. In our case, **Account** defines a common attribute (_balance) and the various functions that manipulate it. Other attributes and methods may be shared as well. We say in this case that the class is partially concrete (or partially abstract).

With partially abstract classes, the challenge is to find the appropriate method granularity to maximize the volume of concrete code that can be shared. Generally speaking, by breaking an abstract method into smaller pieces, we might succeed in finding a piece of code that is shared by the subclasses. This was referred to as dimension splitting in Section 8.5.1. For example, we might realize that there is a lot in common between the processing of payments by the various account types, and decide to break the registerPayment(...) method into two parts: (1) a common part, in terms of intent and code, which is factored up the hierarchy; and (2) a part that has the same intent for all the subclasses, but whose implementation differs. We make the new variable part as an abstract method.

In our banking example, we could write the method registerPayment as follows:

```
(1)   void registerPayment(Payment aPayment) {
(2)     updateBalance(aPayment);    // Common to all types of
                                    // accounts
(3)     updateCreditsAndCharges(); // Depends on type of account
(4)   }
```

In this case, registerPayment(Payment) is no longer abstract (pure virtual, in C++), but updateCreditsAndCharges() is. Figure 11.21 shows the new code structure.

This is the most common way of using abstract classes: a class that factors out common behavior of several subclasses, in *intent* (method signatures) and in *some* of the *implementations*. As a method of implementing program families, abstract classes combined with subclassing may be characterized as follows:

```
class Account {
  float _balance;
  ...
public:
  virtual void registerPayment(
    Payment aPayment) {
    updateBalance(Payment);
    updateCreditsAndCharges();
  }

  virtual void updateBalance(
    Payment aPayment) {
    ...;
  }

  virtual void
    updateCreditsAndCharges()=
0;
  ...
}


class CheckingAccount:public
Account{
  ...
public:
  virtual void updateCreditsAnd-
    Charges() {
    ...
  }
  ...
}
```

```
class SavingsAccount: public
Account{
  ...
public:
  virtual void updateCreditsAnd-
    Charges() {
    ...
  }
  ...
}

class CreditMargin:public
Account{
  ...
public:
  virtual void updateCreditsAnd-
    Charges() {
    ...
  }
  ...
}
```

FIGURE 11.21 By splitting register Payment (Payment), we are able to factor out more behavior in the abstract class.

Ergonomy This method does separate the fixed part of the family from the variable part from the viewpoints of both the family designer and the user.

Safety We identified two safety-related characteristics in Section 8.4.2:

- *Enforcing the Constancy of the Fixed Part.* In this case, this amounts to preventing subclasses from overriding selected aspects in the abstract class. OO programming languages usually do not allow programmers to redefine data fields (instance variables). As for methods, the best they can do is to ensure that the redefinition is conformant with the original version (see Chapter 10). This depends on (1) what is intended to be maintained constant, that is, signatures or behavioral specifications, versus implementation, and (2) the language used. For example, no language prevents the redefinition of implementations—conformant or not. Further, only C++ and Eiffel enforce signature conformance, and only Eiffel enforces some measure of behavioral conformance.

- *Specifying the Variable Parts Intensionally.* First, this method does not limit the methods that can be *added* to a class, and thus, may fail to specify the variable parts altogether. When the variable part is the implementation of an already defined (whether it is implemented or not) method, the specification of that method—in effect, the common part—in terms of either signature or behavior, defines implicitly the range of possible "values" that methods can take, and this technique may be seen as quite effective.

Evolvability

- *Incremental Parameterization or Resolution of an Existing Family.* Subclassing, which is used to relate family members to the description of the family, can also be used to relate an existing family to its subfamilies and superfamilies. In this way, superfamilies can be generated by removing (1) an instance variable, (2) a method implementation (but keeping its specification), or (3) the method altogether (specification included). The opposite operations may be used to generate subfamilies.

- *Shared Maintenance of Common Aspects between a Family and Its Derivative.* It is guaranteed because a family and its derivative will be related by inheritance.

11.2.2 Generic Classes

Recall that a generic class is a class whose specification—and implementation, if one is available—contains a type parameter (see Section 10.1). Genericity is useful in typed languages to support general data structures. For example, instead of defining a linked list structure to contain integer values (e.g.,

IntLinkedList), one to contain strings (**StringLinkedList**), and so on, we could define a *generic* **LinkedList** structure that can contain values of some type T, to be specified when needed. Using Eiffel-like syntax, we could define a generic linked list structure as follows:

```
(1)    class LinkedList[T]
(2)    export successor, predecessor, empty, full,
(3)    ...
(4)    feature
(5)    ...
(6)    successor(x: T): T is
(7)      ...
(8)      do
(9)        ...
(10)     end
(11)   ...
(12)   end--class LinkedList
```

and use the one we need simply by supplying a value for the type parameter at variable declaration time, as in

```
(13)   ...
(14)   myIntLinkedList : LinkedList[INTEGER];
(15)   myStringLinkedList : LinkedList[STRING];
(16)   i,j : INTEGER;
(17)   s,t : STRING;
(18)   ...
(19)   do
(20)     ...
(21)     j := myIntLinkedList.successor(i);
(22)     t := myStringLinkedList.successor(s);
(23)     ...
```

The generic class **LinkedList** can be instantiated for any type T that supports all the operations on elements of the list that are used by **LinkedList**. Genericity is supported in Eiffel, C++, and Ada. Naturally, it is not supported in untyped languages such as Smalltalk and CLOS because all classes are *type-generic*, by default. Further, it is not supported in Java, and that is too bad (see discussion in Section 10.1.4).

In developing **LinkedList**, a developer may have assumed that some operations are supported by the type T, such as comparison operators or arithmetic operators. This restricts the set of legal types to those that support these operations. The specification of genericity comes in two flavors: (1) *constrained genericity*, where the requirements of the type parameter are explicitly—and declaratively—stated; and (2) *unconstrained genericity*, where such requirements are only implicit in the generic code [Meyer 1988]. Ada (and classic

Ada) supports constrained genericity. The specification of the generic *package* **LinkedList** would look something like this:

```
(1)   generic type T is private;
(2)     with function "=" (a,b: T) return BOOLEAN is <>;
(3)     with function "<" (a,b: T) return BOOLEAN is <>;
(4)     ...
(5)   package LinkedList is
(6)     ...
(7)     function successor (X: T) return T;
(8)     ...
(9)   end LinkedList.
```

In this case, we explicitly say that **LinkedList** can be instantiated for any type T that supports the operators = and < with the specified signatures. LIL [Goguen 1986], a formal specification language inspired from Ada, supports semantically richer specifications for type parameters. C++'s templates and Eiffel's earlier version of genericity were unconstrained. The current version of Eiffel supports a limited form of constrained genericity; the developer can require a type parameter to be instantiated to a subclass of a given class. For example, assuming that **Comparable** is a high-level (abstract?) class supporting the operators = and <, by writing

```
(1)   class LinkedList [T → Comparable]
(2)     export successor, predecessor, empty, full,
(3)     ...
(4)     feature ...
(5)       successor (x: T): T is
(6)       ...
```

we restrict the possible values for T to **Comparable** and its subclasses. If **Comparable** is an abstract class, the effect can be quite similar to supporting Ada-like constrained parameters, albeit a bit more cumbersome. For example, we need to make sure that **INTEGER** is a subclass of **Comparable**, if we want **LinkedList** to be instantiable for integers [Meyer 1988], and while it is technically feasible—thanks to multiple inheritance—it is not a good design practice.[4]

Incidentally, abstract classes, polymorphism, and inheritance may be used to simulate genericity; in the **LinkedList** case, we could define a non-generic class **LinkedList** where the type T is bound ("hardwired" or coded) to **Comparable**. Then, wherever an instance of **Comparable** is expected, an instance of any subclass of **Comparable** would do. There remains a problem:

---

[4] Reuse of object-oriented libraries and classes should come only through subclassing, and should not involve adding classes or methods anywhere other than at leaf classes [Kiczales and Lamping 1992].

ensuring the homogeneity of instances of **LinkedList**, such as ensuring that a **String** and an **Integer** cannot be added to the same list. Finally, note that generic classes can be abstract (or *deferred*), combining the two dimensions of variability offered by abstract classes and genericity [Meyer 1990].

Generic classes define program families according to our definition. Conversely, if the variations between the members of a program family can be encapsulated into a type parameter, generic classes are one way to go. As such, they have the following characteristics:

Ergonomy   Generic classes provide a very clean way of separating the shared aspects of the family (the generic code, and the interface of the type parameter) from the variable parts (the actual type and its implementation).

Safety

- Unlike the use of abstract classes, which relies on subclassing to create family members—and hence leaving room for editing family members beyond what was intended—genericity relies on instantiation, and leaves no such room. Thus, family members are guaranteed to share the intended common parts.
- Constrained genericity does support the *intensional* specification of the possible values of the variable part—the type parameter. With unconstrained genericity, illegal types are implicitly rejected during compilation or execution.

Evolvability

- *Incremental Parameterization or Resolution of an Existing Family.* Generic classes can have several type parameters, and type parameters can be added or removed from the definition of a class quite easily. This involves simple editing commands on the class' source code. For example, with unconstrained genericity, transforming an actual type into a type parameter is as simple as: (1) replacing the name of the actual type by a bogus type name, (2) removing the actual type's declaration (if locally defined), and (3) adding the bogus type name to the list of type parameters. With constrained genericity, a little more work is involved. The reverse operations are required to replace a type parameter by an actual type.
- *Shared Maintenance of a Family and Its Derivatives.* Unlike inheritance-based derivation of subfamilies and superfamilies, which offers a built-in code sharing mechanism between a family and its derivatives, there is no corresponding programming language–environment built-in mechanism to support the kind of editing commands required to, for instance, further parameterize an already generic class. This is a commonly recognized

limitation of genericity as a single step or level reuse mechanism. Palsberg and Schwartzbach proposed a combination of inheritance and *type substitution* as a way of supporting language-level mechanisms for supporting incremental parameterization/instantiation of generic classes [Palsberg and Schwartzbach 1990].

Naturally, genericity and abstract classes may be combined to implement program families, combining the flexibility of both mechanisms, but potentially, jeopardizing each other's safeguards. Space limitations do not allow us to explore such combinations.

11.3 METAPROGRAMMING

Levy [1986] states that *"Metaprogramming* [is] defined as creating application programs by writing programs that produce programs." A metaprogram is a program that treats another program as data. Application generators are metaprograms, and building application generators (see Chapter 7, Section 7.2.3) is an example of metaprogramming. As an abstraction and parameterization mechanism, metaprogramming constitutes a culmination of sorts of the techniques presented so far. Recall that our objective has been to find an implementation mechanism for reusable components (or component families) that enables us to

- Implement (realize) as much of the shared aspects of components as possible
- Specify the variable part as precisely as possible, and constrain its development in order to minimize adaptation–effort, to ensure conformance with the intent of the component, and to avoid errors

Going back to the discussion in Section 8.5, and more specifically, our discussion about intensionalization, we go from an enumeration of the variants of a component (extension) to describing the properties satisfied by the variants. Abstract classes and genericity are two ways of describing the variable part in terms of obligations on the custom part of the code that developers must develop. With metaprogramming, we go one step further, and *provide a function that generates the variants*!

Metaprogramming does not require any specific language constructs per se; we can read strings (program specifications) in any language, and print strings (source code of resulting program) in any language. However, depending on how soon we want to be able to execute the generated code, and how complex that code is, things can get pretty complicated. We start by looking at what is involved in building interpreters in general, and comment on the ease with which such interpreters can be built in traditional languages. Next, we take a quick look at reflective languages, which are languages that allow programs to access representations of themselves during run-time, and more specifically, at reflective object-oriented languages.

11.3.1   Building an Interpreter

We have all built interpreters for finite-state automata at one point or another during our college years. In this case, the interpreter takes two parameters, the program to execute, given as a state transition matrix, and the input to that program. This will work for automata with simple data types and simple output functions, or where the range of data types and transition functions that are used in automata is predefined. We will use a simpler example of a rule-based system. This is a system that reads as input a set of production rules in the form CondA ∧ CondB ∧ CondC → doActionA **THEN** doActionB, where CondA, CondB, and CondC are conditions, and doActionA and doActionB are actions. If we were to implement this in C++, CondA, CondB, and CondC could be C++ boolean functions, and doActionA and doActionB, some arbitrary C++ functions. The input format for the rules can be something like

```
BoolFunctionA;BoolFunctionB;BoolFunctionC:ActFunctionA;
  ActFunctionB
BoolFunctionA;BoolFunctionD;BoolFunctionE:ActFunctionC;
  ActFunctionK
```

where the semicolon separating conditions means that they are ANDed, and the colon is used to separate the condition part from the action part. The interpreter would have two tables of functions indexed by function names, a table of boolean functions, and a table of actions. The following code excerpts illustrate what the code for the interpreter might look like

```
(1)   typedef boolean *BOOLEAN_FUNCTION();
(2)   typedef void *ACTION_FUNCTION();
      ...
(3)   Dictionary⟨String,BOOLEAN_FUNCTION⟩* booleanFunctionTable
      = new...;
      ...
(4)   Dictionary⟨String,ACTION_FUNCTION⟩* actionFunctionTable
      = new...;
      ...
(5)   class Rule {
      ...
      public:
(6)     Rule(String ruleText);  // parse a string and extract
                                 the list
                                 // of conditions and actions
      ...
```

```
(7)     CollectionIterator(String)* getConditions();
                                    // return list of conditions
(8)     CollectionIterator(String)* getActions();
                                    // return list of conditions
            . . .
        }
(9)     boolean interpretRuleText(String ruleText) {
(10)       Rule *aRule = new Rule(ruleText);
(11)       boolean conditionPart = true;
(12)       CollectionIterator(String)
                        *conditions = aRule→getConditions(),
                        *actions = aRule→getActions();
(13)       while ((conditions→hasMoreElements()) &
           conditionPart) {
(14)         String boolFuncName = conditions→nextElement();
(15)         BOOLEAN_FUNCTION boolF =
                        booleanFunctionTable→at(boolFuncName);
(16)         conditionPart = conditionPart && (*boolF)();
(17)       }
(18)       if (!conditionPart) return false;
(19)       while (actions→hasMoreElements()) {
(20)         String actionFuncName = actions→nextElement();
(21)         ACTION_FUNCTION actionF =
                        actionFunctionTable→at(actionFuncName);
(22)         (*actionF)();
(23)       }
(24)       return true;
(25)     }
(26)   }
```

Lines (1) and (2) show the definitions of two very simple function types (no parameters), BOOLEAN_FUNCTION and ACTION_FUNCTION. Lines (3) and (4) show the creation of a table that will contain pointers to predefined boolean functions, and action functions, respectively. Lines (5)–(8) show the definition of the class **Rule**, used to represent rule objects. In this case, rule objects are created from a string. We assumed that the constructor of **Rule** parses the input string (a variable of a predefined type **String**), and extracts the conditions and actions. The methods getConditions() and getActions() [lines (7) and (8)] return iterators over collections of function names corresponding to the boolean functions of the condition part of the rule, and the functions of the action part, respectively. The interpreter per se is implemented in the function boolean interpretRule Text(String), which first constructs a rule object from the input string [line (10)], gets the conditions and actions [line (12); sorry, no validation], then evaluates the condition part [lines (13)–(16)]. If the condition part is true, it executes the action part [lines (18) through (22)].

This is an example where the program to be executed or interpreted may be generated *and* executed within the same program run. In terms of flexibility, it doesn't get any better than this. In terms of complexity, it does get an awful lot more complex than this. First, the functions may take parameters, in which case those parameters should be specified in the input format of the rules, and constructed or looked up in the interpreter. Second, different functions may have different signatures, in which case a more general scheme will have to be devised. One possibility would be to have those functions use an array of pointers to objects, and retrieve their parameters from that array, in the same way that the `void main(int argc, char** argv)` C/C++ function works. And then there is the issue that our rules can only refer to predefined functions, and the fact that we cannot in-line simple C/C++ expressions, for example, as part of the actions. Readers can look at useful and interesting ways to extend our rule language and convince themselves that generating and executing program segments in C/C++, in the same (main) program run, can get more and more complicated, all the way to impossible or impractical (not worth the trouble).

If we give up on the requirement that we be able to generate code and execute it within the same program run, then we fall into the mainstream of generation technology, whether for graphical interfaces, for database bridges, and others. In this case, we have two distinct processes: (1) the program generator, which takes as input a representation of the data and functions to be manipulated by the generated program, and generates the code and (2) a separate program that will integrate the generated program, and will run with it as one. Figure 11.22 illustrates the difference between the two paradigms.

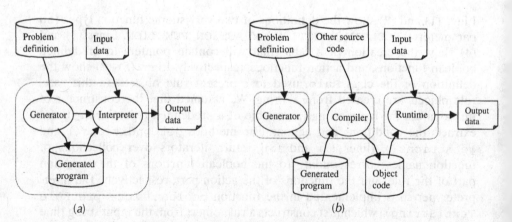

(a)   (b)

FIGURE 11.22 (a) One (or multiple concurrent) process generates the code and executes it; (b) three separate and consecutive processes from code generation to execution.

11.3.2 Computational Reflection and Metaclasses

Our interpreter example above illustrated the need for two mechanisms to implement flexible interpreters efficiently:

- A runtime representation of the programs that we want to execute
- A flexible mechanism for invoking any part of these programs in unanticipated and unplanned ways

The example we studied used a limited form of runtime representation of the programs: two indexed tables pointing to predefined functions. The mechanism used to invoke these functions was C/C++'s built-in mechanism for invoking function variables. These two mechanisms apply, with some restrictions, to procedural code, and they have to be implemented by the developer. Within the context of object-oriented code, we may want to have access to the definition of objects' structure and behaviour during runtime. We discuss object oriented language constructs that support this. There are two general flavors. *Metaclasses*, supported by Smalltalk, CLOS, and some other research languages, are discussed next. The second flavor is that used in the Java language.

11.3.2.1 Metaclass Programming
One way of making type information available during run-time is to make types (classes) as real objects that can be queried during runtime. As objects in their own rights, classes need to have their structure and behavior represented: hence the idea of *metaclasses*; a metaclass is a class whose instances are themselves classes.

Metaclasses have existed in one form or another in Smalltalk throughout its evolution. One of the earlier attempts at formalizing metaclasses may be found in the ObjVlisp model [Cointe 1987], which proposed a unified and minimal model for representing objects, classes, and metaclasses. In this model, the user has the possibility of defining classes by freely specifying their superclass and metaclass, with no limitation. However, existing object-oriented languages are nowhere close to providing such a general scheme. Most typed languages do not provide any representation of classes at run time (C++, Eiffel). Java supports a limited runtime representation of types (see Section 11.3.2.2) but as a read-only repository of typing information. Among untyped languages, CLOS offers, in principle, unlimited access and control, but this lack of restriction makes it difficult to use in practice [Danforth and Forman 1994].

The case of Smalltalk is intermediate: Smalltalk provides a representation of classes as first class objects, but metaclasses have a special status [Briot and Cointe 1989]. In this hybrid model, users have only limited control on metaclasses; they can only add class methods or instance variables, but cannot create their own metaclasses, or decide on the metaclass of a class. However, the language enforces some properties on these metaclasses, in particular, the so-called *parallel inheritance* that ensures, for instance, that creation methods are always inherited properly. An extension of Smalltalk to handle metaclasses according to ObjVlisp was proposed by Briot and Cointe, with the *ClassTalk* system [Briot and Cointe, 1989]. Unfortunately, ClassTalk metaclasses are not compatible with standard Smalltalk classes; in practice, it was not possible to create normal subclasses of ClassTalk classes, making the system difficult to integrate into existing applications. Rivard [1996] proposed an extension of Smalltalk to handle full-fledged metaclasses that seems well integrated with the rest of environment; this solution has yet to make it into a production release of Smalltalk.

On the theoretical front, Graubé [1989] analyzed and criticized full-fledged metaclasses. Graubé identified so-called compatibility problems. These problems arise precisely when users decide arbitrarily which metaclasses to instantiate for their classes. Danforth and Forman proposed an approach based on the dynamic generation of metaclasses that was meant to address these criticisms [Danforth and Forman, 1994]. However, this solution imposes some serious limitations to the practical use of metaclasses [Mili et al. 1995a]. For example, metaclasses representing abstract classes, that is, classes having no instances—and hence, no instance creation methods—cannot be specified. Although the *absence* of a property may arguably not be an inheritable property, it seems to us that no satisfactory solution has yet been put forth that ensures a safe use of metaclasses, beyond the initial Smalltalk proposal.

11.3.2.2 *The Java Model*

Java supports a runtime representation of classes using the *reflection package*. All Java classes and interfaces are represented by instances of the class **Class**. Excerpts of the class **Class** are shown below:

```
(1)  public final class Class implements java.io.Serializable {
(2)    public static Class forName(String className)throws
                           ClassNotFoundException {...}
(3)    public Object newInstance() throws
       InstantiationException, IllegalAccessException {...}
(4)    public native boolean isInstance(Object obj);
       ...
(5)    public Field[] getFields() throws SecurityException {...}
       ...
(6)    public Method[] getMethods() throws SecurityException {...}
       ...
(7)    public native Class getSuperclass();
       ...
     }
```

Line (1) shows that the class is *final*, which means that it cannot be subclassed. The static method forName(String className) returns the class object that represents the class with name className [line (2)]. A side effect of this call is that, if the class has not been loaded into the runtime environment, it will be. The method newInstance() supports the creation of an object of a particular class, given the **Class** object that represents it. For example, after the following code sequence is executed

```
(1)   Class cls = Class.forName("LoanApplication");
(2)   Object loanApp = cls.newInstance();
```

then the variable obj will point to an instance of the class **LoanApplication**, provided **LoanApplication** is an accessible scopewise (e.g., public) and securitywise (e.g., no restrictions were recorded with the security manager), and "instantiable" class (i.e., neither an interface or an abstract class). The method isIntance(Object arg) checks whether arg is an instance of the class or one of its subclasses. For example, the test

```
(3)   if (cls.isInstance(loanApp)) {
(4)      ...
```

will evaluate to true. The method getFields() [line (5)] returns an array of **Field**s, representing all the accessible public fields of the class (or interface), including those inherited from the superclasses. Idem for getMethods() [line (6)]. The method getSuperclass() enables us to navigate the class hierarchy during runtime [line (7)]. We now show excerpts from the classes **Field** and **Method**, both of which implement the interface **Member**, with methods to get the name, the declaring class, and modifiers (**static**, **final**, **abstract**, **public**, etc.). We show the class **Field** first:

```
(1)   public final class Field extends AccessibleObject
      implements Member
      {   ...
(2)       public native Object get(Object obj) throws
              IllegalArgumentException, IllegalAccessException;
          ...
(3)       public native void set(Object obj, Object value) throws
              IllegalArgumentException, IllegalAccessException;
      }
```

We showed two of the most useful methods, the ones that read [line (2)] and write [line (3)] the value of a field on a particular object. The following shows an example code sequence:

```
(1)   Class cls = Class.forName("Applicant");
(2)   Object app = cls.newInstance();
```

```
(3)   Field nameField = cls.getField("name");
(4)   nameField.set(app, "John Doe");
```

Line (4) sets the value of attribute "name" to "John Doe" for the newly created instance of the class **Applicant**. Similarly, the **Method** class is shown below:

```
(1)   public final class Method extends AccessibleObject
      implements Member
      {   ...
(2)      public Class[] getParameterTypes() {...}
         ...
(3)      public Class getReturnType() {...};
         ...
(4)      public native Object invoke(Object obj, Object[] args)
      throws
         IllegalAccessException, IllegalArgumentException, ...);
         ...
(5)   }
```

The methods getParameterTypes() [line (2)], and getReturnType() [line (3)] are self-explanatory. The method invoke(Object, Object[]) [line (4)] invokes the receiver on the first argument (obj) using an array of objects (args) as the parameters. For example, if the class **Applicant** has a public method void setName(String aName), then that method can be invoked as follows:

```
(1)   Class cls = Class.forName("Applicant");
(2)   Object receiver = cls.newInstance();
(3)   Object[] argTypes = new Object[1];
(4)   argTypes[0] = Class.forName("String");
(5)   Method getNameMethod = cls.getDeclaredMethod("setName",
      argTypes);
(6)   Object[] args = {"John Doe"};
(7)   getNameMethod.invoke(receiver, args);
```

Line (5) gets the method object. Note that the method name is not enough, because of overloading. Hence, we have to specify the types of the arguments as an array of **Class** objects [lines (3) and (4)]. Before invoking the method, we also have to prepare the array of parameters [line (6)].

The Java model enables us to do a lot of what Smalltalk metaclasses enabled us to do: being able to (1) query an object about its type during runtime and (2) access an object's state and public functions without a prior knowledge of the object's interface.

However, there is more to metaclasses than the above two functionalities. First, there is the issue of being able to modify the definition of a class *while the program is running*. In Smalltalk, classes are *created* during runtime; class definition is merely the execution of a method on its superclass, asking it to create a subclass of itself. For example, we create **Applicant** as a subclass of **Customer** by executing the following method:

```
(1)  Customer  subclass: #Applicant
(2)            instanceVariableNames: 'assets liabilities'
(3)            classVariableNames: 'applicantCategories'
(4)            poolDictionaries: ''
(5)            category: 'Loan Applications'.
```

The class **Customer** is itself an object, and like all classes, it is a system wide constant called **Customer**! The subclass creation method takes five arguments corresponding to

- The subclass name, represented by the symbol **#Applicant**[5] [line (1)].
- The list of its instance variables ("assets" and "liabilities"), in line (2).
- The list of its class variable names (the equivalent of static data members in C++ and Java).
- Some shared constants (the value corresponding to the keyword **poolDictionaries**, empty in this case).
- A target category, here called **Loan Applications**; a category is like a module, in the sense of organizing classes, but has no semantics associated with it, in terms of visibility or naming.

Once a class is created, new data members and methods may be added to it as in

```
(1)  Applicant addInstVarName: 'employmentIncome'.
(2)  methodName := 'setEmploymentIncome:'.
(3)  newMethodCode := methodName, 'aValue' cr.
(4)  newMethodCode := newMethodCode, 'employmentIncome = aValue.'.
(5)  Applicant compile: newMethodCode category: 'accessors'.
(6)  myApp = Applicant new.
(7)  myApp perform: (methodName asSymbol) with: 5000.
```

Line (1) adds a data member called employmentIncome, and lines (2)–(4) construct a string that represents the method's code. Note that the comma is the concatenation operator for strings—all collections, for that matter—and that sending the message cr to a string [line (3)] appends a carriage return

---

[5] A symbol is like a string, with the following difference. In Smalltalk, two occurrences of the same string, say, "John" and "John", will occupy different spaces in memory, whereas two occurrences of the same symbol will occupy the same memory space. Symbols are typically used as indices in fast access hashtables (**IdentityDictionary**), where equality of reference is used (==) instead of equivalence (=). Examples of such hashtables include the **SystemDictionary**, which contains global constants.

to it. Line (5) invokes the compiler through a two-argument method that takes the source code, and a category name, verifies the syntax of the source code, if successful, compiles it as a method and adds it to the class. As soon as the method is created, we can invoke it on an object of the class [line (7)]. We see here one of several versions of the method "perform," which takes the method name as a symbol (method names are looked up in a method dictionary, much like C++ virtual function tables), and the argument of the method, which is 5000 in this case. This version of perform is a shorthand for a more cumbersome version that takes an array of arguments, much like Java's "invoke" method of the class **Method**.

In Java, it is fairly difficult to modify the definition of a class after it has been loaded: we basically have to rewrite the class loader.[6] Then, there is the issue of adding some behavior to several classes simultaneously. In Smalltalk, because developers can modify metaclasses, they can add state and behaviors to a collection of classes, simultaneously, by taking advantage of metaclasses and metaclass inheritance. In Java, classes are represented by *instances* of the class **Class**, and the class **Class**, is immutable and non-derivable (the **final** keyword, see above).

The question is not whether such advanced functionalities are ever needed, but how often they are needed, and how much do we have to do to overcome the limitations. Advanced to expert Smalltalk developers swear by metaclasses and can't live without them, and that probably accounts for part of the legendary Smalltalk development productivity. In Chapter 14, we will talk about architectural frameworks in general, and about middleware and distribution frameworks in particular, both of which are major consumers of reflection. As we will see, these frameworks rely mostly on predeployment code generation, and are able to do without metaclasses even under high generality requirements. At the same time, most of these frameworks (CORBA, Java RMI, EJB) use a Java-like approach to the extent that they manage run-time repositories of type information.

11.3.3 Implementing Powertypes

We proposed in Section 11.2.3 abstract classes as a way of representing program families; the common aspects of the family are represented as concrete methods of the abstract class, and the variable parts are described as

---

[6] The default behavior of the class loader is to load the "dot class" (e.g., Applicant.class) file only once, the first time the class is needed, but won't be reload it after that, even if reloading is explicitly requested or if the class file changed on disk. To force a reload, we have to redefine the class loader. That is only part of the problem: what do we do with objects created with the old version of the class in those cases where we have just added a data member? Smalltalk nonchalantly migrates them and hopes for the best. However, because the compiled code (bytecodes) of existing methods is remapped (not thoroughly recompiled) to account for new data members, things work out just fine. We suspect that this could be a problem, though, in a distributed environment.

abstract methods (a specification but no implementation) that members of the family—subclasses in this case—have to implement. Abstract classes are adequate, except for the fact that we have limited control on the way the concrete subclasses of the abstract class (i.e., the family members) are created. In particular, we could not enforce semantic conformance of the definition of the abstract methods. We have the same problem of semantic conformance with genericity, which also relies on signature alone.

We can enforce the semantic conformance of members of the family by *generating them* from developer specified parameters—provided, of course, the variations can be reduced to such parameters. An interesting packaging of the generation functionality would make it part of the behavior of the metaclass of the abstract class. In this case, the metaclass would embody the *complete* definition of the family members, constant and variable parts alike, and as such, corresponds to Odell's definition of powertypes (see Section 11.1.4.2). Thus, consider a class C and its metaclass MC. The two classes, together, define a program family where

- Class C, an abstract class, factors out the common behavior of the family members (as in Section 11.2.3).
- The metaclass MC, which, in addition to defining the class C (in the sense that C is an instance of MC), supports (implements) the generation of individual family members as (special) subclasses of C.

In Smalltalk, for example, we can override the subclass creation method (**subclass: . . . category:**) to include additional parameters that correspond to the specific variant of the family, and use those parameters to automatically generate the family member. Compared to using abstract classes alone (see Section 11.2.3), the use of metaclasses and metaprogramming has the advantages described in the following paragraphs.

Ergonomy   *A cleaner separation of the fixed part of the family from the variable part*: unlike abstract classes alone, where the fixed part is by default whatever was not specified as part of the fixed part, in this case the variable parts are embodied in the code of the metaclass.

Safety

- *Enforcing the Constancy of the Fixed Part.* While subclassing still relates a family member to the abstract class—with the possibility of overriding—the use of meta-programming can potentially fully automate the generation of family members, obviating the need for the error-prone manual editing.
- *Specifying the Variable Parts Intensionally.* The use of metaprograms can both circumscribe the variable parts more explicitly than with subclassing alone, and enforce their conformance "by construction."

Evolvability   In addition to the advantages offered by abstract classes (see Section 11.2.3), the use of metaclasses adds one dimension of variability—and maintenance sharing—by encapsulating the description of the variable parts in the metaclass. We can now have two families that share the same fixed part, but whose variable parts may be different, and metaclass inheritance enables us to specify only the difference between the variable parts.

Finally, note that compared to metaprogramming alone, the reliance on classes to represent both the fixed and variable parts of the family is ergonomically superior, hence facilitating both family usage and maintenance.

11.4   DESIGN PATTERNS

Sections 11.2 and 11.3 focused on programming language constructs that support abstraction and parameterization. Those constructs are not always sufficient, and some languages do not support some of them (e.g., metaclasses). In this section, we look at design patterns that provide further mechanisms for abstraction and parameterization. Gamma et al. have viewed design patterns as a set of mechanisms that enable one aspect or another of an object-oriented system fragment to change without affecting other aspects [Gamma et al. 1995]. In some ways, design patterns may all be considered as abstraction mechanisms. In Table 11.1 we show excerpts of their classification [Gamma et al. 1995, p. 30]:

We won't talk about all of these patterns here. Some patterns will be presented as compositional patterns (Chapters 12 and 13), and others will be described along with the architectural frameworks (Chapter 14). Composition patterns are patterns that enable us to compose objects in unanticipated ways. Composability requires abstraction, and the distinction may be difficult to draw. One distinction that we find sometimes useful is to consider composition patterns as patterns that enable us to see different "peers" through similar interfaces, whereas abstraction/generalization patterns enable us to see a class hierarchy of variants through a common interface.

The patterns presented below include those from [Gamma et al. 1995] and others. We group them into structural abstraction patterns and process abstraction patterns.

11.4.1   Structural Abstraction Patterns

11.4.1.1   *A Basic Metamodeling Pattern: Representing Two Levels of Instantiation*
Figure 11.23 shows the object model of a design pattern we used many times to represent class information in C++ during runtime. Implementation-wise, instances of **ObjectType** have two dictionaries: one to hold descriptions of

TABLE 11.1 **Abstraction and Parameterization**

Purpose	Design Pattern	Aspect that Can Vary
Creational	Abstract factory	Families of product objects
	Builder	How a composite object gets created
	Factory method	Subclass of objects to be instantiated
	—	—
Structural	Adapter	Interface to an object
	Proxy	How an object is accessed; its location
	Bridge	Implementation of an object
	—	—
Behavioral	Iterator	How an aggregate's elements are accessed, traversed
	Observer	Number of objects that depend on another object; how the dependent objects stay up-to-date
	Strategy	An algorithm
	Template method	Steps of an algorithm
	Visitor	Operations that can be applied to object(s) without changing their classes

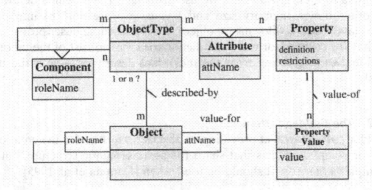

FIGURE 11.23 Simulating metaclasses in a classless language such as C++.

attributes (accessible by attribute name, or attName), that is, instances of class **Property**, and one to hold components, namely, other instances of the class **ObjectType**, accessible by component role name (e.g., leftLeg and rightLeg, both of which could be instances of **Leg**). An actual object will be represented by an instance of the class **Object** or one of its subclasses. Each object (instance of **Object**) will also have two dictionaries, one to hold attribute values (instances of **PropertyValue**, accessible by attName), and one to hold components (instances of **Object** or one of its subclasses, accessible by `roleName`). Objects point to the instance of **ObjectType** that describes them. The class **Object** (and its subclasses) will implement a constructor that takes an instance of **ObjectType** as an argument, from which to initialise the dictionaries. If the classes of objects in the application have no distinguishing behaviour except for the component and attribute access methods, a single class, **Object**, can represent all the classes.

This pattern is similar to Java's reflection package, but focuses on the structural aspects. In addition to attributes, we also provide for a representation of *components*, to stay close to the original object model. It has proven useful for cases where we have to deal with several classes with complex data structures but whose behavior was no, or little, more than structure access; all the access methods can be coded generically as table access methods. It supports the addition of new attributes to existing classes during time, and the addition of new classes altogether. One application area in which this pattern was used was a CAD (computer-assisted design) application that manipulated three-dimensional (3D) objects drawn by the user with a drawing editor. The second application had to do with the processing (analysis and routing) of messages in an avionics message processing system for a major U.S. airline, where incoming messages have unpredictable structure and contents.

An interesting extension of this model is the fact that an *object can have several descriptions*. In essence, by decoupling instances from the language built-in links to their types (since we use artificial types)—which determine, among other things, memory size and layout—we are able to implement multiple classification. Allowing an object to have multiple descriptors simply means that the constructor will build dictionaries that consist of the unions of the dictionaries originating from the individual descriptors—with the usual conflicts!

11.4.1.2 The Builder Pattern

The builder pattern aims at providing an abstract interface for the creation of families of complex objects that share the same semantic structure, but different implementations. It should be used when [Gamma et al. 1995]

- The algorithm for creating a complex object is (or should be) independent of the specific implementations of the parts, and how they are assembled.

- The construction process must allow different internal representations for the composite object.

The builder pattern separates the responsibilities for the creation of complex objects between two classes: (1) the *director*, which embodies the steps of the construction algorithm (the creation of the parts and their high-level assembly); and (2) the *concrete builder*, which implements the individual steps,

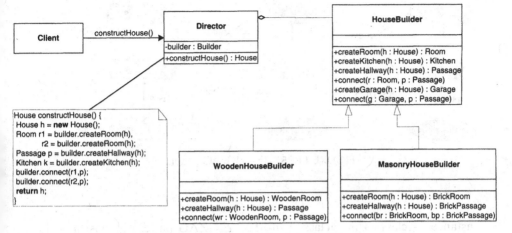

FIGURE 11.24   An illustration of the *builder pattern*.

independently (see Fig. 11.24). We assumed here that we have classes **House**, **Room**, **Passage**, **WoodenRoom**, **BrickRoom**, and so on.

This pattern can be combined with the previous one to parameterize the construction algorithm itself (code of `Director::constructHouse()`) by referring to a structural description of the house (or a different house with a different house plan) of the kind shown in Figure 11.23. Another interesting combination involves the interpreter pattern. In this case, the internal structure of the composite object is represented by sentences from a *structural grammar*, instead of being represented structurally as in Figure 11.23. Then, to build a house, the director parses its description in some language, and then invokes the API (application programming interface) of the builder where each function call may be considered as the semantic action associated with the grammar rule.

11.4.1.3   The ZIGZAG Pattern: Implementing Multilevel Metaclasses

We owe this pattern to Pachet [Pachet and Mili 1994], Sahraoui [1995], Revault et al. [1995], and the MétaGen system. MétaGen is a Smalltalk-based CASE tool generator that generates tools that transform models in a source description language (e.g., analysis model) to models in a target description language (e.g., design or implementation model). MétaGen takes as input a description of a source language, a description of a target language, and set of rules for transforming source language constructs to target language constructs. It outputs a graphical editor for the source language, a transformation procedure, and a graphical editor for the target language [Sahraoui and Revault 1995].

Although Smalltalk supports metaclasses, it supports only one level of metaclasses, and metaclasses have single instances. MetaGen requires several levels of instantiation that cannot be accommodated by Smalltalk's

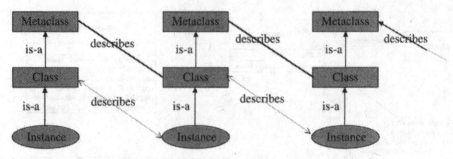

FIGURE 11.25 The ZIGZAG pattern.

instance → class → metaclass chain. The ZIGZAG pattern is illustrated in Figure 11.25.

The basic idea is that in addition to Smalltalk's built-in mechanism for defining and representing metaclasses of user-defined classes, we use an external manual link which allows us to represent class objects by regular instance-objects, which allow us in turn to go up an additional instantiation level. The representation of a class object by an instance is represented by an association describes whereby class objects point to instance objects through a *metaclass instance variable* called describedBy, and instance objects point back through an *instance variable* called describes. Figure 11.26 shows a generic object model for this pattern, and the corresponding Smalltalk class names.

The subclass link between **Metaclass** and **Object** is not an immediate one as there are two classes between the two; **Metaclass → Class Description → Behavior → Object**. Note that in Smalltalk80, developers generally build the hierarchy of classes, and the environment or system generates a parallel hierarchy of metaclasses, which they can then edit by adding properties and methods of classes as objects, namely, metaclass instance variables and methods. For example, the developer creates the class **MetagenObject**, and the system generates its metaclass called **MetagenObject class**. The developer may then add the instance variable describedBy. Developers of Metagen create their classes as subclasses of **MetagenObject**. The system creates the corresponding metaclass as a subclass of **MetagenObject class**, hence inheriting the describedBy variable and the corresponding access methods.

11.4.2 Behavioral Abstraction Patterns

11.4.2.1 The Template Method Pattern
Coplien argued that abstract methods (pure virtual functions in C++) enable us to abstract algorithms: we use the same signature to embody different

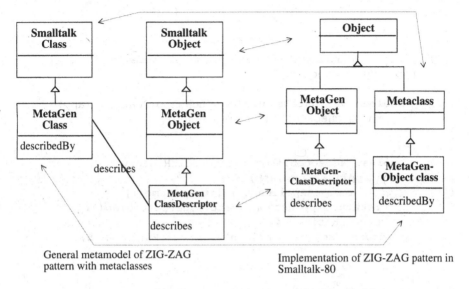

General metamodel of ZIG-ZAG
pattern with metaclasses

Implementation of ZIG-ZAG pattern in
Smalltalk-80

$\longleftarrow$ > : represents correspondence between generic metamodel and Smalltalk's

FIGURE 11.26 ZIZZAG pattern in a language with metaclasses, and in Smalltalk in particular.

algorithms for semantically equivalent functions [Coplien 1999]. The template method pattern enables us to abstract algorithm steps, in those cases where we could have several implementations for the same steps. The following code excerpts are self-explanatory:

```
(1)  abstract class ApplicationHandler {
        ...
(2)    public boolean evaluateLoanApplication(LoanApplication
       lapp){
(3)      if (!evaluateNeedForLoan(lapp)) return false;
(4)      if (!acceptableApplicantCreditHistory(lapp)) return
         false;
(5)      if (!acceptableEmploymentSituation(lapp)) return
         false;
(6)      return true;
       }
        ...
(7)    abstract boolean validateNeedForLoan(LoanApplication
       lapp);
(8)    abstract boolean acceptableApplicantCreditHistory
       (LoanApplication lapp);
(9)    abstract boolean acceptableEmploymentSituation
       (LoanApplication lapp);
```

```
        . . .
      }
(10)
(11)  class StudentLoanApplicationHandler extends
      ApplicationHandler {
        . . .
(12)    boolean validateNeedForLoan(LoanApplication lapp) {
          return checkTuitionInvoice(lapp);
        }
        . . .
(14)    boolean acceptableApplicantCreditHistory
        (LoanApplication lapp) {
(15)      if (lapp.getApplicant().livesAtHome())
(16)        return lapp.getApplicant().getCustodian().
            creditRating> 4;
(17)      return lapp.getApplicant().creditRating > 5;
        }
        . . .
      }
(18)  class MortgageApplicationHandler extends
      ApplicationHandler {
        . . .
(19)    boolean validateNeedForLoan(LoanApplication lapp) {...}
        . . .
      }
```

Note that the various steps of the algorithm need not all be abstract; some may be concrete. Note also that by trying hard enough, it is often possible to turn a case of "same semantics, different algorithm" into a case of a template method by finding higher-level commonalities between algorithms.

11.4.2.2 The Visitor Pattern

In Section 11.1.4.3, we talked about process abstraction as one application of metamodeling. The idea was to factor out a process in terms of a generic algorithm or calculation mapped onto the structure of the problem, and more specifically, the data structure. In the cases that we have seen, the variable part was the data structure and the constant part was the algorithm. Here we talk about the reverse situation, where the constant part is the structure, and the variable part is the actual algorithm. In this case, the algorithms correspond to different operations that we wish to perform on the elements of a complex structure. We illustrate the pattern with a language processing example.

Assume that we are developing a language parser, and that we build a syntax tree composed of different kinds of nodes. Once the syntax tree is built, there are several operations that we could perform on nodes, such as (1) performing semantic validation (e.g., type checking), (2) generating code in another language (e.g., machine language), and (3) optimizing. All of these algorithms involve recursive traversal of the tree. The "normal" way of doing this would code one method per algorithm per node type, as in

```
 (1)   class Node {
 (2)     boolean typeCheck() {...}
 (3)     void generateCode() {...}
 (4)     void optimize(){...}
 (5)   }
 (6)   class ExpressionNode extends Node {
 (7)     boolean typeCheck() {...}
 (8)     void generateCode() {...}
 (9)     void optimize() {...}
(10)   }
(11)   class FunctionCallNode extends Node {
(12)     boolean typeCheck() {...}
(13)     void generateCode() {...}
(14)     void optimize() {...}
(15)   }
```

The problem with this approach is that the addition of a new processing, such as pretty printing, involves making changes to all the class hierarchy, and coding one kind of recursive traversal per node, as different processes may use different traversals.

The solution proposed by the visitor pattern consists of grouping the different node-specific implementations of the new processing in a class, and letting each node-specific implementation traverse the subtree under it as it knows how. The solution is shown below:

```
 (1)  class Node {
 (2)    public abstract void accept(Visitor v);
 (3)  }
 (4)  class ExpressionNode extends Node {
 (5)    public void accept(Visitor v) {
            v.visitExpressionNode(this);}
 (7)  }
 (8)  class FunctionCallNode extends Node {
 (9)    public void accept (Visitor v) {
          v.visitFunctionCallNode(this);}
(10)  }
(11)  ...
(12)
(13)  class Visitor {
(14)    abstract void visitExpressionNode(ExpressionNode n);
(15)    abstract void visitFunctionCallNode(FunctionCallNode n);
(16)  }
(17)  class TypeCheckingVisitor extends Visitor {
(18)    public void visitExpressionNode(ExpressionNode n) {...}
```

```
(19)    public void visitFunctionCallNode(FunctionCallNode n) {...}
(20)    }
(21)    class CodeGenerationVisitor extends Visitor {
(22)    public void visitExpressionNode(ExpressionNode n) {...}
(23)    public void visitFunctionCallNode(FunctionCallNode n) {...}
(24)    }
```

Interestingly, although this pattern handles the addition of new operations easily, it makes the addition of new concrete classes more tedious: a new kind of node (e.g., LoopNode) may require adding one method with signature

```
public void visitLoopNode(LoopNode ln);
```

to each visitor class that we have already defined. This is somewhat to be expected; we have a many-to-many relationship between node types and operation types. We group the operations per node type if we expect stable operations and an evolving set of node types; or per operation type, if we expect a stable set of node types, and an evolving set of operations. Another problem with this pattern is the fact that visitors do the traversal themselves, and thus, may force us to expose more of the internal structure of node classes than we would have wished [Gamma et al. 1995]. One way to alleviate the problem would be to use the iterator pattern to traverse the tree independently of the node type.

11.5 CONCLUSION

To move from a development mode where we craft each component to fit into the so-far-developed ones to a more industrial mode where we build systems from standard components, we need to abstract away as much of the nonessential differences as we can. Nonessential differences are differences that do not deal with intent. Abstraction techniques aim at elevating the description of software to the level of *intent* or *specification* and letting different implementations, in the broad sense of the term (the algorithm, the internal representation, etc.), have a common expression.

In this chapter, we have seen an arsenal of abstraction techniques to be used at both the modeling and programming levels. In both cases, we have to factor out commonalities, in intent and realization, and find a common expression of the variabilities, in terms of intent.

The abstraction techniques that we described for modeling involve few, if any, new modeling concepts. Some of these concepts may be difficult to implement in a particular design or implementation. We advocate going for the most abstract description of a system that we can—but without losing important information—and worry about implementation later. We have shown a set of abstraction techniques to complement built-in language constructs. Some of these techniques are a bit far-fetched, and may not be practical in some situations, for a variety of reasons: (1) scheduling constraints, (2) resource constraints, or (3) performance constraints. Real-life software development is a constant struggle between short-term gain, where the bill comes due later during maintenance and evolution, and long-term gain, where we pay upfront, and hope for later gains. We trust that developers will choose their pain in a way best adapted to their situations.

Chapter 12

Composition Techniques in Object Orientation

If reusable components are the building bricks for building reliable and high quality software, composition techniques constitute the glue or mortar for assembling these components into a coherent and functional whole. In Chapter 7, we identified abstraction and composability as key properties for reusable components. Abstraction has to do with generality and intensional representation of differences (Chapter 11). Abstraction boundaries are modularization interfaces that encapsulate what we believe to be reusable chunks of functionality. Intuitively, composability has to do with the extent to which a variety of functions may be realized by assembling a set of reusable components. The wider the range of behaviors (functions) one can derive from the same set of functions, the better. Abstraction and composability are somewhat contradictory qualities. Abstraction requires exposing as little as possible of the internals of a component. Composability, on the other hand, requires exposing as much of a component as possible, to allow for greater degrees of freedom in recombining it. Composability has to be planned: components are only composable in ways that have been preplanned and built into the design, packaging, and programming. Accordingly, our discussion of composition will be as much about designing and building components as it is about actually composing them.

In the first section, we look in more detail at the underlying issues and at the various tradeoffs. The remainder of the chapter deals with specific techniques for packaging components in such a way as to make them composable. We start (in Section 12.2) with the programming language constructs that are used to support composition. This is done for completeness purposes; in real life, the choice of an implementation language will be dictated by much stronger constraints than composability! Section 12.3 deals with composability at the module level. We will study a number of emerging packaging techniques for packaging functional slices of software applications that cut across the traditional method—class—module structure to provide greater levels of flexibility. Section 12.4 deals with design-level support for composability and composition. In particular, we study some design patterns for building components that are composable by design, as well as design patterns for bridging and composing components that weren't meant to be composed. We go back to our two case studies in Section 12.5 to illustrate some of the techniques discussed in this chapter, and conclude in Section 12.6.

12.1 ISSUES

12.1.1 Composability Requirements

For reusable artifacts to be composable, a number of criteria have to be met. Two components are composable if they are able to communicate and to interoperate. However, if we want these components to be composable with other components, they need to be independent.

Communication and interoperability require that the artifacts use the same "language," in the broadest sense. If the artifacts are analysis-level artifacts, for example, it is important that the same notation (or equivalent notations) be used. If the artifacts are concrete source code or executables, then we have to have the same programming language or, failing that, the same interface protocol such as the same parameter passing modes, the same marshaling protocols, and so on. For example, component object model (COM) components use the same interface language and the same parameter passing (and memory layout) conventions, regardless of the language [Box 1997]. Similarly, components distributed over ORBs may interoperate if each implements the interface that the other expects, but they don't have to use the same programming language.

Once communication problems have been bridged, there remain other considerations for components to interoperate. Garlan and colleagues have shown that interface compatibility is far from sufficient to ensure interoperability of components [Garlan et al. 1995]. Consider the following two classes:

```
class Dispatcher {
  private Queue _taskQueue;
  ...
  public void dispatchNextTask(){
    Task ts =
      (Task)_taskQueue.dequeue();
    ts.run(Task.Priority);
  }
  ...
}
```

```
class Task {
  public static int Priority = 0;
  ...
  public void run(int priority) {
    ...
  }
  ...
}
```

Whoever wrote the dispatcher probably intended the method `run(int)` of **Task** to run in a separate thread.

In this way, the call to `ts.run(Task.Priority)` will return control to the caller (a dispatcher) before the task (`ts`) completes its execution. If, on the other hand, **Task** were written single-threaded, then `ts.run(Task.Priority)` would not return before ts completes, and the application would not function normally. Garlan and his colleagues identified a number of other architecture-related factors that are important to consider for composability.

Regarding independence, it is important that the artifacts be composable without having to change either one, for that would prevent them from being composable with other components. Failing to achieve that, whichever change is required to make two components interoperate has to be low-cost and independent of their core functionalities. The latter can be achieved with proper packaging by separating components into a constant piece with a generic interface, and a bunch of adapters that adapt that interface to specific usage situations.

The last requirement for composability has to do with abstraction, and was discussed in Section 9.1 and in the introductory paragraph of this chapter. The idea is as follows. A reusable artifact embodies a range of behaviors, only a subset of which is made accessible to the outside through the artifact's interface. We would like our artifacts or components to expose all those aspects that are of interest to composition, so that their packaging (or abstraction) does not limit their composability. We may refer to this property as *composability-preserving packaging*. We will examine different facets to the abstraction versus composability preserving property of packaging techniques.

12.1.2   Structural and Behavioral Composition

When we talk about composition, there are two aspects to consider: structural composition and behavioral composition. *Structural composition* deals with the assembly of entities at the data definition level. *Behavioral composition*, on the other hand, deals with the possibility for two components to interact in the process of achieving a higher-level function that is not supported by either component alone. The two are not independent. Depending on the programming paradigm used, the structural composition may be all that is needed to specify the behavioral composition of the components. For example, in a logic-based system, the behavior of a program is embodied in a collection of loosely structured declarative if-then constructs through which loops a rule engine. Putting two sets of rules together is all that is required to get the system to exhibit the *composition* of the *behaviors* of the two programs taken separately. In other words, *structural composition subsumes behavioral composition*. The farther away we move from the declarative paradigm, the more explicit we need to be about the composition. For example, if we are dealing with stateless functions (functions with no side effects on shared data), the only way to get two components (functions) to interact is by having *one call the other.*

We could think of object-oriented programming as half way between a purely declarative programming paradigm and a purely functional paradigm; the methods of an object are composed through their side effects on the object's state data. At the same time, most interactions between objects are mediated through interobject method call. Finally, we should add that structural (data) composition of objects is usually used to let objects see each other so that they may interact over a long period of time, beyond the scope and life of a method call. From our simulation environment, consider the following C++ class definition:

```
class EventHandler: . . . {
  . . .
  Queue⟨Event⟩ _eventQueue;
public:
  void handleNextEvent() {
    Event currentEvent = _eventQueue.dequeue();
    . . .}
  . . .
}
```

Here the many-to-one relationship between events and dispatchers is embodied in a Queue⟨T⟩ variable. This enables an event handler to have access to the events to which it is associated and to invoke behaviors on them. To some extent, the structural composition relationship provides handles for objects to support behavioral composition.

Generally speaking, static associations in object models act as media or *vehicles* for more or less complex behavioral compositions. Different types of static associations imply different patterns of interaction between the associated objects. For example, aggregation often implies propagating some operations from the aggregate to the components.[1] When we delete an aggregate, depending on the semantics of the aggregation, that is, whether it entails existential dependency, we may have to delete the components as well.

Note that in the general case aggregation does not give either the aggregate or the components access privileges to each other's protected data and function members. However, nested classes in C++ and Java do give the nested classes private access privileges. In C++, nested classes can be simulated with external friend classes. Java distinguishes between static and nonstatic internal classes. Nonstatic internal classes are like "appendages" added to objects

---

[1] This is often considered to be the only discernible difference between aggregation and "regular" associations.

of the host class in the sense that they have access to the *values* of the data members of the object within which they were created. The following illustrates internal classes:

```
class Event . . . {
  private int _eventNumber = 0;

  class PriorityLevel {
    private int _normalLevel = 0;
    private int _niceLevel = -10;

    PriorityLevel(int normal, int nice) {
      _normalLevel = normal;
      _niceLevel = nice;
      System.out.println("Priority levels for event #"
+
(L1)        _eventNumber + ": \n" +
          "\t Normal level: " + normal + "\n"+
          "\t Nice level: " + nice);
    }
  }
  Event(int eventNum) {
      _eventNumber = eventNum;
(L2)   new PriorityLevel(1,-20);
  }
}
```

Then, if some piece of code contained the sequence: Event myEvent = new Event(123);, the following will be produced on the standard output:

```
Priority levels for event #123:
  Normal level: 1
  Nice level:   -20
```

The line tagged (L1) in the previous program shows how instances of PriorityLevel are able to access data members of the current object's _eventNumber attribute. Line (L2) shows an instantiation of the internal class within the context of the constructor of **Event**. Just by virtue of it being created within the context of a method on the object event # 123, it has access to its data members. If we wanted to keep referring to this appendage, we would have had to store a reference to it in a data member of the class **Event**-call it _priorityLevel. Then, we would replace (L2) by (L'2):

```
(L'2)  _priorityLevel = new PriorityLevel(1,-20);
```

Static internal classes in Java are like nested classes in C++: they are not appendages of any specific objects of the enclosing class, but they have private access privileges to such objects when they are used as method parameters or local variables.

12.1.3 Abstraction and Granularity

As mentioned in the introduction of this chapter, *composability* of reusable components refers to the range of behaviors that these components can generate when assembled with other components—regardless of the assembly or composition mechanism. *Abstraction*, on the other hand, refers to the extent to which only those properties that should be of concern to the user of the component are exposed. Typically, abstraction is usage-specific; we expose those aspects or features of a component that are relevant to a particular use, or to a family of uses. By focusing on one set of uses, we are bound to make other—perhaps nonanticipated—uses impossible. Hence, composability and abstraction tend to be contradictory.

Consider the example of scrollable lists. In the first graphical libraries (including the first Smalltalk libraries), we had a separate class for scrollable lists and nonscrollable lists; the same for text panes, which could be scrolled in the either/or direction. A scrollable list had a lot of functionalities that were generally useful and had nothing to do with scrolling. We could not use such a functionality alone (or else we would have to pass default values for the parameters that were related to scrolling). More recent versions of graphical libraries have adopted the decorator (or *wrapper*) pattern to "decorate" base classes with additional optional behavior. Decomposing a scrollable list into a list and a scrollable container made for greater reuse of the subcomponents. This did, however, expose some of the interactions between the display of lists and the scrolling that were hidden in the scrollable list abstraction.

This is a general principle; one way of striking a good balance between abstraction and composability is to decompose a component into smaller, yet abstract, subcomponents—we referred to this technique as *splitting* in Section 8.4. The idea here is that we get a wider range of behaviors by replacing some of the subcomponents with other components that have the same interface but different implementations. Further, because the subcomponents are simpler and have smaller interfaces, they impose fewer constraints on their counterparts, and are thus more composable, individually, and as a group—hence one of the premises behind object frameworks. However, by performing this splitting, we expose the interactions between the subcomponents, and add complexity to the component (aggregate) as a whole.

12.1.4 Binding Time

Components may be composed at different times in the software lifecycle. Generally speaking, as a component moves through the lifecycle, some of its properties (aspects or features) are frozen or *bound*, reflecting the choices that we make in the course of the development. As those properties are bound, the component becomes less composable—that is a fact of software life (see Chapter 7). Thus, greater composability suggests that we perform composition as early in the development stage as we can, when the components are still unconstrained, to maximize the range of compositions that we can make. However, by doing so, we leave a lot of work to be done *after* the composition to arrive at a concrete aggregate. Thus, we have to choose between more possibilities for high-cost compositions, and fewer opportunities, but for fairly low cost compositions. Our goal, from a technical standpoint, will be to find ways of packaging software, and to develop composition techniques that allow us to perform the maximum range of compositions, as late in the development lifecycle as possible. Savings in development effort are only half of the story. There are other motivations for seeking late-bound compositions, including decentralized development and ownership of the components that need to be composed, the runtime flexibility, and configurability of the resulting applications, reducing downtime for maintenance, binary compatibility between releases of the same product, and so on.

As we strive for delaying composition time, we should be aware of the performance costs of late-bound compositions. They usually involve additional coordination overhead for the components. Further, they usually preclude various kinds of optimizations, as optimizations typically take shortcuts through the control and/or data flow of a program based on prior knowledge of that flow.

12.2   LINGUISTIC APPROACHES

In this section, we study a number of language-level constructs that support component composition. Most of our discussion is centered around constraints or logic programming, and functional programming, and draws on the discussion in Section 9.3.1. Although these constructs correspond to different programming paradigms, they are interesting for our purposes because of the hybrid object-oriented languages, and because of the non-object-oriented extensions to existing OO languages. The discussion on interobject behavior addresses extensions to object-oriented languages that address the specification of interobject behavior.

12.2.1   Constraint and Logic-Based Programming

With logic-based programming, a program consists of a set of logical of rules, and a set of assertions. An inference engine matches assertions against logical rules, in order to reach new assertions (forward chaining) or hypotheses (backward chaining) that are consistent with the rule base and the set of assertions. Figure 12.1 illustrates this paradigm. The "program" as well as its inputs and outputs are represented declaratively, and are manipulated by a "real" program. A sample logic program is shown below.

```
cousin(x,y):- parent(x,t),sibling(t,s),parent(y,s)
cousin(x,y) :- parent(x,z),parent(y,t),cousin(z,t)
sibling(x,y):- parent(x,z),parent(y,z)
```

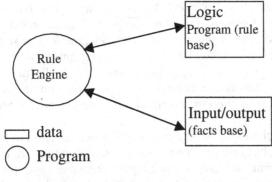

FIGURE 12.1 The rule-based paradigm.

Possible input/output data could be

```
parent(Charles,Elisabeth)
parent(Elisabeth,Mary)
parent(Maggie,Mary)
parent(Mary,Ann)
parent(Dorothy,Ann)
parent(Irene,Dorothy)
parent(John,Maggie)
```

From this program and this input, we can deduce:

```
sibling(Mary,Dorothy):
parent(Elisabeth,Maggie)
cousin(Charles,John)
cousin(Elisabeth,Irene)
cousin(Maggie,Irene)
```

To compose programs in logic, we simply have to "put together" two rule bases, and let the rule engine go through them as a single base. For example, a second rule base might look like

```
grandparent(x,y) :- parent(x,z), parent(z,y)
cousin(x,y) :- parent(x,z),grandparent(z,t),grandparent(y,t)
```

which, with the same inputs, will deduce the following additional facts:

```
cousin(Charles,Irene)
cousin(John,Irene)
```

The interesting thing here is that simply by concatenating the two rule bases, we get all the facts that can be *theoretically* inferred from the combination of the two rule bases. In other words, the packaging of rule bases as simple files is composability-preserving; the knowledge (program) remains composable at the lowest possible granularity level, namely, the logical statement. Moreover, no change has to take place to either "program" to make it composable with the other notwithstanding nomenclature standardization. As mentioned in Section 9.3.1, this is one reason why few implementations of PROLOG support any encapsulation or information hiding mechanism that would hide some rules.

In terms of binding time, the composition of logic programs can be done during runtime; because the "program" is itself data that are manipulated by a inference engine, we can—in principle—compose logic programs during runtime. However, doing this during runtime precludes a number of optimizations that inference engines typically make to speed up execution.

What is valid for logic programming is also valid for constraint programming. In this case, the program is a set of *constraints* on a set of variables, and the input is a set of values for *some* of these variables. A constraint satisfaction procedure propagates the values of bound variables to unbound variables by using the constraints. The following is an example of a constraint program or *constraint satisfaction problem*.

$$\text{Variables: } \{X_1, X_2, X_3, X_4, X_5\}$$
$$\text{Constraints:}$$
$$X_3 < \min(X_1, X_2)$$
$$X_3 + X_4 > X_5$$

The input for this constraint satisfaction problem could be

$$X_1 = 4$$
$$X_5 = 6$$

With these values, there are various families of solutions $\langle X_2, X_3, X_4 \rangle$, including $\langle 5, 3, 4 \rangle$ (or more generally, $\langle X_2 = X_1 + a, X_3 = X_1 - 1, X_4 = X_5 - X_3 + 1 + b \rangle$), $\langle 2, 2, 5 \rangle$ (or more generally, $\langle X_2 = X_1 - a, X_3 = X_2 = X_1 - a, X_4 = X_5 - X_1 + 1 + a \rangle$), and so forth. Typical constraint solvers either stop once they find a solution, or enumerate all the solutions that they find. A constraint satisfaction problem may be composed with another constraint satisfaction problem simply by putting together the two sets of constraints, and letting the solver find values that satisfy both sets of constraints. For example, we could add the constraint: $X_3 > 2$, which would exclude the second family of solutions $(\langle 2,2,5 \rangle)$, and make the problem unsolvable for any $X_1 < 4$. This does not involve making any changes to any of the original "programs," and the solver will find exactly the solutions that would have resulted from designing the two programs as one, from the beginning. In other words, the packaging of constraints is, much like the packaging of logic programs, composability-preserving.

It would appear that logic and constraint programming are ideal for composability. So why isn't logic programming the paradigm of choice for reuse? One of the reasons is abstraction; the packaging mechanisms for logic programs (and constraint satisfaction problems) offer no abstraction, making the paradigm nonscalable. Further, there is the problem of performance. Both logic programming and constraint programming are inefficient. We saw in Section 9.3 that in order to make logic programming abstract or efficient, we have to give up some measure of composability by either exposing fewer of the base rules or compiling the existing rules into new synthetic rules for example, by taking the closure of a long chain of rules.

12.2.2 Functional Composition

Historically, functional composition has been the traditional way of composing software components—mostly code in the beginning. With functional composition, new functions are computed by feeding the outputs of some functions as input(s) to other functions. Functional abstraction abstracts a computation on specific data items into a *function* on a possibly wider domain (see Section 9.3.1). However, by hiding the implementation of this function, we preclude reuse of fragments of this implementation that realize subfunctions. Figure 12.2 shows three different packagings of the same computation, which result in different composability and reusability profiles. Starting with top left corner, we have the original program. The lower left corner shows a first functional abstraction. The resulting function $g(x,y,z,t)$ is fairly usage-specific, and not much reusability results. The final decomposition (right side) identifies two reusable abstractions, namely, the difference between vectors, and the normalized length of a vector.

When talking about functional composition, we should distinguish between two ships: (1) that between float f (float, float) and float g (float, float, float, float) and (2) that between float[] diff(float[], float[]) and float norm(float[]). Relationship 1, which may be referred to a the call relationship, or *functional imbrication*, is actually fairly restrictive. In terms of binding, f (...) is bound to using g (...) or a function with similar *name* and *signature* at coding time. We say that this relationship creates a *lexical binding* between f (. . .) and g (. . .) in the sense that, not only does f (. . .) require a function that computes the norm of the difference of two vectors, but that function has to be called g (. . .). This relationship is, by definition, asymmetric: f (...) depends on g (...), but g (...) does not depend on f (. . .).

Polymorphism in both functional and object-oriented programming languages alleviates the problem created by the call relationship, and delays the binding of the function to a specific implementation until runtime. But the lexical binding remains, and yet, function *names* are *nonessential* properties of functions. Some of the packaging and design techniques discussed later will alleviate or get rid of this binding.

```
float f(float a, float b) {
    float x = getX();
    float y = getY();
    float diffx = x - a,
          diffy = y - b;
    float res = diffx*diffx;
    res += diffy*diffy;
    res = Math.sqrt(res);
    return res;
}
```

```
float f(float a, float b) {
    float x = getX();
    float y = getY();
    return g(x,a,y,b);
}

float g(float x1, float x2,
        float y1, float y2) {
    float  diff1 = x1 - x2,
           diff2 = y1 - y2;
    res =  diff1 * diff1 +
           diff2 * diff2;
    return Math.sqrt(res);
}
```

```
float f(float a, float b) {
    float x = getX();
    float y = getY();
    return g(x,a,y,b);
}

float g(float x1, float x2, float y1,
float y2) {
    float[] vec1={x1,y1};
    float[] vec2={x2,y2};
    return norm(diff(vec1,vec2));
}

float[] diff(float[] v1, float[] v2) {
    float[] v3 = new float[v1.length];
    for(int i=0;i<v1.length;i++)
        v3[i]=v1[i]-v2[i];
    return v3;
}

float norm(float[] v) {
    float res=0;
    for (int i=0;i<v.length;i++)
        res+=v[i]*v[i];
    return Math.sqrt(res);
}
```

FIGURE 12.2 Three packagings of the same functionality, with different reusability profiles.

The relationship between float[] diff(...) and float norm(...) is more interesting. If we forget that the starting point was the function g(...) and assume that we had a library containing float[] diff(...) and float norm(...), and that we had to build a function that computes the norm of the difference between two vectors, then we would have written g(...) as a composition of these two functions. This composability between diff and norm is far less restrictive than the call relationship between f(...) and g(...) because there is no explicit reference from either function to the other. In this case, it so happens that the range (output domain) of one function (diff) is included within the (input) domain of the other, and we were thus able to compose them—in the mathematical sense. In this kind of relationship, the composition code is external to both components. That code can be more or less complex depending on differences in data formats between the two functions, and depending on whichever other computations need to occur in the between. We will refer to this relationship as (mathematical) functional composition.

Interestingly, some researchers have developed software composition programs based on these principles. Robert Hall, of AT&T Bell Labs, had developed a software composition tool that took as input the input/output pairs for the desired program, and that tested various compositions from a library to see which composition would exhibit the desired behavior. Assume, for example, that our reuse library contained the functions `diff(...)` and `norm(...)` mentioned above, as well as a third function, `float[] sum(float[],float[])`, which takes two arrays of floats and returns a single array of floats. A developer (a user of the reuse library) specifies the following input/output pairs:

```
Inputs                    Output
V1=[3,0],  V2=[0,4]       5
V1=[2,2],  V2=[1,2]       1
```

First, because of the types of the inputs and the output, we know that the only possible combinations are `norm(diff(v1,v2))`, `norm(diff(v2,v1))`, or `norm(sum(v1,v2))`. On the basis of the first input → output mapping, all three combinations are possible: V1 − V2 = [3,−4], V2 − V1 = [−3,4], and V1 + V2 = [3,4], and the norm (square root of sum of squares) is 5. If we look at the second set of input/output values, then only `norm(diff(v1,v2))` or `norm(diff(v2,v1))` would produce the output 1; `norm(sum(v1,v2))` would produce 5 again. Thus, in response to the query of the developer, the system answers with these two functions, and lets the user choose or specify additional input/output values to differentiate between the two compositions.[2] Notwithstanding its exponential complexity [Hall 1993, Mili et al. 1994a], this kind of approach is possible only with interpreted languages so that compositions can be generated and tested on the fly. Further, the components should be side-effect-free, or would need to operate in a simulated environment. For the anecdote, Hall tried this approach on lisp functions, and forbade LISP functions with side effects (i.e., used LISP the way it was designed: a purely functional language).

Research curiosities aside, functional composition remains a powerful behavioral composition paradigm, and is the major—but not the only—composition mechanism in object-oriented software. We showed two kinds of composition mechanisms. The first mechanism, called *functional imbrication*, is based on the asymmetric call relationship, and binds the components to each other at coding time, making them fairly dependent. The second mechanism, called *mathematical functional composition*, or functional composition, for short, composes two components or functions by writing glue code that connects the data flows in and out of the components. This kind of composition keeps the two components independent, and make them suitable for a variety of uses.

This dichotomy may seem contrived to the extent that by writing code that glues together two functions, we are creating an imbrication relationship between the glue code and the original functions. In the running example, `diff(...)` and `norm(...)` are composed in a "good way," but are now imbricated in the function that implements the glue code: `g(...)`.

---

[2] In this case, both are valid, of course.

What does this mean in terms of development? Concretely, this means that if we develop components that are meant to collaborate, we should isolate collaboration behavior from what might be called `intrinsic behavior`. Intrinsic behavior is context independent reusable behavior. Collaboration behavior is usage specific context-dependent nonreusable behavior. By separating the two, we increase the reusability of the intrinsic behavior and reduce the extent of the code that is specific to a particular use. Figure 12.3 shows example heuristics for performing this separation. We have a method $f(\ldots)$ in class A that invokes a method $i(\ldots)$ in class B, and a method $h(\ldots)$ in class B that invokes $g(\ldots)$ on A. These dependencies bind big chunks of the two classes together. The idea here is to break those functions that involve coordination [$f(\ldots)$ from class A and $h(\ldots)$ from class B] into smaller collaboration- or context-independent methods [$f_1(\ldots)$, $f_2(\ldots)$ for the case of $f(\ldots)$, and $h_1(\ldots)$ and $h_2(\ldots)$ for the case of $h(\ldots)$]. This heuristic maintains the dependence between the classes A and B, but reduces its scope: greater chunks of A's (B's) functionality may be used with classes other than B (A).

A number of approaches to modeling interobject behavior have gone a step further—they package coordination behavior in entities that are different from the original components. These include work on Thinglab (see previous section) by Alan Borning et al., as well as other work inspired by Thinglab, including our own work on what we called *constraint objects* [Mili et al. 1989, 1990]; a constraint object consists of data and procedures. The data consists of a tuple of objects involved in a particular constraint. The procedures consist of operations that need to be executed to satisfy the constraint, if one of the constrained objects changed state in a way that violated the constraint. A similar concept was proposed by Helm et al. [1990] to describe behavioral dependencies in terms of *contracts*. More recently, we find a similar concept

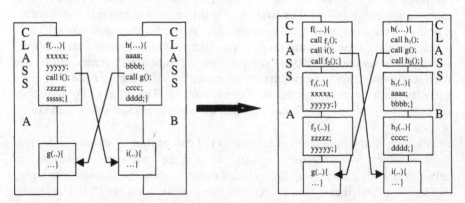

FIGURE 12.3   Breaking up methods that explicitly invoke behavior in collaborating objects.

in *aspect oriented programming* [Kiczales et al. 1997]. We talk about aspect-oriented programming later in the chapter.

12.2.3 Hybrid Object-Oriented and Declarative Approaches

Since the early 1980s, a number of researchers have proposed hybrid approaches that combined logic or constraint programming with object-oriented programming. Logic and constraint programming may be used to describe (and enact) complex relationships and interactions between objects. This was the case for most of the earlier work dealing with languages, tools, and development environments for highly reactive graphical user interfaces. Alan Borning, of the University of Washington, had developed an object-oriented constraint language on top of Smalltalk that supported the specification of complex geometrical constraints between graphical objects [Borning and Duisberg 1986]. Such constraints included the connectivity of a graph, as nodes are moved around, or the relative positions and sizes of geometrical figures, as one of them is moved or resized. Typically, given an initial solution, a constraint solver would detect changes in some of the constrained objects, and propagate those changes to adjacent objects.

One of the authors has worked since the late 1980s on an object-based model of constraints where constraints are represented by classes whose instances represent tuples of objects subjected to the constraint [Mili et al. 1989, 1990]. The instance methods of constraint classes were responsible for enforcing the constraint on a given tuple of objects when state changes in those objects violated the constraint. Unlike the Borning et al. approach, where constraint satisfaction was the responsibility of a single solver, in our approach each constraint had its own domain dependent *satisfiers*. We used an event-based notification mechanism (see Section 12.4.1) to propagate the changes across tuples sharing objects (see Fig. 12.4). This paradigmatic purity came at a very high performance price: the satisfaction of a set of constraints using *relaxation*. In some cases,[3] we were able to derive an analytic solution to a set of constraints.

Helm et al. proposed *contracts* as a way of describing interobject behavior. They view object collaborations as contracts between the participants specified in terms of (1) obligations of the various participants, in terms of the functions that they must support; and (2) interaction sequences, which show the exchange of messages between the participants of the contract in the process of executing the contract. The following excerpt shows the subject-view contract that binds a model (subject) to its views. This is a variation on the *observer*

---

[3] Linear "satisfiers," that is, satisfiers that modified the state variables of constrained objects using a linear function. In this case, we are able to compile a set of "adjacent" constraints into a single constraint.

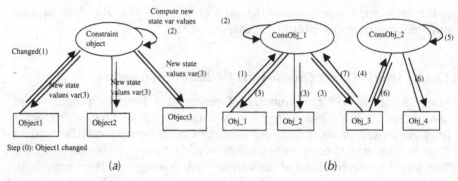

Step (0): Object1 changed

(a)   (b)

FIGURE 12.4   (a) Constraint objects listen for state change events, compute new state variable values for constrained objects, and dispatch the new values; (b) satisfying adjacent constraints using relaxation. `ConObj_1` and `ConsObj_2` take turns at updating objects.

design pattern discussed in Section 12.4.2. The invariant shows the properties that the contract guarantees.

```
contract SubjectView
  Subject supports [
    value: Value
    SetValue(val:Value)+-> δ value {value = val};
                                               Notify()
    GetValue(): Value +--> return value
    Notify() +--> 〈|| v : v ε Views: v +--> Update() 〉
    AttachView(v:View) +--> {v ε Views}
    DetachView(v:View) +--> {v not ε Views}
    ]
  Views : Set(View) where each View supports [
    Update() +--> Draw()
    Draw() +--> Subject -> GetValue()
                         {View reflects Subject.value}
    SetSubject(s:Subject) +--> {Subject = s}
    ]
  invariant
    Subject.SetValue(val) +--> 〈 ∀ v: v ε Views:
                         v reflects Subject.value〉
  instantiation
    〈||v: v ε Views : 〈Subject -> AttachView(v) ||
                         v -> SetSubject(Subject)) 〉
  end contract
```

From this definition, it is not clear whether contracts are used simply for documentation (and perhaps validation) purposes, or whether "contract objects" are used to set up and enforce contracts. We know of no direct implementation of contracts in this form. Ian Holland went ahead and developed a formal model of contracts in the context of his PhD at Northeastern University. The idea of using entities to monitor or enact collaborations between other entities was reincarnated in aspect-oriented programming (AOP) under the name of *dynamic aspects* (see Section 12.3.1). From a commercial product point of view, we know of no commercial implementation of the idea of constraints or contracts, with the exception of a tool kit developed by ILOG Inc. that allows to add a constraint solving component to object-oriented applications. The ILOG Solver[(TM)4] product is a C++ library that supports an application programming interface (API) for specific constraints on C++ objects, and enumerating solutions based on a variety of algorithms. Example applications of the ILOG Solver toolkit include various optimization problems involving scheduling, routing, and complex design problems.

If we consider the knowledge representation side to object-oriented languages' ancestry, it makes sense to consider rule-based extensions to object-oriented languages. Beyond the research prototypes, there have been a number of commercial products that mix the two paradigms. Most products originated as single paradigm products, which later incorporated, more or less successfully, other paradigms to broaden the range of problems for which their product might be applied. ILOG Rules/JRules products are one example where the integration between the object paradigm and the rule-based paradigm has been performed successfully. Assume for example that we have a telecom network management application where we monitor messages coming from various pieces of the network to assess the state of the network. Typically, equipment pieces will be sending messages whether they are functioning properly and not, and even the messages that signal improper behaviour may not warrant attention as the problem will correct itself, or, comes from a bigger problem elsewhere. Message filtering is a big piece to handle, and it involves complex, and sometimes heuristic, logic. Let **MessageHandler** be the class that handles messages, as shown below (in C++):

```
class MessageHandler {
   ...
   StatusType status = AVAILABLE;
public:
   void handleMessage(Message mess);
   void handleErrorMessage(Message mess, PRIORITY pr= 0);
   void handleAdministrationMessage(Message mess);
   ...
}
```

We assume that incoming messages are first handed to handle-Message(Message), which then decides what to do with the message, and dispatches it to the appropriate handler, for instance, handleError-

---

[4] Web site: http://www.ilog.com. Solver is a trademark of ILOG, Inc.

Message(Message,PRIORITY), in case the message turns out an error message that needs attention, or handleAdministrationMessage (Message), which handles accounting and billing messages, and so on. Typically, the handleMessage(Message) method would have fairly complex logic, and that logic would probably evolve. With ILOG Rules, we can delegate that logic to a rule-based agent which will do the proper reasoning and call the proper message handler. The behavior of this agent is described using an OPS5-like syntax, which is translated by a rule compiler into C++ code. The following is an example rule:

```
(defrule repeatErrorMessage default
(1)   ?m:   (Message comesFrom = ?equip time=?t)
(2)         (count > THRESHOLD (Message comesFrom = ?equip
                                        time > ?t-30))
(3)   ?mh:  (MessageHandler status = AVAILABLE)
            ->
(3)         (apply ?mh handleErrorMessage(?m,HIGH))
(4)         (retract ?m)
)
```

This rule is called repeatErrorMessage and has a priority of default. Line (1) matches any instance of class Message that the rule agent was told about "recently"; the condition in line (2) is valid if there are more than THRESHOLD messages on the same piece of equipment that occurred within the last 30 seconds. Line (3) matches any message handler that is currently available. Thus, if there is one recently asserted or known message ?m on a piece of equipment that generated more than THRESHOLD messages over the last 30 seconds, and if there is a message handler ?mh that is available, hand the message ?m to the handler ?mh to process as an error message [line (3)], and forget about message ?m [line (4)].

The rules compiler takes a set of such rules, and generates a rule agent that maintains a "working memory" (a bunch of pointers to C++ domain objects to watch), and that tests the rules on the objects in its working memory, triggering, and eventually firing the rules whose condition part is satisfied. We won't go into the details of the product, but suffice it to say that the rules compiler needs some information about the C++ classes to be able to translate such high-level rule expressions to the C++ code; developers need to provide that information in the rules file. Let **FilteringAgent** be the name of the class generated by the rules compiler; we can rewrite the class **MessageHandler** as follows:

```
class MessageHandler {
  FilteringAgent* myAgent;
  ...
  StatusType status = AVAILABLE;
```

```
public:
   // default constructor. Initialize working memory of rule
   // agent
   MessageHandler() {
      myAgent = new FilteringAgent();
(1)   myAgent->assert(this);
      // assert other info. about the network that the agent
      // needs to reason
(2)   myAgent->assert(...);
   }
   void handleMessage(Message mess) {
(3)   myAgent->assert(mess);
(4)   myAgent->fireAllRules();
   }
   void handleErrorMessage(Message mess, PRIORITY pr= 0);
   void handleAdministrationMessage(Message mess);
   ...
}
```

Line (1) shows how we tell a rule agent about which C++ objects to monitor: using (automatically generated) method `assert`. The message handler lets the agent know about itself, and about other info related to network equipment and parameters [line (2)]. Line (3) shows what the method `handleMessage(Message)` looks like in this case; it "tells" the agent about the new message that arrived, and asks it to do its thing (`fireAllRules` will keep firing rules as long as new facts and conclusions continue to be asserted, and rules keep being triggered).

This specific use of rule agents is simply a realization of the *Strategy* pattern, whereby we delegate the implementation of a complex algorithm to a separate component (for details on the Strategy object, see Gamma et al. [1995]). It also shows a practical way of modeling interobject behavior by reasoning on a set of objects, and triggering actions on some of them.

To conclude, *constraint programming and rule-based programming make useful additions to the object-oriented paradigm as a way of expressing complex business logic that cannot be easily split between a set of interacting objects.* The distribution of responsibilities between objects has always been a thorny point in object-oriented analysis and design. As shown in Chapter 9, object boundaries are not always the best abstraction and encapsulation boundaries for reusable functionalities in general, and composition in particular.

12.3 MODULARIZATION AND PACKAGING APPROACHES

In this section, we discuss a number of approaches to modularization and composition that are within the object-oriented development paradigm, but that propose additional modularization or abstraction boundaries to the usual method, class, and collections of classes (package, namespace). Underlying all these methods is the assumption that there exist some "natural reusable chunks" of functionality that cut across the abstraction boundaries of object-oriented programming. There is emergent consensus in the community that these approaches help package different *concerns* and as such, may be seen as enabling techniques for ensuring a good separation of concerns in software. Aspect-oriented programming deals with *concerns* that cross-cut several classes, which are packaged as *aspects*. Aspects are *woven* into traditional OO programs to inject a concern across a set of classes. Subject-oriented programming considers object-oriented applications as *fusions* or compositions of class hierarchies, each embodying a point of view on the same domain objects. View programming considers classes as time-varying aggregates of *views*, where each view is an instantiation of a generic functional template for the domain object at hand [Mili et al. 1999]. Subject-oriented programming, the oldest of the three approaches [Ossher and Harrison 1992, Harrison and Ossher 1993] has made it into a product, IBM's C++ toolset, and prototype support is available for Java (*HyperJ*). Aspect-oriented programming [Kiczales et al. 1997] has been implemented in Java (*AspectJ*) and is available free of charge. View programming is still a laboratory prototype. We discuss the three approaches in turn. Other approaches that address packaging issues are discussed in Section 12.3.4.

12.3.1   Aspect-Oriented Programming

Aspect-oriented programming recognizes that the programming languages that we use do not support all of the abstraction boundaries in our domain models and design processes. Underlying AOP is the observation that what starts out as fairly distinct concerns at the requirements level, or at the design requirements level (nonfunctional requirements) end up tangled in the final program code because of the lack of support at both the design level and the programming language level, for keeping these concerns separate. With aspect-oriented programming, these concerns may be packaged as *aspects*, which can be woven into any application that has those concerns.

Aspect-oriented programming requires three ingredients:

- A general-purpose programming language for defining the core functionalities of software components
- An *aspect language* for writing *aspects*, specifically, code modules that address a specific concern and that cross-cut various components in the general-purpose language
- An *aspect weaver*, which is a preprocessor that "weaves" or "injects" aspects into the base software components to yield vanilla-flavored components, coded in the general-purpose programming language.

The output of the aspect weaver is next fed into regular programming toolkit (compiler, linker, etc.) to yield the application.

Kiczales et al. have proposed different forms of aspects. The simplest form of aspects, *advisories*, add some piece of code to specific methods identified by more or less complex ⟨method,class⟩ expressions,[5] and may be used to instrument code or to handle some fairly generic functionality (logging, error handling, etc.). The following example shows an aspect used for tracing. In this case, whenever a **Task** is started, suspended, stopped, or resumed, we would like to log a message to that effect. An aspect called *logger* is written to that effect. The aspect states what needs to be added to the core application classes, and where. An *aspect weaver* will "inject" the corresponding pieces of code appropriately.

The aspect language supports other more complex forms of aspects. These include the possibility of specifying class names and method names *intentionally* using more or less complex patterns, and allowing the insertion ("injection") of pieces of code in other points of control of methods. Further, there are other kinds of aspects that add *new* attributes and methods to existing classes. Finally, a third kind of aspects is proposed that handles associations between objects. Such aspects may have their own state variables, and may trigger the execution of a number of methods on the participating objects. These kinds of aspects are similar in intent and mechanism to *constraint objects* [Mili et al. 1990]: monitoring changes in objects' state variables, and requesting actions from the associated objects when some condition holds (or ceases to hold) as a result of a state change.

At the time of writing of this chapter (April 2000), aspect-oriented programming is still evolving, with new features added in regularly, and old features streamlined to yield a more coherent and broadly useful model of aspects. The authors plan the first "official release" of *AspectJ*, a Java implementation of aspect-oriented programming, by summer 2000.

Of the three approaches that we talk about in this section, aspect-oriented programming is the most popular and the one with the greatest following, both in the research community, and in the "trenches" out there. A key factor in the success of AOP is the *simplicity* and *practical usefulness* of some of its constructs.

```
class Task {                          class Task {
    public static int                     public static int
    Priority = 0;                         Priority = 0;
    ...                                   ...
    public void run(int priority) {       public void run(int priority) {
        ...                                   Log.println(
                                                  "Task number "+ taskId +
}
```

---

[5] For example, the class and the method may be specified nominally, or as by properties that they satisfy (e.g., method f(...) of all the classes that implement some interface *I*).

```
public void suspend() {
...
}
public void resume(int
priority) {
...
}
public void stop() {
...
}
...
}
aspect Logger {
  advise
    Task.run(int),
    Task.resume(int),
    Task.suspend(),Task.stop()
{
    static before {
      Log.println(
      "Task number "+
taskId+
      " running at "+
Calendar.time();
    }
  }
}
```

```
          " running at "+
        Calendar.time();
        ...
        }
        public void suspend() {
          Log.println(
          "Task number "+ taskId +
          " running at "+
        Calendar.time();
          ...
        }
        public void resume(int
        priority) {
        Log.println(
          "Task number "+ taskId +
          " running at "+
        Calendar.time();
          ...
        }
        public void stop() {
          Log.println(
          "Task number "+ taskId +
          " running at "+
        Calendar.time();
          ...
        }
        ...
        }
```

The *advisory aspects* (such as the one listed above) are fairly simple to understand, easy to use, and fairly useful. Everybody needs tracing every once in a while in their code. Further, we all have a love–hate relationship with C/C++'s conditional compilation—we love it because it allows us to "inject" source code that is compiled and executed only for certain settings; we hate it because it makes code harder to read and maintain. The advisory aspects keep the advantages of conditional compilation (almost[6]) without the disadvantages of tangling, repetition, or redundancy.

12.3.2 Subject-Oriented Programming

12.3.2.1 Motivation and Principles
Assume that we have developed an application for the local (state) Department of Motor Vehicles (DMV). Such an application might include the classes **DRIVER** (name, license_number, history), **OWNER** (name,

---

[6] With conditional compilation, we can insert conditionally compiled code *anywhere* in the source code. With aspects, we are limited in terms of the insertion points.

vehicle, license),and **VEHICLE**(model, license, serial_number),
with variable access methods, and methods to register vehicles to owners, to
update driving records, check the driving record (history) of a driver—call it
DRIVER::checkHistory(), which returns a number between 1 and 10, say,
1 for poor; and 10 for excellent; and so on. Consider also an application developed for a credit card company (CCC) including the classes **CARDHOLDER**
(name, card_number, history), and **CREDITCARD** (card_number,
owner, balance), with methods to access variables, check the credit history
(**CARDHOLDER**::checkHistory(), which returns a number between 1
and 10, 10 for excellent), and so forth. Consider now how an application
for a car rental agency (CRA) might be developed. We need three basic
classes; **RENTER** (name, driver_license, credit card), **CAR** (model,
license_number, serial number), and **RENTAL** (car, duration,
renter, price), where the price depends on the rental duration, and the
car size, but also on the renter's driving record (e.g., requesting the renter takes
additional insurance) and credit history (e.g., requesting coverage with smaller
deductible); assume that a method **RENTER**::checkHistory() returns a
number between 1 and 10, 10 for excellent. Having written the specifications
(e.g., a C++ header file), we may now see that what a car rental agency calls
a **RENTER** is both a **DRIVER** to the DMV (Department of Motor Vehicles),
and a **CARDHOLDER** to the credit card company, and there is a bit of the functionality in both than can be used to implement **RENTER**. Similarly, a **CAR** for
the rental agency corresponds to a **VEHICLE** for the DMV.

Traditionally, the overlap between the three applications would have been
handled with multiple inheritance; the class **RENTER** is made a subclass of
DRIVER and **CARDHOLDER**, and the class **CAR** is made a subclass of **VEHICLE**.
From this simple example, we can see several disadvantages. First, it would
work only if the applications were developed in the given sequence; if **RENTER**
were specified (and partially implemented) before this overlap was recognized, we would have had to "refactor" the class **RENTER**. Second, **DRIVER**
and **CARDHOLDER** use the instance variable history to refer to different
"histories"; and third, **CAR** and **VEHICLE** use different names (license and
license_number) for the same thing. Other problems and limitations would
appear if **DRIVER** and **CARDHOLDER** had ancestors in their respective applications (same class names, same method names, etc. [Ossher and Harrison
1992, Harrison and Ossher 1993]) .

The subject-oriented approach consists of fusing the different applications
by establishing correspondences between their constituents, *which are external to the code of the individual applications*. This approach allows us to
develop applications separately, in any order, and to compose them in more
flexible ways, and without having to reedit them [Ossher et al. 1995]. In the
car rental agency example, **DRIVER**, and **CARDHOLDER** are fused to yield
the class **RENTER**, with the instance variables (name, license_number,
*driving*_history, card_number, *credit*_history), where name
means the same thing as in the original classes, and where we renamed

DRIVER::history as driving_history and **CARDHOLDER**::history as credit_history. Further, the two original implementations of checkHistory() (**DRIVER**::checkHistory() and **CARDHOLDER**::checkHistory()) have been fused into a new method **RENTER**::checkHistory(), which could return a combination of their results. One such combination is shown below for illustration purposes:

```
int RENTER::checkHistory(){
    return _DMV_checkHistory() + _CCC_checkHistory();
}
```

where _DMV_checkHistory() and _CCC_checkHistory() are also methods of **RENTER** that have the same body as **DRIVER**::checkHistory() and **CARDHOLDER**::checkHistory(), respectively. We could also have in-lined the original methods within **RENTER**::checkHistory(), but this procedure is more involved, and works only with source composition.

12.3.2.2 Subject Labels and Composition

In order to compose applications, we need to first run them through a preprocessor that parses the source code and extracts descriptions of classes, variables, and methods, which support comparisons (establishing correspondences) and combinations (or *compositions*). The set of such descriptions is called a *subject label*, and the preprocessor that extracts them is called *label generator* [Ossher et al. 1995]. A subject label constitutes the subject's *composition interface*. A label contains two kinds of information: (1) *behavioral* or *type* information, used during the matching phase to establish correspondences between subject elements (classes, methods, and variables) and to generate the *types* for the composed subject; and (2) *type ↔ implementation* linkage information, used to generate the implementation for the composed subject from the implementations of its component subjects. For example, classes are represented by the set of instance variables and method signatures, whether they are defined locally or inherited; we refer to this process as *flattening*. Type to implementation information consists of binding, for each class, each method signature to the particular implementation accessible to that class.

Subject composition per se may be seen as consisting of two phases, called *grouping* and *combination*. Grouping identifies the matching parts using default rules, which may be overridden for specific cases. For example, a default class matching rule may consider classes that have the same name to be equivalent. The car rental example illustrates a case where classes having different names may also be considered equivalent. We can also imagine a case where two classes having the same name mean different things. Within matching classes, we may consider that "instance variables (methods) that have the same name and same type (signature) are equivalent, unless otherwise indicated, and with additional cases to be stated explicitly." In the car rental example, we overrode the name matching rule for the instance variable history, and asserted explicitly the correspondence of DMV.**VEHICLE**. license with CRA.**CAR**.license_number.[7] The second step of composition, *combination*, is also defined by default rules, unless otherwise overriden, with additional cases stated explicitly. Combination rules prescribe what to do with constructs that are multiply defined. For the car rental example, we used a "merge" rule for multiply defined classes. Within classes, we may use the set-theoretic union for instance variables and method signatures, provided the variables (methods) whose names match have the same type (signature) as well. The case for multiply defined and implemented methods is the most interesting; we can specify a wide variety of combination techniques for the original implementations. In the car rental example, the resulting **RENTER**::checkHistory() method may return an arbitrary function of the results returned by DMV.**DRIVER**::checkHistory() and CCC.**CARD-HOLDER**::checkHistory() [Ossher et al. 1995].

Work on subject-oriented programming had been going on at IBM Research since the early 1990s. It is our understanding that the work was initially motivated by tool integration concerns: with the surge of interest in computer-aided software engineering (CASE) tools of the late 1980s within the research community, there was also interest into issues related to tool integration [Harrison and Ossher 1993] in general, and work on PCTE (portable common tool interface), in particular. At issue was not only the integration of the modeling notations used but also the integration of the functionalities supported by various CASE tools working in collaboration. From work on combining inheritance hierarchies [Ossher and Harrison 1992] followed the general theory of subject-oriented programming [Harrison and Ossher 1993], and a flexible and powerful subject composition language [Ossher et al. 1995].

In terms of tool support, tools for subject-oriented programming in C++ have been bundled with IBM's VisualAge for C++, since early 1997 (release 4). In 2000, support for subject-oriented programming in Java (called *HyperJ*) was provided free of charge on the Web (see http://www.research. ibm.com/hyperspace/HyperJ/HyperJ.htm). One of the authors of this book has developed prototype support for subject-oriented programming in Smalltalk [Mili et al. 1996].

In terms of conceptual maturity, subject-oriented programming is probably the most mature of the approaches discussed in this section. Most of the problems related to the semantics of inheritance in general, and C++ in particular, have been resolved or, at the very least properly documented. However, compared to the younger but more popular aspect-oriented programming, it has three major disadvantages:

---

[7] Subject qualification is used in the actual formal language used for composition [Ossher et al. 1995], and reflects the hierarchical treelike structure of subject labels.

- From a practical standpoint, the "entry-level" subject composition is too hard. Unlike aspect-oriented programming, which provides very simple features that perform a very useful service (e.g., using advisories to do tracing), subject-oriented programming lacks this gradualness.

- The combination of inheritance hierarchies *is* a difficult problem, regardless of the language. With languages supporting multiple inheritance, we have to deal with the complex semantics of multiple inheritance. Languages that don't support multiple inheritance pose different challenges [Mili et al. 1996].

- Methods may be too coarse-grained to yield effective behavioral compositions. This problem manifests itself for (C++) constructors that have initializers. To avoid interferences between constructors emanating from different subjects, we would have to compose initializers first, and then compose constructor bodies. Similar problems occur with other kinds of computations that have qualitatively distinct stages. Consider the method grantResource(.,.) of class **Process**. This method has two stages: one that consumes the resource [lines (1) and (2)] and one that notifies the rest of the system that the available quantity of resource r has changed. In a multithreaded environment, we would want all the threads running consumeResource to block, and wait until they are "awakened," to do the notification. This way, all the notifications will reflect the true value of resource r:[8]

```
class Process {
   private Hashtable resources;
   ...
   void consumeResource(Resource r, float quantity) {
(1)   resources.put(r,new Float(quantity));
(2)   r.decrement(quantity);
      Thread.suspend();
(3)   notifyAll(r);
   }
   ...
}
```

If we have several methods that need to be composed, we have to make sure that we execute all of their first segments, then all of their second segments, and it is the suspend(...) that does that in this case. Composing similar looking methods would be difficult in this case.

In all fairness, the aspect-oriented people don't solve this problem; they simply don't tackle it. The relationship between aspects and core classes is asymmet-

---

[8] Otherwise, the resource r may be overbooked, if the thread that distributes resources and the threads that consume them interleave. There are simpler ways of doing this in Java, of course, using method synchronization, and wait/notify primitives.

ric, and aspect code "extends" existing code. Kiczales et al. have adapted and enhanced some of the concepts they developed for CLOS (e.g., method wrappers[9]) to affect sub-method-level compositions.

12.3.3 View-Oriented Programming

View-oriented programming is our own homegrown approach to developing object-oriented applications by composing independently developed functional slices. There are interesting differences between view programming and the previous two approaches. First, an essential requirement of our approach is the ability to add and remove views (aspects, subjects) dynamically to an object, that is, during runtime. This is not possible in either aspect-oriented programming or subject-oriented programming, where composition takes place at the source code level before programs are compiled, linked, and run. Most of our intellectual and prototyping effort has gone toward handling this requirement. Other differences are described later after we have explained how our approach works.

In our approach, an application object is considered as an aggregation of components consisting of a *core object* that embodies the application object's basic data and behavior (and unique identity), and a time-varying set of *views*, which are object fragments that add usage-specific or *role*-specific data and functionality. These fragments (views) rely on some of the basic services of the core object. The response of the application object to a message depends on the set of views that are currently attached to it; for any given message and any given point in time, an application object may have zero, one, or several implementations available to it at that time, and these implementations could come from either the core object or the views. In other words, the interface of the application object is defined in terms of the union of the interfaces of the core object and the views that are currently attached to it; the implementations, on the other hand, are the result of the composition of the implementations that come from the core object and the views. Our approach to composing implementations is based on that used in subject-oriented programming.

How does one program with views? Our goal has been to provide conceptual and programming tools to reduce the conceptual and programming overhead for developers who wish to add views to objects. Consider the example of a commercial vehicle (e.g., a van) operated by a department store to make deliveries. Figure 12.5 shows the basic attributes and functionalities of a van, along with two additional views. Let us forget for now how views are implemented—the idea here is to be able to attach and remove/detach the views RollingStock and Transport to a van while the program is

---

[9] Method "wrappers" in CLOS are behavioral fragments that are executed before or after some methods.

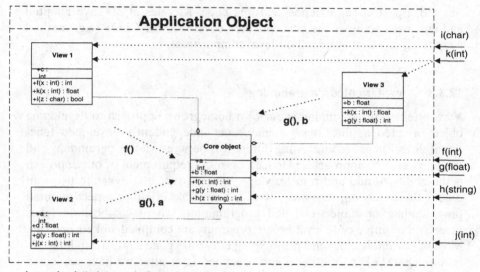

Legend: - dotted arrows indicate delegation links
 - the resulting application object supports all the
   interfaces

FIGURE 12.5   A model of objects with views.

running—and impart on the van at hand the behaviors embodied in these two views:

```
class Van {
  private int serialNumber;
  private float weight;
  private float load;
  private String make;
  ...
  public int getSerialNumber() {
    return serialNumber;
  }
  ...
  public void setWeight(float wt) {
    weight = wt;
  }
  ...
}
view Transport {
  private Route nextRoute;
  ...
  public void scheduleDelivery
    (Package pk,Address
    dest){...}
  public void release() {...}
```

```
view RollingStock {
  private float replacementValue;
  private float residualValue;
  private Date acquisitionDate;

  ...
  public float getResidualValue() {
    return residualValue;
  }
  ...
  public float

  currentYearAmortization(){
    ...}
  ...
}
public void release() {...}
  ...
}
```

We show below the way we would like programmers to write a program that uses these views:

```
. . .
Van myVan = new Van(12346,"Van Duran");
myVan.setLoad(6543);
myVan.attach("rollingStock");
myVan.getResidualValue();
myVan.attach("Transport");
myVan.release();
```

The call to `setLoad()` goes to the core object, whereas `getResidual-Value()` goes to the view "RollingStock". The call to `release()` calls a combination of the implementations provided by "RollingStock" and `Transport`.

For this to work with a typed language, we need to preprocess the preceding code to replace `myVan.getResidualValue()` by the appropriate code sequence that would delegate that call to the "RollingStock" view. In our C++ implementation, views are nothing but C++ classes, and we used aggregation to link core objects to the views that are attached to them. In this case, a translation of the preceding instruction would look like:

```
((RollingStock)myVan.getView("RollingStock")).
    getResidualValue();
```

When a method is implemented by several views, we go through a "composition view" that dispatches to the proper view implementations.

We should note that behavioral extension with delegation causes a well-known design problem known as the "broken delegation problem." Assume that we write

```
myVan.setResidualValue(12000.0f);
```

which gets translated into `((RollingStock)myVan.getView ("RollingStock")).setResidualValue(12000.0f)` and assume that the method `setResidualValue(float val)` is as follows:

```
public void setResidualValue(float val) {
    residualValue = val;
    this.saveInDatabase();
}
```

What does **this** refer to in this function? Obviously, it refers to the object that represents the asset view, and not to the entire application object. If that is what is intended, fine. More often than not, it is not. What is needed in this case is to also save the enclosing object, as well as **this**. So what do we do about this problem?

In our approach, views (view classes) are actually generated from a program template that we call *viewpoint* to adapt the view to the core object (class) on which it will be attached. For example, the view "RollingStock" is an instantiation of a more generic *viewpoint*—say, **Asset**—for the specific case of **Van**'s. The viewpoint **Asset** applies to any domain resource (rolling stock, buildings, computers). Through this instantiation, we can customize the names of the methods supported by the view to the target domain object (**Van**), and also make sure that the view methods "know" how to get the core information from the core object, in case that information is not stored directly in the view (e.g., the serial number). Accordingly, as part of the generation of views, we address the broken delegation problem. In the setResidualValue (**float** val) example, we would have generated the proper code sequence to make sure that the entire object is saved, not just the view [Mili et al. 1999]. Note that in Java, this is less of a problem because we are generating views as *Java (nonstatic) internal classes*, which obviates the need for delegation altogether!

View programming is the less mature of the three technologies presented in this section, and there is no prototype, to date, that people can use on a trial basis, let alone a production environment. Our major difficulty, of course, has been the ability to add and remove views *during runtime*, which requires some complex runtime machinery (data structures and dispatch logic). We have broken the problem into "knowing that views A and B can be added to the class C at run-time" and actually attaching such views during runtime. By allowing our tools to know which views are potentially applicable to a given class in a given program, we were able to overcome a number of hurdles. By further allowing the source classes to be automatically modified (implementing views as internal classes in Java), we remove a significant chunk of difficulties. We continue to seek the right balance between dynamicity and simplicity.

In comparison to aspect-oriented programming and subject-oriented programming, it is interesting to us that the three approaches propose three different dimensions of modularity or *factorization*, which coincide for degenerate cases. First, we should note that both aspect-oriented programming and view programming are *intensional* in the sense that the behavior to be added or composed is specified for an intensionally specified set of host classes. For instance, both *aspects* and *viewpoints* are specified in terms of general properties that their host classes must support. By contrast, subject-oriented programming is *extensional* in the sense that the subjects are target-specific. View programming and subject-oriented programming are orthogonal in the same way that parameterization (parametric polymorphism) and aggregation are orthogonal behavioral extension mechanisms to generalization, but both extend the behavior of individual classes. Aspect-oriented programming is less dogmatic about ways to introduce behavior into existing classes (in every way and place they reasonably can), but it also has mechanisms and constructs for introducing cohesive chunks of interobject behavior. If anything, the AOP people run the risk of "feature creep," where the simplicity advantage is eroded as new constructs are introduced in each release.[10]

12.3.4 Other Approaches

There have been other approaches to building components by composing reusable slices. They are mostly university-based research efforts, and it is unlikely that they would result in commercial products. Don Batory of the University of Texas conducted one of the earlier efforts. His GenVoca system supports the generation of software components by composing or *layering* a select set of components, each providing one cohesive set of services needed by the overall component. They defined *realms* to represent types, and *components* to implement or *realize* those types. The components need not be fully concrete, and may be parameterized by other realms or types. The parameterization relationship defines a dependency between the realms, which in some cases implies a layered structure of the components and realms. In this model, realms *import* interfaces (the type parameters), and *export* interfaces. The exported interfaces include their own, naturally, as well as some imported interfaces. The user of GenVoca will end up with a concrete realization of one realm, where the type parameter has been replaced by an implementer of that type (a component from the corresponding realm). If that implementer has some functionality that is not required by the top most realm (highest layer), but that is needed nonetheless by client programs, one has to find a way of exporting that non-required interface as well. In this example, some of the functionalities of *Container* may need to be exported through the *Access* realm, either for performance optimization purposes (taking shortcuts through software layers), or, simply, because they are needed by another higher-level realm. GenVoca's inherently hierarchical instantiation mechanism creates unnecessary complications; it creates a component by instantiating realms in a bottom-up fashion, at each point "enlarging" the interface of a realm to accommodate whichever functionalities the type parameter happens to have accumulated at that point [Batory and Geraci 1997].

Consider the example of Figure 12.6*a*. Assume that we have one realm, **Container**, which supports two realms, one for random access—call it **Random**—and one for navigation—call it **Navigation**. Normally, we should be able to have a data structure that supports either/or, or both. GenVoca's model forces us to do one of the following:

- Make **Navigation** [**Container**] a component of the realm **Random** (or vice-versa), or

---

[10] At the time of this writing, it is 0.6!

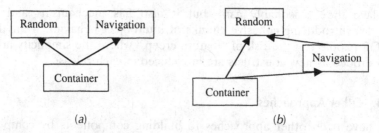

FIGURE 12.6   (a) True functional dependencies between the data structure's aspects; (b) dependency forced by GenVoca.

- Make **Navigation** a parameter of all the components of the realm **Random.**

In other words, it forces the last realm to be instantiated to be the join of all the other ones (see Fig. 12.6b). GenVoca's model works well if the functionalities embodied in the realms truly build on each other like an OSI (Open Systems Interconnect) protocol hierarchy. If they don't, then GenVoca's model is not adequate.

Van Hilst and Notkin of the University of Washington proposed yet another approach [Van Hilst and Notkin 1996]. They tried to support role modeling [Reenskaugh 1995] at the code level. Basically, an application is modeled one collaboration (usecase) at a time. In each collaboration, the application entities play specific roles, and both the static and dynamic models are described in terms of those roles. At design time, we map roles to classes; we could end up with several roles being implemented by the same class (e.g., the different views on a van would normally be mapped into a single class **Van**), and several classes implementing a particular role [Reenskaugh 1995]. The idea proposed by Van Hilst and Notkin carries this concept through code. Van Hilst and Notkin introduced the notion of role components as C++ templates that are parameterized by

- The type of objects to which we are imparting this role
- The other objects that play roles that collaborate with this one

The following is an example of what the header for a role component might look like:

```
template(class WifeType, class SuperType) class Husband:
public Supertype {
    . . . .
}
```

Here, the template class **Husband** defines the role of a husband, providing the attributes and methods that correspond to the role. One such attribute is, for example, to have a wife, and to send messages/interact with her, and thus, the class **Husband** might have a data member that is of type **WifeType**. **WifeType** is a type parameter because it, too, is a role. The class to which this role will be attached is the superclass of **Husband**, which is, itself, a type parameter. Given a class **Man** and a class **Woman**, we could start a husband–wife collaboration as follows:

```
Women* eve = new Woman("Eve");
Husband(Woman,Man)* adam = new
Husband(Woman,Man)("Adam",eve);
if (adam->canSpendTheKidsCollegeMoneyOnSportsCar()) {...}
...
```

In this case, we assumed that **Husband** has a constructor that takes the wife as an argument, and that some of the methods of **Husband** will involve collaboration with the wife object. This method supports defining types on the fly (template instantiation) but does not allow an object to acquire new roles after it has been created.

The nice thing about role components is that they don't introduce any new language constructs or require separate tools, and the technique may be readily used by anyone who wishes to use it! The literature abounds with other approaches. Our purpose is to provide a representative sample that might wet the reader's appetite to find out more, or to follow through developments in this area, until a usable product rolls out.

12.4 DESIGN-BASED APPROACHES

Under design-based approaches, we review a set of design techniques that consist of using features of existing languages in such a way that the resulting components are more composable. We review two such techniques in some detail, event-based composition, and simulated reflection. Then, we review a set of well-known design patterns, classified by the kind of composition problem that they address. Finally, we briefly describe some examples from well-known class libraries and frameworks that show an example (and exemplary) application of these principles.

12.4.1 Event-Based Composition

We saw in Section 12.2.2 that functional composition whereby the method of one component explicitly *calls* methods of the other component is actually fairly restrictive, and creates a *lexical binding* between the two components. With event-based composition, we make sure that the execution of operation f(...) of component requiring A triggers the execution of operation g(...) on component B, without requirily f(...) to explicitly know about

A or explicitly call g (. . .). The general idea here is to view the collaboration between objects as an open "labor fair" at the town square. Components in need of services to be performed come to register or post a "help wanted" request, and components that can perform the service do so, and in some cases, come back to the town square to announce that they were done.

In software terms, this is sometimes referred to as the "publish-and-subscribe" paradigm. Different components (objects) publish some kinds of events. Other components register for those events so that they may be notified when events of those types occur. Figure 12.7 illustrates this paradigm.

We store in a common data structure (dispatch table) which components are interested in which events (event types). Then, whenever a component posts an event, the event dispatcher will consult the dispatch table, and then notify the appropriate components accordingly.

The architecture described here is an "ideal," which may be implemented as described here, and would involve some advanced implementation techniques (multithreading, component middleware, etc.). We will describe some of these technologies in later sections of this Chapter and in Chapter 14. For the purposes of this section, we show a "poor man's realization" of this design for our simulation system problem. What we want here is to coordinate the tasks with the resource managers. We assume that each resource type has a specific resource manager, with its own interface. The idea is that a task may require various resources, and will have to request those resources from the specific resource managers.

We start by showing a naive Java implementation. Here, a task needs to know the various resource managers by name and interface. We assume that all the resource managers are subclasses of an abstract class Resource-

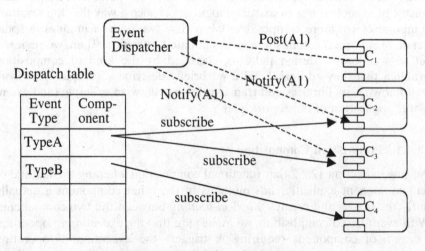

FIGURE 12.7 Event-based composition.

Manager, which has static variables that point to instances of the appropriate resource managers:

```
abstract class ResourceManager {
  public static MemoryManager _memManager;
  public static ConnectionManager _conManager;
    ...
}
class MemoryManager extends ResourceManager {
    ...
  // returns a resource with the appropriate type and size,
  // or null if unsuccessful
  public Resource allocate(MemType mt, int numBlocs) {...}
    ...
}
class ConnectionManager extends ResourceManager {
    ...
  // returns a connection or null if unsuccessful
  public Connection openConnection(ConnectionType cnctype) {...}
    ...
}
class ResourceReq {
  public int type;
  public int qtty;
}
class Task extends ... {
  private Vector _resourceRequirements;
  private Vector _resources;
    ...
  public void start() {
    ResourceReq rreq;
    Resource rs;
    // first acquire resources
    Enumeration res = _resourceRequirements.elements();
    while (res.HasMoreElements()) {
      rreq = (ResourceReq)res.nextElement();
      switch (rreq.type) {
      case MEMORY:
(1)     rs = ResourceManager.
              _memManager.allocate(mt, rreq.qty);
        break;
      case CONNECTION:
(2)     rs = ResourceManager.
              _conManager.openConnection(FDUPLEX);
        break;
      case AUDIODEVICE:
        ...

      default: ...
      }
```

```
      if (rs != null) _resources.add(rs);
      else {
        block(rreq);
        return;
      }
    }
  }
}
  . . .
}
```

Lines (1) and (2) show dependencies between the class **Task** and the class **ResourceManager** and its subclasses. This binds the reusability of **Task** to the context of the **ResourceManager** class, its subclasses, and their interfaces, namely, the signatures and *names* of the methods that they support. An implementation that uses event-based composition would be based on broadcasting requests for resources, and letting the various resource managers satisfy them. The following shows a possible implementation based on this principle where we rewrote the main loop of the method start() and added the method request(ResourceReq):

```
public void start() {
  ResourceReq rreq;
  Resource rs;
  // first acquire resources
  Enumeration res = _resourceRequirements.elements();
  while (res.HasMoreElements()) {
    rs= request((ResourceReq)res.nextElement());
    if (rs != null) _resources.add(rs);
    else {
      block(rreq);
      return;
    }
  }
  . . .
}
  . . .
public Resource request(ResourceReq rreq) {
  return ResourceManager.requested(rreq,this);
}
```

This implementation of request(ResourceReq) calls a static method of ResourceManager that does the actual dispatching:

```
abstract class ResourceManager {
  public static MemoryManager _memManager;
  public static ConnectionManager _conManager;
  . . .
```

```
   public static Resource requested(ResourceReq rreq,Task t){
     switch (rreq.type) {
       case MEMORY:
(1)    return ResourceManager.
                  _memManager.allocate(mt,rreq.qty);
       case CONNECTION:
(2)    return ResourceManager.
                  _conManager.openConnection(FDUPLEX);
       case AUDIODEVICE:
          ...
       default: ...
       }
     }
   ...
   }
```

This design emulates the true event-based composition, and reduces a **Task**'s dependence on the names and interfaces of specific **Resource-Manager**s. That knowledge is now centralized in the **ResourceManager** class, which plays the role of the event dispatcher of our model of Figure 12.8.

If we had been more careful in designing our **ResourceManager**s, perhaps we could have adopted the same interface for all resource managers, regardless of which resource we are requesting. If this had been the case, then instead of the **switch** statement, we would have had a table to consult. We show below what such an implementation could look like:

```
abstract class ResourceManager {
  // This table contains known resource managers indexed by
  // resource type.
  public static Hashtable _managers;
  ...
  public static Resource requested(ResourceReq rreq,Task t){
    ResourceManager rm = _managers.get(rreq.type);
    return rm.requestResource(rreq,t);
  }
  abstract public Resource requestResource(ResourceReq rreq,
                                           Task t);
  ...
}
public class MemoryManager extends ResourceManager {
  ...
  // Do whatever allocate(MemoryType,int) used to do
  public Resource requestResource(ResourceReq rreq, Task t){
    ...}
  ...
}
```

If we adopt a common interface for the resource managers, this means that all the data that are specific to resources and resource managers will need to be carried within the generic **ResourceReq** object. This entails some encoding on the resource requester's end (**Task** objects) to encode the nature of the request, and some decoding on the receiver's end (the **ResourceManager** that will handle the resource request) to extract the required information.

This is a general principle when we try to adopt a uniform communication medium between components, and has been a major reproach of event-based composition; it gets cumbersome as the data that need to be exchanged become complex and recipient-specific. Other disadvantages of this approach include

- The lack of control that developers have over the flow of control in the program
- Performance overhead
- The fact that simple control flow becomes too complicated to implement with event-based composition.

In the example above, things remained reasonably simple because the underlying triggering mechanism between components remains the synchronous method call, and there is a single thread of control. In a truly event-based system, resource requests are run in separate threads from the tasks, which may be blocked while their requests are being processed, and reactivated (through other events) when the various resource managers respond.

For our purposes, it is important to be aware of the design paradigm, of the underlying issues, and ways to emulate it to attain most of the software static design benefits without incurring the costs. The Observer/Observable pattern, and Smalltalk's dependents' mechanism (briefly mentioned in Section 12.4.3) are similar emulations of the pure event-based composition, and yet, achieve most of the static design benefits (independence, low coupling).

12.4.2   Simulated Reflection

Under simulated reflection, we group a bunch of design techniques whereby a component invokes behavior on another component by specifying the service that needs to be performed, but without knowing the name of the methods that invoke that service. And thus, instead of invoking those behaviors directly, we ask the objects to invoke them in the way that they know how. We will look at two examples. The first example is an adaptation of the Observer/Observable pattern in Java. The second example is based on CORBA's method invocation mechanism.

The idea of the Observer/Observable pattern is to maintain a dependence between objects without having the objects know about each other explicitly or know which behaviors to invoke to maintain or enforce the dependence. It has been first used in Smalltalk's model view controller (MVC) framework to keep the view consistent with the state of the model, without requiring the model (e.g., domain classes) to know about the views (interface classes). The Java language provides an implementation of this mechanism using the **Observable** class and the **Observer** interface. The **Observable** class looks like this:

```
class Observable {
    // List of observers. System may also maintain global list
    private Vector _observers;
    // _changed tells whether object has had a change that
    // observers still don't know about
    private boolean _changed = false;
    protected synchronized void setChanged() {_changed = true;}

    public synchronized void addObserver(Observer o) {...}
    public synchronized void deleteObserver(Observer o) {...}
    public synchronized void deleteObservers() {...}
    public synchronized int countObservers() {...}

    // Tell my observers that I changed, and pass change data
    // arg
    public synchronized void notifyObservers(Object arg) {...}
}
```

In turn, the **Observer** interface consists simply of the method

```
    public void update(Observable source, Object data);
```

Thus, if we want to monitor changes in objects of type **A** by objects of type **B**, we make **A** a subclass of **Observable**, and we make sure that **B** *implements* interface **Observer**. The Observer/Observable is best understood in the context of physical simulations, so let us take one such example. Assume that we have an industrial process control application, and that one of the objects being controlled is a turbine. The state of the turbine is displayed on three different views on the operator's console. One view displays the combustion temperature through a thermometerlike scale, the other displays the pressure using a slide bar, and the third displays the speed, through an odometerlike dial. Partial class definitions are shown below:

```
public class Turbine extends Observable {
    private float temperature;
    private float pressure;
    private float speed;
    ...
    public void setTemperature (float newTemp) {
        temperature = newTemp;
        setChanged();
        notifyObservers(new Float(newTemp));
    }
```

```
    public void setPressure (float newPressure) {
      temperature = newPressure;
      setChanged();
      notifyObservers(new Float(newPressure));
    }
    public void setSpeed(float newSpeed) {
      speed = newSpeed;
      setChanged();
      notifyObservers(new Float(newSpeed));
    }
    ...
  }
  class PressureBar extends Bar implements Observer {
    // we assume that 'value' is used to compute the bar
    // height
    private float value;
    private float minValue, maxValue;
    // We don't know what changed, so we will go ahead and
    // redisplay, anyway.
    public void update(Observable source, Object data){
      value = (Turbine)source.getPressure();
      this.repaint();
    }
    ...
  }
  // The graphic class that represents the speed
  class SpeedDial extends Dial implements Observer {
    // we assume that 'value' is used to compute the bar
    // height
    private float value;
    private float minValue, maxValue;
    // We don't know what changed, so we will go ahead and
    // redisplay, anyway.
    public void update(Observable source, Object data){
      value = (Turbine)source.getSpeed();
      this.repaint();
    }
    ...
  }
  // The graphic class that represents the temperature
  class Thermometer extends Scale implements Observer {
    ...
  }
```

This scheme, although obviating the need for application objects to know about their interfaces (views), is somewhat wasteful; all the views are repainted, regardless of whether the state change concerns them. Readers who are familiar with Smalltalk's dependents mechanism are on the edge of their seats—the notifyObservers(...) method (called **changed:with:**) has two parameters, an *aspect*, which is a symbol telling which aspect of the observable has changed, and some change data such as the new value of the aspect that changed. Similarly, the update(...) method has an additional parameter for that aspect. In this case, the two methods would look something like this:

```
class Turbine extends Observable {
  ...
  public void setSpeed(float newSpeed) {
    speed = newSpeed;
    setChanged();
    notifyObservers(Turbine.SPEED, new Float(newSpeed));
  }
  ...
}
class PressureBar extends Bar implements Observer {
  ...
  // Here, we know what changed, so we will only redisplay
  // if we are concerned. Further, we get the
  // value directly from data, without going back to source
  public void update(Observable source, int aspect, Object
  data){
    if (aspect == Turbine.PRESSURE) {
      value = ((Float)data).floatValue();
      this.repaint();
    }
  }
  ...
}
```

When dealing with complex views (e.g., a browser view), the same update(...) method may react to several aspects. For example, the view could be a window that contains a scale object (thermometer), a bar (pressure), and a dial (speedometer), and the same update method will repaint each subcomponent selectively. Note that in this case we would not need to subclass **Dial, Bar,** and **Scale,** since we are handling the update for all three in **TurbineConsole,** as in:

```
class TurbineConsole extends ... implements Observer {
  private PressureBar _bar;
  private Thermomemter _thermom;
  private SpeedDial _dial;
  ...
  public void update(Observable source, int aspect, Object
  data){
    switch(aspect) {
    case Turbine.PRESSURE:
```

```
        _bar.value = ((Float)data).floatValue();
        _bar.repaint();
        break;
      case Turbine.TEMPERATURE:
        _thermom.value = ((Float)data).floatValue();
        _thermom.repaint();
        break;
      case Turbine.SPEED:
        _dial.value =((Float)data).floatValue();
        _dial.repaint();
        break;
      default: {}
      }
    }
    ...
  }
```

This is the approach used in Smalltalk interfaces, for example, and it is not perfect. As a rule of thumb, behavioral extension should not rely on enumerating additional cases in a single monolithic piece of code. Extension should be *conservative*, i.e. it should not affect the existing code.

An alternative solution here is to use reflection. It is so simple in Smalltalk, it is not even fun. We will do it Java style:

```
class TurbineConsole extends ... implements Observer {
  private PressureBar _bar;
  private Thermomemter _thermom;
  private SpeedDial _dial;
  public static Hashtable _methods;
  ...
  public void updateBar(Object data) {
    _bar.value = ((Float)data).floatValue();
    _bar.repaint();
  }
  public void updateDial(Object data) {
    _dial.value = ((Float)data).floatValue();
    _dial.repaint();
  }
  ...
  public void update(Observable source,int aspect, Object
  data){
(1)  Object params[] = new Object[1];
(2)  params[0] = data;
(3)  Method updateMethod =
                   (Method)methods.get(new Integer(aspect));
(4)  updateMethod.invoke(this,params);
    }
  }
  ...
}
```

The idea here is to use Java's reflection package. Recall that in Java, all objects respond to the message getClass(), by returning an instance of class **Class**, which represents the class of the object. That instance of **Class** will also point to descriptions of the attributes and methods of the class, represented by instances of the classes **Field** and **Method**, respectively. Through these instances, we can access the value of a field for a particular object, and invoke a method on a particular object with a particular set of parameters. The above implementation of update shows how we can invoke methods. We assume that the static variable _methods contains a table of update methods the class **TurbineConsole** (updateDial(...), updateBar(...), ...) indexed by the aspect change to which they respond. Line (3) retrieves the **Method** that responds to a particular aspect. All of these methods take one argument of type **Object**. Lines (1) and (2) initialize the array of parameters (one parameter) for these methods. This makes it possible to invoke them transparently line (4).

We could emulate the preceding mechanism in C++, where, instead of **Method** objects, we could store functions (pointers to functions) in the static variable _methods, and invoke them using the usual C/C++ invocation for function variables.

A variation of this scheme is CORBA's *dynamic invocation interface* (DII), whereby client programs can construct requests and invoke them on object references (pointers). One particular implementation that we have been playing with actually uses the DII to implement the skeleton and stub interfaces. CORBA is discussed more at length in Chapter 14. Recall that CORBA's distribution architecture consists of generating, from the same interface definition, a "stub" on the client side, and a skeleton, on the server side. The stub is a proxy that stands for the actual object implementation in client programs, but whose purpose is to forward client requests to the ORB, who in turn will forward it to the implementation. The skeleton maps ORB-channeled requests into explicit method calls on the object implementation. Figure 12.8 shows a simplified version of the architecture.

The stub and skeleton classes generated from the simple IDL interface for Truck are shown below.

```
module Fleet {
  interface Truck {
     attribute string serialNumber;
     attribute float load;
    /** Schedule a truck between dates t1 and t2*/
    void scheduleLoadBetween(in float t1, in float t2);
  };
};
```

The generated Java stub is shown next:

```
package Fleet;
public class _TruckStub extends ObjectImpl implements
```

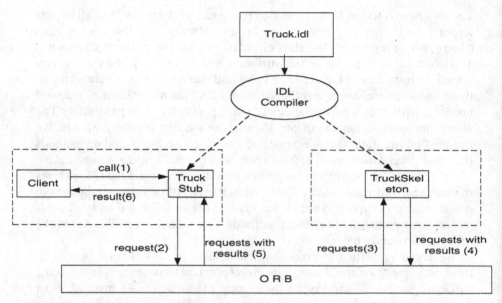

FIGURE 12.8 (Simplified) anatomy of CORBA applications. Data are serialized (byte stream) before being exchanged through the ORB.

```
Fleet.Truck{
  ...
  public String serialNumber() {
(1)  Request _req = _request("_get_serialNumber");
     _req.set_return_type(ORB.init().create_string_tc(0));
     _req.invoke();
     return _req.return_value().extract_string(); }
  public void serialNumber(String value) {...}
  ...
}
```

On the server side, the skeleton class looks like

```
package Fleet;
public abstract class _TruckSkeleton extends
DynamicImplementation
{ ...
(2)  public void invoke(ServerRequest _req) {
(3)    _invoke(_req, this); }
     public static void _invoke(ServerRequest _req,
       _TruckSkeleton _obj) {
(4)    String _opName = _req.op_name();
       Any _ret = _obj._orb().create_any();
       NVList _nvl = null;
(5)    if (_opName.equals("_get_serialNumber")) {
         _ret = _obj._orb().create_any();
```

```
            _req.params(_nvl);
            StringHolderHolder _retHolder =
                    Cnew StringHolderHolder();
(6)         _retHolder.value.value = _obj.serialNumber();
            _ret.insert_Streamable(_retHolder);
(7)         _req.result(_ret);
            return;  }
      if (_opName.equals("_set_serialNumber")) {...}
   }
   ...
   public abstract String serialNumber();
   public abstract void serialNumber(String value);
   public abstract float load();
   public abstract void load(float value);
   public abstract void scheduleLoadBetween(float t1,float t2) ;
}
```

As we can see, on the client side, each method call generates a **Request**, identified by name (a **String**, _get_serialNumber in line (1)), which is then invoked. The request is serialized and transmitted by the ORB to the server side, where it is decoded ("unmarshaled") before the server side object (**_TruckSkeleton**) is asked to invoke the request [line (2)]. The actual invokation [static method _invoke(ServerRequest, _TruckSkeleton)] picks the code sequence to execute based on the request name. Line (5) shows the **if** block for the _get_serialNumber request. Line (6) shows the actual method invocation. Line (7) shows the filling of the result slot of the request.

Because the method void _invoke(ServerRequest, _TruckSkeleton) is generated automatically by the IDL compiler (and so is the rest of the class _TruckSkeleton), code evolution and maintenance is not an issue. But we could imagine, as we did for the interface case, getting rid of the multiple **if** statements, and simply dispatching requests to methods on the basis of some indexed table of methods.[11]

This implementation reminds us of one of the metamodeling patterns seen in the previous chapter. The general idea may be summed up as follows:

- We have two (or more) components that need to interact.
- The components don't know (or we don't want them to know) the exact names and possibly ordering of parameters of the operations of their counterparts.

---

[11] In the turbine graphical interface code, the methods updateBar, updateDial, and so forth, have the same signature, which made the code fairly simple. In the general case, some care must be taken to handle a different number and type of parameters for the various methods invoked using Java's reflection mechanism.

The solution is then to use a declarative (datalike), high-level description of the operations, which may be read during runtime (the idea behind CORBA's DII) and provide a generic mechanism for invoking a method using that declarative high-level description.

12.4.3 Composition Design Patterns

To some extent, all the design patterns help composition in the sense that they introduce abstraction to help components interoperate now and evolve in the future. However, such a statement is not very helpful to the designer who has a specific design problem to solve, and who needs to pick out the design pattern that is most helpful in a particular situation. Let us frame the composition problem as follows. *We have a bunch of components that support complementary functionality, that is packaged at about the right level of granularity* (and hence offers a useful range of compositions) *but that is packaged in a form that makes composition inoperable.* Thus, we have to find ways of bridging the gap created by the packaging of the functionalities.

The design techniques we illustrated in earlier sections are merely variations on well-known design patterns. Our discussion of interobject behavior and contracts [Helm et al. 1990] (see Section 12.2.3) draws on the *mediator* pattern [Gamma et al. 1994]. Event-based composition (Section 12.4.1) illustrates variations on the *observer* and *mediator* patterns. The examples we showed in Section 12.4.2 extend the *observer* pattern, and build on the *proxy* and *command* patterns (the CORBA DII example). In this section, we will discuss two additional compositional patterns, the *adapter* and *bridge* patterns. We have some debate as to whether to include the *composite* and *decorator* patterns. However, the *composite* pattern only deals with the problem of providing a uniform functional interface for recursive aggregates, while *decorator* deals with the problem of extending the behavior of existing objects with additional features dynamically (i.e., while objects are running) and in different combinations of features, while avoiding the proliferation of subclasses.

The *adapter* pattern addresses the following problem: we have two components, A and B, which need to interact. Component B has the functionality that A expects, but has it under a different name/signature. The *adapter* pattern shows how to provide an object that *adapts* the interface of B to the needs of A. Figures 12.9a and 12.9b show two different implementations of the *adapter* pattern.

With the aggregation-based implementation, a concrete subclass of **Window** delegates to the existing implementation, for example, **MyWindow**. With the inheritance-based implementation, a concrete subclass of **Window** also derives from **MyWindow**, which allows it to have access to the actual implementation through **this** instead of through a delegate. The multiple inheritance solution requires, well, multiple inheritance, and thus will work with C++ but not with Java. In Java, a more interesting variant is possible: **Window** could

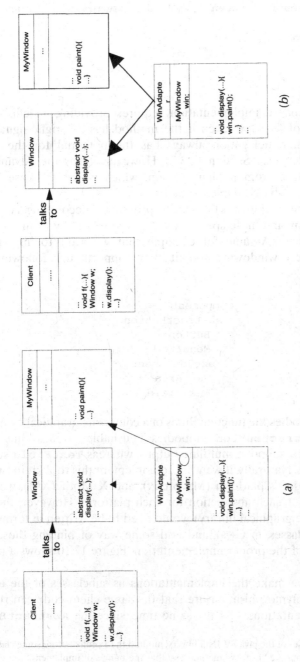

FIGURE 12.9 (a) An aggregation-based implementation of the *adapter* pattern; (b) an inheritance-based implementation of the *adapter* pattern.

be an *interface* instead of a class, in which case **WinAdapter** could be defined as follows:

```
class WinAdapter extends MyWindow implements Window {
  ...
  public void display() {
    paint();
  }
}
```

The aggregation-based implementation requires providing a definition for all the methods of **Window**, even if the method has the right signature in **MyWindow**. Further, delegation always has the potential for the broken delegation problem (see Section 12.3.3). However, it has the advantage of decoupling interface from implementation, which is not the case for the multiple-inheritance-based implementation.

The *bridge* pattern addresses the specific problem of decoupling a type from its implementation, and more specifically, the type hierarchy from the implementation hierarchy. Assume for example that we want to implement a portable (abstract) windowing toolkit that supports the following class hierarchy:[12]

```
             Component
            AbstractButton
              Button
              MenuItem
            TextComponent
              TextArea
              TextField
```

Component embodies the functionalities of a composite graphical component in general. **AbstractButton** embodies "pushable" things that trigger actions. **TextArea** supports multiline output, whereas **TextField** supports single string fields. Naturally, if we want to implement this tool kit in two platforms, say, Microsoft's platform (MS prefix), and X Motif (XM), we would need to implement each abstraction for each platform. However, the client code (that use the graphical library) would need to be written in terms of the types (abstract classes, in C++), and find some way of binding those references to objects of the proper implementation. Figure 12.10 shows a possible implementation.

In this case, we make the implementations as subclasses of the abstract classes and let polymorphism ensure that the same client code can run with different implementations.[13] At the same time, since the **AbstractButton**

---

[12] A (very small) subset of the java SWING library, modulo the J prefix before some class names.
[13] if we use the appropriate "factory" methods, so that the names of implementation classes do not need to show up in the client code. That is the purpose of two additional patterns, the *factory method* and the *abstract factory* pattern [Gamma et al. 1995].

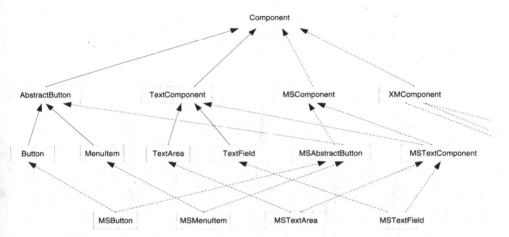

FIGURE 12.10   Multiple implementations of a type hierarchy using inheritance.

class (type) inherits from **Component**, there is a very good chance that **MSAbstractButton** could reuse some of the implementation of **MSComponent**. If the implementation language supports multiple inheritance, platform-specific classes (e.g., **MSTextArea**) could inherit from both their abstraction (**TextArea**) and from the implementation of their superabstraction/type (**MSTextComponent**). However, the code will be hard to maintain, and we need to create a platform-specific implementation for each abstraction, regardless of whether it is truly needed. If the language does not support multiple inheritance (and does not support the separation between types and implementations, see below), we are forced to forego implementation reuse, that is, we cannot make **MSTextArea** inherit from **MSTextComponent**. The bridge pattern prescribes the use of parallel class hierarchies, one for types, which delegates to the proper implementation hierarchy, as shown in Figure 12.11.

Because we have separated the "abstraction" hierarchy from the implementation hierarchy, we can make them vary independently. Indeed, we can reuse implementations a lot more freely without worrying about typing issues, including reusing implementations across platforms. Ironically, the class that represents the common abstraction is *concrete* (it needs to delegate operations) while the class that represents the common implementation is *abstract*. Further, note that the application of this pattern gives rise to another problem: making sure that a client program will use consistent implementations. For example, we need to make sure that if we add a **Button** to a **Component**, both implementations will come from the same platform. The abstract factory pattern addresses this problem. Finally, there is the broken delegation problem, mentioned earlier.

Of course, all of this would be less of an issue in Java, where we can have an *interface* hierarchy that is parallel to the implementation hierarchy. In this

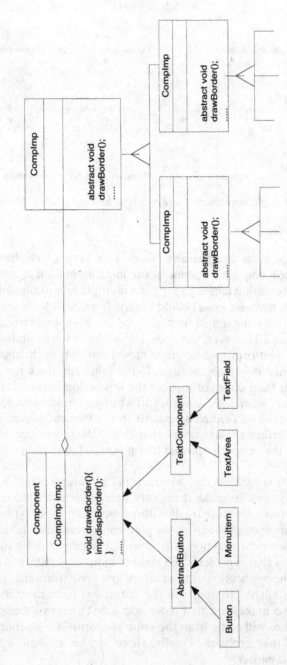

FIGURE 12.11 Decoupling abstraction from implementations so that the two can vary independently.

case, instead of using delegation, we use the implementation relationship. For example, we could have something like this:

```
interface Component {
  public void displayBorder();
  public void displayContents();
  ...
}
interface TextComponent extends Component {
  public void append(String newText);
  ...
}
...
class MSTextComponent implements TextComponent extends
MSComponent
{
  public void append(String newText) {
    ...
  }
  ...
}
```

This would not solve the mutually consistent implementations problem (*abstract factory*), but will take care of the broken delegation problem.

12.5   SUMMARY AND DISCUSSION

Abstraction and composition are at the heart of software reuse. Notwithstanding the issue of whether the reusable components have the right functionality, in this chapter we looked at the different ways to package and compose reusable components, provided they have the required raw material, i.e. the functionality required to generate the desired range of behaviors. We presented three general approaches to the composition problem.

The first set of approaches was noncommittal to a specific programming paradigm. As it turns out, declarative programming approaches provide the most composable packaging of reusable functionality, in terms of least effort required and range of composability. What is interesting about declarative paradigms is the possibility of mixing them with the object-oriented paradigm (Section 12.2.3).

The second set of approaches is object-oriented, but involves new packaging techniques to use in conjunction with object-oriented development. We studied a handful of approaches, which are at different levels of conceptual and development (tool support) maturity. Some are almost ready to use (e.g., aspect-oriented programming, subject-oriented programming), while others are interesting to know about because of the issues they raise, and the novel solutions they bring, which could be applied to similar problems.

The third set of approaches consists of using specific design patterns to address common composability problems. Those approaches are definitely ready to use, involve no new constructs or tools, and should be part of the design arsenal of both application and framework developers. In the next chapter, we will see how we can apply the techniques discussed in this chapter and the previous one, to build highly flexible, configurable, and evolutive application frameworks.

Chapter **13**

Application Frameworks

Reusability is often cited as the major contribution of object orientation to the engineering of software. However, since the late 1980s, it became clear that classes are too small units of reuse to realize the projected or promised benefits [Deutsch 1989]. This is due to two related factors: (1) most classes tend to be rather small in size, and (2) classes seldom perform useful behavior by themselves; they often contribute to a given function by interacting with other objects [Mili et al. 1990]. This led researchers and practitioners alike to look into principles for designing and reusing collections of reusable interacting classes that, together, perform some useful functions [Johnson and Foote 1988, Deutsch 1989].

Developing application frameworks involves the usual tradeoffs between usefulness (general applicability), on one hand and usability (low cost and quality preserving adaptation) on the other. Because they typically cover a lot more functionality than does a single class, they tend to be large, and achieving a given level of usefulness and usability tends to be a lot more complex than in the case of a single class [Fayad et al. 1999]. As coarse-grained reusable components, frameworks require us to use the entire arsenal of abstraction and composition techniques to make sure that they are widely reusable and easily adaptable within the range of their applicability. Documenting and reusing frameworks poses many challenges of its own [Mili and Sahraoui 1999], which have to do in part with the complexity of the artifact and in part with the variety of uses that one can make of a framework, from instantiation, to extension, to emulation [Butler and Denommé 1999].

There is mounting evidence that the construction of application frameworks is a key part of successful reuse strategies [Fayad et al. 1999]. The question is not *whether* to build and reuse frameworks, but rather *how* to build, document, and reuse frameworks. We start by defining what we mean by application framework. In Section 13.2, we talk about technical issues in building and reusing object frameworks. In particular, we talk about component substitutability and component composition. Section 13.3 deals with the process of building frameworks. Section 13.4 goes through a detailed example. We conclude in Section 13.5.

13.1 WHAT IS IN A FRAMEWORK

13.1.1 A First Definition

The reader may find different definitions of application frameworks that stress different aspects of frameworks, including their objective, structure, behavior, and other properties. We start with a simple definition, and refine it as we go along. An application framework may be roughly defined as a set of interacting objects that, together, realize a set of functions. The set of functions defines the area of *expertise* or *competencies* of the framework; we refer to it as the domain of the framework. A *domain* may be either a subset of the *busi-ness domain* (*problem space*), or a subset of the *computing domain* (the *solution space*). A banking application framework implements functions with the *business domain of banking*. The *model view controller* (MVC) framework, developed for the Smalltalk language, covers a subset of the *computing domain*, and more specifically, the *design domain*, by addressing the problem of connecting business logic with GUI (graphical user interface) logic in a way the minimizes the dependencies between the two. Other computing domain frameworks will address *architectural issues*, and some are discussed in Chapter 14.

An application framework may be described by the equation:

$$\text{Application framework} = \text{a blueprint} + \text{component realizations}$$

Most authors will use the term design instead of blueprint. This is perhaps a reflection of the fact that the first application frameworks known to mankind were *computing domain frameworks*, and more specifically, GUI frameworks. However, when we talk about *business frameworks*, the framework identifies *domain classes*, their *interrelationships*, and their *interactions* (analysis level description), and possibly the design and partial realization of such classes, interrelationships, and interactions. In this case, the blueprint can describe either the analysis or the design, or both. Clearly, the earlier in the development lifecycle reuse takes place, the greater the reuse gains. An analysis-only framework (sometimes referred to as a *modeling framework*) typically focuses on analysis level constructs, without making any commitment, designwise, to the way those classes will be implemented. Analysis-only frameworks, or *modeling frameworks* are typically the product of *domain analysis* (see Chapter 8).

In this chapter, we are interested in application frameworks that are designed and partially implemented.

13.1.2   The Anatomy of a Framework

A framework views an application fragment as a set of objects that interact to accomplish a set of domain functions. The definition of a framework must include at least the following:

- A set of participants of the framework
- A set of relationships between the participants of the framework
- A set of interaction scenarios between the participants of the framework

The participants are generally described in terms of *obligations:* each framework participant fulfils a particular role within the framework. That role is often described in terms of an *interface* that the participant must support. The interface consists of a set of properties and method signatures that a component fulfilling that role must implement.

Let us take the example of the MVC framework (see Fig. 13.1): we have three participants, identified as the **Model**, the **View**, and the **Controller**. The **Model** is the part responsible for the application's state and behaviour, and for notifying the other components of state changes. The **view** is the part responsible for the graphical display. The **Controller** is the component that is responsible for reacting to user inputs, and for translating them into actions to be executed on the application side. Formally, the **Model** may be defined by the following interface:

```
interface Model {
    void iChanged(String aspect, Object value);
    Object getState ();
}
```

In this case, any object that plays the role of a model must implement the methods iChanged(String, Object) and getState(). Model objects

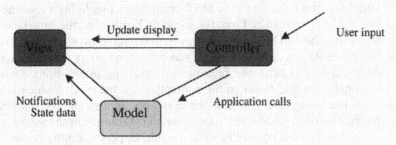

FIGURE 13.1   The model view controller framework.

commit to calling iChanged(String,Object) whenever a state change, deemed worthy of attention, takes place—this commitment is not yet described; see below. The function Object getState() returns a descriptor of the state of the model object that enables the view to update itself. In general, application (business) objects will implement a lot more than iChanged() and getState(), but these functions are required for co-ordinating the model with the view and the controller. Note that although this is a valid Java interface, we are not committing to any particular interface def-inition language; we later see alternative implementations when we talk about specific frameworks.

A possible **view** interface may be defined as follows:

```
interface View {
void update(String property, Object from, Object value);
void display ();
}
```

The view must implement two methods. update(String,Object, Object) is a function that will be called when the model represented by the view (the from argument) had changed with respect to the property property, and with the (new?) value value; display() is the function to be called to display() the view.

An example interface for the controller may be given as follows:

```
interface Controller {
void keyPressed(String key, Point cursorPt);
void leftMouseButtonPressed(Point cursorPt);
void rightMouseButtonPressed(Point cursorPt);
}
```

The functions keyPressed(String,Point), leftMouseButton-Pressed(Point), and rightMouseButtonPressed(Point) are func-tions that a controller must implement to specify the reaction of our MVC application to user input. It is expected that part of the code for these func-tions will call on functions from the model, and functions from the view.

This simplistic presentation of the MVC framework highlights a few impor-tant points about frameworks. First, the mere description of the interfaces of the participants is far too little information to understand how the framework works. Our presentation of the interfaces was accompanied by textual descrip-tions, which explicated both the relationships and the interactions. One of those relationships is that between the controller and the model, which is key to the controller being able to access the corresponding model. We may rep-resent that relationship graphically, such as with UML notation showing a *nav-igable association* from a controller to its model. In programming terms, this relationship could show up as follows:

```
class MyController implements Controller {
    private Model controlledModel;
    private View controlledView;
    ...
    void keyPressed(String key, Point cursorPt){...}
    void leftMouseButtonPressed(Point cursorPt){...}
    void rightMouseButtonPressed(Point cursorPt){...}
}
```

Second, we don't know half the story without seeing the interactions between the various methods. In this particular framework, there are two basic interaction paths through the various components:

$$c.\text{leftMouseButtonPressed()} \rightarrow m.\langle\text{apply function}\rangle$$
$$m.\langle\text{change state}\rangle \rightarrow m.\text{iChanged(stateVar,val)} \rightarrow$$
$$v.\text{update(stateVar,m,val)}$$

The first path indicates the scenario in the case of a user input (left mouse button pressed). The second path indicates an application induced state change, with its effects on the view.

This description of the interaction scenarios is referred to as *message sequences* [Mili and Sahraoui 1999], and is one way of representing the *interaction behavior* or *interobject behavior* that is inherent in the framework. It is not the only one, nor is the description of the behavior complete; there may be invariants to be maintained, postconditions to be verified after message sequences, and so on. The description of interobject behavior is a whole area of research in and of itself [Mili and Sahraoui 1999], and draws on the same formal pool as that of object composition discussed in Section 12.2.3 (see, e.g., Helm et al. [1990]).

So far in this description, we are not saying how the function c.left-MouseButtonPressed(Point) is called when the left mouse button is pressed. Similarly, we are not saying how the function v.update(state-Var,m,val) gets to be called when object m notifies "the world" of its state change. A framework user only cares to know that c.leftMouseButton-Pressed(Point) will be called when the user presses the left mouse button, and then code the method accordingly. This illustrates three further points about frameworks:

- The description of the behavior of the participants is inevitably *incomplete*. This is true not only because the participants may have other behavior that is *not* relevant to the framework but also because some of the framework-related behaviour cannot be specified generically. The preceding two sequences show two examples of incompletely specified participant methods: m.⟨apply function⟩ (first sequence) and m.⟨change state⟩ (second sequence). We later show how we can better refine the specification of the behavior of the framework participants (Section 13.1.3),

- The idea of *inversion of control*[1]—instead of the application-specific code calling reusable code, we have reusable code calling application-specific code, and knowing when that application-specific code will be called, we can put in it whatever it is we want done in certain situations,
- A framework does *not* expose all of its internals. A framework exposes only those parts that need to be customized by the framework users to adapt it to their needs; for a given set of functionalities, the fewer and simpler the parts, the better the framework.

Figure 13.2 illustrates this last point. We don't really know what happens inside, but we know when control gets out of the framework "body," and which methods are called. To some extent, all the information given so far is related to the *framework interface*; the implementation is yet to come.

Referring to the framework equation earlier in this section, a framework includes, in addition to the description of the participants, their relationships, and their interactions, the following:

- A more or less complete implementation of the mechanisms that mediate the interactions between the participants
- For those participants that are application independent, a set of generally useful implementations that may be used to instantiate a framework

The Smalltalk MVC framework includes classes for handling low-level interface events that connect the event management functionalities of the host windowing system with the controllers. Average users need not familiarize themselves with the inner workings of that part of the framework. In automotive terms, these classes embody the *chassis*, which is the block to which connect the various participants, but whose internal composition is of little

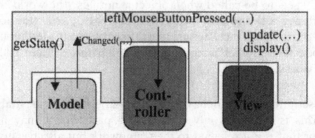

FIGURE 13.2 The participants represent pluggable components into an interaction infrastructure.

---

[1] Also referred to as the Hollywood principle: "Don't call us, we will call you."

interest to the average user. We refer to that part of the framework as the *interaction infrastructure*.

In addition to the interaction infrastructure, a framework will typically come with sample realizations of some of the participants. For the case of Smalltalk, the MVC framework includes an extensive library of *view* classes and their *controllers*. The framework users need to code the model in its entirety—except for the model–view communication mechanism, which is part of the interaction infrastructure. They also have to assemble composite views, and code those parts of the views and the controllers that depend on the application, namely

- Which model method to call in response to any given user interaction
- Which aspects of the model to visualize in the view, and how to update it in response to user input

Figure 13.3 illustrates the relative proportions of each participant that a developer has to build to adapt the framework to a given application domain.

Finally, there is at least another piece of information that the framework user needs to know in order to use the framework: how to assemble the various components. The descriptions of the interactions between the framework's components usually convey more or less thoroughly the behavior of the framework instance at "cruising speed," but often fail to show how it is assembled in the first place. For the MVC, I know what is supposed to happen once the components have been assembled, but how do I get it that far? We refer to these as the *instantiation* scenarios [Mili et al. 1997]. An example instantiation scenario for the MVC is

```
| myModel myView itsController |
"instantiate CheckingAccount"
account := CheckingAccount new.

"create view for account"
myView := MyViewClass new: account.

"set the controller to a MyControllerClass"
myView controller: (MyControllerClass new).
```

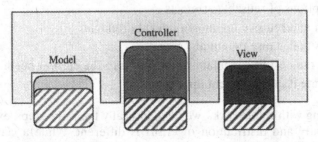

FIGURE 13.3 Relative percentage change to the participants of a framework. The striped portion represents custom code.

Another scenario might skip the last step, as the one argument constructor for **MyViewClass** (**new**: aModel) would assign a default controller to all instances of the views. This piece of information is part of what a developer needs to know about the framework participants and their relationships.

If we summarize what we have said so far, to describe a framework for the purposes of a framework user, we need to specify the following:

- The set of participants of the framework, in terms of the interfaces that they have to support
- The set of relationships between them
- The set of interaction scenarios between the participants that are mediated by the interaction infrastructure of the framework
- The set of instantiation scenarios, showing how to assemble an instance of the framework

A framework *developer* or *maintainer* needs to know a lot more about the framework's inner workings to be able to emulate it or extend it.

In practice, an actual framework will consist of the abovementioned documentation, plus concrete source code for the interaction infrastructure (fixed aspects), a set of partially concrete components that might fulfil the roles of the various participants, as well as a number of generation tools that help realize (concretise) a specific participant on the basis of existing abstract components, and on application specifics, to be supplied by the framework user.

13.1.3 The Framework Reuse Lifecycle

When we develop *with* reusable artefacts, we usually forego the usual analytic processes, and before we go on decomposing a particular artefact (requirement, analysis model, design model, code) into more manageable artefacts, we first look to see if that artefact is not already available, in the desired form or close to it. A number of authors have characterized the (re)use lifecycle for reusable artefacts as follows [Krueger 1992, Mili et al. 1995a]:

1. Specify the need in terms that can be matched against the available descriptions of reusable artefacts.
2. Search and retrieve the most relevant artefacts.
3. Assess their reuse potential.
4. Select the best fit candidate, and adapt it to the current need.
5. Integrate it in the current application.

When dealing with frameworks, we have basically the same steps, except that the complexity and distribution of effort is different. While a class library might have hundreds of classes and methods, a framework user is typically confronted with the choice between a handful (rather than hundreds) of frameworks, and the search and retrieval aspects are not important. Typically, one would evaluate a handful of candidate frameworks on the basis of functional coverage, platform support, quality of documentation, etc.

Thus, the assessment step (step 3) can take a long time, per candidate framework, especially in the final selection stages. It can go from reading the documentation and deciding that a framework is not appropriate, to actually developing prototype applications with the framework to test its various qualities before committing a major development project to it. Typically, in organisations that can afford it, and for major developments, one to two senior developers would be assigned to evaluate a particular framework, and this evaluation may take from a couple of days, to a few weeks. Those developers would report back on their experience accommodating their needs with the candidate frameworks, and a choice is made on the basis of that experience.

Adapting the best-fitting framework to the problem at hand (step 4) means finding realizations for the various participants [Mili and Sahraoui 1999], by selecting concrete components among the ones provided along with the framework, and selecting and adapting application-specific components to adapt them to the roles they would be playing in the framework. Typically, this step involves some hand programming, as well as some program generation using accompanying toolkits. Assessing frameworks involves these very steps, but on a smaller prototypical scale.

Finally, we may liken integration, in the context of frameworks, to implementing various instantiation scenarios that would effectively plug application components into the framework structure.

Frameworks evolve through use. Each reuse instance of a framework will encounter a number of difficulties that identify areas that can be improved, aspects that can be further parameterized, participants that should be further generalized or split, and so on. The framework reuse lifecycle will feed into the framework development lifecycle (see Section 13.3).

13.2 FULFILLING THE FRAMEWORK CONTRACT

At the risk of oversimplifying, if we view the framework as a contract, the *participant interfaces* describe the obligations of the participants, and the interaction scenarios describe the obligations of the framework, as an interaction infrastructure. In this section, we discuss ways to fulfill this contract.

As we mentioned in Chapters 7 and 8, a key concern in developing reusable assets is to identify, isolate, and encapsulate the variabilities within an application domain in such a way as to maximize the common parts, and to constrain the development of the variable part. For the case of object frameworks, given a set of objects that we know we need, and that have to collaborate to a achieve a set of functions, the concern is to break the necessary collaboration between components along lines that will make it possible to

- Implement as much of the common parts as possible.
- Interchange the collaborating components with little or no effect on the rest of the components.

Roughly speaking, we could say that the interaction infrastructure represents the *common aspects* within the functional domain covered by the framework, whereas the *participant interfaces* represent the *variable aspects*. In this section, we discuss the techniques that make it possible to implement the common part, and to enforce the requirements on the variable part.

A key design problem in object frameworks is to handle variabilities. For example, the MVC framework could be seen as answering the following design problem: "suppose that we want to manage the interactions between the model and the view, without having to tie the model classes into the view classes." The mechanism that was devised to manage this interaction is the *dependents* mechanism, later known as the observer/observable design pattern, discussed in Section 12.4. Another concern might be to develop this GUI framework that is portable across platforms. To address this concern, we would separate the computational logic of interface assembly and display from the idiosyncrasies of the APIs of specific platforms. And hence, the bridge and adapter patterns may be used to implement some of the interactions within the framework [Gamma et al. 1995]. Generally speaking, design patterns are used to mediate the interactions within an object framework. This is an indication of both, where to find good design patterns, and how to build good object frameworks:

- Good application frameworks are a source for good design patterns: a good application framework is one that accommodates variation across a wide domain, with little or no effort. By looking at how this was achieved we can find resilient interconnection patterns.
- Once we have identified the components of a framework, and their semantic dependencies, we can minimize the implementation of those dependencies by applying design patterns.

It is natural to confuse design patterns and object frameworks, and explain the difference in terms of granularity; design patterns are design fragments, whereas frameworks are more complex and more complete application fragments. The difference is much starker than that; a *design pattern is a design lesson*, whereas a framework is a *software solution* that *addresses a specific functional domain*, in a way that *may make use of such design lessons*. The didactic aspect of design patterns is their primary goal. The didactic aspect of application frameworks is a useful byproduct for framework developers in the making. Figure 13.4 illustrates this distinction.

Enforcing the framework contract on the participants' side makes use of a set of programming techniques that we present in the remainder of this

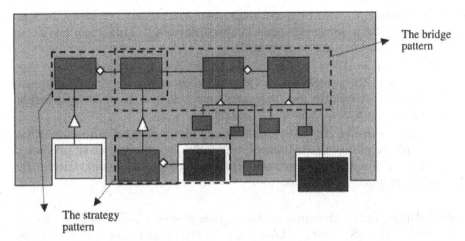

FIGURE 13.4 Frameworks accommodate variabilities by instantiating appropriate design patterns.

section. So far we described participants in terms of the interfaces that they must implement. The common part of the framework, which is typically implemented and provided either as a library or as an executable, refers to these participants somehow. We look at how they are referred to, and what language or design mechanisms we can use to support the substitutability of interfaces for implementations.

13.2.1 Component Substitutability

Most of the earlier frameworks were implemented in Smalltalk and C++. In both C++ and Smalltalk, *obligations* are represented by abstract classes. The code of the common part is represented in terms of these abstract classes. When we select classes to play the roles of specific participants, we use *inheritance, polymorphism*, and *dynamic binding*, to make sure that an instance of the framework will work properly:

> *Inheritance.* The actual participants are subclasses of the abstract classes that represent the participants. Generally speaking, this inheritance relationship serves two purposes:
> - *Type Conformance.* Ensuring the type conformance of the actual participants to what is expected of them in the framework. Inheritance implies subtyping, unless otherwise indicated.[2]

---

[2] If we cancel methods in the derived class, then we are "overriding" the subtyping relationship that comes with inheritance. See Section 10.2.4.

- *Extension.* The abstract classes are not only used to represent obligations but also provide some of the behaviour. In this case, they act as a repository for reusable code.

Polymorphism. By allowing variables of one class to take values belonging to any of the subclasses, we allow the code of the framework that was written generically for the participants' classes to work with actual implementations of those participants,

Dynamic Binding. By delaying the binding of a method call to an actual implementation until runtime, we enable polymorphic code to always invoke the method implementations that are most appropriate to the actual object being used.

We illustrate the combination of these techniques on a small framework that was part of the OSE Library [Dumpleton 1994], a high-quality public-domain C++ library. In process simulation systems, there is a queue of jobs to be executed. A dispatcher retrieves the first job from the queue and executes the code associated with it. Our framework, which we will call OTC_Simulation, offers two general C++ classes; **OTC_Job** and **OTC_Dispatcher**. A potential instance of this framework must include one or more instances of **OTC_Job** (or one of its subclasses), and a single instance of a class that specializes **OTC_Dispatcher**. We represent below the class headers:

```
      class OTC_Dispatcher: . . . {
          Collection(OTC_Job)* jobQueue;
      public:
          OTC_Dispatcher(Collection(OTC_Job)* jobs = null) {
            setJobQueue(jobs);
             ...}

(1)   virtual void log(OTC_Job* job){
            cout << "Executing: "<< job << endl;}

(2)   void setJobQueue(Queue(OTC_Job)* queue) {...}

(3)   int dispatch () {
          int nbJobs = 0;
(3.1)     while (jobQueue->hasMoreElements()) {
(3.2)       OTC_Job* nextJob = selectFirstJob();
(3.3)       nextJob->start();
(3.4)       log(nextJob);
            nbJobs ++;
          }
          return nbJobs;
        }
      ...
      }
```

```
(4)  virtual OTC_Job* selectFirstJob() = 0;
   ...
}
class OTC_Job: ... {

public:
(5)  virtual void start() {
        initialise();
        run();
        end();
        }
(6)  virtual void initialise() = 0;

(7)  void run() {...}

(8)  virtual void end() = 0;
}
```

In this simple framework, one of the visible participants (**OTC_Dispatcher**) assures the coordination with the other participants (**OTC_Job**). Further, the class **OTC_Dispatcher** serves both to describe the obligations of a dispatcher and also to provide parts of the implementation. The heart of the simulation is the nonvirtual method int dispatch() [starting on line (3)]. This method iterates over the collection of queued jobs (3.1), and runs them one by one, logging each job. This method is general, and shouldn't be redefined. The simplest way in C++ to enforce non-redefinability is to declare the method nonvirtual. In this way, the method is statically bound, and code that refers to variables declared of type **OTC_Dispatcher** will call this version, whether the method has been redefined in subclasses or not. For example, if we write

```
(A)  OTC_Dispatcher disp = new MyDispatcher();
     ...
(B)  int numQueuedJobs = disp.dispatch();
```

Then, line (B) above will invoke the version of **OTC_Dispatcher**, regardless of whether **MyDispatcher** has its own version or not. This is not a strong enforcement, because if we had declared disp to be of type **MyDispatcher**, then, **MyDispatcher**'s version will be called. Java has a stronger mechanism for enforcing non-modifiability: the keyword **final**.

Let us continue analyzing the method int dispatch(). To select the next job to execute, we use the method OTC_Job* selectFirstJob() [signature in line (4)], which selects the first job in the job queue according to some priority criteria. This method is pure virtual, meaning that all subclasses of **OTC_Dispatcher** have to provide their own definition. In Java, it would have been declared abstract. In Smalltalk, the conventional way would be to provide an implementation that raises an error, as in

```
selectFirstJob
    self subclassResponsibility.
```

The method void log(OTC_Job) is used to log the execution of jobs. The class **OTC_Dispatcher** provides a default implementation, but subclasses may redefine it. To this end, this method is declared virtual.

Let us now look at the class **OTC_Job**. We have a similar story with the method void start() being overridable and dynamically bound, the method void run() being statically bound (and almost nonoverridable; see above), and methods void initialise() and void end() being undefined and dynamically bound.

Lines (3.2) and (3.3) in method int OTC_Dispatcher::dispatch() illustrate the combination of inheritance, polymorphism, and dynamic binding. An actual instantiation of the framework will use a subclass of **OTC_Job** (*inheritance*), but that is okay, because, thanks to polymorphism, we can assign to nextJob an object from any subclass of **OTC_Job**. And when we invoke the method void OTC_Job::start() on nextJob, we know that it will be the version of the *actual* class of nextJob that will called, thanks to dynamic binding.

A number of authors have argued that inheritance, polymorphism, and dynamic binding are the key to developing frameworks [Lewis et al. 1995]. Of course, we know that these are *not* the only techniques. These are one set of techniques for handling component substitutability. There are other sets of techniques for component substitutability, and a wider range of problems, requiring yet other techniques.

Java supports a clean separation between interfaces and implementations. In Java, the same simulation framework, the participants would be represented with actual Java interfaces:

```
interface Dispatcher {
    public void log(Job aJob);
    public void setJobQueue(Collection queue);
    public int dispatch();
    public Job selectFirstJob();
}

interface Job {
    public void start();
    public void initialise();
    public void run();
    public void end();
}
```

Further, we would have classes that provide a partial implementation of these methods:

```
abstract class OTC_Dispatcher implements Dispatcher {
    private Collection jobQueue;

    public OTC_Dispatcher(){
      this(null);
    }

    public OTC_Dispatcher(Collection jobs){
      setJobQueue(jobs);
    }

(1)  public void log(Job job){
      System.out.println("Executing: "+job);}

(2)  final public void setJobQueue(Collection queue) {
      jobQueue = queue;}

(3)  final public int dispatch () {
      int nbJobs = 0;
      while (jobQueue.hasMoreElements()) {
(4)     Job nextJob = selectFirstJob();
(5)     nextJob.start();
(6)     log(nextJob);
        nbJobs++;
      }
      return nbJobs;
    }

(7)  abstract Job selectFirstJob();
     ...
}

abstract class OTC_Job implements Job {

    public void start() {
      initialise();
      run();
      end();
    }

(8)  abstract void initialise();

(9)  final public void run() {...}

(10) abstract void end();
}
```

There are a few departures from the C++ implementation. First, participants classes do not have to inherit from any particular class: they only have to *implement* the specified interfaces. Second, the provided abstract classes (**OTC_Dispatcher** and **OTC_Job**) refer to each other through the **Dispatcher** and **Job** interfaces [see lines (1), (4), and (7)], and not by name, which would allow them to work not only with each other but also with any other class that implements the corresponding interface. Also, thanks to the **final** keyword [lines (2), (3), and (9)], we are able to enforce the nonmodifiability of methods—provided we implement the participants by extending the provided abstract classes.

Having identified the mechanisms that would allow us to develop or adapt participants, we now turn our attention to issues related to assembling participants to instantiate a framework. It turns out that, despite our best efforts to abstract the roles of the components, we could still be left with implementation-level dependencies between the participant components, which are not adequately expressed by abstract interfaces. For example, in a portable GUI framework that can emulate various native interfaces, there is the implicit assumption that the realization of the **CompositeContainer** widget be compatible with the **TextView** widget, that is, that they both emulate the same native interface. Figure 13.5 illustrates this situation.

In this case, we are saying that out of the possible realizations of **Button** and **Panel**, not all pairwise combinations are possible.

The accepted solution in this case is to have a *factory method* or *factory class* [Gamma et al. 1994]. We illustrate the factory class solution. It consists of including, in the framework, a class whose only purpose is to manufacture objects that play specific roles. By centralizing object creation within a single class, we can more easily enforce constraints such as mutually consistent specializations. In this case, an abstract factory class would look like

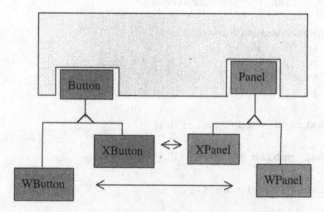

FIGURE 13.5 Mutually consistent specializations.

```
abstract class WidgetFactory {
  abstract public Button getButton();
  abstract public Panel getPanel();
  abstract public ListView getListView();
  ...
}
```

Then, we can have subclasses of the widget factory that would create mutually consistent instances of the various participants, as in

```
class Win32WidgetFactory extends WidgetFactory {
  public Button getButton() {return new WButton();}
  public Panel getPanel() {return new WPanel();}
  public ListView getListView() {return new WListView();}
}
```

and

```
class XWidgetFactory extends WidgetFactory {
  public Button getButton() {return new XButton();}
  public Panel getPanel() {return new XPanel();}
  public ListView getListView() {return new XListView();}
}
```

Of course, languages with some reflection capabilities can do away with subclassing. In Smalltalk, because classes are objects, the concrete implementation of a participant may be used as an instance variable of the factory class. For example

```
Object subclass: #WidgetFactory
  instanceVariableNames:'buttonClass panelClass listClass'
  ...
  !!Method for setting buttonClass!
setButtonClass: aClass
  buttonClass := aClass.!
  ...
  !!Method for returning button!
getButton
  "returns an instance of the class buttonClass"
  ^(buttonClass new).!
  ...
```

In this case, we can create a widget factory instance, assign the proper class objects to the various instance variables, and then ask it to provide instances of these classes.

Java's reflection capabilities are less extensive than Smalltalk's, but it can handle this pattern quite nicely, including as follows:

```
public class WidgetFactory {
  private Class buttonClass;
  private Class panelClass;
  private Class listViewClass;

  WidgetFactory(Class bClass, Class pClass, Class lClass){
    buttonClass = bClass;
    panelClass = pClass;
    listViewClass = lClass;
  }

  public Button getButton() {
    return (Button)bClass.newInstance();
  }

  public Panel getPanel() {
    return (Panel)pClass.newInstance();
  }
  ...
}
```

This implementation assumes that the classes at hand all have a no-argument constructor.

13.2.2 Composition Issues

The participants of a framework collaborate through what we called the *interaction infrastructure* to achieve that function. In an ideal world (or framework), some participants will be framework-usage-specific, while others will be generic framework components. For example, in an idealized MVC framework, view and controller classes would have no connection to model classes, and vice versa. Users of the framework will simply have to pick a view class, a controller class, take one of their model classes, and plug them together. In real frameworks, different participants will implement a different mix of framework-general functionality and usage-specific functionality. In the MVC, model classes have *at least* to implement the method `void iChanged` (`String aspect`, `Object value`), and view and controller classes need to "talk" to model objects. An important challenge for a framework designer is to

- Separate as much as possible framework-general functionality from usage-specific functionality.
- Provide composition mechanisms that are as noncommittal as possible for the composed objects.

If we have a GUI framework whose participants include a model object, and if we want the framework to be used with little change to model objects, we have to make sure that

- The graphic classes need as little access as possible to the model classes, and vice versa.
- Whichever access is needed is mediated in a way that doesn't bind the graphic classes or the model classes.

We don't want the composition of graphical classes to model classes to bind the graphical classes because that means that we need to add usage-specific code to graphical classes. We don't want the composition to bind the model classes, because this means that the model classes can be used only in the context of the GUI framework. Thus, the question becomes how to compose objects without creating dependencies between them.

We have addressed composition issues in Chapter 12, and proposed a variety of composition techniques, including composition design patterns. Some of these patterns may be built into the framework. For example, the MVC framework uses the observer/observable pattern to connect models and views. Other patterns may be used to plug in a class in lieu of a participant when that class does not satisfy the participant's interface. We reproduce below Figure 12.9 from Chapter 12, which shows two alternative implementations of the *adapter* pattern.

Assume that one of the participants is specified with the interface

```
interface Window {
(1)   public void display();
(2)   public void resize(float xFactor, float yFactor);
(3)   public void minimize();
}
```

and assume that I have a class called MyWindow that implements all of these methods, but under different names, or with different signatures:

```
class MyWindow {
   public void display(GraphicsContext gc) {...}
   public void resize(float newX, float newY) {...}
   public void close() {...}
}
```

Then, in order to use the class **MyWindow** as an implementation of the interface **Window**, I could create a subclass as follows:

```
class MyWindowAdapter extends MyWindow implements Window {
(4)   public void display() {
(4.1)   GraphicsContext gc = getDefaultGraphicsContext();
        display(gc);
     }

(5)   public void resize(float xFactor, float yFactor){
        float newX = this.getX()*xFactor,
```

```
        newY = this.getY()*yFactor;
      resize(newX,newY);
    }

(6) public void minimize() {close();}
}
```

Lines (4), (5), and (6) show how we adapted the signatures of functions (1), (2), and (3), respectively. The three functions illustrate situations with different complexities. The easiest is the last one [lines (3) and (6)], where it was only a matter of method name. The case of resize is tricky; although the two functions have the same signature, the parameters don't have the same semantics, and so we need to do parameter conversion. The first function, display(), shows the case where the available implementation has an extra parameter. We assumed here that we can have a default value, but this won't always be the case, and more work may be needed to bridge the two versions. Further, we don't know what the framework code will do with the parameter that we are passing.

The difference between levels of features of a framework and its specific realizations can be problematic. We would want the framework to be feature-laden, and to be as finely tunable as the most advanced host environment. However, we should also provide simpler implementations to accommodate simpler environments. Generally speaking, customisability of the interaction infrastructure of a framework can make the framework code fairly complex.

We conclude this section by addressing a question related to the enforceability of behavioral requirements on the participants. Recall the way we described the collaborations within the MVC framework:

$$c.\text{leftMouseButtonPressed}() \;\rightarrow\; m.\langle\text{apply function}\rangle$$
$$m.\langle\text{change state}\rangle \;\rightarrow\; m.\text{iChanged}(\text{stateVar},\text{val})\rightarrow$$
$$v.\text{update}(\text{stateVar},m,\text{val})$$

In both sequences, we needed to specify the interconnection between method calls, one of which is not known by name. In the second sequence, we wanted to say that any state change function must, one way or another, trigger a call to m.iChanged(stateVar,val). In this case, we could say that state change functions are described *intensionally* instead of *nominally* (by name). Regardless of how the triggering is implemented, we have to worry about making sure that any state change *does* trigger the call to iChanged(). This is a far from trivial design problem, and we discuss a few alternatives below.

Roughly speaking, there are two general strategies. Either we generate the code for methods that modify state variables, or we force the methods that modify state variables to go through our framework supplied code—which makes the appropriate method calls. The latter is generally difficult to enforce, except in reflective environments where we have access to the message dispatching mechanism, and where we can intercept method calls, and prefix (or postfix) them with whichever framework-specific processing we wish. Examples of the first strategy abound in all sorts of frameworks. Typically, developers specify their application-specific classes using some sort of high-level abstract language (e.g., a graphical language or an interface definition language), and the system generates attributes and getter and setter methods, with the appropriate notifications. This is the approach used in most GUI frameworks where event notification code is inserted, where possible, to relieve developers from having to put that code in themselves. Similarly, with distributed objects technology, developers specify their classes using an interface definition language, and a compiler generates the actual code sequences that invoke the RMI (remote method invocation) service instead of executing those methods locally.

Code generation is powerful but has its limitations. First, in most languages, we can override the generated code in a subclass and bypass calls to the framework's interaction infrastructure. Only in Java can we prevent redefinition using the **final** keyword. Second, and most important, by letting the framework toolkit generate part of our application code, we create two problems:

- *Integrating Legacy Application Code into a Framework.* What do we do if we already have application classes that implement a good part of the functionality?
- *Binding Application Code into the Needs of a Specific Framework.* Assume that we have class **Customer**, which we want to visualize through a GUI framework, and persist through a persistence framework. Both framework toolkits will want to generate skeletons of class **Customer**. For example, the method setName(String aName) generated by the GUI toolkit makes sure that the "name" field in the GUI is updated, while the setName(String aName) of the persistence framework makes sure that the name is updated in the database.

There are a range of more or less acceptable solutions to these problems. The first problem can be solved with a variation on the *adapter* pattern and is illustrated in Figure 13.6. We are assuming a C++ framework in this case, and we used the multiple inheritance implementation of the adapter pattern. In Java, **Model** would be an interface, the relation between **ModelCustomer** and **Model** is a realization relationship (ModelCustomer **implements** Model), and iChanged(...) would be generated directly in the class **ModelCustomer**.

This solution would not work in case our **Customer** class is to be used with *two* frameworks. Assume that we wanted our customer objects to be both visualizable and persistent. With multiple inheritance, we need to use the class generated by one framework toolkit as "domain class" (input class) for the next toolkit, as illustrated in Figure 13.7.

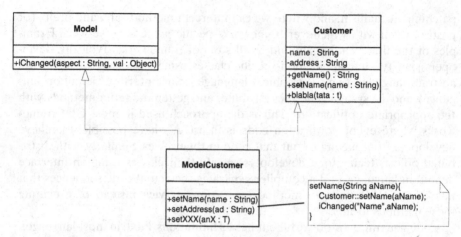

FIGURE 13.6 Generating participant classes from legacy classes to enforce framework interaction model.

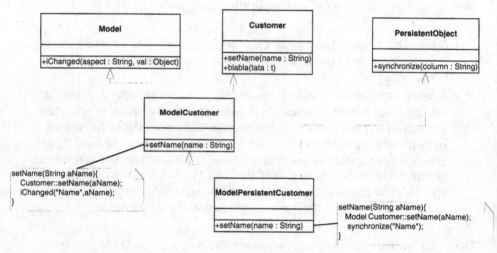

FIGURE 13.7 Cascading generators to play a role in two participants.

Let us now look at the aggregation-based implementation of the adapter pattern, as shown in Figure 13.8.

With this solution, we have, again, the broken delegation problem.[3] Assume that a user is displaying a customer data on a GUI, then modifies the name field, and presses a CONFIRM button, or something of the sort. This will in turn call the method ModelCustomer.setName(String), which will delegate

---

[3] We also have the problem with the cascaded version that we alluded to, for slightly different reasons.

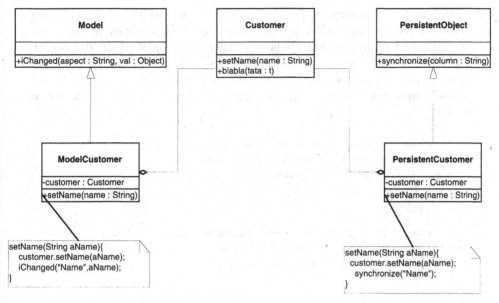

FIGURE 13.8 Handling multiple frameworks with independent aggregation-based adapters.

to `Customer.setName()` and update the view, but it won't trigger the `synchronize("Name")` operation of the persistence framework. And vice versa. Even if we cascade two aggregation-based adapters, as in

```
class ModelCustomer extends Model {
  private Customer customer;
  public void setName(String aName){
    customer.setName(aName);
    iChanged("Name",aName);  }
  ...
}
class PersistentModelCustomer extends PersistentObject {
  private ModelCustomer customer;
  public void setName(String aName) {
    customer.setName(aName);
    synchronize("Name");}
  ...
}
```

the cascade will work only if the name change originated from the persistence framework; if it originates from the GUI framework, the persistence framework won't see it.

This is one type of problem that aspect-oriented programming [Kiczales et al. 1997], subject-oriented programming [Harrison and Ossher 1993], and view-oriented programming [Mili et al. 1999] are supposed to handle: having different framework toolkits to generate their own versions of the same method, and requiring that all be executed when invoked on the object. Subject-oriented programming handles this head-on. In addition to the domain class **Customer**, we would have two framework generated classes whose implementations of the setName(String) method would be as follows:

```
class ModelCustomer extends Model {
  public void setName(String aName){
    iChanged("Name",aName);
  }
  ...
}
class PersistentCustomer extends PersistentObject {
  public void setName(String aName) {
    synchronize("Name");
  }
  ...
}
```

By composing **ModelCustomer** and **PersistentCustomer** with **Customer**, we compose the three implementations of setName(String), with the end result being that all that needs to be done gets done. Aspect-oriented programming would *weave* a *model aspect* and a *persistence aspect* into select methods, to the same effect. View programming would generate a GUI model view and a persistence view from a *GUI model viewpoint* and a *persistence viewpoint*, respectively, to the same effect.

We should qualify our characterization of the pattern of Figure 13.8; it may be appropriate, depending on what needs to get done on both sides. If all the adapters do is—well—adapt, that is, translate a call into another, it will work just fine; it is only when they have side effects that we run into trouble. For instance, there is a very legitimate and powerful use for this pattern in distributed architectures. Recall the high-level architecture of CORBA described in Section 12.4.2, and assume that we have the same business objects, but that two client sites see two different interfaces (with different access privileges, etc). CORBA offers two ways of implementing the server side objects: by inheriting from (extending) the skeleton class generated from the IDL (the *inheritance approach*), or by delegating to it from a *delegator* generated for that purpose (the *tie approach*). When the language does not support multiple inheritance, or when we have two client applications that are used to working with different APIs, then the tie approach is more appropriate, and the delegators (Tie1 and Tie2) generated by the IDL compilers may have different interfaces, but delegate to the same implementation (legacy) object (Imp). Figure 13.9 illustrates this usage. This use of two aggregation-based

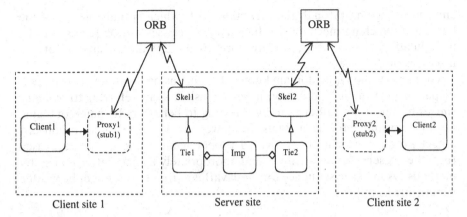

FIGURE 13.9   Using the Tie approach in case a distributed object is seen through different interfaces.

adapters works just fine because the Tie objects do nothing else but unwrap requests, executing them, and wrap back the result.

Before we conclude, we should add that all the abstraction language constructs, techniques, and design patterns (see Chapters 8, 11, and 12) are needed in the context of frameworks to handle participant substitution and composition issues. In this section, we illustrated some of the patterns that address the more recurrent issues, and that are used in novel ways in the context of frameworks. The fact that we didn't illustrate a particular technique or pattern in some detail doesn't mean that it isn't useful in the context of frameworks. One such set of techniques is what we collectively referred to as metamodeling (and metaprogramming) techniques. We briefly illustrate the usefulness of these techniques both for specifying participants intensionally, and for composing them at a high level of abstraction.

We saw in Chapter 11 that we can abstract ("go meta") the description of software artefacts along three dimensions: (1) the representation language, (2) the domain knowledge, and (3) the computational model. "Going meta" along the representation language dimension means, in this case, taking advantage of the programming language's reflection capabilities—if it has any. We saw earlier one instance where having access to the language's reflection capabilities can enforce an interaction sequence on a candidate participant. Indeed, to make sure that every method that causes a state change in the model sends a notification (iChanged(..., ...)), we can intercept method calls and postfix them with the processing that we want. There is a difference here between Smalltalk, a true (if partially) reflective language; and Java, in which reflection is simulated. Smalltalk has a unique dispatching that is accessible and that we can intercept. With Java, we have two dispatching mechanisms: the one built into the virtual machine, which does not need the reflection API, and the one going through the reflection API (which is built on top of the built-in dispatching mechanism). In Smalltalk, classes *are* **Objects**, and by manipulating class objects, we are sure to modify the behaviour of the instances of the class.

Going meta along the domain knowledge dimension means expressing participant requirements and compositions intensionally by referring to *semantic classes* of behaviors, rather than by referring to behaviors by name or signature. For example, the Java Beans framework makes it possible to edit any object property graphically, provided proper naming conventions are used (e.g., the presence of an attribute and appropriately named getter and setter methods). A message sequence for the JavaBeans framework might be written generically as follows:

```
User.entered(text,⟨beanProp⟩) ->
    bean.set⟨beanProp⟩(⟨beanPropType⟩.readString(text))
```

which is basically saying, "if the user is typing text in the field reserved for a bean property, then call the appropriate setter for that property by making sure to convert the string into the actual type of the bean property." Development tools that generate bean editors use Java's reflection API to generate this "generic" sequence, with actual message sequences for the various bean properties.

Finally, going meta along the computational model dimension means being able to express operational parameters of an instantiation of the framework declaratively, much like what Rueping calls *metalevel configuration* [Rueping 1999]. To some extent, the abstract factory pattern is a computational metamodel of the acceptable instantiations of the framework. More complex constraints on the allowable combinations of participant realizations may be expressed in a similar fashion.

13.3 BUILDING FRAMEWORKS

Frameworks are complex reusable artifacts. Building frameworks involves the usual challenges, and more. The *process* for developing frameworks recognizes these challenges. Section 13.2 addressed some of the technical challenges in developing and using a flexible and configurable reusable artifact. In this section, we look more on the process side.

Researchers and practitioners alike agree that (1) frameworks are useful, (2) their development is difficult, and (3) their development benefits from continual improvement based on actual reuse experience. We can agree to that, too. As reusable software artifacts, frameworks have requirements, analysis-level models, designs, and realizations. How do we build each one of these descriptions? Frameworks address functional domains in a way that satisfies a number of design criteria (qualities), namely, flexibility and reuse. The first step in building frameworks is to identify the functional requirements, and most researchers and practitioners agree that this must be the first step in framework development. In domain engineering parlance, this is called *domain scoping* (see Chapter 8).

Regarding the remaining steps, there are two schools of thought, which we may caricature as follows:

1. *The top–down analytic school*, where we develop a framework by performing a domain engineering process, starting with domain analysis, then design, then realization [Aksit et al. 1999]
2. *The bottom–up synthetic school*, where we start by developing an application within the domain of the framework, and then introduce variabilities into it [Shmidt 1999].

The two authors cited will probably object to this characterization as being too reductionist, which is probably true. We illustrate the two schools in this section.

13.3.1   Frameworks as Products of Domain Engineering

In chapter 8 we reviewed a number of domain analysis methods, and studied FODA (feature-oriented domain analysis) in more detail. Recall that in FODA, once we have scoped the domain, we start by building a feature model that shows the various features supported by applications within the domain, showing alternative implementations of the same features (e.g., error logging into a file vs. on the screen), and dependencies and constraints between features [Kang et al. 1990]. For example, some application can have either a terminal interface or a window-based interface, and errors can be logged both to a text file and to the display. We could say that error logging to the display is possible only with window-based interfaces. The information model (static object model) and the operational model (behavioral model) show, among other things, the dependencies between entities and functions or procedures on one hand, and features on the other. For example, two alternative implementations of the logging feature might show up as two subclasses of an abstract class **Logger**, one called **TerminalLogger** and the other, **WindowLogger**.

Existing domain engineering methods recognize that designing and implementing a "domain" has to be incremental, for at least two reasons: (1) to spread out the investment in resources over a tolerable period of time and (2) to road-test the architecture of the domain (or framework) first, before developing a lot of components into that architecture. The question then becomes which parts do we start with?. The answer, from most experts, is to "start with those aspects of the domain that have an influence on the architecture" [Kang et al. 1990, Jacobson et al. 1997]. Our issue might then be how to identify those aspects that most influence the architecture. We find it useful to think of the architecture in terms of two layers: a computational layer and a functional layer. The computational layer underlies all of the functions. The functional layer may be more partitionable than the computational layer, and thus may lend itself better to incremental development. What the experts are saying is: start with those functions that are likely to require *most* or *all* of the computational infrastructure so that the major design tradeoffs will be addressed with the first increment; new functions might be added later, but they should not require a new computational infrastructure, or, the new infrastructure does not depend on the existing one.

For example, suppose that we want to develop a Web-enabled banking framework. In terms of computational infrastructure, mission-critical Web-enabled *business* (banking or otherwise) applications will require

- *Distribution.* The application logic should be location transparent, which means the use or development of a distribution infrastructure,
- *Security.* Communication across the network must be secure, which requires the handling of users, authorizations, certification, encryption, and the like,
- *Transaction Services.* The use of transaction monitors to ensure the ACIDity of distributed transactions,
- *Recoverability.* Distributed logging, mirror sites, and the like.

Because all of these are related, if we want to develop a banking framework incrementally, the first increment should contain the smallest set of functions that will require all four computational services.

The literature abounds with recent experiences with framework development in both industry and R&D labs [Fayad et al. 1999], and a good portion of it falls into this school of thought, namely, viewing framework development as a planned domain engineering process where the framework starts taking shape during the domain analysis phase. Example approaches including those of Aksit et al. [1999], Jacobson et al. [1997], and Fayad and Johnson [1999] have described several other approaches.

13.3.2   Frameworks as Planned Byproducts of Application Development

We have seen in earlier chapters (see Sections 1.3, 4.2, and 7.3) that there is a continuum of approaches to coordinating domain engineering with application engineering. The idea here is that we *grow* frameworks out of subsets of applications within the targeted framework domain. In this approach, we still need to elicit the requirements of the framework. But instead of building it from the top down, we start building applications from the domain, and then start introducing variations in those parts of the applications that concern the domain of interest.

A good number of frameworks originated from R&D labs, and fall into this category, for many reasons. For instance, the work in R&D labs is driven by creativity, trial and error, and risk taking; these R&D "values" are often in contradiction with notions of process, deliverables, documentation, and the like. Also, few R&D labs are interested in investigating the process of building frameworks *as a subject of study*,[4] and thus, studies in the process of building frameworks often come as a post hoc formalization of ad hoc development. These studies have the advantage of embodying true and proven design heuristics.

A representative example of these approaches is *hotspot-driven development* as advocated by Pree [1999] and Schmidt [1999]. A framework "hotspot" is a point of variability within a framework. According to Pree, two applications within the application domain of a framework will differ by the binding of at least one hotspot. The idea here is that we can identify those hotspots early on in the process, but we don't necessarily develop them in the first iteration. The first iteration will solve a specific problem; later iterations will design variability into the identified hotspots. Figure 13.10 illustrates this idea.

The process starts with an identification of the domain of the framework, and requirements for a first application. That implementation is later evolved into a first iteration of the framework where a first point of variability (hotspot) is fully developed; probably that aspect that must often changes from one application to another (step 1). Designing a hotspot means changing a

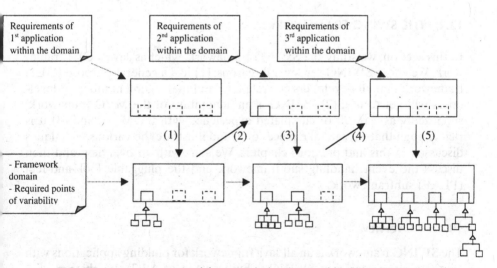

FIGURE 13.10 Incremental framework development by hotspot design.

---

[4] There are a few notable exceptions, of course, like the SEI and the Software Engineering Laboratory affiliated with the University of Maryland, but then these are the places that came up with top–down approaches such as FODA and OO variations thereof.

specific binding of a point of variation (e.g., a terminal logger) into [Schmidt 1999]

1. An abstract description (a generalization) of the aspect of interest, and
2. A number of concrete realizations (including the existing one).

Of course, experience with the framework may identify unanticipated points of variations, which will be implemented along the way [steps (4) and (5)].

There is a close correspondence between *hotspots* and what we called *participants*; most hotspots will lead to the identification of a participant, but there is no one-to-one correspondence. For example, a concrete class at iteration *n* is replaced at iteration *n* + 1 by an abstract class or an interface (depending on the language) and concrete subclasses. The abstract class or interface becomes, in our terminology, a framework *participant*. However, some variations will be handled by parameters. Moreover, a concrete class that is used at a point of variation may be replaced by several collaborating classes, only one of which may be abstract. For example, we could replace the terminal logger by a stream logger (independent of the device), which will be a fully implemented class, and a stream "displayer," which will be abstract with a few concrete realizations, including the **TerminalDisplay**. Thus, the "logger hotspot" was designed as a stream logger (a fixed part of the framework), and a *participant*, which is the abstract class **StreamDisplayer**.

13.4   THE SWING FRAMEWORK

In this section, we study the SWING framework, which is Java's GUI framework. We chose SWING for several reasons: (1) it is a general-purpose (GUI) framework that all developers can relate to, and that a good number of developers will get to use; (2) SWING is an adaptation of the MVC framework, supposedly as a result of cumulated experience with the MVC; and (3) it is rich enough that we can take pieces of it, and illustrate the various techniques discussed in this and previous chapters. We start with an overview, and then discuss the event handling sub-framework and the pluggable look-and-feel (PLAF) subframework.

13.4.1   Overview

The SWING framework is an all Java framework for building applications with graphical user interfaces. SWING is built on top of AWT, the abstract windowing toolkit. The abstract windowing toolkit is *abstract* to the extent that the host windowing environment is abstracted into a set of classes that share the same API, but that have different implementations. AWT makes extensive use of Java *interfaces* (type descriptions) and *abstract classes* to describe windowing systems functionality in a platform independent way. An application written using AWT components on one platform will run on any other platform that has its own implementation of the AWT components, espousing the platform's look and feel. AWT interfaces with the host environment using native code—typically C and C++. Among other things, this meant that the AWT API consists of the lowest common denominator of the various host platforms. This also means that an application can only have the look and feel of its host environment, and won't have the same appearance across platforms. SWING, on the other hand, is entirely Java. It interacts with the host environment through AWT Java components, and it relies only on those AWT classes that are closest to the platform (e.g., **Window**), or that are independent of the platform (**Event**, **Color**, etc.). Figure 13.11 illustrates the distinction. SWING supports a number of features that AWT doesn't, in part because of its independence of the platform, in part because of better architecture.

SWING is considered to be a descendant of the MVC framework, with a twist. A number of experts have noted that Smalltalk's MVC, for example, leads to a strong coupling between views and controllers. For instance, while it is a good idea to separate the display of information (view) from the way a user interacts with that display (controller), controllers were implemented in such a way that they were very tightly coupled with the views. For example, Smalltalk's **MultiListController** is very tightly coupled with the **MultiListView class**, as illustrated in Figure 13.12.

In Smalltalk, controllers control rectangular areas. Default controllers for predefined view classes have different behaviors that depend on the input of the user (pressing a mouse button, dragging the mouse, etc.) *and* on the position of the cursor within the view. As Figure 13.12 shows, the area covered by this multilist widget is thinly sliced into different behavioral areas. The default controller here is too tightly coupled with the view; we can't imagine finding much use for it, outside the context of this view.

Consequently, SWING designers thought that it is not a good idea to separate the interface part into two classes that are spatially collocated, the view and the controller. They decided to group the view and control aspects, but separate another aspect, instead. Figure 13.13 illustrates this distinction.

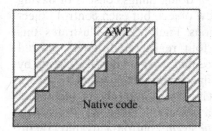 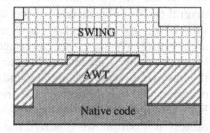

FIGURE 13.11 SWING builds on top of the minimal layer of AWT required to connect to the host environment.

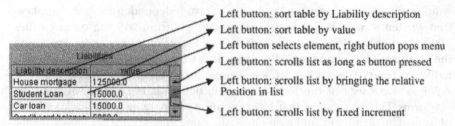

Left button: sort table by Liability description
Left button: sort table by value
Left button selects element, right button pops menu
Left button: scrolls list as long as button pressed
Left button: scrolls list by bringing the relative Position in list
Left button: scrolls list by fixed increment

FIGURE 13.12 Controlling user input depends heavily on the graphical layout (view).

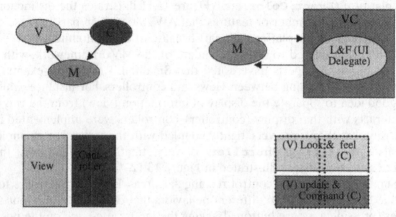

FIGURE 13.13 SWING versus MVC framework: same functionality, different slicing.

In the remainder of this section, we discuss the event handling framework and the pluggable look-and-feel framework.

13.4.2 The Event-Handling Framework

Whereas the MVC assigns one object per (non-composite) view to handle all sorts of user interactions, the SWING way of doing things consists of having several control objects control the same view object, but each control object subscribing to one kind of user interactions. Figure 13.14 illustrates this architecture. We have one interface, and four registered listeners (dotted lines). Basically, user interactions are intercepted as raw interface events by the host windowing systems. Depending on the component on which the event occurred, and the position of the cursor, specific *semantic events* are generated. For example, the **MousePressed** event is a raw event. If the event occurred on top of a button, we generate the *semantic event* "button-activated" (actually called **ActionEvent**); if the event happened on a **JList** within the area of display of the items, then we would have a **ListSelectionEvent**. In

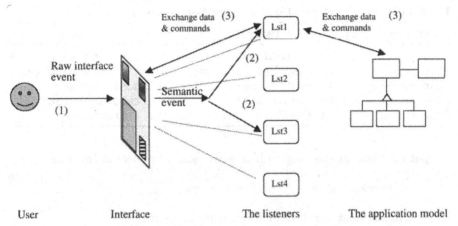

FIGURE 13.14   The event-handling framework in SWING.

Figure 13.14, we show how a user raw event [step (1)] gets translated into a semantic event.

Once the proper semantic event is generated, it is broadcast only to those listeners that care about such events [step (2)]. In Figure 13.14, our interface has four registered listeners, but only two of these (Lst1 and Lst3) care about the new event. These listeners will, in turn, evaluate the current state of both the interface and the application, and may act on the event. We show here the case where listener Lst3 chose to ignore the new event, while Lst1 went ahead and updated both the model and the interface. Listeners have access to the model either through their own state variables, or through data contained in the event.

SWING supports two kinds of events: low-level semantic events—also called *light events* in SWING parlance—and high-level semantic events. We will discuss only high-level events because they embody the structure of the event framework more clearly.

We have already said that listeners register only to certain kinds of events. Well, different kinds of SWING components generate different kinds of semantic events, and so, on any given component, we may register different kinds of listeners. Simple components will typically generate only one kind of high-level semantic event. More complex components may generate several high-level events. For example, **JButton** generates a single high-level event, namely, **ActionEvent**. However, a list may generate two high-level semantic events: one to signal change in list data (e.g., adding or removing elements from the list), and one to signal change in selection. Table 13.1 shows some of the ⟨component, listener, event⟩ associations.

The listeners shown here are actually *interfaces*. A developer who wants a specific listener for an interface component has to implement the corresponding interface. The **ActionListener** interface is shown below:

TABLE 13.1 Some Component-Listener-Event Associations in SWING

Component	Listener	Event
JList	ListDataListener	ListDataEvent
JList	ListSelectionListener	ListSelectionEvent
JButton	ActionListener	ActionEvent
JDocument	DocumentListener	DocumentEvent
JComboxBox	ListDataListener	ListDataEvent

```java
public interface ActionListener extends EventListener {
  /**
   * Invoked when an action occurs.
   */
  public void actionPerformed(ActionEvent e);
}
```

This interface consists of a single function: void actionPerformed (ActionEvent e). The event-handling mechanism (i.e., the *interaction infra-structure*) of SWING guarantees that *if* we register an **ActionListener** on a component, *and* an **ActionEvent** (i.e., a raw event that was translated into an **ActionEvent**) occurs on the component, *then* the method actionPer-formed of the action listener will be called.

Thus, it is up to the developer to put into this function whatever they want to be done when the user performs an action on the component.

Assume that we are creating a **JButton** in our interface with label "Say hello", and that we want the following behavior; if we click on the button, "Hello world" is printed on the standard output. Then, we should first define our action listener:

```java
public class SayHelloListener implements ActionListener {
  public void actionPerformed(ActionEvent e) {
    System.out.println("Hello World");
  }
}
```

According to our framework reuse process (Section 13.1.3), this step consists of selecting or implementing realizations for one of the participants of the framework.

The next step would be to create the button, and attach a **SayHello-Listener** to it:

```java
...
JButton myButton = new JButton();
myButton.setText("Say Hello");
myButton.addActionListener(new SayHelloListener());
...
```

According to our framework reuse process, this is an instantiation scenario; it shows how to assemble the various components. With this, the application is ready to go. Of course, in real life, event listeners will do a lot more than print "Hello world"; they will need to access some of the application data. A starting point may be the event itself, which has an attribute called "source," which points to the interface component from which the event originated. In this new implementation of the method actionPerformed(Action-Event), the variable aButton will point to the **JButton** from which the event originated (we have to cast the return value of getSource() because getSource() returns an **Object**). Usually, from the interface component, we can access the application data.

```
public class SayHelloListener implements ActionListener {
  public void actionPerformed(ActionEvent e) {
    JButton aButton = (JButton)e.getSource();
    System.out.println("Hello World from "+aButton);
  }
}
```

This event-handling framework is fairly common, and may be found, in different flavors, in various GUI frameworks.

Going back to Table 13.1, we see a clear example of three participants, two of which are concrete and provided by the framework, and one of which is abstract (the listener) and has to be developed by the developer. Further, the interaction between these three participants is managed by a fixed and hidden part of the framework that we called the *interaction infrastructure*—in this case the event-handling infrastructure.

13.4.3 The Pluggable Look and Feel Framework

In SWING, the look and feel of applications is delegated to a separate object, for added flexibility. The *look* of a widget has to do with the *visual* attributes such as the color of the border, whether the border is raised or not, the color of the background, the fonts used for text, and so on. Different platforms have different visual attributes, which enable us to immediately distinguish a Motif interface, say, from an MS Windows interface, or an OS/2 interface.[5] The *feel* of the interface is related to user input, and characterizes things such as sensitivity to a three-button mouse, semantics (and timing parameters) of double clicks, and minimum duration for holding keys down to consider them repetitions. All of these "feel" attributes can be parameterized, and each platform has a set of default or preferred values for these parameters. SWING designers decided to encapsulate the look and feel of a GUI into a separate object called *UI delegate*, which can be changed while the application is running. Figure 13.15 illustrates this architecture.

---

[5] Does anybody remember what those are like?

FIGURE 13.15 The look and feel of graphical components is delegated to a separate component managed by the UIManager.

In fact, the UI delegate is defined at the top-level SWING component, namely, **JComponent**, which has an instance variable called ui of type (abstract class) **ComponentUI**. Each subclass of **JComponent** has its own type of UI delegate, which must be a subclass of **ComponentUI**. The name of that class is stored in a String static variable (uiClassID) as shown for the class **JList**.

```
public abstract class JComponent extends ... implements ... {
  ...
  protected transient ComponentUI ui;
  ...
}
public class JList extends JComponent implements ... {
  ...
  private static final String uiClassID = "ListUI";
  ...
}
```

When components are created, their variable ui is initialized with an instance supplied by the **UIManager**. For **JList**, for example, the variable ui will be initialized with an instance of a concrete subclass of **ListUI**.[6] The call sequence for a **JList**, for example, would like this:

```
        ...
        public void setUI(ListUI uiComponent) {
          ui = uiComponent;
          ...
        }
        public void updateUI() {
          setUI((ListUI)UIManager.getUI(this));
        }
```

where getUI() is a static method of the class **UIManager**. For each component, the UIManager can return a UI delegate from a default concrete subclass of **ListUI**, set for all the **JLists** of the current application. Note here that we need to cast the ui component returned by UIManager.getUI(..)

---

[6] Components are not systematically installed with ui components, but for the purposes of this presentation, we will assume that this is the case.

because getUI(...) returns **ComponentUI** (it takes **JComponent** as an argument).

Now, how does the UIManager find the default UI delegate class for a given SWING component? Figure 13.16 gives a simplified overview of the entire class structure.

Basically, for each component type, and each platform, we have one component UI. Thus, for **JList**, we have one subclass of **ListUI** for Windows platforms (let us call it **BasicListUI**), one for Metal, one for OS/2, and so on. For any given platform, the appropriate UI classes for the SWING components are stored within a table managed by a class that is a subclass of the abstract class **LookAndFeel**. For example, for a Windows platform, it is called **BasicLookAndFeel**. Now, the **UIManager** manages a table of such classes. Thus, for a given platform and a given component, the **UIManager** will first find the corresponding **LookAndFeel** class [links (A) and (B)], then, through that class, find the UI class for the component (links (C) and (D)).

When we start an application, we can set the default platform for the look and feel to the current platform on which the application is running. The following code sequence shows a static initialization for the look and feel to be used throughout an applet-launched application:

```
UIManager.setLookAndFeel(
    UIManager.getSystemLookAndFeelClassName());
```

We can get a cross-platform look and feel (the "Java look and feel") with the following initialisation:

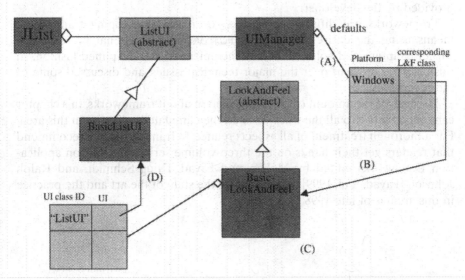

FIGURE 13.16 The overall architecture of the pluggable look and feel.

```
UIManager.setLookAndFeel(
    UIManager.getCrossPlatformLookAndFeelClassName());
```

In essence, what we have here is a reflexion-based two-stage object factory, where the same method

```
public class UIManager {
    ...
    public static ComponentUI getUI(JComponent comp){...}
    ...
}
```

manufactures UI delegates for all sorts of **JComponent**s and all sorts of platforms.

13.5 CONCLUSION

There is growing evidence that application frameworks are an important part of successful reuse. Application frameworks embody domain models, reusable designs, and a significant base of reusable code. By addressing all phases of the development lifecycle, we are able to attain higher levels of reuse, and greater productivity and quality benefits. When reusing frameworks, we typically end up implementing very little code, compared to the code that we reuse without change. On the long and arduous road to program generation, frameworks are the last stop before the terminal. Most frameworks in use today include generators that help generate a good part of the code that has to be provided by the developer.

Frameworks are difficult to develop or reuse. Developing frameworks means using the entire abstraction and composition arsenal presented in earlier chapters, and going at it in an incremental and disciplined fashion. In this chapter, we went over the major technical issues, and discussed some of the process issues.

Because of the amount of literature written about frameworks, this chapter cannot do justice to all the work or to all the cumulated expertise in this area. For a thorough treatment of all aspects related to frameworks, we recommend that readers get their hands on the three-volume series of books on application frameworks edited by Mohammed Fayad, Doug Schmidt, and Ralph Johnson [Fayad et al. 1999], which reflects the state of the art and the practice in this area as of late 1998.

Chapter 14

Architectural Frameworks

Going back to our definition of reusability, large-scale organized efforts at reuse have established that the greatest technical obstacle to reuse is lack of *usability* and not lack of *usefulness*. In particular, there is a lot of useful functionality out there in legacy systems, but most of it does not use the right control paradigm, or doesn't abide by the right interaction protocols, or simply isn't implemented in the right programming language [Garlan et al. 1995, Bass et al. 1998]. In Chapters 11 and 12, we tackled issues related to the techniques that may be used for low-level packaging of software components to make them more easily usable, specifically, to reduce the effort required to adapt a component to a specific use, and to widen the domain over which that effort is still worthwhile. Chapter 13 dealt with the issue of putting those techniques to use in the context of building *application frameworks*, viewed as one way of packaging reusable software artefacts that cover a functional domain.

In this chapter, we are interested in a special kind of framework, which we refer to as *architectural frameworks*. Roughly speaking, an *architectural framework* is an *application framework* whose *functional domain* is the enforcement of a particular *architectural style*. These frameworks are interesting for two reasons: *what they can do* and *how they are built*. We will talk about distribution frameworks and frameworks that support component-based development, because knowledge of these frameworks is now part of the basic arsenal of both the developer and the consumer of reusable software artefacts. What makes these frameworks interesting, from a domain engineering point of view, is the more stringent usefulness requirements (i.e., across application domains), and the kind of solutions that are used to equip them with higher levels of abstraction.

We start the chapter with a general introduction to the notion of architecture and to the role of architectural frameworks. Much of the contents of this first section is based on the book by David Garlan and Mary Shaw, of Carnegie Mellon University [Shaw and Garlan 1996], and the book by Bass, Clements, and Kazman, of the Software Engineering Institute [Bass et al. 1998]. The next section deals with the role of software architecture in software reuse. Section 14.3 discusses issues in architectural frameworks. We then discuss three families of architectural frameworks, the COM family, CORBA, and Java based technologies, in Sections 14.4 through 14.6. We conclude in Section 14.7.

14.1   WHAT IS AN ARCHITECTURE

14.1.1   Definition

According to Bass et al. [1998], p. 23, "The software architecture of a program or computing system is the structure or structures of the system, which comprise software components, the externally visible properties of those components, and the relationships between them."

Most of us think of architecture in terms of diagrams that people draw on corners of paper napkins, or corners of cleared off white boards in meeting rooms, with "DON'T ERASE" written across. They are these mysterious graphs where nodes of various shapes represent software components of different kinds, and where links with different annotations represent relationships of different kinds. They are the diagrams that most people around the table pretend to understand, and very few dare discuss or question beyond the multi-tier-level diagrams that show Web servers, firewalls, Transmission Control Protocol/Internet Protocol (TCP/IP) links, Wireless Application Protocol (WAP) zapons,[1] Internet Inter-ORB Protocol (IIOP) ethers, and few repositories (cylinderlike icons) for good measure; the only reason these *deployment diagrams* are of any value to anybody is the fact that all those around the table tend to have the same architectural experience and are able to reverse engineer those deployment diagrams to similar *software organizations*.

Bass et al. defined software architecture as the high-level design of a software system in terms of software components (modules, subsystems, processes), including their external properties (API, runtime behaviour) and their inter-relationships. Because software tends to be very complex, we need several views of the software that reflect different properties of the software components and different relationships between them, or different decompositions of the software altogether.

Depending on the kind of components and the kind of relationships between them, we have different structures to describe the software:

---

[1] A "zapon" is a broken line like a Z that shows a nonphysical communication link.

- *Module Structure.* In this structure, the nodes represent software modules (packages, classes), and links represent dependency and containment links. For example, a Java package A depends on a Java package B if classes in A refer to classes in B.

- *Conceptual Structure.* In this structure, the components represent functional units of the system, and the relationships between them represent data flows between them.

- *Process Structure.* In this structure, the components represent processes or threads, and the relationships between them represent relationships such as "synchronizes with," "can't run with," "preempts," and "rendezvous with."

- *Calls Structure.* The components are usually "procedures," and the links represent the "calls" or "invokes" relation.

- *Physical Structure.* This represents the mapping of the software onto the hardware. The components represent processing nodes (processors on the same machine or on different machines), and the links represent communication links between the processing nodes. These are sometimes called *deployment diagrams* (see Fig. 14.1).

Each of these structures reflects one aspect of the system and serves different purposes. The module structure may be used to identify dependencies within the parts of the system, and break down system development into as many independent parallel tracks as possible. Figure 14.2 shows an example of module structure using UML notation. The dashed arrows describe dependencies between the modules, meaning in this case that one module needs definitions found in another module. In terms of organizing development, this module structure means that we can have at most four independent teams working on four independent modules (the graphing package, the process ontology package, the machine description package, and the runtime layer), then we have a development bottleneck around the actual simulation package, then we can work on two packages (simulation execution and simulation

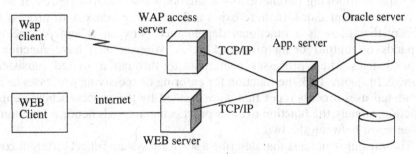

FIGURE 14.1 One of many architectural diagrams (*deployment diagram*).

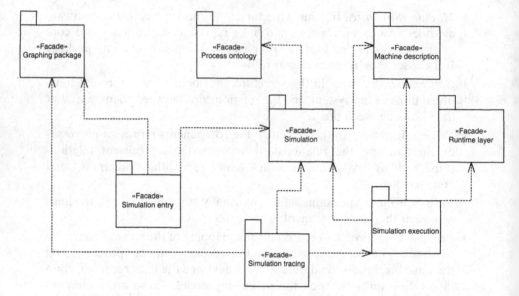

FIGURE 14.2   A module structure for the process simulation framework.

entry), and then we can work on simulation tracing. A two-team configuration, on the other hand, could do {process ontology, machine description}, then {simulation, runtime layer}, then {graphing package, simulation execution}, then {simulation entry, simulation tracing}, assuming that the various packages and teams are of the appropriate sizes. This second configuration appears to be less wasteful of human resources but would spread development over time. Decisions will be made based on nontechnical factors (availability of personnel, needed time to market, existence of other work that can be done by idle development teams, etc.).

The conceptual structure reflects the *functional architecture* of the software in terms of a high-level data flow diagram. An example functional architecture of our simulation framework is shown in the diagram in Figure 14.3. The ellipses represent *processes*. The labeled arrows represent *data flows*, and the capacitor-looking parallel bars—if anybody remembers—represent data stores (persistent data). If there exists a flow from process A to process B, we say that there is a functional dependence between B and A, since B depends on output being produced by A. We can also have functional dependencies when processes communicate through a shared persistent storage. In Figure 14.3, the function for entering or specifying processes to be simulated uses process types that were created by the process schema entry function, namely, the function to enter process metamodels hence, a functional defendence between the two.

The various structures that describe a software system reflect different concerns but ultimately overlap as the same software entities crosscut different

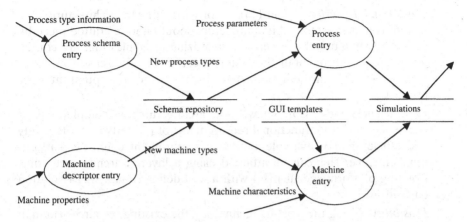

FIGURE 14.3 A partial conceptual model of the process simulation framework.

structures. In our example, the "process entry" function may be implemented using the packages "process ontology," "machine descriptor," "graphing," "simulation," and parts of "simulation entry." If the process entry function were to be implemented as a standalone executable, that executable would have to be built from the compiled code of the aforementioned packages. Other functions would use some of these packages as well. The conceptual model may also overlap with the physical model as different functions may be assigned to different machines. The number and nature of architectural structures required to describe a software system ultimately depends on the application domain, and on the complexity of the application within that domain [Bass et al. 1998]. Bass et al. recommend that designers document a particular structural diagram *only* when that diagram is not trivial and when it adds value (different elements) to the ones already at hand.

14.1.2 Quality Attributes of Architectures

Each software system *has an architecture*, which is the actual organization of the software system as it stands, regardless of how carelessly thought out it was. However, we are able to intuitively recognize *good architectures* from obviously *bad architectures*. There are a lot of architectures in the between, and in this section, we present some of the quality attributes of architectures.

Bass et al. have identified a number of architecture-related quality attributes that help assess the quality of software systems [Bass et al. 1998]. They draw a number of distinctions, including the following important ones: (1) quality attributes of the *architecture* as a *deliverable* in its own right and quality attributes of the *software product* as a whole, but that are influenced by architectural properties.

The quality attributes of a software architecture include

- *Conceptual Integrity.* An important property of the architecture of a system is its consistency. An architecture should not be crafted piece by piece, but should embody general organizing principles that are consistently applied throughout the system. Section 14.1.3 discusses *architectural styles*, which are embodiments of sorts of the conceptual integrity property,

- *Completeness and Correctness.* An architecture is complete if it addresses all the nonfunctional requirements of the software[2] effectively and efficiently. For example, one such requirement could be platform independence. This can be attained using a layered architecture (thus isolating platform specificities) with a well-defined small API (isolation costs little),

- *Feasibility.* Using the existing technology, the existing resources (human and technical), and within the required timeframe.

The three quality attributes are somewhat contradictory. Feasibility often requires shortcuts, which violate conceptual integrity. Further, completeness and conceptual integrity may clash. An example is a perfectly layered architecture where the different layers communicate with only the immediately adjacent layers, have performance penalties, and thus may not address performance requirements (see e.g. [Van Der Linden and Müller 1995]).

Qualities of the software system that are influenced by the architecture may be divided into observable properties of the system during run-time, and properties of the system as the product of development and continued maintenance. Runtime properties include performance (transactions per second), availability (meantime to failure), security, usability, and functionality (the extent to which the product addresses user needs). Not all of these properties are architectural in nature, although a good architecture can only help make things easier.

Qualities of the software system as a product of development and maintenance include variables such as testability, integrability, modifiability, portability, and reusability. *Testability* refers to the ease with which certain system properties may be verified. For example, an event-based architecture with a fixed pool of event handlers cannot guarantee that a given system will be able to handle some hard real-time constraints. Similarly, only an architecture that uses a best-effort message queuing service can avoid deadlocks. In safety-critical software, testability may become the overriding factor in choosing an architecture. The remaining four properties are related to the architecture's accommodation of present-time differences and future evolution, and are tightly related to reuse. They are discussed separately in Section 14.2.

---

[2] Paul Clements disputes the distinction between functional requirements and nonfunctional requirements—which underlies the assumption that they are separable—especially when "nonfunctional" is construed to mean secondary.

14.1.3 Architectural Styles and Connectors

Now that we know what an architecture is, and what quality attributes to seek in an architecture, we look at means of architecting systems in a way that guarantees some of those qualities. There are two ways of going about this: (1) devising an architecture development procedure that takes as input, a prioritised list of architectural quality attributes, and that produces an architecture that satisfies those properties by construction; or (2) studying existing software system architectures with the hope of (a) identifying recurrent architectural styles and (b) finding a reasonably good correlation between these architectural styles and quality attributes. The first alternative is fairly difficult, as software engineering in general remains an a posteriori quantitative science, and thus, architectural design has gone the way detailed design has: *codifying best practices into recognizable abstractions*. That is what *architectural styles* are all about.

Architectural styles are *classes of similarly patterned software architectures*. In Section 14.1.1 we defined software architecture as one or a set of software structures consisting of software components that have externally visible properties, and relationships between them. An architectural style is *a class of architectures* characterized by

- *Component types*, which are component classes characterized by either software packaging properties (e.g., "COM component") or functional (e.g., "transaction monitor") or computational ("persistence manager") roles within an application.
- *Communication patterns between the components*, indicating the kinds of communications between the component types.
- *Semantic constraints*, indicating the behavioral properties of the components individually, and in the context of their interactions.
- *A set of connectors*, which are software artefacts that enable us to implement the communication between the components in a way that satisfies the semantic constraints.

Researchers and practitioners alike have cataloged a number of architectural styles, which are briefly described later in this section.

Bass et al. distinguish between domain reference models and domain reference architectures. A *reference model* is typically the product of domain analysis whereas a *reference architecture* is generally the mapping of a reference model to an architectural style (see Fig. 14.4).

Researchers at Carnegie Mellon University and the Software Engineering Institute have cataloged a dozen or so styles grouped in five families, the *independent components* family, the *data flow* family, the *data-centered* family, the *virtual machines* family, and the *call and return* family. Some members of these families are briefly described below.

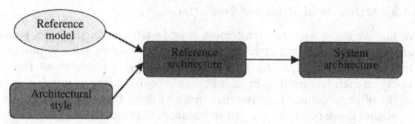

FIGURE 14.4   The role of architectural styles in reuse-centered development.

14.1.3.1 Independent Components

This is a family of architectural styles in which a software system is viewed as a set of independent processes or objects or components that communicate through messages. Messages typically carry data in a more or less standard format, and possibly some description of a task to be performed. Message-based communication allows components to interoperate while retaining control of their own execution, and without having to know each other('s API) in detail. There are two subfamilies, the *event based systems*, and the *communicating processes* family. Under the event-based systems family, we have two styles: the implicit invocation style and the direct invocation style. In the implicit invocation style, we have the publish-and-subscribe style where different components "register" within an event dispatcher as being providers of messages of a certain type (*publish*). Conversely, some components register as being interested in messages of a particular kind (*subscribe*). Components publish their messages through the event manager, which in turn notifies the components that subscribed to that kind of message. Figure 14.5 illustrates this architectural style.

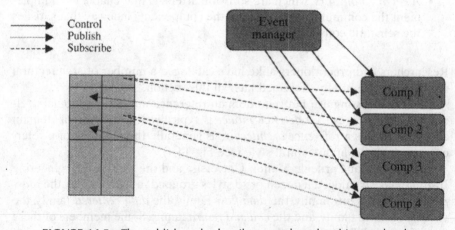

FIGURE 14.5   The publish-and-subscribe event-based architectural style.

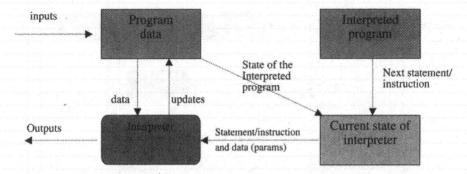

FIGURE 14.6 The virtual machine architectural style.

In the direct invocation style, components talk to each other *nominatively* but do not control each other.[3] A major advantage of the event-based styles is *modifiability, integrability,* and *scalability.*

An example of the communicating processes style family is the client–server style.

14.1.3.2 Virtual Machines

In this family of architectural styles, user programs, instead of running directly on the host hardware machine, are treated as data by a *virtual machine,* which is an abstract machine implemented entirely in software, that runs on top of the actual hardware machine. This architecture has considerable performance penalties but has the advantage of unparalleled portability, and rich control over the execution of user programs. Figure 14.6 illustrates this architectural style.

One known example of this family is the rule-based architectural style, where the interpreted program consists of a rule base, the program data of "facts," and the interpreter, is the inference engine. From the programming language side, both Smalltalk and Java are based on this architecture, which is the key factor behind Java's portability.

14.1.3.3 Data Flow Architectures

Members of this family include batch sequential systems and pipes and filters. In batch sequential systems, different components take turns at processing a batch of data, each saving the result of their processing in a shared repository that the next component can access. Notwithstanding the functional dependencies between the components (e.g., one component needs the results computed by another one), the components are typically asynchronous, and the process can be temporarily interrupted and restarted. With pipes and filters,

---

[3] Typically, components would have their own message-handling logic, and thus each object decides when and how it should handle a specific incoming message.

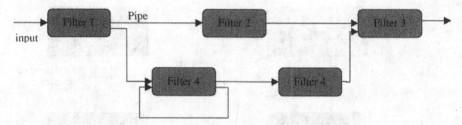

FIGURE 14.7 The pipes-and-filters architectural style.

we have a continuous stream of data piped through a more or less complex structure of processes (filters). Figure 14.7 illustrates this style.

UNIX pipes are one instance of this style, and illustrate its weaknesses: (1) inappropriate for interactive applications, (2) no possibility of error recovery, (3) consume lots of dynamic memory for stateful filters (e.g., a sort filter needs to see all the inputs before starting to output), and (4) imposes a lowest common denominator representation of exchanged data. For example, UNIX pipes can handles streams of lines of text, but nothing more structured than that.

14.1.3.4 Data-Centered Systems

This family of architectural styles consists of having different components communicate through shared data repositories. Communication in this case consists of changing the data accessed by other components. When the data repository is a passive repository (it does not notify interested parties of changes in the data), we have database systems. The components in this case are simply different database applications. When the data repository is an active repository that notifies registered components of changes in it, we have the *blackboard architecture*. In the blackboard model, borne out of AI research in procedural representations and inference models, agents, with limited but specialized intelligence, monitor the state of the blackboard for newly posted work items to which they can respond. Similarly, once an agent completes its work, it posts a message to that effect on the blackboard. Figure 14.8 illustrates this style.

14.1.3.5 Call-and-Return Architectures

These are the architectures that have dominated the software landscape through much of the early decades of software engineering, in part thanks to their simple control paradigm and component interaction mechanism. Bass et al. have identified four styles within this family, *main program and subroutines*, *remote procedure calls*, *object-oriented*, and *layered* [Bass et al. 1998]. We consider the four styles nonorthogonal, with the first two reflecting differences in the control paradigm and run-time behavior, and the last two reflecting two (nonexclusive) packaging techniques. That being said, the four styles are

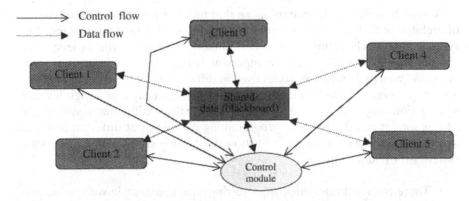

FIGURE 14.8 The blackboard architectural style.

- *Main Program and Subroutine Style.* In this style, programs are modularized based on functional decomposition, and there is typically a single thread of control held by the main program, which is then passed to subprograms, along with some data on which the subprograms can operate,
- *Remote Procedure Call.* This style is an outgrowth of the previous one where some of the subprograms may reside in different processors or machines. The control is still hierarchical, and the communication between callers and callees is typically synchronous,
- *Object-Oriented.* This style emphasizes encapsulation and information hiding, and is predominant with the more traditional strongly typed programming languages. Notwithstanding the typical anthropomorphic object-speak of "objects talking to each other" or "objects sending message to each other," object-oriented systems that are implemented in the more mainstream OO languages (C++, Java) are call-and-return systems at heart. If interobject communication is truly message-based, then we fall into the other styles with more complex mechanisms,
- *Layered.* In this style, functionality is divided into layers of abstraction in such a way that each layer provides services to the layer(s) above it, and uses the services of the layer(s) below it. In its purest form, each layer accesses only the layer below it, but doesn't depend on lower layers. In practice, we have to jump layers for performance reasons (or poor API design).

There are a number of other less common styles, and variations on the existing ones. The catalog of architectural styles is bound to grow like the catalog of design patterns, probably with similarly diminishing returns, as the first styles represent the most commonly useful and recognizable styles.

Researchers and practitioners agree that most software systems use a mix of architectural styles. For example, we could have a personnel management system with a scheduling component, implemented using the independent components style, and a payroll component, using the batch sequential style. We could also have different styles used at different levels of aggregation. For example, a system based on the publish-and-subscribe style at a high level of aggregation may use the object-oriented style within individual components. This is similar to the mixing of programming paradigms at different levels of aggregation that we discussed in Section 9.3. Mixing styles within a software system isn't bad as long as

- There is a solid rationale for preferring a particular style within one part of the system or within one level of aggregation.
- The mix is systematic (has second-order uniformity, e.g., subsystems use the event-based style, and each subsystem is implemented using the object-oriented style, or, *all* signal processing components are pipe-and-filter, and *all* data analysis modules are batch-sequential).
- Differences in style, either across aggregation levels, or across subsystem boundaries have no effect on the overall system.

This last condition is somewhat hard to enforce, as shown by Garlan et al. [1995], since seemingly compatible and interoperable subsystems turned out to be difficult to integrate because of differences in internal control paradigms.

Choosing a style to implement a particular system depends on several factors, not the least of which are fairly down-to-earth ones like the prior experience of the development team, delivery schedules, and resource limitations [Bass et al. 1998]. The *technical* factors concern the level of quality attributes that each style enables us to attain. For example, the event-based systems enable us to achieve a very high level of evolvability, at the expense of performance and complexity.[4] Using the virtual-machine style achieves a very high level of portability, also at the expense of performance and perhaps even testability. Thus, we should prioritize the architectural qualities we would like to achieve, and choose styles accordingly.

Once we have chosen an architectural style for a particular software system, we have to instantiate the style for the software system at hand. This means, among other things:

- Mapping the functional components of the software to the component types of the style
- Implementing the component interaction infrastructure that underlies the style

---

[4] If the logic of the application is complex with lots of conditionals and iteration, dividing it up between components communicating through asynchronous events can be a hair-raising exercise.

A number of software artifacts can be used to implement the component interaction infrastructure of an architecture or a particular style. Those artifacts are often referred to as connectors. *Connectors* could be *design patterns*, such as the observer/observable pattern, which may be used to coordinate objects that have no knowledge of each other's API. They could be programming language constructs such as synchronization or rendezvous constructs, constructs for remote procedure calls, or the language's reflection API, each enabling us to mediate communication between objects. They could also be runnable or running pieces of code, such as CORBA's object request brokers (ORBs), and Java RMI's registries.

In some ways, architectural styles are *specifications of architectures*, whereas connectors are artifacts used to design or implement such specifications. We will define connectors more precisely when we talk about architectural frameworks (Section 14.2.3).

14.2 ARCHITECTURE AND REUSE

Software architecture plays a key role in software reuse, both as an *object* of reuse and as a support infrastructure for reuse. In order to discuss architecture as an object of reuse, we have to look at it from the perspective of a reusable software artefact that has its own development lifecycle. Also, like most reusable artefacts, it has its own fixed part, and its variable parts. Typically, the fixed part is the part that deals with the interaction mechanisms embodied in the architectural style; it may be provided as a language or runtime environment mechanism, or some more abstract service provided by a middleware or an *architectural framework*. The variable part is typically implemented by application-specific components that embody application-specific or domainwide functions. We start this section by examining the lifecycle of a software architecture, viewed as a software artefact. Next, we discuss reusability aspects of architectures. Finally, we discuss issues related to the development and use of architectural frameworks.

14.2.1 The Development Lifecycle of a Software Architecture

In the previous section we discussed *architectural styles* as descriptions of classes of architectures, characterized by component *types*, communication *patterns* between components, semantic constraints and relationships between them. Choosing a style simply means choosing a packaging and a runtime structure that the software will have in the end, but does not get us any closer to achieving that. Next, we have to *design* and *implement* the architecture. In building architecture terms, specifying the architecture consists of doing a quick floorplan whereas designing it consists of choosing the kinds and materials of beams to use, and finally, implementing it consists of manufacturing and assembling the beams.

Depending on the architectural style, *designing* and *implementing* the architecture can be more or less complex. If we are choosing a main-program-and-subroutine-call style, then there isn't much to do to realize the architecture, beyond developing the components themselves; both the packaging of the components (subroutines, functions) and the communication infrastructure (subroutine call) are provided by the host programming language and the runtime system. If we are implementing a publish-and-subscribe architecture, then we have more things to do:

- Designing the API of the components. For example, we could have a single event-handling function that dispatches internally to various functions, or have several event handling functions, one per event type.
- Designing the system's event manager and dispatcher that manages the "subscriptions" of the components, and handles the events they generate.

We could go beyond design and actually *implement* the architecture, for example, by

- Writing abstract classes that implement the event-handling API of the components, and making sure that system components inherit from those classes
- Coding the actual event manager

We refer to the implementation of the architecture as the *computational infrastructure* of the system. What is interesting here is that depending on how we design the architecture, we may even be able to implement the computational infrastructure before any component is actually implemented. In the event-based example, we could implement the computational infrastructure as follows:

```
abstract class Component {
  public void postEvent(Event e) {
    EventHandler.handleEventFrom(e, this); }

  public void publishEventClass(Class eventClass) {
    EventHandler.addPublisher(this, eventClass); }

  public void subscribe(Class eventClass) {
    EventHandler.addSubscription(this, eventClass); }

  abstract public void handleEvent(Event e);
}

public class EventHandler {
  static Hashtable publishers;
  static Hashtable subscriptions;
  ...
```

```
public static void addSubscription(Component comp,Class
evtCls){
   Vector subs = subscriptions.get(evtCls);
   if (subs == null) {subs = new Vector();
     subscriptions.add(evtClas,subs);};
   subs.addElement(comp);
}
...
}

public class Event {
   private Object source;
   private Object data;
   ...
}
```

In this case, a single method (`Component.handleEvent(Event e)`) will take care of dispatching messages to component specific methods, depending on event type and data. We could also imagine hard-coding within the `EventHandler` the component methods that need to be called for each event type, in which case we should wait until all the components have been designed before we implement the architecture.

Figures 14.9 and 14.10 illustrate two possible lifecycle paths for implementing a given architecture, resulting in more or less reuse. In Figure 14.9, we implemented an application-independent (and thus reusable) computational infrastructure.

In Figure 14.10, we had, or chose to bind the analysis model to the architectural style before we did any architecture design or implementation. In this case, the resulting computational infrastructure is specific to the application at hand, or possibly to applications within the same business domain.

14.2.2 Dimensions of Reusability

In light of the previous discussion, let us study architecture as an *object* of reuse. Clearly, we can reuse the *choice of an architectural style*. If for some

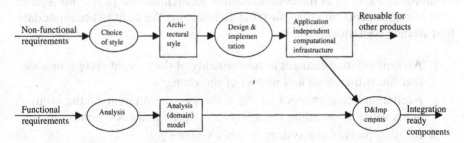

FIGURE 14.9 Implementing a domain independent computational infrastructure.

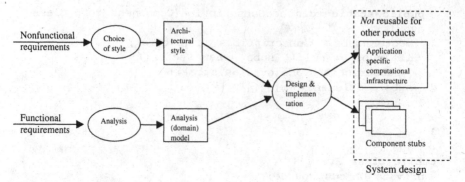

FIGURE 14.10 Binding the computational infrastructure to the analysis model early on.

application A, with its set of technical and nontechnical constraints, we analysed and compared a bunch of architectural styles, and came up with style *S*, then, given another application B with a similar set of technical and nontechnical constraints, we could probably retain style *S* as well, regardless of the functional requirements.

The next level of reuse concerns the *architecture* itself. Here, there are two situations that correspond to the scenarios of Figures 14.9 and 14.10. In Figure 14.9, we would be reusing a computational infrastructure that implements a particular architectural style in a way that is *independent* of the application domain. In Figure 14.9, we are *at least* reusing the computational infrastructure, and if the application B is within the same domain as the application A, then we are also reusing some of the components. In Figure 14.10, B can reuse the design and implementation of the architecture and of the components of A only if B and A are part of the same application domain. When people talk about reuse at the architectural level, they often mean reuse in the scenario of Figure 14.10. Doing reuse at this level is highly effective simply because we are shaving off most of the development lifecycle, for most of the target system.

Consider now architecture as an enabling software artefact for reuse. Here, we consider a system as the combination of an architecture (a *receptacle*) and a set of components that plug into that architecture. We want to accommodate four change scenarios:

1. Accommodating changes in functionality of the current system in a way that limits the scope and impact of the changes
2. Accommodating changes to the software environment of the components while maintaining the system's integrity and good behavior
3. Reusing parts of the system in other systems
4. Reusing third-party parts in the current system

The first two scenarios have as much to do with the component boundaries as they do with the packaging of the components and their interaction mechanisms. This is a general modularization problem. As a general principle, to minimize the effect of change, we need to do two things: (1) finding the smallest component boundary that encapsulates a variable aspect of the system and (2) strive for the lowest coupling between those components and their surroundings. Feature-oriented domain analysis (FODA; see Kang et al. [1990]) suggests that the *features* of a software system be mapped to components so that alternative implementations of the feature can be accommodated by component replacement. Further, both FODA and Jacobson et al.'s RSEB [Jacobson et al. 1997] recommend a layered architecture to group together pieces of the software that have similar change characteristics. Figure 14.11 shows a typical architectural layering. Layered architectures are typically used to accommodate change of internal implementation, but not a change of outside behavior (API). There will be situations, however, where the behavior of a component may need to change. In the event-based style, if we want a component to respond to a different set of events, event dispatch should *not* be hardcoded in the event manager, but should be stored in runtime data structures. Change scenarios 3 and 4 listed above require that the architecture used be a standard or a commonly used one, or failing that, be compatible with standard or commonly used architectures. Scenario 3 means that the system architecture should not be esoteric, intrinsic qualities notwithstanding (low-coupling, late binding, etc.), so that components built into this architecture stand a chance of being reused in other projects within or outside the organization. Scenario

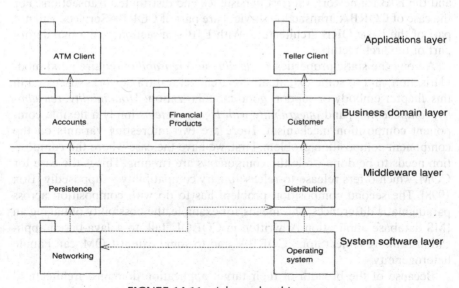

FIGURE 14.11 A layered architecture.

4 is just the converse of the third, we want to the architecture to be able to host third-party components that are written into standard packaging technologies (COM, EJBs, etc.).

14.2.3   Issues in Architectural Frameworks

Architectural frameworks are application frameworks that implement architectural styles in an application or even domain-independent way. Figure 14.9 shows an application development lifecycle where one of the products is an application-independent computational infrastructure that is used as an input for component design. In this section, we briefly discuss the problems that these architectural frameworks try to solve, and the challenges involved in building them.

In Section 14.1, we talked about quality attributes of architectures and how architectural styles, viewed as classes of architectures, are geared toward optimizing some of these attributes. Because architectural frameworks implement the computational infrastructure of architectural styles, we will characterize the services offered by these frameworks in terms of the properties they help optimize. Bass et al. have broken down those properties into run-time observable properties, and static properties of the software product as an artifact. The runtime properties include *performance*, *security*, and *scalability*, and the static properties include things such as *modifiability*, *reusability*, *portability*, *composability*, and *integrability with legacy systems*. Performance and scalability usually imply both *persistence* and *distribution*. Persistence and distribution require support for *distributed transactions*. Most of the architectural frameworks discussed in this chapter support *distribution*. Both CORBA and the EJB framework support persistence and distributed transactions. For the case of CORBA, transaction services are part of CORBAServices, and not part of the basic ORB architecture. With EJB, transactions are a mandatory part of the architecture.

Among the static properties, *portability* and *reusability* require good modularisation, and to some extent, all the architectural frameworks discussed in this chapter embody or support good modularization. *Modifiability*, *reusability*, *composability*, and *integrability with legacy systems* imply a flexible component composition mechanism. There are two interesting variants on the component composition problem. First, we have the case where the composition needs to be done while the components are running. This is the case for COM, which offers release-to-release binary compatibility—supposedly [Box 1998]. The second composition problem has to do with composition across paradigmatic differences. This means, for example, the possibility of having an IMS database application A, written in COBOL, talk to a Java-based application running ObjectStore. CORBA, and to some extent COM, can handle heterogeneity.

Because of the breadth of their target application domains, architectural frameworks have stringent requirements in terms of abstraction and openness;

they must accommodate *all* the applications that wish to implement a particular architectural style or service. First, most of the computational infrastructure should be independent of the target application domain. Second, we should strive for the ability to connect components to the computational infrastructure as late in the process as possible. Finally, we should hide the complexity of the underlying infrastructure away, so that developers only deal with the underlying conceptual model, and not with the implementation details. We will see, through the approaches discussed in the remainder of this chapter, how some of these challenges have been met.

14.3 CORBA

14.3.1 The Problem

Baker [1997] listed a number of problems that faced the industry in the late 1980s:

- Enterprise applications must run on a network of machines, where the functionality is distributed between the machines
- The machines may run different operating systems
- The applications may integrate legacy systems (either legacy data or legacy software components)
- The components may be written in different programming languages or even different programming paradigms

These are the problems that the Common Object Request Broker Architecture (CORBA) was meant to address.

CORBA is an industry standard developed by the Object Management Group, an industry consortium created in 1989 by eleven companies including computer companies (HP, Sun, Data General), telecommunication companies (Philipps Telecommunications N. V., 3COM), and big software users (American Airlines, Canon Inc.), with the mandate "to create a component-based software marketplace by hastening the introduction of standardized object software. The organization's charter includes the establishment of industry guidelines and detailed object management specifications to provide a common framework for application development."[5] The first version of the CORBA standard was produced in October 1991.

We will try to rationalize the CORBA standard by progressively complexifying a simple object-oriented application.

Say we have a decision support system for evaluating loan applications (see Fig. 14.12) from bank customers (instances of **LoanApplication**), and assume that the object that does the assessing is an instance of some

---

[5] From the OMG's mission statement; check http://www.omg.org.

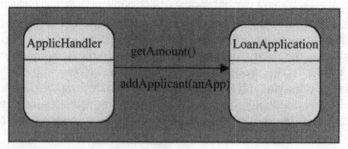

FIGURE 14.12 A simple loan application assessment software.

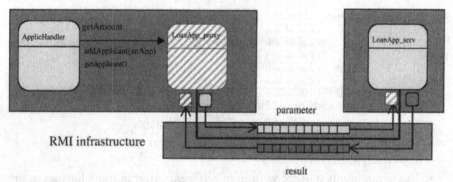

FIGURE 14.13 Achieving location transparency through remote method invocation.

class **ApplicationHandler** that embodies the logic of the business. We see here that both the instance of **LoanApplication** and the instance of **ApplicationHandler** that processes it, reside in the same memory space, on the same machine.

The first challenge that we might have consists of distributing our application among several machines. For example, we could imagine entering the loan application itself on one machine, and performing the business logic (**ApplicationHandler**) on another. There are a number of strategies to distribute data and processing between machines but the approach that provides the best location transparency and that relieves developers from having to worry about remote object access is the approach based on the use of proxies, as illustrated in Figure 14.13. In this case, the application handler "talks" to a local representative (proxy) of the actual loan application object, as if it were local. However, the proxy stores no local state, and method calls are sent through a *remote method invocation infrastructure* to the actual loan application, that is alive and running on a different machine (process), in a different memory address.

The first problem that we are going to face is, of course, the passing of parameters back and forth between the two machines. First, because we are going through a network infrastructure, whatever it is that we are sending must be sent as a bytestream. Therefore, both the name of the method to be called and its parameters must be sent as bytestreams. If the data are simple scalar data (strings, floats, integers), we can send their string representation and recover their value at the other end. If we are passing identityless (see below) structures of such data, then we should probably "stream" them as well. This illustrates a basic mechanism supported by all distribution frameworks: *serialization*. All the classes of a distributed application that may be referenced in more than one site have to be serializable and serialized while traveling through the RMI infrastructure.

If the data consists of objects with identities, then we have to make sure that we pass networkwide identities around, so that wherever they are referenced, we are either talking to the real objects, or to their proxies; we can't have several copies of the same object in different places. This illustrates the need for a sophisticated object *referencing* and object *serialization* and *deserialization* mechanism.

Assuming that this is taken care of, now the question is, how do we start the connection, in the first place. Roughly speaking, we need three things:

1. We have to make sure that the server object is running, or have a way of starting it.
2. We have to be able to locate the running server object.
3. We have to create a proxy for the running server (**LoanApplication**) object.

To locate the server, location transparency dictates that servers not be located based on host address and port number, as is often the case with RPC-based applications, but be located based on logical addresses, which may in turn be related to machine independent identifiers.

The CORBA standard specifies a *naming service* to name objects within a distributed application, and to retrieve them according to that name. A handle on the naming service (myNamingContext) may be used to retrieve an object of a particular type based on its name as in

```
org.omg.CORBA.Object myObject =
    myNamingContext.resolve("MyLoanApp");
LoanApplication myApp =
    LoanApplicationHelper.narrow(myObject);
```

Similarly, we can register objects with the naming service as follows:

```
LoanApplication myApp = new LoanapplicationImp
    (..., ..., ...);
MyNamingContext.bind(itsName,myApp);
```

where itsName is a variable of the appropriate name type. CORBA names may be seen as similar to the tree structures used in IP addresses.

The next thing to be concerned about is to make sure that when a client wants to talk to a named object, that that object is actually alive in some running process. Each named object is associated with a *named server*, which, in turn, is associated with a command to start the process. Thus, when a client asks for an object by name, we look up the name, find the server associated with it, then find the command needed to start the server, execute it, and something from within the server will signal that it is "ready to talk." This illustrates two services: server registration, which is part of the core functionalities; and the *lifecycle service*, which contains advanced functionalities for managing the lifecycle of objects on the server side.

We can now imagine a bunch of services that we would like to support within the context of a distributed application, such as a *security service*, to make sure that only authorized and properly authenticated users are able to access some objects and perform operations on them. If we want to modify several remote objects in a single transaction, the *transaction service* helps coordinate the updates to the various objects. The *relationship service* helps maintain relations between distributed objects, the *persistence service* specifies a generic API for storing and loading objects from persistent storage, and so on.

14.3.2   The Core Architecture

Figure 14.14 shows the trademark overview of CORBA. In this case, we have a client application that needs to talk to remote and/or distributed objects. The distributed object is represented by a proxy on the client side (IDL stubs), which represents an abstract interface between the client program and the inner workings of the distribution infrastructure. Among other things, the so-called IDL stub (proxy) is responsible for translating requests for executing a specific method with a specific set of arguments, into a generically encoded request (bytestream) that can be sent through the wire and unpacked (unmar-

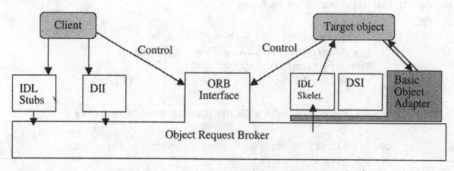

FIGURE 14.14   An overview of the CORBA standard.

shaled) at the server's end. Once the request is reconstructed (by the ORB), we then have to interpret it and dispatch (execute) it. The IDL skeleton does the interpretation and dispatch of requests. If results are to be returned, they are packed back into the request, which is sent back through the wire so that the IDL stub can read the result.

To write the IDL stub (client side proxy) and the IDL skeleton (server-side interpreter and dispatcher of client requests), we need to know only the method signatures: the method name and the types of input. Accordingly, we should be able to generate both the client-side proxy and the server-side interpreter/dispatcher, just from the description of the signatures.

This, plus the fact that we want to be able to have clients and servers written in different languages, led OMG to propose an abstract, implementation language-independent *interface definition language* (IDL) that is sufficiently rich that it can be mapped to a variety of programming languages. Descriptions of distributed objects are then given in this language. The following shows example IDL interfaces for three domain classes:

```
(1)     module Loans {

(2)       typedef float time;

(3)       interface Applicant {
(4)         attribute string name;
(5)         attribute float assets;
(6)         attribute float liabilities;
          };

(7)       interface LoanApplication {
            attribute float amount;
(8)         attribute Applicant mainApplicant;
(9)         attribute sequence(Applicant) coapplicants;

          /** this function adds a co-applicant */
(10)        void addCoapplicant(inout Applicant anApplicant);
          };

          interface LoanApplicationHandler {

          /** this function assesses an application */
(11)        boolean processApplication(in LoanApplication la);

          /** this function withdraws an application */
            void withdrawApplication(in LoanApplication la);
          };
        };
```

Each construct shown here is mapped to a separate programming language construct, depending on the language. A module [line (1)] is mapped to a package in Java, a name space in C++, a category in Smalltalk. An *interface* [lines (3) and (7)] is mapped to a class (sort of) in Java, C++, and Smalltalk, but a **struct** in C. Attributes are also treated differently, depending on the target language. In object-oriented languages, they are mapped to reader/writer functions whereas for non-OO languages (e.g., C) they are mapped to fields of structures or records.

The reader may note that function signatures are given in a similar format to C/C++ or Java, that is, with the return type, followed by the function name, followed by a list of parameters. One difference lies in the passing mode qualifiers (**in**, **out**, **inout**), which have the same meaning as in Ada. This illustrates one of the many subtleties of IDL and its mappings to programming languages.

Designing the IDL involved a delicate balance between putting in it all the useful constructs that are found in target programming languages, and yet, keeping the language abstract and small. The creators of the IDL felt that it should be considered as a *design-level specification of application entities*, and as such, should not be constrained by language limitations, or be caught up in their esoteric constructs [Mowbray and Zahavi 1995]. Passing mode is one of those features that are important to have, even if not all languages support it. Two languages that support it are Ada and C++ (when parameters are given with the & qualifier). Languages that don't support **inout** parameter passing include Smalltalk and Java, in which parameters are passed by value (i.e., copied). When the parameters being passed are pointers to objects—as is the case for all object types in both Smalltalk and Java—this is not a serious limitation because we can still change the attributes of the object even through a copy of the pointer to it. If we want to change the *identity of the object*, then we have a problem. Similarly, if we are passing a scalar parameter, and we want the changes within the function to be reflected outside the function, we also have a problem. For both of these languages, the IDL compiler generates *holder classes* for the types of the parameters that are passed **out** or **inout**, which are passed by value, but which have an attribute of the original type whose value can be changed inside the function. The following shows the holder class for **Applicant**, and the generated Java method that corresponds to the function addCoapplicant(inout Applicant anApplicant) [line (10) above]. **ApplicantHolder** has a public data member value of type **Applicant**. The class (Java interface) **LoanApplication** has a method addCoapplicant(ApplicantHolder anApplicant). The reader can also see how sequences have been mapped in Java (arrays); in C++, a separate class is generated that will allocate memory dynamically.

```
public final class ApplicantHolder implements
                          org.omg.CORBA.portable.Streamable {
    public Loans.Applicant value;
    public ApplicantHolder() {}
```

```
public ApplicantHolder(Loans.Applicant value) {
  this.value = value;
}
...
}

public interface LoanApplication extends org.omg.CORBA.Object {

  public float amount();
  public void amount(float value);
  ...
  public Loans.Applicant[] coapplicants();
  public void coapplicants(Loans.Applicant[] value);

  public void addCoapplicant(Loans.ApplicantHolder anApplicant) ;
  ...
}
```

Before we move on, we should point out one of the differences between the
C++ mapping and the Java mapping. Both the client-side proxies (stubs) and
the server-side objects (skeleton) must support the methods that are specified
in the IDL interface, in addition to supporting a lot of CORBA-specific code.
In C++, the IDL compiler generates an abstract class that has the same name
as the IDL interface (**LoanApplication, Applicant,** etc.), that is inherited by both the client stub and the server-side skeleton. The client stub
and the server side skeleton will also inherit from CORBA specific classes that
implement appropriate generic behaviour for client-side and server-
side objects. This is possible because C++ supports multiple inheritance.
In Java, the common interface for client-side proxies and server side objects
is represented by, well, a Java interface, such as the one shown above (see Fig.
14.15).

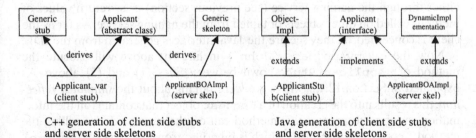

C++ generation of client side stubs   Java generation of client side stubs
and server side skeletons   and server side skeletons

FIGURE 14.15 Alternative generation of client-side and server-side classes from IDL
interfaces.

14.3.3 Handling Method Calls

Now, we turn our attention to the way method calls are handled on both the client side and the server side. OrbixWeb™, a Java-based CORBA product from Iona Software, generated the code excerpts shown below. We will look at the simpler class **Applicant**. The client stub is shown below. We shortened qualified names by removing the org.omg.CORBA package prefix.

```
public class _ApplicantStub extends portable.ObjectImpl
                                implements Loans.Applicant {
     ...
(1)    public String name() {
(2)      Request _req = _request("_get_name");
(3)      _req.set_return_type(ORB.init().create_string_tc(0));
(4)      _req.invoke();
(5)      return _req.return_value().extract_string();
       }

(6)    public void name(String value) {
(7)      Request _req = _request("_set_name");
(8)      _req.add_in_arg().insert_string(value);
(9)      _req.invoke();
       }
     ...
}
```

Before we go over the stub, let us see how it can be used:

```
       /** somehow, I got a handle on a remote loan
          application */
(a)    Applicant myApp = myLoanApplication.mainApplicant();
(b)    myApp.name("John");
```

As we can see, instances of the **_ApplicantStub** will be declared as of type **Applicant** (a Java interface), and as such we can invoke all the functions defined in the **Applicant** interface. However, the actual objects are obtained either through the naming service (see previous section) or as return values of methods called on other objects obtained from the naming service. As far as the client is concerned, all they see are the Java interfaces generated from the IDL.

Now, the call myApp.name("John") in line (b) above will execute the method of **_ApplicantStub** shown between lines (1) and (5) above. As explained in Section 12.4.2, where we were talking about the *simulated reflection*, this results into the creation of a **Request** object that contains all the information required to process this method call on the server side by calling the method _request(String), which is inherited from the class **ObjectImpl** [line (2)]. The class **Request** handles all kinds of requests, and has methods to add return values and parameters. Line (3) shows the call to set/add a return type; line (8) shows a call to add an argument. Once a request is completed, it is invoked. The call to invoke is blocking, in the sense that control returns to the caller only after the call has completed or has thrown an exception on the server side. This is a customisable property; the IDL has a construct to say that a method is nonblocking. Note that the class **Request** is a completely abstract class, with method implementations left to individual vendors. However, we can guess what invoke() does, and that is, call the ORB to which the client is connected so that it forwards the request to the server for execution.

Let us now look at the skeleton (server side), which we simplified slightly:

```
public abstract class _ApplicantSkeleton
        extends org.omg.CORBA.DynamicImplementation {
    ...
    public void invoke(ServerRequest _req){
    _invoke(_req, this);}

    public static void _invoke(ServerRequest _req,
                                  _ApplicantSkeleton _obj){
(1)     String _opName = _req.op_name();
(2)     NVList _nvl = null;

(3)     if (_opName.equals("_get_name")) {
(4)       StringHolder _retHolder = new StringHolder();
(5)       _retHolder.value = _obj.name();
(6)       Any _ret = _obj._orb().create_any();
(7)       _ret.insert_Streamable(_retHolder);
(8)       _req.result(_ret);
(9)       return;}
(10)    if (_opName.equals("_set_name")){
(11)      Any value = _obj._orb().create_any();
(12)      StringHolder value_ = new StringHolder();
(13)      value.insert_Streamable(value_);
(14)      _nvl = _obj._orb().create_list(1);
(15)      _nvl.add_value(null, value, ARG_IN.value);
(16)      _req.params(_nvl);
(17)      _obj.name(value.extract_string());
(18)      return;}
(19)    if (_opName.equals("_get_assets")) {...}
        ...
    }

(20) public abstract String name();
(21) public abstract void name(String value);
(22) public abstract float assets();
(23) public abstract void assets(float value);
(24) public abstract float liabilities();
(25) public abstract void liabilities(float value);
}
```

When a request arrives to the ORB on the server side, it deserializes it, identifies the target object, and creates an instance of `ServerRequest` that will be invoked by the target object using the instance method `invoke(Server-Request)`, which, in turn, calls a static method `_invoke(ServerRequest, _ApplicantSkeleton)`.[6] This method basically extracts the name of the method to be called, and on the basis of the method name, "unpacks" the right parameters (right number, right types), calls the method, stores the results (if any) in the `ServerRequest`, and returns. Lines (3)–(9). show one such sequence for the method `name()` (slightly modified for simplicity). Because the method `name()` returns a string, we create a variable that can hold a string [line (4)]. Then, we set its value field to the result of calling the method `name()`. Lines (6)–(8) make that value the result property of the server request.[7]

Lines (10)–(19) show the same thing for a method that has a parameter. We start by creating a list of parameters that corresponds to the signature of the method as specified in the IDL. This list will help us extract the values of these parameters, we have to keep in mind that the `ServerRequest` is created from a polymorphic, variable-length bytestream sent by the client ORB to the server ORB, and thus, we can unpack it properly only once we know to which method call it corresponds. That is exactly what lines (11)–(16) are doing. Lines (11)–(13) create a variable that will hold the `in` parameter for the method name. Lines (14)–(16) create a template for the parameter list, and submit it to the server request so that it unpacks its bytestream onto that list. Thus, a side effect of the call in line (16) will be that the variable `value` (of type `Any`) will hold the `in` parameter.

The attentive reader could see simpler ways of handling some of this request processing—in the language of their choice. While this code can be perfected, there are two things to keep in mind: (1) this code is generated, and (2) CORBA is supposed to work with much weaker languages. Thus, any CORBA compliant implementation must abide by the CORBA API, even when there are shorter ways of doing things.

The final point about the skeleton here is that we still don't have an implementation of the methods `name()`, `name(String aName)`, and so forth, which are shown as abstract methods here.

14.3.4   Implementing Application Objects

CORBA offers two ways of implementing application objects; one is inheritance-based, and the other is aggregation based. We will discuss them both briefly.

---

[6] This indirection has to do with performance reasons, and also for error handling.

[7] The CORBA type Any is used to store objects of any type (including user-defined types) by basically storing two attributes: (1) the actual value of the object, typically as a bytestream; and (2) a "type" property. Some of this may appear to be an overkill for Java, which has some reflective capabilities, but keep in mind that CORBA is language independent, and so, it must compose with languages with no runtime type information.

In the inheritance-based approach, the actual application objects *inherit* from the generated skeleton. In practice, we have to create an intermediary class (a subclass of the skeleton) from which the actual application object class can inherit, because there is additional generic behavior that is specific to inheritance-based implementations, and that can be generated automatically (various constructors and the _deref() operator). The following excerpt shows the superclass of application objects for the case of inheritance:

```
public abstract class _ApplicantImplBase extends
_ApplicantSkeleton
                                        implements Applicant {
  public _ApplicantImplBase() {
    ORB.init().connect(this);
  }

  public _ApplicantImplBase(String marker) {
    _OrbixWeb.ORB(ORB.init()).connect(this,marker);
  }
  ...
  public Object _deref() {
    return this;
  }
}
```

A subclass of **_ApplicantImplBase** must implement the methods String name(), void name(String aName), and so forth, which were defined in the **Applicant** interface, and also define as abstract methods in **_ApplicantSkeleton**. For example, I can define my class **HMApplicant** as follows:

```
public class HMApplicant extends _ApplicantImplBase {
  private String name;
  private float assets;
  private float liabilities;

  public void name(String aName) {name = aName;}
  public String name() {return name;}

  public void assets(float value) {assets = value;}
  ...
}
```

This approach is simple and works fine in simple cases. However, what if our class **HMApplicant** were to inherit from other classes that are more meaningful from a domain point of view such as **HMPerson**? Because this is Java, single inheritance would force us to forgo the domain superclass, and reimplement its attributes and functions here. In C++, multiple inheritance is not a problem, but we still have a more general problem—we have to modify existing code to make it distributable, even if it is just adding a superclass—it rarely is just that.

Here comes the so-called TIE approach. In this case, the object that interfaces with the ORB *delegates* to the application object, instead of *being* the application object. We show below excerpts of the definition of the "TIE class," adapted from the code generated by OrbixWeb[(TM)8]:

```
public class _tie_Applicant extends _ApplicantSkeleton
                     implements Applicant {
  protected Applicant m_impl;

  public _tie_Applicant(Applicant impl) {
    this.m_impl = impl;
    ORB.init().connect(this);}

  public _tie_Applicant(Applicant impl,String marker) {
    this.m_impl = impl;
    _OrbixWeb.ORB(ORB.init()).connect(this,marker);}

  public String name() {return m_impl.name();};

  public void name(String value){m_impl.name(value);};

  public float assets() {return m_impl.assets();};
  ...
  public Object _deref() {return m_impl;}
}
```

In this case, the class **_tie_Applicant** has a protected attribute of type **Applicant**,[9] to which it delegates all the calls. Now, I can define my application class as follows:

```
public class HMApplicant implements Applicant extends Person {
  private float assets;
  private float liabilities;

  public void assets(float value) {assets = value;}
  ...
}
```

---

[8] OrbixWeb is a trademark of Iona Software, Inc.
[9] The interfaces generated by the IDL to Java compiler contain an additional CORBA-specific method, _deref(). So, in reality, the variable _m_impl is not of type **Applicant**, but rather of another interface, **_ApplicantOperations,** that has all the signatures of the interface **Applicant**, with the exception of the _deref(). The rationale is that, if we are delegating to an object from another class hierarchy, we should not require it to provide CORBA-specific methods.

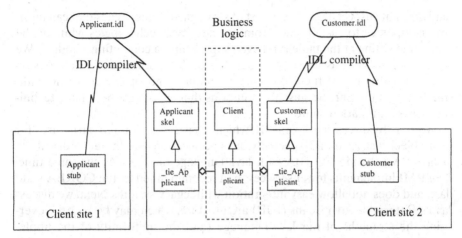

FIGURE 14.16   Offering two views on the same implementation objects using the TIE approach.

where I assumed that I inherited name and its methods from **Person**. If my class **HMApplicant** happened to have the wrong API, but the same func-tionality, I can use any of the alternative implementations of the adapter pattern (see, e.g., Section 12.4).

Some developers might not like the TIE approach because of its reliance on delegation, and the documented *broken delegation problem* (see Section 12.3.3). However, that would not be a problem here because the code that is in the skeleton hierarchy is CORBA-specific whereas the code that is in the application object class hierarchy is application-specific, and there is no danger of finding the same method in both and having to contend with the resulting ambiguity from interpreting the **this** (self-reference).

One great advantage of the TIE approach, in addition to decoupling appli-cation code from distribution code, is the possibility for the same application objects to offer two different interfaces to two different clients. With Java, of course, we would have to go the TIE approach, at least for one of the clients. However, even if multiple inheritance were not a problem, the TIE approach provides a much cleaner and safer solution than the inheritance-based solu-tion (see Fig. 14.16).

14.4   JAVA-BASED TECHNOLOGIES

In this section, we discuss Java-based distribution technologies. The first question that comes to mind is "Why have Java-specific technologies when CORBA is language independent, and is a widely accepted and supported standard?"—especially when the CORBA standard is supported by compa-nies that offer competing technologies (Microsoft, Sun Microsystems). As the reader might suspect, there are a host of strategic business issues that can motivate companies to sustain and promote their own technologies while at the same time sitting at the table (and even supporting) a competing standard. We won't get into those issues, in part because of our ignorance of what goes on in the boardrooms of these companies—industry gossip headlines notwithstanding—and in part because the solutions that we discuss here have technical merits and market share.

We start by discussing Java RMI, which is Java's take on infrastructures for Java object distribution. Expectedly, Java applications are easier to distribute in Java RMI than in CORBA with Java language bindings. At the same time, Java RMI implements fewer services than recommended by the CORBA standard and does not allow easy integration with legacy systems. Next, we discuss Java's Enterprise Java Beans (EJB) architecture, which may be seen as leveraging the strengths of the Java language (and the uniformity of the implementation language across clients and servers) to provide more services, this time, than the CORBA standard.

14.4.1   Java RMI

Java RMI is very similar in principle to CORBA except that it is (much) simpler. With Java RMI, we have to specify the interfaces of the distributed objects, and the server implementations of those interfaces, and let the Java RMI compiler (`rmic`) generate the corresponding stub and skeleton implementations. The major difference with CORBA is that the interfaces are actual Java interfaces. The following shows example interfaces for

LoanApplications and **Applicant**s.

```
public interface LoanApplication extends java.rmi.Remote {
  public Applicant getApplicant() throws RemoteException;
  public void setApplicant(Applicant mainApplicant)
                                    throws RemoteException;
  public float getAmount() throws RemoteException;
  public void setAmount(float amount) throws RemoteException;
  ...
  public Enumeration getCoapplicants() throws RemoteException;
  public void addCoapplicant(Applicant anApplicant)
                                    throws RemoteException;
  ...
}

public interface Applicant extends java.rmi.Remote {
  public String getName() throws RemoteException;
  public void setName(String aName) throws RemoteException;

  public float getIncome() throws RemoteException;
  public void setIncome(float income) throws RemoteException;
}
```

The Java interfaces have to extend the interface **java.rmi.Remote**, and all of their methods must throw the exception **RemoteException**. The interface **java.rmi.Remote** does not define any functionality but identifies a common supertype to all classes whose methods can be invoked remotely. The class **UnicastRemoteObject** provides one commonly useful implementation of this interface, with functions to export a remote object (i.e., generate a client stub that can receive requests on behalf of clients), to deserialize and clone itself.

A possible implementation of **Applicant** is shown below:

```java
public class ImpApplicant extends UnicastRemoteObject
                          implements Applicant {
  private String name;
  private float income;

  public ImpApplicant(String name, float income) throws
                                          RemoteException {
    this.name = name;
    this.income = income;
  }

  public String getName() throws RemoteException {
    //TODO: implement this loans.Applicant method;
    return name;
  }

  public void setName(String aName) throws RemoteException {
    //TODO: implement this loans.Applicant method;
    name = aName;
  }
  ...
}
```

Note that the implementation class implements the **Applicant** interface, and extends the **UnicastRemoteObject**. We show below excerpts from the stub implementation of **Applicant**, generated by the compiler **rmic**:

```java
package loans;
public final class ImpApplicant_Stub extends RemoteStub
    implements loans.Applicant, Remote {
  private static final java.rmi.server.Operation[] operations = {
  new Operation("float getIncome()"),new Operation("String
    getName()"),...
  };
  ...
  public ImpApplicant_Stub(RemoteRef ref) {super(ref);}
  ...
```

```
// implementation of getIncome()
public float getIncome() throws java.rmi.RemoteException {
  try {
    RemoteCall call = ref.newCall((RemoteObject)this,
                           operations, 0, interfaceHash);
    ref.invoke(call);
    float $result;
    try {
       ObjectInput in = call.getInputStream();
       $result = in.readFloat();}}
    catch (java.io.IOException e) {
      throw new UnmarshalException("error unmarshalling
      return", e);}
    finally {
       ref.done(call);}
    return $result;
    }
  catch (RuntimeException e) {
      throw e;}
  catch (RemoteException e) {
      throw e;}
  catch (Exception e) {
      throw new UnexpectedException("undeclared checked
      exception", e);}
}
```

This code closely resembles the stub code for CORBA. The equivalent to a CORBA **Request** is Java RMI's **Call**, which is constructed piece by piece, and then invoked.[10] The invocation of the call may cause a **RuntimeException** (a virtual machine exception), a **RemoteException** (communications exception), or a general undeclared user exception.

Much like the CORBA standard, Java RMI supports a naming service, which enables servers to register named objects, and clients to look up those objects, and bind to them, when they start. The following shows code excerpts for the server-side registration of objects, and the client-side lookup and binding:

```
package loans;
import java.rmi.*;

public class LoansServer {
    ...
    public static void main(String[] args){
    ImpApplicant anApplicant;
```

---

[10] There is another invocation model in Java RMI. We choose to show this one to emphasize the similarity between Java RMI and CORBA.

```
        ImpLoanApplication anApp;
        try {
(1)       anApplicant = new ImpApplicant("John
            Belushi",10000f);
(2)       anApp = new ImpLoanApplication(anApplicant,20000f);
(3)       java.rmi.Naming.rebind("The application",anApp);}
        catch (Exception g){
          System.out.println("Exception thrown:" + g);}
        }
}
```

Lines (1) and (2) show the creation of objects that will live in the server side. Line (3) registers the loan application under the name The application, so that it may be accessed from elsewhere. The following shows the simplest client that we can think of:

```
package loans;
import java.rmi.*;
public class LoansClient {
    ...
    public static void main(String[] args) {
      ...
      // get remote reference to object "The application"
(1)   String objectName = "rmi://hafedh/The application";
(2)   LoanApplication loanApp = null;
      try {
(3)     loanApp = (LoanApplication)Naming.lookup(objectName);}
      catch (Exception e) {
        System.out.println("Exception looking up object:" + e);}
      try {
(4)     Applicant anApplicant = loanApp.getApplicant();
(5)     anApplicant.setIncome(30000f);
        System.out.println("Called remote method on:"+
          anApplicant);
      }
      catch (RemoteException e) {
        System.out.println("Caught an exception: " + e);}
      }
}
```

Line (1) shows the name of the object that we are looking up. In this case, it is the name of the local machine (hafedh), but could be any valid URL (uniform resource locator), and any port number (instead of the default port number for the RMI registry, which is 1099). Lines (2) and (4) show declarations for the remote objects *in terms of the remote interfaces defined in the beginning*; in other words, the developer is shielded from implementation

details, and does not know that the object returned by `Naming.`
`lookup(objectName)` is actually an instance of `ImpLoanApplica-`
`tion_Stub`. In line (4), we retrieve the applicant using the (remote) method
`getApplicant()`. Note that we need to hook up to only one named object
(e.g., a factory object), and from that object, we can pull out as many objects
as we want.

14.4.2 The EJB Architecture

The following excerpt is from Sun Microsystems's EJB specification:
[1998b]

> The Enterprise Java Beans architecture is a component architecture for the
> development and deployment of object-oriented distributed enterprise-level
> applications. Applications written using the Enterprise Java Beans architecture
> are scalable, transactional, and multi-user secure. These applications may be
> written once, and deployed on any server platform that supports the Enterprise
> Java Beans specification.

Enterprise Java Beans (EJB) is an application-independent architecture for
the development and deployment of object-oriented distributed applications.
The term *architecture* is used loosely here, because EJB is not specific to a particular software system, but is more like the *specification of a computational
infrastructure*, if we refer to the software architecture lifecycle of Figure 14.9.
In this section, we give a high-level description of the EJB architecture,
give a small example, and illustrate some of the more interesting design
artefacts used by EJB-compliant computational infrastructures (EJB-enabled
middleware).

The EJB specification includes a number of services that must be implemented by an EJB-compliant infrastructure that go beyond the basic distribution capabilities of Java RMI and the core of CORBA [Monson-Haefel
1999]. The so-called primary services of the EJB architecture are

1. *Object Distribution*. The ability to build an application consisting of collaborating objects that may reside in different memory spaces, and doing
   so in a location-transparent way.
2. *Naming*. The ability to locate objects based on symbolic, rather than
   absolute hardware/software names.
3. *Concurrency*. The ability to manage concurrent access to a distributed
   object, and preventing several processes from corrupting shared data.
4. *Transactions*. The ability to isolate the execution of pieces of code that
   modify shared data so that they can be treated as an atomic operation.
5. *Security*. The ability to selectively allow access to functionality based on
   user profiles.

6. *Persistence.* The ability to save shared data in persistent storage, allowing client programs to have a consistent and persistent view of the data.

We should note that all of theses services are specified as part of the CORBA architecture. However, whereas with CORBA, application developers have to invoke these services explicitly using the CORBA specified API, services 3–6 are offered pretty much behind the scenes for the case of an EJB-compliant computational infrastructure, freeing developers to concentrate on the development of business functions [Monson-Haefel 1999]. In order to benefit from these services, applications must satisfy a number of conditions and adhere to a number of conventions. The combined set of these constraints and conventions forms the so-called *EJB component model*, which describes the contract between the developer of an EJB-enabled application and the implementer of an EJB-compliant computational infrastructure.

The EJB architecture is best understood in the context of multitier client–server applications (see Fig. 14.17).

Client programs communicate with EJB servers using some remote method invocation infrastructure (Java RMI, IIOP, etc.). The distributed objects live in the EJB servers, and the client programs access them through proxies. These objects are persistent in databases through JDBC connections, and thus, the link from EJB servers to database servers is vendor-independent.

The EJB architecture distinguishes between two types of components: entity beans and session beans. *Entity beans* are used to implement data-rich, persistent, and shared business objects. They would typically show up as domain classes during analysis-*entities*, if we use UML's class categories. These objects (beans) are supposed to be loaded up and saved to persistent storage, they are supposed to be concurrently shared between several client programs.

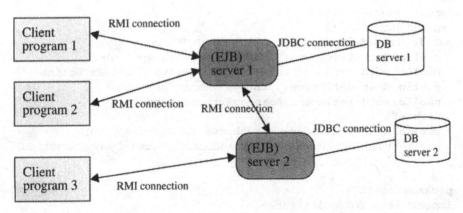

FIGURE 14.17 Implementing multitier client–server applications with the EJB architecture.

By contrast, session beans implement complex business logic that involves several objects, and that cannot be delegated to any object in particular. Typically, *session beans* would implement *use cases* [Monson-Haefel 1999], specifically, a sequence of interactions between the user, through a client program, and the system (server-side application). Session beans are not shared between client programs—at least, not as far as the client program is concerned—and are transient; when the client program terminates, the session bean disappears. There is a further distinction between stateless session beans, which may be thought of as classes with methods, but no data members, and stateful beans, which do have data members that are (or may be) modified by the various functions. A stateless session bean does not remember the functions that have been called on it before, whereas a stateful session bean does, through modifications to the data members. Like stateless session beans, stateful session beans are transient. They are, however, handled differently by the EJB server's resource manager.

We will look at the example of an entity bean corresponding to our loans application. As with CORBA and Java RMI, we have to specify an interface that represents the client view of the application object. In this case, we have to specify *two* interfaces: the *remote interface*, which represents the business object, per se, and the *home interface*, which represents a factory object that supports the creation and initialization of business objects, from runtime-supplied arguments, or from the contents of the database. The home interface may also include a bunch of methods that help locate objects in persistent storage based on various attributes. Implementations of these methods will typically include SQL (Structured Query Language) statements addressed to the database server through the JDBC connection; other persistence mechanisms may be used to the same effect. We show below the remote and home interfaces for an **Applicant**:

```
package testEJB;
import javax.ejb.*;
import java.rmi.*;
public interface Applicant extends EJBObject {
  public String getName() throws RemoteException;
  public void setName(String aName) throws RemoteException;
  public float getIncome() throws RemoteException;
  public void setIncome(float anIncome) throws
  RemoteException;
  public String getAddress() throws RemoteException;
  public void setAddress(String address) throws RemoteException;
}

package testEJB;
import java.io.Serializable;
import java.rmi.RemoteException;
import javax.ejb.*;
```

```
public interface ApplicantHome extends EJBHome {
  public Applicant create(String name,float inc) throws
                            CreateException, RemoteException;
  public Applicant findByPrimaryKey(ApplicantKey aKey) throws
                            EJBException, RemoteException;
}
```

The remote interface has to extend the interface **EJBObject**, and the home interface has to extend the interface **EJBHome**. The interface **EJBObject** includes, among other things, the method boolean isIdentical (EJBObject p0) and Object getPrimaryKey(). When objects reside in the same memory space, we can test equality by comparing memory locations (using ==). However, within client programs, two calls to create(String,float) on an **ApplicantHome** may return two proxies of the same domain object, and we need to find a way that tests whether they are identical that does *not* rely on memory addresses. A default implementation of **EJBObject** will compare primary keys, which brings us to the class **ApplicantKey**. This is a class that must be provided that represents the primary key of entities of this type (i.e., the remote interface); a primary key is a combination of attribute (data member) values that uniquely *identify* objects. Primary key classes have to satisfy certain conditions; they must implement the interface **Serialisable**, and provide their own definition of boolean equals(Object) and int hashCode().

In addition to defining the various interfaces, we have to provide an implementation for the business object, namely, of the the interface **Applicant**. In most EJB vendor implementations, the server-side version of **Applicant** would look something like this:

```
public class ApplicantEJB implements EntityBean {
  private String name;              // domain data
  private String address;        // domain data
  private float income;            // domain data

  protected void storeInDB(){...}
  public String getName() throws RemoteException {return name;}
  public void setName(String aName) throws RemoteException {
  name = aName;}
  ...
  public ApplicantKey ejbCreate(String name, float sum) throws
                            CreateException, RemoteException {
    this.name = name;
    this.income = sum;
    storeInDB();
    ApplicantKey key = new ApplicantKey();
    key.name = name;
    return key;
}
```

```
public void ejbPostCreate(String name, float sum) throws
                CreateException, RemoteException {...}

public ApplicantKey ejbFindByPrimaryKey(ApplicantKey aKey)
throws
                EJBException, Exception, FinderException {...}

public void ejbActivate() throws EJBException,
RemoteException{...}

public void ejbPassivate() throws EJBException,
RemoteException{...}

public void ejbRemove() throws RemoveException,
EJBException,
  RemoteException {...}

public void ejbLoad() throws EJBException, RemoteException {...}

public void ejbStore() throws EJBException, RemoteException {...}

public void setEntityContext(EntityContext parm1) throws
                EJBException, RemoteException {...}

public void unsetEntityContext() throws EJBException,
                RemoteException{...}
}
```

This class, like all entity bean classes, must implement the remote interface (**Applicant**) and a variation of the home interface (**ApplicantHome**). Instead of the method Applicant create(String,float), we have here the method ApplicantKey ejbCreate(String, float), and instead of the method Applicant findByPrimaryKey(ApplicantKey), we implement the method ApplicantKey ejbFindByPrimaryKey(Applicant-Key). This version of the bean class implementation does not correspond to the skeleton implementation, as shown for the case of CORBA and Java RMI. This version of **ApplicantEJB** corresponds to the TIE class in the TIE approach of CORBA; the server-side skeleton of the class **Applicant** (not shown here) *delegates* to an instance of **ApplicantEJB**. Figure 14.18 shows the class structure.

The methods ejbPostCreate(), ejbRemove(), ejbLoad(), ejb-Store(), ejbActivate(), and ejbPassivate() are callback methods that will be called by the EJB server when the appropriate event has occurred. For example, after the creation of an EJB object, the EJB server will call the method ejbPostCreate() on that EJB object. It is up to us to put in that method whatever processing needs to take place right after we created the object (e.g., registering for a kind of application messages). Similarly,

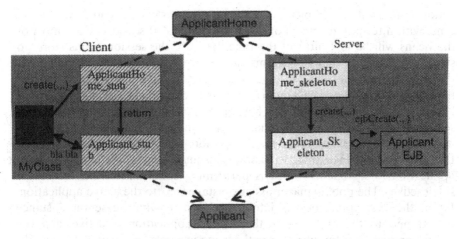

FIGURE 14.18   Overall structure of an EJB-based client–server program.

`ejbRemove()` is a method that will be called when the database record that corresponds to the receiver (the current EJB object) is about to be deleted. `ejbStore()` and `ejbLoad()` notify the EJB object that its state is to be saved onto, or loaded from the database (for the case of entity beans); similarly for `ejbActivate()` and `ejbPassivate()`, for serializing session beans. `setEntityCon  for  text(EntityContext)` sets the context (environment) of an entity bean so that EJB servers can query it about it.[11] `unsetEntityContext()` dereferences the entity bean in preparation for garbage collection.

One interesting aspect of the EJB architecture, from a design point of view, is its resource management infrastructure. Typically, an EJB server will service hundreds, if not thousands, of client sessions simultaneously. For session beans, this means thousands of instances, each one servicing a client program. These session beans may, in turn, reference several entity beans, which need to be synchronized with the contents of the database. If we maintain the ⟨one client⟩–⟨one session bean + several entity beans⟩ correspondence, having several thousand simultaneous connections—as is common with mass electronic commerce sites—will lead to significant performance degradation. The solution advocated by the EJB architecture borrows from the way traditional transaction monitor systems handle database connections between clients and servers: connection pooling. In this case, the EJB server performs *instance pooling*. Let us illustrate instance pooling for the case of stateless session beans.

Let us assume that we have 10,000 simultaneous client connections to a system—on the low end for systems such as eBay, Amazon, or the airline reser-

---

[11] A similar `setSessionContext(SessionContext)` exists for session beans.

vation system Sabre™. Typically, the client programs would be idle most of the time, with intermittent bursts of activity. With 10,000 session beans, most of the beans will be idle most of the time. Because the session beans store no state, and because client programs don't access EJB objects directly (but through aggregation from the server-side skeletons), it is envisageable to have fewer session beans, and pass them around between the clients on an as needed basis. Hence, it may be possible to handle 10,000 client sessions with only 1000 session bean instances. The rationale here is that (1) 1000 instances take up less space then 10,000 and (2) dynamic memory allocation takes up more time than method calls. Figure 14.19 illustrates instance pooling. We have two client applications, only one of which is performing computations on the server side (active). The pool manager assigns instance "a" to the active application. Later, the first application is idle (panel II), in which case the instance is returned to the pool. Later, the second application is active, and the corresponding skeleton object gets the same instance "a" (panel III). Finally, both are active, and the pool manager gets a new session instance from the pool (panel IV).

Instance pooling is also used for entity beans. In this case, the EJB server maintains a pool of instances for each type (class). For example, we could have 1000 instances of **ApplicantEJB**, and 500 instances of **LoanApplicationEJB**. Getting an entity bean instance in and out of the instance pool means that it may change identity; the same instance can represent "John Doe" for client program 1 from time t_1 to time t_2, and "Jane Smith" from time t_3 to time t_4. It is assumed here that the time it takes to create each object, and the cost of establishing database connections, is much higher than the time it takes

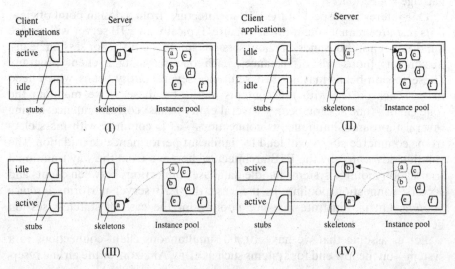

FIGURE 14.19 An illustration of instance pooling. (Adapted from [Monson-Haefel 1999].)

to read values in and out of the database. This, and savings in runtime memory (requiring less swaps), enable an EJB server to support many more client applications simultaneously.

The ways in which the various other services are implemented are also very instructive, and call on a variety of design techniques, some of which were illustrated in Chapters 11 and 12. The reader is encouraged to study these and other examples of general-purpose architectural frameworks as a source for good design practices and patterns.

14.5   THE COM FAMILY

Don Box defined COM as an architecture for "component reuse that allows dynamic and efficient composition of systems from independently developed binary components" [Box 1998]. Microsoft's *Component Object Model* started out with a different set of motivations from the almost contemporaneous CORBA, and the much more recent Sun's Enterprise Java Beans. Don Box neatly summarizes the purpose of the COM architecture: the dynamic composition and reuse of binary components; distribution aspects came in later. Further, it seems to have followed a much different thought process. It appeared to us that CORBA and Sun's EJB seem to have followed a top–down process, starting out with a set of desirable architectural properties, and ending up with a consensual (especially for the case of CORBA) and abstract specification of architectural services. By contrast, COM seems to have followed a bottom-up process whereby the COM specification is the a posteriori formalization of a more or less coherent set of design techniques aimed at resolving practical problems. This pragmatism is often used by COM's proponents as a proof of COM's groundedness [Box 1998] but also by COM's detractors as an indication for its lack of conceptual purity and too low level of abstraction [Szyperski 1999]. For our purposes, COM is interesting from two perspectives: (1) as an enabling technology for reusable components, and (2) as a source for good design idioms. Because of its history and its C/C++ lineage, COM is more complex and more low-level than the technologies discussed previously. Consequently, because of space limitations, we cannot possibly do justice to either perspective, but we will try to do a bit of both to give the reader an idea about the underlying philosophy and some of the design principles of the COM architecture. The interested reader is urged to read Don Box's excellent book on COM [Box 1998].

To motivate the COM architecture, we heavily and shamelessly draw on Don Box's own introduction to the topic from his book [Box 1998]. Roughly speaking, COM was developed to address two problems:

- Component reuse and interoperability at the binary level
- Release to release binary compatibility, namely, binary compatibility of different implementations of the same (or equivalent) functionality

Software reuse has long focussed on source-level reuse; the same source component is integrated wherever it is needed, and compiled and linked with its client code. If an application uses more than one executable, the same reusable code will be compiled and linked in each executable. This results in "code bloat." Further, whenever a new version of that reusable code is deployed, all the client programs need to be recompiled. Dynamically linked libraries (DLLs) were invented for this purpose; instead of the reusable code being compiled and statically linked into the client code, its compiled version is loaded and linked into client programs on demand during runtime (or program startup). However, this leaves two problems related to interoperability and evolution:

- *Differences in Compiler Technology.* Different vendors will implement the same language features differently, leading to binary level incompatibilities,[12]
- *Different Versions of the Same Reusable Components.* If we extend a reusable component, we change its binary representation in a way that may invalidate whichever assumptions client programs had about the class. For example, if we add a private data member to an existing class to cache the results of some expensive computations, we change the memory requirement for on-the-stack variables of this class. This means that client programs will need to be recompiled, even though the interface (API) of the class does not change.

These two problems meant that we have to find a component model that (1) focused on the external behavior of components, regardless of implementation; and (2) could represent that behavior in a vendor and even language-independent way. Having already introduced CORBA, the jaded reader might say "duh!" However, historically, COM was developed at the same time (from 1988 to 1993). Further, Microsoft designers had to contend with existing applications and technologies [e.g., object linking and embedding (OLE)]. We start by describing some of the general principles, and the C++ language binding in particular.

In COM, the behavior of software components is described by *interfaces* written in a language-independent interface definition language, similar in spirit and lineage to CORBA IDL. A COM component may implement several interfaces, as shown in Figure 14.20. The component **Customer** in this case implements five different interfaces: **IUnknown**, which is a compulsory interface for all COM objects; **IPersistentStorage**, which is a predefined COM interface that embodies required callbacks for persistence services; and three domain-specific interfaces, which correspond to the different

---

[12] Language standards attempt to standardize language semantics, but they will often leave vendors the choice of implementation. For example, different C++ compilers use different techniques for generating unique names of overloaded functions (the so-called name mangling).

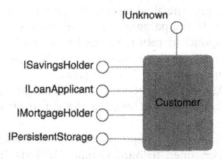

FIGURE 14.20 A COM component.

roles a particular customer may play within the context of a banking application.

A major underpinning of the COM architecture is the separation between *interfaces*, which are implementation and even language-independent behavioral descriptions, and *implementations*. Client programs need know only the interfaces they need to use the component, and in so doing, are shielded from implementation changes. Further, because client programs need see only the interfaces that they need, an existing component may be extended with new interfaces without affecting existing clients. This is a unique and powerful feature of the COM architecture, and corresponds to using the TIE approach in the CORBA architecture to let server-side object implementations implement different combinations of interfaces to client programs.

The following excerpt shows an example of what a COM IDL interface might look like:

```
[
uuid(07F27B6D-6229-11D4-BE4B-8F57EAB8544C),
version(1.0)
]
interface ILoanApplicant: IUnknown {
  HRESULT setName([in] const char* name);
  HRESULT getName([out, retval] char* name);
  HRESULT getIncome([out,retval] float* income);
  HRESULT setIncome([in] float income);
  HRESULT addAsset([in] IAsset anAsset);
};
```

What is between square brackets consists of *attributes*. The interface `ILoanApplication` has two attributes: `uuid()`, which is a globally unique identifier for the interface generated by development tools (a combination of machine hardware address and machine clock), and `version()`, which indicates the version of the interface. All methods "return" an HRESULT, which is the type representing the return error code for the corresponding method.

Method parameters are specified using the familiar type declarations. In addition, we can specify the parameter passing mode ([in] or [out]) and whether they correspond to return values of the corresponding functions. The method addAsset() takes another interface as argument, namely, **IAsset**, which is supposed to be defined elsewhere. COM interfaces may be extended using single inheritance. The reasons why COM interfaces shouldn't support multiple inheritance, and why we can get away with it, will appear shortly.

In C++, COM interfaces are mapped to C++ classes where all the methods of the interface are mapped to pure virtual functions. Implementations of these interfaces are regular C++ subclasses, in the same way that remote object implementations are subclasses of server-side skeleton classes for the case of CORBA. A C++ class can implement several interfaces. A possible implementation of the interface shown above could look like this (in a simplified form):

```
class Customer : public IUnknown, public ISavingsHolder, public
IPersistentStorage, public ILoanApplicant, public
IMortgageHolder {

  char* name;
  float income;
  ...
  float mortgageValue;
  ...
public:
  virtual HRESULT STDMETHODCALLTYPE setName(const char* name)
  {...}
  virtual HRESULT STDMETHODCALLTYPE getName(char* name) {...}
  ...
  virtual HRESULT STDMETHODCALLTYPE getMortgageValue(float*
  val){...}
  virtual HRESULT STDMETHODCALLTYPE setMortgageValue(float
  val){...}
  ...
}
```

In this case, the implementation will inherit from all the classes generated for the interfaces it is supposed to implement.

Figure 14.21 shows the memory layout for the classes **ILoanApplicant**, **IMortgageHolder**, and **Customer**. The memory location vptr refers to the pointer to the table that contains the pointers to the virtual function calls. Remember that in C++, only virtual function calls are bound dynamically, and for this reason, objects have a pointer to the implementations of these functions that are appropriate for their class. In C++, objects are laid out, first by putting the members of the superclass(es), then by putting the local members

ILoanApplicant   Customer

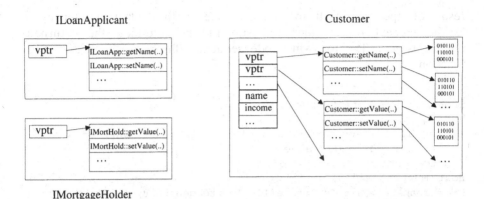

IMortgageHolder

FIGURE 14.21   Memory layout of interfaces and implementations.

of the class. When we upcast an instance of a class to one of its supertypes (say, **ILoanApplication**), we get the offset that corresponds to the beginning of the memory area provided for the members of that superclass. Because in this case all the superclasses are abstract with no data members, the virtual pointers corresponding to the various superclasses are contiguous, and their relative position is unaffected by how many data members are defined in the current class. This is true regardless of the C++ compiler (because it is a part of the language specification). If this sounds too detailed an explanation for how COM achieves implementation independence, it is. However, it is a faithful rendition of the motivations and thought processes that underlie the technology [Box 1998].

Because C++ has no built-in garbage collector, programs must manage the memory of the objects they create. Also, because typically COM objects do not live in the same process as their clients, and because they may service several clients, client programs cannot delete objects they no longer need, but can only notify those objects that they no longer need them. This is done through reference counting: two methods that all COM objects must support are AddRef(), which increments the reference count of an object, and Release(), which decreases the reference count by one. These methods are part of the **IUnknown** interface, the root interface for all COM interfaces. In particular, Release() should *normally* physically delete the object when the counter reaches zero. Client programs, on the other hand, are responsible for calling AddRef(), when they add a pointer to the object, and Release() when they are done with it. Another mandatory method that is part of the **IUnknown** interface is the method (IDL):

HRESULT QueryInterface([in] REFIID riid, [out] void** ppv);

This method queries an object (an implementation) for a particular interface identified by riid, and if the object supports the interface, it returns the result of upcasting itself to that interface in the out parameter ppv. If the current object does not support the interface, the returned pointer is null. The following code sequence illustrates the use of this function:

```
ILoanApplicant *loanApp= . . . ;
HRESULT hr;
// see if loanApp understands IMortgageHolder, and if yes,
// get its mortgage value
IMortgageHolder *mortH = 0;
float mortValue=0.0;
hr = loanApp->QueryInterface(IID_ImortgageHolder,(void**)&mortH);
  if (SUCCEEDED(hr)) {
    hr = mortH->getValue(&mortValue);
    ...
  }
```

Runtime typing makes it possible for the component provider to extend an existing component to provide new functionality, and for client programs to use that functionality, if they are aware of it, and if the particular object they are working with happens to support it.

Because client programs see only interfaces of pure abstract classes, they have no way of creating objects through those interfaces. Thus, COM component developers must provide an object that creates instances of the implementation class. These are called *class objects* (much like Java's **Class** instances), and they must support methods that are similar in spirit to EJB's home interface. To this end, COM offers the **IFactoryClass** interface, which class objects must implement. For example, we could define an interface for factory class for **ILoanApplication** called **ILoanApplicationFactory**, which extends the interface **IFactoryClass**, and implement such a class. Because only one instance of such a class is needed, the class—call it **CLoanApplicationFactory**—can implement the *singleton* design patterns [Gamma et al. 1995]. But then, how do we create instances of class objects? Well, we have to boostrap the process somewhere, and COM uses a mechanism that is similar to the one used by the previous technologies; a server application creates a class object and registers it with the *service control manager* (SCM) so that client programs can access it using a predefined function called CoGetClassObject(...), which takes, among other arguments, the interface of the factory class (in this case **ILoanApplicationFactory**), the name of the specific implementation class (in this case **CLoanApplicationFactory**). The SCM plays the same role as the implementation repository manager in CORBA, and is responsible for some of the functionalities that are part of the lifecycle services in CORBA. COM also supports a sophisticated (or, should we say, complex) naming service using *monikers*, some form of persistence, a complex concurrency control (the notion of *apartments*), security, and distribution (DCOM). Also, it supports a limited version of CORBA's dynamic invocation interfaces.

The path taken by Microsoft seems to be convergence of services with other competing technologies by generalizing or abstracting earlier implementations into fully specified services (basically, MIDL interfaces). Also, interoperability with other technologies (CORBA-based, Java-based) has been on the agenda of both Microsoft and vendors of other technologies, at a time when companies don't want to be locked in the technology of the day, or of a particular vendor.

14.6 SUMMARY AND DISCUSSION

Large-scale organized efforts at reuse have established that the greatest technical obstacle to reuse is lack of *usability* and not lack of *usefulness*. In particular, there is a lot of useful functionality in legacy systems, but most of it does not use the right control paradigm, or doesn't abide by the right interaction protocols, or simply isn't implemented in the right programming language [Garlan et al. 1995, Bass et al. 1998). These are all architectural issues.

A good software architecture is worth reusing. As such, it should be properly motivated, well thought out, thoroughly evaluated, and thoroughly documented. Section 14.1 defined the vocabulary of architecture, and presented some of the distilled architectural knowledge in terms of architectural styles and connectors. Three of the many qualities of a software architecture are the reusability, evolvability, and interchangeability of the components that can plug into it. In other words, a good architecture can be an enabler for reuse. Both perspectives on architecture were discussed in Section 14.2.

The rest of the chapter dealt with what we called *architectural frameworks*, which are application frameworks designed and built to support a particular architectural style. A common characteristic of these frameworks is that they are business-domain-independent, and should be able to handle any application that chooses to adopt the underlying style, with little or no overhead; developers can concentrate on business logic, and let the framework components handle the architectural aspects. Separating function from computation is the holy grail of software reuse; functions can be specified regardless of the underlying computational infrastructure, and computational infrastructures can be developed regardless of what gets computed "on them." Application development then becomes a matter of instantiating implementation-independent business components and assembling them onto a common computational infrastructure.

We discussed three such frameworks (or families of frameworks): CORBA, Java-based technologies (with a greater focus on distribution than on components), and COM. These families are interesting for two reasons. First, ideally, they should be part of the technical arsenal of software architects and senior developers. The discussion in this chapter gives only a glimpse over these technologies—the interested reader will have to study the original sources cited in the Bibliography (especially Baker [1997], Bass et al. [1998], Box [1998], Garlan et al. [1995], Monson-Haefel [1999], Mowbray and Zahavi [1995], and Szyperski [1999]) to gain a deeper understanding and a practical knowledge of these technologies. The second reason why these frameworks are interesting relates more to how they were built, and the set of design techniques they bring to bear. We are not interested in comparing these technologies feature by feature. We are more interested in the similarities to gain insight into alternative solutions to the same design problem, modulo some language differences. These frameworks also illustrate some of the design tensions between performance and abstraction, between generality and readiness, and other distinctions.

A major design problem faced by the three technologies is to separate behavioral specifications from implementations. All three use different constructs to represent behaviors and implementations. With Java-based technologies, which are targeted for Java-only applications, both constructs are part of the language (*classes* and *interfaces*). Both CORBA and COM use a language-independent *interface definition language* (IDL). All three technologies use descriptions of the business functionalities in terms of interfaces, and generate language-specific implementation stubs and skeletons that bridge business function invocations with the underlying computational infrastructure. Generation technology has implications in terms of the development lifecycle; technologies that involve generation mean that the choice of an architecture has to be made before the business logic code is actually compiled or the executable is built (linked). This adversely affects the dynamic evolution of applications that adopt this architecture. Fortunately, all of these technologies have some form of support of reflection; the implementation of a particular architectural service for a business component does not need to be compiled in, but can rely on type information that is available at runtime. For example, to persist a yet unheard of object, all we have to do is to query the object for its persistent fields, serialize the values of these fields, and generate on-the-fly SQL queries that will save them onto a database. Support for reflection depends in part on how much type information is available during runtime, and on the host language itself. With Smalltalk, this is trivial. With Java, it is still fairly simple. With C++, some ingenuity is required, but is still eminently feasible. In all cases, executing code through the reflection API is more costly, and the various technologies strike different balances between code generation and relying on the reflection API. Other services use other design techniques and patterns and language constructs. We hope to have illustrated enough of them to encourage the student of architecture to dig deeper into these technologies as a source of design expertise.

14.7 FURTHER READING

Most of the material in this chapter is taken from professional books or on-line manuals that deal with specific technologies or products. The reader is encouraged to double-check that these sources are still up to date in terms of providing an accurate snapshot of the state of a particular technology. Given the pace of evolution in this area, we are resigned to the fact that some of these references will be obsolete by the time you get your hands on this book.

Part V

Application Engineering

Whereas domain engineering is concerned with the development of reusable assets, application engineering is concerned with the development of applications using those assets. The availability of reusable assets may change the way we develop software, in terms of both process and development tasks and heuristics. With the generative approach, large portions of the target application are generated from requirements-level operational parameters, automating a number of development steps. With the building blocks or composition-based approach, savings occur at the later stages of development and at a more "local" level, but new tasks are needed to identify, adapt, and compose the so-adapted reusable components.

In Chapter 15, we provide an overview of the impact of reuse on application engineering for both the generative and the compositional approach. Chapters 16 and 17 focus on the composition-based approach, and discuss in some detail two new development steps required by the compositional approach: (1) component selection and retrieval and (2) component adaptation and integration.

Chapter 15

Application Engineering

In Section 15.1, we provide an overview of the impact of reuse practice on the development of applications. Section 15.2 presents a generic development life-cycle for composition-based application engineering.

15.1 APPLICATION ENGINEERING PARADIGMS

In Section 1.4, we identified two general paradigms for reuse: the compositional paradigm versus the generative paradigm. In the *compositional paradigm*, new applications are developed by *composing* smaller software components, some or most of which are reusable components taken from a reuse library. In the *generative paradigm*, we develop new applications (or significant parts thereof) by feeding abstract, specification-level parameters to a *processor* that generates the application according to those parameters. In fact, these are only extreme points along a continuous spectrum reflecting different maturity levels of the application domain and of the development organization.

The various points along the compositional–generative axis may be characterized by the kind of reusable assets that are available. Toward the compositional end, there is the implicit assumption that our reusable assets consist mainly of a set of fairly independent components (or component clusters) that are packaged in a way that maximizes their usability (see Chapter 7). However, we assume that the components are fairly architecture-neutral in the sense that their use does not impose a specific *functional architecture* on the application at hand. In this case, the application engineer will *first* design the *application architecture*, and then select a component from the library on the basis of the functionality that it provides and on the extent to which it can be integrated into the overall architecture. Here, *integrability* refers to *functional integration* (the component plays a useful role in the overall functional architecture; see Section 14.1) and to *infrastructure integration* in the sense of plugging into the *computational infrastructure* (see Section 14.2). In the extreme case, the availability of reusable components that abide by a particular component model (e.g., COM, EJB; see Sections 14.3–14.5) may influence the choice of the computational infrastructure, but ultimately, the functional architecture is the responsibility of the application engineer.

Toward the generative end, all except a very few aspects of the application are left to the application engineer to specify, typically by making a few menu selections and filling out a few forms. Thus, the functional architecture, the computational infrastructure, and most of the components are provided. The application engineer is left to fill out only a few stubbed-out components (classes, methods, procedures).

Between these two extremes, we find situations where most of the functional architecture is available in advance, where the computational infrastructure is also available, and where a good number of components that play a role in the functional architecture and that plug into the computational infrastructure are also available.

Application engineering in this case is similar to framework instantiation discussed in Section 13.1, only on a wider scale. In software reuse jargon, this is the application engineering phase of *product-line engineering*. The three paradigms represent different maturation levels, of the application domain, of the organization's expertise in that domain, and of the organisation's development processes. Figure 15.1 illustrates this point. The goal, of course, is to move an organization (or an application domain) toward the righthand side of Figure 15.1.

Part VII of this book deals with specific points along this spectrum. Chapter 21 discusses *component-based software development*, which falls on the lefthand side of Figure 15.1. Chapter 23 deals with *COTS-based development*, which is a special case of component-based development when the components are commercial off-the-shelf (COTS) components, and Chapter 22 deals with *product line engineering*, which falls in the middle of the spectrum between generative and composition (right of middle of Fig. 15.1).

15.2   APPLICATION ENGINEERING LIFECYCLES

A software lifecycle is a model for organizing, planning, and controlling the activities associated with software development and maintenance [Peters 1987]. For the most part, a lifecycle identifies development tasks, and identifies and standardizes intermediary work products (deliverables), and review and evaluation criteria. When we talk about software reuse, there are two life-

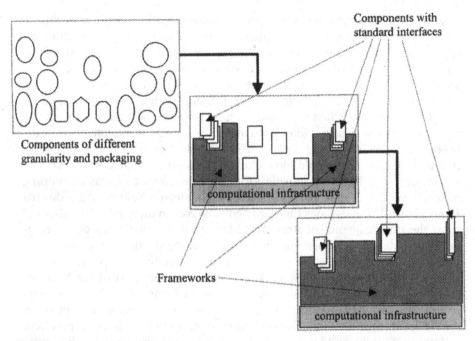

FIGURE 15.1 Moving from a component/composition-based approach toward a generative approach.

cycles to consider: (1) the lifecycle for developing reusable assets and (2) the lifecycle for developing with reusable assets. Chapters 4, 7, and 8 discussed the lifecycle for developing reusable assets, and a spectrum of relations between that lifecycle and the lifecycle for developing *with* reusable assets. In this chapter, we focus on the lifecycle for developing with reusable assets.

The first question that comes to mind is whether the availability of a base of reusable assets modifies the underlying lifecycle. This depends on both the reuse approach used—along the compositional ↔ generative dimension—and on the development methodology used. With the compositional approach, both the reusable assets and the products developed with them are software components. Building new applications with reusable components need not follow a lifecycle radically different from building new applications without reusable components. One criticism leveled at the waterfall lifecycle is that each lifecycle stage is influenced mainly by the previous stages (top–down), while the existence of reusable components requires some sort of a look-ahead procedure to identify opportunities for reuse and take advantage of them [Simos 1990, Henderson-Sellers and Edwards 1990]. We believe this to be mainly a documentation issue; reuse has traditionally meant reuse of small code fragments that have little or no lifecycle documentation. If analysis information were stored in components libraries, for example, analysts could identify opportunities for reuse at the analysis level without looking at the actual code of reusable components. The point has been made, though, that object-oriented software development requires a mix of top–down and bottom–up approaches [Henderson-Sellers and Edwards 1990]. This is explained by the premise that an object-oriented development lifecycle needs to combine application and domain engineering in order to attain reuse objectives [Henderson-Sellers and Edwards 1990]. The application engineering part of the lifecycle proceeds in a top–down fashion from requirements gathering to high-level system design. Domain engineering consists of building "clusters" (libraries or layers [Meyer 1990]) of classes, starting with the lowest level (building blocks) that would most likely be needed no matter what the final system design is like, and moving up to application-specific classes, looping back on system design, or even analysis [Henderson-Sellers and Edwards 1990]. Figure 15.2 illustrates this paradigm. The roman numerals (I, II, III, etc.) show the time sequence of steps. This lifecycle shows that some of the components that are developed may be useless in case they don't implement any useful subsystem of the application(s) at hand (no match at step III), in which case we either revise our system decomposition (upper part of diagram), or revise our component aggregations (lower part of diagram). The proponents of this lifecycle acknowledge that it may be wasteful in resources, but stress the fact that it leads to much shorter time-to-market cycles for new products.

Other OO-induced lifecycle changes have been proposed in the literature that are motivated by considerations other than reuse, such as managing the risks inherent in switching to a new development technology [Pittman 1993].

The situation is markedly different with the generative approach. The effect of using the generative approach for software development is much easier to assess; the generative approach shortens traditional lifecycles through automation [Martin 1985]. Application generators, for example, obviate the need

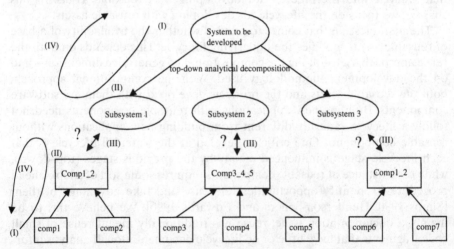

FIGURE 15.2 A hybrid top–down bottom–up development lifecycle that takes into account the existence of reusable assets.

for specifying the software requirements: designing, coding, and testing, of big chunks of applications [Levy 1986]. Executable specification languages and transformational systems obviate the need for designing, coding, and testing, but developers still need to produce precise formal specifications of the desired system [Agresti 1986]. Application generators have experienced some commercial success in the 1980s in the MIS area. Most of these generators were geared toward data processing where the input is usually the specification of data sources and output format (forms) and the output is a database application that queries the data source and displays the results of the query. Application generators have received little attention in the literature, perhaps because the areas where they have been successfully used are too narrow or considered not exciting by researchers, or because researchers don't like solved problems! There is still ongoing research in general-purpose generational technology (automatic programming) in the form of *executable specification languages*. In the context of reuse, we note Simos's work on application-specific specification languages (ASLs), and what he calls domain lifecycle [Simos 1990]. He sees ASLs as the culmination of the maturation of an application domain, or an organization's expertise in that domain. The maturation starts with small reusable code components and moves toward more abstract representations and more complex constructs until an entire application domain is covered [Simos 1990].

On a smaller scale, we have all used, at one point or another UNIX's Lex and Yacc tools, which generate language compilers from a specification of the grammar of the language. Further, since the early 1990s, the distinction between the generative and compositional approaches started to vanish, with the advent of visual programming environments. The object-oriented drag-and-drop visual editors for building user interfaces or database connectors exemplify this approach. Typically, developers select components from a palette and position them on a canvas that reflects some view of the structure of the software to be developed—for graphical user interfaces (GUIs), it is the actual layout of the interface! The editor enables developers to configure the components by specifying some of their customizable attributes. It will also generate the glue code that implements the software structure visualized by the canvas. For example, a GUI editor will generate the code to create the widgets (window objects) and to position them relative to their container as positioned by the developer.

Successful reuse practice today falls in the middle between the generative approach and the compositional approach, specifically, toward product-line engineering. In this case, we can considerably shorten the earlier phases of software development. For instance, for the case of requirements and analysis, we only have to specify what distinguishes a product of the line from others. As for architecture, it is usually product-line wide, and thus, we are left with the selection of components to plug into the architecture, and the creation of the missing components. In practice, we will find that different parts of our product line will be better understood than others (see middle step in Fig.

15.1), and the engineering of a given application will involve a mix of the three paradigms. However, the trend is toward automation; richer libraries obviate the need to develop new components, and standardized application programming interfaces and component models make it easier to generate greater portions of application code, using such facilities as introspection, interface registries, and the like (see Chapter 14).

15.3   APPLICATION ENGINEERING DEVELOPMENT TASKS AND HEURISTICS

Software development can be considered as a problem-solving activity, where the problem is to find a software implementation that satisfies a set of user requirements. Cognitive scientists and AI theorists alike consider recall as an essential part of human problem solving [Rumelhart and Norman 1983, Lenat et al. 1990].

Broadly speaking, when faced with a problem, we first perform a "rote recall" to see if we haven't solved the problem before [Lenat 1990]. When that fails, we start looking for analogical (similar) problems that we might have already solved, and adapt their solution to the problem at hand [Carbonell 1983]. When that fails, we fall back on general analytic problem-solving knowledge and skills [Lenat et al. 1990]. Most development methodologies are analytic in nature, and fall back immediately on general problem-solving knowledge and heuristics such as divide and conquer, and successive refinements. Researchers recognize that "informal reuse" (i.e., in developers' heads) has always been taking place, whereby the base of reusable knowledge is "acquired" individually by developers through experience [Barnes and Bollinger 1991]. To some extent, "formal" software reuse in general, and the compositional approach in particular, recognize the earlier recall-based phases of problem solving, and aim at formalizing them and providing computer support for them.

Challenges to supporting reuse within development methodologies include (1) identifying reuse tasks and the skills required to perform those tasks [Maiden and Sutcliffe 1993], (2) providing methodological and tool support for these tasks [Mili et al. 1994a, Morel and Faget 1993], and (3) integrating reuse activities into the normal workflow of developers [Fischer 1987, Mili et al. 1994a]. The reuse tasks depend heavily on the reuse approach used along the compositional–generative axis. With the generative approach, the reuse tasks consist of specifying the desired application in a high-level language [executable specification language, fourth-generation language (4GL), etc.], and the required cognitive skills need not be different from those required of traditional development methods. With the building block approach, developers try to build a system that satisfies a set of requirements by using as many existing components (or developing as little code) as possible. For any part of the target system, developers must [Fischer 1987, Ramamoorthy et al. 1988, Mili et al. 1994a, Maiden and Sutcliffe 1993]: (1) formulate the requirements of the part in a way that supports retrieval of potentially useful reusable components, (2) understand the retrieved components, and (3) if the retrieved components are sufficiently close to the needs at hand, and are of sufficient quality, then adapt them. If no component is found that matches perfectly or closely the given requirements, developers may fall back on general-purpose analytic heuristics to decompose the system (or part thereof) into smaller parts for which steps 1–3 may be reiterated [Ramamoorthy et al. 1988].

The search-and-retrieval problem benefits from a large body of work in the area of document retrieval, and is be discussed in more detail in Chapter 16. For the time being, we note that the focus is shifting from being able to sift through thousands of reusable components, to a more knowledge-intensive kind of retrieval that operates on fewer and bigger components, where the results of search combine retrieval, explanation, and adaptation of reusable assets.

Component and program understanding represents an important part of both the mental effort and the cost factor, in reuse [Fischer 1987, Maiden and Sutcliffe 1993] and maintenance [McClure 1992]. Component understanding can mean three things (criteria): (1) understanding what it does, (2) understanding how it does it, and (3) understanding how to modify it in such a way that it does something a little different. In a reuse-and-maintenance context, some abstract implementation-independent component documentation should accom-modate criterion 1, obviating the need for reusers to browse through actual code—thus obviating the need for criterion 3. For components whose adaptation and extension has been properly planned, the amount of knowledge needed for criterion 3 can be very small, compared to what it would take to explain how the component works, specifically, criterion 2; the knowledge required for criterion 3 corresponds to documenting what Krueger called the variable part of component abstractions [Krueger 1992]. It is reasonable to assume that if a component is to be modified in a unanticipated (or not properly parameterized) fashion, one might need to delve into the minute details of the component, and the knowledge required for criterion 3 may be comparable to that required for criterion 2. However, studies have shown that reusers are able to edit and adapt components with only a sketchy understanding of how they work [Maiden and Sutcliffe 1993]; whether that is desirable or not is another issue.

Program understanding involves the recognition of high-level abstract patterns amid complex and detailed structures. Studies have shown that experts and novices use different approaches to program understanding [Maiden and Sutcliffe 1993], suggesting that reusers and maintainers may need training in program understanding or the support of tools that help them understand programs [Fisher 1987, McClure 1992, Maiden and Sutcliffe 1993].

Component understanding is the first step toward component adaptation. Unplanned component adaptation constitutes a textbook case in analogical problem solving [Carbonell 1983]. Analogical problem solving is used when the mapping from problem to solution cannot be characterized intensionally, but such that some <problem,solution> pairs are known for which elements in the solution space (software artifacts) can be traced to elements in the problem space (requirements). A new problem (NP) is solved by first matching it to a known problem–solution pair <KP,KS>, and then using the difference between NP and KP to infer the difference between KS and the actual solution of NP (NS). Analogical problem solving is unsound in the sense that a problem–solution pair NS is not guaranteed to solve the problem NP; if we modify a component using this kind of reasoning, we lose any assurances that the modified version does what it says (verification), and what we want it to do (validation). It is inherently unsound because it relies on an incomplete knowledge (partial extension) of the problem $\rightarrow$ solution mapping. This kind of technique is only used in the constrained context of transformational systems [Baxter 1992] or for informal software artifacts for which not much else can be done [Maiden and Sutcliffe 1992].

In terms of tool support and integration, there is a fairly wide consensus that tools for reuse tasks should integrate seamlessly into CASE environments [Fischer 1987, Maiden and Sutcliffe 1992, Morel 1993, Mili et al. 1994a]. Typical reuse functionalities such as search and copy + edit should be available to developers in a modeless fashion, and should not distract them from their normal workflow (see, e.g., Mili et al. [1994a]). Broadly speaking, reuse-oriented CASE environments should be viewed as problem-solving aids, to be used as extensions of developers' mental workspace, rather than a rigid formalism requiring constant translation back and forth to that mental workspace. This entails, among other things, enabling developers to custom-tailor their development environments, and providing them with proactive development aids and tools [Fischer 1987]. The former is made possible by offering fine-grained development functionalities that developers may combine and sequence at will [Morel 1993].

Much of the earlier work on knowledge-based component understanding and adaptation was based on the implicit assumption of whitebox reuse. The idea here is that reusers will adapt the components that match closely but not exactly their needs, and to this end, they need to study the entrails of the reusable components that they are working with. A number of factors make this feel as if it is less of an issue today than it was in 1990, such as (1) advances in component packaging technology make it possible to reuse components in a blackbox fashion requiring little or no adaptation; (2) there is a proliferation of such components in the market today, and there are plenty of opportunities for reuse; (3) the source code of these components may not always be available; and (4) the complexity and size of such components are typically such that any unplanned adaptation is more trouble than it is worth.

There are cases, however, where whitebox reuse is still needed and economically and technically viable: in the area of framework instantiation (see Chapter 13). The learning curve for frameworks is still a big impediment to their use [Fayad and Schmidt 1997], and any help along these lines is welcome. The techniques presented in the preceding paragraphs are still eminently relevant, but the focus should shift from function-level understanding to understanding complex structural and inter-object-level interactions.

Chapter **16**

Component Storage and Retrieval

The successful deployment of software reuse is critically dependent on the ability to classify and retrieve reusable software assets in an efficient, precise manner. Efficiency is crucial because in order for software reuse to be practical, its attending overhead must be controlled. Precision is even more crucial because retrieving an irrelevant asset may cause much loss of productivty; the programmer may spend an inordinate amount of effort trying to adapt the asset, approaching or exceeding the effort to develop a substitute from scratch, or may spend much time analyzing the asset, only to find that it is best to discard it and develop a custom component from scratch.

In this chapter, we discuss the storage, classification, and retrieval of software assets for the purpose of software reuse; we refer to such storage structures as *software libraries*. In Section 16.1, we introduce some concepts and terms that pertain to software libraries, and discuss means to characterize and assess them. In Section 16.2, we discuss issues that arise in the design and deployment of software libraries, and we briefly review the main families of software libraries that are in use today (both in industry and as research prototypes).

16.1 AN INTRODUCTION TO SOFTWARE LIBRARIES

In this section we introduce some terminology that we use in this chapter to discuss the storage and retrieval of software assets; then we discuss how to characterize storage and retrieval methods, and how to assess such methods.

16.1.1   Terminology for Storage and Retrieval

A *software library* is a set of software assets that are maintained by an organization for possible *browsing* and/or *retrieval*; while *software assets* are typically source code units, they could be other assets, such as specifications, designs, documentation, or test data. Also, although the most common application of software libraries is software reuse, it is not necessarily the only application. The difference between *browsing* and *retrieval* is that while the latter consists in identifying and extracting assets that satisfy a predefined *matching condition*, the former consists in inspecting assets for possible extraction, without predefined criterion. In this chapter, we focus our attention on *retrieval*, although we may occasionally discuss browsing techniques.

Because retrieval depends on matching a candidate asset against a user *query*, the representation of both the query and the asset is an important consideration. Queries can be represented in a number of different ways, including natural-language patterns and templates (for *information retrieval methods*; see Section 16.2.3), lists of keywords (for *descriptive retrieval methods*; Section 16.2.3), sample input/output data (for *operational semantics methods*; Section 16.2.3), input/output signature or functional description (for *denotational semantics methods*; Section 16.2.3), or designs or program patterns (for *structural methods*; Section 16.2.3). Assets have an even wider range of representation than queries, since they usually include a reference to the actual asset. The representation of the asset is typically substantially more abstract than the asset itself, and is made purposefully abstract to capture the important or salient features of the asset while overlooking minor or irrelevant details; in the information retrieval literature, the representation of the asset is referred to as the asset's *surrogate*. For the sake of efficiency, the matching condition between a query and an asset typically involves the asset's surrogate, rather than the asset itself.

We distinguish between two aspects in the activity of *asset retrieval*, whereby the library is scanned for identification of *relevant* assets: *navigation*, which determines which assets are visited and/or inspected, and in what order; and *matching*, which determines the condition under which an asset is selected. Brute-force navigation consists in visiting all the assets of the library in an arbitrary order; this occurs in particular when the *storage structure* of the library is a flat organization. More elaborate navigation methods are possible when the storage structure has a meaningful organization. Matching consists in testing a condition that involves a given asset to determine whether the asset must be selected. We distinguish between two conditions: the *relevance criterion*, which is the condition under which an asset is considered to be relevant with respect to a query; and the *matching condition*, which is the condition under which an asset is selected. In practice, these two conditions may be different. If the relevance condition is too complex to be automatically tested or if the asset's surrogate is too abstract to afford a precise characterization of relevant assets, one may choose a matching condition that is weaker than the relevance condition; on the other hand, whenever a high degree of retrieval precision is required, one may select a matching condition that is stronger than (i.e., logically implies) the relevance criterion. In other words, the matching condition can be seen as an implementation of the relevance criterion.

We distinguish between (at least) two overall objectives of an *asset retrieval* operation: *exact retrieval*, whose purpose is to identify library assets that satisfy the submitted query with respect to every aspect (functional correctness, architectural assumptions, interaction protocols, resource requirements, etc); and *approximate retrieval*, whose purpose is to identify library assets that can be modified with minimal effort to satisfy a submitted query. Exact retrieval fits in the lifecycle of *blackbox reuse*, whose phases are (1) *exact retrieval*, whereby correct assets are identified and retrieved; (2) *assessment*, whereby retrieved assets are evaluated with respect to the query to select that which provides the best fit; (3) *instantiation*, whereby the selected asset is duly specialized to fit the purpose of the query at hand; and (4) *integration*, whereby the instantiated asset is integrated into its host system and submitted to some form of integration testing. Approximate retrieval fits in the lifecycle of *whitebox reuse*, whose phases are (1) *approximate retrieval*, whereby assets that approximate the query are identified and retrieved; (2) *assessment*, whereby retrieved assets are evaluated with respect to the query to select that which minimizes the expected modification effort; (3) *modification*, whereby the selected asset is duly modified to fit the purpose of the query at hand; and (4) *integration*, whereby the instantiated asset is integrated into its host system and duly tested. We distinguish between two patterns of program modification: (1) *generative modification*, which consists in reusing the design of an asset while rewriting the lower levels of its hierarchical structure; and (2) *compositional modification*, which consists in using the building blocks of the retrieved asset and combining them in a new design structure to satisfy the query at hand.

It may be worthwhile to illustrate the distinction between *retrieval goal*, *relevance criterion*, and *matching condition* by means of an example. If we consider the method of software storage and retrieval by signature matching, we could conceivably define two possible retrieval goals: either our retrieval goal is that retrieved components be correct with respect to the submitted query, or it is that retrieved components have the same signature as the submitted query. If we are interested in a component that computes the depth (height) of a binary tree we may submit the signature *binarytree, naturalnumbers.* For the sake of argument, assume that the method returns a component that computes the depth of a binary tree and a component that computes the number of nodes of a binary tree. Under the first retrieval goal, only one component is deemed relevant (the first), whereas under the second, both are deemed relevant. Precision and recall (which count the number of relevant assets that are or are not retrieved) cannot be defined unless a retrieval goal is agreed on. On the other hand, to illustrate the distinction between *relevance criterion* and *matching condition*, consider the storage–retrieval method that operates by behavioral sampling. Here, the relevance criterion is typically that the candidate component be correct with respect to the reuser's intent, and the matching condition is (only) that the candidate component behave satisfactorily on the data sample provided by the reuser; clearly, these are different conditions, as an asset may well satisfy the latter and fail to satisfy the former.

16.1.2 Assessment Criteria

We define a set of criteria that we use to assess and compare storage and retrieval methods. We discuss in turn technical criteria, managerial criteria, then human criteria; for each criterion, we attempt to present a quantitative metric to measure it or, failing that, a discrete set of ratings.

16.1.2.1 Technical Criteria

We identify six technical evaluation criteria, which are discussed in turn below:

- *Precision.* The precision of a retrieval algorithm is the ratio of relevant retrieved assets over the total number of retrieved assets; this is a number that ranges between 0 and 1. Under the hypothesis that all library assets are visited (e.g., exhaustive navigation), we get perfect precision (=1) whenever the matching condition logically implies the relevance criterion. This can be achieved in particular by letting the matching condition be *false*, which means that no assets are returned (hence no irrelevant assets are returned). When concrete quantitative data are not available to quantify the precision of a storage–retrieval method, we may, instead, assign values in a discrete five-value rating [*very low* (VL), *low* (L), *medium* (M), *high* (H), *very high* (VH)], where *VH* refers to perfect precision and *VL* refers to very poor precision.

- *Recall.* The recall of a retrieval algorithm is the ratio of relevant retrieved assets over the total number of relevant assets in the library; this is a number that ranges between 0 and 1. Under the hypothesis that all library assets are visited (e.g., exhaustive navigation), we get perfect recall (=1) whenever the relevance criterion logically implies the matching condition. This can be achieved in particular by letting the matching condition be *true*, which means that all library assets are returned (hence no relevant assets are forgotten). Under the same conditions as those cited above, we may use a five-value rating scale where *VH* stands for perfect recall and *VL* stands for very poor recall.

- *Coverage Ratio.* The coverage ratio of a retrieval algorithm is the average number of assets that are visited over the total size of the library; this is a number that ranges between 0 and 1. The brute-force exhaustive navigation produces a coverage ratio of 1, but more elaborate algorithms may take advantage of the storage structure to exclude portions of the library from consideration without affecting recall. Ideally, in order to preserve recall, they must ensure that no excluded portion of the library contains any relevant assets. Again, we may use a five-value rating scale rather than a numeric scale, where *VH* stands for an exhaustive coverage and *VL* stands for a very selective coverage.

- *Time Complexity per Match.* The time complexity of a match measures the number of computation steps that are required to match the query against a library asset; we represent this measure by the $O(N)$ notation, where N is some measure of size of the query. To simplify comparisons, we define the following scale for this measure:

Very Low	Low	Medium	High	Very High
Constant	Linear	Polynomial	Exponential	Unbounded

This measure, along with coverage ratio, can be used together to estimate the time performance of a retrieval algorithm.

- *Logical Complexity per Match.* The performance of a retrieval method has to be considered against the complexity of performing a match under this method; the more complex the match, the more one would expect from the method (in terms, e.g., of precision and recall). Also, the logical complexity of a retrieval method is important because it is a determining factor of the method's automation potential. We derive a five-value rating scale for logical complexity:

Very Low	Low	Medium	High	Very High
Simple boolean	Compound boolean	Simple predicate	Compound predicate	Second-order predicate

- *Automation/Automation Potential.* An important criterion in the success of a storage and retrieval method is the potential that the method be automated. We derive a five-value rating scale to this effect:

Very Low	Low	Medium	High	Very High
Nonautomatable	Requires a major effort	Requires a nontrivial effort	Automatable with some effort	Trivially automatable

16.1.2.2 Managerial Criteria

We identify the following managerial criteria, which we use subsequently to assess storage–retrieval methods.

- *Investment Cost.* This criterion reflects the cost of setting up a software library that implements the proposed method, prorated to the size of the library. Because we expect that the largest portion of this cost stems from manpower effort, we propose to measure the cost in person-months. To prorate this cost to the library size, we measure the criterion in terms of

$$\frac{\text{person-months}}{1000 \text{ assets}}$$

If we encounter a situation where there are nonnegligible costs that are not manpower-related, we may include them using an estimate of conversion factor (e.g., \$10,000 is equivalent to one person-month). In the absence of precise quantitative data, we may use a five-value rating scale where *VL* refers to a very low investment cost (can be amortized in the short run, even with limited use) and *VH* refers to a very high investment cost (can be amortized only under the condition of intensive long term use).

- *Operating Cost.* This criterion reflects the yearly cost of operating a software library, prorated to the size of the library. For the reasons that we discussed above, we represent this cost in person months; because time appears in both the numerator and the denominator of our ratio, it can actually be canceled, and we are left with a ratio of full-time software person (FSP; see Boehm [1981]) per 1000 assets:

$$\frac{\text{FSP}}{1000 \text{ assets}}$$

If we encounter a situation where there are non-negligible costs that are not manpower-related, we may include them using an estimate of conversion factor (\$10,000 per month is equivalent to one FSP). In the absence of precise quantitative data, we may use a five-value rating scale where *VL* refers to a very low operating cost (a fraction of a full-time software person for a large library) and *VH* refers to a very high operating cost (more than one full-time software person for a few hundred components).

- *Pervasiveness.* This criterion reflects the extent to which the proposed method is used in research and development. The five-value rating scale that we propose for this criterion is as follows:

Very Low	Low	Medium	High	Very High
Not used	Barely used	Some use	Widely used	Routine use

- *State of Development.* This criterion reflects the state of development of the method at hand: whether it is a mere speculative idea or a fully operational industrial product. The five-value rating scale that we propose for this criterion is as follows:

Very Low	Low	Medium	High	Very High
Speculative idea	Laboratory prototype	Experimental product	Industrial product	Fully supported supported product

16.1.2.3 Human Criteria

We identify two human criteria that we can use to evaluate storage and retrieval methods for software libraries.

- *Difficulty of Use.* We derive the following five-rating scale to assess difficulty of use.

Very Low	Low	Medium	High	Very High
Trivial	Easy	Nontrivial	Difficult	Very difficult

- *Transparency.* This criterion reflects to what extent the operation of the asset library depends on an understanding of how the retrieval algorithm works. This criterion overlaps to some extent with *difficulty of use*, but also differs from it in the following sense: The more transparent the algorithm, the easier it is to modify the implementation algorithm without affecting users. We have derived the following five-value rating scale to assess transparency:

Very Low	Low	Medium	High	Very High
Detailed knowledge	Good knowledge	Some cognizance	Slight cognizance	Perfect transparency

16.1.3 Characterizing a Storage–Retrieval Method

Methods for the storage and retrieval of software assets in software libraries abound in the field. In order to understand these methods and have a sound basis for comparing them, we introduce a classification method that allows us to characterize each method by a number of (nearly) orthogonal features. These features are presented and discussed in this section.

- *Nature of the Asset.* The most important feature of a software library is, of course, the nature of assets that are stored therein. The most typical asset is code (whether source code or executable code), but other kinds of assets are also possible, such as specifications, designs, test data, and documentation. Some library methods are restrictive, in the sense that they work for a single kind of asset, whereas others may work for a wide range of assets.

- *Scope of the Library.* Another crucial feature of a software library is the scope of the library: whether the library is expected to be used within a single project, within an organization, or on a larger scale. In order to use a software library effectively, a reuser must share some common knowledge with the maintainer of the library (pertaining, e.g., to the interpretation of terminology, the representation of assets, the form and meaning of error messages), and with other users. If this common knowledge is general (so that any reuser is likely to have it), then one expects the library to have a large scope; the more specialized this knowledge, the smaller the scope.

- *Query Representation.* A software library can be characterized by the form that queries submitted to the library must take. Among possible options we may mention: a formal functional specification, a signature specification, a behavioral sample, a natural-language query, or a set of keywords.

- *Asset Representation.* The representation of assets is an important feature of a library, not only because it dictates what form user queries take but also because it determines how retrieval is performed. In a perfectly transparent library, the representation of an asset is irrelevant to the user, but no library is perfectly transparent. Among the possible values of this attribute, we mention formal specifications, signature specifications, a set of keywords, the source text, the executable code, and requirements documentation.

- *Storage Structure.* The most common storage structure in software libraries is *no structure* at all; software assets are stored side by side with no meaningful ordering between them. Whereas in traditional database systems entries are ordered by their identifying keys, it is difficult to define a general key that can be used to order software assets in a meaningful way. There are some exceptions; some libraries that are based on formal specifications order assets by the refinement ordering between their specifications, and AI-based software libraries define semantic links between assets.

- *Navigation Scheme.* This attribute is correlated to that of *storage structure*, because to a large extent, the storage structure determines the navigation scheme. In flat storage structures, the only possible pattern of navigation is the brute-force exhaustive search of all the entries. Whenever the assets are arranged on some nontrivial structure, this structure can be used to help orient the search toward those assets that are most likely to satisfy the query—and steer it clear of those that are known to be irrelevant or are thought unlikely to be relevant.

- *Retrieval Goal.* To fix our ideas, we discuss this feature in the context when the library assets are programs. In principle, the goal of a retrieval operation is to find one or several programs that are correct with respect to a given query. If this retrieval operation fails to turn up candidate programs, one may want to perform another retrieval operation, with the lesser ambition of finding programs that approximate the query, with the expectation that we must modify the (selected) retrieved programs. Depending on whether we are interested in generative modification or compositional modification, the goal of the retrieval operation changes considerably. Under generative modification, we are interested in programs whose design can be adapted to solve the query; under compositional modification, we are interested in programs whose components can be combined to solve the query.
- *Relevance Criterion.* The relevance criterion defines under what conditions a library asset is considered to be relevant for the submitted query with respect to the predefined retrieval goal. For example, if the query is a functional specification and the retrieval goal is correctness with respect to the query, then the relevance criterion is that the library asset be correct with respect to the submitted query.
- *Matching Condition.* The matching condition is the condition that we choose to check between the submitted query and a candidate library asset to decide whether the asset is relevant. Ideally, the matching condition should be equivalent to the relevance criterion, but this is not always so; if the asset's surrogate (the representation of the asset) is too abstract, and/or if the relevance criterion is too intractable, these two criteria may differ significantly.

To summarize this section, in Table 16.1 we present a table of all the attributes discussed above, along with a tentative (not necessarily exhaustive) indication of the values that each attribute may take.

16.1.4 Exercises

1. (A) Give an example of compositional modification and an example of generative modification.

2. (B) Consider the six technical criteria that we use to assess storage and retrieval methods. Identify and discuss correlations between pairs of such criteria; for example, discuss in what sense we can consider that precision and recall are correlated.

3. (A) Characterize a storage–retrieval method that is easy to use but not transparent, and one that is difficult to use but perfectly transparent.

TABLE 16.1   Attributes of a Software Library

Attributes	Characterization
Nature of asset	Source code, executable code, requirements specification, design description, test data, documentation, proof
Scope of usage	Within a project, across a program, across a product line, across multiple product lines, worldwide
Query representation	Functional specification, signature specification, keyword list, design pattern, behavioral sample
Asset representation	Functional specification, signature specification, source code, executable code, requirements documentation, keywords
Storage structure	Flat structure, hypertext links, refinement ordering, ordering by genericity
Navigation scheme	Exhaustive linear scan, navigation hypertext links, navigating refinement relations
Retrieval goal	Correctness, functional proximity, structural proximity
Relevance criterion	Correctness, signature matching, minimizing functional distance, minimizing structural distance
Matching criterion	Correctness formula, signature identity, signature refinement, equality and subsumption of keywords, natureal-language analysis, pattern recognition

4. (A) In what sense are the features *storage structure* and *navigation scheme* correlated? In what sense are these features orthogonal?

5. (A) Use an example to illustrate the difference between *retrieval goal* and *relevance criterion*. Use an example to illustrate the difference between *relevance criterion* and *matching condition*.

6. (C) Consider two retrieval methods, say, M_0, M_1, whose precision and recall are respectively p_0, p_1 and q_0, q_1.

   (a) Derive the precision and recall of the method that consists in applying M_0 first, then applying M_1 to the output of M_0.

   (b) Consider the four cases that may arise from comparing the precisions of the methods and their recalls, and discuss in which order the methods must be applied if we wish to maximize precision.

   (c) Same question, if we wish to maximize recall.

7. (B) Consider two methods, as in problem 6 above. Derive the precision and recall of the method that consists in selecting all the components that are retrieved simultaneously by both methods.

8. (B) Consider two methods, as in problem 6. Derive the precision and recall of the method that consists in selecting all the components that are retrieved by at least one of the methods.

16.2 CLASSIFYING SOFTWARE ASSETS FOR STORAGE AND RETRIEVAL

16.2.1 Obstacles to Software Assets Classification

To the same extent that software assets classification is critical to success, the ability to store, classify, and retrieve software assets is also notoriously difficult. Cataloging nonsoftware assets for convenient classification and retrieval is generally easy, and is widely supported by a wide range of efficient, finely tuned, technologies. The cataloging of software assets is, however, quite another matter, for the following reasons:

- *Software assets are very information-rich.* A software asset cannot be fully characterized unless we have information about its function, its structure, its input and its output formats, its interaction protocols, its architectural assumptions, its system requirements, its hardware requirements, its compiler requirements (if it is in source form), its operational characteristics, its resource requirements, the design information that it embodies, and other attributes. Each attribute has a wide (potentially infinite) range of possible values, hence making classification virtually impossible. In addition, the number of relevant attributes and the width of each attribute create such a large and unwieldy search space that matching between a query and an asset is also virtually impossible. Generally, it is possible to control complexity by means of the tried-and-true device of abstraction; but the next premise seems to rule out this possibility.

- *Software assets can be arbitrarily similar.* Two software assets residing in the same repository can be arbitrarily similar. This arises whenever the same repository contains successive versions of the same product, platform-specific versions of some product, or other variations of the same product. The representation of these assets must be sufficiently detailed to reflect such differences, and retrieval algorithms must be sufficiently precise to recognize these differences. This precludes liberal use of abstraction mechanisms to control complexity.

- *Lack of meaningful relations between assets.* Structure is a prerequisite for organized search in a large space. Traditionally, two devices can be used to structure large catalogs for the purpose of classification and retrieval:

  An Equivalence Relation. When the catalog is structured by an equivalence class, the retrieval proceeds by first identifying a class, then identifying an asset within the class. Examples of such a structure include a department store catalog, the Yellow Pages, or (perhaps more relevant) a catalog of hardware components; the table of contents of these catalogs lists the equivalence classes.

  An Ordering Relation. When the catalog is structured by an ordering relation, the retrieval proceeds by inspecting assets in a predefined order until we find an asset that matches the query or determine (halfway through the catalog) that no asset that satisfies the query can be found beyond the current position (hence no asset that satisfies the query can be found in the catalog). Examples of such a structure include a bookstore's catalog, ordered by ISBN numbers.

The trouble with software assets is that they do not lend themselves to an equivalence structuring nor (much less) to an order-based structuring. It is possible, in some limited cases (e.g., a catalog of common datatypes), to partition the set of assets in an equivalence like manner (e.g., the stacks, the queues, the heaps); it is virtually impossible to apply this pattern to general sets of software assets (that stem from arbitrary domains, from an arbitrary combination of heterogeneous domains, from an arbitrary collections of assets). Also, the fact that assets range over a continuum of functionality means that a given asset may partake on (hence share common properties with) more than one partition—which precludes transitivity (a prerequisite for equivalence).

It is equally unrealistic to define a meaningful ordering relation among arbitrary software assets. One could possibly define an ordering based on the subsumption relation (that some component is more general than another, has more functional features, etc.)—but this deals with only one attribute (functionality) of software assets, and is a sparse ordering (i.e., has few arcs) for arbitrary collections of assets. One could also conceivably assign arbitrary numeric identifiers to assets and order them according to the numeric ordering of their identifiers. The difficulty with this option is, of course, that one cannot expect users to submit their queries in terms of numeric identifiers—most typically, queries take the form of combinations of requirements.

As a result of these premises (and perhaps others), there is no generally accepted solution to the crucial problem of storing, classifying, and retrieving software assets for the purpose of software reuse. This matter has been the subject of active research since the mid-1980s and has generated many sophisticated ideas, but few practical general solutions. On the other hand, practitioners have been relying primarily on low-tech solutions, that offer no measurable quality of service guarantees.

16.2.2 Issues in Software Storage and Retrieval

In this section, we analyze issues that arise in the design of a scheme for software storage and retrieval. This analysis is intended to enable the reader to assess and compare storage and retrieval schemes.

- *Assets that Abstract a Function.* What gives these assets their worth is the function that they compute, and the service that this function renders in host systems. Archetypical examples of such assets are mathematical routines (e.g., in FORTRAN) and ADT implementations (e.g., in Ada); there is some debate whether these should be considered instances of reuse or merely extensions of the programming language, but we will adopt the first view, for the sake of this example. The user of such assets has no cognizance of their structure, and uses them on the basis of their advertised function.

- *Assets that Abstract a Structure.* What makes these assets worthwhile is the structure they have, and the problem-solving experience that this structure embodies. Archetypical examples of such assets include programming cliches [Rich 1898], design patterns [Buschmann et al. 1996, Gamma et al. 1994, Pree 1995], and requirements cliches [Reubenstein and Waters 1991].

This dichotomy has a profound impact on many aspects of software reuse, which we discuss in turn below.

- *How Assets Are Represented.* An asset that embodies a function should be represented by a function that abstracts its most relevant functional (semantic) properties, whereas an asset that embodies a structure should be represented in a way that highlights its relevant structural (syntactic) properties.

- *How Assets Are Matched.* An asset that embodies a function is matched against a query by testing its functional properties against the functional requirements of the query, using some form of subsumption or equivalence relation. Matching an asset that embodies a structure is totally different, in terms of both how the query is represented and how the asset is analyzed to determine its relevance with respect to the query.

- *How Assets Are Developed.* Design for blackbox reuse is primarily a specification issue, and is determined by the generality of the asset's specification and the genericity of its implementation. Design for whitebox reuse is primarily a design issue, and is determined by such design qualities as modularity, simplicity, and structuredness. Lifecycles of design for reuse to depend a great deal on which reuse policy the asset is designed for (blackbox vs. whitebox).

- *How Assets Are (Re)used.* By definition, assets that embody a function may only be used for blackbox reuse, where the user has no cognizance of the internal structure of the asset. Assets that embody a structure may or may not have a function associated with them; typically, they are geared toward whitebox reuse.

16.2.3   Classifying Software Libraries

Using the attributes listed in Table 16.1, we have divided the existing library organizations into six classes, which we will discuss in the sequel. Each class corresponds to a distinct pattern of attribute values and includes all the library organizations that fit the pattern; whenever we discuss a class, we present the pattern of attributes that characterize it. We have identified six classes of storage–retrieval methods, which we present below, in the order of increasing technological sophistication.

- *Information Retrieval Methods.* These methods depend on a textual analysis of software assets. It is important to acknowledge that the storage and retrieval of software assets is simply a specialized instance of information storage and retrieval. Hence it is important to discuss these methods, and possibly highlight their shortcomings. If traditional information retrieval methods were adequate in dealing with software assets, there would be little incentive to investigate other methods.

- *Descriptive Methods.* These methods depend on a textual description of software assets. While information retrieval methods represent assets by their source text, descriptive methods rely on an abstract surrogate of the asset, typically a set of keywords, or a set of facet definitions. This has a profound impact on the design as well as the performance of retrieval algorithms.

- *Operational Semantics Methods.* These methods depend on the operational semantics of software assets; they can be applied to executable code, and proceed by matching candidate assets against a user query on the basis of the candidates' behavior on sample inputs. These constitute an elaboration on information retrieval methods, in the sense that they exploit a unique feature of software assets, namely, their executability.

- *Denotational Semantics Methods.* These methods depend on the denotational semantic definition of software assets; unlike operational methods, denotational methods can be applied to non-executable assets (such as specifications). They proceed by checking a semantic relation between the user query and a surrogate of the candidate asset. The surrogate of the software asset can be a complete functional description, a partial functional description, or a signature of the asset.

- *Topological Methods.* The main discriminating feature of topological methods is their goal, which is to identify library assets that minimize some measure of distance to the user query. This feature, in turn, has an impact on the relevance criterion, and hence on the matching condition; whether an asset is relevant cannot be decided by considering the query and the candidate asset alone, since the outcome depends on a comparison with other assets.

- *Structural Methods.* The main discriminating feature of structural methods is the nature of the software asset they are dealing with. Typically, they do not retrieve executable code, but rather program patterns, which are subsequently instantiated to fit the user's needs. This feature, in turn, has a profound impact on the representation of queries and assets, as well as on the relevance criterion, which deals with the structure of assets and queries rather than their function.

16.2.4 Exercises

1. Consider bibliographic references dealing with *information retrieval* methods; see those cited in Section 16.3 (below), as well as more recent references.

   (a) Produce a characterization of this family of methods, by filling out the Table 16.2.

   (b) Produce an assessment of this family of methods, by filling out Table 16.3.

2. Same exercise, for *descriptive methods*.

3. Same exercise, for *operational methods*.

4. Same exercise, for *denotational methods*.

TABLE 16.2   Summary Characterization

Attributes	Characterization
Nature of asset	
Scope of usage	
Query representation	
Asset representation	
Storage structure	
Navigation scheme	
Retrieval goal	
Relevance criterion	
Matching criterion	

TABLE 16.3   Summary of Assessment

Technical						Managerial				Human	
Precision	Recall	Covariance Ratio	Time compliance	Logical compliance	Automation	Inventory cost	Operation cost	Pervasiveness	Development state	Difference of use	Transparency

5. Same exercise, for *topological methods*.

6. Same exercise, for *structural methods*.

16.3 FURTHER READING

The most natural techniques to apply to the problem of software asset storage and retrieval are, naturally, information retrieval techniques. Understandably, the earliest techniques were based on information retrieval ideas. These include work by Frakes and Nejmeh [1987a, 1987b], Maarek and co-workers [Maarek and Berry 1989, Maarek et al. 1991], and Helm and Maarek [1991]. More software-specific approaches, encompassing a wide range of assets, were taken by Maiden and Sutcliffe [Maiden and Sutcliffe 1992, 1993, 1994; Maiden et al. 1995]. Devanbu et al. [1991] borrow techniques from knowledge engineering and artificial intelligence to build a knowledge base that contains PBX (public branch exchange) software assets. The work of Clifton and Li [1995] as well as that of Mittermeir and Lydia [1995] can be considered as instances of information retrieval methods. It is reasonable to consider that hypertext methods are specialized forms of traditional information retrieval methods; they differ by their ability to deal with multimedia documents, and their ability to work across computing sites. The work of Lucarella and Zanzi [1996] fits this characterization. Other hypertext approaches include the works of Isakowitz and Kaufmann [1996] and Poulin and Werkman [1995]. Poulin and Werkman [1995] describe a reusable software library (RSL) interface and a search tool using Mosaic. ASSET (Asset Source for Software Engineering Technology) [ASSET 1993] is a software library organized by the Advanced Research Projects Agency (ARPA) under the STARS program.

Descriptive methods are based on the observation that the simplest way to describe an asset is to attach to it a (set of) keyword(s) [Matsumoto 1993]. The approach most widely discussed in the reuse literature of descriptive methods is the *faceted approach* introduced by Prieto-Diaz [1985, 1991] and Prieto-Diaz and Freeman [1987]. Related to the faceted approach is the notion of the four-dimensional classification cube proposed by Mittermeir and Rossak [1987, 1990] and Hochmueller [1992]. Another extension of the basic concepts of keyword-based classification is classification by weighted term spaces or by fuzzy relations [Karlsson 1995].

Operational methods are based on the simple observation, first made by Podgurski and Pierce [1992, 1993] that a software component can be uniquely identified within a large software library on the basis of its behavior on few randomly selected sample inputs. R. J. Hall [1993] discusses a number of weaknesses in the basic behavioral sampling (BS) technique of Podgurski and Pierce [1992], and proposes means to cope with them. Atkinson and Duke [1995] combine the behavioural sampling idea of Podgurksi and Pierce [1992] with the lattice structuring idea of Mili et al. [1994] to produce a software library organization for the storage and retrieval of classes, in the sense of object oriented programming. Chou et al. [1996] present a behavior-based storage and retrieval technique for object-oriented software components. Park and Bais [1997] introduce a version of behavioral sampling where input samples are neither statistically selected (as in the Podgurski–Pierce [1992] paper) nor user-selected (as in Hall's [1993] paper); rather, they are selected on the basis of an inductive argument on the input domain.

Denotational methods are based on a semantic representation of software assets; retrieval takes place by matching the semantic representation against a similarly denoted query. Perry and Popovich [Perry 1989, Perry and Popovich 1993] introduce a prototype of a software library, where software assets are represented by predicates that define their main functional features and interface characteristics. Rittri [1989] proposes a method for software component storage and retrieval that applies to modules written in a functional language and is based on signature matching. Rittri later [1992] improves the recall of his method by weakening the matching condition. Runciman and Toyn [1989] propose a similar solution, which uses polymorphic type systems to define criteria of signature matching in the context of functional programming, and provides independence of the number of arguments. Rollins and Wing [1989] present a software library of ML (machine language) components whose specifications are written in λ-PROLOG following a Larch-like [Guttag et al. 1985] two-tiered approach; they use λ-PROLOG's inference capability to automate component retrieval. Gaudel and Moineau [Moineau and Gaudel 1991, Moineau and Gaudel 1991] introduce a *theory of software reusability* on the basis of algebraic specifications of software components that implement abstract data types. Moineau and Gaudel [1991] illustrate the proposed theory by means of an operational system for component retrieval, called *ReuSig*, which deals exclusively with signature matching aspects. A specialized version of this system, which deals with Ada components, is discussed in another paper [Badaro and Moineau 1991] under the name *ROSE-Ada*. Cheng and Jeng [1992a], discuss an organization of a software library that is based on formal specifications of components and queries. Their software library is organized into a two-layered hierarchy by means of a clustering algorithm, where the top layer places together related software components. Chang and Jeng extended their work later that year [Cheng and Jeng 1992b] by investigating matching criteria that attempt to minimize measures of distance between the query at hand and candidate library components, and they extended it further 3 years later [Jeng and Cheng 1995] by defining matching criteria between components, and between methods. Boudriga et al. [1992] discuss the design of a software library based on relational specifications of components and queries, and on an ordering of library components by a refinement ordering relation. An experimental prototype of this design is given by Mili et al. [1994]. Steigerwald [1992] discusses a system that is geared toward prototyping real-time embedded systems. Zaremski and Wing [1993, 1995a] discuss signature matching as a mechanism for retrieving software components from a software library.

Zaremski and Wing [1993, 1995b] extend their work on signature matching by investigating specification matching. Penix and Alexander [1995] advocate a formal specification-based, domain-theory-oriented, approach to software component retrieval. They extend their work the next year [Penix and Alexander 1996] by considering a variety of matching criteria and refining the definition of features. Recognizing that most specification matching algorithms fail to perform satisfactorily in practice, due to the bottleneck of theorem proving, Fischer et al. [1995] propose a stepwise filtering procedure that starts with high recall and low precision, and ends with high precision and low recall. While all software libraries discussed so far deal with executable software components, the library of Massonet and Van Lamsweerde [1997] contains requirements specifications. To the extent that they can be considerd as *software assets*, theorem proofs can be considered as possible entries of software libraries; Ihrig and Kambhampati [1995] and Kolbe and Walther [1995] discuss organizations of libraries of proofs.

Topological methods are charecterized by the fact that they retrieve assets by minimizing some measure of distance to the query. Ostertag et al. [1992] present an AI-based library system which is based on a hybrid approach, including the faceted index approach [Prieto-Diaz 1990] and the semantic network approach [Wood and Sommerville 1988, Devanbu et al. 1991]. This system retrieves assets that minimize the estimated adaptation effort required to adapt the asset to satisfy the query. Spanoudakis and Constantopoulos [1993, 1994] introduce a conceptual modeling language, which they use to represent queries and assets, and define a measure of structural distance between queries and assets. Girardi and Ibrahim [1994a, 1994b] introduce a structural measure of distance between software assets, and use it to perform retrieval in a software library. Penix and Alexander [1995, 1996] discuss a formal specification-based method for the storage and retrieval of software components in a software library. In order to improve the recall of their method, they make provisions for approximate retrieval whenever exact retrieval fails to produce assets, or produces too few. Faustle et al. [1996] propose a classification and retrieval method for object oriented repositories, based on the use of fuzzy logic. Labed Jilani et al. [1997] present four measures of semantic distance that refelect four different interpretations of what it means for a component to approximate a query. Components and queries are represented by relational specifications, and the measures of distance take their values in a partially ordered set (rather than the set of real numbers).

Structural methods select library assets, not on the basis of their function, but rather on the basis of their structure and/or their design. Beginning in 1976, Rich and colleagues [Rich and Schrobe 1976, 1978; Rich and Waters 1990; Waters 1981, 1982] discuss a long-term research project titled *The Programmer's Apprentice*. From a retrieval standpoint, this project is interesting because it includes a library of programming cliches, which are symbolic representations of structural features of software assets. Building on the results achieved with the *Programmer's Apprentice*, Rich and Waters [1988] discuss research ideas towards the *Design Apprentice*. Reubenstein and Waters [1991] present the *Requirements Apprentice*, an automated assistant for requirements acquisition. Paul and Prakash [1994] discuss the retrieval of source code from a software library using structural information. They define a sophisticated language-dependent notation to represent structural patterns of source code, and define a pattern matching mechanism that determines whether a piece of source code matches a given pattern. This chapter is drawn from a survey of software libraries presented by Mili et al. [1998].

Chapter 17

Reusable Asset Integration

Application engineering with reusable assets involves the search and retrieval of reusable assets that satisfy a specified set of requirements, which was discussed in the previous chapter, followed by the integration of those assets into the system at hand. Chapters 11 and 12 discussed a number of techniques for packaging reusable object-oriented components in a way that makes this integration cost-effective and quality preserving. Chapter 13 showed some examples of well-packaged reusable assets (application frameworks) in the graphical user interfaces domain, and Chapter 14 discussed examples of integration infrastructures, both of which draw on the techniques presented in Chapters 11 and 12. However, these techniques do not solve all of the integration problems, nor should we expect all reusable software to be packaged according to those techniques. In this chapter, we look at the integration problem from the viewpoint of the application engineer, whether the proper abstraction and composability mechanisms have been built into the components or not.

We start by discussing the various reusable asset integration paradigms. Recall that reusability is the combination of two properties: *usefulness* and *usability*. To be equally usable (usable with same amount of effort) across their range of usefulness, reusable assets need to be stored in a parameterized, non–fully realized form. Reusable asset integration then consists of two distinct steps: (1) *asset (component) instantiation*, which consists of deriving a usage-specific concrete realization of the reusable asset (Section 17.1); and (2) *asset composition*, which consists of composing the newly instantiated concrete realization into the application at hand (Section 17.2). Next, we discuss general issues related to the reliance on reusable software for the development of new applications. Our discussion is, for the most part, independent of the reuse paradigm along the compositional versus generative dimension. In particular, we make no distinction between general component-based software development, COTS-based development, or product-line engineering; paradigm-specific issues are discussed in Chapters 21 and 22. For the purposes of this chapter, we will use the terms *software asset* or *software component* (or simply *component*) interchangeably. However, the reader should be aware that in Chapter 21, the term *software component* will take on a special meaning and refer to a specific packaging of reusable software assets.

17.1   ASSET INSTANTIATION PARADIGMS

Recall the anatomy of a reusable component, shown in Chapter 7, which we reproduced in Figure 17.1. Component instantiation consists of selecting a concrete realization for the fixed part, among the ones available in the reuse repository, and providing an implementation of the variable part, either by selecting among variants in the repository, or by providing one variant, one way or another.

Note that a good packaging, that is, a clean separation of the fixed part from the variable part, makes it possible to instantiate a reusable asset without modifying it in any way. However, depending on whether the intended use was a preplanned one, and the range of variation, instantiation may involve a range of techniques, from a simple selection among library variants, to the specification of some generation parameters, to actually writing code by "filling in the blanks" at predetermined places in the asset. The different instantiation mechanisms have different cost profiles, and can be more or less semantic-preserving. Of course, our preference would be for a free, semantic-preserving component instantiation mechanism! However, the cost of developing such reusable assets usually stands in the way of achieving effortless and semantically correct instantiations. We review the range of techniques below.

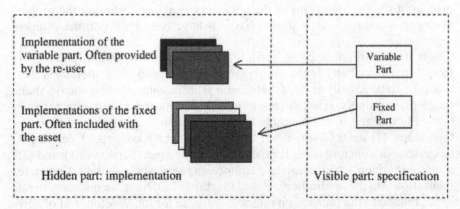

FIGURE 17.1   Anatomy of a reusable component.

17.1.1 Component Selection

We include component selection for the sake of completeness. In this case, the reuse repository comes with a variety of implementations that are semantically and behaviorally equivalent, and the reuser has to select one of the implementations. We have all downloaded freeware from a WB site, and had to select executables based on supported platforms. In this case, the reusable component provider has gone through the trouble of generating all the variants that are needed, and component instantiation is effortless in this case. Other instances of selection include selecting among various releases of the same reusable component. This is an issue only to the extent that we need to record such dependencies for proper configuration management (see Chapter 5 and Section 17.3.2).

17.1.2 Component Generation

With component generation, the reusable component consists of a generic template and a generator. The reuser specifies values for the template parameters, and the generator produces a usage-specific version of the reusable component. In Chapter 11, we reviewed various component generation techniques, including generic classes, metaprogramming, and metaclass programming. With generic classes, the template is merely the generic class (generic package, in Ada, class template in C++), and the generator is simply the underlying programming language compiler. Visual editors are also generators in the sense that they translate spatial relationships between graphical objects laid on its canvas (high-level input) into actual code that implements the software analog of these spatial relationships.

In terms of instantiation effort, component generation is rather inexpensive. In terms of semantic correctness, the generated code is typically correct by construction—although formally proving that it is may be an intractable mathematical problem. In this sense, component generation is an ideal reuse technology. However, building generators is a costly proposition, and for this reason, generators are usually limited to well-circumscribed and well-understood domains. And as mentioned in Chapter 15, generation is usually the last evolutionary step in reuse technology.

17.1.3 Component Specialization

To create an application-specific component from a generic component using specialization, the user extends an existing functionality at a given point of entry (also called *hotspot* in framework parlance). Entry points for specialization may be

- *Partial Implementation.* Some library components could be developed to implement some behavior but provides interfaces for other behavior without implementing them. For example, if the component is a C++ class, some methods of the class are implemented and other methods are left for the reuser to implement. In this case, the user implements a partially abstract component.

- *Overriding*. Some library components provide default implementation for the entire behavior of the component. The implementation language that is used to develop the library component could have support for overriding mechanisms. For example, in Java the application-specific class could inherit from a library class and the user could override a (non-final) default behavior of one or more of its methods.

- *Plug-ins*. Developers add functions to coarse-grained components by writing plug-ins. A plug-in registers its services with the component. The component calls the plug-in whenever its services are required.

As shown in Chapter 10 and Section 11.2.1, partial implementation and overriding are fraught with danger because there is no easy way of enforcing semantic conformance of the partial implementation (or the override) to the intent of the component. Kiczales and Lamping [1992] have shown that, in the context of object-oriented libraries, documenting the interfaces of the various classes is utterly insufficient to guarantee proper extension of class libraries. This is less of a problem with plug-ins, since the code of plug-ins is not supposed to call the code of the host component.

We should mention that component specialization is the overriding mechanism for component instantiation in object-oriented software development. Further, depending on the granularity of the reusable asset, one or more instantiation mechanisms may be used. In particular, framework instantiation (see Section 13.2) typically involves a mix of these mechanisms.

17.2 ASSET COMPOSITION PARADIGMS

Chapter 12 dealt thoroughly with composition techniques, from the component provider perspective. We studied language-level support for composability as well as design patterns and novel packaging techniques. In this section, we look at the composability problem from the perspective of the component reuser. We first discuss composition scenarios, going from the perfect case where a reusable component has the right functionality and interface, to the worst-case and all-too-common scenario where a reusable component supports (most of) the right functionality, but does not necessarily have the right interface. In Section 17.2.2, we discuss a range of composition mechanisms, by highlighting their strengths and weaknesses.

17.2.1 Composability Scenarios

Assume that we want to integrate two instantiated components together, that is, make them interact with each other in a given application. For the purposes of the discussion of component interaction, we use the following terms:

- *A solicitor (client)*—the component that has the current execution control and is initiating a request for a particular service.
- *A provider (server)*—the component that is called to provide a certain service through the execution of some procedures (methods).

This distinction is merely a tool that is useful for analyzing component interactions and for pinpointing the obligations and expectations of the various components within a system. However, we shouldn't assume that the client is the application code and the server is the reusable asset code; as we know, with application frameworks (Chapter 13), the reusable code usually "calls" the application-specific code (the Hollywood principle). In fact, components are always described in terms of the interfaces that they support, and in terms of the interfaces that they require, and so they typically play both roles vis-à-vis different parts of an application.

We identify four composability scenarios, discussed below:

Scenario 1: Exact Match. The provider has exactly the functionality and interfaces required by the solicitor (see Fig. 17.2).

This ideal situation requires no effort on the part of the reuser beyond writing the client program. In some cases, the client program may even be written in terms of an abstract provider (server), and the binding of the actual provider to the abstract provider becomes simply a matter of loading the right implementation in the runtime environment. Depending on the technology used, this may mean loading the class file (in Java; see Chapter 11 for examples of dynamic class loading and instantiation), loading the DLL (e.g., in a Windows environment) programmatically, or registering a COM component that implements a particular interface (see Chapter 14).

Scenario 2: Extra Services. The provider has more services than needed by the solicitor but the required services are exactly matched (see Fig. 17.3).

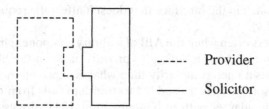

Provider

Solicitor

FIGURE 17.2 A symbolic diagram for exact-match pattern.

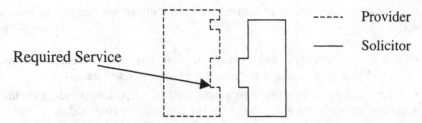

Required Service

- - - - - Provider

———— Solicitor

FIGURE 17.3   A symbolic diagram for extra service pattern.

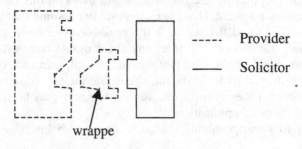

- - - - - Provider

———— Solicitor

wrappe

FIGURE 17.4   A symbolic diagram for a modifiable provider.

This is the equally trouble free case since there is no composition overhead. In Java, the "implements" relation between classes and interfaces "transfers-through" the extends relationship between interfaces, meaning that if class A implements interface I_1 and interface I_1 extends interface I_2, then A implements I_2 as well. The same for COM components (see Section 14.5). This is generally not a problem except for configuration management purposes; other clients may use the extra services from the same component, and one should not assume that if one client is okay with a replacement (e.g., down to an earlier version that implements just the required services), the others should be, too. When the reusable assets are source code components, extra functionality may also hurt because of executable footprint and general performance considerations (memory consumption, computational overhead).

Scenario 3: Modified Services. The provider has to be modified to provide the exact-match interface of the solicitor; this usually occurs in case of slight mismatch in the interface that doesn't affect the requested services (see Fig. 17.4).

This occurs often when the API of a library component has more parameters than the client is willing to provide or when the library component API has a finer granularity than what is expected by the client. An additional software layer is added to translate calls from one format to another. The adapter pattern [Gamma et al. 1995], discussed in Section

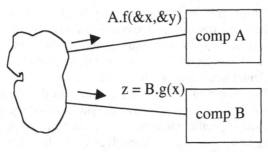

FIGURE 17.5 Gluing.

12.4, handles this kind of situation. There is composition overhead in this case, but the composition code is fairly straightforward, and may even be generated.

Scenario 4: Complementary Services. In the first three scenarios, the solicitor (client) performs a function that is useful for the application at hand, and to perform that function, it needs the services of the (provider). In this scenario, the functionality that we wish to support is not part of the API of the solicitor, and we must compose two components by writing glue code that combines the functionalities of the components. This is functional composition in the true sense, and the gluing code is the embodiment of the composite function. A glue example could be a fragment that pulls a request from a component A, changes or reformats it (while maintaining its semantic content), and submits it to another component B. In this particular case, gluing is needed because of incompatibility of control. In Figure 17.5, we assumed that component A supports a function $f(x,y)$ that modifies both input parameters, and we want to call $g(.)$ on x after it has been processed by $A \cdot f(x,y)$; we can't pipe $A \cdot f()$ into $B \cdot g(.)$, we have to write separate code that makes both calls.

This definition of glue is oriented more toward programmatic constructs. In an architectural sense, the glue may not be a code fragment. It can be a construct in an architecture description language to specify the connectors or the connection mechanism between components such as a constraint between the state variables of two components [Allen and Garlan 1997].

17.2.2 Composability Media

17.2.1 Direct Composition
In this category applications are built from components interacting directly with each other. In this case, components are knowledgeable of the existence of other components and their services and directly invoke these services.

Direct composition creates strong interface-level coupling between components, and is generally discouraged. Given n components that must interact with each other, direct composition requires that we support $n \times n = n^2$ interfaces [Mowbray and Zahavi 1995]. In particular, adding a single component may require implementing up to n additional interfaces.

In Chapter 12 we saw a number of design patterns that help reduce interface coupling, either by abstracting away idiosyncrasies of specific implementations (e.g., platform-specific implementations, as with the *adapter* pattern), or by abstracting away interfaces themselves (e.g., the *observer/observable* pattern). For instance, if we standardize component interfaces, we have n interfaces, one per component. To achieve interface standardization, component interactions must be mediated through some sort of software bus. We discussed event-based composition in Chapter 12, and discussed integration frameworks (middleware) in Chapter 14. We revisit and discuss middleware-mediated composition next.

17.2.2.2. Middleware-based Integration

The evolution of component integration technologies such as CORBA, DCOM, and Enterprise Java Beans facilitates the integration of components. When using a middleware for integrating components, the integrator uses an underlying infrastructure that hosts all components. In this case, components don't directly invoke each other through their implementation interfaces, but may invoke each other through publicly published interfaces in a framework-specific services repository. Applications developed on top of CORBA [OMG 1998], DCOM [DCOM 1998] and Enterprise Java Beans fall under this category (see Sections 14.3–14.5). Both CORBA and COM go one step further and make it possible to invoke component functionality through a generic API (called DII, for dynamic invocation interface, in CORBA), making it possible for a component to invoke services during runtime it didn't know about at startup.

17.3   ISSUES IN INTEGRATING COMPONENTS

Developing with reusable assets raises a number of issues that traditional software development does not face. We classify issues in integrating components under the following categories:

Component Issues. These are technical issues as related to components themselves, which include component interfaces, testing, and modeling.

Process Issues. These are issues and problems in the integration process, which include, but are not limited to, intercomponent communication, composition mechanisms, and adaptation techniques.

Quality Issues. These are issues in evaluating the quality (nonfunctional attributes) of components and how the quality attributes of an application can be assessed as components are integrated.

17.3.1 Component Issues

17.3.1.1 Cataloging and Documentation

Several researchers have long tackled the problem of constructing libraries of reusable code assets and defining storage, retrieval, and browsing algorithms. Reuse libraries are thought of as collections of code assets. Components, are not necessarily code assets. Binary components, specification components, and design components are several examples of diverse forms of components. Each component technology has its own library. For instance, Java has its library of SWING components and Java Beans. CORBA implementations are packaged with a set of reusable components implementing common services. Lessons from research in libraries of reusable code assets could be useful in guiding the development of component libraries and creating a component market.

Cataloging and documentation techniques are confronted by configuration management problems such as maintaining several versions (upgrades) of the same component. Understanding the functionality of a component and its behavior is not a trivial problem. Intensive documentation is not a sufficient solution; other solutions such as experimentation with the component, application examples, browsing components (its advertised capability), and recordability (logging component events) could be beneficial [Vigder et al. 1996].

Good component documentation is important for minimizing integration problems. Providing component users with useful reuse documentation, such as component use cases, would make them aware of the benefits and consequences (e.g., adaptation effort) of reusing and selecting a component.

17.3.1.2 Testing and Certification

Several issues arise when certifying a component, mainly the assessment of the testing and certification techniques. Several testing techniques are commonly practiced, for example, blackbox testing, fault injection, and operational system testing [Voas 1998b]. Testing a component includes the vendor side tests and the customer acceptance tests. Other issues include the assessment of the potential errors and effects that a component causes on other components. In case of critical applications (e.g., mission-critical software), a rigorous certification process is conducted on any acquired component [McDermid 1998]. A good component is characterized by having a certificate and a documentation of test cases that are exercised on the component.

In traditional software development, testing is done at the unit level and followed by integration and system testing. In component-based development where components are integrated together, testing becomes more difficult. Components are tested individually by the construction team (viz., domain engineers or by the vendor in case of commercially acquired components). The context in which a component operates changes from one application to another. This might initiate a recertification or re-testing plan for the acquired component depending on the context in which it is used.

17.3.1.3 Managing Upgrades

A good component has few versions and lives through few upgrades. Multiple versions and upgrades raise several issues: how different versions are maintained, whether an upgrade should be considered a new component, and how the upgrade should be performed to maintain compliance with the old version interfaces. The following are possible problems that occur on component upgrade (Chapter 5 further explains management of component upgrades):

- Upgrades may have undesirable extra functionalities.
- Component upgrade may not match the desired upgrade for the application under development.
- Replacing old versions with new versions in current applications is a difficult task.
- System upgrade (e.g., new hardware) may preclude continued usage of older versions.

17.3.2 Process Issues

17.3.2.1 Development Process Model

A simple model for component-based software development is discussed by Brown and Wallnau [1996], extended in another publication [CBSE 1999], and summarized in Chapter 21. This model is a simple reference model for key activities of the development process. As mentioned in Chapter 15, traditional software development models are not applicable to component-based software development because several activities are introduced that are not addressed in traditional models. Component retrieval and composition mechanisms as well as techniques to integrate components are new activities in a component-based development approach (see Chapter 21). The following features are specific for component integration that influences a different process model:

Interface-Centric. The emphasis in component integration is component interfaces because they play the major role in gluing and plugging components together.

Programming Language Dependence. Programming languages provide different techniques to instantiate components and differ in the way a component references another component.

Compositional. The development process is a composition mechanism in which we assemble applications from components rather than develop and implement them from scratch. For component integration, we develop only glue or wrapper codes, which consequently should be minimized.

Separation of Concerns. An application that is developed from components relies heavily on the separation of concerns and functionalities of the individual components. This is required to decrease dependability between components and hence improve the system maintainability.

17.3.2.2 Selection of Components

As mentioned in Chapter 15, traditional development techniques typically work in a top–down fashion where the analysis and design phases lead to specifications of components or software to be developed. However, when we develop with reusable software components, we have to familiarize ourselves with existing components (in-house or commercial) before analyzing the system at hand. The idea here is that with this knowledge, we will try to break the system down into its components along the boundaries of the components that we already have, thereby saving on analysis, design, and development. If all we have is a library of container classes, bottom–up development is not much different from programming in a high(er)-level language. Practically, we cannot build a system from the ground up, just starting with requirements on one hand, and container classes on the other. Accordingly, we usually end up iterating between a top–down approach and a bottom–up approachs. We can do bottom–up system architectural design if the components we are dealing with are subsystem-level components, and not implementations of stack.

Among other things, this means maintaining documentation for reusable assets at different levels of development so that they may be assessed for their appropriateness to synthesize a software system or subsystem. By the same token, we should be open-minded about revising the requirements slightly, if that enables us to put a product on the market a few months ahead of schedule [Bass et al. 1998].

17.3.2.3 Maintenance

A component-based software is developed by integrating a variety of components supplied from heterogeneous sources. Maintaining such software is not a traditional task of determining how maintenance of a function affects another function using conventional impact analysis methods. Maintenance practice becomes harder because of the unavailability of source code, as in the case of using COTS components.

17.3.3 Quality Issues

17.3.3.1 Reliability

Application engineering with reusable components is touted as an approach toward improving application quality and improving software maintainability and reliability by integrating high-quality reusable components. However, ensuring the reliability of a software application is a difficult task, even when pretested and trusted software components are integrated together to develop the application. As a result, several techniques have emerged to estimate and analyze the reliability of applications developed as an assembly of components. These can be categorized as [Yacoub et al. 1999]:

> *System-Level Reliability Estimation.* Reliability is estimated for the application as a whole, for example, using integration testing and/or system level architecture evaluation.
>
> *Component-Based Reliability Estimation.* Application reliability is estimated using the reliabilities of individual components and their interconnection.

The first approach treats the software system as a unit. This approach may not be suitable for applications developed from integrating components because it does not consider compositional and integrative properties of systems and does not accommodate the reliability growth and measurement of individual components. As for the second approach, two issues arise: (1) estimating the reliability of individual components and (2) analyzing the reliability of the application by aggregating the reliabilities of constituting components.

Another problem arises when reusing a component is the severity of modifying the source code, and how these modifications affect the reliability of the component and of the component-based system in general. Models and techniques to analyze and estimate the reliability of component systems are research areas that deserve further attention.

17.3.3.2 Performance

Component-based systems often experience performance degradation when compared to optimized systems developed from scratch. This is a result of using an underlying integration framework or architecture for component interactions or using wrappers and glue code for integration. Even when components interact directly through procedural call, optimization of the performance of the application is not necessarily obtained by optimizing the performance of its individual components, since a different breakdown of functionality may possibly yield a much more efficient implementation.

17.3.3.3 Security

There are several issues related to overall security of an application defined in terms of the security of individual components. There is the issue of modeling component security and how components interaction preserves the security of the overall application. Many software components are designed without factoring in security issues; some other components are developed with strict constraints on security such as firewalls or encryption software. When integrating these components together, the problem arises as to how to assess the overall security of the application. Some issues are related to security risks in component design, procurement, integration, and maintenance [Lindquist and Jonsson 1998]. Other issues are related to types of security risks such as access to unauthorized resources or services, unauthorized access, and abusing authorized privileges [Zhong and Edwards 1998]. Another problem is defining how to prevent security-broken components from compromising the overall application security. A security framework of component-based system security is badly needed.

Part VI

Managerial Aspects of Software Reuse

Software metrics in general and software reuse metrics in particular, allow the software engineer to quantify reuse related processes and products, to define quality goals for processes and products, and to monitor and control the attainment of these goals. We introduce software reuse metrics in Chapter 18, classifying them tentatively into component engineering metrics, domain engineering metrics, application engineering metrics, and finally corprate level metrics. Costs and benefits can be viewed as special cases of metrics; in Chapter 19 we attempt to quantify the component-level costs and benefits associated with reusable assets. In Chapter 20 we use these quantitative metrics to derive an integrated ROI-based model for software reuse. Even though software reuse carries the promise of substantial gains in productivity and quality, its application does not always ensure that gains can actually be achieved. Rather, its potential benefits must be carefully weighted against costs related to its deployment. The ROI models that we discuss in this part are intended to quantify the costs and benefits involved in reuse-related decisions, so as to provide a rational basis for decision making. Also, they highlight what measures need to be taken and what param eters need to be fine-tuned in order to make reuse happen.

Chapter 18

Software Reuse Metrics

Metrics play an important role in software engineering in general, and in software reuse in particular; they allow the engineer to measure quality, to define quality goals, and to monitor the realization of these goals. In this chapter, we give a brief introduction to some salient software engineering metrics, then we focus on software reuse metrics; we discuss in turn metrics related to reusable assets, then metrics related to reuse-based software projects, and finally metrics related to organizations that practice software reuse.

18.1 SOFTWARE ENGINEERING METRICS

Before we discuss reuse-specific metrics, we briefly present an overview of software metrics in general.

18.1.1 Attributes and Metrics

When we discuss software metrics in general, and software reuse metrics in particular, it is important to distinguish between (software) *attributes* and (software) *metrics*. While attributes represent features we are interested in, metrics represents the means we have to quantify these attributes—however partially or however imperfectly. It is important, as we discuss metrics in this chapter, to keep this distinction in focus. To illustrate this distinction, consider the following example. We are interested in the *understandability* of a software component, because we feel that this feature is a good indication of its modifiability and ultimately its reusability (in a whitebox reuse context). We have some analytical evidence, borne out by further empirical evidence, to the effect that the component's volume is significantly correlated to its understandability. Yet it would be wrong to equate understandability with volume, for two reasons:

- *There is more to understandability than volume.* Understandability is dependent not only on complexity (which is reflected by volume, albeit partially) but also on such other features as: the clarity of the asset's structure, the integrity of the asset's design, the adequacy of its comments, and the relevance of its documentation.
- *There is more to volume than understandability.* Volume is correlated not only to understandability but also to such attributes as: complexity, reliability, fault density, and cohesion.

In summary, attributes are the features that we *want* to measure, and metrics are the quantities that we *can* measure. We hope that every attribute can be mapped onto one or more metrics, but this is neither always possible nor, indeed, necessary.

18.1.2 Structural Metrics

Structural metrics of software products are metrics that reflect the structure of the product, namely, its representation rather than its contents, or its form rather than its function. The most obvious structural metric of a computer program is, of course, its size. The size of a program is typically measured in terms of lines of code, although one may argue that the number of tokens is a more faithful measure, since it takes into account variations in line length. A number of standards exist for determining what to count as a line of code, and typical standards provide the following criteria:

- All programming statements are included in the line count, including such statements as program and procedure headers, data declarations, and type declarations.
- Blank lines and comment lines are not included.
- Single lines that include block delimiters (begin, end) or keywords (if, then, else) are counted.

A more faithful and more stable (representation-independent) way to measure program size is to use lexical tokens. We view a program as a huge expression made up of operators and operands, and we measure its size by means of four quantities:

n_1: number of unique operators
n_2: number of unique operands
N_1: number of occurrences of operators
N_2: number of occurrences of operands

Operands include constants and variables; operators include arithmetic and logical operators, comparison operators, punctuation symbols, and control structure keywords. If we let $n = n_1 + n_2$ and $N = N_1 + N_2$, then the program is viewed as a sentence of length N in a language of size n. Using Shannon's information theory, we find that under the hypothesis that all symbols are equally likely to occur at any position of the sentence, the quantity of information (entropy) carried by the program is

$$V = N \times \log(n)$$

This quantity is called the *volume* of the program.

There is more to the structure of a program than merely the number of its lines or the number of its tokens. For a given length, a program may be more or less complex. To account for this variation, we consider the *cyclomatic complexity* of a program, which is derived on the basis of the program's flowgraph, and uses the following formula:

$$c = e - n + 2$$

where e is the number of edges and n is the number of nodes in the flowgraph. Graph theory provides that, if the flowchart is a planar graph, then this expression $e - n + 2$ represents the number of regions in a planar representation of the flowchart.

Empirical studies show that both the volume of a program and its cyclomatic complexity have significant correlations with meaningful aspects of program behavior such as fault density and required testing time.

18.1.3   Functional Metrics

While structural metrics are easy to collect, they are not necessarily meaningful and can be abused arbitrarily; it is easy to imagine two programs that have the same length (or the same volume, or the same cyclomatic complexity) but have widely varying degrees of usefulness or widely varying degrees of functionality. *Functional metrics* address this shortcoming by focusing on the function provided by the program rather than the source text of the program. The most common functional metric is the *function point*, which is given by the following formula:

$$FP = T \times \left(0.65 + 0.01 \times \sum_{i=1}^{14} F_i \right)$$

where T is evaluated by means of information given in Table 18.1 and factors F_i are determined by means of the rating scale given in Table 18.2, for each of the following criteria:

TABLE 18.1 Estimating Factor *T* in *FP* Formula

Parameter	Count	Simple	Medium	Complex	Term
Number of user inputs	×	3	4	6	=
Number of user outputs	×	4	5	7	=
Number of user inquiries	×	3	4	6	=
Number of files	×	7	10	15	=
Number of external interfaces	×	5	7	10	=
Total, *T*					

1. Does the system require reliable backup and recovery?
2. Are data communications required?
3. Are there distributed processing functions?
4. Is performance critical?
5. Will the system run in an existing, heavily utilized operational environment?
6. Does the system require on-line data entry?
7. Does the on-line data entry require the input transaction to be built over multiple screens or operations?
8. Are the master files updated on line?
9. Are the inputs, outputs, files, or inquiries complex?
10. Is the internal processing complex?
11. Is the code designed to be reusable?
12. Are conversion and installation included in the design?
13. Is the system designed for multiple installations in different organizations?
14. Is the application designed to facilitate change and ease of use by the user?

Table 18.2, which provides estimates of the average number of lines of source code that are required to build one function point in various programming languages, substantiate our earlier discussion to the effect that lines of code do not faithfully reflect the amount of functionality provided by a program.

Note that, by its very definition, the function point metric can be computed on the requirements document of the program, rather than on the program itself. This is quite fitting for a *functional* (vs. structural) metric; because it deals with the function of the program rather than its structure, this metric can be

TABLE 18.2   Ratings Scale for F_i Factors

0	1	2	3	4	5
No influence	Incidental	Moderate	Average	Significant	Essentail

Programming Language	Average $\dfrac{LOC^a}{FSP}$
Assemler	300
COBOL	100
FORTRAN	100
Pascal	90
Ada	70
OO Languages	30
4G Languages	20
Code generators	15

[a](lines of code)/(number of full-time software people).

derived without looking at the program itself, but by inspecting a description of its function (which the requirements document is).

18.1.4   Exercises

1. (A) In order to justify the cost of a software product, a software provider may claim that the product either requires a great deal of effort to develop or provides a great deal of useful functionality. Use counterexamples to show that the size of the product cannot be used to support either claim (i.e., give an example of a large program that does not cost much to produce, and a large program that is not very useful). Comment.

2. (A) In order to justify the cost of a software product, a software provider may claim that the product either requires a great deal of effort to develop or provides a great deal of useful functionality. Discuss how a function point measure is a better reflection of development effort, and a better reflection of useful functionality than lines of code.

3. (A) Consider the following Pascal program; compute its volume and its cyclomatic complexity:

```
program trysort(input, output);
    procedure quicksort
        (first, last: indextype);
    var
        i, j:
        pivotindex: indextype;
```

```
                    temp,
                    pivotvalue: valuetype;
               begin
               {splitting the array}
               if first<last then
                 begin
                 i:= first; j: last;
                 pivotindex:= (first+last)/2;
                 pivotvalue:= a[pivotindex];
               repeat
                 while (a[i]<pivotvalue)
                   do i:= i+1;
                 while (a[j]>pivotvalue)
                   do j:= j-1;
                 if i<=j then
                   begin
                   temp:= a[i];
                   a[i]:= a[j];
                   a[j]:= temp;
                   i:= i+1;
                   j:= j-1
                   end
                 until i>j;
                 {array is now split}
                 quicksort(first,j);
                 quicksort(i,last);
                 end;
               end;
            begin
            quicksort
            end.
```

4. (B) Consider a management information system whose relevant information is available to you, and that is written in one of the languages cited in
   Section 18.1.3 (Assembler, COBOL, FORTRAN, Ada, Pascal, OOL, 4GL).
   Estimate its FSP metric and its LOC metric; compare the ratio between
   these figures and the figure given in Section 18.1.3.

18.2 COMPONENT ENGINEERING METRICS

In this section we address the issue of what makes a software asset reusable.
As a default, we consider that *asset* refers to an arbitrary software product,
although sometimes our discussion deals with programs or program parts. We
distinguish between three kinds of attributes that make a software asset
reusable:

- *Concept.* The first attribute that makes an asset reusable is the concept that it embodies, irrespective of how this concept is represented.
- *Content.* For a given concept, a reusable asset may be more or less reusable depending on *how* it embodies this concept.
- *Context.* For a given concept and a given implementation thereof, an asset may be more or less reusable depending on the complexity of the context that it requires to operate.

These three features are the subject of Sections 18.2.1–18.2.3; in Section 18.2.4, we present some exercises.

18.2.1 Concept

We have identified two attributes that are related to the concept of a reusable asset:

- *Generality.* A concept is all the more *general* that it admits many useful instantiations or specializations. We distinguish between two forms of generality: *structural generality* and *functional generality*. To illustrate functional generality, consider that a routine that sorts arrays of arbitrary length, arbitrary record structure, arbitrary ordering key, in an arbitrary order (increasing or decreasing) is more (functionally) general than a routine that sorts integer arrays of length 100 in increasing order. To illustrate structural generality, consider that a program pattern such as

```
function reduce (a: array [indextype] of scalartype):
  scalartype;
var
  i: indextype;
  begin
  reduce:= neutral_elt;
  for i:=1 to N do
    reduce:= reduce op a[i]
  end;
```

can be specialized to compute the sum of an array (neutral_elt=0, op=+), the product of an array (neutral_elt=1, op=*), the maximum element of an array (neutral_elt=-∞, op=max), and the minimum of an array (neutral_elt=-∞, op=min), to cite only a few. With features such as currying (in functional languages) and using functions and operations as parameters (e.g., in Ada), it is possible to view some forms of structural generality as instances of functional generality; the distinction is, nevertheless, helpful for the purposes of our discussion.
- *Usefulness.* The usefulness of an asset in a particular application domain reflects the frequency with which the asset is needed in that application domain. Generality contributes to usefulness but is distinct from it—

while generality is intrinsic to the asset, usefulness is relative to an application domain; the same asset may be useful in an application domain and much less useful in another.

18.2.2   Content

Whereas the concept of an asset reflects its essence, the *content* of an asset reflects how this essence is embodied in a concrete artifact. Three families of attributes define content; we discuss them in turn below.

- *Functional Attributes*. Functional attributes reflect the faithfulness with which the asset embodies its concept. We have identified two functional attributes: reliability and correctness. Clearly, an asset that has these features has a better reuse potential than one that does not.
- *Structural Attributes*. Structural attributes reflect the quality of the asset's representation, and are meaningful reusability attributes to the extent that reuse may involve analyzing, understanding, or adapting the asset. We have identified two structural features: understandability and adaptability. While the former makes it easy to analyze an asset for the purpose of blackbox or whitebox reuse, the latter makes it easy to adapt an asset for the purpose of whitebox reuse.
- *Operational Attributes*. We have identified one operational attribute: efficiency. A reuser who is seeking an efficient implementation of some concept may want to discard an asset that does not satisfy the declared efficiency requirement, even if it satisfies functional and structural requirements—hence efficiency does affect the reuse potential of an asset.

18.2.3   Context

Whereas concept attributes deal with the essence of an asset and content attributes deal with the intrinsic qualities of the asset's representation, *context* attributes deal with the ability to integrate the asset within its host environment. Most context attributes are very dependent on the (programming) language in which the asset is represented. Programming languages can profoundly affect context attributes through such features as scoping rules, intermodular control, and information hiding. We have identified three context attributes, which we discuss in turn below.

- *Genericity*. Genericity reflects the ease with which an asset can be instantiated and specialized. This attribute is not to be confused with generality—whereas generality is a characteristic of the concept, genericity is a characteristic of the concept's representation; whereas generality is decided in the requirements specification phase (of the devlopment of the asset), genericity is decided at the implementation phase. Genericity supports generality, and is contingent on a programming language that provides constructs for genericity as well as a programming discipline that makes use of these constructs.

- *Interoperability*. Interoperability is the ability of an asset to interact with other components of a host software system in a seamless manner, or the ability to adapt the asset with minimal effort to achieve the same goal.
- *Portability*. Portability is the ability of an asset to operate on a wide variety of computer platforms. It can be seen as an instance of interoperability, where the host software system is a computer platform, but raises sufficiently distinct issues to be considered a separate attribute.

Generality, a concept attribute, and genericity, a context attribute, both enhance the reusability of an asset. In Chapter 20, we will see how these attributes are quantified in concrete terms, in an equation that reflects the reuse benefits of the asset.

18.2.4 Exercises

While this section purports to discuss software reuse *metrics*, all we have done so far is discuss *attributes*. In the following exercises, we discuss how to derive metrics to reflect the attributes that are of interest to us.

1. (B) One can take a very concrete view of a metric, "a metric is the association of a number to a feature," or a very abstract view, "a metric is a partial ordering." Discuss these views; find examples where associating a number is not only difficult or impossible but is also meaningless. Consider also that it is possible to define a metric as a vector of numeric values; in what sense does this define a partial ordering?

2. (A) Discuss how currying in functional languages can be used to cast structural generality as functional generality. Give an example.

3. (A) Discuss how the ability to use functions and operators as parameters in Ada can be used to cast structural generality as functional generality. Give an example.

4. (A/B) Give an example of a generic asset that is not general, and an example of a general asset that is not generic. Comment.

5. (B) Consider concept attributes. Discuss how to quantify these attributes using existing metrics or new metrics. Keep in mind the questions raised in exercise 1.

6. (B) Consider content attributes. Discuss how to quantify these attributes using existing metrics or new metrics. Keep in mind the questions raised in exercise 1.

7. (B) Consider context attributes. Discuss how to quantify these attributes using existing metrics or new metrics. Keep in mind the questions raised in exercise 1.

18.3   APPLICATION ENGINEERING METRICS

In Section 18.2 we discussed asset related software metrics, which revolve around the issue of how to measure the reuse worthiness (or reuse potential) of a software asset. In this section we discuss project-level metrics, which revolve around the issue of the extent to which a software development project makes use of software reuse and the extent to which a software development project contributes to the corporate effort in software reuse. Such issues are relevant to the extent that one may want to enforce reuse standards within an organization, or assess maturity levels of development projects, or reward contributions to the corporate reuse effort, or, for example, trace gains in software quality or programmer productivity to the deployment of reuse practices.

18.3.1   Project-Level Functions

We have identified three project-level objective functions that a project manager must endeavor to optimize; we briefly present them below.

* *Reuse Distribution.* This metric considers the overall size of the application produced by the software development project and divides it up into the following categories:

  New code—percentage of code developed specifically for this application.

  Reused code, verbatim—percentage of code reused verbatim from a corporate reuse library.

  Adapted code—percentage of code reused from a corporate reuse library, after adaptation.

  Two remarks arise from this definition: (1) the percentage cited in this definition are typically size percentage, measured in lines of code (but of course other measures than size can be used, such as volume and function points.) and (2) irrespective of which measure is used in computing the percentages, the percentages must be interpreted with caution. Consider, for example, a project where we have found that 20% of the LOC size is reused verbatim and 80% is developed from scratch. Even if we neglect the cost of integrating the reused code, and even if we neglect the nonlinear effects of software costs, we cannot claim that we have saved 20% of the development effort. The reason for this is that most typically, the size of a reused asset is larger than the size of the code we would have written if the reusable asset were not available. See exercise 1.

- *Project-Level Return on Investment.* While the corporation has a stake that all projects make use of reusable assets and produce reusable assets, individual projects have to balance the benefits of reuse against other short-term considerations, such as changes in the group's operational procedures, risk that project staff be distracted by the introduction of the software reuse technology but do not benefit from it (e.g., they spend too much time looking for reusable assets and fail to find any), and overhead caused by producing reusable assets. The decision to apply software reuse in any one project is not straightforward; there are cases where, from the project's viewpoint, the potential risks outweight the benefits. The project-level ROI quantifies this decision by providing estimates of risks and benefits and matching them in an ROI equation; this will be discussed in detail in Chapter 20.
- *Reusable Code Percentage.* This metric reflects the amount of code contributed by the individual project to the corporate software reuse library, as a percentage of the size of the application produced by the project. This metric can be used to reward individual projects; the challenge of a project manager is to optimize this metric without undue burden on the project team, and without derailing the project goals.

18.3.2 Exercises

1. (B) Consider a software application of size 100 KLOC (kilolines of code), for which we have found the following reuse distribution.
   - New code: 80%
   - Reused code, verbatim: 20%
   - Adapted code: 0%

   We estimate that the cost of integrating the 20-KLOC reused software into the application is equal to the cost of developing a product of 5 KLOC; further, we estimate that if we had to develop the whole product from scratch, its size would have been 94 KLOC (rather than 100 KLOC). Using basic COCOMO (constructive cost model) and assuming an organic development mode, estimate the cost of developing this product with reuse and without reuse. What percentage of effort was saved with reuse? Conclude.

2. (B) Consider a software application of size 100 KLOC, for which we have found the following reuse distribution.
   - New code: 30%
   - Reused code, verbatim: 20%
   - Adapted code: 50%

We estimate that the cost of integrating the 20-KLOC reused software into the application is equal to the cost of developing a product of 5 KLOC; further, we estimate that the cost of modifying the adapted code and integrating it into the application is equal to the cost of developing a product of 40 KLOC from scratch; finally, we estimate that if we had to develop the whole product from scratch, its size would have been 89 KLOC (rather than 100 KLOC). Using basic COCOMO and assuming an organic development mode, estimate the cost of developing this product with reuse and without reuse. What percentage of effort was saved with reuse? Conclude.

18.4   DOMAIN ENGINEERING METRICS

Domain engineering metrics reflect to what extent the domain engineering effort is successful, by quantifying the level of demand experienced by domain assets, the level of efficiency of the library, and the degree of usefulness of domain assets.

18.4.1   Reuse Means: Software Library Metrics

In order to justify the creation or the existence of a software reuse library, one must make a case for the level of use of the library in the organization's day to day operations. We have identified three metrics that reflect the level of library traffic.

- *Number of Accesses to the Library.* This is a straightforward indication that the library is playing an important role in the organization's day to day operations.
- *Number of Retrievals from the Library.* This is clearly more meaningful than the number of accesses, even though it is not itself an indication of library usefulness—since a component may have been retrieved and subsequently discarded.
- *Library Efficiency.* This quantity is defined as the ratio of the number of reused assets that have been extracted from the library per unit of time (e.g., a year) over the total size of the library. For a unit of time as long as a year, this figure should be near 1.

It may be tempting to consider that the second metric (number of retrievals) subsumes the first (number of accesses), and hence can override it in practice. In fact, it is best to maintain both measures because the first ultimately reflects the level of faith that application developers have in the reuse initiative, whereas the second measure reflects on the quality of reusable assets. Hence, in a way, the first metric reflects the perception (by application engineers) of library quality, whereas the second metric reflects the actual library quality.

18.4.2 Exercises

1. (B) Let AL, RL, and LE be (respectively) the number of accesses to the library, the number of retrievals from the library, and the library efficiency observed on a domain engineering operation. We wish to formulate guidelines for how to take corrective measures depending on the values of these metrics. If we take two discrete ratings for each metric (*low* and *high*), we obtain eight distinct outcomes; for each outcome, propose corrective actions.

2. (R) Expand the discussion of this section by proposing further domain metrics, perhaps metrics related to the quality of domain analysis, or domain scoping.

18.5 ORGANIZATION LEVEL METRICS

In this section we discuss metrics that reflect the corporate involvement in software reuse, or the corporate maturity with respect to software reuse.

18.5.1 Reuse Impacts: Productivity Gains

The first and most obvious way to quantify the impact of reuse on a corporate operation is to consider the distribution of reused and original code in the total quantity of code produced per unit of time. If the unit of time is the year and the amount of code is measured in KLOC, then we obtain the following distribution table, which we refer to as the *yearly reuse distribution by size*.

Category	Percentage
New code	%
Reused code, verbatim	%
Internal	%
External	%
Adapted code	%
Internal	%
External	%

Under *reused code* and *adapted code*, we distinguish between code that is developed in house (referred to as *internal*) and code that is acquired from outside sources (referred to as *external*). These two sources of code obey different cost equations, and hence ought in principle to be considered separately.

We ignore for a moment the distinction between internal and external sources of reusable (or adaptable) code, and we let C_n, C_r, and C_a respectively represent the ratios of new code, reusable code, and adaptable code in an application. As we will discuss in Chapter 19, the cost of developing a line of code with verbatim reuse averages 0.20 times the cost of developing a new line from scratch; further, we find that the cost of developing a line of code by adaptation is on average 0.67 times the cost of developing a new line from scratch. Consequently, if we assume linear development costs (which is reasonable only for small-size products), we find that the cost of developing a product with reuse distribution (C_n, C_r, C_a) is a linear function of

$$C_n + 0.2 \times C_r + 0.67 \times C_a$$

subject to the constraint: $C_n + C_r + C_a = 1$. See also exercise 2.

Reuse distribution is not an end in itself; it is interesting only to the extent that it helps to improve the overall organization's productivity. We introduce the *reuse leverage metric* as the ratio between the productivity of the organization (lines of code per year) with reuse over its productivity without reuse. Because of the potential inflation in the line count that stems from reusable code, one must beware that actual productivity gains (in terms of functionality, or market value) may be less than the reuse leverage claims them to be.

18.5.2 Exercises

1. (A) Consider the cost equation given above for a system whose reuse distribution is (C_n, C_r, C_a) under the hypothesis of linear costs. Give examples of how this equation can be used to make reuse/new development decisions and reuse/adaptation decisions.

2. (B) COCOMO equations [Boehm 1981] provide that in order to derive the cost of a multicomponent software system, we first estimate the development effort using the overall size estimate, then we prorate the overall effort to each component according to its size. Hence the effort of component A in a system made up of components A, B, and C is obtained (under basic COCOMO, assuming organic mode) as

$$E(A) = \frac{A}{A+B+C} \times 2.4 \times (A+B+C)^{1.05}$$

Given a system S whose reuse distribution is (C_n, C_r, C_a), give a precise formula of its cost (that does not assume linear costs).

18.6 FURTHER READING

Boehm [1981] presents counting rules for lines of code and shows how this metric can be used to estimate software costs and manage software projects. Token-based metrics, introduced by Halstead [1977], have become routine textbook material [Sommerville 1995, Pressman 1992]. The cyclomatic complexity metric is due to McCabe [1976] and the function points metric was initially developed by Albrecht [1979] to deal with MIS applications and later extended by Albrecht and Gaffney [1983] to cover other kinds of software applications. For a general treatment of software metrics, consult Fenton [1991], and for a thorough discussion of software reuse metrics, consult [Poulin 1997a]. Asset-level software metrics are also discussed in the literature [Boetticher et al. 1993, Caldiera and Basili 1991, Chen and Lee 1993, Chen et al. 1995, Karlsson 1995, Hislop 1993, Karlsson et al. 1992, Mayobre 1991, NATO 1991, RAPID 1990, Selby 1989, Stalhane 1995, Torres and Samadzadeh 1991]. Project-level metrics are discussed by Poulin [1997], who refers to models by Frakes and Terry [1994], Balda and Gustafson [1990], Henderson-Sellers [1993], Poulin and Caruso [1993], and DISA/JIEO/CIM [1993]. Organization-level metrics presented in this chapter are due to Poulin et al. [Poulin 1997, Poulin and Werkman 1994].

Chapter 19

Software Reuse Cost Estimation

The ability to estimate, predict, and monitor lifecycle costs is an integral part of a successful software process, including a software reuse process. We submit that in software reuse (as in software engineering in general), most decisions can ultimately be rationalized by means of economic considerations. Software cost estimation deals with deriving estimates of cost and schedule for a software product on the basis of an estimate of its expected size. While one may argue that it is not necessarily easier to estimate the expected size of a product than to estimate its expected development effort and schedule, we submit that cost and schedule equations are useful beyond cost estimation, as they help us understand, analyze and quantify the various cost factors, and their effect on final costs. In this chapter we discuss cost estimation in the context of software reuse, by focusing in turn on component engineering (developing for reuse) and then application engineering (developing with reuse). First, we present a brief overview of software cost estimation in the context of custom development, using the popular COCOMO cost model, due to Boehm [Boehm 1981].

19.1 SOFTWARE ENGINEERING ECONOMICS: COCOMO

COCOMO (for constructive cost model) is a software cost estimation model that derives estimates for the cost and schedule of a software development project on the basis of an estimate of the size of the software product to be developed. This model is geared primarily toward the development of software products *from scratch* (rather than by adapting or reusing existing products) and applies to projects that follow the waterfall lifecycle. This model is actually the aggregate of three submodels: *basic COCOMO*, *intermediate*

COCOMO, and *detailed COCOMO*; these differ by their target precision as well as (consequently) the range of cost factors that they involve.

19.1.1 Basic COCOMO

The COCOMO model distinguishes between three modes of software development, and provides different cost and schedule equations for each:

- *Organic Mode.* This mode characterizes software development projects that are typically carried out in house by a development team who is familiar with the application domain of the product, is accustomed to work together on this type of product, and is empowered to (re)negotiate product requirements (e.g., dropping out some requirements clauses) and process requirements (e.g., reporting delivery date, or revising the development budget). Typical projects developed under this mode involve simple *applications*.

- *Embedded Mode.* This mode characterizes software development projects that are typically carried out for an outside customer (or for the market at large). Typically, such projects involve complex products that require technological innovations, and hence are developed without prior experience with similar products. Also, such projects are typically subject to contract obligations or market pressures; hence their process and product requirements are not subject to renegotiation. Typical projects developed under this mode involve *systems* products.

- *Semidetached Mode.* This mode characterizes software development projects that have a combination of organic and embedded features, or features that are halfway between organic and embedded values. Typical projects developed under this mode involve *utility* products.

The following equations provide for each development mode (or, equivalently, for each kind of software product), the estimated development effort (E, in person-months) and the estimated development schedule (T, in months) as a function of the estimated product size (S, in thousand lines of code).

Product Family	Development Effort	Development Schedule
Organic	$E = 2.4 \times S^{1.05}$	$T = 2.5 \times E^{0.38}$
Semidetached	$E = 3.0 \times S^{1.12}$	$T = 2.5 \times E^{0.35}$
Embedded	$E = 3.6 \times S^{1.20}$	$T = 2.5 \times E^{0.32}$

COCOMO provides an estimate of the yearly maintenance effort as a linear function of the development effort, using a factor called the *annual change traffic* (ACT):

$$E_{MAINT} = ACT \times E$$

A typical value for ACT is 0.15; each year, one spends 15% of the application's development cost in maintenance. We will revisit this figure when we assess quality gains of reusable assets, in terms of the savings in maintenance costs.

19.1.2   Intermediate COCOMO

Basic COCOMO uses only two cost factors: the estimated size of the software product and its expected development mode (organic, embedded, semidetached); consequently, basic COCOMO estimates are not precise, and can be used only to produce order-of-magnitude assessments of the expected development costs. Intermediate COCOMO builds on basic COCOMO by introducing more cost factors and delivering better precision. Specifically, intermediate COCOMO derives the development effort (E) as the product of two factors

$$E = \text{EAF} \times E_{\text{NOM}}$$

where E_{NOM} (nominal effort) is derived from the estimated size and the expected development mode, and EAF (effort adjustment factor) is derived from the additional cost factors. The equations of nominal effort (as a function of the estimated size S and the expected development mode) are

Product Family	Development Effort
Organic	$E_{\text{NOM}} = 2.8 \times S^{1.05}$
Semidetached	$E_{\text{NOM}} = 3.0 \times S^{1.12}$
Embedded	$E_{\text{NOM}} = 3.2 \times S^{1.20}$

As for the effort adjustment factor (EAF), it is derived from 15 cost factors, which are divided into four families:

- *Product Attributes.* These are product-related attributes that are known to have an impact on the development cost of the product, and include

  RELY—the required reliability of the product,

  CPLX—the complexity of the product,

  DATA—the size of the database that the product manipulates (in relation to the size of the software product).

- *Platform Attributes.* These are attributes that pertain to the equipment used for developing the software product, and include

  TIME—execution time constraint,

  STOR—main storage constraint,

  PVOL—volatility of the platform (how often during the development lifecycle the development platform changes),

  TURN—computer turnaround time.

- *Personnel Attributes.* These are factors that pertain to the development staff (programmers, analysts, engineers), and include

  ACAP—analyst capability,

  PCAP—programmer capability,

  AEXP—application Experience,

  PEXP—platform experience,

  LTEX—language and tool experience.

- *Project Attributes.* These are project-related attributes that are known to have an impact on the development cost of the product, and include

  MODP—use of modern programming practices,

  TOOL—use of software tools,

  SCED—required development schedule (in relation to the estimation given by the schedule equation).

The effort adjustment factor is derived from these cost factors in a three-step process:

1. We assign a discrete rating to each cost factor, ranging from *very low* to *very high*.
2. Using Table 19.1, we convert these ratings into numeric values.
3. We obtain the effort adjustment factor by multiplying all the numeric values that we find for all 15 cost factors.

If we let M_i, for $i \in \{\text{RELY,CPLX}, \ldots ,\text{SCED}\}$, be the numeric value derived from Table 19.1 for cost factor i, then the intermediate COCOMO estimate of the development effort is

$$E = \prod_{i=\text{REKY}}^{i=\text{SCED}} M_i \times E_{\text{NOM}}$$

This is a more precise cost estimation formula than basic COCOMO, and often falls within 20% of the actual cost.

19.1.3 Detailed COCOMO

Detailed COCOMO builds on intermediate COCOMO by recognizing that the impact of a cost factor varies from one phase to the next. For example, analyst capability (ACAP) has a greater impact on the requirements analysis phase and product design phase than on the programming phase; conversely, computer attributes have a greater impact on the programming phase than on the requirements analysis product or design phases. To account for this variance, we consider that for each cost factor i, where $i \in \{\text{RELY,CPLX}, \ldots , \text{SCED}\}$, and for each rating (from *very low* to *extra high*), we should give— not a single effort multiplier value, but rather a vector of values, one for each

TABLE 19.1   Conversion of Cost Factors into Numeric Values

Cost Factor	Very Low	Low	Nominal	High	Very High	Extra High
RELY	0.75	0.88	1.00	1.15	1.40	—
CPLX	0.70	0.85	1.00	1.15	1.30	1.65
DATA	—	0.94	1.00	1.08	1.16	—
TIME	—	—	1.00	1.11	1.30	1.66
STOR	—	—	1.00	1.06	1.21	1.56
PVOL	—	0.87	1.00	1.15	1.30	—
TURN	—	0.87	1.00	1.07	1.15	—
ACAP	1.46	1.19	1.00	0.86	0.71	—
AEXP	1.29	1.13	1.00	0.86	0.71	—
PCAP	1.42	1.17	1.00	0.86	0.70	—
PEXP	1.21	1.10	1.00	0.90	—	—
LTEX	1.14	1.07	1.00	0.95	—	—
MODP	1.24	1.10	1.00	0.91	0.82	—
TOOL	1.24	1.10	1.00	0.91	0.83	—
SCED	1.23	1.08	1.00	1.04	1.10	—

phase of the lifecycle. COCOMO encompasses five phases of the lifecycle: requirements analysis (RA), product design (PD), detailed design (DD), coding and unit testing (CT), and integration testing (IT). Also, it provides a distribution of nominal development effort across phases; hence the nominal effort of phase j, for $j \in \{RA,PD,DD,CT,IT\}$, is given by the formula

$$E_{NOM}(j) = E_{NOM} \times \rho_j$$

where E_{NOM} is derived according to the formulas given for intermediate COCOMO for the development mode at hand, and ρ_j is the ratio of nominal development effort devoted to the phase j for the given development mode. The adjusted development effort for phase j is then obtained by multiplying the nominal effort for the phase by the effort adjustment factor for the phase:

$$E(j) = \prod_{i=REKY}^{i=SCED} M_i^j \times E_{NOM}(j)$$

where M_i^j is the effort multiplier of cost factor i ($i \in \{RELY,CPLX, \ldots SCED\}$) at phase j ($j \in \{RA,PD,DD,CT,IT\}$). The overall cost estimate is then

$$E = \sum_{j=RA}^{j=IT} E(j)$$

Even though it is considerably more complex than intermediate COCOMO, detailed COCOMO is not much more precise; hence this model is rarely used, and in fact rarely investigated.

19.1.4   Exercises

1. (B) One can generally justify the cost of an artifact either by the cost of producing the artifact or by the service rendered by that artifact. Show, using examples as needed, that the metric of *lines of code* is neither a faithful reflection of cost nor a faithful reflection of service rendered. Discuss the appropriateness of using *lines of code* as a basis for estimating software costs. (Why do we still use it?) Discuss alternatives.

2. (A) Consider a software product whose estimated size is $S = 80$ (80,000 lines of code). Using basic COCOMO, estimate its development effort (in person-months) under each one of the three development modes. Draw conclusions on the importance of choosing the correct mode and the existence of three modes (as opposed to a continuum of modes, and corresponding equations).

3. (A) The *productivity range* of a cost factor is the ratio between its largest value and its smallest value in Table 19.1. Compute the productivity ranges of all the cost factors on intermediate COCOMO, and rank them in decreasing order. Draw practical lessons from this ranking.

4. (B) Explain why the effort equations of basic COCOMO are different from the nominal effort equations of intermediate COCOMO. Give an interpretation for the ratio of coefficients in these equations for each development mode. (*Hint*: Consider that there is a statistical correlation between development mode and mean effort adjustment factor.)

19.2   COMPONENT ENGINEERING ECONOMICS

One key argument of software reuse is that reusable assets provide better productivity, quality, and time to market than assets developed for custom use. In this section, we seek to quantify these three gains in economic terms:

- Productivity gains can be quantified by the difference in development costs that stems from reusing existing assets versus developing custom assets from scratch.
- Quality gains can be quantified by the difference in maintenance costs that stems from reusing existing assets versus developing custom assets from scratch.
- Time-to-market gains can be quantified by the difference in development schedule that stems from reusing existing assets versus developing custom assets from scratch.

These gains do not come for free, of course; they are balanced against higher asset development costs, and nontrivial organizational overheads. We discuss these costs and benefits in the sequel.

19.2.1   Development for Reuse

It is widely accepted that a reusable asset costs more to develop than an *equivalent* (in a sense that remains to be defined) custom-tailored asset. We recognize two propositions that justify this claim:

- *Size inflation*—a reusable asset is typically of bigger size than an equivalent custom-developed asset.
- *Unitary reuse overhead*—the development cost of one line of reusable code is higher than the development cost of one line of custom-tailored code.

The combination of these two propositions produces a significant cost overhead for reusable assets. For the purposes of our discussion, we consider that a reusable asset R is *equivalent* to a custom-tailored asset C if an application developer may consider using R to fulfill the function of C, or/and if an asset developer may consider developing R (for reuse) as a substitute for developing C (for single use).

The proposition of size inflation can be justified by the following premises:

- A reusable asset will satisfy not only specific requirements of one particular application but a wide range of requirements, which must be anticipated and duly provided for.
- A reusable asset must be generic, that is, have appropriate linguistic features that enable the (re)user to create specific instances of the asset, to satisfy application-specific requirements.

On the other hand, the proposition of unitary reuse overhead can be justified by the following premises:

- A reusable asset must be thoroughly validated, because it is expected to be used in a wide range of systems; hence the stakes of its failure are all the more consequential.
- A reusable asset must be carefully documented, since it is expected to come under closer scrutiny by people who may be totally ignorant of its design rationale.

To quantify the cost increase that stems from these propositions, Poulin [1997] introduces the factor of RCWR (relative cost of writing for reuse), which is the ratio of the cost of developing a reusable asset over the cost of developing an equivalent custom-tailored asset. Table 19.2 summarizes the results of empirical studies that attempt to measure this factor. Many of these findings produce values of RCWR around 1.50.

When reusable assets are developed as part of a domain engineering effort, we must take into account the cost of domain analysis, and distribute this cost

TABLE 19.2   RCWR: Relative Cost for Writing for Reuse

Source	RCWR
Bardo	1.15–1.25
Reifer [1997]	1.10–1.36
Caldwell	1.25–1.30
Lim [1998]	1.11–1.80
Gaffney and Cruichshank [1992]	1.50
Poulin [1997a]	1.50
Jones [1994]	1.50
Pant et al. [1996]	1.55
Favaro [1996]	1.00–2.20
Tracz [1995]	1.60
IBM	1.25–2.00
Lockheed Martin	1.86
Margano and Rhoads [1992]	2.00

TABLE 19.3   RUSE Cost Factor: Ratings and Effort Multipliers

Very Low	Low	Nominal	High	Very High	Extra High
No reuse	Reuse across project	Reuse across program	Reuse across product line	Reuse across multiple product lines	
1.00	1.15	1.33	1.53	1.75	

over the domain assets. To this effect, we introduce the factor of *relative cost of domain engineering* (RCDE). This ratio differs from (exceeds) RCWR in that it includes not only the cost of developing a reusable component to meet some specification (which is reflected by RCWR) but also the cost of determining that a component that meets such a specification is reuse worthy. Empirical studies by Gaffney and Cruickshank [1992] give values of RCDE between 1.5 and 2.5; we let the default value of this ratio be 2.0.

COCOMO 2.0 further recognizes that the excess cost of developing for reuse is dependent on the expected scale of reuse. To this effect, it introduces the cost factor RUSE, whose ratings and effort multipliers are given in Table 19.3. Table 19.3 shows that the expected scale of reuse of a given reusable asset can have an impact as large as 75% on the development cost.

19.2.2   Quality Gains

Deploying a reusable asset in an application yields not only productivity gains (in terms of savings in development costs), but also quality gains. One way to quantify quality gains is to consider that the improvement in quality results in lower maintenance costs, and to estimate the maintenance cost differential of the application over a predefined period of time. If we let $E_{\text{MAINT}}(y)$, $E_{\text{MAINT}}^{\text{BB}}(y)$, and $E_{\text{MAINT}}^{\text{WB}}(y)$, be the maintenance effort at year y of (respectively) a custom-tailored asset, a reusable asset used in blackbox form, and a reusable asset used in whitebox form, then we typically have the following inequalities for all y:

$$E_{\text{MAINT}}^{\text{BB}}(y) < E_{\text{MAINT}}^{\text{WB}}(y) < E_{\text{MAINT}}(y)$$

The rightmost inequality stems from the premise that reusable assets cost less to maintain because they are developed with greater care; the leftmost inequality stems from the premise that the quality features that are built into a reusable asset are better preserved under blackbox reuse than under white-box reuse. The quality gains achieved at year y by the blackbox (respectively, whitebox) reuse of the asset are denoted by $\text{QG}^{\text{BB}}(y)$ [respectively, $\text{QG}^{\text{WB}}(y)$] and defined by

$$\text{QG}^{\text{BB}}(y) = E_{\text{MAINT}}(y) - E_{\text{MAINT}}^{\text{BB}}(y)$$
$$\text{QG}^{\text{WB}}(y) = E_{\text{MAINT}}(y) - E_{\text{MAINT}}^{\text{WB}}(y)$$

If we take a fixed-term view, whereby we are interested in the quality gains cumulated over a predefined amount of time (say, Y, measured in number of years), then we introduce cumulative quality gains measures for blackbox reuse and whitebox reuse:

$$\text{CQG}^{\text{BB}}(y) = \sum_{y=1}^{Y} \text{QG}^{\text{BB}}(y)$$

$$\text{CQG}^{\text{WB}}(y) = \sum_{y=1}^{Y} \text{QG}^{\text{WB}}(y)$$

We now focus on ways to quantify these functions. To this effect, we consider COCOMO's equation for maintenance effort (Section 19.1), and consider that the same equation applies to reusable assets, in addition to custom-tailored assets—but possibly with different values of the *annual change traffic*

$$E_{\text{MAINT}} = \text{ACT} \times E$$
$$E_{\text{MAINT}}^{\text{BB}} = \text{ACT}' \times E$$
$$E_{\text{MAINT}}^{\text{WB}} = \text{ACT}'' \times E$$

where ACT, ACT', and ACT" are the annual change traffic of (respectively) custom-tailored assets, blackbox reused assets, and whitebox reused assets. As we have discussed earlier, it is reasonable to consider that maintenance costs are typically lowest for a blackbox reused asset, followed by the maintenance costs of a whitebox reused asset, followed by the maintenance costs of a custom-tailored asset. This translates into the following inequality between ACT factors:

$$\text{ACT}' < \text{ACT}'' < \text{ACT}$$

Typically, COCOMO takes for ACT the default value of 0.15; in the absence of better information, we will usually take the default value of 0.10 for ACT″ and 0.07 for ACT′.

19.2.3 Productivity Gains

At the component engineering level, productivity gains can be quantified by assessing how valuable the asset is for application developers. We must first recognize that how valuable an asset is to a developer depends on whether the developer intends/expects to use the asset under blackbox reuse or under whitebox reuse. We reflect these quantities by what we call *blackbox price* (denoted by P^{BB}) and *whitebox price* (denoted by P^{WB}). These quantities must be sufficiently low to make the reuse option more attractive for the application developer than the custom development option. In order to quantify this premise, we consider the costs of custom development costs against the costs of blackbox reuse and whitebox reuse costs, and infer conditions on (respectively) blackbox price and whitebox price. In order to take into account quality gains as well as productivity gains, we consider the cumulated quality gains of the asset over a limited term, say, Y.

In order for blackbox reuse to be preferable to custom development, the blackbox price P^{BB} must satisfy the following condition:

$$\text{INS} + P^{BB} < E + \text{CQG}^{BB}(Y)$$

where INS is the cost of asset instantiation and E is the cost of asset development from scratch (which we have saved by opting for reuse); for the sake of argument, we consider that retrieval costs are negligible. Poulin [1997b] writes the term INS as

$$\text{INS} = \text{RCR} \times E$$

where RCR (relative cost of reuse) is found, according to empirical investigations, to be about 0.20. Also, if we assume (as does COCOMO's maintenance equation) that annual maintenance effort is the same from year to year, we use the default values we have presented earlier for the ACT of blackbox reusable assets, and we take $Y = 3$, we can write the term $\text{CQG}^{BB}(Y)$ as follows:

$$\text{CQG}^{\text{BB}}(Y) = 3 \times (0.15 - 0.07) \times E = 0.24 \times E$$

This yields the following upper bound on P^{BB}:

$$P^{\text{BB}} < (1.0 + 0.24 - 0.20) \times E = (1.04) \times E$$

If the benefits of blackbox reuse are to be divided equally between the producers and the consumers of the reusable asset, we find $P^{\text{BB}} = 0.52 \times E$.

Likewise, in order for whitebox reuse to be preferable to custom development, the whitebox price P^{WB} must satisfy the following condition:

$$\text{ADP} + P^{\text{WB}} < E + \text{CQG}^{\text{WB}}(Y)$$

where ADP is the cost of asset adaptation and E is the cost of asset development from scratch (which we have saved by opting for reuse); for the sake of argument, we consider that retrieval costs are negligible. If we assume (as does COCOMO's maintenance equation) that annual maintenance effort is the same from year to year, we use the default values we have presented earlier for the annual change traffic of white box reusable assets, and we take $Y = 3$, we can write the term $\text{CQG}^{\text{WB}}(Y)$ as follows:

$$\text{CQG}^{\text{WB}}(Y) = 3 \times (0.15 - 0.10) \times E = 0.15 \times E$$

In order to estimate the cost of asset adaptation, we refer to a chart due to Selby [1989], which plots the relative cost of adaptation as a function of the portion of source code that has been modified. This factor, which we denote by RCA (relative cost of adaptation), can be derived from the chart in Figure 19.1 by taking the integral of the curve between 0 and 1. We find

$$\text{RCA} = (0.125 \times (0.05 + 0.55) \times 0.5 + 0.5 \times (0.55 + 0.70) \times 0.5$$
$$+ 0.375 \times (0.70 + 1.00) \times 0.5) = 0.67$$

This yields the following upper bound on P^{WB}:

$$P^{\text{WB}} < (1.0 + 0.15 - 0.67) \times E = (0.48) \times E$$

If the benefits of whitebox reuse are to be divided equally between the producers and the consumers of the reusable asset, we find $P^{\text{BB}} = 0.24 \times E$. Note that with this whitebox price, the benefit achieved by an application developer is also $0.24 \times E$. This is not a large benefit, especially if we consider it against the backdrop of reuse-related risks, reuse overheads, and the cost of asset retrieval (which we have conveniently neglected). In light of these observations, it is not difficult to imagine circumstances in which reuse initiatives fail to reap benefits, or in fact end up causing losses.

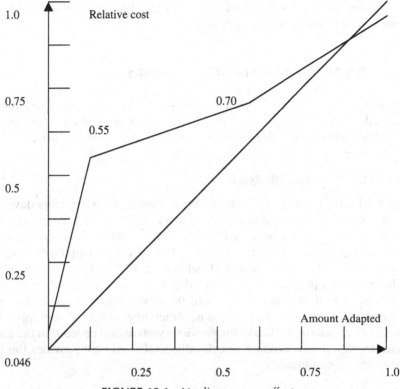

FIGURE 19.1   Nonlinear reuse effects.

19.2.4   Time-to-Market Gains

To be fair, reuse does yields benefit not only in terms of productivity (application development costs) and quality (lower maintenance costs) but also in terms of time to market (delivering the application in a short time). Time to market can be quantified by the difference between development schedule of custom-tailored asset and the time required to retrieve and instantiate (blackbox reuse)/adapt (whitebox reuse) a reusable asset. The development schedule for custom-tailored software can be assessed using COCOMO's schedule equations. The schedule of retrieval and instantiation/adaptation is so organization-specific that it is impossible to propose generic estimates; it can be estimated by inspecting organization-specific processes.

19.2.5   Exercises

1. (B) The equation on P^{BB} derived in Section 19.2.3 stems from comparing the cost versus the benefit of the reuse option. We can, alternatively, derive the same equation by comparing the overall lifecycle costs (including development costs and limited-term maintenance costs) of the reuse option

versus the custom development option. Proceed in this manner and show how you can find the same equation.

19.3 APPLICATION ENGINEERING ECONOMICS

Whereas component engineering economics deals with the costs and benefits associated with developing a reusable asset, application engineering economics deals with developing applications using reusable assets.

19.3.1 Development with Reuse

When a software product is developed from scratch, we estimate its development cost using its estimated size, S. But when the development of the product involves reused code, we must make provisions for taking into account code that was developed from scratch with code that has been adapted from existing code. COCOMO 2.0's approach [Boehm et al. 1995] is to consider that the development of a product of size S by adaptation of existing code is equivalent (in terms of development effort) to the development from scratch of a new product of size $S' = f(S)$, for some function f. Given S', we apply the nominal effort equation given in the previous section and proceed in the same manner as with a new product. Specifically, COCOMO 2.0 provides the following conversion equation:

$$S' = f(S) = S \times \frac{1}{100} \times (\mathrm{AA} + \mathrm{SU} + 0.4 \times \mathrm{DM} + 0.3 \times \mathrm{CM} + 0.3 \times \mathrm{IM})$$

where AA = *assessment and assimilation*—a factor reflecting the effort of assessment and assimilation required to integrate the reused code into the host software product; ranges between 0 (if no effort is required) and 8 (if extensive module test and evaluation is required) and varies by increments of 2.

SU = *software understanding*—a factor reflecting the software understanding effort required to reuse the existing code at hand; varies by increments of 10 between 50 for poorly structured, poorly documented, obscure code and 10 for well-structured, well-documented, clearly written code.

DM = *design modified*—a factor measuring the percentage of the reused code's design that was modified as part of its adaptation.

CM = *code modified*—a factor measuring the percentage of the reused component's source code that was modified as part of its adaptation.

IM = *integration modified*—a factor measuring the percentage of the reused component's integration testing that had to be redone following its adaptation.

Using the estimate of size-equivalent S', we can derive the cost of adapting asset C of size S by the formula

$$\text{ADP} = \delta(S')$$

where δ is the effort estimation function that we choose to use; in the absence of better information, we take basic COCOMO's equation for the organic mode.

In the absence of the detailed information required by COCOMO 2.0, we can use the formula discussed earlier to estimate adaptation effort:

$$\text{ADP} = \text{RCA} \times E$$

where E is the cost of custom development; the default value for RCA is 0.67.

19.3.2 Productivity Gains

We consider an application A made up of three components: a reusable asset B that is reused verbatim (blackbox); a reusable asset W that is reused after adaptation (whitebox); and a component C that is custom-tailored for the purposes of this application. The case where A includes more than three components can be derived analogously; also, for the sake of presentation, we use the same symbol to represent components and their sizes.

If we neglect the size inflation that stems from reuse, we find that the cost of developing this application from scratch can be written as

$$E = \delta(B + W + C)$$

Productivity gains can be assessed by contrasting this cost against the cost of developing A with reuse. The cost of reusing B verbatim can be formulated as the cumulative cost of retrieval, acquisition, and instantiation:

$$\text{RET} + P^{\text{BB}} + \text{INS}$$

The cost of reusing W in whitebox reuse can be formulated as the cumulative cost of retrieval, acquisition, and adaptation:

$$\text{RET} + P^{\text{WB}} + \text{ADP}$$

The cost of developing part C from scratch can be formulated using traditional cost models as $\delta(C)$. The cost of integrating components B, W, and C into a unique application can be formulated as the difference between the development cost of $B + W + C$ and the individual development costs of B, W, and C:

$$\delta(B + W + C) - [\delta(B) + \delta(W) + (C)]$$

The application-level productivity gain achieved from software reuse, denoted by PG_α for application α, can then be formulated as the difference between custom development cost and development with reuse:

$$PG_\alpha = \{\text{definition}\}$$
$$\delta(B+W+C)-((\text{RET}+P^{BB}+\text{INS})+(\text{RET}+P^{WB}+\text{ADP})$$
$$+[\delta(C)]+[\delta(B+W+C)]-[\delta(B)+\delta(W)+\delta(C)])$$
$$= \{\text{simplifying, rearranging}\}$$
$$\delta(B)-(\text{RET}+P^{BB}+\text{INS})+\delta(W)-(\text{RET}+P^{WB}+\text{ADP})$$

Interestingly, the overall application level productivity gain is the sum of the productivity gains (development effort savings) of B and W, since C is developed from scratch either way. By referring to the default values of P^{BB} and INS [as fractions of $\delta(B)$] and the default values of P^{WB} and ADP (as fractions of $\delta(C)$), we can rewrite the above expression as

$$\delta(B) \times 0.28 + \delta(W) \times 0.09 - 2 \times \text{RET}$$

For B and W small enough, and RET large enough, this expression can be dangerously close to zero, even less than zero—not to mention the fact that our model makes no provision for reuse risks.

19.3.3   Quality Gains

Application-level quality gains can be derived from component-level quality gains, for all the components that are used in the application. Better-quality reusable assets translate into less corrective maintenance as far as these assets are concerned. Also, better documentation for the reusable assets translates into lower maintenance costs, per maintenance action, across all types of maintenance (corrective, perfective, adaptive). Given an application α, we let BB_α and WB_α be (resp.) the multiset of reusable assets that have been used in the development of application α; because these are multisets, the same asset may appear more than once, in the same multiset. The quality gains at year y for application α can be captured by the following formula:

$$QG_\alpha(y) = \sum_{\gamma \in BB_\alpha} QG^{BB}(y) + \sum_{\gamma \in WB_\alpha} QG^{WB}(y)$$

From this formula, we can derive the (limited-term) comulative quality gains achieved from software reuse of an application α, or the net present value of quality gains (if we scale down future gains by the discount rate). In the next chapter we discuss how we can use this *quality gains* function to build a ROI model at the application level.

19.3.4 Time-to-Market Gains

Shortened time to market carries two benefits for the application developer:

- *Increased Sales Volume*. With shortened time to market, the project will start collecting benefits earlier. For a fixed term (Y), collecting earlier means also collecting more.
- *Increased Market Share*. By getting to market earlier, the project has the potential of securing a bigger share of the market, by virtue of its exclusive (if temporary) access to users.

While it easy to quantify gains that stem from sales volume, it is much more difficult to quantify those that stem from market share.

19.3.5 Exercises

1. (B) Consider a reusable asset C of size $S = 40$ KLOC; we are interested in comparing the two alternative methods that we have to estimate its adaptation costs:

   (a) Compute the adaptation effort of component C using COCOMO 2.0's equation, taking the following values for the relevant cost factors:

   $$AA = 4$$
   $$SU = 30$$
   $$DM = 20$$
   $$CM = 20$$
   $$IM = 10$$

   (b) Compute an estimate of its adaptation effort using the formula $ADP = RCA \times E$, where E is derived by means of basic COCOMO's effort equation.

   (c) Compare and conclude. Note that we normally apply the second method only if the information required to apply the first method is unavailable.

2. (B) Consider the two formulas discussed in Section 19.3.1 for estimating adaptation costs of software components. We pose $DM = CM = IM$, and we let AA and SU take median values ($AA = 4$, and $SU = 30$). For what value of DM are the two formulas identical? Comment.

3. (A) Work the details of the formula given in Section 19.3.2 for application-level productivity gains; justify all the steps.

4. (A) Propose realistic data for which the productivity gains formula given in Section 19.3.2 produces a value of zero.

5. (R) Catalog reuse related risks at the application level. Consider, for example, such contingencies as application developers attempting retrievals

and failing to find satisfactory assets; or retrieving assets, only to find subsequently that these are not adequate for their purposes. How can these risks be integrated in the model discussed in Section 19.3.2?

6. (A) Quantify time-to-market benefits that stem from increased sales volume.

7. (R) Discuss models for time-to-market benefits that stem from increased market share.

19.4   FURTHER READING

The original COCOMO model is due to Boehm [1981]. COCOMO 2.0 is due to Boehm et al. [1995]. Many of the constants used as default options in this chapter are due to Poulin [1997b], who derives these constants by synthesizing a wide range of past empirical experiments. The chart we have used to derive the RCA factor is due to Selby [1989].

Chapter 20

Software Reuse Return on Investment

Software reuse is dependent on the seamless cooperation of many parties in an organization, and it will happen only if all the parties involved in this co-operative process can achieve the corporate reuse goals at the same time as they are achieving the goals that are mandated for themselves or their teams.

In order to model this multiparty, multicriterion situation, we take the following modeling decisions.

- There are four parties in the software reuse process: the corporate management, which has a stake in seeing the reuse program reap benefits for the corporation; the domain engineering team, which has a stake in seeing its domain engineering products reused; the application engineering teams, which have a stake in producing applications with low cost, high quality, and short time to market; and the component developers, who have a stake in seeing their components reused widely.

- Each party has to take decisions as part of the software reuse process. Corporate management must decide whether to initiate a corporate reuse program, and in the affirmative must make strategic decision about upfront investment costs, investment cycles, and discount rates; the domain engineering team regularly makes decisions about whether to initiate a domain engineering activity, by considering domain analysis costs, asset development costs, and expected pervasiveness of the proposed domain in the corporate business plan; project teams regularly make decisions about whether to apply reuse in a development project, and must consider risks and benefits of reuse for their project; component developers regularly make decisions about whether to build a reusable asset for a specific function, and must consider the development costs against the potential benefits.

- The four parties can model their decisionmaking process in economic terms, following an investment cycle. At the corporate level, corporate management commits resources to initiate a reuse program, and expects to reap benefits in terms of better product quality, higher productivity, and shorter time to market; at the domain engineering department level, the reuse department commits resources to initiate a domain engineering initiative and expects to reap benefits by *selling* (internally if needed) reusable assets to project teams; project teams commit resources and take risks to adopt a reuse discipline, and expect to reap benefits in terms of productivity, quality, and timeliness of project completion; component developers commit resources to develop a reusable asset, and expect to reap benefits by *selling* the asset to project teams, internally if needed.

- The four economic decisions can be quantified by ROI functions. These economic functions enable the decisionmaker to make binary decisions, and quantify to what extent the selected decision is justified.

- In order for reuse to happen in an organization, relevant cost factors must be fine-tuned so that the ROIs of all the parties are positive.

This puts to rest the premise that one can make reuse happen by lecturing or preaching to concerned parties. Rather, the corporation must set up reward–reporting–accounting mechanisms to ensure that the corporate goals are reached at the same time as the goals of individual parties and teams.

20.1 MODELING INVESTMENT DECISIONS

20.1.1 Investment Cost Factors

An investment decision can be analyzed and quantified by five cost factors, which we review briefly below.

- *Investment cycle*, denoted by Y, measured in number of years, typically ranging between 3 and 5, counted from a start date, which we denote by SD.

- *Discount rate*, denoted by d, is an abstract quantity typically ranging between 0.10 and 0.20; it reflects the time value of money (if we consent to spend a dollar today, we expect to get back at least $(1 + d)$ dollars within a year to make the sacrifice worthwhile).

- *Investment costs*, denoted by IC, and measured in person months. We use the person-months as the unit of measurement because most costs that arise can best be quantified as personnel effort; when, occasionally, we encounter costs that are more naturally quantified in monetary terms, we use a default ratio to convert them to person months.

- *Episodic benefits*, at year y, for $SD + 1 \leq y \leq SD + Y$, denoted by $B(y)$, and measured in person-months.
- *Episodic costs*, at year y, for $SD + 1 \leq y \leq SD + Y$, denoted by $C(y)$, and measured in person-months.

For the sake of uniformity, we take the following notational conventions, which we may occasionally use throughout the chapter:

- We extend function C to year SD, and we pose $C(SD) = IC$.
- We extend function B to year SD, and we pose the default value $B(SD) = 0$. There are situations where we want to assign $B(SD)$ a value different from zero; but zero is the implicit value when no other value is specified.

We further extend this convention by considering that for years prior to the start of the cycle (SD), both $B(y)$ and $C(y)$ are zero.

20.1.2 Economic Functions

The literature on engineering economics provides a wide range of economic functions that can be used to assess the worthiness of an investment decision; we review these briefly below.

- *Net present value* (NPV), measured in person-months, and defined by

$$NPV = -IC + \sum_{y=SD+1}^{SD+Y} \frac{B(y) - C(y)}{(1+d)^{y-SD}}$$

An investment is worthwhile whenever the NPV exceeds zero; it is all the more attractive that NPV is larger. Using the conventions introduced above, we can write the NPV formula as

$$NPV = \sum_{z=0}^{Y} \frac{B(SD+z) - C(SD+z)}{(1+d)^{z}}$$

For the purposes of this study, we adopt this latter definition of NPV, because it gives us more latitude to decide how to define $B(SD)$ and $C(SD)$.

- *Return on investment* (ROI), defined by (the dimensionless formula)

$$ROI = \frac{NPV}{IC}$$

The ROI formula recognizes that investments involve risks, and that our estimates are not always accurate, and hence prorates the net present value (potential payoff) with the investment cost. For the same value of NPV, the investment is all the more worthwhile that IC is relatively smaller.

- *Profitability index* (PI), defined by (the dimensionless formula)

$$PI = \frac{1}{IC} \times \sum_{z=1}^{Y} \frac{B(SD+z) - C(SD+z)}{(1+D)^z}$$

This quantity prorates the potential profit with respect to the investment cost. An investment is worthwhile whenever PI exceeds 1, and is all the more attractive that PI is greater.

- *Average rate of return* (ARR), defined by the dimensionless formula

$$ARR = \frac{PI}{Y}$$

It prorates the profitability index by the number of years in the investment cycle.

- *Average return on book value* (ARBV), defined with respect to an *amortization schedule* of the investment cost over the investment cycle. We model the amortization schedule by means of a function $Am(y)$ that satisfies the equation $\sum_{z=1}^{Y} Am(SD+z) = IC$, and we define ARBV by

$$ARBV = \frac{1}{Y \times IC} \times \sum_{z=1}^{Y} \frac{B(SD+z) - C(SD+z) - Am(SD+z)}{(1+d)^z}$$

Favaro [1996] discourages the use of this function, because it is vulnerable to many accounting distortions and too many subjective factors. Although we agree with Favaro's assessment, we do include it for now, for the sake of completeness, and we usually take $Am(y) = IC/Y$ for all $y: SD + 1 \le y \le SD + Y$.

- *Internal rate of return* (IRR), defined as the value of d that makes the net present value zero, namely, the solution in d of the following equation:

$$\sum_{z=0}^{Y} \frac{B(SD+z) - C(SD+z)}{(1+d)^z} = 0$$

An investment is worthwhile if IRR is smaller than the corporate discount rate (determined by corporate management as a strategic decision).

- *Payback value* (PBV), defined as the shortest investment cycle that makes the net present value nonnegative, that is, the smallest integer value in Y such that

$$\sum_{z=0}^{Y} \frac{B(SD+z)-C(SD+z)}{(1+d)^{z}} \geq 0$$

An investment is worthwhile is PBV is smaller than the amount of time that corporate management is willing to wait for the investment cost to be amortized.

20.1.3 Exercises

1. (A) Provide closed forms for the following quantities.

(a) $\sum_{x=1}^{X} \frac{1}{(1+d)^{x}}$.

(b) $\sum_{x=1}^{X} \frac{x}{(1+d)^{x}}$.

(c) $\sum_{x=X}^{X'} \frac{1}{(1+d)^{x}}$.

(d) $\sum_{x=1}^{X} \frac{x}{(1+d)^{x}}$.

2. (A) What do you infer about an investment decision whose NPV is very high (say, 200 person-months), and whose ROI is very low (say, 0.20)? Is it worth the investment?

3. (A) Under what condition on ARR is an investment profitable?

4. (A) Under what condition on ARBV is an investment profitable?

5. (A) Assume that the quantity $B(y) - C(y)$ is independent of y, for $y > SD$, and write it as a linear function of IC, for example

$$B(y)-C(y) = \lambda \times IC$$

Derive PBV as a function of IC and λ. Compute concrete values of PB for selected values of λ (e.g., 0.10, 0.20, 0.30), given that $d = 0.15$.

20.2 SOFTWARE REUSE INVESTMENT DECISIONS

A corporate software reuse initiative involves many stakeholders: corporate managers, domain engineering teams, application engineering teams, individual producers of reusable assets. Each stakeholder has a distinct ROI equation, which can be characterized by analyzing the cost factors that we have discussed in Section 20.1.1. In this section, we discuss these cost factors, and investigate how they can be estimated in practice. For the sake of simplicity, we focus our discussion on factors IC, $B(y)$, and $C(y)$, since factors Y and d are uniform within a corporation, and hence are the same for all stakeholders; also, their derivation (a strategic corporate decision) raises no special issue. This section shows how these costs are cascaded from one investment cycle to the next; this cascade effect is illustrated in Figure 20.1 and Table 20.1.

20.2.1 Component Engineering Investment Cycle

We review in turn the three cost factors of investment costs, episodic benefits, and episodic costs, as they apply to the component developer. The investment decision we are dealing with here is whether to develop a reusable asset to

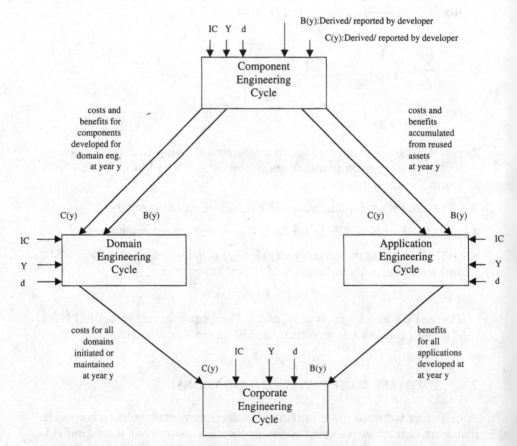

FIGURE 20.1 Cascade of costs through investment cycles [IC—upfront investment costs; *Y*—investment cycle (in years); *B(y)*—benefits at year *y*; *D*—discount rate; *C(y)*—costs at year *y*].

TABLE 20.1   Balance Sheets

Year, y	Cost, $C(y)$	Benefit, $B(y)$
	Component Balance Sheet	
$y = \mathrm{SD}$	Development for reuse	—
$y > \mathrm{SD}$	Residence costs + maintenance	Sales to projects
	Domain Balance Sheet	
$y = \mathrm{SD}$	Domain analysis + asset development	—
$y > \mathrm{SD}$	Asset development + concentrated domain analysis	Asset sales to projects
	Application Balance Sheet	
$y = \mathrm{SD}$	Purchase of reusable assets	Development cost savings
$y > \mathrm{SD}$	—	Quality gains
	Corporate Balance Sheet	
$y = \mathrm{SD}$	Infrastructure	—
$y > \mathrm{SD}$	Domain costs	Application benefits

satisfy a tentatively specified set of requirements; the decision will hinge on how much it costs to develop this asset, how much savings project teams will achieve by reusing it, and with what frequency we expect this asset to be needed in future development projects. Relevant costs are cataloged as follows:

- *Investment Costs.* The upfront investment costs involved in component engineering include the costs of development for reuse, and the costs of reuse certification and library insertion. Specifically, the investment cost of the component engineering investment cycle, which we represent as the episodic cost at year SD, can be quantified by the following equation:

$$C_y(\mathrm{SD}) = \mathrm{ER} + \mathrm{LI}$$

where ER is the estimated cost of development for reuse and LI is the cost of certification and library insertion. In the absence of more accurate information, ER can be estimated by estimating the cost of development from scratch, E (using traditional cost estimation models) and prorating it with the RCWR factor (relative cost of writing for reuse, for which we have discussed default values in the previous chapter), specifically, $\mathrm{RE} = E \times \mathrm{RCWR}$.

- *Episodic Costs.* The episodic costs at year y, for $\mathrm{SD} + 1 \le y \le \mathrm{SD} + Y$, can be quantified by the following equation:

$$C_\gamma(y) = OC(y) + MN_\gamma(y)$$

where $OC(y)$ is the component's share of the yearly cost of operating the library and $MN_\gamma(y)$ is the maintenance cost of component γ at year y. The term $OC(y)$ can trivially be quantified by dividing the labor costs of operating the library by the size of the library, and is realistically independent of γ—although it could conceivably depend on y (e.g., by virtue of economy of scale phenomena, as the size of the library increases). The term $MN_\gamma(y)$ can be quantified by means of COCOMO-like maintenance effort equations; it is, of course, dependent on the component, and may well depend on the year (e.g., decrease as the component improves, or increase as the component grows larger). Note that this term is different from the maintenance effort we mentioned in the previous chapter in our discussion of component-level quality gains. In quantifying quality gains, we are measuring the maintenance costs that are incumbent on the end user of applications, whereas in this discussion we are interested in the maintenance costs that are incumbent on the component developer, which include such aspects as versioning and release management. Another way to distinguish between these maintenance cost factors is to consider that maintenance costs that are used to quantify quality gains are those that are charged against the application team (and/or their customers or end users) and maintenance costs that are included in a component's episodic costs are those that are charged against the domain team (specifically, against the component developer's account).

- *Episodic Benefits.* These are the much-touted gains in productivity and quality that stem from reuse. Gains in productivity can be quantified by subtracting reuse costs from custom development costs. Custom development costs can be derived using traditional cost estimation models. Reuse costs can be derived using the multitude of empirical results that are available nowadays. Gains in quality can be quantified in person-months by equating them with the gains in maintenance costs integrated over the relevant lifetime of the reusable products [H. Mili et al. 1999a, Mili 1996]. Episodic benefits at year y, for $SD + 1 \le y \le SD + Y$, can be quantified by the following equation:

$$B_\gamma = \text{freq}(y) \times P_\gamma^{BB}(y) + \text{freq}'(y) \times P_\gamma^{WB}(y)$$

where $\text{freq}(y)$ = frequency of blackbox use of the component at hand at year y [depending on whether y is in the past or in the future, $\text{freq}(y)$ can be collected from reuse data or estimated on the basis of expert judgment]

$P_\gamma^{BB}(y)$ = blackbox sale price of component γ (this quantity must be low enough to encourage application developers to acquire it, yet high enough to ensure that the component's return on investment is positive) freq$'(y)$ = frequency of whitebox use of the component at hand at year y [depending on whether y is in the past or in the future, freq$'(y)$ can be collected from reuse data or estimated on the basis of expert judgment]

$P_\gamma^{BB}(y)$ = whitebox sale price of component γ

20.2.2 Application Engineering Investment Cycle

We review in turn the three cost factors of investment costs, episodic benefits, and episodic costs, as they apply to the manager of an application engineering development project. The investment decision we are dealing with here is whether to adopt reuse in a given development project; the decision will hinge on how much of a match there is between the project's needs and the available reusable assets, and how much of an overhead reuse adoption involves for the project. The investment cycle of application engineering has some special features, which we review:

1. We assume that an application development project takes place well within a year, and hence all the development costs can be modeled as upfront investment costs, or, equivalently, as episodic costs at year SD.

2. The costs of application development with reuse have to be balanced against the cost of custom development of an equivalent application; we model this situation by means of a nonzero value for the benefit function at year SD.

With these two qualifications in mind, we review the costs involved and discuss how to quantify them.

- *Investment Costs.* The costs of reuse adoption include the cost of training, tool acquisition, and the operational impact of reuse processes. The operational risks that stem from reuse adoption include the following contingencies:

  Components can be retrieved without being relevant, if the library's retrieval procedure does not have good precision.

  Components can be retrieved and be deemed relevant, but prove subsequently to cost too much to adapt and integrate.

  All of these costs can be quantified in person months, specifically the person-months wasted because of the distractions caused by poor retrieval precision or poor quality reusable assets. At year SD, the application engineering costs for application α are the costs of acquiring reusable assets, which we write as

$$C_\alpha(\text{SD}) = \sum_{\gamma \in \alpha} PR_\gamma$$

where PR_γ is the price of component γ. Depending on whether component γ is used *blackbox* or *whitebox* in developing application α, we find $PR_\gamma = P_\gamma^{BB}$, or $PR_\gamma = P_\gamma^{WB}$.

- *Episodic Costs.* For years subsequent to the cycle's start date (SD), episodic costs are zero:

$$C_\alpha(y) = 0,\, SD+1 \le y \le Y$$

- *Episodic Benefits.* At year SD, the benefit derived from reuse is the cost savings achieved by using reusable assets rather than writing custom code. This is the application level productivity gain achieved from reuse, which we have discussed in the previous chapter. We find

$$B_\alpha(SD) = PG_\alpha$$

The episodic benefits of subsequent years, $y > SD$, can be quantified by the quality gains achieved from reuse, which we have discussed in the previous chapter. We find

$$B_\alpha(SD) = QG_\alpha(y)$$

20.2.3 Domain Engineering Investment Cycle

We review in turn the three cost factors of investment costs, episodic benefits, and episodic costs, as they apply to the manager of a domain engineering initiative. The investment decision we are dealing with here is whether to initiate a domain engineering effort in a tentatively specified application domain; the decision hinges on how much development activity is expected in the future within the specified domain, and how much effort is involved in performing domain analysis and design for reuse. Relevant costs are cataloged as follows:

- *Investment Costs.* The upfront investment costs of domain engineering are the (nontrivial) costs of domain analysis, asset development (for reuse), and asset cataloging. We can quantify them by adding the domain analysis costs to the investment costs of all the components that are developed at year SD as part of the domain engineering effort. Quantitatively, we write

$$C_\delta(SD) = DA + \sum_{\gamma \in \delta} C_\gamma(SD)$$

The first term of this equation represents the domain analysis costs; the second term represents the development and cataloging costs of all the domain assets that are developed at year SD. Even though the sum quantifier covers all the domain assets, only assets that are created at year SD are accounted for, since the other assets (that are created in subsequent years) have zero cost for year SD.

- *Episodic Costs.* Episodic costs of the domain engineering cycle at year y, for $SD + 1 \le y \le SD + Y$, are the sum of the episodic costs of all the components that are developed at year y as part of the domain. Specifically

$$C_\delta(y) = \sum_{\gamma \in \delta} C_\gamma(y), \quad y \ge SD+1$$

The convention that $C_\gamma(SD) = IC$ provides, with respect to the formula of $C_\delta(y)$ that if several components of a domain are developed over several years, they are duly discounted against the appropriate years. This, in turn, means that we do not have to assume that all the components of a domain have to be developed at once, at the beginning of the domain engineering cycle.

- *Episodic Benefits.* Episodic benefits of the domain engineering cycle at year y, for $SD + 1 \le y \le SD + Y$, are the sum of the episodic benefits of all the components that are developed as part of the domain. Specifically

$$B_\delta(y) = \sum_{\gamma \in \delta} B_\gamma(y), \quad y \ge SD+1$$

20.2.4 Corporate Investment Cycle

We review in turn the three cost factors of investment costs, episodic benefit, and episodic costs, as they apply to the corporate manager. The investment decision we are dealing with here is whether to initiate a corporate software reuse program; the decision will hinge on the expected infrastructure costs, the operational impact of reuse introduction, and the expected volume of development activity. Relevant costs are cataloged as follows:

- *Investment Costs.* The upfront investment costs of the corporate investment cycle include the cost of building a reuse infrastructure and initiating a reuse program, which include purchasing and installing a repository to hold reusable assets; required hiring, personnel training, and operational modifications within the corporation; and eventually, the cost of initially populating the reuse library. All these costs can be computed or estimated at the beginnings of the corporate investment cycle, yielding the value of $C_\rho(SD)$.

- *Episodic Costs.* The corporate episodic cost at year y, $SD + 1 \le y \le SD + Y$, is the cumulative episodic cost of all the domain engineering activities that are active in a given year. It also includes the cumulative upfront cost for all development projects and domain engineering initiatives that started on the given year. This can merely be written as

$$C_\rho(y) = \sum_{\delta \in \rho} C_\delta(y), \quad SD+1 \le y \le SD+Y$$

- *Episodic Benefits*. The corporate episodic benefit is the cumulative application engineering benefit of all the projects that are in progress on a given year:

$$B_\rho(y) = \sum_{\delta \in \rho} B_\delta(y), \text{SD} + 1 \le y \le \text{SD} + Y$$

The cascade pattern by which costs are propagated from one decision cycle to the next is highlighted in Figure 20.1. This figure illustrates how the various viewpoints are related to each other, and how the cost parameters can be fine-tuned to ensure that all viewpoints are satisfied. Figure 20.1 complements Table 20.1 by showing the cost table of each investment cycle, for the start date (SD) and for subsequent dates ($y > $ SD).

Note that the corporate level benefits are the cumulative benefits reaped from application engineering, while the corporate-level costs are the cumulative costs incurred from domain engineering. One may want to ask what happened to domain engineering benefits and application engineering costs. The answer lies in the way in which costs and benefits are tallied in Table 20.1: the benefits of domain engineering, which are "Asset sales to projects," cancel out the costs of application engineering, which are "Purchase of reusable assets." At the corporate level, this transfer of assets (and reverse transfer of credit) is an internal operation, which represents neither a gain nor a loss. If the domain engineering activity were selling assets outside the corporation, and/or the application engineering activity were purchasing assets from outside the corporation, then this delicate balance would be broken, and we would have to redefine corporate costs and corporate benefits as the cumulative costs and benefits of both domain engineering and application engineering.

20.2.5   Exercises

1. (A) The formulas of the corporate investment cycle depend on the premise that all reusable assets are for private corporate consumption (no sale to outside developers) and that all reusable assets used in application development come from corporate domain engineering (no outside procurement). Lift in turn each one of these hypotheses and show how the corporate return on investment formula is affected.

2. (B) It is tempting to think that, in the same way as the costs and benefits of a domain are obtained from adding the costs and benefits of the assets in the domain, the costs and benefits of an application are obtained from adding the costs and benefits of the assets that make up the application. Explain why such is not the case.

3. (B) Consider several possible arrangements of maintenance contracts between developers and users of reusable assets. Analyze the impact of each arrangement on (a) quality gains achieved by application engineering and (b) episodic costs charged against component developers and domain engineering.

4. **(B)** We have argued repeatedly throughout this book that reusability is made up of two attributes, which are usefulness and usability. Consider the component level ROI and show how these attributes are quantified.

5. **(R)** In order for software reuse to happen in an organization, all the stakeholders have to find that reuse is in their best interest. In this exercise, we wish to use the ROI (return on investment) models as a framework to investigate how to make reuse happen.

   (a) Identify all the cost factors that arise in the ROI cycles and that can be controlled at the corporate level.

   (b) Using a single function (e.g., the net present value), write a system of equations to the effect that all the net present values are positive.

   (c) Discuss how to use this system of equations to derive the controllable factors. Adjust the list of controllable factors as necessary.

   (d) Solve the same system, this time maximizing the corporate net present value while keeping all the other net present values positive.

6. **(R)** Review the various organizational structures that are possible in software reuse (see Chapter 4). Analyze the impact that these structures may have on the ROI formulas.

20.3 FURTHER READING

There has been a great deal of research on the economics of software reuse, and a large number of economic models have been proposed [Balda and Gustafson 1990; Barnes and Bollinger 1991; Boehm et al. 1995; Bollinger and Pfleeger 1990; Bowes et al. 1992; CSE 1999; Coulange 1998; Favaro 1996; Favaro et al. 1998; Frakes and Terry 1994; Frazier 1993; Gaffney and Cruickschank 1992; Gaffney and Durek 1989; Guerrieri et al. 1989; Henderson-Sellers 1993; Jones 1994; Kain 1994; Kang and Levy 1989; Karlsson et al. 1992; Leach 1997; Lim 1992, 1994, 1996; Malan 1993; Malan and Wentzel 1993; Margano and Rhoads 1992; Mayobre 1991; Melo et al. 1995; Mili 1996; NATO 1991; Pant et al. 1996; Poulin 1997a, 1997b; Poulin and Caruso 1993; Raymond and Hollis 1991; Reifer 1997; Schach 1994; Schach and Yang 1995; Schimsky 1992; Stevens 1993].

Interestingly, even though these models appear to be dealing with the same problem (software reuse cost estimation), they in fact differ significantly from each other. Some of the features that distinguish between these different cost models include the following:

* *Investment Cycle.* We recognize that most decisions that arise in the practice of software reuse can be modeled as return on investment decisions. Also, we have identified four distinct investment cycles, which we have briefly introduced above: the *corporate* investment cycle, the *domain*

engineering investment cycle, the *application engineering* investment cycle, and the *component engineering* investment cycle. Each of these cycles is subject to a specific economic rationale, and can be quantified by means of a variety of economic functions.

- *Economic Function.* Favaro [1996] identifies five different functions that an investment assessment model may want to consider: *net present value*, *payback value*, *average return on book value*, *internal rate of return*, and *profitability index*. Traditional textbook references on engineering economics [Berney and Garstka 1984; Horngren 1981; Van Horne 1983; Viscione 1984] discuss other relevant functions that pertain to investment cycles.

- *Cost Factors.* For a given investment cycle and a given economic function, the set of cost factors that are taken into account in a cost model is the most important feature of the model; this feature specifies what aspects of the reuse decision we want to consider.

- *Reuse Organization.* Several organizational models are possible in software reuse [Caldiera and Basili 1991; Coulange 1998; Fafchamps 1994]; the organizational structure has some impact on how costs are determined, charged, and accounted for. Many cost models assume specific organizational structures, but virtually none make this assumption explicit.

- *Scope.* Some models consider a punctual decision, whereas others consider a long term investment cycle; some models limit the investment cycle on the basis of technical considerations (life expectancy of a reusable asset), while still others limit the cycle on the basis of strategic considerations (e.g., investment must pay off within 3 years, investment cycle driven by market considerations).

- *Hypotheses.* Some cost models neglect integration costs, and assume that the cost of building an aggregate of two components is the sum of building each; some cost models assume that software development costs are linear in the size of the product; some cost models fail to take into account the discount rate of resources; some cost models ignore quality gains and focus on productivity gains; some (virtually all) cost models ignore the inflation of code size that stems from software reuse, when in fact reusable code tends to be larger than code developed for a specific single use (due to requirements of generality); finally, virtually all cost models ignore time-to-market benefits that stem from software reuse.

- *Viewpoint.* Many parties are involved in a software reuse initiative; these include the corporate executives, the producer staff, the consumer staff, the library managers, and component providers. Each of these parties has a specific outlook, a specific objective function to optimize, specific constraints, and specific responsibilities—all of which influence the party's interpretation of economic equations.

References on engineering economics, where the interested reader is referred for more information on investment analysis, include discussions on economics Berney and Garstka 1984; Horngren 1981; Van Horne 1983; Viscione 1984].

Part VII

Software Reuse Technologies

Practicing software reuse involves implementing a set of changes to the development of software at the organizational, managerial, and technical levels. Part II of this book talked about the organizational changes. Parts III, IV, and V dealt with the technical aspects, and Part VI dealt with the economic and econometric aspects.

Implementing a reuse program means making choices and tradeoffs along each of these dimensions. If we were to characterize reuse programs as points in this multidimensional (multiaspect) space, we would get a practically infinite (or a finitely impractical) number of approaches. Luckily, there emerged trends, which correspond to specific combinations of these different aspects, that are representative of industry practice, either because they have a certain conceptual cohesion, or through best of breed, natural selection process. These are *component-based software development* (CBSD), *product-line engineering* (PLE), and *COTS-based development*. The three are not orthogonal, and have a lot of common issues and solutions. However, they represent interesting combinations that are worth studying. These specialized forms of reuse are described in the next three chapters.

The following table compares the various forms along a number of dimensions:

A Comparison of CBSE, COTS, and PLE Along the Organizational, Technical, and Economic Dimensions

Aspect	Component-Based Software Engineering	COTS-Based Development	Product Line Engineering
Organizational			
Primary interactions	Involvement of component and application engineers. Library retrieval	Strong relationship with third party (component vendor)	Strong involvement of domain engineers
Primary reuse skills	Component engineer Application engineer Reuse librarian	Reuse manager	Domain engineer Architect
Technical			
Integration	Compositional with other components. Generative	Compositional only	Compositional into domain architecture. Generative
Constraints	Components comply with component model (not necessarily domain constraints)	Components comply to application constraints	Components comply to domain architecture constraints
Support service responsibilities	Application engineers	Component vendor	Domain engineers
Packaging	Binary source code may be available and modifiable	Binary black box components	Reference architecture, middleware infrastructure; guidelines; binary components; source code
Retrieval	Public or domain libraries	Commercial advertisement	Domain libraries
Implementation technology	Defined by component model	Not controllable	Defined by reference architecture.
Economical			
Component acquisition	Adapt	Buy	Instantiate
Market scope	Driven by ROI from an application developer perspective	Driven by ROI from the component provider perspective	Driven by ROI from the domain engineering perspective
Economical motivations	Common component models	Common market	Common design and architecture.

Chapter 21

Component-Based Software Engineering (CBSE)

Component-based software engineering is a special case of software engineering *for* and *with* reusable assets; reusable assets have a special packaging, and are referred to as *components*. The term "component" is hopelessly overloaded, and has been used to refer to reusable assets for as long as we have been talking about reuse [McIlroy 1970]. The component ideal envisioned by reuse researchers, practitioners, and preachers is one of reusable assets that are self-contained, fairly independent concrete realizations, that require little or no customization (plug and play) and that provide well-defined services to the applications in which they integrate [Cox 1990]. Advances in software development methods and in software packaging techniques have made this component ideally attainable, if not fully realized. This chapter looks at the nature of components, and at the specific processes and issues in building, acquiring, and using components in application development.

From a development point of view, components embody the best of breed in terms of abstraction and composition. To this end, component technology employs the most advanced abstraction (e.g., introspection; see Sections 11.3 and 11.4) and composition techniques (see Section 12.4). Among other things, this often means that, at the very least, the components have to abide by an interface standard. More typically, in addition to standardized interfaces, their interaction will be mediated through a separate software layer (middleware, called *computational infrastructure* in Chapter 14; see Sections 14.3–14.5).

From a process point of view, component-based development is interface-centric and centered around integration. Interoperability with legacy subsystems that do not abide by the chosen interface standard poses new challenges.

From an economic point of view, component-based development is a viable alternative to other development approaches if there is a dynamic component market with broad offerings and competitive pricing. Because components rely on component models, the acceptance and standardization of these models is of utmost importance. As we saw in Chapter 14, the industry is not short of standards! Different component technology vendors have wisely chosen to ensure interoperability of the standards while they try to dominate the market, making it conceivable, if not entirely practical, for technology consumers to make rational decisions.

In the next section, we define components. Component models are described in Section 21.2. Section 21.3 provides an overview of the lifecycles for component-based development. Issues specific to component-based development that have not been addressed in Chapter 17 are discussed in Section 21.4. References and suggestions for further reading are given in Section 21.5.

21.1 COMPONENTS

With the growing literature on CBSE [Szyperski 1999, CBSE 1999, D'Souza and Wills 1998, Bosch et al. 1997], the term *software component* is overloaded with multiple definitions, close to the point of making the term devoid of meaning. We start by discussing some of the definitions, and settling on a working definition for the purposes of this chapter. Section 21.1.2 discusses the structure components in terms of the interfaces it has with its environment. Section 21.1.3 gives a list of desirable characteristics of components.

21.1.1 What Is a Component

Brown and Wallnau acknowledge in their workshop summary [Brown and Wallnau 1998, CBSE 1999] the multitude of definitions of software components and further analyze the variances in terms of granularity, context dependence, and autonomy. Several authors define a component in different contexts. Some of these definitions are:

1. A component is an encapsulated, distributable software package with well-defined interfaces [CBSE 1999]. The encapsulation attribute implies the self-containment property of a component and its provision of some considerable functionality. The interface attribute implies the ability to compose components.

2. A software component is a unit of composition with contractually specified interfaces and whose context dependencies are all explicited. A software component can be deployed independently and is subject to composition by third party [Szyperski and Pfister 1997]. This definition covers technical aspects

of a component: independence, contractual interfaces, and composition. It also covers some market-related aspects such as deployment by third parties. The fact that a component can be *deployed* means that a component embodies executable or loadable code, which precludes a great many kinds of reusable assets such as source-level class libraries, reference architectures [Szyperski 1999], and other assets that need to be transformed (compiled, generated) in some way before they are made part of a running system.

3. A component is a coherent package of software implementation that [D'Souza and Wills 1998] (a) can be independently developed and delivered, (b) has explicit and well-specified interfaces for the services it provides, (c) has explicit and well-specified interfaces for the services it expects from others, and (d) can be composed with other components, perhaps customizing some of their properties, without modifying the components themselves. In addition to the independent development and the clear specification of services and dependencies, this definition stresses again the notion that a component is not to be changed. However, unlike Szyperski's definition, it does not insist on the components being deployable as is. The Unified Modeling Language (UML 1.3) defines a component type, components, and a component instances. A component type is part of UML's metamodel and is used to describe different kinds of components, such as source components, library components, resource components, and executables. Components represent packagings of such software artifacts, and may be seen as units of relatively independent deliverables. A component instance represents a runtime implementation unit and may be used to show implementation units that have identity at runtime, including their location on processing nodes. These definitions are somewhat orthogonal to the previous ones since they focus on lifecycle issues. Sametinger [1997] gives a superset of these definitions; see paragraph 4 (below).

4. Reusable software components are self-contained, clearly identifiable pieces that describe and/or perform specific functions, have clear interfaces, appropriate documentation, and a defined reuse status. Sametinger claims that this definition conforms to the definitions given in the NATO standard for the development of reusable software components [Brown 1994]. The fact that a component may either *describe* or *perform* specific functions means that Sametinger includes in his definition things such as reusable specifications, analysis models, and the like, making component-based development indistinguishable from general development with reusable assets.

Conspicuously absent from the definitions given above is the reference to any implementation technology. This is no accident, and there is a wide consensus that components are not objects, and need *not* be implemented with objects. In terms of granularity, components are typically larger than classes. According to Steel [Steel 1996], the success of component software—which is not necessarily object-oriented—over objects is due the to the coarser granularity of components. *Object-oriented components* are typically implemented as a set of classes where one of the classes plays the role of a façade for the remaining classes in the component; COM components are like that.

21.1.2   The Anatomy of a Component

Typically, we describe components in terms of interfaces that provide access to their functionality. Several languages are used to describe component interfaces, including module interface languages (MILs), interface definition languages (IDLs), and architecture description languages (ADLs). Regardless of the notation and semantics of an interface description language, one can classify component's interfaces according to possible interactions with the surrounding artifacts and environment. Figure 21.1 illustrates a high-level model of a component that explicitly defines its interaction with other components and with the platform on which it executes.

We distinguish the following model elements:

1. *Internals (Private Aspects)*. This part represents internal information and structure of a component. It provides the actual functionality of the component as exposed by its interface. This element is private to the component and is not exposed to any other component or to the platform on which it runs. The component internals embody implementation decisions, and are or should be hidden from other components. The interfaces should reveal as little as possible about the inner working; only the necessary functionalities are exposed.

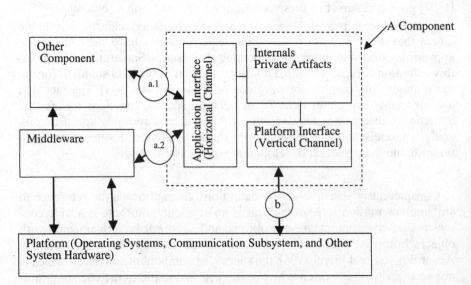

FIGURE 21.1   A component model with emphasis on interactions with other artifacts.

2. *Application Interfaces*. These interfaces define the interactions with other application artifacts such as other components or applications. Such interfaces represent the import/export relationships with other components (or the middleware) with which the component interacts. A set of exported interfaces represents the functionality that this component can provide. A set of imported interfaces represents the functionalities that the component requires from external components in the process of performing its own functionalities. These interfaces are sometimes called *horizontal channels* as they specify the interaction with other peer components and application entities irrespective of the platform or hardware on which they run. The inspection of horizontal channel interfaces enables us to identify the structure of messages sent/received from other component, study timing issues as related to requests coming in/from the component, and discover incompatibilities in data formats and types and incompatibilities in the message protocol (synchronous, asynchronous, publish and subscribe, etc.). Notice that a component may export several interfaces. For instance, there will be instances where different clients may need different sets of services, which may all be conveniently implemented by the same component. The circumstance where components are extended is a special case of this situation; clients written into an older release may see one interface, whereas clients written into the new release may want to use the new services as well. All the integration frameworks discussed in Sections 14.3–14.5 support the extension of interfaces, with COM addressing this problem head on, since it was one of the motivations behind the technology (see Section 14.5). As for import interfaces, they may appear to contradict the independence property of components. In fact, independence should be interpreted in a broader sense. First, it is not reasonable to demand total independence of components; a component should not have to carry with it a database management system, say! Rather than total independence, we should understand independence in terms of (1) *explicit* and *documented* dependencies and (2) *graceful degradation of service*, when a dependent component is not available.

3. *Platform Interfaces*. These interfaces define the component interaction with the platform on which it executes. A platform may be characterized by the hardware (a specific processor, memory, communication equipment, and probably other hardware as well), the operating system, including the runtime environment, access to peripherals, communication subsystems, and so forth. Component portability relies on a layering strategy of such interfaces so as to maximize the parts of a component that do not depend on the platform. The virtual machine paradigm is one that ensures complete portability of components; only the virtual machine needs to be rewritten from one platform to another, regardless of the component (see Section 14.1.3). Alternatively, component developers may generate different components, one for each platform, but generate each component by assembling software layers that depend more or less on the platform. For example, the same component may

be provided for SunOS (operating system), with two variants, one for SPARC (Scalable Processor Architecture) machines, and one for Intel machines (hardware).

Platform interfaces are sometimes called *vertical channels* because they show vertical interaction with lower layers of software, as opposed to interactions with other peer components. The inspection of vertical channel interfaces enables us to identify integration issues related to detecting and responding to operating system and communication events, interactions over communication channels, and understanding hardware dependencies and portability to other platforms.

21.1.3 What Makes a Good Component

A component is first, and foremost, a reusable asset. As such, it is no different from other assets, and it should be

- *Well Documented.* It should be documented for reuse, including integration documentation.
- *Cohesive.* A component should encapsulate at one level of abstraction exactly one nontrivial purpose, such as a function or a structure.
- *Independent (Low-Coupling).* A component should be as independent as possible from other components. Minimizing dependence on other components makes a component more useful and easily interoperable.
- *Useful.* A component should have a set of use cases and situations in which it was previously used or needed. The documentation of core components provided by domain engineers should keep information about the history of usage of the component in other software products.
- *Certified.* A good software component has test suites and benchmarks that can be used for independent verification. A good component should have a certificate endorsed by the supplier or by a trustable third party.

However, because of its form (executable, binary), and its usage mode (black-box reuse), a component should also satisfy the following properties:

- *Composable.* To quote Szyperski, "Components are for composition" [Szyperski 1999, p. 3]. Whereas source components may be reused by adaptation, components are fundamentally intended for composition, without any modification. A component should provide the necessary capabilities to be composed with other component. We may value customizability with general reusable assets, but such is not the case with components, except for some operational parameters that may be specified/accessible at startup.

- *Having Well-Defined Interfaces.* This is a desirable property of code components in general, and even more so for components, since they are meant for external composition.

- *Conforming to a Component Model.* In principle, by conforming to a component model, a component may interact (compose) with any component that conforms to the same component model. Conformance to a component model is one way of achieving the previous two qualities: composability and well-defined interfaces, provided the component model is a good one, of course. We discuss component models in the next section.

- *Secure.* Security relates to the extent to which a component defines and manages access privileges to its internal constituents. We should keep in mind that components are typically accessed using some RPC or RMI (remote procedure call or remote method invocation) protocol, and for this reason, they (their memory) are not owned by the process that invokes them. Following the adage that a processing chain is as secure as the weakest link, and because components are not meant to be modified, it is important that components have built-in security mechanisms that may be tailored to the specific usages/users of the component.

21.2 COMPONENT MODELS

21.2.1 What Is a Component Model

Intuitively, a component model is model or *a template* for defining components with the context of a particular software architecture style. In Chapter 14, we defined architectural styles as families of software architectures that may be characterized by *components types*, *communication patterns* between components of these types, *semantic constraints* on the behaviors of components individually and collectively, and *connectors*, which are software artifacts that enable us to mediate communication between components. A component model, then, specifies one or several component types, and defines the contracts that components of these types need to satisfy to offer their services to, and use the services of, other components of systems architected using this style. While the notion of a component model is architectural in nature, within the context of component systems, *component models* may be defined in terms of component *interfaces* that are described in fairly precise and formal interface definition languages—including *programming languages*, as is the case for the EJB component model (see Section 14.4.2) where the component model is defined in terms of *Java* interfaces. Recall, from Section 14.2.1, that a *software architecture* is the instantiation of an *architectural style* for a domain-specific *functional architecture*, and that in some cases, we are able to implement the computational infrastructure that is embodied in an architectural style, enabling a late binding of the functional architectural to the architectural style. In this context, a *component model then becomes the set of interfaces that a functional component needs to implement, in order to plug into the computational infrastructure that implements a particular style*!

Typically, component models will define obligations in two ways:

- *Intensively*, for application or domain-specific functionality. Examples of *intensively* specified obligations include CORBA's requirement that the business functions of distributed components be expressed in CORBA IDL. However, CORBA does not prescribe *what* functions to specify. Similarly, the EJB architecture prescribes that we define a *home interface* for EJB, but don't specify what lookup methods we have to support.
- *Extensively*, for functionality that interfaces with the computational infrastructure. For example, the JavaBeans component model prescribes that components implement specific introspection functions. Also, the EJB architecture prescribes that we provide implementations for some specific methods that interface with the container (e.g., ejbStore(), ejbLoad(), ejbRemove()). COM requires that COM components implement the QueryInterface(. . .) function.

A component model specifies not only interfaces but also the semantics of the functions that implement those interfaces! Component models may be judged according to how well documented those semantics are, and how strictly they are enforced. The next section looks at the issues that component models would ideally address.

21.2.2   Things that Component Models Should Address

Practitioners and researchers alike have uncovered a number of situations where components that would appear compatible at first glance (by looking at their signatures) in fact turn out to be incompatible [Garlan et al. 1995, Shaw 1995]. These are called *architectural mismatches*. Ideally, a component model should be sufficiently precise to address the sources of these mismatches. Researchers have identified the sources of mismatches by looking at the assumptions that components may make about their role in an interaction with other components [Shaw 1995; DeLine 1999a, 1999b]. We review these assumptions in turn.

21.2.2.1   Data Representation

Two components should agree on the representation of the data they exchange. The representation of data is usually implemented as datatypes. Two components can share a common type system or agree on a low level (greatest common denominator) representation of the data items exchanged between them. Alas, in practice, when the components are written in different programming languages, we will typically find that the highest common denominator is the bytestream!

21.2.2.2   Data Transfer
Components encounter mismatches in the direction of data flow as well as the sequence of data transfer. Practical examples of such mismatches include the traditional push/pull dichotomy, which specifies whether the component pushes the data to another or it waits for other components to pull its data. A component that is developed for the push mode will not work in the pull mode.

21.2.2.3   Transfer Protocol
A transfer protocol describes how the data are transferred between components and specifies how the components interact to effect a transfer. Example interactions include procedure-based callbacks, direct invocations, and event-based interactions. Transfer protocols are ripe for mismatches, both in the number and order of individual transfers of data, and in terms of transfer of control.

21.2.2.4   State Persistence
Some components are stateless, such as static library systems of mathematical procedures. Other components retain their states (e.g., stateful session beans in EJB, entity beans, most CORBA objects). State persistence may be an assumption made by a client (calling) component about the server (supplier) component. This assumption possibly produces unexpected results if the server turns out to be stateless. Typical examples include using a stateless session bean that should have been deployed as a stateful one.

21.2.2.5   State Scope
State scope defines the extent of the exposure of the component's internal state. For example, a document editor component allows other external components to have access to portions of a document, the whole document, or the editor itself. When two components disagree on the portion of the state that a component exposes, this causes packaging mismatches.

21.2.2.6   Failures
The technique to report component failures may differ from one component to another. For instance, failures are possibly reported as exception events. Other components may assume that their failure status is reported using a global error number with enumerated values. Gluing together components with different failure mechanisms causes mismatches.

21.2.2.7   Connection Establishment
The technique by which a connection between components is established and is torn down differs according to assumptions that are made by a component

developer. For instance, in the object-oriented paradigm the initialization and connection establishment between components is made possible using references or pointers.

21.2.3 Example Component Models

All the architectural frameworks discussed in Chapter 14 have an underlying component model. Depending on the set of services offered by each framework, the component model may be more or less exhaustive.

The CORBA component model started out as a component model for distributed objects (a "wiring standard," as Szyperski calls it), which was more or less fully described in Chapter 14. OMG has been working on standardizing a number of other more advanced services from the beginning, and the result is the *Object Management Architecture* (OMA), which specifies, in addition to basic distribution services, things such as security services, trader service, and relationship service. Typically, each one of these services comes with its own required interfaces, which augment the basic component model.

In Java, we have the JavaBeans component model, which is basically a component model for customizable reusable components, the EJB component model, which is the set of obligations that classes must satisfy to take advantage of the services of EJB servers. We have seen some of those obligations in Chapter 14 (Section 14.4). Java RMI also has an inherent component model for remote objects. Other Java technologies (e.g., JINI) have their own component models that may address specific application areas.

COM, of course, stands for component object model (and not *common*), which evolved in two directions, with COM+ toward a simpler component model for in-process components, and DCOM for distributed COM. Various other middleware technologies come with their own component models in terms of interfaces to support, and services to plug into.

The reader should note, though, that component models are not only about integration infrastructures. Domain-specific component frameworks all carry implicit component models. For example, the OpenDoc framework, which may be seen as a framework for building applications as compositions of embeddable editors, has a component model based on the *document* abstraction. *Document parts* have to implement a complex interface (ODPart).

21.3 COMPONENT-BASED SYSTEM DEVELOPMENT (CBSD)

The concept of designing and developing applications from a set of components is not new. Since 1970, several approaches have emerged that make use of components to build applications. Each approach has its own perspective of what constitutes a component. What is really new is the large-scale software development and sharing of components and architectures. The increase in scale and scope requires integration processes that produce component-based systems in a short time-to-market frame. The driving forces for finding new efficient techniques to develop component-based software are triggered by

- The increased development of large-scale applications, which include distributed applications
- The rapid development of new technologies that support integration and composition
- The increasing competition between software companies to deliver products to the market in record times to meet ever-shrinking windows of opportunity

To find efficient techniques to build component-based systems, we have to understand the overall development process and the activities involved in the process.

In the remainder of this section, we first start by describing a component-based development lifecycle that represents the consensus of several researchers and practitioners in the field (consensus report of the Second International Workshop on Component-Based Software Engineering [CBSE 1999]). Next, we address the issue of component granularity: what should be the ideal size of a component. As we will see, there is no optimal granularity; it depends on the perspective that we take. From a production management perspective, a good component size is one that corresponds to a good-sized project deliverable. From a run-time perspective, a good component size may be one that can run in a separate process and that uses an "average amount of resources" and so forth. The different perspectives are presented in Section 21.3.2.

21.3.1 CBSD Process

Developing component-based systems does not follow the traditional software development process in which requirements are analyzed and components are identified. Such a process is essentially a failure for component software. This is because it simply ignores the existence of reusable components and tries to find a match to components that are newly identified by the analyst. When a mature component market exists, the development process will be concerned with acquiring components (in house or commercially) rather than constructing them.

Regardless of the multitude of component definitions, we can still identify and categorize the activities in a component-based development approach (see Fig. 21.2). The way each activity is conducted depends heavily on the nature and type of the component. In the following, we focus on the set of activities that are practiced in component-based system development in general [CBSE 1999]. These activities are the integration of several software reuse concepts that we have discussed in pervious chapters.

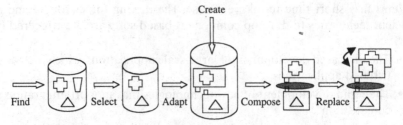

FIGURE 21.2   Activities in component-based development.

Find. The process of finding components defines how to document and create repositories of components. Finding a component is an activity in the domain engineering phase. Domain engineers mine families of similar products to document core components. Part III, on domain engineering, further explains how to acquire components through domain analysis, in-house development, reverse engineering, or commercially.

Select. We select specific components from a repository in order to use them in component-based software development. The selection process is usually related to library (repository) retrieval and browsing techniques and algorithms that are discussed in Chapter 16.

Adapt. Adaptation is the process of customizing selected components to satisfy user requirements in the new context in which the component is used. Adapted components are amended to address the source of conflict with other components or with the underlying integration framework. There are several techniques to adapt and customize a component for integration with other components or with the underlying framework or architecture. Some of these techniques were discussed in Chapter 17.

Create. In component-based system development, it is sometimes possible that the selected components do not fully satisfy the application requirements even after adaptation. In such cases, the product integrator has to develop and create new components for this specific application. This situation is avoided by extensive domain analysis techniques that document common generic components and their application-specific variations as discussed in Chapter 8.

Compose. Composition is an assembly-and-integration process. The effort of integration depends on the nature of the component to be integrated. For example, if components are subroutines, the development effort for integration is large because we have to integrate a large number of them; if components are anchor packages, integration will be in the form of writing macros to adapt the package; and if components are COTS, we develop glue code for integration, which could be difficult. Some composition techniques for object-oriented components are discussed in Chapter 12.

Replace. The replacement process is related to product maintenance. Component-based systems evolve over time to fix errors in components and add new functionalities. The old version of the component is swapped out and a modified version is swapped in. This is often referred to as *component upgrade*. This process addresses several problems such as version management of components, preserving the same component interface across versions, identifying additional adaptation requirements, and other configuration management problems. Versioning is usually a problem associated with COTS components as discussed in Chapter 23.

21.3.2 Component Granularity

Components partition systems and system development in various ways. Components represent units of development, of runtime, of distribution, of cost, and so forth. Szyperski [1999] identified a number of *dimensions* along which components may represent units of things. To mention a few:

Abstraction Dimension. Abstraction implies the levels of details encapsulated within the component. These details define functionality, resources, structure, or state. Objects are abstractions of functionality and state. Patterns are abstractions of a set of interacting classes. Architectures are abstractions of the whole system structure. Another way to view abstractions is the level of the component deployment in the development lifecycle. For instance, components can be analysis units, design units, or specific code units.

Management Dimension. The management dimension can include the cost of a component. Many investment models partition the system into a set of components to study the cost of each and the effect of the cost on the overall system cost. Components can be defined as decomposition units on which accounting is based. Another management dimension could be the deliverable units. Usually management is concerned about which units the production team delivers and which units are acquired commercially. Components can be those units.

Business Dimension. At a business level, components can be the units of dispute. When a component-based system fails, the failure is traced to errors and faults in one or more of its constituting units. If these units are supplied by different parties (third partieds for commercially acquired components), then these parties tend to blame each other for the failure. Components can be units for resolving such disputes. Similarly, components can be units on the maintenance dimension.

Compilation Dimension. Component-based systems are seldom compiled in one piece. Instead, individual units are usually compiled separately and plugged (loaded) into the system. Components can play the role of these individually compiled units.

Distribution Dimension. In a distributed component-based environment, components live on different processors or machines, and interact with each other remotely. When considering a distributed environment as such, components can be considered the units that are distributed and placed remotely.

21.4   ISSUES IN DEVELOPING WITH COMPONENTS

Component-based development faces the same set of challenges faced by general application engineering with reusable assets, as discussed in Section 17.3. In addition to those issues, we have issues that are specific to component-based development by virtue of the nature of components (independent, deployable units), the nature of the architecture (or architectural style) that they impose, and the process with which they are typically acquired [Hayes 1998, Kroeker 1998, Krieger and Adler 1998, Brown and Wallnau 1998, Weyuker 1998]. We discuss these issues below. Some are more technical in nature, and are discussed first. Business issues are discussed in Section 21.4.2.

21.4.1   Technical Issues

21.4.1.1   Interfaces
To qualify a software artifact as a component, its interfaces to other application artifacts should be clearly defined. We classified component interfaces as platform interfaces and application interfaces (see Section 21.1.2). Whereas platform interfaces deal with the host environment (operating system and hardware), application interfaces deal with interaction with other components. Component interfaces depend on the nature of the component itself. Component interfaces can also be classified as outgoing or incoming. An interface can define services provided by the component (exported services). Components can also acquire services from other application components (imported services). The DCOM model is one of the few models that clearly distinguishes between the exported and imported services of a component. Moreover, the distinction between interfaces at different development levels is essential. Architectural interfaces have different characteristics from implementation and programmatic interfaces [Allen and Garlan 1997]. Another issue that deserves further investigation is that different component technologies define different types of interfaces. CORBA has its own IDL, DCOM has its own COM IDL, and Java technologies use Java interfaces. Commonalties and differences between these IDLs should be used to guide research on a standard, architectural, interface definition language.

21.4.1.2   Development Process Model
A simple model for component-based software development was discussed by Brown and Wallnau [1996], extended in another publication [CBSE 1999], and

summarized in Section 21.3.1. This model is a simple reference model for key activities of the development process. Vigder et al. [1996] identify the differences between traditional development and component-based development. For our purposes, we identify the differences between application engineering with general reusable assets, and component-based development:

- *Interface-Centric.* The emphasis in CBSD is component interfaces because they play the major role in gluing and plugging independently *deployed* components [D'Souza and Wills 1998].
- *Programming-Language-Independent.* Unlike source code assets, which are integrated into an application using the application's development environment (editors, compilers, linkers, packagers), components in the sense of this chapter are used as binaries, or more generally, as readily deployable executables. This means that we should be able to "talk" to a component regardless of the programming language in which it was implemented, which may be more or less problematic, depending on differences between languages (see, e.g., Section 10.3 on inertoperability of OO programming languages).
- *Compositional.* The development process is a composition mechanism in which we assemble applications from components rather than develop and implement them from scratch. Bottom–up development with little or no room for customization is a challenging intellectual activity, and often leads toward changing our requirements in creative ways to take advantage of the existing components.
- *Separation of Concerns.* An application that is developed from components relies heavily on the separation of concerns and functionalities of the individual components. This is required to decrease dependability between components and hence improve the system maintainability.

21.4.1.3 Integration
The process of integrating components together to satisfy the application functionality is crucial to CBSD. There are two kinds of integration:

- *Static integration*: integration during development.
- *Dynamic integration*: integration during runtime. Runtime integration is concerned with the way in which components collaborate at runtime and how each component has control over the operation in a specific period of time.

Static integration is more an issue of type consistency, and is usually easy to predict and enforce. Runtime integration, however, involves a lot of architectural detail that may not be visible (or documented) through the static interface. Section 21.2.2 enumerated a number of sources of runtime mismatches. An adaptation of one or more components may be inevitable. Adaptation involves extending (specializing) the component to satisfy the application requirements. Several types of adaptation techniques exit such as wrapping, glue code, or mediators (see Section 17.2).

21.4.1.4 Integrating Legacy Software

In component-based development a single component model may pervade an entire application or a major subsystem of an application. Abiding by that component model may cause backward-compatibility problems with legacy subsystems. This can be a problem.

Some people consider CORBA as an integration architecture, first and foremost [Mowbray and Zahavi 1995]. Generally speaking, legacy systems and subsystems are wrapped within component shells that abide by the underlying component model. In CORBA, there is no telling as to how an IDL interface is implemented on the server side. In principle, an IDL interface may be used to generate OO proxies and procedural servers.

21.4.2 Business Issues

21.4.2.1 Component Market and Standards

Standardization is a good approach for developing a common component market. Standards are beneficial in defining common interfaces and infrastructure for interoperation between components and component-based systems. A standard helps in establishing a marketplace; however, a market helps in establishing a standard as well. For example, the Object Management Group (OMG) has taken the approach of standard before market by defining standards of component interfaces and interaction protocols such as the IIOP and IDL. Several companies have been developing market products in conformance to that standard, and hence a market has been established on the basis of these standards. The Microsoft DCOM and ActiveX have taken the market-before-standard approach by encouraging and promoting reuse of components through products such as VBXs (Visual Basic Controls), then after the component approach has gained interest by users, the standardization role became in effect. To clearly evaluate each approach, business models are essential. These models are currently not available.

21.4.2.2 Market Scope, Scale, and Standardization

The market for component software varies in scope and scale. By *scale* we mean the number of market sectors that the component serves. For instance, a component that is developed for World Wide Web applications has a wide scope because a lot of businesses can deploy the component. On the other hand, a component developed for automated teller machines (ATMs) has a narrower scope, namely, the banking sector. By *scale* we mean the market volume. For instance, a component developed for ATM applications, although scoped by the banking sector, has a wide scale (many users). On the other side, a component developed for space shuttle control system has a smaller scale (few users). The criteria to scope or scale the market are not clearly distinguishable. Standardization is a difficult problem in markets with large scope and scale. In markets with large scope, it is hard to develop a component with services required by many users and at the same type provide the flexibility by which the component can be adapted. In a market with large scale and limited scope, it is less likely that good and cost-effective solutions exist within a short period of time.

21.5 FURTHER READING

Component-based software engineering is the topic of discussion and debate in many forums. Perhaps the most focused discussions are held during the First and Second International Workshop on CBSE held in conjunction with ICSE'98 and ICSE'99. A comprehensive discussion about the topic and its relation to object-oriented concepts is exhaustively covered by Syzperski [1999].

For more information on Java technologies, we refer the reader to the Java-Soft Web site (http://www.javasoft.com). For information on DCE (distributed computing environments), we recommend a paper by Schill [1993]; further information is available from the DCE Web site (Open Group Web site: http://www.opengroup.org/tech/dce/). Information about CORBA standards can be found on the OMG Web site (http://www.omg.org/). Szyperski [1999] has compared the three major component technologies, including their common features and differences. For more information on component packaging mismatches, we recommend the work by Robert DeLine [1999a, 1999b]; for architecture mismatch issues, we recommend the studies by Garlan et al. [1995] and Shaw [1995].

Chapter 22

Product-Line Engineering (PLE)

Product-line engineering is a specialized form of software reuse that promises productivity, quality, and shorter time to market in developing similar products in the same domain. This emerging reuse technology has potential impact on software engineering practice. It deserves special attention for several reasons:

1. It has good potential for bringing a software reuse program to a successful outcome. The most crucial success factor of any software reuse initiative is the availability of carefully designed, thoroughly validated software assets. With its emphasis on domain analysis and development for reuse for a particular set of products, product-line engineering is geared toward meeting this goal.

2. It has an integrated development lifecycle where application engineering and domain engineering processes and their interaction are guided by a set of products in a specific domain.

3. It provides a mechanism for scoping the domain by using a set of products to be developed within the product line. In domain engineering, it is usually difficult to define a scope for the domain; a product-line approach defines an economic way of scoping the domain.

4. It raises technical challenges. The deployment of product-line engineering requires a profound understanding of a variety of topics, including domain definition, domain analysis, derivation of generic domain architectures, identification of commonalties and variabilities in product families, and identification and specification of domainwide software assets.

One objective of PLE is to facilitate the production of similar products in the same domain through a composition of common domain artifacts. We might ask how we can make the composition of these domain artifacts faster and easier. Software architecture is often the solution because it embodies earliest design decisions for the product line and provides a framework within which reusable components can be developed and integrated. In this chapter, we discuss the basic concepts of product-line engineering, its lifecycle, and how the PLE lifecycle covers several aspects of software reuse. We discuss software architectures for product lines and summarize examples of PLE approaches.

22.1   PLE AND SOFTWARE REUSE

Software development methods that are used to engineer systems are continuously improving. Historically, software engineers treated each new project as a single development effort that discarded the use of previous experiences and assets produced when building other software systems. Instead, PLE views many systems within the context of similar systems built in the past, exploiting the commonalties and engineering the appropriate differences. Additionally, existing assets must be reengineered for reuse and new ones must be developed with a reuse perspective.

Whereas the creation of variations in a single system requires large investment in understanding new requirements, redesigning, recoding, and retesting, the creation of product lines initially invests in supporting these variations so that the effort in understanding and accommodating new requirements, redesigning, or recoding new members of the family is minimized. There is always the tradeoff between optimizing software assets for a particular product and optimizing it for reuse across several products. It is seldom possible to create generic assets that are widely reusable in multiple applications. Therefore, the domain should be scoped with a family of products in mind. PLE offers this scoping mechanism by managing the creation of reusable artifacts that apply to a specific set of products.

Organizations can produce new releases and versions of a product by using architectures and components from prior releases or versions. Product-line engineering is different. The first key difference concerns the production of a related set of products; within a product line an organization develops multiple products, and each has its own cycles of release and version. The evolution of a single product must be considered within a broader context, specifically, the evolution of the product line as a whole and not as variations of its earlier version. This is because the evolution of a product version could affect the common reference architecture and the set of components used by other products. The second key difference is that production of a product in the family is from a common asset base. Each product in the product line can be produced by taking advantage of analysis, design, code, testing, planning, training, and a host of other activities that have already been performed for previous products in the product line. This is far different from mere code reuse, which is often the case in producing new releases from a single product.

PLE is a streamlined integration of several aspects of software reuse. It embodies technical aspects, such as, domain and application engineering phases that are scoped by a family of products. It embodies economic aspects where the return on investments on domain models is paid back with reuse in developing products in the same family. It also embodies organizational aspects where the organization of domain and application engineering teams and their interaction is important.

Software development economics requires approaches that are able to reduce the cost of development, deployment, and lifecycle maintenance of software products. Investment in a set of products that belong to the same domain is a basic approach to reduce cost. Software reuse discipline does not focus on the development of particular cases, but instead motivates using existing assets to the extent possible. An asset is a candidate for reuse in another product if the required asset has similarities with the product that already uses the asset. Thus, an organization has an economic incentive to structure its marketable products such that they have functional and structural similarities. Amortizing the investment across more than one product is an approach that targets reducing the overall cost of development of all products in the family. From a marketing viewpoint, a product line is a group of similar products within a market segment. A product family is a set of products sharing common features, which could be common designs, architecture, or standards. Reuse is maximized by building products from common product family assets, including the architecture, design, components, and domain models. This improves the economies of production. Although not a standard practice, the technical means for achieving software reuse based on product lines are fairly well established [Brownsword and Clements 1996]. The basic technical means to create a product line include

- *Domain Analysis*. Domain models for the product line should be produced in order to identify the commonalities and variations among the family members.
- *Software Architecture*. A standard skeletal infrastructure that servers as the reference architecture should be developed. The reference architecture is adopted to all members of the product line.
- *Development Process*. The process is based on two folds: domain engineering and application engineering with precise definition of all the elements produced and the interaction between the two phases defined.

22.1.1 Exercises

1. **(B)** From your reading of Chapters 21 and 23, discuss how product-line engineering, as a specialized form of reuse, is different from component-based software engineering.

2. (B) Elaborate on the difference between product-line engineering and engineering of a single product with multiple releases and versions.

22.2 PLE LIFECYCLE

22.2.1 Domain and Application Engineering Aspects

Product-line engineering is concerned with selecting, refining, and establishing technical practices for identifying and exploiting commonalties that exist across software products in a particular domain. There is a tremendous market pressure to develop products that are variants of a core product in a short time-to-market constraint. Organizations address this challenge by following a product line approach to support the development of similar products in the same domain. Product-line approaches enable organizations to manage product development efforts according to the product line software engineering principles and disciplines.

As illustrated in Figure 22.1, the technical aspects of PLE can be classified into *domain engineering* and *application engineering*. *Domain engineering* includes activities such as domain analysis and definition, development of a domain (reference) architecture, and development of domain (core) assets (components). *Application engineering* includes application requirements analysis, instantiation of the reference architecture, instantiation and customization of domain components, and component-based development. Architectures play an essential role in the product line lifecycle. Domain engineers analyze domain models to define a reference (domain) architecture. These domain models are the results of one of various domain analysis tech-

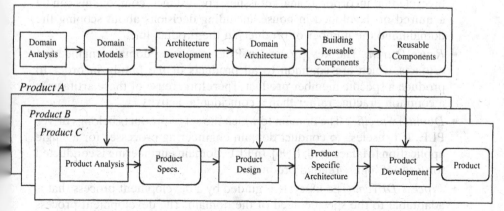

FIGURE 22.1 The PLE lifecycle as domain and application engineering phases.

niques as discussed in Chapter 8. In application engineering, the reference architecture is instantiated to develop a product specific architecture based on the product specification and domain models.

Architectural decisions are made at early stages of the product-line lifecycle. Architecture decisions can have an impact on the quality of the family of products. If the software architecture is not carefully developed, it may be unlikely to either satisfy system requirements or accommodate variability among products in the family. Good architectures are necessary to produce high-quality products and to increase development and maintenance productivity and predictability. Evaluation and analysis of architectures for product families is another essential activity that becomes more crucial in the PLE context. The challenges to an analysis–evaluation technique stem from its specificity to the architecture-level abstractions rather than borrowing design-level methods and from the fact that we analyze and evaluate a domain architecture rather than a product-specific architecture.

22.2.2   Attributes of a PLE Lifecycle

According to the general lifecycle shown in Figure 20.1, it is obvious that the development lifecycle for a product family has specific characteristics that distinguish it from traditional software lifecycles. The development lifecycle is

- *Architecture-Based.* Architectural decisions are made at early stages of the lifecycle. Domain engineers endeavor to develop a reference architecture that is instantiable in several products. Good architectures are necessary to produce high-quality products that belong to the family.

- *Economically Driven.* A PLE technical process is driven by nontechnical market forces. Multiple decisions are taken along the development lifecycle that incorporate market issues. For instance, components can be acquired or developed in house, including decisions about scoping the domain and the number of products in the product line.

- *Reuse-Driven.* The key process in PLE is reusing domain engineering artifacts, which are common to all products of the family, in order to produce a specific member product. Therefore, reuse of these artifacts is a common practice rather than a coincidental activity.

- *Domain-Specific.* The domain to which the set of products belongs drives PLE. It is useless to conduct domain engineering processes for a single application [Malaca et al. 1996]. In PLE, domain engineering is conducted for a set of highly related products.

- *Process-Driven.* The lifecycle is guided by a development process that is adaptable to the specific need of the domain. The development process is usually supported by tools to facilitate analysis and development. Although the process is not unique, there is a set of common high-level activities that is usually exercised in most PLE lifecycles regardless of the way these activities are conducted. The main feature of this process is the intensive interaction between domain engineers and application engineers to reuse all possible domain artifacts throughout the production process.

- *Producer–Consumer Relationship.* The development lifecycle has two main phases: the domain engineering phase, which is considered the production of common artifacts (producer), and the application engineering phase, which consumes these artifacts to develop products in the family (consumer). Such a tight relationship maximizes the productivity and benefits sought of a product line.

22.2.3 Success Factors

Several experiences in PLE [Malaca et al. 1996, Dikel et al. 1997, Bosch 1999, Bass et al. 1999] acknowledge that the key success factors for an organization adopting product-line software development discipline are:

- *Domain-Specific Expertise.* An organization should consult deep domain expertise to catalog commonalties and variabilities in the domain.
- *Architectures.* An organization should establish an architecture rhythm by developing a well-defined architecture for the family, adopting architecture styles, and architecture patterns.
- *Configuration Management.* The domain analyst provides a reliable technique to maintain versions of domain artifacts and to manage feedback from application producers.
- *Business Models.* An organization pursuing a product line approach establishes a solid business case through which managers are committed to the high initial investment with the expectation of long-term benefits.
- *Scoping the Domain.* The domain should be wide enough that the return on investment is clear but yet narrow enough that the technical production of domain artifacts is feasible.
- *Avoid the "Least Common Denominator" Concept.* One way to ensure that domain assets are reusable is to define, design, and develop the least common assets among products in the domain. This is not rarely the solution, however. Products in the family should be able to use or do not use specific assets as well as adapt common assets.
- *Managing Requirements in the Product-Line Context.* A product-line approach to software-intensive systems requires that the system analyst distinguish between those requirements that are common to all products

in the family and those that are specific to a particular product. In addition to this distinction in the nature of requirements, a requirements traceability mechanism should be used to identify the relationship between requirements and to trace them to software assets used in the development of products in the family.

- *A Separate Domain Engineering Unit.* Success stories of adopting a PLE approach sometimes acknowledge that two separate groups should be established for application and domain engineering. However, other stories advocate one technically managed unit. This factor is very dependent on the organization and the size of the effort invested in a product line.

Architectures are the most deserving focus of a product-line approach. The report of the second Workshop on Development and Evolution of Software Architectures for Product Families 1998 [Clements and Weiderman 1998] acknowledges the importance of software architecture for product families. The following section discusses software architecture aspects that are mostly related to PLE.

22.2.4 Exercises

1. (A) Given the PLE lifecycle, identify and explain whether each of the following activities belongs to the application engineering phase, domain engineering phase, or both (use Fig. 22.1 as reference for your reasoning).
   (a) Reengineering
   (b) Asset adaptation
   (c) Asset generators
   (d) Architecture evaluation
   (e) Asset library management.

22.3 PRODUCT-LINE ARCHITECTURES

22.3.1 Software Architectures and Product-Line Architectures

Software development based on architectures shifts the focus toward architectural elements such as components and connectors, where connectors are treated as top-level constructs. Software connectors can be as simple as procedure calls. They can also be as elaborate as client–server protocols, links between distributed databases, or middleware.

The difference between software architecture in general and product-line architecture (PLA) is that in PLE we develop a domain (reference) architecture that is used by all products in the family. Such architectures should be robust, flexible, and highly customizable to facilitate the instantiation of the core architecture in multiple products. The architecture for a product line provides the framework and context for developing and reusing reusable software assets and defining/managing the required engineering processes. It is often harder to develop a reference architecture than traditional development of an application architecture. This is due to the need to represent variations across products in the family by flexible elements defined within the reference architecture. A robust and repeatable configuration process for variation management is often needed.

22.3.2   Conformance and Synchronization in PLAs

In a product line, the reference architecture is instantiated in the development of each product in the family. Instantiating a reference architecture in a specific product often includes:

- Instantiating the common connectors and components of the reference architecture. This process defines the architecture in the application context rather than the domain context.
- Identifying architectural elements that are specific to the product under development. Elements that are deferred from the domain design and implementation phases can now be completed.
- Validating the application architecture for the specific product in hand and verifying the conformance of that specific architecture to the domain architecture.

The instantiation of a reference architecture produces a product-specific architecture. The management of the reference architecture and its instances is a core activity in the PLE lifecycle. New issues also arise in the evaluation of reference and product-specific architectures when compared to the evaluation of a single application architecture. The most relevant issues are:

- Measuring the conformance of an instantiated architecture to the reference architecture; specifically, determining how products are verified with respect to the product line architecture. It is important to quantify to what extent a product instance satisfies all the constraints imposed by the domain architecture.
- Synchronizing product architectures with new releases of the product-line architecture and identifying how the modifications and maintenance of a PLA affect the products already on the market. Product-line architectures evolve from their initial design. This evolution results from the desire to incorporate technological changes, repair existing problems, or add new functionalities. This evolution could cause configuration management problems and hence products should be synchronized with the new release of a product-line architecture.

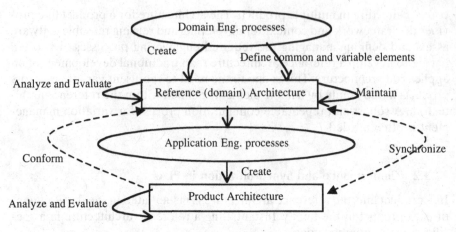

FIGURE 22.2   Product-line and product-specific architectures.

Figure 22.2 illustrates the activities concerning software architectures in a PLE context: creation, synchronization, conformance, and evaluation.

22.3.3   Evaluating Architectures

There is an increasing demand for evaluating software architectures. The work in the field has primer contribution from the Software Engineering Institute (SEI) at Carnegie Mellon University [SEI 2000, Carriere et al. 1999], the European ESPRIT initiative [Linden 1998], and the Center for Software Engineering at the University of Southern California [USC 2000]. Architecture analysis and evaluation techniques have focused mostly on application architecture with little emphasis on product-line reference architectures. The evaluation techniques developed for evaluating specific product architecture can be extended and applied to reference architectures, but there are specific additional requirements and issues that arise in the context of product families, for example, synchronization, conformance, and accommodating uncertainties in architecture evaluations. These uncertainties are introduced because of the incomplete nature of a product-line architecture that gives flexibility in instantiating the architecture in several products.

22.3.4   Exercises

1. (B) The SAAM (software architecture analysis method) [Kazman et al. 1994] and ATA (architecture tradeoff analysis) (ATA home page: http://www.sei.cmu.edu/ata/ata_init.html) are two architecture analysis and evaluation methods. Discuss the applicability and limitations of these methods as applied to analysis and evaluation of product-line architectures instead of a software architecture in general.

2. (B) PLAs evolve by time as discussed in Section 22.3.2. Identify reasons of evolution of a PLA. For each case, discuss the impact of the evolution on the architecture elements. Illustrate your discussion using examples (when possible).

22.4   PLE APPROACHES

Product-line engineering is gaining the interest of organizations as one of the most promising forms of software reuse. To this extent, several PLE approaches have evolved to deliver on such promises. These approaches are all instances of the family-oriented discipline that PLE introduces. Perhaps the best-known approaches are the SYNTHESIS methodology by the Software Productivity Consortium (SPC), the product-line framework by the Software Engineering Institute (SEI), the family-oriented abstraction, specification, and translation (FAST) by Lucent Technologies, and the product-line software engineering (PuLSE) methodology by Fraunhofer Institute for Experimental Software. This section highlights the most salient features of the Synthesis approach by SPC and the product-line practice by SEI as examples of PLE approaches.

22.4.1   The SYNTHESIS Approach

SYNTHESIS is a methodology for constructing software systems as instances of a family of like systems having similar descriptions. SYNTHESIS views a domain as a business area whose objectives are fulfilled by a family. It defines a program family as a set of programs that have common properties. It views the creation of program versions not as successive modifications to previous versions, but as derivations from a common abstraction. A family of similar work products having some variabilities are represented by an adaptable work product, using means provided by abstraction-based reuse. Instances of each work product are derived to generate a particular system product. SYNTHESIS consists of two integrated and iterative subprocesses: application engineering and domain engineering. SYNTHESIS's work products are produced using a process of domain engineering that generates standardized and reusable work products including code and documentation. Domain engineering also defines a template application engineering process. On the other hand, application engineering puts emphasis on requirements and engineering decisions describing a particular system, given a family of such systems.

SYNTHESIS can be applied in either an "opportunistic" mode, focusing on existing reuse opportunities within the works product of a traditional application engineering lifecycle; or in a comprehensive "leveraged" mode, fully deploying the SYNTHESIS methodology throughout a program or product line. The type of synthesis process that an organization can adopt is dependent on the context in which the organization staff works. This context is governed by three concerns: business objectives, system engineering practice, and the objectives of software engineering processes. Since the leveraged mode represents a matured product-line process, we focus in the following discussion on this mode.

22.4.1.1 Domain Engineering in Leveraged SYNTHESIS

Domain engineering provides application engineering projects with the ability to create an accurate model of any product in the scope of the domain. Domain engineering organizes and directs resources to accomplish the business objectives of an organization. Moreover, it provides leverage by which projects within a domain can deliver a product more effectively (see Fig. 22.3). As an iterative process, domain engineering in SYNTHESIS involves the following activities:

1. *Domain Management.* This is an activity for managing business area resources to achieve the organization's business objectives. More precisely, domain management plans, monitors, and controls the use of domain resources to provide standardized process and product family for a domain of interest.

2. *Domain Analysis.* This activity studies and formalizes a business area as a domain in order to standardize and leverage knowledge of how recurring and varying customer requirements affect the form and content of a product. In SYNTHESIS, the scope of a domain is a business decision based on evaluations of available expertise and potential business opportunities. The domain analysis activity consists of the following three steps:

   a. *Domain Definition.* This activity is an informal description of the systems in the business area of the domain. A domain definition establishes conceptual basis and bounds and determines whether planned development and evolution of the domain is viable relative to the organization's business objectives. It provides a basis for determining, informally, whether a system is properly within that scope.

   b. *Domain Specification.* This is a specification of a product family and an associated application engineering process for constructing members of the family. In other words, domain specification creates a precise specification of the problems and solutions that are supported by the domain and defines an application engineering process that is used to build a product in the domain.

   c. *Domain Verification.* This activity ensures the correctness, consistency, and completeness of domain engineering work products.

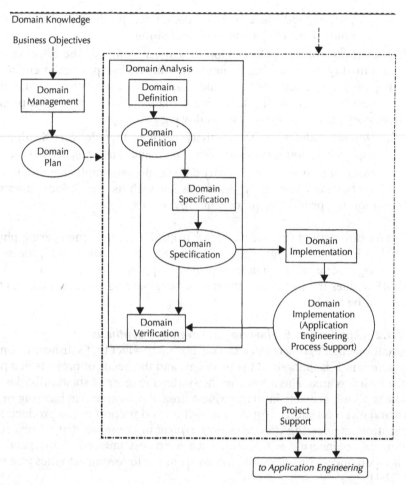

FIGURE 22.3 Domain engineering in leveraged synthesis (adopted from SPC [1993]).

d. *Domain Implementation.* Domain implementation activity consists of two steps:

(1) *Product Implementation.* A product implementation consists of adaptable components (including code, documentation, and support for verification–validation) and procedures that are used to create deliverable application engineering work products according to an application model that describes the product.

(2) *Process Support Development.* This is the infrastructure supporting the practice of application engineering by defining: the policies and procedures by which application engineers produce a work product (the application engineering process), automated support for efficient performance of the application engineering

process, and the associated use of the product implementation component of domain implementation.

3. *Project Support.* A project support activity evaluates the effectiveness and quality of domain implementation for use by application engineering projects. It provides customer support to application engineering projects in understanding and using domain implementation. The project support activity consists of the following two steps:

   a. *Domain Validation.* This activity certifies that deliverable domain implementation satisfies application engineering projects' needs.

   b. *Domain Delivery.* This activity delivers domain implementation to an application engineering project, assists with its use, and identifies the required product or process improvements.

The main observation that we can draw from the domain engineering phase of SYNTHESIS is that it integrates technical aspects (products and processes) and managerial aspects (planning, project support, etc.). Moreover, SYNTHESIS defines the product of the domain engineering and recommends the process to be used in application engineering.

22.4.1.2 Application Engineering in Leveraged Synthesis

Application engineering creates and supports a product that satisfies customer requirements. It is tailored to the problems and the needs of projects in a particular business area. This allows for the systematic reuse of standardized work products within projects in that business area. Application engineering organizes and directs resources for the production and support of the product. The application engineering process is *prototypical* in the sense that an objective of domain engineering is to define such a process tailored to the needs of the domain under consideration. It consists of the following activities (see also Fig. 22.4):

1. *Project Management.* This activity plans, monitors, and controls project resources to deliver a product.

2. *Application Modeling.* This activity resolves decisions to specify a required product, based on an analysis of customer requirements, and evaluates it with respect to technical constraints or constraints imposed by customers.

3. *Application Production.* This activity creates a standardized product and the associated delivery support work products in compliance with an application model.

4. *Delivery and Operation Support.* This activity delivers the application product to the customer, supports its use, and evaluates its effectiveness.

The salient feature that we observe in the application engineering phase of SYNTHESIS is that the process is a prototype. The domain engineering phase

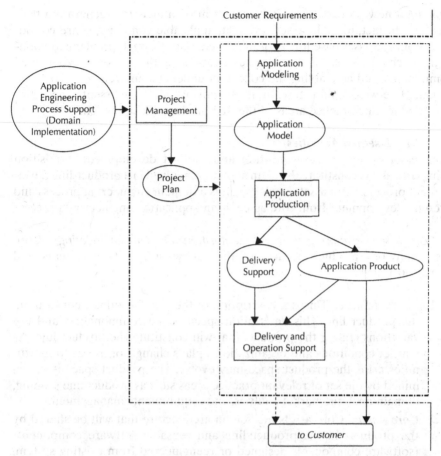

FIGURE 22.4 Application engineering in the leveraged SYNTHESIS methodology (adopted from SPC [1993]).

can modify the prototype process and define new steps according to the domain under consideration.

22.4.2 The Product-Line Practice

The product-line practice (PLP) initiative by the Software Engineering Institute (SEI) helps in facilitating and accelerating the transition to sound software engineering using a product-line approach. The objective of the PLP initiative is to provide organizations with an integrated business and technical approach to multi-use of software assets. In PLP, a software product line [Clements and Northrop 1998, Bass et al. 1999] is defined as a set of software systems sharing a common, managed set of features that satisfy specific needs of a particular market segment or mission. Using a product-line approach, building a new product (system) becomes more a matter of generation than creation. In fact, to build a new product, applicable components are considered from the asset base for tailoring as necessary through preplanned variation mechanisms such as parameterization, adding any new needed components, and assembling the collection under the umbrella of a common product-line-wide architecture. In this section, we highlight essential activities and product-line practice areas of the SEI product line approach.

22.4.2.1 Essential Activities

Core asset development–acquisition and product development–acquisition using core assets constitute the main activities involved in a product-line development process. Core asset development is a domain engineering process and product development from core assets is an application engineering process.

Core Asset Development and/or Acquisition (Domain Engineering) Core asset activities produce or acquire the following objects [Clements and Northrop 1998]:

1. *Product Space.* This is a description of the initial products constituting the product line. This description specifies the commonalties and the variations among the products that will constitute the product line. As market conditions and organization's plans change, or as new opportunities arise, the product space may evolve. The product space is determined by the set of relevant practice areas such as product line scoping, domain analysis, market analysis, and requirements management.

2. *Core Assets.* Core assets include an architecture that will be shared by the products in the product line and reusable software components (software components designed or reengineered from existing system, requirements statements, documentation and specifications, schedules, budgets, and test plans). The development and acquisition of core assets takes the following inputs:

   a. *Product Constraints.* These constraints deal with the kind of commonalties and variations that exist among the products in the family.

   b. *Production Constraints.* These constraints deal with the production process, for example, constraints on whether COTS components should be used.

   c. *Styles, Patterns, and Frameworks.* These include the architectural building blocks that are relevant and meet the product and production constraints.

   d. *Production Strategy.* This constraint discusses the approach that will be used to build the product line, for example, top–down or bottom–up approaches.

   e. *Inventory of Preexisting Assets.* This includes libraries, frameworks, algorithms, tools, and components that could be utilized.

Other practice areas that are relevant to produce the core assets include architecture exploration and definition, architecture evaluation, requirements management, risk management, component development, and testing.

3. *Production Plan.* The production plan describes how the products are developed from the core assets and specifies the kind of approach to be used in building the product line. It also defines a plan to collect data in order to feed metrics to measure organizational improvement representing the result of the product-line practice.

Product Development or Acquisition (Application Engineering) The product space, the core asset list, the production plan, and the requirements for individual products constitute the input factors on which the product development/acquisition activity is dependent. The creation of products can affect:

- *The Product Space.* In some cases people who define the scope may not have envisioned a product of the product line, and so, its production will affect the product space.
- *Core Assets.* Existing similarities between a new product and others may be exploited to create new core assets.
- *Production Plan.* New system generation procedure may be added in order to enhance the production efficiency, following the production of new products in the field.
- *Requirements for Specific Products.* Indeed, some customers may change their requirements to bring them in line with the product line scope and, so, to take great profit of the advantages within the product line.

Management The structure of the enterprise is responsible for the success or failure of the product-line effort. Organizations adopting a product-line approach should manage the architecture, core assets, and products of the product line. In addition, management of the organization's external interfaces for the product line is required. Indeed, new different relationships with customers and suppliers must be introduced and strengthened. Another important function of the management is to create an adoption plan describing the desired state of the organization, which deals with the production of products in the family and how to meet this state using a specific strategy.

22.4.2.2 *Product-Line Practice Areas*
In addition to the set of essential activities that PLP defines for a product-line approach, PLP identifies other practice areas that are useful in a product-line approach. This section highlights areas of expertise and practice [Clements and Northrop 1998] that are essential for successfully developing, deploying, and maintaining a software product line in the SEI PLP approach.

Software Engineering Practice Areas   Critical software engineering technologies that come into effect for product-line development include:

1. *Domain Analysis.* Domain analysis in PLP delivers domain models. Domain models capture the commonalities and variability of related software systems in the domain and define the common high-level requirements and areas of variations for a class of systems. Domain analysis determines the scope of the target products and identifies key common features and their variations across current, future, and competitor systems. PLP recommends the following practices for domain analysis:

   a. *Domain Identification.* Domain identification is determining the domains embodied in the products that an organization delivers to its customers. In PLP, domains are areas of expertise needed to create products.

   b. *Domain Selection.* Domain selection entails choosing one or more domains for subsequent domain modeling, based on selection criteria that include business goals, perceivable return on investment, availability of people and resources, and management support.

   c. *Domain Scoping.* Domain scoping is determining the boundary of the domain and its relationship to other domains.

   d. *Domain Modeling.* Domain modeling is analyzing a set of previously delivered applications in the target domain, capturing and representing the commonalities and variability of the domain capabilities provided by these applications in a model, incorporating new domain requirements into the model, and creating a domain terminology dictionary.

   Domain models, which are the output of domain analysis, constitute an input to the domain design phase of domain engineering and support the creation of another core asset: a high-level software architecture spanning multiple systems. Partitioning the architecture into subsystems as well as determining its important quality attributes are guided by the domain model.

2. *Mining Existing Assets (Reengineering).* This activity deals with how useful artifacts (architectures, domain models, software components, design documentation, etc.) can be extracted from existing legacy systems. Mined assets must be well structured and documented, and must provide clear and general interfaces. When used in a product line, mined assets must fit into a reference architecture. Mined assets can be added to the asset library when they do not require extensive renovation. The highly desirable assets are those that can be used with little or no change, have well-defined interfaces, and have been used over long periods of time.

3. *Developing and Maintaining a Reference Architecture.* The architecture exploration defines the software architectural style for the product line, which defines the type of components in the architecture and both their data and control interactions. All the individual products of a product line would have a common architectural structure even if all perform different functions from the other, and perform those functions in different ways. For product-line architectures, documentation is an issue. Both the architecture of each product and that of the product line must have documentation. For the latter, the documentation describes how to build a product (tailoring, extracting from a library, setting parameters, etc.) as well as the issues surrounding architectural conformance and instantiation of the product-line architecture for a particular product. In addition, this documentation should be more formal and complete to be reused for multiple products. Product development is based on one of the instance architectures created by the architecture for each new product.

Technical Management Practice Areas

1. *Metrics and Tracking.* Metrics provide the quantitative data necessary to make informed value judgments and give guidance for the product-line practices, such as defining criteria for identifying viable product-line components. Moreover, metrics provide organization-level insight, such as the economics of traditional versus product line development within the organization. Compared to the standard software development practices, the use for metrics for product lines is more important. First, product lines constitute a new method of doing business, and are able to achieve substantial gains over a sustained period of time. Thus, a measurement program is essential to measure the improvement anticipated by the product-line approach and to provide justification of the investment. Second, there is a distinction between core assets and specific products, which requires a comprehensive measurement program to measure both core asset and application development. In a product-line approach, the measurement practice must address the process for building, evolving, and sustaining assets as well as the process for building, enhancing, and sustaining products.

2. *Product-Line Scoping.* Product line scoping defines the space of products constituting the product line and developed from core assets. It identifies the commonality that members share and the way in which they vary from each other. Product line scoping requires understanding the potential commonalities and variations across current and future systems in the product line. Scoping a product line requires modeling of the product line context that takes into account existing product constraints such as a set of computing platforms to run the products or the set of features provided by these products. Moreover, the system attributes distinguishing products in the product line must be documented.

Organizational Management Practice Areas

1. *Organizational Structure.* The organizational structure reflects the division of roles and authority to form groups each carries a set of specific responsibilities in a product-line effort. In a product-line approach, projects have to develop production systems utilizing a set of core assets. Organizational structures are needed to create and manage these core assets. Management of the product-line core assets, including components, the reference architecture, and domain models, should be applied in a long-term lifecycle to meet the organization objectives. To manage these assets, many aspects should be taken into account such as ownership of the architecture and decisions about architectural style and the built-in variability of components. In PLP, applications are developed following a component-based integration process. The development process starts with an existing architecture, and uses some existing components. The organization structure should take into consideration the following set of responsibilities: (a) negotiating customer requirements in order to situate new products within the scope of the family, (b) utilizing the core asset base in building new products, and (c) the core asset owners are involved in order to evolve new capabilities regarding deficient core assets for a new product.

2. *Other Practice Areas.* Other practice areas that belong to organizational management include building and communicating a business case, funding, market analysis, developing and implementing an acquisition strategy, training, customer and supplier interface management, risk management, and technology forecasting.

22.4.3 Product-Line Approaches

It appears from the brief discussion on the two product-line engineering approaches, SYNTHESIS and the PLP approach, that PLE is a promising paradigm for software development that integrates several aspects of software engineering in general and software reuse in particular for the purpose of increasing productivity, increasing quality, and decreasing time to market.

Whereas the set of activities and processes of product-line approaches are fairly widely understood and acknowledged, each PLE approach has its own features and recommended emphasis and practices. The SYNTHESIS approach emphasizes the technical aspects of the two PLE phases—domain engineering and application engineering—and the process of defining and integrating activities of the two phases. On the other hand, PLP clearly separates the technical aspects, organizational structures, and the management aspects of a PLE lifecycle.

22.5 FURTHER READING

Several governmental and industrial organizations have undertaken PLE initiatives; the following are references to some of these initiatives.

- Fraunhofer-Gesellschaft Institutes, Fraunhofer Institute for Experimental Software Engineering IESE in Kaiserslautern: the PuLSE project (Germany) (http://www.fhg.de/)
- NASA/WVHTCF Software Optimization and Reuse Technology (SORT) program (http://www.sort.wvhtf.org/)
- The Air Force Materiel Command's Electronic Systems Center (ESC) at Hanscom Airforce Base (http://www.hanscom.af.mil/)
- The Software Productivity Consortium, *The Synthesis Approach, Reuse-Driven Software Processes Guidebook*, version 2.0.3 (http://www.software.org/)
- The Software Engineering Institute (SEI), Third Product Line Practice Workshop, Carnegie Mellon University (http://www.sei.cmu.edu/publications/documents/00.reports/ootr024.html)
- The family-oriented abstraction, specification, and translation (FAST) process, at Lucent Technologies [Weiss and Lai 1999]

Vigder et al. [1996] identify the differences between traditional development and component-based development. Some issues regarding maintaining systems developed from COTS, free OTS, and in-house libraries are discussed by Voas [1998c].

Chapter 23

COTS Based Development

COTS based software development is the process of building software applications from commercially available software components. This is an increasingly popular paradigm for software development, but one that is not without risks and associated costs. In this chapter, we analyze this paradigm as a specialized form of software reuse and discuss how to deploy it in practice.

23.1 COMMERCIAL OFF THE SHELF SOFTWARE

23.1.1 Definition and Background

A *COTS product* is an executable software product that has the following characteristics:

- It is sold, leased, or licensed to the general public.
- Buyers, lessees, and licensees have no access to the source code, hence can only use the product as a black box.
- It is offered by a vendor who has created it and is typically responsible for its maintenance and its upgrades.
- It is available in multiple identical copies (within the same version) on the market.

There are a number of advantages to use COTS products in software development. But also a number of subtle (and unsubtle) pitfalls. Among the advantages are:

- *Gain in Cost.* Because the product is produced once and used multiple times, it can be sold for an arbitrarily small fraction of its development cost.
- *Gain in Operational Quality.* Because the product is widely used by a broad segment of users, it is typically thoroughly tested and debugged, hence its quality is much better than any one user can afford.
- *Gain in Functionality.* While the community of users may have widely varying backgrounds, the developer of the COTS product can be arbitrarily expert in the application domain of the product, hence offer more functionality and quality than any individual user.
- *Gain in Time to Market.* Because the product is readily available on the market it can be acquired and deployed immediately. By contrast, users who contemplate developing alternative custom-made products can count on a lengthy lifecycle time, and run the additional risk of schedule overruns.
- *Gain in Maintenance Overhead.* Multiple users of a COTS product not only share the cost of developing the product, they also share the cost of its long-term operation and maintenance. The vendor is typically responsible for its corrective maintenance (in terms of removing faults uncovered by users), its perfective maintenance (in terms of upgrades), and its adaptive maintenance (in terms of enhancements requested by the user community).

We will see in the sequel of this chapter, that despite all its advantages, COTS based software development is no panacea; it is advantageous under very specific conditions, and needs to be applied upon careful consideration of a wide range of issues.

23.1.2 COTS and CBSD

Component-based software development and COTS based software development are both compositional approaches to software development, and one could consider that COTS development is a special case of CBSD. In this section, we discuss some of the salient differences between COTS development and CBSD; we characterize these differences by keywords, to help the reader remember them and refer to them. Most of these differences stem from the fact that COTS components are *necessarily* developed by third parties, with what that entails in terms of customizability, access privileges, and economic profile.

- *White Box versus Black Box Reuse.* Whereas with CBSD the user/system developer can practice white box reuse in addition to black box reuse, in COTS development the user/system developer is often restricted to black box reuse because of some contractual agreement with the component vendor. An implication of this observation is that while components (re)used under CBSD can be integrated by means of modifying their source code, COTS components can only be integrated by means of wrapper code (code that preprocesses their input or postprocesses their outputs).

- *Copyright Privileges.* Whereas in CBSD the user/system developer acquires source code, in COTS development the user/system developer acquires the services of executing the asset. Consequently, whereas under CBSD the system produced by a system developer is the property of the system developer, under COTS development the COTS vendor maintains copyright privileges on the COTS components of the system.

- *Maintenance.* Whereas in CBSD the user/system developer is responsible for maintaining the acquired components, under COTS development the maintenance of COTS products is the responsibility of the vendor. An implication of this observation is that while under COTS development both development costs and maintenance costs are shared among users, in CBSD only development costs are shared.

- *Retrieval Criteria.* Whereas COTS components are retrieved by exact retrieval criteria, CBSD components can be retrieved by exact criteria or approximate criteria; in addition, the latter can be retrieved by virtue of functional criteria or structural criteria (whereas the former have no visible structure for the purposes of retrieval). Consequently, a software component that is made available under CBSD has a potentially higher reuse frequency than a functionally equivalent COTS component.

These observations justify, among others, why we have chosen to discuss COTS development as a separate chapter, rather than a subsection of component based software development.

23.1.3   Exercises

1. Consider that you need a program that sorts arrays in decreasing order and all you have available is a component that sorts arrays in increasing order. Discuss how you would make use of the available component if it were a COTS component. Propose a more efficient solution under CBSD (where the source code is available). Discuss verification and validation under each solution.

2. Consider that you need an assembler for an assembly language that has macros, and all you have available is an assembler that does not handle macros. Discuss how you would make use of the available component under the hypotheses of COTS development; then of CBSD.

3. Consider that you need an optimizing compiler for a high level programming language, and all you have is a non-optimizing compiler. Assume that

the desired optimizations require access to an intermediate representation of the program semantics. Discuss whether you can make use of the available asset under the hypothesis of COTS development, and CBSD. Discuss and compare the economics of both solutions, and contrast them to the solution of developing a compiler from scratch (using compiler generators).

23.2 A LIFECYCLE FOR COTS BASED DEVELOPMENT

Consider that we are given a set of system requirements and are expected to develop a system to satisfy these requirements, using possibly COTS products from some existing repositories (vendor catalogs). Once the requirements are analyzed, captured, and specified in some (formal or informal) notation, we may proceed in one of two ways to design the system:

1. *Bottom Up Design.* In this approach, we first acquaint ourselves with available COTS components, analyze their relationship to the proposed system, prospect how these products can be deployed to design the system, then draw a system design that takes the best advantage of these available COTS components.

2. *Top Down Design.* In this approach, we first acquaint ourselves with the requirements specification, then we proceed with system design following a top down discipline, and check at each step of the design whether the leaves of the design structure can be satisfied by existing COTS products.

To make use of existing COTS components and existing integration technologies, the system designer often follows a bottom up approach in which acquaintance is a main activity.

If we factor out the design discipline, which is a software design issue more than a software reuse issue, we find the following sequence of phases: (1) *selection* from a wide range of candidate assets; (2) *integration* in the host system after determining that the asset is adequate for the intended purpose; (3) *verification and validation* of the COTS product within its new operating environment; and (4) *maintenance* of the COTS product, as well as impact of its maintenance on host systems. These issues are discussed in the remainder of this section.

23.2.1 COTS Selection

Generally speaking, COTS based development is a desirable option whenever we value functionality and ease of use over reliability and integrity. Because a COTS product is intended for a large body of users, it has features to satisfy a wide range of needs, hence typically has ample functionality. Also, because a COTS product is developed with the expectation that it will be amply amortized by the sheer size of its user community, it is fully loaded with features that facilitate its operation and enhance its widespread use. Yet, they cannot be used in systems with stringent reliability requirements, due to possible mismatches between the functionality provided by the COTS developer and the expectations of system designers who (re)use the COTS product. Because they are used in contexts that were not necessarily known to the COTS designer at design time, COTS products may fail to behave according to the expectations of the system designer who is (re)using them—even when they are deemed reliable according to the requirements of the COTS designer. Finally, because they do not stem from a coherent, carefully fine-tuned design, but are composed of predefined assets and glue code, COTS based systems may lack the integrity and simplicity that characterize good designs.

The selection of a COTS component is contingent upon three orthogonal conditions:

1. *Quality.* Reusable assets in general, and COTS assets in particular, are expected to meet high standards of quality; standards include the traditional software qualities of reliability and efficiency. For the purposes of COTS development, we also need ease of integration and upgradability; the former seeks to control/minimize development costs, whereas the latter seeks to control/minimize maintenance costs (as we may want to take advantage of subsequent upgrades of the COTS products we use).

2. *Fitness.* The question of fitness takes two different forms depending on the design discipline being adopted in the design of the application system. Under top down design, the question is whether the component satisfies the predefined functional requirements that are expected by the host system. Under bottom up design, the question is whether the component may be used towards building a layered implementation of the application system.

3. *Interaction.* Not only do we have to ensure that candidate COTS products satisfy expected functional requirements when they are integrated into a host system (which is what the condition of fitness deals with), we also have to ensure that they do not interact with other functions of the system.

Ultimately, we must, before proceeding any further in considering a candidate COTS component, answer the question of whether it is better to (re)use the COTS component or develop a custom-made component from scratch.

23.2.2 COTS Integration

Many aspects of COTS components integration are the same as the integration of a source code component in the context of component based software development; hence we defer those aspects to Chapter 21, where these issues are discussed in some detail. We focus, in this section, on those aspects that are COTS-specific.

- *Interface Matching.* In order to combine two separately developed COTS products into a single system, we must ensure that their interfaces match. Because we have no access to their internal source code, this can only be done by means of *wrappers*, or *glue code*, which perform such tasks as formatting inputs and outputs, preprocessing inputs, postprocessing outputs, providing default values where needed, controlling exceptional conditions, and so on.
- *Functional Matching.* While it is important to ensure that a selected component does satisfy the required functional properties, it is also important to ensure that it does not have extra functional features, which may (if left unchecked) interfere with other functions of the system. This means that, in case the COTS product has excess functionality, that extra code must be written *around* the product to filter out excess functionality and ensure that it does not interfere with other parts of the system.
- *Intercomponent Communication.* Because under the COTS protocol, the user has no access to the source code, the vocabulary of intercomponent communications is fairly limited. It includes traditional procedure calls, system level capabilities (Unix's pipes, desktops' drag-and-drop, clipboards, cut-and-paste), and data sharing (via data files, databases, and program data areas).
- *Integration Testing.* Again, because under the COTS protocol, the user has no access to the source code, the range of options for integration testing is limited to black box testing of the COTS products.

Software documentation is known to be an important component of any software product. It is even more crucial for COTS products; while the documentation of a source code product is a complement to the source code, the documentation of a COTS product is a substitute for the source code. Because the completeness, timeliness, and precision of the documentation of a COTS product is of the utmost importance strict standards of documentation are required for COTS products.

23.2.3 Verification and Validation of COTS Based Systems

It is reasonable to consider that a COTS product that has been used by several thousand users over several years has been tested far more thoroughly than any amount of regularly scheduled integration testing. Also, a COTS product vendor who anticipates to sell his product by the thousands can consent an amount of verification and validation that no single user can afford. Yet, the verification and validation of COTS products remains a time consuming and nontrivial task. In this section, we discuss the verification and validation

(V&V) of COTS products at application engineering time (when the COTS product is reused), and contrast it to the verification and validation that is performed at domain engineering time (when the COTS product is designed).

- *Difference in Requirements*. While domain engineering V&V deals with the generic requirements of the COTS product as formulated from a domain-wide perspective, the application engineering V&V deals with the specific requirements of the application at hand. In other words, while domain engineering V&V focuses on substantiating vendor claims, application engineering focuses on meeting the specific expectations of the application.

- *Difference in Goals*. While application engineering V&V deals primarily with verification of the selected asset for the purposes of the application at hand, domain engineering V&V deals with two goals: first ensuring that the target requirements are adequate for the purposes of the selected domain; and second, ensuring that the asset satisfies these requirements. Also, application engineering V&V makes up, in effect, for any gap in the precision of the retrieval and selection process. Finally, domain engineering V&V must achieve the goal of *certifying* the COTS product, namely to ensure that it satisfies industry-wide standards of quality.

- *Difference in Methods*. Whereas application engineering V&V is restricted to black box testing, domain engineering V&V can use all the methods of static and dynamic verification. On one hand, application engineering V&V can deploy black box testing using usage pattern information, which is specific to the application at hand, and which is not available at the time of the domain engineering V&V.

Hence, even though COTS products are thoroughly validated by their extensive product testing and their widespread field use, the application engineer is not dispensed from a substantial V&V task; this task must for the most part be repeated whenever he uses a new version of the product.

23.2.4 Maintenance of COTS Based Systems

As long as one only considers development costs when adopting a COTS based development, it is difficult to imagine any situation where using COTS products is not advantageous over custom-made development (assuming the appropriate COTS products are available). The main reason why anybody may want to decline using COTS when such products are available is the consideration of maintenance issues and their associated costs and risks. The main reason why maintenance is such an issue in COTS based development is that the maintenance of a COTS product remains the responsibility of the COTS vendor (rather than the COTS user/buyer/lessee/licensee); this means that the COTS user is using or selling a product that is not completely under his control. This situation has many implications some of which are rather far reaching:

- The acquisition of the COTS product may include clauses to the effect that the vendor provides maintenance and support. Maintenance and support costs must be taken into acount, over the expected lifetime of the host system, to provide a sound *purchase versus develop* decision.
- The user of a COTS based system is not at liberty to evolve his system as he wishes, but is subject to the upgrade schedule imposed by the vendor. Of course, the user may choose not to make an upgrade, but the vendor may also choose not to support older versions indefinitely.
- Each COTS upgrade requires a thorough verification and validation effort by the application engineer, for the reasons discussed in Section 21.2.3. Even *upwards compatibility* does not dispense the application engineer from a thorough verification and validation effort—due to the issues of interaction discussed in Section 21.2.2. The extra functionality of the upgraded COTS product may interfere with other functions of the application system.

The rapid evolution of technology and the rapid changes in business processes amplify the effect of these contingencies. Paradoxically, these contingencies are actually part of an optimistic scenario, which is that the COTS vendor remains in business, and that it keeps supporting the COTS product you acquires; none of which are a certainty.

Before purchasing a COTS product, an organization must make provisions for the case when the vendor goes out of business. At the very least, the buyer must ensure that if the vendor does go out of business, the buyer can acquire the source code of the COTS product. To ensure that the transfer of the source code between an officially defunct company and a former client takes place smoothly, it may be necessary to place the code with a third party, possibly as an escrow.

An organization must also make provisions for the case when the vendor decides to discontinue a product or discontinue servicing it. Such provisions may include transfer of the source code, and/or subcontracting the main-tenance function to a third party.

In a business (such as the software industry) where products regularly outlive their life expectancy and companies are prone to sudden death, these are not vain measures. Note that obtaining the source code is not the end of the buyer's difficulties, but could well be the beginning: it is not necessarily straightforward to maintain a large software product about nothing is known ahead of time.

23.2.5 Cost Estimation for COTS Development

The ability to estimate costs of software products and processes is an integral part of good software engineering. The cost models that we have discussed in Part VI assume that reusable assets are acquired by the organization that develops the host system, and that they are acquired in source form (thereby becoming an integral part of the host system). These premises have an important impact on the costs of COTS based development; hence the models discussed in Part VI cannot be applied to COTS based development. In this section, we briefly describe a COTS specific cost estimation model, called *COCOTS*, which is an outgrowth of the COCOMO model.

COCOTS recognizes that, to be feasible, a COTS based solution must satisfy three lines of constraints: technical constraints, pertaining to the match between system requirements and COTS product functionality; economic constraints, pertaining to the tradeoffs involved in the COTS solution vs. the custom development solution; and strategic constraints, pertaining to the operating environment of the application system under development. Also, COCOTS identifies five sources of cost in COTS based development, which are: the cost of assessing candidate COTS components; the cost of tailoring selected components; the cost of integrating and testing the COTS component into the host system; the cost of increased system level programming due to the volatility of the COTS components; and finally the cost of increased system level verification and validation due to the use of COTS product executable code. COCOTS includes two models, that vary by amount of required data and (consequently) by precision: the *Early Design* COCOTS model relies on few parameters, and is applied early in the lifecycle, when little cost information is available; the *Post Architecture* COCOTS model relies on more parameters, provides better precision, but can only be applied in later phases of the procurement process.

23.2.6 Exercises

1. A COTS vendor provides an optimized compiler for Pascal and a system developer needs a regular (not necessarily optimized) compiler for a subset of Pascal (e.g., dealing with Pascal programs that have no user-defined files). Use this example to illustrate the difference in requirements, goals, and methods between the verification and validation activity done by the COTS vendor, and that done by the COTS user.

2. A COTS vendor provides an optimized compiler for Pascal and a system developer needs a regular (not necessarily optimized) compiler for a subset of Pascal (e.g., dealing with Pascal programs that have no user-defined files). Use this example to illustrate how the use of extra functionality interferes with other functions of the application system. Propose a solution to control this feature interaction.

3. Find an example where excess functionality in a COTS product interferes with other functions of the host application system.

23.3 DEVELOPING COTS CERTIFICATION CRITERIA

COTS-based development promises various advantages but yet carries as many risks. Establishing trust in commercial components is a major challenge. Testing and certification techniques are essential to establish trust in the acquired components and assess the suitability of a COTS component for integration with the rest of the application. The risks become more critical when the COTS component is intended for use in multiple products in the same domain (i.e., in a product line). In this section, we discuss how to develop certification and suitability testing criteria for COTS components. We discuss a hierarchical reference model to guide the process of developing COTS certification criteria and use an example of a database management system (DBMS) to illustrate the use of the model.

23.3.1 Certification Categories

To certify a COTS component, we first need to develop the criteria against which we assess the component. A reference model can be used to identify possible categories under which certification criteria can be developed. In developing the hierarchical model, one can consider:

- *Certification Level.* This category is derived by an *economic investment cycles* rationale [Mili 2000]. Decisions regarding the development or reuse of the COTS components can be rationalized as investment decisions. At the COTS development level, the vendor invests in developing the components and expects a return on investment in commercializing the COTS product for usage in particular domains. At the domain engineering level, domain engineers acquire COTS components and expect to reap the benefits from integrating the COTS component within the product line architecture rather than investing in the development of in-house components. At the application level, application engineers expect a cost reduction by reusing existing reference architecture and the COTS components. Therefore criteria are characterized by the certification level, which is categorized as COTS worthiness, domain pervasiveness, architecture conformance, and application adequacy.
- *Certification Agent.* Several parties can be involved in the COTS certification process; these include the COTS vendor, the domain analyst, the domain engineer, and the application engineer. Certification criteria are developed based on the perspective of these parties.
- *Focus of Certification Criteria.* One can use the C3 model of component-based software, whereby a component can be characterized by its

Certification Dimensions

Certification Level	Certification Agent	Certification Focus	Certification Goals
COTS Worthiness	Vendor	Content	Worthiness
Domain Pervasiveness	Domain Analyst	Concept	Usefulness
Architecture Conformance	Domain Engineer	Context	Usability
Application Adequacy	Application Engineer	Context	Adequacy

Certification Category

FIGURE 23.1 Classification of certification categories along the level, focus, agent, and goal dimensions.

content, concept, and context. The analyst can then develop certification criteria for each of the three focal points.

- *Certification Goal.* Finally the purpose of a certification criteria can evolve around assessing the worthiness, usefulness, usability, and adequacy of the COTS component.

Figure 23.1 summarizes the categories along the four dimensions.

23.3.2 COTS Certification Levels

We can categorize the criteria development according to the certification level (derived from the economic rationale) as follows:

- *COTS Worthiness.* In this category, we develop certification criteria that assess the *worthiness* of a software product to be a COTS component. In order to be considered as a viable COTS component a software product has to meet some intrinsic criteria that deal exclusively with its content.
- *Domain Pervasiveness.* In this category, we develop certification criteria that assess the *usefulness* of the concept of a COTS component. These criteria reflect the viewpoint of the domain analyst who only accepts components that he expects to be often used.
- *Architecture Conformance.* In this category, we develop certification criteria that assess the *usability* of the COTS component in a given product line context. These criteria reflect the viewpoint of the domain engineer who is concerned with minimizing the overhead costs of integrating the COTS component in the product line architecture.
- *Application Adequacy.* In this category, we develop application specific criteria that assess the adequacy of the COTS component in the particular application at hand. These criteria reflect the viewpoint of the application engineer who is concerned with developing an application that belongs to the product line.

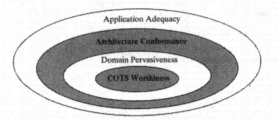

FIGURE 23.2 A hierarchical model for generating COTS certification criteria.

Figure 23.2 shows the hierarchical model for developing COTS certification criteria. The above categories represent a hierarchy of certification criteria for COTS component as used in a product line. For instance, the COTS worthiness category is an assessment of the usefulness of the component and, hence should be assessed for any COTS component. In order to certify a COTS component for a specific domain it has to be certified as a worthy COTS component and a useful component to the domain at hand. Further up the hierarchy, to certify a COTS component as usable in a certain architecture, we must ensure that it is worthy as a COTS component, useful in the domain, and usable in the product line reference architecture. Finally, to certify a COTS component for a specific application in the product line, we have to ensure that it is COTS worthy, useful in the domain, conforming to the domain architecture, and adequate for the particular application we are developing.

In the following section we explain each of the above categories and define subcategories and criteria. Figure 23.3 summarizes a model that was developed in [Yacoub 2000]. We use a running example of a database management system (DBMS).

23.3.3 COTS Worthiness

A component is COTS worthy if it is technically and commercially sound. The criteria for certifying the technical soundness include functional attributes, structural attributes, and operational attributes. Commercially sound components are those that are sold and marketed by credible vendors. Criteria for certifying the commercial soundness include assessment of the vendor development process and the stability of its business.

23.3.3.1 Functional Attributes
Criteria for certifying the functionality of a COTS component should assess the services that the component provides and the quality by which the component delivers these services. Functional attributes reflect the faithfulness with which the component embodies its concept.

Application Adequacy

Application-specific testing and certification

Architecture Conformance

Genericity
Interoperability
  Dependencies on other components
  Required Interfaces
  Provided Interfaces
  Integration Criteria
Portability
  Environment Interfaces
Compliance with Standards

Domain Pervasiveness

Generality
Retrievability
Usefulness

COTS- Worthiness

Functional attributes
  Services
  Quality of Service
    Tolerating failures
    Performance
    Security
    Reliability
Operational attributes
  Efficient Implementation
  User Interfaces
Structural attributes
  Understandability
    Documentation
    Testability
  Adaptability
Vendor and Market attributes
  vendor business stability
  the development process
  obsolescence of the component
  maintenance contract
  marketing trends,
  customer support

FIGURE 23.3   The Hierarchical COTS Certification Model.

Services. COTS testing and certification should include criteria to assess the functions and capabilities that are supported by the COTS component as claimed by the component vendor. This category usually embodies a large portion of the testing and certification criteria.

DBMS Example The DBMS provides the capability to create, maintain, provide access to, and delete data dictionaries. The DBMS supports storage of the following data types: text, alphabetic, alphanumeric, character strings, float, scientific notation, integers, user-defined, date-time combined, logical yes/no used in boolean calculations, binary large objects (BLOBs), multimedia, images, graphics, OLE-object, currency, and hyperlinks to Uniform Resource Locators (URL).

Quality of Service. While the certification of the COTS component services is an assessment of the functionalities supported by the component, the quality of these services (QoS) is a property of the component that deserves further certification. QoS attributes include tolerating failures, such as masking failures and failure recovery; performance attributes, such as response time; security attributes, such as immunity to viruses or access constraints; and reliability attributes, such as the failure history of the component over its operational period.

DBMS Example
Performance criteria. The DBMS provides a query optimizer to choose efficient strategies for evaluating a relational query. The DBMS optimization parameters include the following: CPU utilization, network access paths, indexes, physical clusters, and distributed access paths.

Security criteria. The DBMS can enforce data access controls based on the discretionary access control requirements. The DBMS ensures that access permission to an object by users not already possessing access permissions shall only be assigned by authorized system administrators. The DBMS encrypts user passwords.

Reliability criteria. The DBMS can recover from a corrupted database. The DBMS supports checkpointing/savepointing. The DBMS initiates automatic recovery using the data manager log file to undo or redo transactions.

23.3.3.2 *Structural Attributes*
Whereas certification criteria based on functional attributes assess the functions of the COTS component, certification criteria based on structural attributes assess the COTS component itself. Structural assessment of COTS component is impractical because these component are often used as black boxes. We have identified two of the structural features that possibly could be used to assess the structure of the COTS component even in the absence of source code.

Understandability. A great deal of understandability can be attributed to documentation. Documentation of a COTS component covers how to use the component (e.g., user manual), and how to configure the component (e.g., setup or reference manual). Moreover, the nature of the documentation is also important, for instance, electronic, online, and interactive documentation versus paper-based documentation. There is more to understandability than documentation. Understandability is also dependent on the volume of the component (e.g., its size), the clarity of the component structure, and the integrity of the component structure. A certification criterion that is heavily based on understandability is testability. To support component testability, vendors should supply test oracles or test generators to generate test cases to certify the COTS component.

DBMS Example
   Documentation criteria.   The DBMS has an administrator guide, a reference manual (online, hardcopy), a user manual (online, hardcopy), and tutorials.

Adaptability. COTS certification criteria include assessment of whether the component support adaptation mechanisms for customization purposes with minimal effort and impact on the component content.

DBMS Example The DBMS supports language extensions and server programmability. The DBMS supports the following procedural extensions to SQL: block structure, parameter passing, loop constructs, and conditional checks. The database administrator can view and edit configuration parameters.

23.3.3.3   Operational Attributes
Operational attributes are characteristics of the COTS component as it executes in the operation or run-time environment. We have identified two categories: efficient implementation and user interfaces.

Efficient Implementation. A COTS user who is seeking an efficient implementation of some concept may want to discard a COTS component that does not satisfy the predefined efficiency requirement, even if it satisfies the functional and structural requirements. Hence efficiency does affect the worthiness of a COTS component. Criteria for assessing efficiency include resource brokerage such as files, memory, and so on.

User Interfaces. Some COTS components have user interfaces through which the user interacts directly with the component during operation time. Interfaces that are harder to understand fail the user acceptance tests and decrease the worthiness of a component. A user-friendly interface is more credible.

DBMS Example The DBMS provides a common graphical user interface (GUI) for all COTS database administration tools. A common GUI is used to implement administration user functions. The DBMS provides a GUI to backup and restore the database.

23.3.3.4 Vendor and Market Attributes

As opposed to certification of in-house off-the-shelf components COTS certification involves commercial aspects that pertain to the component vendor. The worthiness of the component is measured by its vendor credentials. Certification criteria based on vendor and market attributes include assessment of

- the vendor business stability, for instance, how long the vendor has been in business and the risks of the vendor going out of business
- the process that is followed in developing the component including the testing and certification process at the vendor site
- obsolescence of the component, namely, what happens if the vendor goes out of business or the component becomes obsolete
- maintenance contract, because in COTS development the maintenance of a COTS product is the responsibility of the vendor usually because of the unavailability of source code
- stability of the component, which includes assessment of the versioning history of the component, frequency of upgrades, and the reasons for upgrade (i.e., more functionality, less defects, etc.)
- marketing trends, which includes assessment of technology issues and market trends and considerations for alternative COTS components in the market
- the availability of customer support and the form of the support (online, phone-based, etc.)

DBMS Example Training and courses offered by the vendor include: administrative and user training onsite or remote. The maintenance and support provided by the vendor include maintenance contract, phone-in technical support, and online support. Version upgrades are included as part of the maintenance contract free of charge.

23.3.4 Domain Pervasiveness

Domain-specific certification criteria are measures for the concept that a COTS component embodies, irrespective of how this concept is represented. The concept of a COTS component reflects its essence. We identified three categories for certifying the concept of a COTS component.

23.3.4.1 Generality

A concept is more general when it admits many useful instantiations or specializations. We distinguish between two forms of generality, *structural* and *functional*. The inability to change the structure of the COTS component, due to limited access to the source code or maintenance agreements with the vendor, makes functional generality more relevant than structure generality.

23.3.4.2 Retrievability

A COTS component that is selected for a particular domain will be stored with other domain components in the component library. Retrievability is a measure of how easy it is to retrieve the component from the library, which can be quantified by the average precision and recall of the retrieval procedures in the component library. Retrievability is not a major concern when a separate library is kept for the product line because of the limited number of components in the library all of which serve the same product line, whereas it is more significant when the component is stored in a general-purpose library. COTS components have no visible structure for the purposes of retrieval, functional retrieval criteria are often used.

23.3.4.3 Usefulness

The usefulness of a COTS component in a particular product line reflects the frequency with which the component is needed in the product line domain. Generality contributes to usefulness but is distinct from it, while generality is intrinsic to the component, usefulness is relative to a product line; the same component may be useful in one application domain and much less useful in another. Certification criteria should assess how frequently the component is used, the number of applications in which it was used, and whether the component has well-known and documented use cases.

23.3.5 Architecture Conformance

For a given concept (domain-specific) and a given implementation (component-specific), a COTS component may be more or less usable depending on the context that it is required to operate within. For example, the context for a COTS component could be the architecture in which it is integrated. Certification criteria should assess the conformity of the component to the architecture constraints. While domain-specific certification criteria assess the essence of a COTS component and the COTS worthiness certification criteria assess the intrinsic qualities of the component's representation, architecture conformance criteria assess the ability to integrate the COTS component with other components in the architecture and with its host environment. We have identified four context attributes, which we discuss in turn below.

23.3.5.1 Genericity

Genericity reflects the ease with which a component can be instantiated and specialized. This attribute is not to be confused with generality, whereas, generality is a characteristic of the concept (a domain property), genericity is a characteristic of the concept's representation (a component property). Assessment of genericity as applied to COTS components is related to how difficult it is to put the component in operation such as installation, un-installation, controlled setup features, and so on.

DBMS Example A comprehensive start-up kit containing the necessary information about installation and use of the product is provided. An administrator/installation guide is delivered with the DBMS component.

23.3.5.2 Interoperability
Interoperability is the ability of a component to interact with other components of the architecture in a seamless manner, or the ability to adapt the component with minimal effort to achieve the same goal. Dependencies on other components (interoperability) can be assessed by the required interfaces and the provided interfaces that the component requires and offers [Yacoub 1999].

DBMS Example The DBMS provides a standard Application Programmers Interface (API) for database administration. The DBMS interoperates with third party desktops to support maintenance. The DBMS interoperates with the following window environments: X-Window, OSF/Motif, OpenLook, Common Desktop Environment (CDE), Windows 3.1, Windows 95, Windows NT. The DBMS interoperates with the following communications protocols: TCP/IP and POSIT. The DBMS sustains client-server connections independent of the database server's hosts and the client applications.

23.3.5.3 Portability
Portability describes the degree to which a component is unconstrained by the choice of execution platforms. The portability of a COTS component is affected by two main factors, the availability of the component on various execution platforms and the similarity of interfaces to the COTS component when hosted on those platforms. Portability is an important consideration, even when the product line has already specified its execution platform. At some point in the evolution of the architecture, it may be desirable to change platforms. Assessing the portability of COTS candidates before product selection can help ensure that this migration is not prohibitively expensive. The COTS candidates are scored based on the number of platforms on which they are supported and the effort the vendor should expend to port the component from one platform to another.

DBMS Example The DBMS supports host/platform file management transparency. The DBMS operates on a variety of UNIX- and/or POSIX-compliant operating systems, that include the following: Sun OS version 4.1 or higher, Sun Solaris, HP-UX, IBM AIX, Windows NT, and DEC Alpha. The DBMS facilitates portability of applications across many different platforms that support the same standards.

23.3.5.4   *Compliance with Standards*

A COTS component should comply with architectural standards in the same domain. Certification criteria assess the level of compliance of a COTS component to these standards. For product line engineering, several Department of Defense (DoD) organizations have recognized that the development of product line reference architectures is an enabler to control software cost and complexity in developing products of the same family. The DoD realizes the importance of architectures for the Defense Information Infrastructure Common Operating Environment (DII COE) [DIICOE 1997]. For government agencies, an important category is to use certification criteria for measuring compliance with the DII COE constraints. For example, a COTS component used in the DII COE environment must be certified against the following DII COE compliance categories:

1. *Runtime Environment.* Measures compliance of the component's fit within the COE executing environment, the amount it reuses COE components, whether it will run on a COE platform, and whether it will interfere with other components.

2. *Style Guide.* Measures compliance of the component's user interface to the style guide. This is to ensure that the proposed component will be consistent with the rest of the COE-based system to minimize training and maintenance cost.

3. *Architectural Compatibility.* Measures compliance of the component's fit within the COE architecture and the component's potential life cycle as COE evolves.

4. *Software Quality.* Assesses a component's program risk and software maturity through the use of traditional software metrics. This can be done using measurements such as lines of code and complexity metrics.

DBMS Example   In the domain of a database management system there are several standards. For example, the DBMS should comply with ANSI X3.135-1992 SQL, FIPS 127-1 SQL and IRDS (FIPS 156). We also certify whether the DBMS implements a Data Definition Language (DDL) supporting the ANSI SQL standard referential integrity features. The DBMS's architecture should follow the ANSI/SPARC Study Group on Database Management Systems' three abstraction levels. The DBMS should also implement a data manipulation language (DML) which should be compliant with ANSI X3.135-1992 SQL and FIPS 127-1 SQL.

23.3.6   Application Adequacy

While the domain-specific criteria deal with generic requirements of the COTS component as formulated from a domain-wide perspective, application specific criteria deal with specific requirements for one particular application of the product line. Application specific criteria focus on meeting the specific expectations of the application. Application engineering certification can deploy black box testing using usage pattern information, which is specific to the application at hand, and which is not available at the time of the domain engineering certification.

Even though COTS components are thoroughly validated by their extensive product testing and their widespread field usage, the application engineer is not dispensed from a substantial certification task; this task must, for the most part, be repeated whenever he uses the COTS component in a new application.

23.4   FURTHER READING

It is difficult, in a short bibliography such as this, to be fair to all the work that has been done in COTS based software development. Three research centers account for a significant portion of the work on COTS; the *Software Engineering Institute* (Pittsburgh, PA), the Canadian *National Research Council* (Ottawa, Ont.), and the University of Southern California's *Center for Software Engineering* (Los Angeles, CA). Some of the sources that we have used to compile a snapshot on the state of the art in COTS based development include the special issue of *Computer* Magazine devoted to COTS [Voas 1998a, 1998b, McDermid 1998, Lindquist and Jonsson 1998, Zhong 1998]; the proceedings of the *1999 International Workshop on Component Based Software Engineering* [CBSE 1999]; an online technical report of USC's Center for Software Engineering on COCOTS [COCOTS 2000]; the proceedings of the 1999 *Symposium on Software Reusability* [Mittermeir 1999]; and a variety of other references [Brown 1998, Chavez 1998, Dean 1997, Mcgraw 1999, Obendorf 1999, Vigder et al. 1996, Voas 1998c].

Appendixes

Appendix A

Software Reuse Resources

A.1 TEXTBOOKS

Some books dedicated to software reuse, as of the date of press, ranked in alphabetical order of their author (see Bibliography for full references).

Bassett [1996]
Biggerstaff and Perlis [1989]
Coulange [1998]
Ezran et al. [1998]
Gamma et al. [1994]
Gautier and Wallis [1990]
Hall [1992]
Hallsteinsen and Paci [1997]
Hooper and Chester [1991]
Jacobson et al. [1997]
Karlsson [1995]
Leach [1997]
Leavens and Sitaraman [2000]
Lim [1997]
McClure [1992]
McClure [1995]
Meyer [1994]
Poulin [1997a]

Pree [1995]

Prieto-Diaz [1991a]

Rada [1995]

Rada [1999]

Reifer [1997]

Sametinger [1997]

Schafer et al. [1993]

Sodhi and Sodhi [1998]

Tracz [1995]

Walton and Maiden [1993]

A.2   WEB SITES

Some Web sites dedicated to software reuse, as of the date of press, ranked by alphabetical order of their URL.

1. *dii-sw.ncr.disa.mil.* Home page of the *Center For Computer Systems Engineering* (CFCSE). Serving as the CFCSE Information Clearing-house, this site provides DISA, DoD program managers, and other users with access to historical data on the DoD Software Reuse initiative (SRI).

2. *www.omg.org.* Home page of the *Object Management Group* (OMG). The OMG was formed to create a component-based software market-place by hastening the introduction of standardized object software. The organization's charter includes the establishment of industry guide-lines and detailed object management specifications to provide a common framework for application development.

3. *rsc.asset.com.* Home page of IEEE's *Reuse Steering Committee.* Responsible for coordinating reuse standards. Operates the *Reuse Library Interoperability Group* (RIG), whose purpose is to draft standards for interoperability of component reuse libraries.

4. *www.ccpl.com.* Home page of the *Command and Control Product Line* (CCPL). The CCPL is a consortium of industrial partners who work under contract of the U.S. Air Force to develop a product line technology for command and control applications. They use a variety of software reuse technologies (product-line engineering, software architectures, component-based software engineering, COTS-based software development) to streamline software composition and development.

5. *www.netron.com.* Home page of *Netron.* Provider of the *NetronFusion* product, described as a software reuse and component-based develop-

ment technology to build flexible components and deliver hybrid architectures with Java clients talking to COBOL servers.

6. *www.iit.nrc.ca.* Home page of the *Institute for Information Technology* of the Canadian *National Research Council.* Performs long-term research on COTS-based software engineering, and other software reuse-related issues. Maintains a bibliography of COTS publications.

7. *www.nplace.wvhtf.org.* Home page of *NPLACE: National Product Line Asset Center.* NPLACE defines criteria for testing COTS products. These criteria are structured in a multilayer hierarchy, ranging from application-specific requirements to general COTS worthiness requirements. Their aim is to standardize COTS certification procedures.

8. *www.reusability.com.* Home page of *Extended Intelligence Inc.* Billed as a *Software Reuse Resource Center for Business.* Offers a variety of services, including reuse products and services, reuse education and training, reuse events calendar, reuse books and papers, reuse information sources, and reuse tips.

9. *www.reuse.com.* Home page of *The Reuse Group.* Offers services in reuse management, reuse personnel, reuse process and methodology, and reuse technology. Maintains a list of reuse resources.

10. *www.sei.cmu.edu.* Home page of the *Software Engineering Institute,* which has long-term research initiatives on many aspects of software reuse, including software architectures, product-line engineering, and COTS-based software engineering.

11. *www.software.org.* Home page of the *Software Productivity Consortium,* which provides a variety of guidebooks and tools on domain analysis, product-line engineering, and software reuse costs.

12. *www.tcse.org.* Home page of the *Technical Council on Software Engineering.* Includes a committee called the *Committee on Software Reuse,* which runs the *ICSR* conferences, the *WISR* workshop series, and the *ReNews* newsletter.

A.3 CONFERENCE SERIES

Following is a list of reuse-specific conferences, ranked by alphabetical order. In the absence of permanent Web sites, we present the site of recent instance; they are usually forward-linked.

1. *ICSR: International Conference on Software Reuse.* Convened in 1991 (ICSR1: Dortmund, Germany), 1992 (ICSR2: Lucca, Italy), 1994 (ICSR3: Rio de Janeiro, Brazil), 1996 (ICSR4: Orlando, FL), 1998 (ICSR5: Victoria, BC, Canada) and 2000 (ICSR6: Vienna, Austria). No permanent Web site. The mirror Web sites of ICSR6 are

http://icsr6.isys-e.uni-klu.ac.at/icsr6/

http://www.spe.ucalgary.ca/icsr6/

Proceedings published by IEEE Computer Society.

2. *Reuse: Reuse Education and Training Workshop*. Annual worskhop held in Morgantown, WV. Convened from 1992 to 1998, with differene themes from year to year.

3. *SPLC: Software Product Line Conference*. Convened for the first time in Denver, CO in August 2000. Organized by the Software Engineering Institute. Conference Web site:

http://www.sei.cmu.edu/plp/conf/SPLC.html.

4. *SSR: Symposium on Software Reuse*. Convened in 1995 (SSR'95: Seattle, WA), 1997 (SSR'97: Boston, MA), 1999 (SSR'99: Los Angeles, CA), and 2001 (SSR'01: Toronto, Ontario, Canada). The mirror Web sites of SSR'99 are

http://csalpha.unomaha.edu/~ssr99/

http://ssr99.ifi.uni-klu.ac.at/ssr99/

Proceedings published by ACM.

5. *WISR: Workshop on Institutionalizing Software Reuse*. Convened in 1988 (Bass Harbor, ME), 1989 (Melbourne, FL), 1990 (Syracuse, NY), 1991 (WISR4: Reston, VA), 1992 (WISR5: Palo Alto, CA), 1993 (WISR6: Owego, NY), 1995 (WISR7: St Charles, IL), 1997 (WISR8: Columbus, OH), and 1999 (WISR9: Austin, TX). The University of Maine maintains a permanent website for the WISR workshop series, at

http://www.umcs.maine.edu/~ftp/wisr/wisr.html

Proceedings are maintained in electronic form on an ftp site at the University of Maine.

6. *ICSE Colocated Workshops*. There is a proliferation of ICSE-colocated workshops that deal with various aspects of software reuse. Some are more permanent than others, and they usually deal with limited-term interests. A sampling of reuse-related workshops colocated with ICSE 2000 includes

- International Software Architecture Workshop
- Continuing Collaborations for Successful COTS Development
- International Workshop on Component Based Software Engineering: Reflection on Practice
- Software Product Lines: Economics, Architectures and Implications

The proceedings of these events are usually published in limited edition, for the purposes of the workshop attendance. The website of ICSE 2000, with which these were colocated, is

http://www.ul.ie/~icse2000.

A.4 SOFTWARE REUSE SURVEYS

We present a list of software reuse surveys, ranked by order of publication. These may report on the state of the art, the state of the practice, or on research perspectives.

Krueger [1992]
Poulin [1993]
Prieto-Diaz [1993]
Mili et al. [1995a]
Zand and Samadzadeh [1995]
Mili et al. [1998]
Poulin [1999]

Appendix B

Term Projects

In this appendix, we present two examples of a software reuse project, each is adequate for a term project in a course on software reuse. We discuss in turn domain engineering aspects then application engineering aspects. As we envision this project, the class may be divided into groups, using one of the team organizations discussed in Chapter 4. If the class is too large, it may be divided into two or more reuse structures, where each individual structure is organized according to one of the patterns discussed in Chapter 4, not necessarily the same organization (so as to compare alternative organizations).

B.1 SIMULATION OF WAITING QUEUES

B.1.1 Domain Engineering

We want to develop a domain-specific library of components for the purpose of producing applications that simulate the behavior of waiting queues. To fix our ideas, we consider that we are dealing with customers lining up at the cash registers of a store, or travelers lining up at check-in counters, or so on. Individual applications vary in a number of ways, including

- *Topology of Service Stations.* The number of service stations may be fixed or variable (in time); we may have one service station or more than one; if there are more than one service station, the service stations may be interchangeable (they deliver the same service) or not (e.g., checkout counters for 10 items or less; checkout counters for more than 10 items).
- *Service Time.* The service time may be constant or variable; if it is variable, it may be determined by the customer or by the service station

or by both (e.g., customer determines amount of service needed, and service station prorates that with its own productivity factor); also, if it is variable, it may be subject to a maximum service value (as is the case in CPU dispatching algorithms); when the maximum is reached, the customer may be thrown out, queued at the end of the queue where it was, or considered as a new arrival.

- *Topology of Queues.* A single queue; multiple interchangable queues; multiple queues with different service categories (each customer may line up at queues of a given category).
- *Types of Queues.* First-in/first-out (FIFO) queues; last-in/first-out queues; priority queues; limited-size queues.
- *Arrival Distribution.* Markov distribution; Poisson distribution; clustered distribution (if the service stations are immigration posts at an airport, then passenger arrivals are clustered around/after flight arrivals).
- *Dispatching Policy.* Customers are assigned to queues at random, and may not change queues after the first assignment; customers are assigned to the shortest queue on arrival and may not change queues subsequently; customers assigned to the shortest queue on arrival and switch queues to take the shortest subsequently, until they are served.
- *Measurements.* Average waiting time; standard deviation of waiting time (as a measure of fairness); maximum waiting time; throughput.

The object of this domain engineering exercise is to develop a set of library components that can be easily combined to produce any queue simulation we may want; samples of such simulations are discussed in the next section.

B.1.2 Application Engineering

The application engineering team may participate in the definition of reusable assets (but typically not in their implementation); once the assets are defined (there is no need to wait until the assets are developed), the application team develops applications (by combining the projected assets) to satisfy the following requirements. Once their development task completed, they are expected to produce feedback on the adequacy of the asset library.

1. *CPU Dispatching.* We want to simulate the behavior of a CPU dispatching mechanism. We are interested in measuring fairness and throughput. There is a single priority queue, with maximum service time (quantum service, Q); once a process has exhausted its service time, it is queued back, with an increased priority.
2. *Self-Serve Carwash.* We have a set of self-serve interchangeable carwash stations. Arriving cars line up at the shortest queue (queues of equal length are interchangeable) and do not change queues

subsequently; queues are FIFO, of course. Service is limited to a maximum value (but may take less time), and cars are expected to clear the station once the maximum time has expired. Arrival distribution is markovian. We are interested in monitoring maximum waiting time (we dont want anybody to leave before being served) and throughput (we want to serve as many people as possible).

3. *Checkout Counters.* We have a number of checkout counters at a supermarket, some of which are reserved for shoppers with 10 items or less. Shoppers with 10 items or less line up in the shortest express check-out queue; others line in the shortest queue reserved for them. Once they are lined up in some queue, shoppers do not leave the queue until it is their turn. Service time is determined by the shopper (size of the shopper's cart) and by the productivity of the cash register attendant (a factor p between, say, l and h, where $0 < l \leq 1 \leq h < 2$). Arrival rate is markovian distribution. The number of stations increases whenever the longest queue exceeds a threshold value L and decreases by one whenever the number of stations of each category is greater than one and the length of one queue is zero. Whenever a new cash register is open, shoppers at the end of the queue rush to line up at the station (talk of fairness!) until the length of the queue equals the shortest current queue of the same type (express checkout, regular checkout). We are interested in average waiting time and fairness.

4. *Immigration Posts.* We have a number of immigration stations at an airport, some of which are reserved for nationals, the others are for foreign citizens. There are two queues: one for nationals, the other for foreigners; each queue feeds into the corresponding set of stations, and there is no transfer between queues. The number of stations that handle nationals increases by one whenever the length of the nationals' queue exceeds some value, say, L; and the number of stations that handle foreigners increases by one whenever the length of the foreigners' queue exceeds some other (larger?) value, say, M. The arrival rate is a clustered distribution, as passengers come by planeloads. Service time for nationals is constant, and service time for foreigners is determined by the passenger and by the productivity of the immigration agent attendant (a factor p between, say l and h, where $0 < l \leq 1 \leq h < 2$). We are interested in monitoring throughput.

5. *Checkin Counters.* We have two FIFO queues for passengers at an airline checkin station: a queue for first class and a queue for coach. We have two categories of service stations: first class and coach; the number of stations does not change for the length of the experiment. The duration of the service is the same for all passengers and all stations of the same class, but differs from first class to coach. The arrival rate is markovian distribution; passengers line up at their designated queue and do not leave it until they are served. Whenever one queue is empty, the corresponding service stations may serve passengers of the other

queue (typically first-class stations serve coach passengers when no first-class passengers are waiting). We are interested in monitoring the average waiting time and the maximum waiting time for each class of passengers.

6. *Round-Robin Dispatching.* Same as example 1, but with a FIFO queue; processes that exceed their time quantum are inserted at the back of the queue. Discuss the option to create this application by modifying the application produced for the example presented in 1 and compare it to the option to create this application directly from the library of assets.

7. *Self-Serve Carwash, Arbitrary Service Time.* Same as example 2, but without limit on the service time. Discuss the option to create this application by modifying the application produced for the example presented in 2 and compare it to the option to create this application directly from the library of assets.

8. *Fair Checkout Counters.* Same as example 3, but whenever a new counter is open, it is filled by shoppers at the front of the longest queues (although in practice they are least motivated to go through the trouble, their queue swapping will probably minimize average waiting time and maximize fairness). Discuss the option to create this application by modifying the application produced for example 3 and compare it to the option to create this application directly from the library of assets.

9. *Multiqueue Immigration Posts.* Same as example 4, but with one queue for each post; use the policy of example 4 for queue swapping when a new post is created. Assume also that passengers go from queue to queue whenever their position in the current queue is farther (from the head) than the length of another queue. Discuss the option to create this application by modifying the application produced for example 4 and compare it to the option to create this application directly from the library of assets.

10. *Fair Multiqueue Immigration Posts.* Same as example 9 with the policy of example 8 for queue swapping when a new post is created. Consider the option to create this application by modifying the solution produced for example 9, then consider the option to create this application by modifying the solution produced for example 8, and compare them to the option to create this application directly from the library of assets.

B.2 LIBRARY SYSTEMS

B.2.1 Domain Engineering

This sample product line concerns *libraries*. We include video libraries as an example of variance. This section describes a generic library and delineates the scope of the domain. Later sections will describe three specific applications in this product line.

An abstract library consists of a (usually large) number of *items* stored at one or more locations. A library has *customers*. There are two primary actions which are performed:

- *Removal* of an item from the library by a customer (the item is said to be *on loan*).
- A customer can *return* an item that he or she has removed in the past.

Additionally the library system must provide a means to allow customers to search for a given item by various keywords. For example, a video library might allow for search by title, year, or genre. Auxiliary operations (some of which may or may not be relevant for a given product in the line) include

- *Adding* and *deleting* customers.
- *Adding* and *deleting* items. A new book is added when it is acquired by the library. A book is deleted when it is either lost, or unusable (for example, videos wear out).
- Customers *pay* money under certain circumstances.
- A customer may not be allowed to remove an item. The specific borrowing policies vary from product instance to product instance.
- Some libraries allow a customer to place a *hold* on an item. The item is set aside for a given period of time, and during that time only the customer in question can remove the item. If the item is currently on loan, it can be returned and is then set aside. In this case, the time period begins when the item is returned.

Additionally, in the case where the library consists of more than one storage location a number of operations relate to location:

- A customer can request an *interlibrary loan* where an item held at a different storage facility is transfered to the given storage facility. Conditions, costs, and so on will vary among product instances.
- The search facility needs to allow searching by storage facility. In some cases only the local facility is shown (by default), and in others the items at all storage facilities should be shown.

B.2.1.1 Variabilities
In addition to the variabilities noted above the following areas provide for significant variability between product instances:

- *Database platform*—the implementation of the library system may need to use an existing database implementation.

- *Item type (and properties)*—the properties associated with, say, a video are different from the properties associated with a book.
- *Borrowing policies*—who can borrow? How many items can be borrowed at once? Under what conditions are borrowing rights modified?
- *Late penalties*—what happens when items are not returned in time?
- *Recall policies*—what happens when a hold is requested on item which is on loan? Is a request for prompt return sent to the customer who holds the item?
- *Hold policies*—who can place holds? When do holds expire?
- *Money*—does it cost money to become a customer? To remove an item? To place a hold? To return an item late?
- *Membership*—are there different classes of members? University libraries often allow postgraduates and staff to loan more items than undergraduates.
- *Reports (individual, systemwide)*—customers may desire reports on their status (how much money they owe, what items they have on loan etc.). A library may desire a systemwide report (e.g., how many items are on loan, how many items have been loaned and returned, how much money has been collected from various sources).
- *Interlibrary loan.*
- *Scale (size)*—number of facilities and number of books.

B.2.1.2   Commonalities
- *Customers*—general data (name, phone, etc.), money issues, limitations (e.g., how many items can be borrowed at once etc.)
- *Items*—*data*: location, status. *Operations*: (hold), loan, return.
- *Search*—engine, user interface.
- *Reports*—does there exist any commonality here?

B.2.2   Application Engineering

B.2.2.1   Library Application 1: Small Book and CD Library
This small library provides recreational books and CDs to the student population at a school. All students are automatically members (at no cost) and can borrow up to five books and up to three CDs at a time. Books must be returned within a month and CD within a week. Failure to do so will suspend borrowing rights for the students but no fine is incurred.

The library system consists of two components; a search component available to students will run on a bank of PCs. The library database runs on a PC on the librarian's desk and the librarian handles removal and return of books. Note that the search components need to access the librarian's PC to be able to report on the status of a book or CD. No holds are allowed, and since only a single location exists, interlibrary loans are irrelevant. Books have the following properties: title, author, publisher, year, genre. CDs have the following properties: title, composer, artist, works, genre.

B.2.2.2 Library Application 2: Large University Library

This library provides for the students and staff in a midsize university. There are a number of library branches—the catalog searches all of these. Since the branches are all on campus, there is no need for interlibrary loans. Students can borrow up to 16 books at a time, each of which must be returned within a month. Staff members can borrow any number of books for up to 2 months. Holds can be placed only by staff members. If a hold is placed on a book that is on loan, a letter (or email) is sent to the person who has the book. Likewise, letters and emails are sent when a book becomes overdue by 2 weeks, 6 weeks, 10 weeks, and so on. Borrowing rights are suspended when books become overdue, and there is a fine of $2 per book per week overdue beyond the 4th day of the month. For example, two books returned 5 weeks late incur a fine of $2 \times (5 - 4) \times 2 = $4. No books can be borrowed if there are unpaid fines.

In addition to books, the libraries have a fine collection of journals and periodicals that can be borrowed only by postgraduate students or staff and for a period of only 2 days. Items have the following properties:

- Books: author, title, year, publisher.
- Journals: title, year, volume, number, publisher

The library operates numerous terminals that can be used to search the catalog and place holds (on provision of card number). Additionally, Internet access to the catalog is possible. The university council requires a monthly report indicating library usage in terms of books borrowed and returned broken down by category of customer (staff, postgraduate, undergraduate).

B.2.2.3 Library Application 3: Video Library

Although this video library is part of a chain, it operates independantly. Note that at some future point, it may be desirable to link with other video stores so videos at other locations can be searched and ordered by an inter-store loan mechanism.

Videos have the following properties: title, director, producer, genre, date of release, actors, rating, shelf number. Customers pay a yearly membership. Reminders are mailed out a month before membership expires. A customer may not borrow videos if the return date is past the expiration date of their membership. Videos are shelved by category with the exception of new releases. A video is considered to be a new release for the first 3 months after it arrives at the store. The computer system needs to generate a daily list of videos that need to be moved from the new release shelves to the shelves corresponding to their genres. At this time the shelf number corresponding to the video is updated.

Video hire is according to the following rates:

Term	Rate
Daily[a]	$3 per day
New release	$5 for one day
Weekly[a]	$12 per week
Value pack[a] (three videos)	$25 per week

[a]Excludes new releases.

Videos are charged when they are returned. A "late" return is simply charged for the appropriate period of time. Customers are limited to having at most seven videos out on loan at a given time.

The store clerks have two terminals that can be used interchangeable to add new videos, check in and check out videos, and search the collection. Also, there are a number of terminals in the library that customers can use to conduct searches.

The borrowing history of each customer is stored, and the store plans to introduce an automated personalized recommendation scheme in the future.

The system produces monthly reports documenting:

- The number of customers
- The number of new (nonrenewing) customers
- Money collected broken down into the categories: membership money collected, video loan payment (not new release), video loan (new release).
- Table of top 30 videos (judging by the number of times loaned out)

The system also maintains a list of "old" videos. These are tested for defects and retired if they are hard to view. A video is moved to the old list when it has been in store for 3 years or when a customer complains about the quality of the video. In the latter case, the customer is given a refund if the video is found to be defective.

Bibliography

Abelson, R., and P. Abelson, "Concepts for representing mundane reality in plans," in *Language, Thought, and Culture: Advances in the Study of Cognition*, D. Bobrow and A. Collins, eds., Academic Press, New York, 1975, pp. 273–309.

Addy, E., "A framework for performing verification and validation in reuse-based software engineering," *Ann. Software Eng.* **5**:279–292 (1998).

Agresti, W. W., "What are the new paradigms?" in *New Paradigms for Software Development*, W. W. Agresti, IEEE, 1986, pp. 6–10.

Aharonian, G., "Starting a software reuse effort at your company," *ReNews—Electron. Software Reuse Newsl.* **1**:3 (Sept. 1991).

Aksit, M., and L. Bergmans, "Obstacles in object-oriented software development," *Proc. OOPSLA'92*, Oct. 18–22, 1992, ACM Press, Vancouver, BC, Canada, 1992, pp. 341–358.

Aksit, M., B. Tekinerdogan, and F. Marcelloni, "Deriving frameworks from domain knowledge," in *Building Application Frameworks—Object-Oriented Foundations of Framework Design*, M., Fayad, D. C. Schmidt, and R. E. Johnson, eds., Wiley, New York 1999, pp. 169–198.

Albrecht, A. J., "Measuring application development productivity," *Proc. SHARE/ GUIDE IBM Application Development Symp.*, IBM Corp., 1979, pp. 83–92.

Albrecht, A. J., and J. E. Gaffney, "Software function, lines of code and development effort prediction: A software science validation," *IEEE Trans. Software Eng.* **SE-9**(6):639–647 (1983).

Allen, R., and D. Garlan, "Formalizing architectural connection," *Proc. ICSE'16*, Sorrento, Italy, May 16–21, 1994, pp. 71–80.

Allen, R., and D. Garlan, "A formal basis for architectural connection," *ACM Trans. Software Eng. Meth.* **6**(3):213–249 (July 1997).

ASSET 1993, *Asset Submittal Guidelines*, Tech. Report SAIC-92/7625-00, version 1.2, ASSET, Morgantown, WV, Dec. 1993.

Atkinson, S., and R. Duke, "A methodology for behavioral retrieval from class libraries," *Austral. Comput. Sci. Commun.* **17**(1):13–20 (Jan. 1995).

Badaro, N., and T. Moineau, "Rose-ada: A method and a tool to help reuse ada code," *Proc. Ada Eur. Conf.*, Springer-Verlag [Lecture Notes in Computer Science (LNCS)], Vol. 499), 1991.

Baker, S., *CORBA* Distributed Objects Using ORBIX, Addison-Wesley, Reading, MA, 1997.

Balda, D. M., and D. A. Gustafson, "Cost estimation models for the reuse and prototype software development lifecycles," *ACM SIGSOFT Software Eng. News* **15**(3):42–50 (July 1990).

Balzer, R., "A 15 year perspective on automatic programming," *IEEE Trans. Software Engineering,* **SE**(11):1257–1268 (Nov. 1985).

Barnes, B. H., and T. B. Bollinger, "Making reuse cost effective," *IEEE Software* **8**(1):13–24 (Jan. 1991).

Basili, V. R., and G. Caldiera, "A reference architecture for the components factory," *ACM Trans. Software Eng. Meth.* **1**(1):53–80 (Jan. 1992).

Basili, V. R., G. Caldiera, F. McGarry, R. Pajerski, G. Page, and S. Waligora, "The software engineering laboratory: An operational software experience," *Proc. 14th Internatl. Conf. Software Engineering,* Melbourne, Australia, May 1992, pp. 370–381.

Basili, V. R., G. Caldiera, and H. D. Rombach, "The experience factory," *Encyclopedia of Software Engineering,* Wiley, New York, 1994.

Bass, L., R. Celements, S. Cohen, L. Northrop, and J. Withey, *Product Line Practice Workshop Report,* Tech. Report CMU/SEI-97-TR-003, June 1997.

Bass, L., P. Clements, and R. Kazman, *Software Architecture in Practice,* Addison-Wesley, Reading, MA, 1998.

Bass, L., G. Campbell, O. Clements, L. Northrop, and D. Smith, *Third Product Line Practice Workshop Report,* Tech. Report CMU/SEI-99-TR-003, ESC-TR-99-003, March 1999.

Bassett, P. G., "Frame-based software engineering," *IEEE Software,* 9–16 (July 1987).

Bassett, P. G., *Framing Software Reuse: Lessons from the Real World,* Prentice-Hall/Yourdon Press, Upper Saddle River, NJ, 1996.

Bassett, P. G., "How to solve the reuse problem," *Proc. 5th Internatl. Conf. Software Reuse,* IEEE Computer Society, Los Alamitos, CA, 1998, pp. 373–374.

Batory, D., L. Coglianese, M. Goodwill, and S. Shaver, "Creating reference architectures: An example from avionics," *Proc. Symp. Software Reuse,* Seattle, WA, April 1995.

Batory, D., "Subjectivity and genvoca generators," *Proc. 4th Internatl. Conf. Software Reuse,* Orlando, FL, April 1996.

Batory, D., and B. J. Geraci, "Composition validation and subjectivity in genvoca generators," *IEEE Trans. Software Eng.* **23**(2):67–82 (Feb. 1997).

Batory, D., B. Lofaso, and Y. Smaragdakis, "Jts: Tools for implementing domain specific languages," *Proc. 5th Internatl. Conf. Software Reuse,* Victoria, BC, Canada, June 1998.

Batory, D. S., T. Y., Leung, and T. E. Wise, "Implementation concepts for an extensible data model and data language," *ACM Trans. Database Syst.* **13**(3):231–262 (Sept. 1988).

Baxter, I. D., "Design maintenance systems," *Commun ACM* **35**(4):73–89 (April 1992).

Bayer, J., J.-M. DeBaud, O. Flege, P. Knauber, R. Laqua, D. Muthig, K. Schmid, and T. Widen, "PuLSE: A methodology to develop software product lines," *Symp. Software Reusability, SSR'99*, Los Angeles, May 1999.

Berlack, H. R., *Software Configuration Management*, Wiley, New York, 1992.

Berney, P. R., and S. J. Garstka, *Accounting: Concepts and Applications*," Richard D Irwin, Inc., Homewood, IL, 1984.

Biggerstaff, T. J., and C. Richter, "Reusability framework, assessment and directions," *IEEE Software* 41–49 (July 1987).

Biggerstaff, T. J., and A. J. Perlis, *Software Reusability, Vol. 1: Concepts and Models*, ACM Press, New York, 1989.

Bobrow, D., "Dimensions of representation," in *Representation and Understanding: Studies in Cognitive Science*, D. Bobrow and A. Collins, eds., Academic Press, New York, 1975, pp. 1–34.

Bobrow, D., and D. Norman, "Some principles of memory schemata," in *Representation and Understanding: Studies in Cognitive Science*, D. Bobrow and A. Collins, eds., Academic Press, New York, 1975, pp. 131–150.

Boehm, B. W., *Software Engineering Economics*, Prentice-Hall, Englewood Cliffs, NJ, 1981.

Boehm, B. W., B. Clark, E. Horowitz, C. Westland, R. Madachy, and R. Selby, "Cost models for future software lifecycle processes: COCOMO 2.0.," *Ann. Software Eng.* **1**:57–94 (Sept. 1995).

Boetticher, G., K. Srinivas, and D. Eichmann, "A neural net-based approach to software metrics," *Proc. 5th Internatl. Conf. Software Engineering and Knowledge Engineering*, San Francisco, CA, June 1993, pp. 271–274.

Bollinger. T. B., and S. L. Pfleeger, "Economics of reuse: Issues and alternatives," *Inform. Software Technol.* **32**(10):643–652 (Dec. 1990).

Borning, A., and R. Duisberg, "Constraint-based tools for building user interfaces," *ACM Trans. Graphics*, **5**(4):345–374 (Oct. 1986).

Bosch, J., C. Szyperski, and W. Weck, *Report on 2nd Internatl. Workshop on Component-Oriented Programming* (WCOP'97) (in conjunction with ECOOP'97), Jyväskylä, Finland, June 9, 1997.

Bosch, J., "Product-line architectures in industry: A case study," *Proc. 21st Internatl. Conf. Software Engineering* (ICSE'99), Los Angeles, CA, May 1999, pp. 544–554.

Boudriga, N., A. Mili, and R. T. Mittermeir, "Semantic-based software retrieval to support rapid prototyping," *Struct. Programming* **13**:109–127 (1992).

Bowes, R. J., T. R. Huber, and R. O. Saisi, *Informal Technical Report for the Software Technology for Adaptable, Reliable Systems (STARS) Acquisition Handbook—Final*, Tech. Report, DSD Laboratories Inc., for Airforce Material Command, Hanscom Air Force Base, MA, Oct. 1992.

Box, D., *Essential COM*, Addison-Wesley, Reading, MA, 1998.

Brachman, R. J., and J. G. Schmolze, "An overview of the KL-ONE knowledge representation system," *Cogn. Sci.* **9**:171–216 (1985).

Braun, C. L., *Domain Specific Software Architectures, Command and Control, Domain Model Report*, CDRL CLIN 0006, Contract DAAB07-92-C-Q502, GTE Federal Systems Division, 1992.

Braun, C., "Organizing for the effective reuse of commercial off-the-shelf (COTS) software," *JICS'98 Proc.*, Vol. III, Oct. 1998, pp. 503–506.

Briot, J. P., "Actalk, a testbed for classifying and designing actor languages in the Smalltalk-80 environment," *Proc. Eur. Conf. Object-Oriented Programming* (ECOOP'89), *Lecture Notes in Computer Science* (LNCS), Springer-Verlag, 1989.

Briot, J. P., and B. P. Cointe, "Programming with explicit metaclasses in Smalltalk-80," *OOPSLA'89*, 1989, pp. 419–432.

Briot, J. P., and P. Cointe, "An experiment in classification and specialization of synchronization schemes," in *Proc. 2nd Internatl. Symp. Object Technologies for Advanced Software* (ISOTAS'96), LNCS 1049, 1996, pp. 227–249.

Brown, A., and K. Wallnau, "Engineering of component-based systems," in *Component Based Software Engineering*, A. W. Brown, ed., Software Engineering Institute, IEEE Computer Society, 1996.

Brown, C., *NATO Standard for the Development of Reusable Software Components*, Public Ada Library, 1994. (http://wuarchivewustl.edu/languages/ada/docs/nato_ru/).

Brown, C., "Organizing the effective reuse of commercial off the shelf (COTS) software," *Internatl. Joint Conf. Information Systems*, Durham, NC, Oct. 1998, pp. 503–506.

Brown, W., and K. Wallnau, "The current state of CBSE," *IEEE Software* 37–46 (Oct. 1998).

Brownsword, L., and P. Clements, *A Case Study in Successful Product Line Development*, Software Engineering Institute, Carnegie Mellon University, CMU/SEI-96-TR-016, Oct. 1996.

Buschmann, F., R. Meunier, H. Rohnert, P. Sommerlad, and M. Stal, *Pattern Oriented Software Architecture: A System of Patterns*, Wiley, New York, 1996.

Butler, G., and P. Dénommé, "Documenting frameworks," in *Building Application Frameworks—Object-Oriented Foundations of Framework Design*, M. Fayad, D. C. Schmidt, and R. E. Johnson, Wiley, New York, 1999, pp. 495–504.

Caldiera, G., and V. Basili, "Identifying and qualifying reusable software components," *IEEE Comput.* **24**(2):61–70 (Feb. 1991).

Capers Jones, T., "Reusability in programming: A survey of the state of the art," *IEEE Trans. Software Eng.* **SE-10**(5):488–494 (Sept. 1984).

Carbonell, J., "Learning by analogy," in *Machine Learning*, R. Michalskim J. Carbonell, and T. Mitchell, eds., Tioga Publishing, Palo Alto, CA, 1983, pp. 137–161.

Cardelli, L., and P. Wegner, "On understanding types, data abstraction, and polymorphism," *ACM Computing Surveys* **17**(4) (1985).

Carriere, S., R. Kazman, and S. Woods, "Assessing and maintaining architectural quality," *Proc. 3rd Eur. Conf. Software Maintenance and Engineering*, 1999, pp. 22–30.

CBSE 1999, *Proc. 1999 Internatl. Workshop on Component-Based Software Engineering*, in conjunction with 21st Internatl. Conf. Software Engineering (ICSE99), Los Angeles, CA, May 16–22, 1999.

Champeaux, D. de, D. Lea, and P. Faure, "The process of object-oriented design," *Proc. OOPSLA'92*, Oct. 18–22, 1992, ACM Press, Vancouver, BC, Canada, 1992, pp. 45–62.

Charette, R. N., *Software Engineering Risk Analysis and Management*, McGraw-Hill, New York, 1989.

Charette, R. N., *Applications Strategies for Risk Analysis*, McGraw-Hill, New York, 1990.

Chavez, A., C. Tornabene, and G. Wiederhold, "Software component licensing: A primer," *IEEE Software* 47–53 (Sept./Oct. 1998).

Chen, D. J., and P. J. Lee, "On the study of software reuse using C++ components," *J. Syst. Software* **21**(1):19–36 (1993).

Chen, Y. F., B. Krishnamurthy, and K. P. Vo (1995) "An objective reuse metric: Model and methodology," *5th Eur. Software Engineering Conf.*, Sitges, Spain, Sept. 1995, pp. 109–123.

Cheng, B. H. C., and J. J. Jeng, "Formal methods applied to reuse," *Proc. WISR-5*, Palo Alto, CA, 1992 (1992a).

Cheng, B. H. C., and J. J. Jeng, "Reusing analogous components," *Proc. IEEE Internatl. Conf. Tools with AI*, Nov. 1992 (1992b).

Chou, S. C., J. Y. Chen, and C. G. Chung, "A behavior-based classification and retrieval technique for object oriented specification reuse," *Software Pract. Exper.* **26**(7):815–832 (July 1996).

Cleaveland, C. T., "Building application generators," *IEEE Software* 25–33 (July 1988).

Clements, P., and L. Northrop, *A Framework for Software Product Line Practice*, version 1.0, Software Engineering Institute, Carnegie Mellon Univ., Pittsburgh, PA, Sept. 1998.

Clements, P., and N. Weiderman, *Report on 2nd Internatl. Workshop on Development and Evolution of Software Architectures for Product Families*, Tech. Report CMU/SEI-98-SR-003, Carnegie Mellon Univ., Pittsburgh, PA, May 1998.

Clifton, C., and W.-S. Li, "Classifying software components using desgn characteristics," *Proc. 10th Knowledge-Based Software Engineering Conf.* (KBSE'95), D. Setliff and H. Reubenstein, eds., Boston, MA, Nov. 1995, IEEE CS Press, 1995, pp. 139–146.

Coad, P., and E. Yourdon, *Object-Oriented Analysis*, 2nd Ed., Prentice-Hall, Englewood Cliffs, NJ, 1991.

COCOTS, 2000, Center for Software Engineering (http://sunset.usc.edu/COCOTS/cocots.html).

Cointe, P., "The ObjVLisp kernel: A reflexive LISP architecture to define a uniform Object-oriented system," in *Meta-Level Architectures and Réflexion*, P. Maes and D. Nardi, eds., North-Holland, Amsterdam, 1987, pp. 155–176.

Coleman, D., P. Arnold, S. Bodoff, C. Dollin, H. Gilchrist, F. Hayes, and P. Jeremaes, *Object-Oriented Development: The Fusion Method*, Prentice-Hall, Englewood Cliffs, NJ, 1994.

COM 1995, Microsoft Corporation, *The Component Object Model Specification*, version 0.9, Oct. 24, 1995 (http://www.microsoft.com/com/default.asp).

Cook, W. R., "Interfaces and specifications for the smalltalk-80 collection classes," *Proc. OOPSLA'92*, ACM Press, Vancouver, BC, Canada, Oct. 18–22, 1992, pp. 1–15.

Coplien, R., *Multiparadigm Software Development in C++*, Addison-Wesley, Reading, MA, 1999.

Coulange, B., *Software Reuse*, Springer-Verlag, London, UK, 1998.

Cox, B. J., "Planning the software revolution," *IEEE Software* **7**(6):25–35 (Nov. 1990).

(CSE 1999) Center for Software Engineering, *COCOTS*, Tech. Report, Univ. Southern California, Los Angeles, CA, June 1999.

(CTA 1990) Computer Technology Associates, Inc., *JIAWG Reuse System Description*, Ridgecrest, CA, 1990.

Dahl, M. B., and K. Nygaard, *Simula Common Base Language*, Tech. Report S-22, Norwegian Computing Center, 1970.

Danforth, S., and I. R. Forman, "Reflections on metaclass programming in SOM," *Proc. OOPSLA'94*, Portland, OR, 1994, pp. 440–452.

Darden, L., and R. Rada, "Hypothesis formation using part–whole interrelations" in *Analogical Reasoning: Perspectives in Philosophy and Artifical Intelleigence*, D. Helman, ed., Netherlands, 1998.

(DCOM 1998) *Component Object Model*, 1998.
(home page: http://www.microsoft. com/com/dcom.asp).

Dean, J. C., and M. R. Vigder, "System implementation using commercial-of-the-shelf (COTS) software," in *Proceedings of the 1997 Software Technology Conference* (STC '97), Salt Lake City, UT, April 28–May 3, 1997.

Dean, J. C., "Timing the testing of cots software products," paper presented at 1st International ICSE Workshop on Testing Distributed Component Based Systems, Los Angeles, CA, May 1999.

Debaud, J., and P. Knauber, "Applying PuLSE for software product line development," paper presented at European Reuse Workshop, ERW'98, Nov. 1998.

DeLine, R., "A catalog of techniques for resolving packaging mismatch," *Proc. Symp. Software Reusability (SSR'99)*, Los Angeles, CA, May 1999 (1999a).

DeLine, R., "Avoiding packaging mismatch with flexible packaging," *Proc. 21st Internatl. Conf. Software Eng. 1999 (ICSE'99)*, Los Angeles, CA, May 1999, pp. 97–106 (1999b).

Deutsch, L., "Design reuse and frameworks in the Smalltalk-80 programming system," in *Software Reusability*, Vol. II, T. J. Biggerstaff and A. J. Perlis, ACM Press, Vancouver, BC, Canada, 1989.

Devanbu, P., R. Brachman, P. Selfridge, and B. Ballard, "Lassie: A knowledge-based software information system," *Commun. ACM* **34**(5):34–39 (May 1991).

Diaz, O., and N. W. Paton, "Extending ODBMSs using metaclasses," *IEEE Software* **11**(3):40–47 (May 1994).

DIICOE97, Defense Information Infrastructure (DII) Common Operating Environment (COE), *Baseline Specifications*, Joint Interoperability and Engineering Organization, Defense Information Systems Agency, April 29, 1997.

Dikel, D., and D. Kane, S. Ornburn, W. Loftus, and J. Wilson, "Applying software product-line architecture," *IEEE Comput.* **30**:49–55 (Aug. 1997).

DISA/JIEO/CIM 1993, *Software Reuse Metrics Plan*, Tech. Report 4.1, Defense Information Systems Agency/Joint Interoperability Engineering Organization/ Center for Information Management, Aug. 1993.

(Domain 1999) *Domain Engineering: A Model-Based Approach*, Tech. Report, Software Engineering Institute, Carnegie Mellon Univ., Pittsburgh, PA, 1999 (http://www.sei.cmu.edu/domain-engineering).

D'Souza, D. F., and A. C. Wills, *Objects, Components, and Frameworks with UML: The Catalysis Approach*, Addison-Wesley, Reading, MA, 1998.

Dumpleton, G., *OSE—C++ Library User Guide*, Dumpleton Software Consulting Pty. Ltd., Parramatta, Australia, 1994.

Edwards, S. H., "Common interface models for reusable software," *Internatl. Journal of Software Eng. Knowl. Eng.* **3**(2)193–206 (June 1993).

Edwards, S. H., and B. W. Weide, "WISR8: 8th Annual Workshop on Software Reuse Summary and Working Group Reports," *Software Eng. Notes* **22**(5):17–32 (Sept. 1997).

Ernst, G. W., R. J. Hookway, J. A. Menegay, and W. F. Ogden, "Modular verification of data generics," *Comput. Lang.* **16**(3/4):259–280 (1991).

Ernst, G. W., R. J. Hookway, and W. F. Ogden, "Modular verification of ada abstractions with shareable realizations," *IEEE Trans. Software Eng.* **20**(4):288–307 (April 1994).

Estep, J., and S. Hissam, *CARDS Technical Concept Document*, Lockheed Martin Tactical Defense Systems Ref. N. STARS-VC-B009/001/00; ASSET Collection No. ASSET_A_586, Feb. 1994.

Ezran, M., M. Morisio, and C. Tully, *Practical Software Reuse: The Essential Guide*, Valtech, Paris, France, 1998.

Fafchamps, D., "Organizational factors and software reuse," *IEEE Software* **11**(5):31–41 (Sept. 1994).

Faget, J., and J. M. Morel, "The reboot environment," *Proc. 2nd Internatl. Workshop on Software Reusability*, March 1993.

Faustle, S., M. G. Fugini, and E. Damiani, "Retrieval of reusable components using functional similarity," *Software Pract. Exper.* **26**(5):491–530 (May 1996).

Favaro, J., "A comparison of approaches to reuse investment analysis," *Proc. 4th Internatl. Conf. Software Reuse*, Orlando, FL, April 1996, pp. 136–145.

Favaro, J. M., and K. R. Favaro, "Strategic analysis of application framework investments," in *Building Application Frameworks*, M. Fayad, D. C. Schmidt, and R. E. Johnson, eds., Wiley, New York, 1999, pp. 567–697.

Favaro, J., K. Favaro, and P. F. Favaro, "Value based software reuse investment," *Ann. Software Eng.* **5**:5–52 (1998).

Fayad, M., and D. C. Schmidt, "Object-oriented application frameworks," *Communications of the ACM*, **40**(10):32–38 (Oct. 1997).

Fayad, M., and R. E. Johnson, *Domain Specific Application Frameworks*, Wiley, New York, 1999.

Fayad, M., D. C. Schmidt, and R. E. Johnson, *Building Application Frameworks*, Wiley, New York, 1999.

Fenton, N. E., *Software Metrics: A Rigorous Approach*, Chapman & Hall, London, 1991.

Fischer, B., M. Kievernagel, and G. Snelting, "Deduction-based software component retrieval," paper presented at IJCAI Workshop on Reuse of Proofs, Plans and Programs, Montreal, Quebec, Canada, June 1995.

Fisher, G., "Cognitive view of reuse and design," *IEEE Software*, 60–72 (July 1987).

(FODA 1999) *Feature Oriented Domain Analysis* (FODA), Bibliography, 1999 (http://www.sei.cmu.edu/domain-engineering/FODA_bib_ref.html).

Forman, I., S. H. Danforth, and H. H. Madduri, "Composition of before/after meta-classes in SOM," *Proceedings of OOPSLA 1994*, Portland, OR, October 2333-63, 1994.

Fowler, M., *A Comparison of Object-Oriented Analysis and Design Methods*, Tutorial Notes, TOOLS USA '93, Santa Barbara, CA, August 2–5, 1993.

Frakes, W. B., and B. A. Nejmeh, "An information system for software reuse," *Proc. 10th Minnowbrook Workshop on Software Reuse*, Minnowbrook, NY, 1987 (1987a).

Frakes, W. B., and B. A. Nejmeh, "Software reuse through information retrieval," *Proc. 20th Annual Hawaii International Conf. System Sciences*, Kona, HI, Jan. 1987, pp. 530–535 (1987b).

Frakes, W. B., and T. Pole, "An empirical study of representation methods for reusable software components," *IEEE Trans. Software Engineering*, 1–23 (Aug. 1994).

Frakes, W. B., and C. Terry, "Reuse level metrics," *Proc. 3rd Internatl. Conf. Software Reuse*, W. B. Frakes, ed., Rio de Janeiro, Brazil, Nov. 1994, pp. 139–148.

Frazier, T., "Economics of software reuse, working group report," paper presented at 2nd Reuse and Education and Training Workshop, Morgantown, WV, Oct. 1993.

Freeman, P., "Reusable software engineering: Concepts and research directions," in *Tutorial: Software Reusability*, IEEE Computer Society, 1987, pp. 10–23.

Freeman-Benson, B. N., "Kaleidoscope: Mixing objects, constraints, and imperative programming," *Proc. OOPSLA'90*, ACM Press Ottawa, Oct. 21–25, 1990.

Gabriel, R. P., "The failure of pattern languages," *J. Object Oriented Programming*, 84–88 (Feb. 1994).

Gaffney, J. E., and T. Durek, "Software reuse—key to enhanced productivity: Some productivity models," *Inform. Software Technol.* **31**(5):258–267 (June 1989).

Gaffney, J. E., and R. D. Cruickschank, "A general economics model of software reuse," *Proc. Internatl. Conf. Software Engineering*, Melbourne, Australia, May 1992, pp. 327–337.

Gamma, E., R. Helm, R. Johnson, and J. Vlissides, *Design Patterns: Elements of Reusable Object Oriented Software*, Addison-Wesley, Reading, MA, 1995.

Garlan, D., R. Allen, and J. Ockerbloom, "Architectural mismatch: Why is reuse so hard," *IEEE Software* **12**(6) (special issue on software architecture): 17–26 (Nov. 1995).

Gaudel, M. C., and T. Moineau, "A theory of software reusability," *Lecture Notes in Computer Science*, Vol. 300, Springer-Verlag, 1991, pp. 115–130.

Gautier, R. J., and P. J. L. Wallis, eds., *Software Reuse with Ada*, IEEE Computing Series, 16, Peter Perengrinus Ltd., May 1990.

Gennari, J. H., P. Langley, and D. Fisher, "Models of incremental concept formation," in *Machine Learning: Paradigms and Methods*, J. Carbonell, ed., MIT Press, Amsterdam, The Netherlands, 1990, pp. 11–62.

Girardi, R., and B. Ibrahim, "Automatic indexing of software artifacts," in *3rd Internatl. Conf. Software Reuse*, W. B. Frakes, ed., Rio de Janeiro, Brazil, Nov. 1994, pp. 24–32 (1994a).

Girardi, R., and B. Ibrahim, "A similarity measure for retrieving software artifacts," in *6th Internatl. Conf. Software Engineering and Knowledge Engineering*, W. Berztiss, ed., Jurmala, Latvia, June 1994, pp. 89–100. (1994b).

Glass, R. L., *Building Quality Software*, Prentice-Hall, Englewood Cliffs, NJ, 1992.

Godin, R., and H. Mili, "Building and maintaining analysis-level class hierarchies using Galois lattices," *ACM SIGPLAN Not.* **28**(10):394–410 (1993); *OOPSLA'93* (Washington, DC, Sept. 26–Oct. 1, 1993).

Goguen, J. A., "Parameterized programming," *IEEE Trans. Software Eng.* **SE-10**(9): 528–543 (Sept. 1984).

Goguen, J. A., "Reusing and interconnecting software components," *Computer* 16–28 (Feb. 1986).

Goguen, J. A., "Parameterized programming and software architecture," *Proc. 4th Internatl. Conf. Software Reuse*, Orlando, FL, April 1996, pp. 2–10.

Goldberg, A., and D. Robson, *Smalltalk80—The Language*, Addison-Wesley, Reading, MA, 1989.

Graubé, N., "Metaclass compatibility," *OOPSLA'89*, New Orleans, pp. 305–316.

Guerrieri, E., L. A. Lashway, and T. B. Ruegsegger, "An acquisition strategy for populating a software reuse library," paper presented at Natl. Conf. Software Reusability, Washington, DC, July 1989.

Guttag, J. V., J. J. Horning, and J. M. Wing, "An overview of the Larch family of specification languages," *IEEE Software*, **2**(5):24–36 (Sept. 1985).

Hall, P. A. V., *Software Reuse and Reverse Engineering in Practice*, Chapman & Hall, London, 1992.

Hall, P., and R. Weedon, "Object-oriented module inter-connection languages," in *Advances in Software Reuse*, March 24–26, 1993, IEEE Computer Society Press, Lucca, Italy, 1993, pp. 29–38 (selected papers from the 2nd Internatl. Workshop on Software Reusability).

Hall, R. J., "Generalized behaviour-based retrieval," *Proc. Internatl. Conf. Software Engineering*, Baltimore, MD, May 1993.

Hallsteinsen, S., and M. Paci, *Experiences in Software Evolution and Reuse: Twelve Real World Projects*, Springer-Verlag, 1997.

Halstead, M. H., *Elements of Software Science*, North Holland, Amsterdam, 1977.

Harandi, M. T., ed., *Proc. Symp. Software Reuse*, Assoc. Computing Machinery, Boston, MA, May 1997.

Harms, D. E., and B. W. Weide, "Copying and swapping: Influences on the design of reusable components," *IEEE Trans. Software Eng.* **17**(5):424–435 (May 1991).

Harris, D., H. Reubenstein, and A. S. Yeh, "Recognizers for extracting architectural features form source code," in *Proceedings of the Second Working Conference on Reverse Engineering*, IEEE Computer Society Press, 1995, pp. 252–261.

Harrison, W., and H. Ossher, "Subject-oriented programming: A critique of pure objects," Washington, DC, Sept. 26–Oct. 1, 1993, *Proc. OOPSLA'93*; *SIGPLAN Not.* **28**(10):411–428.

Harston, R., "User-interface management control and communication," *IEEE Software* 62–70 (Jan. 1989).

Hautamaki, A., "Points of view and their logical analysis," *Acta Philosophic Fennica*, Vol. 41, Helsinki, Finland, 1986.

Hayes, L., "Don't take anything for granted in component development," *Datamation* (June 1998).

Helm, R., I. Holland, and D. Gangopadhyay, "Contracts: Specifying behavioral compositions in object-oriented systems," *Proc. OOPSLA'90*, Oct. 22–25, 1990, ACM Press, Ottawa, Canada, 1990.

Helm, R., and Y. S. Maarek, "Integrating information retrieval and domain specific approaches for browsing and retrieval in object-oriented class libraries," *Proc. OOPSLA'91* **26**(11):47–61 (Oct. 1991).

Henderson-Sellers, B., and J. M. Edwards, "The object-oriented systems life cycle," *Communications of the ACM*, **33**(9):143–159 (Sept. 1990).

Henderson-Sellers, B., "The economics of reusing library classes," *J. Object Oriented Programming* **6**(4):43–50 (July/Aug. 1993).

Hess, J. A., W. E. Novak, P. C. Carroll, S. G. Cohen, R. R. Holibaugh, K. C. Kang, and A. S. Peterson, *A Domain Analysis Bibliography*, Tech. Report CMU/SEI-90-TR-3, Software Engineering Institute, Jan. 1990.

Hetzel, W. C., *The Complete Guide to Software Testing*, Wiley, New York, 1993.

Hewitt, C., "Actors: How to use what you know," *Proc. 4th Internatl. Joint Conf. Artificial Intelligence*, 1975, pp. 189–198.

Hislop, G., "Using existing software in a software reuse initiative," paper presented at 6th Annual Workshop on Software Reuse, Oswego, NY, Nov. 1993.

Hochmueller, E., *AUGUSTA—Eine reuse-orientierte Software Ent wick lungsum gebung zur Erstellung von Ada-Applikationen*, PhD thesis, Univ. Klagenfurt, Austria, May 1992.

Holibaugh, R., Joint Integrated Avionics Working Group (JIAWG), *Object-Oriented Domain Analysis Method* (JODA), CMU/SEI-92-SR-003 (1992).

Hooper, J. W., and R. O. Chester, *Software Reuse: Guidelines and Methods. Software Science and Engineering*, Plenum Press, New York, June 1991.

Horgan, J., and A. Mathur, "Software testing and reliability," in *Handbook of Software Reliability Engineering*, M. R. Lye, ed., McGraw-Hill, New York, NY, 1996, Chapter 13, pp. 531–566.

Horngren, C. T., *Introduction to Management Accounting*, 5th ed., Prentice-Hall, Englewood Cliffs, NJ, 1981.

Horowitz, E. C., and J. B. Munson, "An expansive view of reusable software," *IEEE Trans. Software Eng.* **10**(5):477–487 (1984).

Hunter, R., *Once is Not Enough: Requirements for a Sustainable Reuse Program*, Gartner Group Strategic Analysis Report, Gartner Group, Inc., R-480-103, 1996.

IEEE 610.12-1990, *IEEE Standard Glossary of Software Engineering Terminology*, The Institute of Electrical and Electronics Engineers, Inc., New York, 1990.

IEEE 1059-1993, *Guide for Software Verification and Validation Plans* (*ANSI*), The Institute of Electrical and Electronics Engineers, Inc., New York, 1993.

IEEE 730.1-1995, *Guide for Software Quality Assurance Plans* (*ANSI*), The Institute of Electrical and Electronics Engineers, Inc., New York, 1995.

IEEE 1042-1987 (R1993), *Guide to Software Configuration Management* (*ANSI*), The Institute of Electrical and Electronics Engineers, Inc., New York, 1997.

IEEE 730-1998, *Standard for Software Quality Assurance Plans*, The Institute of Electrical and Electronics Engineers, Inc., New York, 1998a.

IEEE 828–1998, *Standard for Software Configuration Management Plans*, The Institute of Electrical and Electronics Engineers, Inc., New York, 1998b.

IEEE 829-1998, *Standard for Software Test Documentation*, The Institute of Electrical and Electronics Engineers, Inc., New York, NY, 1998c.

IEEE 1012-1998, *Standard for Software Verification and Validation*, The Institute of Electrical and Electronics Engineers, Inc., New York, 1998d.

Ihrig, L., and S. Kambhampati, "Automatic storage and indexing of plan derivations based on replay failures," paper presented at IJCAI Workshop on Reuse of Proofs, Plans and Programs, Montreal, Quebec, Canada, June 1995.

Intrator, Y., and H. Mili, *Getting More Out of Your Classes: Building Families of Programs in OOP*," Tech. Report 234. Dep. Math and Computer Science, Univ. Quebec at Montreal. May 13, 1994.

Isakowitz, T., and R. J. Kauffman, "Supporting search for reusable software objects," *IEEE Trans. Software Engin.* **22**(6):407–423 (June 1996).

Isoda, S., "Experiences of a software reuse project," *J. Syst. Software* **30**(3):171–186 (Sept. 1995).

Jacobson, I., and F. Lindstrom, "Re-engineering of old systems to an object-oriented architecture," *Proc. of OOPSLA 1991*, Phoenix, AZ, October 1991.

Jacobson, I., M. Griss, and P. Jonsson, *Software Reuse: Architecture, Process and Organization for Business Success*, Addison-Wesley, Longman, Harlow, UK, 1997.

Jaffe, D. T., and C. D. Scott, *Getting Your Organization to Change: A Guide for Putting Your Strategy into Action*, Crisp Publications, Menlo Park, CA, 1999.

Jawarski, A., F. Hills, T. Durek, S. Faulk, and J. Gaffney, *A Domain Analysis Process*, Software Productivity Consortium, Jan. 1990.

Jeng, J. J., and B. C. H. Cheng, "Specification matching for software reuse: A foundation," *ACM Symp. Software Reuse*, Seattle, WA, April 1995, pp. 97–105.

Jimenez-Perez, G., and D. Batory, "Memory simulators and software generators," *Proc. Symp. Software Reuse*, Boston, MA, May 1997.

Johnson, R. E., and B. Foote, "Designing reusable classes," *J. Object-Oriented Programming* (Aug./Sept. 1988).

Johnson, R. E., "Documenting frameworks using patterns," *Proc. OOPSLA'92*, Vancouver, BC, Oct. 18–22, 1992, ACM Press, Vancouver, BC, Canada, pp. 63–76.

Johnson, R. E., "Why a conference on pattern languages," *Software Eng. Notes* **19**(1): 50–52 (Jan. 1994).

Jones, C., "Economics of software reuse," *IEEE Comput.* **27**(7):106–107 (July 1994).

Joos, R., "Software reuse in an industrial environment," *Proc. 4th Annual Workshop on Software Reuse (WISR 4)*, Nov. 1991 (ftp://gandalf.umcs.maine.edu/pub/WISR/wisr4).

Kain, B. J., "Measuring the roi of reuse," *Object Mag.* **4**(3):48–54 (June 1994).

Kang, K. C., and L. S. Levy, "Software methodology in the harsh light of economics," *Inform. Software Technol.* **31**(5) (June 1989).

Kang, K., S. Cohen, J. Hess, W. Novak, and A. Peterson, *Feature-Oriented Domain Analysis (FODA) Feasibility Study*, Tech. Report CMU/SEI-90-TR-021, Software Engineering Institute, Nov. 1990. (www.sei.cmu.edu/publications/documents/ 90.reports/90.tr.021.html).

Karlsson, E. A., G. Sindre, and T. Stalhane, *Techniques for Making More Reusable Components*, Tech. Report 41, REBOOT, June 1992.

Karlsson, E. A., *Software Reuse: A Holistic Approach*, Wiley, New York, 1995.

Karlsson, E. A., and J. Brantestam, "Generic reuse development processes," in *Software Reuse: A Holistic Approach*, E. A. Karlsson, ed., Wiley, New York, 1995, pp. 253–270.

Kazman, R., L. Bass, G. Abowd, and M. Webb, "SAAM: A method for analyzing the properties of software architectures," *Proc. Internatl. Conf. Software Engineering* (ICSE'94), May 1994, pp. 81–90.

Kiczales, G., and J. Lamping, "Issues in the design and documentation of class libraries," *Proc.* OOPSLA'92, Oct. 18–22, 1992, ACM Press, Vancouver, BC, Canada; *SIGPLAN Note* **27**(10):435–451 (1992).

Kiczales, G., J. Lamping, and C. Lopez, "Aspect-oriented programming," *Proc. Eur. Conf. Object-Oriented Programming (ECOOP)* (Finland), Springer-Verlag, June 1997, LNCS 1241.

Kolbe, T., and C. Walther, "Proof management and retrieval," paper presented at IJCAI Workshop on Reuse of Proofs, Plans and Programs, Montreal, Quebec, Canada, June 1995.

Koltun, P., and A. Hudson, "A reuse maturity model," *Proc. 4th Annual Workshop on Software Reuse (WISR 4)*, Nov. 1991. (ftp://gandalf.umcs.maine.edu/pub/WISR/ wisr4/).

Krieger, D., and R. Adler, "The emergence of distributed component platforms," *IEEE Comput.* 43–53 (March 1998).

Krishnamurthy, S., and A. P. Mathur, "On the estimation of reliability of a software system using reliabilities of its components," *Proc. ISSRE'97*, Albuquerque, NM, Nov. 1997.

Kroeker, K., "Component technology," *IEEE Comput.* **31**:132–133 (Jan 1998).

Krueger, C. W., "Software reuse," *ACM Comput. Surv.* **24**(2):131–183 (June 1992).

Kuwabara, K., T. Ishida, and N. Osato, "Agentalk: Coordination protocol description for multiagent systems," *ICMAS'95*, 1995, pp. 455–461.

Labed Jilani, L., R. Mili, and A. Mili, "Approximate retrieval: An academic exercise or a practical concern," *Proc. 8th Annual Workshop on Software Reuse*, March 1997.

Lampson, B., "How software components grew up and conquered the world," Keynote Address in *Proc. 21st Internatl. Conf. Software Engineering 1999 (ICSE'99)*, Los Angeles, CA, May 1999.

Leach, H., *Software Reuse*, McGraw-Hill, New York, 1997.

Leavens, G. T., and M. Sitaraman, eds., *Foundations of Component-Based Systems*, Cambridge Univ. Press, March 2000.

Lenat, D. B., and R. V. Guha, *Building Large Knowledge-Based Systems: Representation and Inference in the CYC Project.* Addison-Wesley, 1990.

Lenat, D., V. Ramanathan, A. Guha, K. Pittman, D. Pratt, and M. Shepherd, "CYC: Towards programs with common sense," *Commun. ACM* **30**(8)(special issue on natural-language programming):30–49 (Aug. 1990).

Levy, L. S., "A metaprogramming method and its economic justification," *IEEE Trans. Software Eng.* **SE-12**(2):272–277 (Feb. 1986).

Lewis, R. O., *Independent Verification and Validation, A Life Cycle Engineering Process for Quality Software*, Wiley, New York, 1992.

Lewis, T., G. Andert, P. Calder, E. Gamma, W. Pree, L. Rosenstein, K. Schmucker, A. Weinand, J. M. Vlissides, *Object-Oriented Application Frameworks*, Manning Publications, 1995.

Lieberherr, K. J., P. Bergstein, and I. Silva-Lepe, "From objects to classes: Algorithms for object-oriented design," *J. Software Eng.* **6**(4):205–228 (1991).

Lim, W. C., "A cost justification model for software reuse," *Proc. 5th Workshop on Institutionalizing Reuse*, Univ. Maine, Orono, Oct. 1992.

Lim, W. C., "Effects of reuse on quality, productivity and economics," *IEEE Software* 11(5):23–30 (Sept. 1994).

Lim, W. C., "Reuse economics: A comparison of seventeen models and directions of future research," *Proc. 4th Internatl. Conf. Software Reuse*, Orlando, FL, April 1996, pp. 41–50.

Lim, W. C., *Managing Software Reuse: A Comprehensive Guide to Strategically Reengineering the Organization for Reusable Components*, Prentice-Hall PTR, Upper Saddle River, NJ, 1998.

Linden, F., ed., "Development and evolution of software architectures for product family," paper presented Second at 2nd Internatl. ESPRIT ARES Workshop, Springer, LNCS 1429, 1998.

Lindquist, U., and E. Jonsson, "A map of security risks associated with using COTS," *IEEE Comput.* 31(6):60–66 (June 1998).

Linn, M. C., and M. J. Clancy, "Can experts' explanations help students develop program design skills," *J. Man-Machine Stud.* 36:511–551 (1992).

Linton, M., J. Vlissides, and P. Calder, "Composing user interfaces with interviews," *IEEE Comput.* 8–22 (Feb. 1989).

Lipkis, T. A., "A KL-ONE classifier," *Proc. 1981 KL-ONE Workshop*, J. G. Schmolze and R. J. Brachman, eds., Bolt Beraneck and Newman Inc., June 1982, pp. 128–145.

Liu, S. S., and A. N. Wilde, "Identifying pobjects in a conventional procedural language: An example of data design recovery," in *Proceeding of the Conference on Software Maintenance*, IEEE Computer Society Press, 1990, pp, 266–271.

Livadas, P. E., and P. K. Roy, "Program dependence analysis," in *Proceedings of the Conference on Software Maintenance*, IEEE Computer Society Press, 1992, pp. 356–365.

Lowry, M., A. Philpot, T. Pressburger, R. Waldinger, and M. Stickel, "Amphion: Automatic programming for the naif toolkit," *NASA Sci. Inform. Syst. Newsl.* 31:22–25, (Feb. 1994).

Lubars, M. D., *Wide-Spectrum Support for Software Reusability*, IEEE Computer Society Press, 1990, pp. 275–281.

Lubars, M., G. Meredith, C. Potts, and C. Richter, "Object-oriented analysis for evolving systems," *Proc. 14th Internatl. Conf. Software Engineering*, ACM Press, Melbourne, Australia, May 11–15, 1992, pp. 173–185.

Lucarella, D., and A. Zanzi, "A visual retrieval environment for hypermedia information systems," *ACM TOIS* 14(1):3–29 (Jan. 1996).

Maarek, Y. S., and D. M. Berry, "The use of lexical affinities in requirements extraction," *Proc. 5th Internatl. Workshop on Software Specification and Design*, Pittsburgh, Pa, May 1989.

Maarek, Y. S., D. M. Berry, and G. E. Kaiser, "An information retrieval approach for automatically constructing software libraries," *IEEE Trans. Software Eng.* 17(8):800–813 (Aug. 1991).

Maiden, N. A. M., P. Mistry, and A. G. Sutcliffe, "How people categorise requirements for reuse: A natural approach," *Proc. RE '95, 2nd IEEE Internatl. Symp. Requirements Engineering*, New York, March 1995, pp. 148–155.

Maiden, N. A. M., and A. G. Sutcliffe, "Exploiting reusable specifications through analogy," *Commun. ACM* **35**(4)(special issue on CASE):55–64 (April 1992).

Maiden, N. A. M., and A. G. Sutcliffe, "Requirements engineering by example," RE '93, *Proc. 1st Intlernatl. Symp. Requirements Engineering*, IEEE CS Press, 1993, pp. 104–112.

Malaca, R., R. L. Stuckey, and D. Gross, "Managing domain specific product line development," *IEEE Software* **13**:57–67 (May 1996).

Malan, R., *Software Reuse: A Business Perspective*, Tech. Report, Hewlett-Packard Laboratories, Feb. 1993.

Malan, R., and K. Wentzel, *Economics of Reuse, Revisited*, Tech. Report HPL-93-31, Hewlett-Packard Laboratories, April 1993.

Malenfant, J., "On the semantic diversity of delegation-based languages," *ACM SIGPLAN Not.*, V 30, N 10, OOPSLA'95 Proc., Austin, TX, Oct. 1995, pp. 215–230.

Margano, J., and T. E. Rhoads, "Software reuse economics: Cost benefit analysis on a large scale ada project," *Proc. Internatl. Conf. Software Engineering*, Melbourne, Australia, May 1992, pp. 338–348.

Martin, J., *Fourth Generation Languages—Volume I: Principles*. Prentice-Hall, Englewood Cliffs, NJ, 1985.

Martin, J., and J. Odell, *Object-Oriented Methods: A Foundation*, Prentice-Hall, Englewood Cliffs, NJ, 1997.

Massonet, P., and A. Van Lamsweerde, "Analogical reuse of requirements frameworks," *Proc. 3rd IEEE Internatl. Symp. Requirements Engineering*, Annapolis, MD, Jan. 1997, pp. 26–37.

Matsumoto, Y., "A software factory: An overall approach to sw production," *Proc. ITT Workshop on Reusability in Programming*, Newport, RI, 1993.

Mayobre, G., "Using code reusability analysis to identify reusable components from software related to an application domain," *Proc. 4th Internatl. Workshop on Software Reuse*, Reston, VA, Nov. 1991.

McCabe, T. J., "A complexity measure," *IEEE Trans. Software Eng.* **SE-2**(4):308–320 (1976).

McClure, C., *The Three R's of Software Automation: Reengineering, Repository, Reusability*, Prentice-Hall, Englewood Cliffs, NJ, 1992.

McClure, C., *Experiences in Organizing for Software Reuse*, Tech. Report, Extended Intelligence, Inc, Chicago, IL, 1995.

McDermid, J., "The cost of COTS," *IEEE Comput.* **31**(6):46–52 (June 1998).

McGraw, G., and J. Viega, "Why COSTS software increases security risks," paper presented at 1st International ICSE Workshop on Testing Distributed Component Based Systems, Los Angeles, CA, May 1999.

McIlroy, D., "Mass produced software components," *Software Engineering Concepts and Techniques: NATO Conf. Software Engineering*, in J. M. Buxton, P. Naur, and B. Randell, eds., Petrocelli/Charter, New York, 1969.

Mellor, S., *The Shlaer-Mellor Method*, ACM Press, Washington, DC, Sept. 26–Oct. 1, 1993; tutorial notes, OOPSLA'93.

Melo, W. L., L. C. Briand, and V. R. Basili, *Measuring the Impact of Reuse on Quality and Productivity in Object Oriented Systems*, Tech. Report TR-95-2, Univ. Maryland, Dept. Computer Science, Jan. 1995.

Meyer, B., in *Object-Oriented Software Construction*, Prentice-Hall International, 1988.

Meyer, B., "Lessons from the design of the Eiffel Libraries," *Commun. ACM* **33**(9):69–88 (Sept. 1990).

Meyer, B., *Reusable Software: The Base Object Oriented Component Libraries*, Prentice-Hall, Englewood Cliffs, NJ, 1994.

Mili, A., R. Mili, and R. Mittermeir, "Storing and retrieving software component: A refinement based approach," *Proc. Internatl. Conf. Software Engineering*, Sorrento, Italy, May 1994, pp. 91–100 (1994a).

Mili, A., E. Addy, and S. Yacoub, "A case study in software reuse," *Software Quality J.* (1999) (1999b).

Mili, A., R. Mili, and R. Mittermeir, "A survey of software reuse libraries," *Ann. Software Eng.* (1998).

Mili, A., and S. Yacoub, "A comparative analysis of domain engineering methods: A controlled case study," paper presented at the International Workshop on Software Product Lines: Economics, Architectures, and Implications, in conjunction with the 22st Internatl. Conf. Software Engineering (ICSE2000) Limerick, Ireland, June 4–11, 2000.

Mili, A., S. Fowler, R. Gottumukkala, and L. Zhang, "An integrated cost model for software reuse," *in Proc. of the 22nd Interntl. Conf. Solftware Engineering*, Limerick, Ireland, June 4–11, 2001, to appear. (Also available as a technical report, West Virginia University, Nov. 1999 http://www.csee.wvu.edu/reuseroi.)

Mili, H., *Building and Maintaining Hierarchical Semantic Nets*, doctoral dissertation, George Washington Univ., Washington DC, Aug. 1988.

Mili, H., *Object-Oriented Design Using Relation Objects*, Tech. Report, Univ. Québec à Montréal, Sept. 1989.

Mili, H., J. Sibert, and Y. Intrator, "An object-oriented model based on relations," *J. Syst. Software* **12**:139–155 (May 1990).

Mili, H., and R. Rada, "A model of hierarchies based on graph homomorphisms," *Comput. Mathe. Appl.* **23**(2–5):343–361, (1992).

Mili, H., and H. Li, "Data Abstraction in SoftClass, an OO CASE Tool for Software Reuse," *Proc. TOOLS'93*, B. Meyer, ed., Prentice-Hall, Santa Barbara, CA, Aug. 2–5, 1993, pp. 133–149.

Mili, H., and H. Li, *Class Design as a Late Binding of Structure to Semantics, or Having your Cake and Eating It Too*, Tech. Report 235. Dep. Math and Computer Science, Univ. Quebec at Montreal, May 13, 1994.

Mili, H., R. Rada, W. Wang, K. Strickland, C. Boldyreff, L. Olsen, J. Witt, J. Heger, W. Scherr, and P. Elzer, "Practitioner and SoftClass: A comparative study of two software reuse research projects," *J. Syst. Software* **27** (May 1994) (1994b).

Mili, H., F. Mili, and A. Mili, "Reusing software: Issues and research directions," *IEEE Trans. Software Eng.* **21**(6):528–562 (June 1995) (1995a).

Mili, H., F. Pachet, I. Benhyaya, and F. Eddy, "Report on the OOPSLA'95 Workshop on Metamodeling," *Addendum to OOPSLA'95 Proc.*, *ACM SIGPLAN Not.* 1995 (1995b).

Mili, H., R. Godin, E. A. Ki, and H. Mcheick, "Representing and retrieving reusable components," Technical Report 96–25, Dept. C. S., UQAM, 1996.

Mili, H., "On behavioral modeling in object-oriented programming," *J. Syst. Software* **34**(1):105–121 (July 1996) (1996a).

Mili, H., W. Harrison, and H. Ossher, "Supporting subject-oriented programming in Smalltalk," *Proceedings of TOOLS USA '96*, Santa Barbara, CA, July 29–August 2, 1996 (1996c).

Mili, H, H. Sahraoui, I. Benyahia, "Representing and querying reusable object-oriented frameworks," *Proc. 1997 Symposium on Software Reusability (SSR '97)*, ACM, New York, May 1997, pp. 110–120.

Mili, H., and H. Sahraoui, "Describing and Using Frameworks," in *Building Application Frameworks—Object-Oriented Foundations of Framework Design*, M. Fayad, D. C. Schmidt, and R. E. Johnson, eds., Wiley, New York, 1999, pp. 523–561.

Mili, H., and F. Pachet, "Metamodeling for multidimensional reuse," in *Proceeding of the Maghrebian Conference on Software Engineering and AI (MCSEAI '2000)*, 1–3 November, 2000, Fes, Morocco, pp. 29–39.

Mili, R., *Return on Investment of Reusable Components: Analytical and Empirical Approaches*, Tech. Report, Univ. Ottawa, Ottawa, Ontario, Canada, Dec. 1996 (1996b).

Minsky, M., "A framework for representing knowledge," in *The Psychology of Computer Vision*, P. H. Winston, ed., McGraw-Hill, New York, 1975.

Minsky, M., *The Society of Mind*, Simon & Schuster, New York, 1986.

Missaoui, R., H. Sahraoui, and R. Godin, "Migrating to an object-oriented database using semantic clustering and transformation rules," *Knowl. Data Eng.* **27**(1):97–113 (1998).

Misra, S. K., and P. J. Jalics, "Third-generation versus fourth-generation development," *IEEE Software*, **5**(4):8–14 (July 1988).

Mittermeir, R. T., and W. Lydia, "Abstract visualization of software: A basis for a complex hash-key," in *Advances in Intelligent Computing*, B. Bouchon-Meunier, R. R. Yager, and L. A. Zadeh, eds., LNCS 945, Springer, 1995, pp. 545–554.

Mittermeir, R., and A. Mili, eds., *Proc. 1999 Symp. Software Reusability*. ACM, Los Angeles, CA, May 1999.

Mittermeir, R., and W. Rossak, "Software bases and software archives, alternatives to support software reuse," *Proc. Fall Joint Computer Conf. '87*, Dallas, TX, Oct. 1987, pp. 21–28.

Mittermeir, R. T., and W. Rossak, "Reusability," in *Modern Software Engineering*, P. A. Ng Peter and R. T. Yeh, eds., Van Nostrand Reinhold, 1990, pp. 205–235.

Moineau, T., and M. C. Gaudel, "Software reusability through formal specifications," in *Proc. 1st Internatl. Workshop on Software Reusability*, R. Prieto-Diaz, W. Schaefer, J. Cramer, and S. Wolf, eds., in Tech. Reports UniDo, Memo 57, Dortmund, Germany, 1991, pp. 202–212.

Monson-Haefel, R., *Enterprise Java Beans*, O'Reilly & Assoc., 1999.

Moore, J. M., and S. C. Bailin, *Domain Analysis: Framework for Reuse*, IEEE Computer Society Press, 1991, pp. 179–203.

Morel, J.-M., and J. Faget, "The REBOOT environment," in Selected papers from the Second International Workshop on Software Reusability, Lucca, Italy, March 24–26, 1993, *Advances in Software Reuse*, IEEE Computer Society Press, 1993, pp. 80–88.

Morisio, M., M. Ezran, and C. Tully, "Introducing reuse in companies: A survey of European experiences," *Proc. 5th Symp. Software Reusability*, Association for Computing Machinery, May 1999, pp. 3–9.

Mostow, J., and M. Barley, "Automated reuse of design plans," *Proc. Internatl. Conf. Engineering Design*, Boston, MA, 1987.

Mowbray, T., and R. Zahavi, *The Essential CORBA: Systems Integration Using Distributed Objects*, Wiley, New York, 1995.

Myers, B. A., "User-interface tools: Introduction and survey," *IEEE Software* 15–23 (Jan. 1989) (special issue on user interfaces).

Neighbors, J. M., "The DRACO approach to constructing software from reusable components," *IEEE Trans. Software Eng.* 564–574 (Sept. 1984).

Nada, N., *Gmu Software Reuse Survey*, Tech. Report http://www.cs.gmu.edu/nada/survey/,Georges Mason Univ., March 1998.

(NATO 1991) *Standard for the Development of Reusable Software Components*, Tech. Report 18, NATO, Aug. 1991.

Obendorf, T., "Investigating COTS based systems," Birds of a Feather Session, 1999 International Conference on Software Engineering, Los Angeles, CA, May 1999.

Odell, J., *Powertypes*, in *Report on the OOPSLA '95 Workshop on Metamodeling*, H. Mili, F. Pachet, I. Benhyaya, and F. Eddy, eds., Austin, TX, October 1995. (See http://www.info.uqam.ca/Labo Recherche/Larc/metamodeling-wshop.html.)

(ODM 1993) *Software Technology for Adaptable Reliable Systems (STARS)—Organization Domain Modeling (ODM)*, Vol. I, *Conceptual Foundations, Process and Work Product Descriptions*, version 0.5, Unisys STARS Tech. Report STARS-UC-05155/001/00, STARS Technology Center, Arlington, VA, July 1993.

Ogando, R. M., S. S. Yau, and N. Wilde. "An object finder for program structure understanding," *J. Software Maint.* **6**(5):261–283 (1994).

(OMG 1998) Object Management Group, *The Common Object Request Broker: Architecture and Specification*, revision 2.2, 1998.
(http://www.omg.org/corba/ corbaiiop.html).

Opdyke, W., *Refactoring Object-Oriented Frameworks*, PhD thesis. Univ. Illinois at Urbana-Champaign, 1992.

Ossher, H., and W. Harrision, "Combination of inheritance hierarchies," *SIGPLAN Notices*, **27**(10): 25–40, Proceedings of OOPSLA '92, Vancouver, B.C., October 18–22, 1992.

Ossher, H., W. Harrison, F. Budinksy, and I. Simmonds, "Subject-oriented programming: Supporting decentralized development of objects,' Proceedings of the 7th IBM Conference on Object-Oriented Technology, Santa Clara, CA, July 1994.

Ossher, H., M. Kaplan, W. Harrison, A. Katz, and V. Kruskal, "Subject-oriented composition rules," *Proc. OOPSLA'95*, ACM Press, Austin, TX, Oct. 15–19, 1995, pp. 235–250.

Ostertag, E., J. Hendler, R. Prieto-Diaz, and C. Braun, "Computing similarity in a reuse library system: An AI-based approach," *ACM Trans. Software Eng. Meth.* **1**(3):205–228 (July 1992).

Pachet, F., and H. Mili, "Text generation with CYC," *Proc. 2nd World Congress Expert Systems*, Lisbon, Portugal, Jan. 10–14, 1994.

Palsberg, J., and M. I. Schwartzbach, "Type substitution for object-oriented programming," *Proc.* ECOOP/OOPSLA'90, Ottawa, ON, CANADA, Oct. 21–25, 1990, pp. 151–160.

Pant, Y., B. Henderson Sellers, and J. N. Verner, "Generalization of object oriented components for reuse: Measurement of effort and size change," *J. Object Oriented Programming* **9**(2):19–31,41 (May 1996).

Park, Y., and N. Bai, *Generating Samples for Component Retrieval by Execution*, Tech. Report, Univ. of Windsor, Windsor, Ontario, Canada, 1997.

Partsch, H., and R. Steinbruggen, "Program transformation systems," *Comput. Surv.* **15**(3):399–436 (Sept. 1983).

Paul, S., and A. Prakash, "A framework for source code search using program patterns," *IEEE Trans. Software Eng.* **SE-20**(6):462–475 (June 1994).

Paulk, M. C., B. Curtis, M. B. Chrissis, and C. V. Weber, *Capability Maturity Model for Software*, version 1.1, Software Engineering Institute, CMU/SEI-93-TR-24, Feb. 1993.

Penix, J., and P. Alexander, "Design representation for automating software component reuse," *Proc. 5th Internatl. Workshop on Knowledge Based Systems for the (Re)Use of Software Libraries*, Nov. 1995.

Penix, J., and P. Alexander, *Efficient Specification Based Component Retrieval*, Tech. Report, Univ. Cincinnati, Knowledge Based Software Engineering Laboratory, ECECS, July 1996.

Penrose, R., *The Emperor's New Mind*, Oxford Univ. Press, 1989.

Perry, D. E., "The inscape environment," *Proc. 11th Internatl. Conf. Software Engineering*, IEEE Computer Society Press, 1989, pp. 2–12.

Perry, D. E., and S. S. Popovich, "Inquire: Predicate-based use and reuse," *Proc. Knowledge Based Software Engineering Conf.*, Chicago, IL, Sept. 1993.

Perry, W. E., *Quality Assurance for Information Systems: Methods Tools, and Techniques*, Wiley, New York, 1991.

Peters, L., *Advanced Structured Analysis and Design*, Prentice-Hall, Englewood Cliffs, NJ, 1987.

Podgurski, A., and L. Pierce, "Behaviour sampling: A technique for automated retrieval of reusable components," *Proc. 14th Internatl. Conf. Software Engineering*, ACM Press, New York, 1992, pp. 300–304.

Podgurski, A., and L. Pierce, "Retrieving reusable software by sampling behavior," *ACM Trans. Software Eng. Meth.* **2**(3):286–303 (July 1993).

Poulin, J., *A Survey of Approaches to Reusability Metrics*, Tech. Report, IBM Corp., April 1993.

Poulin, J., *Measuring Software Reuse: Principles, Practices and Economic Models*, Addison-Wesley, Reading, MA, 1997 (1997a).

Poulin, J. S., "The economics of software product lines," *Internatl. J. Appl. Software Technol.* **3**(1):20–34 (March 1997) (1997b).

Poulin, J., "Reuse: Been there, done that," *Commun. ACM* **42**(5):98–100 (May 1999).

Poulin, J. S., and J. M. Caruso, "Determining the value of a corporate reuse program," *Proc. IEEE Computer Society Internatl. Software Metrics Symp.* Baltimore, MD, May 1993, pp. 16–27 (1993a).

Poulin, J. S., and J. M. Caruso, "A reuse metrics and return on investment model," *Advances in Software Reuse: Proc. 2nd Internatl. Workshop on Software Reusability*, Lucca, Italy, March 1993, pp. 152–166 (1993b).

Poulin, J., and K. J. Werkman, "Software reuse libraries with mosaic," *Proc. 2nd Internatl. World Wide Web Conf.: Mosaic and the Web*, Chicago, IL, Oct. 1994, pp. 17–21.

Poulin, J., and K. J. Werkman, "Melding structured abstracts and the world wide web for retrieval of reusable components," *Proc. Symp. Software Reuse*, Seattle, WA, April 1995, pp. 160–168.

Pree, W., *Design Pattern for Object Oriented Software Development*, Addison-Wesley, Reading, MA, 1995.

Pree, W., "Hot-spot driven development," in *Building Application Frameworks: Object Oriented Foundations of Framework Design*," M. E. Fayad, D. C. Schmidt, and R. Johnson, Wiley, 1999, pp. 379–394.

Pressman, R., *Software Engineering: A Practitioner's Approach*, 3rd ed., McGraw-Hill, New York, 1992.

Prieto-Diaz, R., *A Software Classification Scheme*, Tech. Report, Univ. California, Irvine, Irvine, CA, 1985.

Prieto-Diaz, R., "Domain analysis for reusability," *Proc. COMPSAC'87*, IEEE Press, 1987, pp. 23–29.

Prieto-Diaz, R., "Classification of reusable modules," *Software Reusability*, Vol. I: *Concepts and Models*, in T. J. Biggerstaff and A. J. Perlis, eds., Frontier Series. ACM Press/Addison Wesley, Reading, MA, 1990.

Prieto-Diaz, R., *Domain Analysis*, IEEE Computer Society Press, 1991 (1991a).

Prieto-Diaz, R., "Implementing faceted classification for software reuse," *Commun. ACM* **34**(5):88–97 (May 1991) (1991b).

Prieto-Diaz, R., *Reuse Library Process Model*, Tech. Report 03041-002, STARS, July 1991 (1991c).

Prieto-Diaz, R., "Making software reuse work: An implementation model," *Software Eng. Notes* **16**(3):(1991); ACM SIGSOFT (1991d).

Prieto-Diaz, R., "Status report: Software reusability," *IEEE Software* **10**(3):61–66 (May 1993).

Prieto-Diaz, R., and G. Arango, *Domain Analysis and Software System Modeling*, IEEE Computer Society Press, 1991, pp. 179–203.

Prieto-Diaz, R., and P. Freeman, "Classifying software for reusability," *IEEE Software* **4**(1):6–16 (Jan. 1987).

Quick, M., and R. Cortes, *CARDS Library Operations Policies and Procedures*, Vol. II, Lockheed Martin Tactical Defense Systems Ref. No. STARS-VC-B004/001/00; ASSET Collection No. ASSET_A_585, Feb. 1994.

Rada, R., *Software Reuse*, Ablex Publishing, Liverpool, UK. Sept. 1995.

Rada, R., *Reengineering Programs: How to Reuse Programming to Build New State of the Art Software*, Glendale Publishing, Jan. 1999.

Ramamoorthy, C. V., V. Garg, and A. Prakash, "Support for reusability in genesis," *IEEE Trans. on Software Engineering*, **14**(8):1145–54 (Aug. 1988).

(RAPID 1990) *Rapid Center Standards for Reusable Software*, Tech. Report 3451-4-012/6.4, US Army Information Systems Engineering Command, October 1990.

Raymond, G. E., and D. M. Hollis, "Software reuse economics model," *Proc. WADAS'91: 7th Washington Ada Symp.*, Summer SIGAda Meeting, McLean, VA, June 1991, pp. 141–155.

Reenskaug, T., *Working with Objects*, Prentice-Hall, Englewood Cliffs, NJ, 1995.

Reifer, D. J., *Practical Software Reuse*, Wiley, New York, 1997.

Reubenstein, H. B., and R. C. Waters, "The requirements' apprentice: Automated assistance for requirements acquisition," *IEEE Trans. Software Eng.* **SE-17**(3):226–240 (March 1991).

Revault, N., H. Sahraoui, G. Blain and J.-F. Perrot, "A metamodeling technique: The metagen system," *Proceedings of TOOLS Europe 1995*, Paris, France, 1995.

Rich, C., and H. E. Schrobe, *An Initial Report on Lisp's Programmer's Apprentice*, Tech. Report MIT/AI/TR-354, Massachusetts Institute of Technology, Cambridge, MA, Dec. 1976.

Rich, C., and H. E. Schrobe, "An initial report on lisp's programmer's apprentice," *IEEE Trans. Software Eng.* **SE-4**(11) (Nov. 1978).

Rich, C., and R. C. Waters, "The programmer's apprentice: A research overview," *IEEE Comput.* **21**(11):10–25 (Nov. 1988).

Rich, C., and R. C. Waters, *The Programmer's Apprentice*, Addison-Wesley, Reading, MA, 1990.

Rittri, M., "Using types as search keys in function libraries," *Proc. Conf. Functional Programming Languages and Computer Architectures*, Wesley, Reading, MA, Addison 1989.

Rittri, M., *Retrieving Library Identifiers via Equational Matching of Types*, Technical Report 65, Programming Methodology Group, Dept Computer Science, Chalmers Univ. Technology and Univ. Goteborg, Goteborg, Sweden, 1992.

Rivard, F., "Smalltalk: A reflective language," in *REFLECTION'96*, San Franscico, CA, April 21–23 1996, G. Kiczales, ed., 1996 (http://www.emn.fr/deptinfo/rivard/perso/informatique/reflection96/reflection96.htm).

(RLPM 1991) Software Technology for Adaptable, Reliable Systems (STARS) Program, *Reuse Library Process Model*, Electronic Systems Div., Air Force Systems Command, USAF, Hanscom AFB, MA, 1991.

Rollins, E. J., and J. Wing, "Specifications as search keys for software libraries," *Proc. Conf. Functional Programming Languages and Architectures*, Sept. 1989, pp. 173–183.

Rosch, E., "Principles of categorization," in *Cognition and Categorization*, E. Rosch and B. B. Lloyd, eds., Lawrence Erlbaum Assoc., Hillsdale, NJ, 1978.

Rueping, A., "Managing class dependencies," in *Building Application Frameworks— Object-Oriented Foundations of Framework Design*, M. Fayad, D. C. Schmidt, and R. E. Johnson, eds., Wiley, New York, 1999, pp. 325–344.

Rumbaugh, J., M. Blaha, W. Premerlani, F. Eddy, and W. Lorensen, *Object-Oriented Modeling and Design*, Prentice Hall, Englewood Cliffs, NJ, 1991.

Rumelhart, D., and D. Norman, *Representation in Memory*, Center for Human Information Processing, La Jolla, CA, June 1983.

Runciman, C., and I. Toyn, "Retrieving reusable software components by polymorphic type," *Proc. Conf. Functional Programming Languages and Computer Architectures*, Addison-Wesley, 1989, Reading, MA.

Sahraoui, H. A., Application de la meta-modelisation a la generation des outils de conception et de mise en oeuvre des bases de donnees, PhD Thesis, Universite Paris 6, June 1995.

Sahraoui, H. A., H. Lounis, W. Mélo, and H. Mili, "A concept formation based approach to object identification in procedural code," *J. Aut. Software Eng.* **6**(4):387–410 (1999).

Sametinger, J., *Software Engineering with Reusable Components*, Springer-Verlag, 1997.

Sanyal, S., V. Shah, and S. Bhattacharya, "Framework of a software reliability engineering tool," *Proc. HASE'97*, 1997.

Schach, S. R., "The economic impact of software reuse on maintenance," *J. Software Maint. Research Pract.* **6**(4):185–196 (July/Aug. 1994).

Schach, S. R., and X. F. Yang, "Metrics for targeting candidates for reuse: An experimental approach," *Proc. ACM Symp. Applied Computing*, 1995, pp. 379–383.

Schafer, W., R. Prieto-Diaz, and M. Matsumoto, *Software Reusability*, Prentice-Hall, Englewood Cliffs, NJ, 1993.

Schank, R., "The structure of episodes in memory," *Language, Thought, and Culture: Advances in the Study of Cognition*, D. Bobrow and A. Collins, eds., Academic Press, New York, 1975, pp. 237–272.

Schill, A., "DCE—the OSF distributed computing environment," *Proc. Internatl. DCE Workshop*, Karlsruhe, Germany, Springer-Verlag, Oct. 1993.

Schimsky, D., "Software reuse—some realities," *Vitro Tech. J.*, **10**(1):47–57 (1992).

Schmidt, H. A., "Framework design by systematic generalization," in *Building Application Frameworks—Object-Oriented Foundations of Framework Design*, M. Fayad, D. C. Schmidt, and R. E. Johnson, eds., Wiley, New York, 1999, pp. 353–378.

Schwanke, R. W., "Intelligent tool for re-engineering software modularity," *Proc. Internatl. Conf. Software Engineering*, 1991, pp. 83–92.

(SEI 2000) *The Product Line Engineering Practice* (*PLP*) *Initiative*, Software Engineering Institute, Carnegie Mellon Univ., Pittsburgh, PA (http://www.sei.cmu.edu/ plp/plp_init.html).

Selby, R. W., "Quantitative studies of software reuse," in *Software Reusability*, T. J. Biggerstaff and A. J. Perlis, eds., Addison-Wesley, Reading, MA, 1989.

Shaw, M., "Architectural issues in software reuse: It's not the functionality, it's the packaging," *Proc. Symp. Software Reusability* (SSR'95), 1995.

Shaw, M., and D. Garlan, *Software Architecture: Perspectives on an Emerging Discipline*, Prentice-Hall, Upper Saddle River, NJ, 1996.

Shlaer, S., and S. Mellor, *Object-Oriented Systems Analysis: Modeling the World in Data*, Yourdon Press, Englewood Cliffs, NJ, 1992.

Simon, H., and A. Ando, "Aggregation of variables in dynamic systems," *Econometrica* **29** (1961).

Simos, M. A., "Organization domain modeling (ODM): Formalizing the core domain modeling life cycle," *ACM SIGSOFT Software Eng. Notes*, **20**(SI):196–205 (Aug. 1995); also reprinted in *SSR '95. Proc. 17th Internatl. Conf. Software Engineering, Symp. Software Reusability*, 1995.

Simos, M. A. "The domain-oriented software life cycle: Towards an extended process model for reusability," in *Software Reuse: Emerging Technology*, W. Tracz, ed., IEEE Computer Society Press, 1990, pp. 354–363.

Sindre, G., R. Conradi, and E. D. Karlsson, "The reboot approach to software reuse," *J. Syst. Software* **30**(3):201–212 (1995).

Sitaraman, M., "A class of mechanisms to facilitate multiple implementations of a spe-cification." *Internatl. Conf. Computer Languages*," IEEE, April 1992, pp. 182–191.

Sitaraman, M., "On tight performance specifications of object oriented software," *Internatl. Conf. Software Reuse*, IEEE, Nov. 1994.

Smaragdakis, Y., and D. Batory, "Implementing reusable object oriented components," *Proc. 5th Internatl. Conf. Software Reuse*, Victoria, BC, Canada, June 1998.

Snyder, A., "Inheritance and the development of encapsulated software systems," in *Research Directions in Object-Oriented Programming*, MIT Press, Boston, MA, 1987, pp. 165–188.

Sodhi, J., and P. Sodhi, *Software Reuse: Domain Analysis and Design Process*, McGraw-Hill, New York, 1999.

(SofTech 1993) SofTech, Inc., *Domain Analysis and Design Process, Version 1*, Document 1222-04-210/30.1, DISA-CIM Software Reuse Program Office, 1993.

Sommerville, I., *Software Engineering*, 5th ed., Addison-Wesley, Reading, MA, 1995.

Spanoudakis, G., and P. Constantopoulos, "Similarity for analogical software reuse: A conceptual modelling approach," *Proc. CAiSE '93*, LNCS Vol. 685, June 1993.

Spanoudakis, G., and P. Constantopoulos, "Measuring similarity between software artifacts," *Internatl. Conf. Software Engineering and Knowledge Engineering*, W. Berztiss, ed., Jurmala, Latvia, June 1994.

(SPC 1993a) *Reuse Adoption Guidebook*, version 2.0.5, SPC-92051-CMC, Software Productivity Consortium, Herndon, VA, 1993.

(SPC 1993b) *Reuse-Driven Software Processes Guidebook*, version: 2.0.3, Software Productivity Consortium, Herndon, VA, Dec. 1993 (1993b).

Sprott, D., "Components in the ERP market," *Compon. Strat. Mag.* 18–22 (Nov. 1998).

Stacy, W., and J. MacMillian, "Cognitive bias in software engineering," *Commun. ACM* **38**(6):57–63 (1995).

Stalhane, T., "Development of a model for reusability assessment," *Proc. 2nd Symp. Software Quality Techniques and Acquisition Criteria*, Florence, Italy, May 1995, pp. 111–123.

Steel, J., *Component Technology*, IDC White Paper (Part One), International Data Corp. London, 1996.

Steigerwald, R. A., "Reusable component retrieval with formal specifications," *Proc. 5th Annual Workshop on Software Reuse*, Palo Alto, CA, Oct. 1992.

Stevens, B., "Linking software reengineering and reuse: An economic motivation," *CASE Trends* 24–36 (March 1993).

Stroustrup, B., in *The C++ Programming Languages*, Addison-Wesley, Reading, MA, 1986.

(Sun 1998a) Sun Microsystems, Inc., *JavaBeans*, Graham Hamilton, ed., version 1.01, July 24, 1997.

(Sun 1998b) Sun Microsystems, Inc., *Enterprise JavaBeans Specification*, version 1.0, March 1998 (http://java.sun.com/products/ejb/docs.html).

Sutcliffe, A. G., and N. A. M. Maiden, "Domain modeling for reuse," *3rd Internatl. Conf. Software Reuse*, Rio de Janeiro, Brazil, Nov. 1994, IEEE CS Press, pp. 169–177.

Sward, R. E., and T. C. Hartrum, "Extracting objects of legacy imperative code," in Proceedings of IEEE Automated Software Engineering Conference, 1997, pp. 98–106.

Szyperski, C., *Component Software: Beyond Object-Oriented Programming*, Addison-Wesley, Reading, MA, 1999.

Tarr, P., H. Ossher, W. Harrison, and S. N. Sutton, "N Degrees of separation: Multidimensional separation of concerns," in Proceedings of the 21st International Conference on Software Engineering, Los Angeles, May 16–22, 1999, pp. 107–109.

Thomason, R. H., J. F. Horty, and D. S. Touretzky, *A Calculus for Inheritance in Monotonic Semantic Nets*, CMU-CS-86-138, Carnegie-Mellon Univ. Pittsburgh, PA, 1986.

Torres, W. R., and M. H. Samadzadeh, "Software reuse and information theory based metrics," *Proc. 1991 Symp. Applied Computing*, Kansas City, MO, April 1991, pp. 437–446.

Tracz, W., "Domain analysis working group report," *Software Eng. Notes* (July 1992).

Tracz, W., "LILEANNA: A parameterized programming language," in *Advances in Software Reuse* (selected papers from the 2nd Internatl. Workshop on Software Reusability, Lucca, Italy, March 24–26, 1993), IEEE Computer Society Press, 1993, pp. 66–78.

Tracz, W., *Confessions of a Used Program Salesperson*, Addison-Wesley, Reading, MA, 1995.

Ungar, D., and R. B. Smith, *Self: The Power of Simplicity*, Proceedings of OOPSLA '87, Orlando, FL, October 4–8, 1987, pp. 227–242.

Ullman, J., *Elements of ML Programming—ML97 Edition*, Prentice-Hall, Englewood Cliffs, NJ, 1998.

USC 2000, Center for Software Engineering, Software Architecture research center at University of Southern California, 2000 (http://sunset.usc.edu/Soft_Arch/SwArch.html).

Van Der Linden, F. J., and J. K. Müller, "Creating architectures with building blocks," *IEEE Software* **12**(6):51–60 (Nov. 1995).

Van Hilst, M., and D. Notkin, "Using role components to implement collaboration-based designs," *Proceedings OOPSLA '96*, San Jose, Ca, October 6–10, 1996, ACM SIGPLAN Not., **31**(10):359–369.

Van Horne, J. C., *Financial Management and Policy*, 6th ed., Prentice-Hall, Englewood Cliffs, NJ, 1983.

Verner, J., and G. Tate, "Estimating size and effort in fourth-generation development," *IEEE Software*, **5**(4):15–22 (July 1988).

Vigder, M. R., W. Gentleman, and J. Dean, "COTS software integration: State of the art," Tech. Report 39198, Institute for Information Technology, National Research Council Canada, 1996 (http://www.sel.iit.nrc.ca/abstracts/NRC39198.abs).

Vigder, M. R., and J. Dean, "An Architectural Approach to Building Systems from COTS Software Components," *Proc. 1997 Center for Advanced Studies Conference* (CASCON97), Toronto, Ontario, Canada, Nov. 10–13, 1997.

Viscione, J. A., *Financial Analysis: Tools and Concepts*, Publications Div., National Association of Credit Management, New York, 1984.

Vitaletti, W. C., and R. Chhut, *Domain Analysis Guidelines*, SofTech, Inc., May 1991.

Voas, J., "The challenges of using COTS software in component based development," *IEEE Comput.* **31**(6):44–45 (June 1998) (1998a).

Voas, J., "Certyifying off the shelf software components," *IEEE Comput.* **31**(6):53–59 (June 1998) (1998b).

Voas, J., "Maintaining component based systems," *IEEE Software* 22–27 (July/Aug. 1998) (1998c).

Voas, J., "The software quality certification triangle," *Crosstalk* **11**(11):12–14 (Nov. 1998) (1998d).

Wallace, D. R., and R. U. Fujii, "Software verification and validation: An overview," *IEEE Software* **6**(3):10–17 (May 1989); *Software Verification and Validation: Its Role in Computer Assurance and Its Relationship with Software Project Management Standards*, NIST Special Publication 500-165, National Institute of Standards and Technology, Gaithersburg, MD, 1989.

Wallnau, K., ed., *International Workshop on Component Based Software Engineering*. SEI, Los Angeles, CA, May 1999.

Walton, P., and N. Maiden, eds., *Integrated Software Reuse: Management and Techniques*, Unicom Applied Information Technology. Ashgate Publishing, May 1993.

Waters, R. C., "The programmer's apprentice: A session with kbemacs," *IEEE Trans. Software Eng.* **SE-7**(11):1296–1320 (Jan. 1981).

Waters, R. C., "The programmer's apprentice: Knowledge based program editing," *IEEE Trans. Software Eng.* **SE-8**(1):1–12 (Jan. 1982).

Wegner, P., "The object-oriented classification paradigm," in *Research Directions in Object-Oriented Programming*, MIT Press, Boston, MA, 1987, pp. 479–560 (1987a).

Wegner, P., "Varieties of reusability," in *Tutorial: Software Reusability*, Peter Freeman, 1987, pp. 24–38 (1987b).

Wegner, P., "Dimensions of object-oriented modeling," *Computer* **25**(10)(special issue on object-oriented computing):12–20 (Oct. 1992).

Weide, B. W., S. H. Edwards, D. E. Harms, and D. A. Lamb, "Design and specification of iterators using the swapping paradigm," *IEEE Trans. Software Eng.* **20**(8):631–643 (Aug. 1994).

Weiss, D. M., and C. T. R. Lai, *Software Product-Line Engineering: A Family-Based Software Development Process*, Addison-Wesley, Reading, MA, 1999.

Weyuker, E., "Testing component-based software: A cautionary tale," *IEEE Software* 54–59 (Oct. 1998).

Williamson, M., "Cultural issues: Avoiding the point of no reuse," *CIO Mag.* **4**:5 (March 1, 1997).

Winograd, T., "Frame representations and the declarative-procedural controversy," in *Representation and Understanding: Studies in Cognitive Science*, editors D. Bobrow and A. Collins, eds., Academic Press, New York, 1975, pp. 185–210.

Wirfs-Brock, R., Wirfs-Brock, B. W., and L. Wiener, in *Designing Object-Oriented Software*, Prentice-Hall, Englewood Cliffs, NJ, 1990.

Wood, M., and I. Sommerville, "An information system for software components," *SIGIR Forum* **22**(3):11–25 (1988).

Yacoub, S., B. Cukic, and H. Ammar, "Scenario-based reliability analysis of component-based software," *Proc. 10th Internatl. Symp. Software Reliability Engineering* (ISSRE'99), Boca Raton, FL, Nov. 1–4, 1999, pp. 22–31.

Yacoub, S., H. Ammar, and A. Mili, "A model for classifying component interfaces," Second Interntl. Workshop on Component-Based Software Engineering, in conjunction with the 21st Interntl. Conf. on Software Engineering (ICSE '99), Los Angeles, CA, May 17–18, 1999.

Yacoub, S., A. Mili, C. Kaveri, and M. Dehlin, "A hierarchy of COTS certification criteria," in Proc. of the First Software Product Line Conference (SPLC 1), Denver, CO, August 28–31, 2000.

Yeh, A. S., D. R. Harris, and H. B. Reubenstein, "Recovering abstract data types and object instances from a conventional procedural language," *2nd Working Conf. Reverse Engineering*, IEEE Computer Society Press, 1995, pp. 252–261.

Yellin, D., and R. Strom, "Interfaces, protocols, and the semi-automatic construction of software adaptors," *Proc. OOPSLA'94*, Portland, OR, Oct. 1994, ACM Press, Vancouver, BC, Canada, 1994, pp. 176–190.

Zand, M., and M. Samadzadeh, "Software reuse: Current status and trends," *J. Syst. Software* **30**(3):167–170 (Sept. 1995).

Zand, M., and M. Samadzadeh, *Software Reuse Research: Are We on the Right Track?* Tech. report, Univ. Oklahoma, Norman, OK, 1998.

Zaremski, A. M., and J. M. Wing, "Signature matching: A key to reuse," *Proc. SIGSOFT'93: ACM SIGSOFT Symp. Foundations of Software Engineering*, **SEN** **18**(5):182–190 (Redondo Beach, CA, Dec. 1993).

Zaremski, A. M., and J. M. Wing, "Signature matching: A tool for using software libraries," *ACM Trans. Software Eng. Metho.* **4**(2):146–170 (April 1995) (1995a).

Zaremski, A. M., and J. M. Wing, "Specification matching of software components," *Proc. SIGSOFT'95: 3rd ACM SIGSOFT Symp. Foundations of Software Engineering*, **SEN 20**(4):6–17, ACM Press, New York, Oct. 1995 (1995b).

Zhong, Q., and N. Edwards, "Security controls for COTS components," *IEEE Comput.* **31**(6):67–73 (June 1998).

Index